T0189258

Lecture Notes in Computer Science 14455

Founding Editors

Gerhard Goos
Juris Hartmanis

Editorial Board Members

The series Lecture Notes in Computer Science (LNCS), including its subseries Lecture Notes in Artificial Intelligence (LNAI) and Lecture Notes in Bioinformatics (LNBI), has established itself as a medium for the publication of new developments in computer science and information technology research, teaching, and education.

LNCS enjoys close cooperation with the computer science R & D community, the series counts many renowned academics among its volume editors and paper authors, and collaborates with prestigious societies. Its mission is to serve this international community by providing an invaluable service, mainly focused on the publication of conference and workshop proceedings and postproceedings. LNCS commenced publication in 1973.

Paolo Ciancarini · Angelo Di Iorio ·
Helmut Hlavacs · Francesco Poggi
Editors

Entertainment Computing – ICEC 2023

22nd IFIP TC 14 International Conference, ICEC 2023
Bologna, Italy, November 15–17, 2023
Proceedings

Springer

Editors
Paolo Ciancarini 🆔
University of Bologna
Bologna, Italy

Angelo Di Iorio 🆔
University of Bologna
Bologna, Italy

Helmut Hlavacs 🆔
University of Vienna
Vienna, Austria

Francesco Poggi 🆔
Italian National Research Council (CNR)
Rome, Italy

ISSN 0302-9743   ISSN 1611-3349 (electronic)
Lecture Notes in Computer Science
ISBN 978-981-99-8247-9   ISBN 978-981-99-8248-6 (eBook)
https://doi.org/10.1007/978-981-99-8248-6

This Springer imprint is published by the registered company Springer Nature Singapore Pte Ltd.
The registered company address is: 152 Beach Road, #21-01/04 Gateway East, Singapore 189721, Singapore

Paper in this product is recyclable.

Preface

We are proud to present the conference proceedings of the 22nd edition of the IFIP International Conference on Entertainment Computing (ICEC 2023) in this edited LNCS volume. The conference was hosted by the Department of Computer Science of the University of Bologna in Bologna, Italy, during November 15–17, 2023. As the longest lasting and prime scientific conference in the area of entertainment computing, ICEC brings together researchers and practitioners with diverse backgrounds in order to connect, share, and discuss both recent and potential future developments in this field. Considering the broad range of topics represented in our 2 keynotes, 35 papers in the main tracks, 4 workshops, and 2 tutorials, ICEC 2023 served as a lively forum for multidisciplinary exchange to advance our understanding of entertainment computing and all related areas.

Overall, we received a total of 85 submissions from authors spread all over the world. The works collected in this volume discuss the latest findings in the areas of game experience, player engagement and analysis, serious gameplay, entertainment methods and tools, extended reality, and game design. All papers underwent double blind peer review with at least 3 reviews per paper. This resulted in 13 accepted full papers and 5 short papers, 8 work-in-progress papers, 7 interactive entertainment demonstrations, 2 student competition papers, and 5 papers for workshops and tutorials. Additionally, a special section on aesthetics and empowerment includes 10 peer-reviewed papers.

We thank all members of the Program Committee, composed of 84 experts from more than twenty different countries, for their hard work, timeliness, and help in ensuring the high quality of the presented proceedings.

A special thank goes to the keynote speakers Roberto Bresin from the KTH Royal Institute of Technology and Ekaterina Prasolova-Førland from the Norwegian University of Science and Technology (NTNU).

We would also like to thank all the Organizing Committee members, who gave us valuable insights, as well as the ICEC Steering Committee. Many thanks also go to the International Federation for Information Processing (IFIP) and the Associazione Italiana per l'Informatica ed il Calcolo Automatico (AICA) for their continuous and precious support.

We would like to express our gratitude to everyone who supported us in hosting this year's conference and to all participants for making ICEC 2023 a successful event.

September 2023

Paolo Ciancarini
Angelo Di Iorio
Helmut Hlavacs
Francesco Poggi

Organization

General Chair

Paolo Ciancarini · University of Bologna, Italy

Program Chairs

Angelo Di Iorio · University of Bologna, Italy
Helmut Hlavacs · University of Vienna, Austria

Work in Progress Chairs

Andrea Giovanni Nuzzolese · Italian National Research Council (CNR), Italy
Erik van der Spek · Eindhoven University of Technology,
The Netherlands

Workshops Chairs

Jannicke Baalsrud Hauge · The Royal Institute of Technology (KTH),
Sweden
Barbara Göbl · University of Vienna, Austria

Tutorials Chair

Allegra De Filippo · University of Bologna, Italy

Interactive Entertainment and Experiential Works Chairs

Jerome Dupire · Conservatoire National des Arts et Métiers,
France
Andrea Poltronieri · University of Bologna, Italy

Student Game and Interactive Entertainment Competition Chairs

Erik van der Spek   Eindhoven University of Technology,
                                    The Netherlands
Mara Dionisio   University of Madeira— ITI/LARSYS, Portugal

Doctoral Consortium Chair

Esteban Clua   Universidade Federal Fluminense, Brazil

Local Chair

Andrea Poltronieri   University of Bologna, Italy

Proceedings Chair

Francesco Poggi   Italian National Research Council (CNR), Italy

Publicity Chair

Marco Ferrati   University of Bologna, Italy

Steering Committee

Jannicke Baalsrud Hauge   The Royal Institute of Technology (KTH),
                                    Sweden
Jorge Cardoso   University of Coimbra, Portugal
Esteban Clua   Universidade Federal Fluminense, Brazil
Rainer Malaka   University of Bremen, Germany
Erik van der Spek   Eindhoven University of Technology,
                                    The Netherlands

Program Committee

Jannicke Baalsrud Hauge	The Royal Institute of Technology (KTH), Sweden
Matthew Barr	University of Glasgow, UK
Barbara Rita Barricelli	Università degli Studi di Brescia, Italy
Nicole Basaraba	Maastricht University, The Netherlands
Regina Bernhaupt	ruwido, Austria
Fernando Birra	Universidade NOVA de Lisboa, Portugal
Joseph Alexander Brown	Thompson Rivers University, Canada
Carlos Caires	University of Saint Joseph, Macao
Jorge Cardoso	University of Coimbra, Portugal
Elin Carstensdottir	University of California Santa Cruz, USA
Paolo Ciancarini	University of Bologna, Italy
Esteban Clua	Universidade Federal Fluminense, Brazil
João Cordeiro	School of Arts, Portuguese Catholic University, Portugal
Nuno Correia	Universidade NOVA de Lisboa, Portugal
Drew Davidson	Carnegie Mellon University, USA
Allegra De Filippo	University of Bologna, Italy
Angelo Di Iorio	University of Bologna, Italy
Mara Dionisio	University of Madeira, Portugal
Ralf Doerner	RheinMain University of Applied Sciences, Germany
Heiko Duin	University of Bremen, Germany
Jerome Dupire	Conservatoire National des Arts et Métiers, France
Kai Erenli	UAS BFI Vienna, Austria
Gerald Estadieu	Faculty of Arts and Humanities, University of Saint Joseph, Macao
Marco Ferrati	University of Bologna, Italy
Pablo Figueroa	Universidad de los Andes, Colombia
Mateus Finco	Universidade Federal do Rio Grande do Sul, Brazil
Stefan Goebel	TU Darmstadt, Germany
Pedro González Calero	Universidad Politécnica de Madrid, Spain
Barbara Göbl	University of Vienna, Austria
Helmut Hlavacs	University of Vienna, Austria
Robin Horst	RheinMain University of Applied Sciences, Germany
Hiroyuki Iida	Japan Advanced Institute of Science and Technology, Japan

Naoya Isoyama	Otsuma Women's University, Japan
Jinyuan Jia	Tongji University, China
Philipp Jordan	University of Hawaii at Manoa, USA
Nicolas Jouandeau	Paris8 University, France
Mohd Nor Akmal Khalid	Japan Advanced Institute of Science and Technology, Japan
Christoph Klimmt	Department of Journalism and Communication Research, Hanover University of Music, Drama, and Media, Germany
Kei Kobayashi	Nagoya City University, Japan
Troy Kohwalter	Universidade Federal Fluminense (UFF), Brazil
Sahra Kunz	Escola das Artes - Universidade Católica Portuguesa, Portugal
Michael Lankes	Upper Austria University of Applied Sciences, Hagenberg, Austria
Jingya Li	Beijing Jiaotong University, China
Qingde Li	University of Hull, UK
Sheng Li	Peking University, China
Penousal Machado	University of Coimbra, Portugal
Rainer Malaka	University of Bremen, Germany
Delfina Sol Martinez Pandiani	University of Bologna, Italy
Filipa Martins de Abreu	University of Saint Joseph, Macao
André Miede	Hochschule für Technik und Wirtschaft des Saarlandes, Germany
Michela Mortara	CNR imati Ge, Italy
Wolfgang Mueller	University of Education Weingarten, Germany
Andrea Nuzzolese	Italian National Research Council (CNR), Italy
Carla Patrão	University of Coimbra, Portugal
Andre Perrotta	Centre for Informatics and Systems of the University of Coimbra, Portugal
Johannes Pfau	Universität Bremen, Germany
Francesco Poggi	Italian National Research Council (CNR), Italy
Andrea Poltronieri	University of Bologna, Italy
Maria Popescu	Carol I National Defence University, Romania
Kjetil Raaen	Høyskolen Kristiania, Norway
Theresa-Marie Rhyne	Consultant, USA
Teresa Romão	Faculdade de Ciências e Tecnologia/Universidade NOVA de Lisboa, Portugal
Licinio Roque	University of Coimbra, Portugal
Alessandro Russo	CNR ISTC, Italy
Che Mat Ruzinoor	Universiti Utara Malaysia, Malaysia
Anthony Savidis	Department of Computer Science, University of Crete and ICS-FORTH, Greece

Andreas Scalas   CNR IMATI Genova, Italy
Nikitas Sgouros   University of Piraeus, Greece
Edirlei Soares de Lima   Breda University of Applied Sciences,
                                   The Netherlands
Erik van der Spek   Eindhoven University of Technology,
                                   The Netherlands
Ioana Andreea Stefan   Advanced Technology Systems, Romania
Elif Surer   Middle East Technical University, Turkey
Cristina Sylla   University of Minho, Portugal
László Szécsi   Budapest University of Technology and
                                   Economics, Hungary
Heinrich Söbke   Bauhaus-Universität Weimar, Germany
Daniel Thalmann   Ecole Polytechnique Fédérale de Lausanne,
                                   Switzerland
Zhang Ting   Zhejiang University, China
Mai Xuan Trang   Phenikaa University, Vietnam
Kai Tuuri   University of Jyväskylä, Finland
Xiaosong Yang   Bournemouth University, UK
Cheng Yao   Zhejiang University, China
Nelson Zagalo   University of Aveiro, Portugal
Leijing Zhou   Zhejiang University, China

Contents

Entertainment Methods and Tools

Extended Reality

Game Design

Interactive Entertainment

Student Game Competition

Workshops

Workshop: Aesthetics and Empowerment

Tutorials

Game Experience

Dynamic Difficulty Adjustment by Performance and Player Profile in Platform Game

Marcos P. C. Rosa[1]([✉]), Carla D. Castanho[1], Tiago B. P. e Silva[1],
Mauricio M. Sarmet[2], and Ricardo P. Jacobi[1]

[1] University of Brasília, Brasília, Brazil
`mpcayres96@gmail.com`, {`carlacastanho,jacobi`}`@unb.br`
[2] Federal Institute of Education, Science and Technology of Paraíba, Paraíba, Brazil

Abstract. The Dynamic Difficulty Adjustment (DDA) of games can play an important role in increasing the player engagement and fun. This work investigates the different mechanisms of a DDA system for a platform game to adequately adapt its difficulty level and keep the player in a state of flow. The proposed adjustment varies the size of the platform and the height of the jump, comparing different approaches from the game systems. Tests were made with sample groups, in which participants answered questionnaires and had their data collected for research purposes. The results indicated that the difficulty of platform games can be estimated by the components of the levels, including correlation between the difficulty and player performance data. In addition, player profiles were predicted from raw game session data and used with machine learning methods to define difficulty progression. Finally, the DDA models were able to adjust the game difficulty to the players, decreasing the dispersion between the performance data and keeping the player in a state of flow, especially when using a feed forward neural network to progress difficulty based on the player's profile.

Keywords: dynamic difficulty adjustment · platform game · player profile · machine learning · game telemetry · flow

1 Introduction

The requirements and rules to make good games need to adapt to the new scenarios, creating fun games for each consumer profile. New mechanisms are required to cover a diversity of players and allow games to target users with different skill levels and preferences.

Boredom or frustration can be caused by non-adaptive games by not assessing the match between the degree of challenge and the player profile [3]. In contrast to the pre-established difficulty levels, the Dynamic Difficulty Adjustment (DDA) is an emerging technique that seeks to adapt the difficulty of a game during its execution according to the skills of each player [1].

P. Ciancarini et al. (Eds.): ICEC 2023, LNCS 14455, pp. 3–16, 2023.
https://doi.org/10.1007/978-981-99-8248-6_1

There is a field of study in the DDA area to define robust metrics and rules for adaptation in relation to the concept of flow and the pattern of game systems [2,17]. Furthermore, few studies apply machine learning outside the context of NPC adaptation or associate adaptation with player characteristics other than their ability, such as specific characteristics of player profiles.

For the present work, the objective is to increase the robustness of the metrics for measuring difficulty and component analysis, generalizing them to be used in platform games. For the construction of the proposed model, game balancing will be analyzed in relation to generic components of platform games and the corresponding difficulties. Also, the efficiency of computational methods for estimating the difficulty of individual components and game levels will be investigated.

Thus, the estimated difficulty will be compared with that experienced by the players, allowing a better assessment of the DDA in all analyzed variations. With this, the models will be compared, finding out which ones have comparatively superior results and if all are significantly better than the game without applying adjustments. For this, the state of flow and the adequacy of the difficulty will be evaluated, according to questionnaire responses and the dispersion of game data captured during test sessions.

Considering the objectives presented, a 2D platform game will be adapted according to the most common components of this genre. In addition, the game will be adjusted in order to progress according to the difficulties experienced by each player, trying to keep it in an suitable difficulty range.

The game will have a DDA that analyzes the player's performance by heuristic functions or by machine learning, relating the progression of difficulty with the player's profile. Furthermore, this work will present the correlation between raw game data with the difficulty experienced and the player's profile, in addition to the use of characteristics related to difficulty from the player profiles to improve the DDA method.

In a second instance, tests will evaluate the DDA applied to configure the size of platform components and jump height. Finally, tests will investigate the use of machine learning and the association of player profiles with the difficulty experienced, verifying the metrics for measuring the flow state and the adequacy of the difficulty in studies with the application of DDA. In this scenario, a comparison will be made between the DDA with heuristic functions and with an artificial neural network (ANN).

2   Related Work

Difficulty in automatically generated 2D platform games has been investigated by Mourato et al. [12]. A method of measuring difficulty based on the probability of success in completing a level was proposed for this context, with the difficulty of individual components made by a jump success probability model.

From there, commercial games had their difficulty mapped and the results of difficulty measured and tested with participants were similar. Also, regarding content generation [11], the transformation of simple paths into challenges with complex structures was elaborated, changing components in strategic locations.

In turn, the dynamic balancing of difficulty in a puzzle game was the subject of study by Hawkins et al. [5]. They sought to meet different skill levels and maintain satisfaction according to the characteristics of the player's profile, depending on the affinity for challenges and risks. A modeling technique known as particle filtering was used, being applied to model various skill levels and to consider the risk profile of the player.

In the context of machine learning, neural networks can be used to improve adaptability proposals in games. Or et al. [13] proposed a DDA method that optimized the user experience by considering other players and game rules. It was based on a deep neural network that minimized the loss of user experience function. Furthermore, experiments in a puzzle game outperformed manual heuristics made by game designers.

On the other hand, the work presented by Rosa et al. [14] had the development of a hybrid DDA, including performance and affective data, for a platform game. This work investigated if the DDA mechanism appropriately adapted its difficulty level and kept the player in a state of flow. The three approaches (performance, affective and hybrid) were compared to verify the efficiency of each model, with the affective state of the player estimated through the electrodermal activity (EDA) of the skin.

The results indicated that the three DDA models were able to adjust the gameplay difficulty to the players when varying platform size. Specifically about the performance-based DDA system, the variation of platform size and of jump height were tested independently and together, verifying the adequacy of difficulty in the adaptations. However, the improvement of the player's state of flow was not verified.

3   Methodology

The present work deals with the development of a DDA system for platform games. For this, it was performed the improvement of difficulty estimation methods, the definition of a technique to recognize player profiles and the application of DDA through categorized player profiles.

Thus, based on the studies of [2,4] a cyclic diagram of the DDA model was made (Fig. 1). There are four interconnected systems that refer to the raw data of the Player, the Monitoring of these metrics, and the corresponding Analysis and Control Systems of the components that will be adjusted.

This work updates the measurement of the difficulty based on platform components [12], and revisits the concepts and results for a system-based DDA [14], noting that all systems must be independently tested. For this context, metrics were determined to measure the flow state [6,9] and the player profile [8], based on the literature review and analysis of the participants' responses.

Several adaptations were made to the open-source game *The Explorer: 2D*, developed by *Unity Technologies*. Changes in the game were made to create

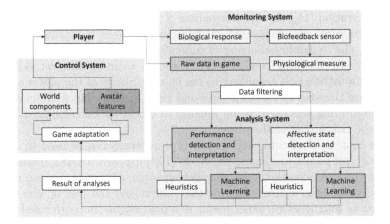

Fig. 1. Cyclic diagram of the system-oriented DDA.

levels, adjust game components to the proposal, implement communication with external tools, distribute for multiple devices, and enable game adaptation:

- Control System: adaptation of platform sizes on the horizontal and vertical axes (Fig. 2); of the avatar's jump height (Fig. 3); and of the combinations of these two adaptations.
- Analysis System: analysis based on heuristics, considering the difficulty experienced by the player; and based on the machine learning method by feed forward ANN, considering the difficulty experienced and the player's profile.

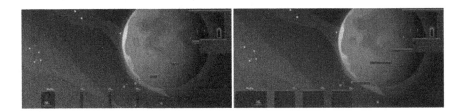

Fig. 2. Illustration of platform size adaptation, showing the original level and the adaptation that decreases the difficulty level.

In addition, the efficiency of computational methods that estimate the game difficulty was evaluated. For that, the platform difficulty was computed from the probability of success of a jump [12,14]. The jump corresponds to a parabola and the probability of success comes from the horizontal and vertical error of the parabola from an origin point in relation to a given end point. Besides, based on equations of kinematic physics, new jump configurations were included: jump

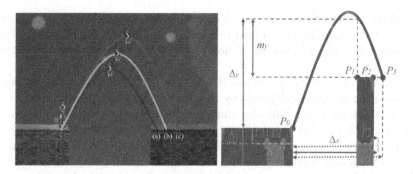

Fig. 3. Illustration of the difference in difficulty for jump height, being (a) minimum jump height, (b) medium and (c) maximum. Followed by an updated graphical representation of the jump's margin of error.

impulse speed, variation of angle or direction in the jump, and platforms with an end before the point of the jump parabola destination, as shown in Fig. 3.

Further, it was sought to cover the difficulty for game components other than platforms. These difficulties were calculated by the inverse of the sum of the component's characteristic attributes, such as enemy health and attack range, the space occupied by a trap, and the distance to be covered by a mobile object. Having measured each individual component difficulty, the level difficulty is calculated by multiplying the average component difficulty and a inverse proportion of the number of components, prioritizing the global mean while still considering the level size. In this way, the method is able to calculate the total difficulty of a level for any platform game, associating generic components of multiple platform sub-genres (platforms, obstacles, movement aids, collectibles and triggers), as described by Smith [15].

Considering the robustness of the DDA method, rules were defined for the Control System, such as the equal prioritization of changes on the x and y axes, and the change of origin according to the nearest point. Also, adaptations must have spatial limits to maintain design standards, avoid conflicts in the map, and prevent the existence of unreachable components.

The focus of the study was on tailoring the difficulty to each player and keeping it in a state of flow when investigating DDA models in platform games. It is observed that smaller platforms or shorter distances between platforms, and smaller jump heights represent greater difficulty. With that, the game was modified based on the data related to the prediction of the difficulty experienced by the player, and the general progression of the difficulty was fixed for a heuristics model and made from the categorization of the player between player profiles of the Hexad model [10] for a ANN model.

While data was captured and analyzed in real time, the adaptation was applied only before the start of the level or when the player died to avoid the DDA from being too noticeable to the player. If the player experience was considered harder than the desired for the level by the Analysis System, the Control System adapted the level to be easier, and vice versa. Also, the individual components were adapted by adding the difference between its estimated difficulty and the experienced difficulty to prevent outliers, such as ten easy components and one very difficult.

In both models, the experienced difficulty was determined based on death rate, execution of successful jumps by the player, and time played in a level. In the heuristics model, this difficulty varies according to the sum of the inverse of the number of levels (for the difficulty progression) raised by the inverse of the three input variables (to express the difficulty based on the player performance).

The ANN model used a supervised learning method for classification. Thus, a feed forward ANN was encoded with three attributes in the input layer and one attribute in the output layer (experienced difficulty or player profile). ANN training was performed with the backpropagation algorithm and the sigmoid activation function, considering the data scale always between 0 and 1 and running 1000 times with the learning rate updated according to the sum of squared errors.

Moreover, the Hexad model associates systems with user personalities and is based on studies on human motivation and types of players, having a significant association with the Big Five global personality factors model [7]. In this context, there are six types of profiles [16]: Achiever (motivated by mastery); Socialiser (by relatedness); Philanthropist (by purpose); Free Spirit (by autonomy); Player (by reward); and Disruptor (by change).

The player profile was limited to the Free Spirit or Achiever profiles of the Hexad model. Considering that players of the Achiever profile seek mastery, they prefer a greater challenge in the game compared to Free Spirit players. Thus, the player profile was determined considering proximity to Achiever over Free Spirit from input data of the amount of collectibles gathered, the execution of ranged attacks compared to melee attacks, and the time walking towards the level exit, without exploration. This value was used to determine how much the difficulty should progress when starting each level in the ANN model.

4   Experiments

Three experiments were conducted, with remote execution (whether on a computer or mobile phone) and participation of players with different skill levels and familiarity with games. The first test intended to verify the improvement made in the difficulty estimation method that involves more platform configurations and other components of the genre. In addition, the objective was to investigate the efficiency of computational methods to recognize the player profiles of the Hexad model and the difficulty experienced in this work, statistically correlating the extracted game data with the actions of the players.

Therefore, the game contained 8 levels, testing different components and difficulty situations for platform games. The levels were planned to contain generic platform game components in order to ascertain their difficulty. Fifty-one volunteers aged between 15 and 55 years participated in the experiment. Additionally, data from this test were used to train the neural network.

The second test aimed to apply more robust metrics to the performance-based DDA, verifying whether the system keeps the player in a state of flow and has a better result in adapting the difficulty to the user. The comparison tests of DDA Control System models needed to stimulate different reactions, testing metrics and perception instruments.

For this, the game presented 10 levels with extremes of difficulty, as the questionnaires related to the state of flow did not have significant differences between the DDA models tested in [14]. That is, by presenting levels alternating between easy and difficult, it is expected to avoid co-variance between the difficulty progression of the level design and the adaptations performed by the Control System.

Four adaptation models in the Control System were compared: (1) without the application of DDA, (2) with platform size adaptation, (3) with jump height adaptation and (4) with combined platform size and jump height adaptation. 112 volunteers participated in this experiment, 28 for each model tested, with ages ranging from 15 to 55 years. In this context, the following hypothesis was verified for the proposed models:

Theorem 1. *A DDA system combining platform and jump height adaptation provides adequate difficulty and keeps the player in a state of flow.*

In the third test, the objective was to use machine learning to improve the DDA Analysis System by recognizing the player profile and estimating the difficulty. Thus, it was verified the ability of a DDA system to integrate machine learning and use characteristics of the player's profile to keep the player in a state of flow and reduce the dispersion between the performance of different players.

The game presented 8 levels with extremes of difficulty and three models of the Analysis System were compared: (1) without the application of DDA, (2) with analysis based on heuristics and (3) with analysis based on machine learning. 69 volunteers participated, with 23 testing each model and ages ranging from 18 to 45. It is noted that only one model in the Control System was applied, being the combined DDA of platform size and jump height adaptation. Thus, the following hypothesis was defined:

Theorem 2. *A DDA system with machine learning, that defines the adaptations by the difficulty experienced and by the player's profile, provides adequate difficulty and keeps the player in a state of flow.*

All tests had questionnaires, applied at the beginning and end of the game session to, respectively, capture sociodemographic data and verify the hypotheses of each experiment. The first level of each test was a tutorial, with due attention to present different components and without the application of DDA. Furthermore, each experiment had different volunteers and the test conditions were specified beforehand to ensure that participants had the same information and chances to complete the game.

5   Discussion

5.1   Investigation of Difficulty Estimation and Player Data

In the first experiment, the player was asked to describe the difficulty experienced in the level numerically in values from 0 to 10 at the end of each level, as shown in Fig. 4. The estimated difficulty and that obtained by the average informed by the players have less difference between their values in the new method, with the estimated values always within the first and third quartiles reported by the participants. Thus, it shows that they maintain a significant proportion, with results superior to those presented by the previous method of [14].

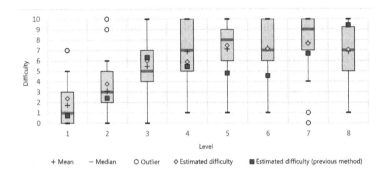

Fig. 4. Box-plot with the average difficulties informed in the questionnaire and the values estimated by algorithms in the first experiment.

It is also observed that the percentage of participants who complete a level decreases in cases of high difficulty or with the presence of puzzles, and the DDA aims to reduce the number of dropouts. Moreover, other metrics were measured at the end of each level, following the standard Likert scale with values between 1 and 7. Among the data analyzed, it was found that when too easy or too difficult, boredom and frustration increased for the average player, needing to maintain a standard of difficulty according to the player's skills.

For this, a selection of resources supervised by filtering with numerical input and categorical output (Free Spirit or Achiever) was performed using ANOVA selection. All game data were tested and the most relevant statistical tests obtained to predict the profiles were: percentage of collectibles gathered, time walking in the opposite direction to the end and number of ranged attacks.

These actions are related to the exploration and mastery profile, with the player using the game time to perform more activities in the level and to carry out actions in a planned way. Therefore, it was possible to identify performance variables that are significantly related to Free Spirit or Achiever profiles, which were used in the neural network.

Additionally, a supervised selection of resources was made with data related to the difficulty experienced by the player, with numerical input and output (difficulty between 0 and 1) and using the Pearson selection. All game data were tested and the most relevant statistical tests were obtained for: percentage of successful jumps, time played and death rate. Thus, these parameters can predict the difficulty experienced by players, usable in heuristics and in the neural network of the DDA Analysis System for subsequent tests.

5.2   Comparison Between DDA Control System Models

In the second experiment, the adequacy of the difficulty was confirmed in relation to the decrease in the dispersion of the performance of different players. In this sense, the variation of all data collected from the game was investigated, observing that the averages improved and had less deviation when a DDA model was used, as seen in Fig. 5.

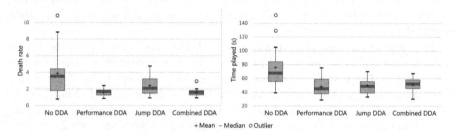

Fig. 5. Box-plot with average death rate and time played per level by participants in the second experiment, divided by the DDA Control System model.

The death rate and time played averages were always smaller and the successful jumps average higher when applying some DDA model, especially the platform DDA. While the performance improvement is generally positive for players, this is not a direct indication that the model is better than others. A game can only facilitate so that it always gets better results from the players. In turn, the decrease in dispersion between performances is a more complex factor to be achieved, as it is directly dependent on the players' skills.

To compare the means between the 4 groups, the ANOVA technique was used, with a significance level of 0.05. Thus, all values obtained significant variation between means, with the hypothesis that the difficulties are equal rejected in multiple cases, such as the proportion of successful jumps, the death rate and the average time played for each level by the participants. It shows that the combined DDA was the one that presented the lowest deviation among all the models for all the collected data, followed by the platform DDA, the jump DDA and, in the end, without DDA.

Moreover, there was a higher number of completed levels (ending without using the function to give up the level) when using combined DDA (98%) compared to platform DDA (96%), jump DDA (90%) and without DDA (87%). This indicates that the application of performance adjustments can be associated with players' resilience.

At the end of the game session, questions were asked about the players' experience, difficulty adequacy and flow state. It was noted that the means were significantly different when using the ANOVA technique with a significance level of 0.05. First, it was verified how the players described their own performance, with the best averages for the platform (5.52) and combined (5.42) DDA than of the game without DDA (4.47). For participants with a predilection for games with easy difficulty, the difference was more significant when comparing the game without DDA (2.66) with the platform (4.25), jump (5) and combined (5) DDA.

The greatest fun happened in the game with platform DDA (5.47), followed by the jump DDA and combined DDA (5.05), and without DDA (4.64). Also, the lowest boredom and frustration were with the platform DDA (2.87; 2.47), followed by the combined DDA (3.10; 3.10), without DDA (3.35; 3.94), and the jump DDA (3.88; 4.17). It is noted that the jump DDA may not be ideal for use in future tests as it had a negative impact on users' responses, while the other models demonstrate consistency.

To compare the difficulty, it was asked whether the game suited the user's skills and the difficulty increased progressively. The results were worse for the game without DDA (3.17; 4.11) and better for the platform DDA (5.26; 5.47). When analyzing the flow state, it was asked if the player worried about failing, had control of his actions, lost track of time, had automatic actions, and was focused on the game. The means without DDA (5.41; 3.88; 2.88; 4.82; 3.88) were worse in all questions, with the best results varying for each question between models, mostly in the combined DDA (4.10; 5.79; 4.05; 5.47; 5.53).

Theorem 1 was confirmed by providing adequate difficulty and keeping players in a state of flow in a game with a model combining adaptation of platform size and jump height. In this sense, there was significance in the difference between means for the flow state, which had not occurred in the tests of [14]. That is, the adaptations were not causing significant variance in the results related to the flow state in such tests due to the stimulus provided by the levels not having a significant difference. This change was successful and made it possible to corroborate the flow state measurement format through questionnaires and game data.

5.3   Comparison Between DDA Analysis System Models

In the third experiment, the suitability of the difficulty for the different models of the Analysis System was verified. Thus, all data collected from the game was analyzed in order to identify if there was less dispersion for the DDA models. The data that had the greatest decrease in dispersion and improvement in the average of the participants were for the percentage of successful jumps, percentage of collectibles gathered, death rate and time played, shown in Fig. 6.

To compare the means between the 3 groups, the ANOVA technique was used, with a significance level of 0.05. All values obtained significant variation between means, and the hypothesis that the difficulties are equal was rejected.

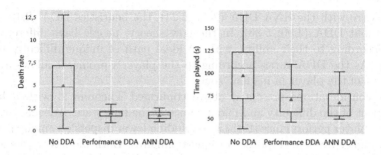

Fig. 6. Box-plot with average death rate and time played per level by participants in the third experiment, divided by the DDA Analysis System model.

Specifically on the death rate and the time played, it had a greater reduction in the average to complete each level and a smaller dispersion when the ANN model was applied compared to the other models.

One data that improved only with the neural network DDA was the percentage of collectibles gathered, which associates with the adequacy of the challenge progression by the player's profile and correlated motivation to complete additional tasks in the levels. Furthermore, there was a higher number of completed levels when using the ANN model (98%) compared to the heuristics model (95%) e without DDA (87%).

Analyzing specific profiles, it was noted that the percentage of successful jumps is higher for players of the Achiever profile when no DDA is applied and that this average increases for both profiles (Achiever and Free Spirit) when a DDA model is applied. It is also observed that the heuristics DDA maintains a wide variation in the percentage of collectibles gathered for the Free Spirit profile, although there is improvement for the Achiever profile. However, this is improved and have less dispersion for both profiles by applying neural network DDA.

The same questionnaire of the second experiment was applied at the end of the game, with all the means being significantly different when using the ANOVA technique with a significance level of 0.05. In first instance, it was investigated how the players described their own performance, with the ANN model having a higher average (6.36) than the heuristics (5.65) and without DDA (4.24).

Regarding difficulty, the dispersion was lower and the results were better for the ANN model referring to adequacy and progression (6.53; 6.05) compared to the heuristics model (5.83; 5.81) and without DDA (3.12; 2.92). The questions referring to the state of flow (worry about failing, control of actions, loss of track of time, automatic actions, and focus on game) were also worse in all questions without DDA (5.23; 3.37; 2.79; 3.80; 4.01), with the best results being for the ANN model (2.81; 6.34; 6.56; 6.72; 6.61) than of the heuristics model (3.22; 5.43; 5.66; 5.87; 5.04).

Fun occurred more in the game with RNA DDA (6.53), than by the heuristics DDA (6.06) and without DDA (4.12). Moreover, the lowest boredom and frustration were with the RNA DDA (2.12; 2.24), the heuristics DDA (2.12; 2.54) and without DDA (4.00; 5.36). In the flow theory, people have different flow zones according to their ability, with no ideal path of unique difficulty in the activity. As the DDA varies according to the player's profile, it allows a more precise fit of the player in his flow zone.

The considerations presented above confirmed Theorem 2, with a better adjustment of the difficulty and maintenance of the flow state. Adequacy can be noted by player performance statistics, including lower dispersion among players, and by higher average responses on questionnaires. Both models were successful in their proposal, but there were superior results with the neural network Analysis System adapting the progression by the player's profile.

6   Conclusion

Studies of Dynamic Difficulty Adjustment are growing in scope of themes and works carried out. However, few researches adapt as part of a game system or include characteristics of player profiles for adaptation. Therefore, this work proposed improvements to methods of difficulty estimation and player profile prediction for usage in a DDA system.

The focus was on tailoring the difficulty to each player and keeping it in a state of flow when investigating DDA models in platform games. With that, the game was modified based on the data related to the prediction of the difficulty experienced by the player and the general progression of the difficulty was made from the categorization of the player between the Free Spirit and Achiever profiles of the Hexad model.

From the analyzed results, the DDA system was capable of adapting the difficulty and keeping the player in a state of flow for a platform game, with reduced performance dispersion among players and improved responses given by participants regarding flow and difficulty adequacy and progression, with a significant difference between means. In particular, the difficulty was found to be more adequate when using models that only adapt platforms or that combine the adaptation of platforms and the jump height.

In turn, it was found that a DDA system, with analysis performed by a feed forward ANN, is capable of adjusting the difficulty and keeping the player in a state of flow for a platform game when applying characteristics of the player profile for progression of difficulty. In this context, a decrease in the dispersion of player performance and an improvement in the answers regarding the flow and difficulty were observed, with a significant difference between means and better results for the model with neural network than with heuristics analysis. It was also verified that performance can be superior with DDA, including a higher frequency of players completing levels.

Future work include adaptation with affective state captured by different physiological signals and the usage of machine learning techniques for analysis. Furthermore, other neural network models and machine learning methods can be tested and compared to predict the player profile and the difficulty experienced.

The difficulty can be also analyzed as influenced by the design of the game, with the investigation of puzzles, specific missions and content that challenge the player. Finally, adaptability can be applied in other contexts, such as players' health, where DDA can be integrated in studies that apply games to rehabilitation, memory training or increase of attention, for instance.

References

1. Andrade, G., Ramalho, G., Gomes, A.S., Corruble, V.: Dynamic game balancing: an evaluation of user satisfaction. American Association for Artificial Intelligence (2006)
2. Bontchev, B.: Adaptation in affective video games: a literature review. Cybern. Inf. Technol. **16**(3), 3–34 (2016)
3. Chang, D.M.J.: Dynamic difficulty adjustment in computer games. In: Proceedings of the 11th Annual Interactive Multimedia Systems Conference (2013)
4. Chen, J.: Flow in games (and everything else). ACM Mag. **50**(4), 31–34 (2007)
5. Hawkins, G., Nesbitt, K., Brown, S.D.: Dynamic difficulty balancing for cautious players and risk takers. Int. J. Comput. Games Technol. **2012**, 1–10 (2012)
6. Jackson, S., Marsh, H.: Development and validation of a scale to measure optimal experience: the flow state scale. J. Sport Exerc. Psychol. **18**, 17–35 (1996)
7. John, O.P., Srivastava, S.: The big five trait taxonomy: history, measurement, and theoretical perspectives. In: Handbook of Personality: Theory and Research, pp. 102–138 (1999)
8. Krath, J., von Korflesch, H.F.O.: Player types and game element preferences: investigating the relationship with the gamification user types HEXAD scale. In: Fang, X. (ed.) HCII 2021. LNCS, vol. 12789, pp. 219–238. Springer, Cham (2021). https://doi.org/10.1007/978-3-030-77277-2_18
9. Kyriazos, T., Stalikas, A., Prassa, K., Galanakis, M., Flora, K., Chatzilia, V.: The flow short scale (fss) dimensionality and what mimic shows on heterogeneity and invariance. Psychology **9**, 1357–1382 (2018)
10. Marczewski, A.: User types. In: Even Ninja Monkeys Like to Play: Gamification, Game Thinking, and Motivational Design, pp. 65–80 (2015)
11. Mourato, F.J.S.V., Birra, F., Santos, M.P.: Difficulty in action based challenges: success prediction, players' strategies and profiling. In: Proceedings of the 11th Conference on Advances in Computer Entertainment Technology, pp. 1–10 (2014)
12. Mourato, F.J.S.V., Santos, M.P.: Measuring difficulty in platform videogames. In: 4ª Conferência Nacional em Interação Pessoa-Máquina (2010)
13. Or, D.B., Kolomenkin, M., Shabat, G.: DL-DDA - deep learning based dynamic difficulty adjustment with UX and gameplay constraints. In: 2021 IEEE Conference on Games (CoG), pp. 1–7 (2021)
14. Rosa, M.P.C., et al.: Dynamic difficulty adjustment using performance and affective data in a platform game. In: Stephanidis, C., et al. (eds.) HCII 2021. LNCS, vol. 13094, pp. 367–386. Springer, Cham (2021). https://doi.org/10.1007/978-3-030-90238-4_26

15. Smith, G., Cha, M., Whitehead, J.: A framework for analysis of 2D platformer levels. In: Sandbox 2008 Proceedings of the 2008 ACM SIGGRAPH Symposium on Video Games, pp. 75–80 (2008)
16. Tondello, G., Wehbe, R., Diamond, L., Busch, M., Marczewski, A., Nacke, L.: The gamification user types Hexad scale. In:Proceedings of the 2016 Annual Symposium on Computer-Human Interaction in Play, pp. 229–243 (2016)
17. Zohaib, M.: Dynamic difficulty adjustment (dda) in computer games: a review. In: Advances in Human-Computer Interaction, pp. 1–12 (11 2018)

A Data-Driven Classification of Video Game Vocabulary

Nicolas Grelier[✉] and Stéphane Kaufmann

Focus Entertainment, Paris, France
{nicolas.grelier,stephane.kaufmann}@focusent.com

Abstract. As the video game industry is a novel and fast-changing field, it is not yet clearly understood how players speak about games. We use the user-generated tags of the video game digital distribution service Steam to better understand what words are essential to players for describing a game. Our method is data-driven as we consider for each game on Steam how many players assigned each tag to it. We introduce a new metric, the priority of a Steam tag, that we find interesting in itself. This enables us to categorise Steam tags based on their importance in describing games according to players.

Keywords: Taxonomy · Steam tags · Players

1 Introduction

In the last two decades, game analytics has gained a lot of interest [15]. According to Su, Backlund and Engström, "game analytics is the process of identifying and communicating meaningful patterns that can be used for game decision making" [15]. They present a classification of game analytics into four groups: game development analytics, game publishing analytics, game distribution channel analytics and game player analytics. In this paper, we focus on game player analytics. Our aim is to understand the vocabulary used by players to speak about video games. More precisely, we are interested in finding what are the most important words for describing video games according to players.

In our study, we rely exclusively on Steam tags: groups of words that players can freely assign to games. Some examples are *Strategy*, *Card Battler*, *Agriculture*, *Ninja*, *Difficult* and *Free to Play*. In total, as of May 2023, there exist 427 Steam tags. For a more comprehensive explanation of Steam tags, please refer to Subsect. 1.3.

1.1 From Beliefs to Facts

In [4], Drachen *et al.* observe that game analytics "is in its infancy and the available knowledge is heavily fragmented, not the least due to Game Analytics interdisciplinary nature and the lack of knowledge sharing between academia

P. Ciancarini et al. (Eds.): ICEC 2023, LNCS 14455, pp. 17–30, 2023.
https://doi.org/10.1007/978-981-99-8248-6_2

and industry". They add that "the root cause of these problems is the lack of a framework for organizing current knowledge and prioritising interesting problems" [4]. They introduce the concept of *stylised facts* for mobile game analytics (although we believe that the concept is essential to game analytics in general) in order to better connect industry and academia.

However, they argue that the available knowledge and data are too fragmented and incomplete to establish stylised facts. Thus, they introduce two "proto-stylised fact concepts which describe situations where less empirical validation is available: *beliefs* and *hypothetical stylised facts*" [4]. The aim is to "provide a roadmap for structuring current knowledge and building towards a situation where stylised facts can be generated and validated". Beliefs are statements supported by virtually no empirical evidence, whereas hypothetical stylised facts are supported by some empirical evidence. However, they are still not stylised facts, since "while there may be some available empirical evidence supporting these hypothetical stylised facts, it is clearly not enough to rigorously, generally, support them". Establishing hypothetical stylised facts help in obtaining stylised fact, which is essential for the research field (see [4] for a detailed argumentation).

In this paper, we provide empirical evidence for a hypothetical stylised fact. We aim at presenting our findings in a quantitative manner, and to provide an interpretation of the metric we introduce.

1.2 Taxonomy Definition

In Sect. 3, we present a data-driven taxonomy of all Steam tags. This consists in doing a hierarchical classification, where we divide the tags into categories, referred to as "taxa". We classify Steam tags based on their importance in describing games, and propose ideas on how to further refine the taxonomy into subcategories in future work.

1.3 The Steam Tags

In this paper, we rely solely on Steam data. More precisely, we study the user-generated tags on Steam. As of May 2023, there exists a total of 427 tags that players have assigned to the 50757 games in Steam. Those tags, consisting of groups of words or acronyms like *Action RPG*, *MOBA* or *Open World*, are freely assigned to games by players, who can also invent new ones. Steam provides a taxonomy of Steam tags [14], on which we rely in Sect. 3 for identifying what tags are considered as genre tags.

There exist many papers relying on Steam data, for instance Steam players reviews [7,10,11,13,18] or Steam user accounts [2,3,8,12]. Some of these studies use Steam tags, but they are only used as tools for filtering games, and are not the topic of study. To the best of our knowledge, there are only three papers that truly study Steam tags per se. First, Windleharth *et al.* do in [17] a conceptual analysis of Steam tags. They discuss and classify Steam tags into categories, some containing many elements like Gameplay genre, and some containing only one element like Relationships which contains only the tag *Remake*. A second paper that studies Steam tags is [6], in which Li and Zhang examine how genre tags are related to each other. Finally, in [5], Li uses correlation between Steam tags related to gameplay to obtain a list of 29 "factors". Those factors are not necessarily Steam tags but rather groups of highly correlated Steam tags. For instance, the factor *Rogue* contains the Steam tags *Dungeon Crawler*, *Rogue-like* and *Rogue-lite*. We argue in Sect. 2 why the notion of priority of Steam tags that we introduce in this paper can be beneficial to their studies, as it is more reliable and interpretable.

All players are free to assign to games some of the already-existing Steam tags, or even to add new ones. For a game, Steam shows "tags that were applied to the product by the most users". Steam shows at most 20 tags for any game, sorted by decreasing order of number of players who assigned the tag. The exact number of players who assigned a tag is not directly shown on Steam, but can be found in the page source code. To obtain the data of how many players assigned a tag to a game, we used SteamSpy's API.

1.4   Our Contributions

Our research aims to answer the following questions:

- What metric can be used to measure the importance of a Steam tag in describing video games?
- How can we identify which Steam tags are considered essential by the Steam community using data-driven methods?

We are interested in these questions because understanding player community language benefits developers' communication about their games. Gaining insights into crucial topics with high player impact is advantageous even in early game creation.

In Sect. 2, we introduce the new metric "tag priority" that gauges a tag's importance in describing a game. We present a hypothetical stylised fact that tags with high priority are seen as essential by players (see Sect. 2 for the formal definition and statement of the fact). Conversely, tags with low priority are interesting to players but not crucial for describing the game. We observe that most essential tags are genres, along with a few additional ones. We conduct an analysis to understand the reasons behind the essentiality of these tags. Surprisingly, we also note the existence of non-essential tags that are nonetheless assigned to most games.

1.5   Methodology

We introduce in Sect. 2 the priority of a Steam tag for a game. It is a natural candidate for a metric that would describe how essential a tag is. We note that there are two possible interpretations of this metric: the first is that it measures a tag's essentiality in describing a game, which is our desired outcome. The second interpretation is that it measures the strength of the consensus that the tag is an appropriate descriptor for the game. We provide multiple examples where the second interpretation of the metric does not apply, which reinforces our argument that the priority score reflects a tag's essentiality. Thus, by demonstrating cases where the consensus-based interpretation is not applicable, we motivate the use of tag priority as a measure of a tag's importance in describing a game.

The tag priority metric assigns a score to a tag for a given game. To assess a tag's overall importance, we consider its priority across all games to which it is assigned. By plotting the priority histograms of the Steam tags we identify distinct patterns, which allows us to define a taxonomy of Steam tags according to their priority histograms over all games.

Although we were unable to provide an entirely algorithmic approach to categorise priority histograms, we developed an ad-hoc solution by evaluating the priority medians of tags across all games to which they are assigned. Using defined thresholds on priority medians, we categorise tags as low, medium, or high priority in our taxonomy of tag essentiality. Those thresholds were chosen by relying mainly on our own expertise of the video game industry. While acknowledging the subjective nature of our decision, we provide justifications for our threshold selections to the best of our ability.

2   The Priority of Steam Tags

In [6], Li and Zhang defines a graph that aims to accurately represent the Steam tags. There is one vertex per tag, and two tags are connected by an edge if they are both assigned to a same game. The edges are weighted according to how many games have both tags assigned to them. The authors discard some edges by using the "Narrow by tag" feature in Steam. We find the authors' results difficult to interpret due to their chosen methodology. First, it is not clear what the Steam "Narrow by tag" feature does. Additionally, the authors connect two tags T and T' with an edge even if for the game G to which they are both assigned, the tag T is the most assigned tag to G and T' is the least assigned tag to G, without discussing the rationale behind this decision. It seems wrong to us to connect the two tags with an edge since T is apparently essential for describing G whereas T' is not so much relevant.

In [5], Li computes correlation between tags. The analysis is more precise than in [6] since when a tag T is assigned to a game, a weight is associated to T. If for a given game G, the tag T is the tag most assigned to G, then T obtains a weight of 20. If G has 20 tags and T is the least assigned, it obtains a weight of 1. More generally, the n-th most assigned tag obtains a weight of $20 - n + 1$. We point out two issues. First, Li does not discuss whether it makes sense to use these weights, and how to interpret them. Secondly, the distributions of the number of players who assigned tag varies greatly over all games. For instance, the two most assigned tags to the game *HITMAN 2* are *Stealth* (10373 players) and *Assassin* (819 players). The ratios of the number of players for these tags is therefore $819/10373 \approx 0.08$. If we do the same with the game *Golf It!*, we find that the most assigned tag is *Multiplayer* (249 players) and the second most assigned is *Mini Golf* (243 players). This time, the ratio is $243/249 \approx 0.98$. With Li's method, those ratios would be $19/20 = 0.95$ for both games [5].

In this section, we define, interpret and study a new metric, that will be used in the next section for the taxonomy. It is a more refined version of what was proposed by Li [5]. For each Steam tag, we define what we call its *priority* for a given game.

Table 1. A fictional example of tags assigned to a game with their priorities

tag	number of players	priority
Adventure	1000	1
Puzzle	750	0.75
2D	500	0.5
Atmospheric	100	0.1
3D	0	0

Definition 1. The priority of a tag T for a given game G is a score that ranges from 0 to 1. Let t_T denote the number of players who assigned to the game G the tag T. Similarly, let $t_{\max}$ denote the maximum over all tags assigned to G of the number of players who assigned the tag. The priority of T for G is equal to $t_T/t_{\max}$. A fictional example is shown in Table 1.

In particular, any game with at least one tag has a tag with priority 1: the tag that was assigned to it by the largest number of players. If a tag was not among the 20 most assigned tags to a given game, then its priority is 0 (recall that Steam only shows the 20 most assigned tags). We choose this metric as we are interested in identifying how players think about games. Let us consider all positive priorities over all games and tags. We compute a mean of 0.60, a median of 0.61 and a standard deviation of 0.28. This shows that the priority contains some information, as the standard deviation is quite high. There are two compatible reasons as to why not all tags have the same priority for a given game G. First, it may be that some players assign much fewer tags than other players. This would imply that the tags with highest priority correspond to what players consider to be essential for describing G. The second reason would be that players do not perfectly agree on what tags are best suited to describe G. This second reason would imply that the tags with highest priority are what players agree upon for describing G, and that their opinions diverge on the tags with low (but non-zero) priority. We present several examples where the second reason cannot apply, demonstrating that the first reason is the primary factor. Based on this empirical evidence, we propose the following hypothetical stylised fact:

Hypothetical Stylised Fact 1. *For a given game G, the tags with highest priority correspond to what players consider to be the most essential for describing G.*

We provide empirical evidence supporting Hypothetical Stylised Fact 1. The fact is hypothetical as defined in [4] because our methods for supporting it cannot establish it for good. This could be done if we had access to a database of the tags assignment per player, but this is not publicly available.

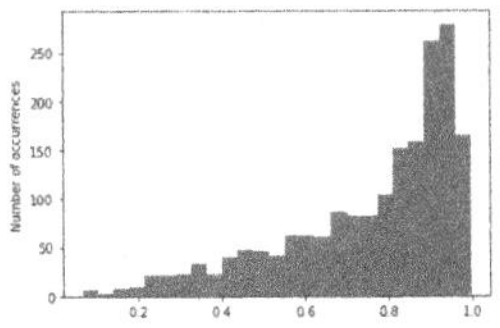

(a) Histogram of the ratios of the priority of *Shooter* over the one of *FPS* for the 1867 games whose *FPS* priority is higher than the one of *Shooter*.

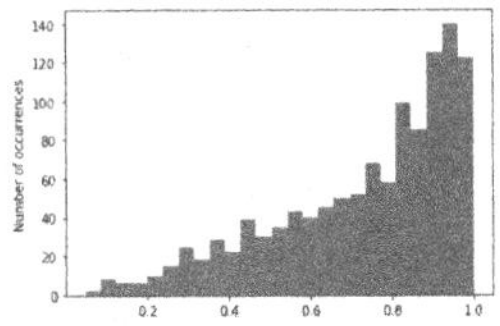

(b) Histogram of the ratios of the priority of *Co-op* over the one of *Online Co-Op* for the 1171 games whose *Online Co-Op* priority is higher than the one of *Co-op*.

Fig. 1. Some empirical evidence for Hypothetical Stylised Fact 1.

We consider two tags: *Shooter* and *FPS*. "FPS" stands for "first-person shooter", and is a subgenre of shooter game [1,16]. Therefore, anyone who thinks that a given game G is an FPS would also agree that it is a shooter game. We consider all of the 1867 games to which both tags *Shooter* and *FPS* are assigned, with *FPS* having the highest number of players. If Hypothetical Stylised Fact 1 were wrong, for each game we should have very similar priorities for both tags. Indeed, all players who assigned the tag *FPS* would also assign the tag *Shooter*. In contrast, we believe that some players assign only a few tags, corresponding to what they consider most essential. Under this hypothesis, we would expect some players to only assign the tag *FPS*, but not the tag *Shooter* as it is less important to them, or because they consider it to be already implied by the tag *FPS*. The histogram in Fig. 1a illustrates the ratios between the priority of *FPS* and *Shooter*. We observe a long tail phenomenon; also the mean is equal to 0.76 and the median to 0.83. This implies that for half of the considered games, less than 83% of those players who assigned the tag *FPS* also assigned the tag *Shooter*.

We apply the same method for the tags *Online Co-Op* and *Co-op*[1]. Obviously, a game with an online co-op mode thereby contains a co-op mode. However, when we consider the 1171 games to which both tags *Online Co-Op* and *Co-op* are assigned, with *Online Co-Op* having the highest number of players, we observe again a long tail phenomenon in Fig. 1b. The mean is equal to 0.73 and the median to 0.80. The natural explanation to this long tail phenomenon and to these low means and medians is Hypothetical Stylised Fact 1: Many players assign only a few tags to a game, selecting the ones they consider most essential. We have shown here the results for only two pairs of tags, for which the numbers of corresponding games were important (1867 and 1171, respectively). We tested other pairs, and for all of them we obtained similar results, but due to lack of space we do not show them here. Also, the number of games was significantly lower. Some examples of those pairs are *Top-Down Shooter* and *Top-Down* (655 games), *Football* and *Sports* (165 games), *Traditional Roguelike* and *Rogue-like*[2] (102 games).

We point out an issue that we discovered concerning the priority. Although we still believe the notion to be of interest, and that it brings useful information, we think that the notion could be refined and improved in future work. It seems that for some reason unknown to us, the priority of some tags behave erratically. Let us consider for instance the tag *Free to Play*. We consider three free to play games: *Dota 2*, *Team Fortress 2* and *Counter-Strike: Global Offensive*. For the first two games, *Free to Play* has a priority of 1. However, the second tag with highest priority for *Dota 2* is *MOBA* with a priority of 0.33, whereas for *Team Fortress 2* it is *Hero Shooter* with a priority of 0.99. It is quite intriguing to us how the priorities of the second tags with highest priorities can be so different. This phenomenon occur regularly with the tag *Free to Play*. We do not understand why the priority of the second most assigned tag can differ so much, when both games are equally free to play. We fear that for *Dota 2*, the tag *Free to Play* pushes all other priorities to very low values, thereby introducing noise in the data. Concerning *Counter-Strike: Global Offensive*, the priority of *Free to Play* is 0. The reason for this can be easily understood: The game was released in 2012 and made free to play only in 2018. We believe that the tags were mostly assigned soon after the release of the game, and that is why *Free to Play* is not amongst the 20 most assigned tags. This motivates even further the fact that the method should be refined, with a particular emphasis on the tag *Free to Play*.

3   A Taxonomy of Steam Tags

In this section, we categorise all of the Steam tags through a taxonomy. In Sect. 2, we defined the notion of priority of a tag for a game, and established

---

[1] Steam tags are case sensitive. We follow the Steam capitalisation which may differ from tag to tag.

[2] Once again we follow the spelling of Steam, where rogue-like is not always written with a hyphen.

that it contained some information. In particular, we gave empirical evidence for Hypothetical Stylised Fact 1, stating that for a given game G, tags with high priorities correspond to what players consider to be the most essential for describing G. In this section, we consider tags one by one, and for each tag we look at its priority distribution over all games for which the priority is non-zero. This allows us to define the taxa into which we classify the Steam tags.

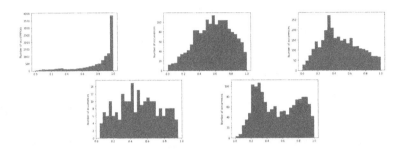

Fig. 2. Histograms of the priorities of *Strategy*, *Hand-drawn* and *Comedy* (Top); *Politics* and *PvE* (bottom).

Interestingly, the priority histograms of the Steam tags exhibit roughly five different shapes, out of the infinitely many shapes that could have occurred. We show them in Fig. 2. We find:

1. **Very high priority peak**: e.g. *Strategy* with a peak around a priority of 1. The number of occurrences decreases exponentially fast for lower priorities,
2. **Bell curves with high priority**: e.g. *Hand-drawn* whose histogram is similar to a bell curve centred around a priority of roughly 0.5,
3. **Bell curves with low priority**: e.g. *Comedy*, whose histogram is similar to a bell curve centred around a priority of roughly 0.4,
4. **Constant curves**: e.g. *Politics* with a rather uniform distribution,
5. **Two Phases**: e.g. *PvE* with two peaks in the histogram.

Thanks to Hypothetical stylised Fact 1, we infer that tags whose histograms are like the one of *Strategy* are exactly those that players consider essential for describing games. Up to a few exceptions, those tags are either not mentioned at all, or are the most assigned to a game. On the contrary, tags whose histograms are like the one of *Comedy* are those that players do not consider essential for describing games. While remaining tags may be essential for certain games, they are typically not among the most frequently assigned or least frequently assigned tags.

It seems not trivial to find an algorithm that would identify in which class does a tag belong using its priority histogram. This is a question that we leave for future work. However, recall that we are mainly interested in finding which tags are essential, and which tags are not, for players to describe games. Thus, in this paper we simplify our task, and divide the Steam tags into three taxa: High priority tags, Medium priority tags and Low priority tags.

3.1   Low Priority Tags

According to Hypothetical Stylised Fact 1, those tags correspond to what few players deem interesting for describing a game, and that is not essential. We define the taxon as the set of tags with a priority median of 0.45 or less. While we acknowledge that the choice of this threshold may not be perfectly justified, we offer a rationale to support it. In Steam's taxonomy [14], there is a taxon named *Themes & Moods*, mainly comprised of tags with the lowest priority medians. There is another taxon called *Features*, where the priority medians are close to the overall average of all Steam tags. The threshold of 0.45 provides a reasonable separation between these two taxa, exemplified by the *Themes & Moods* tag *Old School* with a priority median of 0.449275 and the *Features* tag *Tutorial* with a priority median of 0.450450. In total, there are 80 tags in the Low priority tag taxon.

Table 2. Tags with the lowest priority medians.

tag	priority median	number of games
Masterpiece	0.18	6
Epic	0.20	106
TrackIR	0.20	31
Vikings	0.22	45
Reboot	0.23	11
Mod	0.24	62
Addictive	0.24	409

Table 3. Low priority tags that are most assigned to games.

tag	priority median	number of games
Singleplayer	0.36	23376
Multiplayer	0.42	6371
Retro	0.43	4748
VR	0.44	4696
Difficult	0.39	4404
Great Soundtrack	0.31	4245
Co-op	0.39	3153

We present in Table 2 the tags with the lowest priority medians, along with the number of games to which they are assigned. One could argue that we do not have enough data to deal with tags that are assigned to very few games. However, for the taxon of Low priority tags, we think that if a tag was seldomly assigned, it supports even more the claim that this tag is not what players deem most essential for describing a game. Nonetheless, among the Low priority tags, there are some that are assigned to thousands of games. We show them in Table 3. We find those tags especially interesting. Players do not use those tags as their primary descriptors for a game, yet they are still assigned to many games. This gives us an interesting learning: Having a low priority does not mean that the tag applies only to a few games. It just means that the tag is not essential for describing a game.

3.2 High Priority Tags

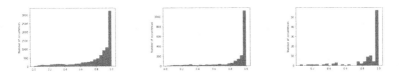

Fig. 3. Histograms of the priorities of *RPG*, *Racing* and *Roguelike Deckbuilder*.

Before defining the taxon of High priority tags, we first present in Fig. 3 a few more priority histograms of tags that are in this taxon. These histograms roughly look like Dirac functions centred at 1. We want to define our High priority tags taxon as the set of tags whose histograms look similarly to those three. We observe that all tags with such priority priority histogram that are related to gameplay are genre tags, and that nearly all tags commonly accepted as genre have such priority histograms. This is using the definition of genre tags from Steam's taxonomy [14]. In future work, we intend to investigate this phenomenon further and explore potential methods for subdividing this taxon into several subcategories, one of which will contain genre tags.

To allow for some wiggle room, we decided to define the taxon as the set of tags whose priority median is sufficiently high, at least 0.574803, and whose maximum value in the histogram is obtained for a priority of at least 0.765644. The median threshold was chosen so that the tag *Twin Stick Shooter* would be in that taxon, as its priority median is exactly that value, but not *Underground* and *Conversation* that were following. Indeed, *Twin Stick Shooter* is considered as a genre tag whereas the two others are not [14]. The maximum value threshold was chosen such that *Tabletop* would be a High priority tag, but not *2.5D* and *Lore-Rich* that were following. Likewise, *Tabletop* is a genre tag wheras the two others are not [14]. With this definition, we have 155 High priority tags.

3.3 Medium Priority Tags

We have one last taxon for all of the remaining 192 tags. Recall that Fig. 2 depicted five shapes of histograms, three of them corresponding to Medium priority tags. Figure 4 depicts other examples of histograms with such shapes. We have curves that look like bell curves, as with *2D*, curves that look rather constant, like the one of *Open World*, and curves with two peaks, like the one of *Choices Matter*.

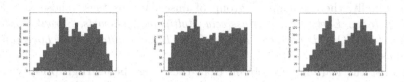

Fig. 4. Histograms of the priorities of *2D*, *Open World* and *Choices Matter*.

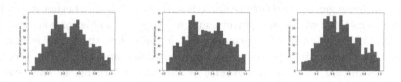

Fig. 5. Histograms of the priorities of *1990's*, *Military* and *Robots*.

In the list of tags with priority histograms similar to that of *Choices Matter*, we also find tags like *PvP*, *PvE* and *Turn-Based*. These tags share a common characteristic: They can be crucial features in some games while being less essential in others. For example, it is often the case in visual novels that *Choices Matter* is the most essential feature. However, in certain games, players have limited choices that may, for instance, only affect the ending cinematic. In these cases, choices still matter to some extent but are not the primary reason for playing the game. A similar pattern can be observed for tags like *PvP*, *PvE*, and *Turn-Based*. Therefore, we anticipate finding two categories of games for these tags: those in which they are essential and those in which they are not. This distinction is clearly reflected in their priority histograms, which exhibit two peaks. This further supports the validity of Hypothetical Stylised Fact 1.

We were not able to obtain further findings with the study of the two other shapes. Figure 5 depicts three histograms of other Medium priority tags. Observe that they are all similar to the one of *2D*. However, we do not see any similarity between *2D*, *1990's*, *Military* and *Robots* beyond the fact that they are Medium priority tags. It seems to us that in this case, the shape of the histogram does not bring us any further insight.

3.4   Some Interesting High Priority Tags

As mentioned in Subsect. 3.2, all High priority tags related to gameplay are genre names: *Adventure*, *RPG*, *Farming Sim* and so on. Furthermore, nearly all tags commonly understood as genre tags, for instance in Steam's tags taxonomy [14], are in the High priority tags taxon. We plan to examine this topic more closely in future work. In addition to genre tags, we find tags related to products that are not video games, e.g. *Utilities*, *Video Production*, *Audio Production*, and so on. Finally, there remains a group of miscellaneous tags. Those are: *Free to Play*, *Indie*, *Early Access*, *Massively Multiplayer*, *e-sports*, *Sexual Content*, *Nudity*, *LGBTQ+*, *Dinosaurs*, *Mechs*, *Cats*, *Experimental*, *Noir*, *Lovecraftian* and *Western*.

We list the learnings we obtain from these tags being High priority tags. Unsurprisingly, players care about whether the game is free. We indeed expect players to mind how much they have to pay for a game, which is why *Free to Play* is a High priority tag. Secondly, the tags *Indie*, *Early Access*, *Massively Multiplayer* and *e-sports* provide a lot of information about the type of game, even though those are not genres. Players know better how much money was invested into the game, whether the game is entirely finished, whether it involves a lot of interactions with other players, and whether it is made for e-sports. The latter tag in itself is full of information. It implies that the game is hard to master, that it has a multiplayer mode, and that it is competitive. The presence of the tags *Sexual Content* and *Nudity* is also not surprising, as they can be important filters for players to know whether they want to play a game. Next, we have the tags *LGBTQ+*, *Dinosaurs*, *Mechs* and *Cats*[3] which are themes that players think to be so important that they are worth mentioning right away when describing a game. Similarly, *Experimental*, *Noir*, *Lovecraftian* and *Western* are ambiances of high importance for players when describing a game. We believe that game developers can benefit from knowing that these themes and ambiances matter particularly to players.

4   Conclusion

We introduced the concept of priority of Steam tags and demonstrated its relationship to players' perceptions of games. Moreover, our approach enabled us to create a data-driven taxonomy about tags essentiality. We list some further improvements that can be made to our study. We stated that the notion of priority might need to be refined in order to be more consistent, by taking the example of the tag *Free to Play*. Although considering priority histograms allowed us to define an interesting taxonomy, this method has some limit. In future work, we plan on defining an algorithmic method that would identify the shape of a priority histogram. Furthermore, we observed that High priority tags related to gameplay are genre tags, and that nearly all tags commonly understood as genre tags are High priority tags. We plan on studying further this phenomenon. Lastly, it is important to acknowledge a limitation of our method, which is its inherent bias towards games available on Steam. We recognise that this bias may

---

[3] Interestingly, players are more interested in cats than in dogs. Indeed *Cats* has a median priority of 0.60 with a maximum value in the histogram at 0.96, whereas for the tag *Dog* those values are 0.56 and 0.45, respectively.

impact the generalisability of our findings. Also, we note that our computations assume an equal impact for all games. However, according to Orland [9], in 2014, over a quarter of registered games on Steam had never been played. Thus, we believe it would be beneficial to consider player engagement metrics, such as the number of players or total hours played, and to weight games accordingly in our computations.

References

1. Adams, E., Rollings, A.: Fundamentals of Game Design (Game Design and Development Series). Prentice-Hall, Inc. (2006)
2. Baumann, F., Emmert, D., Baumgartl, H., Buettner, R.: Hardcore gamer profiling: results from an unsupervised learning approach to playing behavior on the Steam platform. Procedia Comput. Sci. **126**, 1289–1297 (2018)
3. Becker, R., Chernihov, Y., Shavitt, Y., Zilberman, N.: An analysis of the Steam community network evolution. In: 2012 IEEE 27th Convention of Electrical and Electronics Engineers in Israel, pp. 1–5. IEEE (2012)
4. Drachen, A., Ross, N., Runge, J., Sifa, R.: Stylized facts for mobile game analytics. In: 2016 IEEE Conference on Computational Intelligence and Games (CIG), pp. 1–8. IEEE (2016)
5. Li, X.: Towards factor-oriented understanding of video game genres using exploratory factor analysis on Steam game tags. In: 2020 IEEE International Conference on Progress in Informatics and Computing (PIC), pp. 207–213. IEEE (2020)
6. Li, X., Zhang, B.: A preliminary network analysis on steam game tags: another way of understanding game genres. In: Proceedings of the 23rd International Conference on Academic Mindtrek, pp. 65–73 (2020)
7. Lin, D., Bezemer, C.P., Hassan, A.E.: An empirical study of early access games on the Steam platform. Empir. Softw. Eng. **23**(2), 771–799 (2018)
8. O'Neill, M., Vaziripour, E., Wu, J., Zappala, D.: Condensing steam: distilling the diversity of gamer behavior. In: Proceedings of the 2016 Internet Measurement Conference, pp. 81–95 (2016)
9. Orland, K.: Steam tags (2014). https://arstechnica.com/gaming/2014/04/steam-gauge-addressing-your-questions-and-concerns/
10. Petrosino, S., Loria, E., Kainz, A., Pirker, J.: The panorama of Steam multiplayer games (2018–2020): a player reviews analysis. In: FDG 2022: Proceedings of the 17th International Conference on the Foundations of Digital Games, pp. 1–7 (2022)
11. Pirker, J., Loria, E., Kainz, A., Kopf, J., Dengel, A.: Virtual reality and education-the Steam panorama. In: FDG 2022: Proceedings of the 17th International Conference on the Foundations of Digital Games, pp. 1–11 (2022)
12. Sifa, R., Drachen, A., Bauckhage, C.: Large-scale cross-game player behavior analysis on Steam. In: Eleventh Artificial Intelligence and Interactive Digital Entertainment Conference (2015)
13. Sobkowicz, A., Stokowiec, W.: Steam review dataset-new, large scale sentiment dataset. In: Proceedings of the Tenth International Conference on Language Resources and Evaluation (LREC 2016) Workshop Emotion and Sentiment Analysis, pp. 55–58 (2016)
14. Steamworks: Steam tags (2021). https://partner.steamgames.com/doc/store/tags#13

15. Su, Y., Backlund, P., Engström, H.: Comprehensive review and classification of game analytics. SOCA **15**(2), 141–156 (2021)

16. Voorhees, G.: Chapter 31: Shooting. In: Wolf, M.J., Perron, B. (eds.) The Routledge companion to video game studies, chap. 31, pp. 251–258 (2014)

17. Windleharth, T.W., Jett, J., Schmalz, M., Lee, J.H.: Full Steam ahead: a conceptual analysis of user-supplied tags on Steam. Cataloging Classif. Quart. **54**(7), 418–441 (2016)

18. Zuo, Z.: Sentiment analysis of steam review datasets using Naive Bayes and decision tree classifier (2018)

Prov-Replay: A Qualitative Analysis Framework for Gameplay Sessions Using Provenance and Replay

Leonardo Thurler[✉][ID], Sidney Melo[ID], Esteban Clua[ID], and Troy Kohwalter[ID]

Universidade Federal Fluminense, Niterói, Rio de Janeiro, Brazil
{lpthurler,sidneymelo}@id.uff.br, {esteban,troy}@ic.uff.br

Abstract. The usage of game data to analyze relevant information and possibilities about the game has been widely explored by academia and industry. Hence, numerous techniques exist for collecting data with distinct objectives. Among the strategies employed for analyzing gameplay sessions, the collection and analysis of provenance data emerge as prominent. In this paper, we improve provenance approaches through a Prov-Replay conceptual framework. Our framework uses provenance data providing an interactive provenance graph visualization synced with a replay to help to understand the context of gameplay events. To validate Prov-Replay, we applied this framework in an under-development commercial game, collecting real game session data and performing a test with the game developers.

Keywords: Game Provenance · Provenance Graph · Game Telemetry · Game Analysis · Provenance Graph Visualization · Game Replay · Unity

1 Introduction

Since the early 2000s, there has been significant interest in utilizing game data, commonly referred to as game telemetry, to explore valuable insights and opportunities related to a game. This attention has been observed in both academic and industry domains [1,2,4]. This strategy is being used for insights about many different game aspects like balancing game experience [20], behavioral analysis [15] and improving game monetization [4].

Kohwalter et al. [9] introduced a conceptual framework called Provenance in Games (PinG) as a means to leverage game telemetry. Their main objective is to collect provenance data that, when analyzed, is able to provide feedback to the developers and/or players, allowing them understand the cause-effect relations of players' decisions. Since then, there have been several works deepening and using these frameworks for various purposes [3,11,12,15,16]. Nevertheless, one of the major challenges encountered in studies involving the analysis of game

© IFIP International Federation for Information Processing 2023
Published by Springer Nature Switzerland AG 2023
P. Ciancarini et al. (Eds.): ICEC 2023, LNCS 14455, pp. 31–40, 2023.
https://doi.org/10.1007/978-981-99-8248-6_3

provenance graphs is the comprehension of the contextual information associated with the graph to understand the cause-effect relations. Motivated by this issue, the present work introduces Prov-Replay, a conceptual framework that suggests a new approach to analyze provenance graphs on games. This framework combines a provenance tracker module and provenance graph viewer controller integrated with a replay module, which is able to facilitate user analysis by visualizing both the provenance graph and game state in game space, allowing understanding of the entire context of a desired moment.

Our experiment results demonstrate that, when using our conceptual framework fundamentals, it is possible to improve both efficiency and effectiveness of qualitative analysis processes by providing effective ways to capture and access important information enabling a more informed qualitative analysis.

This paper is organized as follows: Sect. 2 presents some of the related work in the areas of game data analysis and visualization. Section 3 provides background information to present PinG conceptual framework and issues to consider when making a replay system. Sections 4 and 5 present our proposed Prov-Replay conceptual framework and its implementation through PinGU Replay. Section 6 presents the results of our case study. Finally, Sect. 7 presents our conclusions and some considerations for future work.

2   Related Work

Kleinman et al. detail various approaches to game data visualization in their work [8], emphasizing the significant growth of spatiotemporal visualization techniques. They highlight that such visualizations play a crucial role in assisting human analysts in deriving meaningful insights from context-sensitive information, providing positive reactions from users [7,14,22]. More closely to our proposal, Kuan et al. [14] presented a study with an analysis process with an interactive, spatiotemporal visualization system for analyzing battle information from StartCraft 2[1] Their analysis involved utilizing their custom-developed tools in conjunction with an official replay system provided by the game. However, this work is limited only to real-time strategy (RTS) games. Moreover, the presented information depends on an external tool and does not display the data inside the game space.

Kohwalter et al. [13] presented the ProvViewer[2], a visualization tool for provenance graphs generated using the PROV-N notation [19]. This tool displays data in a two-dimensional (2D) visualization and provides several options such as filters, merging, highlighting, and collapsing information that facilitates the visualization and analysis. Although ProvViewer provides visualization and facilitates data analysis, it also has some limitations, such as presenting all data collected from a 3D game space in a 2D visualization, making some information difficult to understand. Another limitation is the impossibility of verifying the state of game elements at a specific moment in the graph.

---

[1] https://starcraft2.com/.

[2] http://gems-uff.github.io/prov-viewer/.

3   Theoretical Background

Kohwalter et al. [3] provide an easy way to collect provenance data. They implemented the Provenance in Games for Unity (PinGU), a provenance gathering framework for the Unity[3] game engine based on the PROV model [6] and the PinG framework [9]. In the provenance context, there are three vertex types: Entities, Agents, and Activities. Entities represent objects without autonomous behavior, like items, weapons, and static obstacles in the environment. Agents represent objects capable of making decisions or have some responsibilities in the game, like players, enemies, and Non-playable characters (NPCs). Activities are actions or events that occur throughout the game. Edges within the graph represent the various types of relationships that can exist between vertex elements.

Wagner [21], Montville [18], and Engel [5] show some issues to consider when making a replay system. The two most popular approaches to making a replay system are: state-based and input-based. The state-based strategy captures a sequence of states from desired game elements. The input-based strategy consists of capturing an initial state from game elements and a sequence of inputs that can update their state values. Both strategies have advantages and disadvantages: the input-based needs less memory space than the state-based since it requires saving less information to reproduce replay. On the other hand, state-based is a more versatile strategy because it can be applied to non-deterministic and deterministic games.

4   Prov-Replay

In this paper, we propose a new conceptual framework named Prov-Replay to perform interactive analysis through gameplay sessions using spatiotemporal visualization techniques synchronized with replay. Our solution provides a visual representation of the provenance graph inside the game level space, allowing users to configure rules to interactivity manipulate the graph, making it possible to omit or highlight desired elements during the analysis process (Fig. 1).

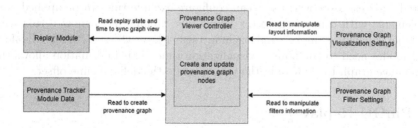

Fig. 1. Prov-Replay high-level architecture.

---

[3] https://unity.com/.

Our architecture has some key elements:

The **Replay module** can use any replay strategy, such as input-based or state-based, as detailed by Engel [5]. Still, the strategy needs to reproduce a faithful gameplay session replay. This is necessary to allow users to see the states of any objects that might impact the gameplay experience and player decisions, understanding the whole context information.

The **Provenance Tracker module** gathers provenance information about gameplay sessions. We use the existing PinG conceptual framework [9] to capture and store the provenance data.

The **Provenance Graph Viewer Controller** plays a crucial role in creating and updating provenance graph nodes that are synchronized with the replay. It also manages other elements involved in this process to enable the manipulation and visualization of the provenance graph.

The **Provenance Graph Visualization Settings** allows the user to configure and create presets with information for the graph layout, which provides functionalities to highlight desired elements using rules to colorize and resize provenance graph elements. The visualization strategy is based on using different shapes and colors for vertices. Vertices shape are used to map semantic concepts from the provenance: activities (rectangle), entities (circles), and agents (pentagons). Colors are used to highlight vertices and show edges' relationship intensity. The edge value, if any, defines the intensity and is more common on influences (i.e., relations with wasInfluencedBy type).

Provenance Graph Filter Settings allows the user to configure and create presets with information related to filters in the displayed graph. The filter provides functionalities that show or hide specific provenance graph elements using rules and time configurations. We created two filters mode: Exclude and Include. The *Exclude filter* mode uses a top-down visualization strategy, where the provenance graph excludes only information that matches user-configured rules and presents everything else. The user can configure much information to exclude, like vertex label, type, object name, object tag, edges relations (i.e., Source and Target), labels, type, and all vertex information linked by relation. The *Include filter* mode uses a bottom-up visualization strategy, where the provenance graph shows only information that matches user-configured rules. The user can configure vertex labels to show and define whether it displays relations that involve desired vertices. Moreover, users can configure exclude rules to be applied only on elements with configured vertex labels (i.e., Configure to show vertex with the label "SpawningSmoke" and exclude tags "Player02" and "SmokeMissile"). Both modes need to configure a visualization time. This information allows the provenance graph to show only the vertex inside the defined time offset.

5   PinGU Replay

In order to validate Prov-Replay, we created a visualization tool for the Unity game engine named PinGU Replay that incorporates the elements of our conceptual framework. Since Unity is not a deterministic game engine, we created a state-based replay module to reproduce a faithful replay. PinGU [10] is our provenance tracker module, so all provenance data of activities, agents, entities, and their relations are collected by PinGU and processed by the provenance graph viewer controller. These implementations are discussed in more detail in the following sections.

5.1 Replay Module

The ReplayController, plays a pivotal role in replay module. It handle the various tasks associated with recording and reproducing replays. It takes charge of processing replay readings, configuring the necessary settings, and creating saved objects. The configuration of the game replay storage data consists of four stages. *First stage* consist in identify and configure ReplayObject and Replay-Transform components on game objects that represent agents and entities. The *second stage* consists in creating a ReplaySettings scriptable. This file contains configurations to generate replay files, replay save data frequency, and reference to replay objects prefabs. The *third stage* creates a game object in the scene to act as a controller for the replay system. This game object will have two attached components: Replay Controller and Replay Data Serializer, which references the ReplaySettings. The *last stage* consists in updating code to use ReplayController methods to start and stop recording and save replay data into a file.

5.2 Provenance Graph Viewer Controller

This module uses PinGU provenance data to generate an interactive provenance graph and syncs this graph visualization with the replay module. To visualize the provenance graph, we must create a game object in the scene to act as a controller for the provenance graph viewer system. This game object is attached to the Provenance Graph Viewer Controller component, responsible for setting the PinGU provenance data and configure visualization and filter settings. Figure 2 illustrates examples using some layout and filter settings.

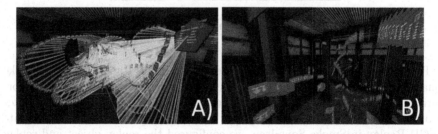

Fig. 2. A) Shows all provenance graph elements using exclude filter without any rule and custom color. B) Use include filter mode to show vertex with the label "Firing-MachineGun", and change color by vertex tag: "Player01" (red) and "Player02" (blue). (Color figure online)

6   Case Study

6.1   Research Hypotheses

In order to assess the efficiency and effectiveness of Prov-Replay, we formulated two research hypotheses (RH). Subsequently, we collected responses from game developers and conducted an analysis to validate our hypotheses.

- **RH 1** - The visualization of the graph with the replay provides more information about the context and allows more in-depth qualitative analysis;
- **RH 2** - Visualizing the provenance graph with the replay allows the user to quickly identify points with relevant events. Thus, users can visit them without watching and making notes about the entire session replay.

6.2   PinGU Replay Integration in Smoke Squadron and Data Collect

Smoke Squadron[4] is a local multiplayer arcade flight battle game under development by the indie game studio Ops Game Studio[5], which provided access to game source code to capture provenance data and realize experiments. The game match consists of players controlling a small remote airplane. Players must battle each other using machine guns, missiles, and a solid smoke trail that kills at touch. The match ends when one of the players loses all his lives (Fig. 3).

Fig. 3. Screenshot of Smoke Squadron game.

Previously, Melo et al. [17] integrated the PinGU framework into Smoke Squadron to collect provenance data. The study details all the provenance information that PinGU collects in this game, considering the most relevant attributes to our proposal the Label, Type, Date, Object Name, and Tag. To integrate PinGU Replay in Smoke Squadron, we configured the replay object and replay transform components on the following game elements: players' airplanes and pick-up items, Missiles, and Smokes.

---

[4] https://www.facebook.com/smokesquadrongame/.
[5] https://opsgamestudio.com/.

Following, we conducted a playtest with seven male players, aged between 22 and 34 years old, with intermediate to advanced skills in games. The playtest session lasted 4 h and generated 32 game sessions. We then manually selected two specific sessions that we considered that contain rich data to be analyzed by game developers. The first selected session had 114 s of duration, where both players were still learning how to play. The resulting provenance graph has 3422 edges and 2465 vertices. The second session has 343 s of duration, where both players were already more experienced in the game. Finally, the resulting provenance graph has 12749 edges and 8912 vertices.

6.3 Smoke Squadron Developers Using PinGU Replay

We conducted an analysis session with 3 Smoke Squadron game developers. Although they all know game design, their primary functions are 3D Artist, Programmer, and Game Designer/Producer. This distribution of primary functions allowed us to analyze the tool with three different and complementary user profiles. Each analysis session lasted 2 h and was divided into seven steps. We introduce participants to the experiment roadmap and objectives in the *first step*. In the *second step*, the participants had 15 min to analyze the first game session using only the replay module without any information about the provenance graph. In the *third step*, we introduce participants to provenance concepts and show how to use the interactive provenance graph module of PinGU Replay[6]. In the *fourth step*, the participants had 15 min to analyze the first game session again, but using replay with interactive provenance graph visualization; the objective of this step is for participants to confirm previously analyzed information and to acclimate themselves to how to use the visualization tool. In the *fifth step*, the participants had 30 min to analyze the second game session using all PinGU replay features. In the *sixth step*, the participants answered questions about their experience in analyzing the game using only the replay and using the replay with graph visualization, as well as the positive and negative aspects and how we could improve PinGU Replay. In the *final step*, we conducted a small interview to find out if they believed the tool could help them improve future projects they are developing.

6.4 Analyzing Game Developers' Answers

To evaluate Prov-Replay, we analyzed the responses of game developers and checked our defined hypotheses.

About **RH 1**, we claim that our approach provides a better understanding of game sessions. When using only the replay to analyze game sessions, all game developers remained in doubt about the causes of player deaths, whether players collected items, and whether the MachineGun weapon hit players. Due to this confusion, they answered some of these questions incorrectly, either because of a lack of clarity or not being able to observe the moment of the replay in

---

[6] https://drive.google.com/file/d/1GUUIUutwI9TN7lThpNvP9MfE6qkLkHNl/view.

which it happened. When they used provenance graph data and visualization with replay information, they could confirm their assumptions by filtering out all moments that these events happened during the game session and checking provenance relation. This allowed them to fix some of their responses and update their conclusions. Consequently, they agreed that the graph played a crucial role in enhancing their understanding of the context and confirming their initial assumptions. Regarding **RH 2**, our findings confirm that the utilization of provenance graph data and visualization facilitates the rapid identification of key points that contain significant events. As a result, this significantly assists users in their analysis process. When game developers analyzed the second session in the *fifth step*, two out of three developers started their analysis using the graph to visualize the desired information and answer the questions directly. In contrast, the other developer preferred to watch the entire replay to understand how the session went. However, as soon as the game developer started answering the questions, they also used the graph to see the desired moments and analyze them again. Furthermore, their answers confirmed that they all believe that the graph made it easier to locate the desired events and provided a faster way to find the moments that should be analyzed.

Furthermore, the developers expressed specific areas for improvement, with a primary focus on the process of provenance collection. This happens because a specialist, instead of the developers, instrumented the provenance collection. In an ideal scenario, this collection should be instrumented by the developers, making the analysis process even easier. However, another important point to note is that the developers were not aware of provenance in games, and even not knowing and not participating in the collection instrumentation, they managed to benefit from the tool even with little training. Other mentioned improvements were related to tool usability and performance.

7   Conclusion

In this paper, we presented and validated the Prov-Replay conceptual framework. We created PinGU Replay and applied it in Smoke Squadron, collecting real game session data and performing a test with the game developers.

Later, we analyzed game developers' answers to check our research hypotheses. After this analysis, we concluded that Prov-Replay could improve both efficiency and effectiveness of the qualitative analyses process since it provides means for better understanding of the whole game context information and easy identification of relevant events, which aids users' analysis process.

As future work, we intend to improve visualization performance, add more features in filter submodules such as automatic collapses, and implement all Prov-Replay features to be accessible at game runtime, allowing players to analyze game. We also intend to test different game genres.

References

1. Andersen, E., Liu, Y.E., Snider, R., Szeto, R., Popovic, Z.: Placing a value on aesthetics in online casual games, pp. 1275–1278 (2011). https://doi.org/10.1145/1978942.1979131
2. Calvo-Morata, A., Rotaru, D.C., Alonso-Fernández, C., Freire-Morán, M., Martínez-Ortiz, I., Fernández-Manjón, B.: Validation of a cyberbullying serious game using game analytics. IEEE Trans. Learn. Technol. 13(1), 186–197 (2020). https://doi.org/10.1109/TLT.2018.2879354
3. Costa Kohwalter, T., Gresta Paulino Murta, L., Walter Gonzalez Clua, E.: Capturing game telemetry with provenance. In: 2017 16th Brazilian Symposium on Computer Games and Digital Entertainment (SBGames), pp. 66–75 (2017). https://doi.org/10.1109/SBGames.2017.00016
4. El-Nasr, M., Drachen, A., Canossa, A.: Game Analytics: Maximizing the Value of Player Data (2013)
5. Engel, T.: Creating a replay system in unity (2020). https://www.kodeco.com/7728186-creating-a-replay-system-in-unity. Accessed 01 May 2023
6. Gil, Y., Miles, S.: Prov model primer (2010). https://www.w3.org/TR/prov-primer/. Accessed 01 May 2023
7. Halabi, N., Wallner, G., Mirza-Babaei, P.: Assessing the impact of visual design on the interpretation of aggregated playtesting data visualization. In: Proceedings of the Annual Symposium on Computer-Human Interaction in Play. CHI PLAY '19, pp. 639–650. Association for Computing Machinery, New York, NY, USA (2019). https://doi.org/10.1145/3311350.3347164
8. Kleinman, E., Preetham, N., Teng, Z., Bryant, A., Seif El-Nasr, M.: "what happened here!?" a taxonomy for user interaction with spatio-temporal game data visualization. Proc. ACM Hum.-Comput. Interact. 5(CHI PLAY) (2021). https://doi.org/10.1145/3474687
9. Kohwalter, T., Clua, E., Murta, L.: Provenance in games (2012)
10. Kohwalter, T., Clua, E., Murta, L.: Reinforcing software engineering learning through provenance, pp. 131–140 (2014). https://doi.org/10.1109/SBES.2014.16
11. Kohwalter, T., Figueira, F., Serdeiro, E., Da Silva Junior, J.R., Murta, L., Clua, E.: Understanding game sessions through provenance. Entertain. Comput. 27 (2018). https://doi.org/10.1016/j.entcom.2018.05.001
12. Kohwalter, T., Murta, L., Clua, E.: Provchastic: understanding and predicting game events using provenance (2020)
13. Kohwalter, T., Oliveira, T., Freire, J., Clua, E., Murta, L.: Prov viewer: a graph-based visualization tool for interactive exploration of provenance data, pp. 71–82 (2016). https://doi.org/10.1007/978-3-319-40593-3_6
14. Kuan, Y.T., Wang, Y.S., Chuang, J.H.: Visualizing real-time strategy games: the example of Starcraft II. In: 2017 IEEE Conference on Visual Analytics Science and Technology (VAST), pp. 71–80 (2017). https://doi.org/10.1109/VAST.2017.8585594
15. Melo, S., Kohwalter, T., Clua, E., Paes, A., Murta, L.: Player behavior profiling through provenance graphs and representation learning, pp. 1–11 (2020). https://doi.org/10.1145/3402942.3402961
16. Melo, S., Paes, A., Clua, E., Kohwalter, T., Murta, L.: Detecting long-range cause-effect relationships in game provenance graphs with graph-based representation learning. Entertain. Comput. 32, 100318 (2019). https://doi.org/10.1016/j.entcom.2019.100318

17. Melo, S.A., Clua, E., Paes, A.: Heterogeneous graph dataset with feature set inter-section through game provenance (2021)
18. Montville, A.: Implementing a replay system in unity and how I'd do it differently next time (2014). https://www.gamedeveloper.com/programming/implementing-a-replay-system-in-unity-and-how-i-d-do-it-differently-next-time. Accessed 01 May 2023
19. Moreau, L., Missier, P.: Prov-n: the provenance notation (2012). https://www.w3.org/TR/prov-n/. Accessed 01 May 2023
20. Pedersen, C., Togelius, J., Yannakakis, G.: Modeling player experience for content creation. IEEE Trans. Comput. Intell. AI Games **2**, 54–67 (2010). https://doi.org/10.1109/TCIAIG.2010.2043950
21. Wagner, C.: Developing your own replay system (2004). https://www.gamedeveloper.com/programming/developing-your-own-replay-system. Accessed 01 May 2023
22. Wallner, G., Halabi, N., Mirza-Babaei, P.: Aggregated visualization of playtesting data. In: Proceedings of the 2019 CHI Conference on Human Factors in Computing Systems. CHI '19, pp. 1–12. Association for Computing Machinery, New York, NY, USA (2019). https://doi.org/10.1145/3290605.3300593

Player Engagement and Analysis

Seligman's PERMA Model in Video Games – The Positive Influence of Video Games on Well-Being

Gary L. Wagener[✉] and André Melzer

University of Luxembourg, 11 Porte Des Sciences, 4366 Esch-sur-Alzette, Luxembourg
gary.wagener@uni.lu

Abstract. In the past, research on video games has focused on negative gaming aspects and its potential risks, particularly regarding players' well-being. Based on Seligman's PERMA model (2011), which links the fulfillment of different factors (*Positive Emotions, Engagement, Relationships, Meaning, Accomplishment*) to flourishing mental-health, the present research examined positive video game effects on the different PERMA factors and well-being. It investigated how well-being varies across gaming-related factors such as different player types (i.e., *High Performers, Casual Players, Highly Involved Players,* and *Crafters*) and time spent playing video games. Additionally, gender differences were assessed for time spent playing, video game status, and genre preferences. In an online-survey, 963 active gamers provided self-reports about their gaming habits, player characteristics, and well-being. Time spent playing video games was not related to well-being. Furthermore, Highly Involved Players had the significantly lowest scores on PERMA factors and well-being, which may have meaningful implications for future research on problematic gaming. There were no gender differences in playing time or the importance of video games in players' lives. However, there were some gender differences in genre preferences, with men preferring shooters and role-playing games, and women preferring more sandbox games or simulations. This is important as it suggests that the gender gap in active gamers may finally be closing, allowing women to benefit from the positive effects of video games just as much as men.

Keywords: PERMA model · well-being · video games · gender differences · player types

1 Introduction

In the past, research on video games has mainly focused on negative aspects of gaming (e.g., violent video game effects on aggression [2–7]) and the potential risks of video game exposure (e.g., problematic gaming [8]) [9]. However, there has also been a recent rise of research on positive aspects and effects on well-being of video game exposure [1, 10, 11].

"Gaming may be among the most efficient and effective means by which children and youth generate positive feelings" [1]

P. Ciancarini et al. (Eds.): ICEC 2023, LNCS 14455, pp. 43–58, 2023.
https://doi.org/10.1007/978-981-99-8248-6_4

This is becoming increasingly relevant with billions of video game players [12], and because even more people, across all demographics, started playing video games during the COVID-19 pandemic [13–15]. Therefore, it is important to look at VG effects, particularly regarding well-being and who may benefit from playing video games.

1.1 Video Games and Well-Being

In recent decades, there has been increased focus on the link between video game play and well-being, defined in the PERMA model (explained in more detail below) as a combination of positive emotions, engagement, positive relationships, meaning, and accomplishment [16]. For example, a study by Johannes and colleagues, using a combination of objective player data and self-reports, found a positive relationship between interactive exposure to casual video games and affective well-being [17]. However, the motivation why people play video games, and their need satisfaction from playing, were closely related to well-being [17]. Other research found a positive relationship between moderate gameplay (7 to 10 h per week) and mental-health [10, 18]. People who scarcely play or do not play at all (0 to 6 h per week) do not receive the positive benefits of video games and show poorer results on mental-health. Additionally, people playing excessively (more than 10 h per week) show increases in problematic behaviors (e.g., somatic symptoms, detrimental effects on social interactions and relationships, and generally lowered mental-health) [10, 18]. Excessive video game exposure may lead to increased risks for problematic gaming disorder characterized by impaired control and functional impairment, showing similar prevalence to comparable substance-related addictions [8]. Similar results report that moderate amounts of video game play is associated with positive benefits for social and emotional well-being [19].

Research during the COVID-19 pandemic also revealed that gaming can provide players with several benefits for well-being: cognitive stimulation, reduced anxiety and stress, positive effects on mood and mental-health, and positive effects on socialization and social interactions [20].

However, it is important to examine not only the general effects of video games, but also the underlying mechanisms and who they are more or even less pronounced in. Positive video game effects, for example, might depend on certain personality traits and game characteristics [21]. For these potential positive video game effects, Seligman's positive psychology model for well-being [16] could provide a theoretical framework.

1.2 The PERMA Model

In Seligman's positive psychology model for well-being [16], he postulates that well-being is composed of five elements: Positive Emotion (i.e., feelings of happiness and satisfaction), Engagement (i.e., being fully invested and immersed, feeling senses of flow in an activity), Relationships (i.e., positive social relations and interactions), Meaning (i.e., feeling a sense of purpose, fulfilment, and larger-than-self), and Accomplishment (i.e., a sense of achievement and satisfaction) [10]. Taken together, this combines to the PERMA model.

Applied to video games, gaming offers the possibility of improving psychological well-being, as they may contain features of the PERMA model [10]. For example, people use video games to elicit positive emotions and to reduce stress, relax, and regulate their emotions [11, 13, 14, 22]. They actively engage in video game play to improve their mood and feel better, depending on personality and game characteristics [21].

Furthermore, VG are highly engaging, leading to feelings of increased immersion and flow-experiences [10, 23]. Highly engaged players of World of Warcraft, for example, reported increased life satisfaction and decreased stress levels as a result of playing the game [23]. However, this can be moderated by the time spent playing video games [10]. Playing for increased amounts of time can lead to more negative effects and increased risks for problematic behaviours.

Another key gaming motivation is for social purposes, to play with friends and/or to make new friends [24]. During the COVID-19 pandemic, video gaming was even promoted as a tool to stay socially connected [15]. In their review on the relationship between social video gaming and well-being, Bowman and colleagues concluded that social interactions in video games can make people feel less lonely and increase social bonding [25]. Unlike negative social interactions like trolling or toxicity, video games can increase well-being through the effects of positive social interactions [25].

Moreover, video games can provide not only hedonic pleasure, but also meaning, that is, eudaimonia. This includes emotional and moral content, which can also lead to self-reflection, social connectedness, and increased nostalgic feeling [26]. These eudemonic experiences in video games have a positive impact on the well-being of players, as they induce positive psychological involvement and interaction [26, 27], especially for highly involved players [28]. These meaningful experiences can allow players to cope with negative experiences [26].

In addition, video games provide opportunities to acquire new skills, improve already learned skills, and fulfil the psychological need for competence [10, 29]. In this line, video games can provide players with a sense of accomplishment, one of the more prominent gaming motives [24]. The sense of achievement and goal attainment in turn is positively associated with well-being [10].

1.3 Gaming Motivation

As stated above, positive video game effects might be dependent not only on game characteristics but also on players' characteristics. Reasons why people play are as diverse as the games themselves, varying across genders, cultural settings, and personality profiles [30]. Even though gaming prevalence are almost equal across genders [13, 14], gaming preferences and experiences are not. Women feel as competent with video gaming than men, but actually play less [31, 32] and prefer social games, simulations, and puzzles [33]. Women also tend to treat video games as a less important hobby than men [33]. Also, they are less susceptible than men to negative video games effects [10].

Gaming motives are also important factors to consider when evaluating the impact of video games on well-being. Gaming motivation might be a key moderator of the relationship between video game play and well-being [34]. Some researchers argued that positive effects of video games could be rooted in self-determination theory, linking psychological well-being of players with the fulfilment of the basic motives and psychological needs for competence, autonomy, and relatedness [35]. This could be also in line with previous research showing the importance of engagement as well as achievement and accomplishment in video games [10].

Other researchers divided players into different player types with specific personality characteristics, gaming motives, and game preferences [24, 36]. Recently, four distinct player types with different profiles for gaming motives and game preferences were identified [24]: *Casual Players* who play predominantly for enjoyment motivation, *High Performers*, who play predominantly for achievements and competition, *Crafters*, who play for exploration and achievement, and *Highly Involved Players* with highest levels of gaming motivation who play predominantly for escapism. These player types play for specific gaming motives and could therefore experience different benefits to their well-being. For each, different PERMA factors could play a greater or lesser role, providing a potentially complex picture of the video game effects on well-being.

Identifying which characteristics are important to whom and what effects video games may have on certain types of players could be essential for research on the positive effects of video games on well-being.

1.4 Hypotheses

In an online survey, the following hypotheses and research questions were investigated:

Moderate play time has a positive relation to well-being, while less as well as extensive play time is not or even negatively related to well-being, respectively (**H1**). Furthermore, compliance with the PERMA factors has a positive association with well-being (**H2**). Considering gender differences, men and women differ in game preferences, gaming experience, and video game status (**H3**). In addition to the hypotheses, we also examined whether the well-being of the four player types depended on the number of PERMA factors they met (**RQ1**). Lastly, do different player types also differ in their PERMA profile (**RQ2**)? For example, highly involved players may be more likely to play to satisfy the need for engagement and meaning, whereas casual gamers may play primarily to experience positive emotions.

2 Methods

2.1 Participants

The study was promoted through social network sites (e.g., Facebook groups, Discord servers, Instagram stories) and interactive online gaming sites (e.g., Twitch). Only active video gamers who speak either German or English were able to participate. Participants who reported playing video games for less than half an hour per week were excluded. A total number of 1586 people took part. Based on their data, participants were assessed for careless responding. Those with unusually short completion time (i.e., relative speed index ≥ 2) [37], straightlining (i.e., ≥ 15 identical ratings in a row and an average longstring of ≥ 5) [38], and/or extremely high or low response variability [39] were excluded, resulting in a remaining valid sample size of $N = 963$.

Among those participants, 70.2% were male (n = 676), 29.6% female (n = 285), one participant was diverse, and another participant indicated "other" without further specification. Participants were aged between 18 and 34 years ($M = 25.18$; $SD = 3.42$). Participants played video games for an average of 14.60 h a week ($SD = 12.89$; min $= 0.50$, max $= 75.00$).

2.2 Gaming Habits, Motivation and Player Types

Participants were asked how much time they spent on average per week playing video games on any device. Furthermore, participants had to rank the status of video games in contrast to other hobbies and leisure activities (e.g., sports) from least to most important. Also, 10 game genres with short descriptions[1] were presented to participants and they then ranked the three genres they play most often from most to least played.

The four player types retrieved from Holl et al. [24] were used to divide video game players into four categories (see Table 1). Participants were asked to actively choose which of the four player types presented with brief explanations would best describe them. Distribution of player types are presented in Table 1.

Table 1. Description of player types and distribution of player types in the present sample.

Player Type	Explanation	Motivation	Frequency	Percent
Casual Player	Play casually and enjoy games and do not play primarily for achievement or competition	lowest means for all gaming motives, but high on boredom and enjoyment motivation	$n = 271$	28.1
High Performer	Players who want to achieve things, compete, and show their skills	high motivation for aggression, prestige, and competition, but lowest motivation for enjoyment	$n = 398$	41.3
Crafter	Players who enjoy creating and achieving things by building and crafting	low aggression, prestige, and escapism motivation, but high in achievement, creativity, and enjoyment motivation	$n = 172$	17.9
Highly Involved Players	Players who are fully focused on stories and achievements	highest overall motivation and highest motivation for escapism	$n = 122$	12.7

2.3 Well-Being and PERMA

The World Health Organization's Well Being Index (WHO-5) was used [40], which is composed of five items (e.g., 'I have felt cheerful and in good spirits.'). The WHO-5

---

[1] Taken from https://www.hp.com/us-en/shop/tech-takes/video-game-genres.

measures well-being over the past two weeks on a scale ranging from 1 = *at no time* to 5 = *all the time*. Internal consistency of the scale was very good (α = .89). The PERMA-Profiler [41], a brief measure of the PERMA model that consists of 15 questions (3 items per PERMA domain; e.g., *In general, how often do you feel joyful*) was used. The response options range from 0 = never to 10 = always. In the present study, participants were asked to think about their time playing video games when answering the items. The overall internal consistency of the PERMA-Profiler was excellent with α = .94 (Positive emotion: α = .77; Engagement: α = .76; Relationships: α = .79; Meaning: α = .78; Accomplishment: α = .76).

2.4 Procedure

The online survey was conducted via the platform SosciSurvey[2]. In the first part of the survey, participants gave informed consent first and then provided some demographic information (e.g., age, gender). Participants were also asked if they considered themselves as active gamers (*yes* or *no*). The second part of the survey focused on gaming habits: Gaming experience, video game status, and gaming genres were assessed. In the third part, participants completed the WHO-5 items, the PERMA profiler, and indicated their player type.

At the end of the questionnaire, participants were thanked and could take part in a raffle of one of ten coupons each worth 20 Euros by providing a valid email address, which was stored separately from all other data.

3   Results

3.1   H1: Effects of Play Time on Well-Being

There was no significant correlation between average time spent playing video games per week and well-being according to the WHO-5, $r = -.01$, $p = .668$.

Next, participants were divided into three groups according to indications in [10]: low users (less than 7 h per week; $n = 359$), moderate users (7 to 10 h per week; $n = 122$) and high users (more than 10 h per week; $n = 482$).

First, a one-way ANOVA with user groups as independent variable (low users vs. moderate users vs. high users) and WHO-5 score as dependent variable was calculated. Levene's test of homogeneity was significant, and therefore Welch's test was used. There was a significant difference between the three groups for WHO-5 score, $W(2, 334.34) = 6.21$, $p = .002$, $\eta^2 = .01$. Looking at pairwise comparisons, low users ($M = 22.12$; $SD = 4.13$) had significantly higher WHO-5 scores than moderate users ($M = 20.61$; $SD = 5.02$), $Mdiff = 1.51$, $SE = 0.51$, $p = .010$, 95% CI [0.28, 2.75]. Furthermore, low users also had significantly higher WHO-5 scores than high users ($M = 21.26$; $SD = 5.38$), $Mdiff = 0.87$, $SE = 0.34$, $p = .035$, 95% CI [0.05, 1.69]. However, there was no difference between moderate and high users, $p = .577$.

For a more detailed look at the relationship between user group and well-being, bivariate Pearson correlations were calculated for the average time spent playing video

---

[2] https://www.soscisurvey.de/en/index

games per week and the WHO-5 score for the three user groups. For low users ($M =$ 2.92; $SD = 1.60$), there was a weak significant negative correlation with well-being: $r = -.12$, $p < .05$. For moderate users ($M = 8.89$; $SD = 1.33$), there was a significant moderate positive correlation with well-being, $r = .29$, $p < .01$. For high users ($M = 24.73$; $SD = 10.84$), the correlation with well-being was negative but non-significant, $r = -.08$, $p = .06$.

3.2 H2: The Compliance with the PERMA Factors Has a Positive Association with Well-Being

First, bivariate Pearson correlations were calculated between the PERMA factors and the WHO-5 score (see Table 2).

Additionally, a linear regression model with the WHO-5 score as outcome variable and the five PERMA factors entered at the same step, to determine which factor contributed most to the prediction of well-being, was significant, $R^2 = .20$, $SE = 4.41$, $F(5, 957) = 48.87$, $p < .001$. Table 3 shows that Meaning and Accomplishment, next to Engagement, had the greatest impact on well-being. In this model, both Positive Emotions and Relationships did not significantly predict the WHO-5 score.

Table 2. Bivariate Pearson correlation coefficients and significance level for the PERMA factors and the WHO-5 score

	WHO-5 score	
	r	p
Sum PERMA	.45	< .001
Accomplishment	.41	< .001
Engagement	.40	< .001
Positive Emotions	.40	< .001
Meaning	.41	< .001
Relationships	.39	< .001

Table 3. Linear regression coefficients of the five PERMA factors on the outcome of the WHO-5 score.

	b	SE	t(957)	p	95% CI
Accomplishment	0.31	0.16	2.42	.016	0.08, 0.71
Engagement	0.31	0.16	1.97	.049	< 0.01, 0.62
Positive Emotions	0.20	0.17	1.15	.249	-0.14, 0.53
Meaning	0.40	0.15	2.60	.009	0.10, 0.70
Positive Relationships	0.26	0.15	1.65	.100	-0.05, 0.56

3.3 H3: Men and Women Differ in Game Preferences, Gaming Experience, and Video Game Status

A one-way ANOVA revealed no significant difference between men ($M = 14.32$; $SD = 12.38$) and women ($M = 15.29$; $SD = 14.03$) for average hours per week spent playing video games, Welch's $F(1, 479.57)^3 = 1.02$, $p = .312$, $\eta2 < .01$.

This was also the case for video game status (scale from 1 to 9) as dependent variable. Again, there was no difference between men ($M = 3.97$; $SD = 2.77$) and women ($M = 4.01$; $SD = 2.61$), Welch's $F(1, 585.64) = 0.05$, $p = .824$, $\eta^2 < .01$.

For game genre preferences, men featured in their top 3 mostly the Multiplayer Online Battle Arena (MOBA) genre with 37%, the Role-Playing Games (RPG) and Action Role-Playing Games (ARPG) with 35.1%, and Shooters (first-person and third-person shooters) with 33.8%. For women, however, the 3 most featured game genres differed. In their top 3, they listed MOBA's with 43.6%, Sandbox games with 32.4% and RPG with 31,7%. Additionally, Shooters ranked first among men (12.7%), while RPG ranked first among women (14.3%).

3.4 RQ1 and RQ2: Does the Well-Being of the Four Player Types Depend on the Number of PERMA Model Factors They Fulfil? Do Different Player Types Differ in Their PERMA Profiles?

For High Performers, there were low correlations across all PERMA factors. The strongest correlation with well-being was shown for Accomplishment ($r = .27$, $p < .01$) and Meaning ($r = .29$, $p < .01$), and the weakest for Positive Emotion ($r = .24$, $p < .01$). For Casual Players, well-being was strongest correlated with Positive Emotion ($r = .62$, $p < .01$) and weakest with Relationships ($r = .56$, $p < .01$). For Crafters, well-being was most strongly correlated with Engagement ($r = .55$, $p < .01$) and Meaning ($r = .56$, $p < .01$), while the weakest correlation was with Accomplishment ($r = .49$, $p < .01$). Highly Involved Players had moderate correlations across all the factors of the PERMA model with the strongest correlation with Positive Emotion ($r = .45$, $p < .01$) and the weakest correlation with Relationships ($r = .38$, $p < .01$).

Next, a multivariate analysis of variance using Pillai's trace showed that there was a significant difference between the 4 gamer types on the 5 factors of the PERMA model, $V = 0.8$, $F(15,2883) = 5.30$, $p < .001$ (see Fig. 1). Bonferroni corrected pairwise comparisons showed that, for example, High Performers had significantly higher scores for Accomplishment, Positive Emotions, and Engagement[4]. Interestingly, Highly Involved Players had the significantly lowest scores across all PERMA factors, even for Meaning and Engagement. The full table for the pairwise comparisons is available in the electronic supplement and/or can be send upon request.

Additionally, an ANOVA showed a significant difference across the player types on the sum score of the PERMA profiler, Welch's $F(3, 378.23)^5 = 16.68$, $p < .001$, $\eta^2 = .06$. The means are displayed in Fig. 2. Bonferroni corrected pairwise comparisons are displayed in Table 4.

---

[3] Levene's test of homogeneity of variances was significant ($p = .007$).

[4] For engagement, there was no difference between High Performers and Casual players.

[5] Levene's test of homogeneity of variances was significant ($p = .024$).

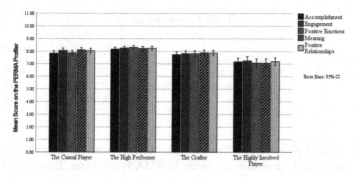

Fig. 1. Mean scores for the five PERMA factors for the four player types.

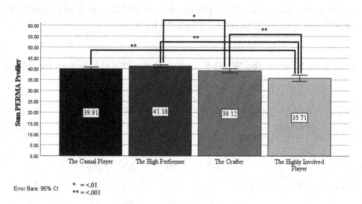

Fig. 2. Sum scores for the PERMA Profiler for the four player types

Table 4. Bonferroni adjusted pairwise comparisons between the four player types and the total score of the PERMA Profiler.

		Mdiff	SE	p	95% CI
Casual Player	High Performer	−1.27	0.55	.125	−2.72, 0.18
	Crafter	0.80	0.68	1.00	−1.00, 2.59
	Highly Involved Player	**4.20**	0.76	**< .001**	2.20, 6.20
High Performer	Casual Player	2.27	0.55	.125	−0.18, 2.72
	Crafter	**2.07**	0.64	**.007**	0.39, 3.74
	Highly Involved Player	**5.47**	0.72	**< .001**	3.57, 7.37
Crafter	Casual Player	−0.80	0.68	1.00	−2.59, 1.00
	High Performer	**−2.07**	0.64	**.007**	−3.74, 0.39
	Highly Involved Player	**3.40**	0.82	**< .001**	1.23, 5.58

(continued)

Table 4. (*continued*)

		Mdiff	SE	p	95% CI
Highly Involved Player	Casual Player	**−4.20**	0.76	**< .001**	−6.20, −2.20
	High Performer	**−5.47**	0.72	**< .001**	−7.37, -3.57
	Crafter	**−3.40**	0.82	**< .001**	−5.58, -1.23

Across the four player types, there were moderate to strong correlations between the WHO-5 score and the total score of the PERMA Profiler (see Table 5). Also, there were significant differences across the four player types for the WHO-5 score, Welch's $F(3, 410.84) = 4.37$, $p = .005$, $\eta^2 = .01$ (see Fig. 3). Bonferroni corrected pairwise comparisons are provided in Table 6. Highly Involved Players had significantly lower WHO-5 scores than Casual Players and High Performers.

Table 5. Correlations between the WHO-5 score and the PERMA factors for the four player types.

Correlation with WHO-score for:	SUM PERMA Profiler	ACC	ENG	PE	Meaning	Positive Relationships
	r	r	r	r	r	r
Casual Player	.66	.60	.59	.62	.57	.56
High Performer	.29	.27	.25	.24	.29	.27
Crafter	.61	.49	.55	.50	.56	.51
Highly Involved Player	.49	.44	.42	.45	.39	.39

All correlation coefficients displayed reached significance on the .001 level.
Note: ACC = Accomplishment, ENG = Engagement, PE = Positive Emotions.

Table 6. Bonferroni corrected pairwise comparisons between the four player types and the WHO-5 score.

		Mdiff	SE	p	95% CI
Casual Player	High Performer	0.40	0.39	1.00	−0.62, 1.42
	Crafter	0.54	0.48	1.00	−0.73, 1.80
	Highly Involved Player	**1.75**	0.54	**.007**	0.33, 3.16
High Performer	Casual Player	−0.40	0.39	1.00	−1.42, 0.62
	Crafter	0.14	0.45	1.00	−1.05, 1.32
	Highly Involved Player	**1.35**	0.51	**.048**	0.01, 2.69

(*continued*)

Table 6. (*continued*)

		Mdiff	*SE*	*p*	95% CI
Crafter	Casual Player	−0.54	0.48	1.00	−2.59, 1.00
	High Performer	−0.14	0.45	1.00	−3.74, -0.39
	Highly Involved Player	1.21	0.58	.223	−0.32, 2.75
Highly Involved Player	Casual Player	**−1.75**	0.54	**.007**	−3.16, -0.33
	High Performer	**−1.35**	0.51	**.048**	−2.69, -0.01
	Crafter	−1.21	0.58	.223	−2.75, 0.32

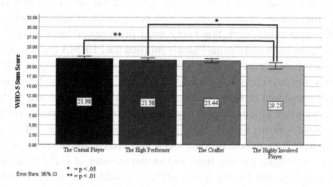

Fig. 3. WHO-5 total score for the four player types.

4 Discussion

The current study aimed to identify the effects of video game play on well-being across different player groups under the framework of Seligman's PERMA model. Furthermore, gender differences for gaming exposure, genre preferences, and the status of video games in the lives of participants were assessed. In addition, it was hypothesized that time spent playing video games is associated with player well-being.

Following Jones et al. [10], it was hypothesized that gaming would have a positive effect on well-being. However, this was thought to be moderated by play time with moderate usage having a positive effect of well-being while low and high usage having no or negative effects. The present results could not confirm this. There was no significant relationship between time spent playing video games and general well-being. Low users, however, had significantly higher well-being than moderate or high users. For moderate users, there was a positive relationship between time spent playing and well-being, indicating that if moderate users spent more time playing, general well-being increases. Previous research has found that time spent playing video games is not a good predictor of video game effects on well-being [17]. Recently, Vuorre and colleagues [42] linked objective player behavior data of about forty thousand gamers obtained from seven game publishers with self-reported well-being data. They concluded that play time appears to be unrelated to well-being, but that factors like gaming motivation play a far greater role in this regard [42]. Other factors such as need satisfaction may also be more important factors in predicting gaming experiences and player well-being [32]. This was also found in the present study and could explain the complex picture of the impact of play time on well-being, even though only correlative assumptions can be made. Similar research on the relationship of learning outcomes, wellbeing, and gaming motivation showed as well that players' eudaimonic motives and need satisfaction like need for self-realization are linked to well-being [47].

In contrast to time spent playing video games, meeting the PERMA factors for Accomplishment, Meaning, and Relationships predicted well-being for active video game players. The fulfillment of these factors (i.e., the sense of accomplishment, the experience of eudaimonia, and the cultivation of positive relationships) provided by playing video games could be essential to the well-being of active gamers. In addition, there were significant associations between well-being and the fulfillment of the PERMA factors for all player types, with this being most pronounced for Casual Players and Crafters. High Performers and Casual Players fulfilled the PERMA factors most strongly, while Highly Involved Players achieved the significantly lowest scores, who also had the significantly lowest scores for general well-being. This may indicate that players who are deeply immersed in video games and play out of a heightened motivation for escapism may be more susceptible to negative effects of video games on their well-being. For example, gaming disorder may be caused by seeing video games as the only remedy for negative personal conditions, and it may lead to impairments in daily life, a reduced ability to regulate gaming time and an impairment of social relationships [8]. This could also explain why Highly Involved Players had low scores on PERMA factors and the lowest scores on Relationships, as they may have greater difficulty having and/or regulating positive social interactions and relationships.

However, it should be noted that the present study only tests correlative relationships, which can therefore also be inversely related. Thus, low well-being could also lead to increased video game use due to efforts to compensate for well-being, which in turn has a negative effect on well-being. Slater et al. [43] postulated a corresponding reciprocal relationship in their Downward Spiral Model for the effects of violent video games. A more detailed examination of the relationships should be given special consideration in future research on the clinical effects of gaming and gaming disorders.

Gender differences in gaming genres were confirmed: men preferred genres like shooters and RPGs, while women preferred casual puzzles and sandbox games [33, 44]. It is interesting to note that the most popular gaming genre across genders were MOBAs. In addition, however, no gender differences were found for time spent playing video games and video game status. In contrast to previous research [31–33], this is reflected in recent reports of large-scale surveys [13, 14]. Although gaming still presents some gender barriers for women, and women generally prefer other media forms such as social media to video games [45], this may not be the case for active female gamers. As women turn to the hobby of video gaming, the gender gap between active male and female gamers could dissolve. Women may still be less encouraged to take gaming up as a hobby and play male-dominated game genres such as shooters [46], but once they overcome these gender barriers, women can positively benefit from playing video games and they play as much as men. This could be particularly important for video game developers and game advertisements aimed at a female audience.

Finally, the PERMA factors of Accomplishment, Engagement, Positive Emotions, Meaning, and Positive Relationships were hypothesized to be related to well-being. Although there were substantial differences between player types, meeting the PERMA factors was generally associated with increased well-being. From this, a complex picture of the effects of video games on well-being emerges. Future research could more closely examine the effects of psychological need satisfaction through video game play to better understand its effects and its users. Also, prior research showed similar results using the theoretical framework of the self-determination theory [48] which is similarly based on positive psychology than the PERMA model. In the future, it could be useful to compare both approaches for their influence on and predictive value for players' well-being.

Some important limitations must be mentioned. No causal conclusions can be drawn from the present study. Future experimental and longitudinal studies need to examine the correlative results of the current online survey in more detail. From the results, we do not know the direction of the association between video game play, need satisfaction, and/or well-being. In addition, it would be interesting to compare active to non-active or passive gamers and people who do not play video games at all. For example, exposure to video games is not only limited to active play but can also take the form of watching others play video games online. This could have several implications for people's psychological need satisfaction and thus their well-being. In the present study, only active video game players were assessed. For this study, active video gamers were defined as individuals who spent at least half an hour per week playing video games. This may have had a detrimental effect on recruitment, including possible sample bias.

In summary, the present study highlights the importance of considering differentiated factors such as gender, gaming motivation, and player types when examining the effects of video games on well-being. Time spent playing video games may not be a valid predictor of well-being alone. Rather, who plays video games, for what reasons, and what someone expects to get out of gaming may have broader implications for gamer well-being. Furthermore, gender differences could only be found for in preferences for certain game genres, indicating a possible trend reversal in which gender differences and gender roles in video games no longer play the same role as before. Playing video games can have positive effects on the well-being of players and different types of players benefit from playing video games. This is true for female gamers as well as for male gamers. This finding is likely to have major implications for future gaming research that examines the positive and/or negative effects of video gaming.

References

1. Granic, I., Lobel, A., Engels, R.C.M.E.: The benefits of playing video games. Am. Psychol. **69**, 66–78 (2014). https://doi.org/10.1037/a0034857
2. Ferguson, C.J.: Blazing angels or resident evil? Can violent video games be a force for good? Rev. Gen. Psychol. **14**, 68–81 (2010). https://doi.org/10.1037/a0018941
3. Ferguson, C.J.: Do angry birds make for angry children? A meta-analysis of video game influences on children's and adolescents' aggression, mental health, prosocial behavior, and academic performance. Perspect. Psychol. Sci. **10**, 646–666 (2015). https://doi.org/10.1177/1745691615592234

4. Ferguson, C.J.: Aggressive video games are not a risk factor for future aggression in youth: a longitudinal study. J. Youth Adolescence **48**, 1439–1451 (2019)
5. Anderson, C.A., et al.: Violent video game effects on aggression, empathy, and prosocial behavior in eastern and western countries: a meta-analytic review. Psychol. Bull. **136**, 151–173 (2010). https://doi.org/10.1037/a0018251
6. Calvert, S.L., et al.: The American psychological association task force assessment of violent video games: science in the service of public interest. Am. Psychol. **72**, 126–143 (2017). https://doi.org/10.1037/a0040413
7. Prescott, A.T., Sargent, J.D., Hull, J.G.: Metaanalysis of the relationship between violent video game play and physical aggression over time. Proc. Natl. Acad. Sci. U.S.A. **115**, 9882–9888 (2018). https://doi.org/10.1073/pnas.1611617114
8. Stevens, M.W., Dorstyn, D., Delfabbro, P.H., King, D.L.: Global prevalence of gaming disorder: a systematic review and meta-analysis. Aust. N. Z. J. Psychiatry **55**, 553–568 (2021). https://doi.org/10.1177/0004867420962851
9. Przybylski, A.K., Weinstein, N.: How we see electronic games. PeerJ. **4**, e1931 (2016). https://doi.org/10.7717/peerj.1931
10. Jones, C., Scholes, L., Johnson, D., Katsikitis, M., Carras, M.: Gaming well: links between videogames and flourishing mental health. Front. Psychol. **5**, 00260 (2014)
11. Villani, D., Carissoli, C., Triberti, S., Marchetti, A., Gilli, G., Riva, G.: Videogames for emotion regulation: a systematic review. Games Health J. **7**, 85–99 (2018). https://doi.org/10.1089/g4h.2017.0108
12. Newzoo: PC & Console Gaming Report 2023 (2023)
13. Electronic Software Association: 2021 Essential facts about the video game industry (2021)
14. Electronic Software Association: 2022 essential facts about the video game industry (2022)
15. Toledo, M.: Video Game Habits & COVID-19. https://papers.ssrn.com/abstract=3676004 (2020). https://doi.org/10.2139/ssrn.3676004
16. Seligman, M.E.P.: Flourish: a visionary new understanding of happiness and well-being. Free Press, New York, NY (2011)
17. Johannes, N., Vuorre, M., Przybylski, A.K.: Video game play is positively correlated with well-being. R. Soc. open sci. **8**, rsos.202049, 202049 (2021). https://doi.org/10.1098/rsos.202049
18. Allahverdipour, H., Bazargan, M., Farhadinasab, A., Moeini, B.: Correlates of video games playing among adolescents in an Islamic country. BMC Pub. Health **10**, 286 (2010). https://doi.org/10.1186/1471-2458-10-286
19. Kutner, L., Olson, C.: Grand theft childhood: the surprising truth about violent video games and what parents can do. Simon and Schuster (2008)
20. Barr, M., Copeland-Stewart, A.: Playing video games during the COVID-19 pandemic and effects on players' well-being. Games Cult. **17**, 122–139 (2022). https://doi.org/10.1177/15554120211017036
21. Reinecke, L.: Mood management theory. In: Rössler, P. (ed.) The International Encyclopedia of Media Effects, pp. 1–13. Wiley-Blackwell (2017)
22. Reinecke, L.: Games and recovery: the use of video and computer games to recuperate from stress and strain. J. Media Psychol. **21**, 126–142 (2009). https://doi.org/10.1027/1864-1105.21.3.126
23. Snodgrass, J.G., Lacy, M.G., Francois Dengah, H.J., Fagan, J., Most, D.E.: Magical flight and monstrous stress: technologies of absorption and mental wellness in Azeroth. Cult. Med. Psychiatry **35**, 26–62 (2011). https://doi.org/10.1007/s11013-010-9197-4
24. Holl, E., Sischka, P., Melzer, A.: Development and Validation of the Motivation to Play Scale (MOPS). Presented at the International Communication Association Conference, Paris (2022)
25. Bowman, N.D., Rieger, D., Tammy Lin, J.-H.: Social video gaming and well-being. Curr. Opin. Psychol. **45**, 101316 (2022). https://doi.org/10.1016/j.copsyc.2022.101316

26. Daneels, R., Bowman, N.D., Possler, D., Mekler, E.D.: The 'Eudaimonic Experience': a scoping review of the concept in digital games research. MaC **9**, 178–190 (2021). https://doi.org/10.17645/mac.v9i2.3824

27. Reinecke, L., Oliver, M.B.: The Routledge Handbook of Media Use and Well-Being: International Perspectives on Theory and Research on Positive Media Effects. Routledge (2016)

28. Snodgrass, J.G., et al.: Positive mental well-being and immune transcriptional profiles in highly involved videogame players. Brain Behav. Immun. **82**, 84–92 (2019). https://doi.org/10.1016/j.bbi.2019.07.035

29. Ryan, R.M., Rigby, C.S., Przybylski, A.: The motivational pull of video games: a self-determination theory approach. Motiv. Emot. **30**, 344–360 (2006). https://doi.org/10.1007/s11031-006-9051-8

30. Ratan, R.A., Chen, V.H.H., Degrove, F., Breuer, J., Quandt, T., Williams, P.: Gender, Gaming Motives, and Genre: Comparing Singaporean, German, and American Players. IEEE Trans. Games **pp**, 1 (2021). https://doi.org/10.1109/TG.2021.3116077

31. Hamlen, K.R.: Re-examining gender differences in video game play: time spent and feelings of success. J. Educ. Comput. Res. **43**, 293–308 (2010). https://doi.org/10.2190/EC.43.3.b

32. Johnson, D., Gardner, J., Sweetser, P.: Motivations for videogame play: predictors of time spent playing. Comput. Hum. Behav. **63**, 805–812 (2016). https://doi.org/10.1016/j.chb.2016.06.028

33. Phan, M.H., Jardina, J.R., Hoyle, S., Chaparro, B.S.: Examining the role of gender in video game usage, preference, and behavior. Proceed. Hum. Factors Ergon. Soc. Annual Meeting **56**, 1496–1500 (2012). https://doi.org/10.1177/1071181312561297

34. Halbrook, Y.J., O'Donnell, A.T., Msetfi, R.M.: When and how video games can be good: a review of the positive effects of video games on well-being. Perspect. Psychol. Sci. **14**, 1096–1104 (2019). https://doi.org/10.1177/1745691619863807

35. Przybylski, A.K., Rigby, C.S., Ryan, R.M.: A motivational model of video game engagement. Rev. Gen. Psychol. **14**, 154–166 (2010). https://doi.org/10.1037/a0019440

36. Bartle, R.: Hearts, clubs, diamonds, spades: players who suit MUDs 27 (1996)

37. Leiner, D.J.: Too fast, too straight, too weird: non-reactive indicators for meaningless data in internet surveys. Survey Res. Methods **13**, 229–248 (2019). https://doi.org/10.18148/SRM/2019.V13I3.7403

38. Schonlau, M., Toepoel, V.: Straightlining in Web survey panels over time. Survey Res. Methods **9**, 125–137 (2015). https://doi.org/10.18148/SRM/2015.V9I2.6128

39. Dunn, A.M., Heggestad, E.D., Shanock, L.R., Theilgard, N.: Intra-individual response variability as an indicator of insufficient effort responding: comparison to other indicators and relationships with individual differences. J. Bus. Psychol. **33**, 105–121 (2018). https://doi.org/10.1007/s10869-016-9479-0

40. WHO: Wellbeing measures in primary health care/the Depcare Project. WHO Regional Office for Europe: Copenhagen (1998)

41. Butler, J., Kern, M.L.: The PERMA-Profiler: a brief multidimensional measure of flourishing. Intnl. J. Wellbeing. **6**, 1–48 (2016). https://doi.org/10.5502/ijw.v6i3.526

42. Vuorre, M., Johannes, N., Magnusson, K., Przybylski, A.K.: Time spent playing video games is unlikely to impact well-being. R. Soc. open sci. **9**, 220411 (2022). https://doi.org/10.1098/rsos.220411

43. Slater, M.D., Henry, K.L., Swaim, R.C., Anderson, L.L.: Violent media content and aggressiveness in adolescents: a downward spiral model. Commun. Res. **30**, 713–736 (2003). https://doi.org/10.1177/0093650203258281

44. López-Fernández, F.J., Mezquita, L., Griffiths, M.D., Ortet, G., Ibáñez, M.I.: The role of personality on disordered gaming and game genre preferences in adolescence: gender differences and person-environment transactions. Adicciones **33**, 263–272 (2021). https://doi.org/10.20882/adicciones.1370

45. Leonhardt, M., Overå, S.: Are there differences in video gaming and use of social media among boys and girls?—A mixed methods approach. IJERPH **18**, 6085 (2021). https://doi.org/10.3390/ijerph18116085

46. Lopez-Fernandez, O., Williams, A.J., Griffiths, M.D., Kuss, D.J.: Female gaming, gaming addiction, and the role of women within gaming culture: a narrative literature review. Front. Psychiatry **10**, 00454 (2019)

47. Vahlo, J., Välisalo, T., Tuuri, K.: Informal learning and wellbeing outcomes of gameplay and their associations with gameplay motivation. Front. Psychol. **14**, 1176773 (2023). https://doi.org/10.3389/fpsyg.2023.1176773

48. Türkay, S., Lin, A., Johnson, D., Formosa, J.: Self-determination theory approach to understanding the impact of videogames on wellbeing during COVID-19 restrictions. Behav. Inf. Technol. **42**, 1–20 (2022). https://doi.org/10.1080/0144929X.2022.2094832

The Meaning of Life (in Video Games)

Fausto Mourato[1]([✉]) [iD], João Morais[1] [iD], and Edirlei Soares de Lima[2] [iD]

[1] ESTSetúbal, Instituto Politécnico de Setúbal. Campus do IPS, 2914-508 EstefanilhaSetúbal, Portugal
{fausto.mourato,joao.morais}@estsetubal.ips.pt
[2] Academy for Games and Media, Breda University of Applied Sciences, Breda, The Netherlands
soaresdelima.e@buas.nl

Abstract. This paper explores how the concept of life has been used in video games through time. Life is an essential element in different types of action games and several nuances have been used to provide various types of emotions and effects during gameplay. However, the details and patterns have not been extendedly analyzed. Primarily, we survey works regarding the description and formalization of game analysis with emphasis on works in which the concepts have impact in the arguably accepted notion of life. Multiple examples are provided to show different approaches to the concept of life and the impact of such approaches in overall gameplay, namely in the game difficulty and emotions. The examples are then generalized, resulting in a proposal of framework to describe life representation in games. The proposed framework was evaluated in a user study, having participants with gaming culture (professionals, academics, and students of game development courses). Each participant was assigned with the task of fitting a preselected set of games within the framework. The results indicate good coverage of the main concepts with satisfactory consistency.

Keywords: Game Terminology · Life · Game Design · Game Analysis

1 Introduction

The challenge of formally analyzing games is present since their establishment as a popular medium. Some media have more concrete methods (for instance, music theory has very systematic methods to define concepts such as rhythm, harmony, and melody) while others are more abstract and conceptual (for instance, one can recall the art piece that consists of a banana taped on a wall [1]).

Regarding core game design process, one of the pioneer approaches is the MDA (Mechanics-Dynamics-Aesthetics) Framework [2], which formalizes the consumption and the design of games, presenting a formal way to bridge the two parts of the process: designers and players. The MDA Framework is a solid reference that brought attention to important aspects of the design process and is widely used and adapted. However, some of its elements lack some pragmatism to be widely used in the industry. Additionally,

© IFIP International Federation for Information Processing 2023
Published by Springer Nature Switzerland AG 2023
P. Ciancarini et al. (Eds.): ICEC 2023, LNCS 14455, pp. 59–71, 2023.
https://doi.org/10.1007/978-981-99-8248-6_5

the MDA is flexible and adjustable. For instance, it starts with a set of aesthetics that is explicitly stated to be nonexclusive and modifiable. While this flexibility allows different mindsets, it also compromises systematization.

One of the main efforts to systematize video game concepts is the Game Ontology Project (GOP) [3], which can be summarized as a hierarchy of concepts abstracted from an analysis of many specific games. The work "identifies the important structural elements of games and the relationships between them, organizing them hierarchically" [3]. In this paper we focus the study of a particular aspect used in video games since their dawn: the concept of life. This concept is indeed pointed in the GOP hierarchy under the top-level entry "rules". Examples are presented, but there is room for improvements and research, as this is a core element of gameplay. As will be further discussed in Section II, some game design books also describe life and present use cases but, in general, there is a lack of a defined set of terms to allow the establishment of game design patterns. This is precisely the main goal of this work: present a framework to describe the structure of lives in video games (where applicable) and to analyze how different configurations within that structure can impact gameplay.

The paper is organized as follows: Sect. 2 reviews related work previous attempts to formalize the concept of life in video games; Sect. 3 presents the proposed framework through a description of its main components, which are decomposed in a set of attributes with specific data types; Sect. 4 describes the methodology and results of the user study conducted to validate the proposed framework; Sect. 5 presents concluding remarks and a discussion of our results and future works.

2 Related Work

2.1 Initial Concept of Life

The basic notion of life in video games is widely perceived and supported by literature. Orland et al. [4] provide a dictionary of gaming terms for the press where life is described as a play-turn that a player has between the start and the end of play. The GOP [3] defines life as something to "represent a measure of opportunities that a player has to succeed in the game". Rouse III [5] refers to lives as a finite number of tries before the "game over" state, which is the ultimate penalty for running out of lives. Lecky-Thomson [6] details the concept of lives and presents some examples. Space Invaders is referred as the pioneer where lives soften the impact of losing similarly to having multiple balls in a pinball machine. Checkpoints and saving are terms that are also presented as work as a continuation of the concept. Additionally, other features related to the concept of lives are identified, namely: defensive armor, power-ups, weapons, or ammunition that somehow cancels or softens the usual penalty associated to being hit (this feature is corroborated by Fullerton [7]), and items or power-ups that allow (re)gaining life (this feature is also referred by Moore [8]).

2.2 More Than Just Life: Hit Points and Health Points

The concept of health is commonly referred similarly to the notion of life in gaming literature. It can be seen as an evolution of basic principles of multiple retrying options, with more variants. It is normally designated by the acronym HP, standing either for Health Points or Hit Points [9]. In both cases, it represents the "total amount of damage a unit can withstand before being rendered incapable of participating in combat" [8]. This is valid for players, that will lose the game, opponents that will be overcome by the player, and even objects within the environment [10].

The notion of HP presents different benefits for game design and gameplay, such as simplifying the design process and rule balancing, and is a simple and effective way that "both players and computers can easily work and understand" [11]. It is also effective to give the feeling of progression by making the player start with a small number of points that can increase during the game [12]. Additionally, it is possible to stack extra rules or expand the concept to allow more complex systems that a set of hardcore players enjoy (e.g., the health points can be associated with different parts of the body, armor, or equipment). It is also common to have some mechanism of additional protection that prevent or reduce the loss of health points when the player is hit. They can take the form of shield, armor, or any another equipment, but the common notion is that is something that protects the player in case of being hit.

2.3 Other Approaches for Life Representation

The basis of the concept of life played an important role in the early days of video games, providing a desire to avoid the finality of the player character's death and inciting players to spend more coins in arcades (increasing the final profit [13]). With the evolution of games, it also evolved and gained different purposes, such as expanding gameplay, evoking emotions, providing monetization methods, etc. Many contemporary games do not use a direct representation of life as an isolated element, but combine different approaches for life, health (or hit) points, and protections. Also, life is represented differently among games and there are distinct interpretations and meanings to allow retries. For instance, in the Uncharted series (2007 - 2017) "life" is a luck meter of being critically hit and in the Assassin's Creed series (2007 – 2020) it is a measurement of synchronization with past events. With all the existing possibilities, the main concepts are informally used and perceived but there is a lack of formalization and systematization of the main existing entities and their attributes.

3 Proposed Framework

Considering the literature review on the different representations of life, including variations of game genre, style and even development limitations, we have analyzed how the different concepts stack on the gameplay structure, and extracted the interdependency among them. As a result, we identified the whole existence of a gaming character in an action game to be decomposable with the following four elements: Credit; Life; Energy; Protection. These elements provide different levels to handle the consequences of failing challenges within a game and will be described next.

Credit – Represents the access to play a game session and is an allowance to enter or be kept in the game world, regardless of the features of the player's character. This top-level concept gets its roots in arcade machines, in which inserting a coin would allow one game credit to play the game with its respective rules (e.g., number of tries, time, or other restrictions). Though the existence of credits is strongly associated with the monetization model of the arcade machines, it is still applicable nowadays. Normally, games that are bought with a premium model provide infinite credits, but many free games have a monetization model that include the notion of credit, where watching ads replaced coins as currency. Credits are composed by the following attributes:

- Mechanism, that describes how players earn credits and has the following values: Infinite; Payment (limited); Payment (without limits); Predefined value (of 2 or more); One credit only.
- Penalty, stating what happens when the player loses a credit. This enumeration has the following values: seamless continue; respawn on the same position; respawn at a previous checkpoint; level restart.

Life – Represents the possibility of retrying the challenges of the game. While credit is focused on the world, the concept of life has focus on the player. A new life implies the existence of a new instance of the player in the world, in which the last instance was lost (died, was destroyed, etc.). As we have seen in the literature review, the essence of this concept is present since the early days of gaming and is universally considered in gaming culture. Even though it makes more sense in the context of living characters, the popularity of the term allows its usage for any other type of representation in a game, such as vehicles, or even in more abstract scenarios such as quizzes. The element life is composed by the following attributes:

- Mechanism, defining the way for its representation and having one of the following alternatives: One; Multiple; Infinite.
- Penalty, stating what happens when the player loses a life. This enumeration has the following values: seamless continue; respawn on the same position; respawn at a previous checkpoint; level restart.
- Methods to earn life, which present the different ways to obtain additional lives during gameplay and can be described as a multiple selection enumeration with the following values: Performance (for instance the player's score); Pick-up; Tradable.

Energy – Represents the capability that allows players to sustain injury, damage or partially fail a challenge without implying the death or destruction of their avatar. In our literature review we have observed that the most common designation for such type of representation is HP, standing both for Health Points and Hit Points. In both cases, the designation has some restrictions. Health implies a living character and is not adequate for vehicles and other non-living entities controlled by the player. Hit implies damage through physical threats on the level and may not depict well situations in which the character is poisoned, is stepping on a hazardous surface, or other similar situations that can happen in any video game. Therefore, for our framework, we propose the use of the broader term energy, composed by the following attributes:

- Mechanism, defining its representation and having the following values: continuous; discrete; hidden (with feedback for critical levels); hidden (without any feedback); inexistant (player loses one life directly when is hit).
- Penalty, stating what happens when the players lose energy. This enumeration has the following values: seamless continue; visual feedback; impact on movement.

- Regeneration methods, which present the different ways to restore some (or the totality) of the player's energy. They can be described as a multiple selection enumeration having the following values: automatic (regenerated with time according to a specific rate); through equipment; pick-up; tradable; items.

Protection – Refers to the player's capability to prevent, be immune, or mitigate the effects of something that, in regular cases, would result in loss of energy. This is specifically an external optional layer that protects the player, in opposition to energy that is internal to the player. Protection has the following set of attributes and features:

- Mechanism, representing the behavior of the player protection mechanism, which can be: a time-interval; a specific amount; based on endurance; inexistant (players lose energy whenever they are hit).
- Type, representing the degree of protection given to a player, which can have the following values: full (full protection against all threats); partial (only protecting from a specific set of threats – e.g., only from magical damage).
- Penalty, stating what happens when the players lose part of their protection. This is an enumeration with the following values: seamless continue; visual feedback; impact on movement.
- Regeneration methods, which present the different ways to restore some (or the totality) of the player's protection. They can be described as a multiple selection enumeration having the following values: automatic (regenerated with time according to a specific rate); through equipment; pick-up; tradable; items.

Regarding the methods to earn life, energy and/or protection we referred the terms pick-up, item, equipment and tradable. For this matter, a pick-up should be considered as something that the player collects and use immediately, in opposition to items or equipment that are carried in an inventory and used when the player wants (for items) or selected for continuous use (for equipment). Tradable refers to items or equipment that can be exchanged for something directly obtainable in the game (for instance, the player can collect coins that are used in a store to buy life/energy/protections).

A visual representation of the concepts used in our framework is presented in Fig. 1. Credit provides entrance to the game world and protection, energy, and life are all focused on the Player and act as layers to handle threats. Each layer acts sequentially, filtering the potential damage of the threats that hit the player. An initial layer of protection filters and/or absorbs the damage. In case of partial filtering or absorption, the remaining effects of a certain threat can pass to the next layer, which will receive the remaining damage (i.e., part of the damage will be absorbed by the protection layer). Running out of Energy implies losing a Life, which does not occur with the Protections, that are external elements (players can run out of protection without losing energy or lives, but if they run out of energy, they lose a life). In the same manner, running out of lives implies losing one Credit.

Our framework aims to cover the main alternatives that were used in games to represent life to allow the player to fail and retry in action video games. As this first creation has its natural shortcomings, it intends to cover a large set of games that could be expanded in the future while enlightening the contours of its applicability. Currently, we have perspectives that the framework can be used in the following scenarios:

- Study of existing games, to analyze and compare games and extract design patterns that are used to create some kind of emotional responses.
- Development of new games, as it serves as a checklist of features that must be defined for a regular action game.
- Development of game-like experiences outside gaming context, where having proper game design and game culture knowledge is useful, such as gamification [14] and serious games [15].

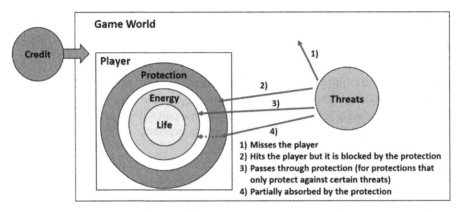

Fig. 1. Representation of the main concepts of the framework.

4 Evaluation

4.1 Goal and Methodology

The proposed framework aims to allow analyzing existing games and compare them regarding life representation. Such comparisons push a better understanding about game design patterns that promote certain effects regarding challenge and difficulty. Also, it aims to aid the design process, promoting a guide to cover the different aspect to consider. Considering these goals, we conducted a study to analyze and evaluate the completeness and consistency of the proposed framework.

The evaluation procedure adopted in the study consists of asking participants to fit popular single-player action games within the framework. This experiment was conducted with academics, professionals, and students with a connection to game development area. We consider that a game fits the framework if it is possible to describe its approach regarding life representation with the elements of a framework by filling a form, without requiring additional explanations. The percentage of analyzed games that fit the framework represents an indication of its completeness. Consistency is analyzed by comparing different responses within the same game (the similarity of the responses indicates the consistency of the framework).

The set of games used in the experiment aims to represent the general gaming history and multiple genres where life is an important gameplay element (for instance, graphical novels were not considered). For this matter, we started with a list containing the best games of each year for the most popular magazines. Games that could not fit the action genre were removed (i.e., games where life is not a relevant element of the gameplay). In addition, games that represent a continuation of a franchise were also removed (except in cases where significant gameplay differences are known).

The framework was tested by 43 participants, including game development students from two different universities, professors, and industry professionals. At the beginning of the experiment, participants were briefed about the goal and the concepts of the framework, and then they were asked to anonymously fill a form where they could select a game (from the selected set of games) and classify the different features of the game within the concepts of the framework. In the form, every main component (credit, life, energy, and protection) had a free text field in which the participants could indicate game features that were special and could not be described only by the terms of the framework. The participants could fill the form many times as they want for different games. In total, we received 87 analyses for the selected set of games. After excluding games with less than three different analyses, we obtained a study set with a total of 82 analysis covering the 16 different games (an average of 5 analysis for each game) that will be explored thereafter.

4.2 Results and Discussion

To analyze the results, we compared the answers obtained for the questions related to the different elements of the framework in each game. For the evaluation of the consistency, each element of the framework was tagged as:

- **Consistent (C)**: for cases in which all responses were the same.
- **Inconsistent (I)**: when responses were different without a recognizable pattern.
- **Arguable (A)**: for situations in which the responses were not the same but there is a plausible and meaningful cause for that. These cases will be further discussed.
- **Not Applicable (N/A)**: when another answer cancels the meaning of the element (for instance, with infinite lives, the ways to increment life does not apply).

The results obtained in the comparison of the answers for each element of our framework are presented in Tables 1, 2, 3, and 4 (each table contains de results regarding credits, lives, energy, and protection, respectively).

Initially, we were expecting to analyze mainly the percentage of consistent cases within the domain of applicable features to evaluate the consistency of our framework. However, the percentage of consistent elements was below our expectations (around 65%). This made us observe with more detail the possible causes of potential inconsistent cases and we have identified multiple justifications that do not imply bad consistency. Some of them also show the potential of the framework to incite further studies. These cases were tagged as Arguable and represent the following situations:

1. **Some responses mix multiple versions of a franchise or platform** – In some games, in which Doom was the most obvious one, the responses were divided into two obvious clusters with barely identical answers in each cluster. By observing the differences between the groups, we could imply that some responses considered the original version of Doom, while the others considered the 2016's version.

2. **Having infinite retries was not clear** – In contemporary games with premium models, it is common to have infinite lives and/or credits. For instance, in Uncharted, the player dies and restarts in a checkpoint, without any limit. There was a natural confusion within participants in interpreting this situation as 1 credit with infinite lives or infinite credits with only 1 life. Based on the definition of our framework, we consider that these situations mean infinite lives, as the player effectively dies in the game, but the right of play is not revoked for that.

3. **Participants forgot some details** – Typically, in responses regarding methods to regenerate energy or protection, some details were missing in the analyses. One situation that occurred multiple times was having some participants stating that energy or protection could be gained with pick-ups and items, while a few only referred pick-ups. These cases reflect that some analyses are incomplete.

4. **Different game modes** – As some participants stated in the comments, some games, particularly multiplayer, have different game modes and the answer depends on the considered mode. Some inconsistencies of Counter-Strike, League of Legends, and Overwatch are due to this fact.

5. **Difficulty levels** – As claimed in a few comments of the participants, sometimes the difficulty level implies different approaches in the framework features. Before beginning the tests, we have already thought about difficulty, as it is straightforward to perceive that the definition of the features depends on that. One obvious example is having a different number of energy blocks for different difficulty levels. However, the differences might be stronger. A game with a harder mode based on permadeath has two different approaches for life mechanism, an easier one with some or infinite lives, and another one with only one life. In these cases, different difficulty levels should be considered as different game versions.

6. **Different types of projectiles inflict different reaction on the player** – Regarding the penalty for losing energy, there were some inconsistencies, in which some responses for the same game stated that there was impact on gameplay, and other stated that there was no impact. This happened specially on shooting games, which made us identify the fact that, in some games penalty of losing energy may depend on the type of threat. For instance, being hit by a pistol bullet may not imply impact on the player movement but being hit by a rocket will.

7. **Visual feedback penalty is ambiguous** – We have identified some inconsistencies in which, for the same game, different participants stated that the game has visual feedback for being hit while others did not. There are different possible causes for this, as the subtilty of feedback or misinterpretations of what this may mean. We believe that is important to clarify this term in the future, especially to expand the term to any type of feedback (for instance, audible feedback).

8. **Different characters may imply strong differences in gameplay** – Regarding Overwatch, some participants stated in the comments that the game characters are associated with classes and that different classes imply different features. For instance, one class might have an energy regeneration method that is different from another class. This might be the main reason of the inconsistency of this feature. Regarding game analyses, we consider that cases of specific character classes, as well as stated with difficulty settings, should be analyzed as different games. This means that playing with a character of a certain class results in a different game in comparison to playing

with a character of another class. While this consideration might be arguable, we can consider it for evident cases in which the player can choose or use characters with very distinct abilities. For instance, the multiplayer mode of Sonic puts the players in control of very different characters, as the second player plays with Tails, a character that can fly, also having infinite lives.

Table 1. Overview of the results regarding Credits.

Game	Mechanism	Penalty	Comments
Doom	Arguable	Arguable	No
Counter-Strike	Consistent	Consistent	Multiple
Super Mario Bros	Arguable	Arguable	No
Uncharted 4	Consistent	N/A	No
LittleBigPlanet	Inconsistent	Inconsistent	No
League of Legends	Consistent	Consistent	Multiple about the increase of cost for credit
God of War	Arguable	Consistent	No
Overwatch	N/A	N/A	No
Diablo II	Consistent	Consistent	1 about difficulty levels
Sonic Hedgehog	Consistent	Consistent	Multiple
GTA V	N/A	N/A	No
The Last of Us	N/A	N/A	No
Tomb Raider	N/A	N/A	No
Donkey Kong	Arguable	Arguable	No
Frogger	Consistent	Inconsistent	No
Prince of Persia	Consistent	Consistent	No

Table 2. Overview of the results regarding Life.

Game	Mechanism	Penalty	Comments
Doom	Arguable	Arguable	No
Counter-Strike	Consistent	Consistent	Multiple
Super Mario Bros	Arguable	Arguable	No
Uncharted 4	Consistent	N/A	No
LittleBigPlanet	Inconsistent	Inconsistent	No
League of Legends	Consistent	Consistent	Multiple about the increase of cost for credit
God of War	Arguable	Consistent	No

(continued)

Table 2. (*continued*)

Game	Mechanism	Penalty	Comments
Overwatch	N/A	N/A	No
Diablo II	Consistent	Consistent	1 about difficulty levels
Sonic Hedgehog	Consistent	Consistent	Multiple
GTA V	N/A	N/A	No
The Last of Us	N/A	N/A	No
Tomb Raider	N/A	N/A	No
Donkey Kong	Arguable	Arguable	No
Frogger	Consistent	Inconsistent	No
Prince of Persia	Consistent	Consistent	No

Table 3. Overview of the results regarding Energy.

Game	Mechanism	Penalty	Increment	Comments
Doom	Consistent	Consistent	Arguable	No
Counter-Strike	Inconsistent	Inconsistent	Consistent	Multiple
Super Mario Bros	Inconsistent	Inconsistent	Consistent	No
Uncharted 4	Consistent	Consistent	Consistent	No
LittleBigPlanet	Inconsistent	Inconsistent (completeness)	Consistent	No
League of Legends	Consistent	Inconsistent	Consistent	Multiple about stealing energy
God of War	Consistent	Consistent	Consistent	2 referring regenerative item
Overwatch	Consistent	Consistent	Inconsistent	Multiple about being revived and the existence of classes
Diablo II	Consistent	Consistent	Inconsistent	Multiple, specifying the increment methods
Sonic Hedgehog	Consistent	N/A	N/A	1 about rings as protection
GTA V	Consistent	Consistent	Consistent	1 referring regenerative item
The Last of Us	Consistent	Consistent	Consistent	No
Tomb Raider	Consistent	Consistent	Inconsistent	No

(*continued*)

Table 3. (continued)

Game	Mechanism	Penalty	Increment	Comments
Donkey Kong	Consistent	N/A	N/A	No
Frogger	Consistent	N/A	N/A	No
Prince of Persia	Consistent	Inconsistent	Consistent	No

Table 4. Overview of the results regarding Protection.

Game	Mechanism	Representation	Penalty	Type	Absorption	Increment	Comments
Doom	A	A	C	C	C	C	No
Counter-Strike	C	C	I	I	I	I	Multiple
Super Mario Bros	A	A	A	A	A	A	No
Uncharted 4	C	N/A	N/A	N/A	N/A	N/A	No
LittleBigPlanet	C	N/A	N/A	N/A	N/A	N/A	No
League of Legends	A	A	A	A	A	A	Multiple(a)
God of War	C	N/A	N/A	N/A	N/A	N/A	2 (b)
Overwatch	C	C	A	A	A	A	Multiple(c)
Diablo II	I	I	I	I	I	I	1 (c)
Sonic Hedgehog	C	C	C	C	C	C	1 (d)
GTA V	C	C	C	C	C	I	1 (a)
The Last of Us	C	N/A	N/A	N/A	N/A	N/A	No
Tomb Raider	C	N/A	N/A	N/A	N/A	N/A	No
Donkey Kong	C	N/A	N/A	N/A	N/A	N/A	No
Frogger	C	N/A	N/A	N/A	N/A	N/A	No
Prince of Persia	C	N/A	N/A	N/A	N/A	N/A	No

C – Consistent; I – Inconsistent; A – Arguable; N/A – Not Applicable
(a) referring which items protect. (b) about using the shield in gameplay.
(c) about the existence of classes. (d) stating that there are 2 different protections.

The identification of some of the previous cases let us retag some of the features as arguable instead of inconsistent, reducing the initial set of inconsistencies to around 25%. If we divided the analyses for Doom into two different games this value would lower to 20%, resulting in 80% of arguable consistency.

For the evaluation of completeness, we analyzed the comments of the open fields of the form. Most of them were descriptions of what they have considered and do not imply a lack of completeness of the framework. For instance, in different answers, the participants stated that some games have pick-ups to restore energy, and in the open fields they listed which pick-up are those. Still, within the comments, we were able to identify three main limitations of the framework, which are described next.

Lives associated to checkpoints – Little Big Planet raised this limitation, as the game has a different life system. In this game, when the players die, they return to a checkpoint, obviously represented as circular marks. The number of lives is associated to checkpoints, meaning that the player can reappear N times in each checkpoint. Also, there are different types of checkpoints, providing 3, 6 or infinite respawns. The framework does not have a definition for this mechanic.

Specific multiplayer modes – Some multiplayer games provide different modes, which lie outside of the representability of the framework. Examples of such cases include game modes based in a last man standing concept, popularized in battle royale games as Fortnite; games consisting of rounds with teams that adopt a paintball mechanic, which forces players to wait for a new round when they die; and team-based games that offer the possibility of having players healing other players.

Stealing energy – Some participants referred in the comments that in League of Legends, one specific way to regain energy is by stealing it from other characters. This aspect was not in the framework.

5   Conclusions

In this paper we explored the different representations of life in video games. While this is a widely used terminology, there is a lack of formal definitions to characterize it. Therefore, we have defined a framework to describe life related concepts. The concepts of the framework were presented and discussed with students of 3 different universities with game development courses, and it was particularly interesting to gather their opinions and observe the fomented discussions. For instance, the rings in the game Sonic raised various debates about if they should be considered energy or protection. This was surely a positive effect, as well as the fact that, in the end, after exploring the impact on gameplay, they normally converged to a consensus.

In our study, we analyzed a set of popular games within the framework to understand its consistency (similarity between analysis) and completeness (most of the situations are describable within the framework). For 80% of the analyzed features, the framework is arguable consistent, a promising result, as this is, as far as we know, the first strong effort on this subject. We have also identified the causes for some of the inconsistencies, so improved versions of the framework can already be envisaged.

Regarding completeness, we have identified three cases where games presented mechanics that did not fit the framework. Considering that 16 games were analyzed within four main classifications, and that the identified cases apply to only one of the categories, the issues are related to only 3 cases (out of 64). The situations of having lives associated with checkpoints and stealing energy from characters is something to be included in a next version of the framework, to improve its completeness. The limitations regarding multiplayer modes require a more in-depth study.

The set of games used to validate our framework was defined starting from a list of the best games for each year, selected by reputable video game journalists or magazines.

This choice provided a neutral and unbiased test set but left out an important segment of the game market, which is the mobile gaming market. The concept of credit was popular in arcade games and lost its presence in games in home consoles. However, the monetization models based in ads, common in free games for mobile platforms, brought a new approach to credits that is worth studying. Future research should also consider the versions and platforms of the games being analyzed, which can lead to comparisons of how the same games are represented in multiple platforms.

Finally, further developments should also consider a possible improvement regarding the description of the framework with a more formal mechanism and/or language. This might also lead to studies analyzing if more formal representations can contribute to a better understanding of the framework concepts.

Acknowledgements. This paper is financed by Instituto Politécnico de Setúbal.

References

1. Bryzgel, A.: The $120,000 banana: how to have your art and eat it. The Conversation. https://theconversation.com/the-120-000-banana-how-to-have-your-art-and-eat-it-128571. Accessed 30 May 2023
2. Hunicke, R., Leblanc, M., Zubek, R.: MDA: a formal approach to game design and game research. In: Proceedings of the Challenges in Game AI Workshop, 19th National Conference on Artificial Intelligence. AAAI Press, San Jose, CA (2004)
3. Zagal, J. P., Bruckman, A.: The game ontology project: supporting learning while contributing authentically to game studies. In: Proceedings of the 8th International Conference on International Conference for the Learning Sciences - Volume 2 (ICLS'08). International Society of the Learning Sciences, pp. 499–506 (2008)
4. Orland, K., Thomas, D., Steinberg, S.: The Videogame Style Guide and Reference Manual. Lulu.com, Morrisville, NC (2007)
5. Rouse III, R.: Game Design: Theory and Practice (2nd ed.). Jones & Bartlett Learning, Burlington, MA (2004)
6. Lecky-Thomson, G.: Video Game Design Revealed. Course Technology, Boston, MA (2007)
7. Fullerton, T.: Game Design Workshop: A Playcentric Approach to Creating Innovative Games, 4th edn. A K Peters/CRC Press, Natick, MA (2018)
8. Moore, M.: Basics of Game Design. A K Peters/CRC Press, Natick, MA (2011)
9. Carreker, D.: The Game Developer's Dictionary: A Multidisciplinary Lexicon for Professionals and Students. Cengage Learning, Boson, MA (2012)
10. Brathwaite, B., Schreiber, I.: Challenges for Game Designers. Charles River Media, Boston, MA (2008)
11. Adams, E., Dormans, J.: Game Mechanics: Advanced Game Design. New Riders, Indianapolis, IN (2012)
12. Adams, E.: Fundamentals of Game Design, 2nd edn. New Riders, Indianapolis, IN (2009)
13. Rogers, S.: Level Up! The Guide to Great Video Game Design, 2nd edn. John Wiley & Sons, Hoboken, NJ (2014)·
14. Huotari, K., Hamari, J.: Defining gamification. In: Proceeding of the 16th International Academic MindTrek Conference on - MindTrek ' vol. 12, p. 17 (2012)
15. Prensky, M.: Digital Game-Based Learning. Paragon House, St Paul, MN (2007)

Method for Training Player Emotion in a Custom FPS Game Using Heart Rate

Shuo Zhou^(✉) and Norihisa Segawa

Kyoto Sangyo University, Kyoto, Japan
{zhoushuo3,sega}@acm.org

Abstract. As a part of e-sports, first-person shooter (FPS) games are extremely competitive and playable, and many players devote their time and energy to them. Within these intense gaming scenarios, players must maintain composure and exhibit precise control over their mouse or controller. However, not all players possess the ability to regulate their emotions effectively. It is all too common for players to succumb to overwhelming stress during a game, resulting in costly errors and ultimately, defeat. Therefore, it becomes imperative to discover methods for training players to manage their emotions and maintain a state of calm while engaged in FPS games. In this study, we propose a new training approach: using heart rate analysis to gauge a player's stress levels during gameplay and employing it as a parameter to help them adjust their emotions and remain composed. To evaluate the viability of this method, a series of experiments and evaluations were conducted. The experimental results provide evidence to support the notion that training with heart rate can effectively assist players in stress control during a custom FPS game.

Keywords: Heart Rate · Emotion · Stress · FPS game · Train · PulseSensor · Arduino

1 Introduction

In recent years, an increasing number of players have participated in e-sports entertainment events and competitions [1] [2]. Although the e-sports category is not considered a sport in the traditional sense, it has a large user base and business value. As a part of e-sports, first-person shooter (FPS) games are extremely competitive and playable, and many players devote their time and energy to them. For players, control and experience in the game are important, as these elements directly affect their score in the game [3]. To enhance the in-game control and compensate for the lack of experience, players often need to spend time improving their game skills [4] [5]. Various training software for FPS games have powerful features for situational simulation and customization, and players can improve their gaming skills by training repeatedly using such software [6].

In addition to mastering shooting techniques, emotional control also plays a vital role for players in FPS games [7]. In high-intensity situations, where swift

© IFIP International Federation for Information Processing 2023
Published by Springer Nature Switzerland AG 2023
P. Ciancarini et al. (Eds.): ICEC 2023, LNCS 14455, pp. 72–80, 2023.
https://doi.org/10.1007/978-981-99-8248-6_6

elimination of enemies is crucial to survival, players must maintain composure and exhibit precise control of their mouse or controller. However, not all players are adept at managing their emotions effectively. Novice or average players can easily succumb to excessive stress during gameplay, leading to costly mistakes and potential defeat. Therefore, it becomes essential to explore methods for training players to regulate their emotions and remain calm while immersed in FPS games.

Previous studies have indicated the potential of using biological information to analyze the physical and psychological state of players in the game and using the information to optimize the player's control in the game and improve the gaming experience [8,9]. Among the various biological indicators, heart rate is considered particularly effective in real-time stress analysis [10]. Therefore, we propose a novel training approach: using heart rate analysis to gauge a player's stress levels during gameplay and using this data as a parameter to guide players in adjusting their emotions and maintaining a calm state.

Our objective is to train players through a customized FPS game that integrates real-time heart rate monitoring. By doing so, players can acquire the skills necessary to regulate their emotions, maintain composure, and ultimately reduce control mistakes, thus improving their overall gaming experience.

2   System Composition

Here, we build a system for training emotion in a custom FPS game based on the player's heart rate in real-time (Fig. 1).

2.1   System Implementation

During gameplay, the player's primary task involves shooting at targets using the mouse. In this proposed system, the player's heart rate will be continuously monitored in real-time. The change in the player's heart rate will serve as a parameter to adjust the speed of the target's movement within the game. Consequently, when the player's heart rate is within a normal range, the motion

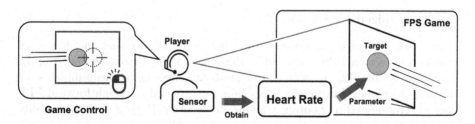

Fig. 1. In a custom FPS game, the target changes speed based on the player's heart rate. The higher the player's heart rate, the faster the speed of the target. In the game, the player needs to stay as calm as possible and defeat the target as soon as possible.

of the target will remain manageable, allowing the player to successfully hit the target. However, as the player's heart rate rises due to increased stress, the target's speed will correspondingly increase, posing a greater challenge for the player to hit accurately. Thus, throughout the game, players will be compelled to regulate their emotions, maintaining a calm state and ensuring their heart rate remains within a normal range, enabling them to effectively hit the target. By implementing this system, players can be trained to control their emotions while engaged in the game.

2.2 Obtain Heart Rate

To acquire the player's real-time heart rate data during the game, we developed a device using the Arduino Uno microcontroller and the heart rate sensor called PulseSensor [11] (Fig. 2). The PulseSensor (Fig. 2(a)(b)) is inexpensive and easy to set up. By attaching the heart rate sensor to the player's wrist (Fig. 2(d)), we are able to continuously gather real-time heart rate data throughout the engagement from the player during the FPS game. This data allows us to analyze the player's stress level and monitor changes in their heart rate.

Fig. 2. The device used to obtain the real-time heart rate. (a) Front of PulseSensor. (b) Back of PulseSensor. (c) Connection between the Arduino and the PulseSensor. (d) Attaching the sensor on the player's wrist.

2.3 Customized FPS Game

To establish a connection between the player's heart rate and the game, we developed a custom FPS game using Python and the Ursina engine (Fig. 3). The Ursina engine [12], an open-source platform, offers numerous templates for designing 3D games. Leveraging this engine, we created a straightforward FPS game and configured a shooting training mode using Python. We successfully integrated the Arduino device with the game, enabling us to measure, analyze, and display the player's real-time heart rate fluctuations during gameplay.

Within the game, the player operates the mouse to aim at a target that moves dynamically. To simulate the experience of a typical FPS game, we designed

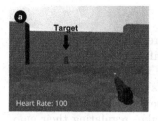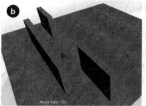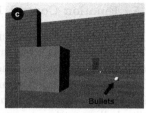

Fig. 3. A custom FPS game. (a) The target in the game is a blue square that moves at a speed that changes based on real-time heart rate. (b) The target moves in front of a wall, and part of its motion path is covered by two other walls. (c) In the game, the target will continuously shoot at the player, and the player needs to dodge bullets to counterattack. (Color figure online)

a scene featuring two walls that partially obstruct the player's view, allowing them to observe the target only within a fixed window. This setup emulates the challenge of shooting and was used to simulate a typical FPS game where the player needs to shoot at a fast-moving target. The target follows an accelerated linear path, moving back and forth. The game provides customization options for the number, size, direction, health, and initial speed of the targets. When the game starts, the target will shoot at the player, the player needs to dodge the bullets while shooting at the target. When a bullet successfully hits a target, the target's health diminishes. The game concludes ends when the target's health reaches zero. At the end of the game, the system automatically calculates the time taken by the player to defeat the target from the beginning of the gameplay session.

2.4 Connected Heart Rate and Target Speed

To facilitate emotion control training, we established a direct correlation between the player's real-time heart rate and the speed of the target's motion. Before the game started, the device records the player's average heart rate under normal conditions, which serves as their resting heart rate benchmark. At the beginning of the game, the target moves at an initial speed determined by the player's reaction time. As the player experiences increased stress from failing to hit the target swiftly, the target's speed will become faster with the rise in heart rate. For instance, consider a player with a resting heart rate of 70 beats per minute (bpm). In this scenario, we set the target's initial speed to 10. During gameplay, for every 5-unit increase in the player's heart rate, the target's speed increases by 5 units as well. Consequently, if the player's heart rate elevates to 100 bpm due to stress, the target's speed will reach 40 (four times the initial speed), significantly impeding the player's ability to hit the target. Conversely, when the player consciously tries to calm down and their heart rate decreases, the target's speed gradually decreases, eventually returning to normal levels.

2.5 Emotion Control Training

During the game, the player's heart rate fluctuates in response to their emotions. When players feel the pressure to defeat the target swiftly, their heart rate tends to increase. This makes the target's speed accelerate and more difficult to hit. This can lead to a detrimental cycle where the player's control becomes compromised, resulting in a progressively more difficult game experience. To overcome this challenge, players must recognize that staying calm, regulating their emotions, and maintaining a smooth shooting technique are key to achieving rapid target defeat. By adopting this approach, players can actively train themselves in-game and develop the ability to effectively manage their emotions.

3   Evaluation of the Proposed Method

This study focuses on constructing a real-time heart rate-based system for emotion training in a customized FPS game. To assess the viability of this training method, a series of experiments were conducted. Firstly, it was crucial to verify the feasibility of employing heart rate as a training parameter. Subsequently, a controlled experiment was conducted to illustrate the effectiveness of the heart rate-based training method compared to conventional repetitive training approaches.

3.1 Experimental Method

In the custom game detailed in Sect. 2.3, we established a target with a health point (HP) value of 100. Each successful hit from time the participant results in a deduction of 10 HP from the target. In the game, the target's speed is set to 10 and the participant must defeat the target as quickly as possible. At the beginning of the experiment, we first recorded the time taken by the participant to complete the game 5 times. The participant then performed 20 training sessions. When the training session is over, the participant completes the game 5 more times and the time taken will be recorded. The participant's real-time heart rate during each game will be recorded.

For experiments, we use the following two training methods (Fig. 4).

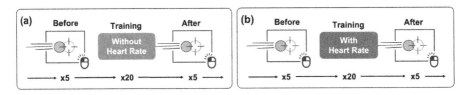

Fig. 4. Two training methods. (a) Training without heart rate (repetitive training). (b) Training with heart rate.

Without Heart Rate: During the training sessions, the participant followed a training method that did not incorporate the use of heart rate. In this method, the speed of the target within the game remained constant at 10, and the participant engaged in repetitive gameplay without any adjustments based on heart rate fluctuations.

With Heart Rate: The participant underwent heart rate-based training. In this method, the speed of the target within the game changes dynamically adjusted based on the participant's heart rate, as described in Sect. 2.4. The objective for the participant was to successfully complete the game while consciously maintaining a state of calmness and striving to keep their heart rate as close to normal as possible.

In this study, only the author's data (a male, 27 years old, with experience in FPS games) was collected because the study is still a work in progress.

3.2 Experiment 1: Feasibility of the Training Method Using Heart Rate

Before comparing the results of the two methods, we need to confirm that the method of training in a custom FPS game using heart rate is feasible. We recorded the time taken by the participant to beat the target before and after training with the heart rate and the average heart rate of the participant during the game. The results (Fig. 5) showed that the participant spent an average of 17.36 s and an average heart rate of 90 bpm the five times before training, while the participant spent an average of 12.91 s and an average heart rate of 77 bpm the five times after training.

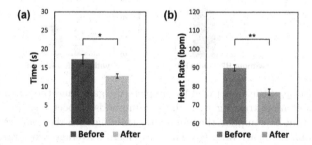

Fig. 5. Comparison between the time taken by the participant to complete the game and the mean heart rate before and after training. (a) After training, the average time taken by the participant to complete the game decreased by 4.45 s. (b) After training, the average heart rate of the participant during the game decreased by 12 bpm.

A Mann-Whitney U test was used to test the validity of the method of training using heart rate. We first compared the time taken by the participant to complete the game before and after training. The significance level was set at 5% (a two-tailed test). According to the statistical analysis, the u-value was 23.0, and the p-value was 0.0317. The test results confirmed that the participant took significantly less time to defeat the target after training with heart rate compared to before. We then compared the mean heart rate of the participant during the game before and after training. The significance level was set at 1% (a two-tailed test). According to the statistical analysis, the u-value was 25.0, and the p-value was 0.0079. The test results confirmed that the increase in the participant's heart rate during the game was controlled after training with heart rate compared to before.

Experimental results showed that training using heart rate could improve the player's self-control of their stress level in this custom FPS game.

3.3   Experiment 2: Control Experiment

To determine the effectiveness of the heart rate-based training method compared to the non-heart rate method (repetitive training), the participant underwent training using both approaches. The participant's time to defeat the target and average heart rate during the game were then compared. The results (Fig. 6) showed that the participant spent an average of 15.20 s and an average heart rate of 86 bpm to complete the game five times after training without the heart rate, while the participant spent an average of 12.91 s and an average heart rate of 77 bpm to complete the game five times after training with the heart rate.

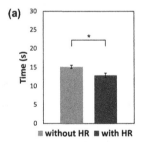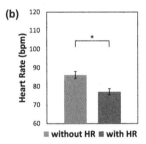

Fig. 6. Comparison of the time taken to complete the game and the average heart rate of the participant after training with the two methods respectively. (a) The participant's average time to complete the game after training with the heart rate was 2.29 s less than without the heart rate. (b) The participant's average heart rate during the game after training with the heart rate was 9 bpm less than without the heart rate.

The Mann-Whitney U test was used to test whether there was a significant difference between the results of training using the two methods. The significance level was set at 5% (two-tailed test). We first compared the time taken by the participant to complete the game after training using the two methods. According to the statistical analysis, the u-value was 23.0 and the p-value was 0.0317. The test result confirmed that the participant trained using the heart rate method spent significantly less time defeating the target compared to the method trained without the heart rate method. We then compared the mean heart rate of the participant during the game after training using both methods. According to the statistical analysis, the u-value was 23.0 and the p-value was 0.0361. The test results confirmed that the participant trained with the heart rate method had better-controlled increases in heart rate during the game compared to that without the heart rate method.

Experimental results showed that training with heart rate allows players to better control their stress in customized FPS games compared to training without heart rate.

3.4   Discussion

In this section, we conduct a series of experiments to verify that training with heart rate in a custom FPS game could help players control their stress. We first verified that training using heart rate could help the participants control their heart rate to defeat the target quickly. Then, we demonstrated in a controlled experiment that a training method using heart rate was more effective than not using heart rate (repetitive training). These experiments collectively provide evidence supporting the notion that training with heart rate can effectively assist players in stress control during a custom FPS game.

4   Conclusion and Future Work

In this study, we propose a method for training player emotions using heart rate in FPS games. Our experimental findings confirm that this heart rate-based training can aid participants with stress and help the participant to control during a custom FPS game. Nevertheless, it is important to acknowledge certain limitations of our study: (1) Data collection was restricted to the authors, and we did not conduct broader experiments. (2) The experiments were limited to a custom game and did not involve existing FPS games. (3) The experiment duration was short, and the long-term sustainability of the training effects was not assessed. (4) Heart rate is only one possible parameter to observe stress in players.

In conclusion, this study represents an ongoing effort, and the effectiveness and generalizability of the heart rate-based method for training player emotions in FPS games remain topics for future investigation. However, our study introduces a novel approach to training player emotions. When future studies were completed, we believe that this method could be applied to other games and sports. This study could provide a reference for such investigations.

As for future work, we will conduct further experiments to collect data from more participants to verify the effectiveness of the training method using heart rate in general. In addition, we will also use some existing FPS games to further validate the effectiveness of the method. Whether the training effect can be retained in the long term will also be investigated in the future long-term process.

References

1. Parry, J.: E-sports are not sports. Sport, Ethics Philosophy **13**(1), 3–18 (2019)
2. Abanazir, C.: Institutionalisation in e-sports. Sport Ethics Philos. **13**(2), 117–131 (2019)
3. Depping, A.E., Mandryk, R.L., Li, N., Gutwin, V., Vicencio-Moreira, R.: How disclosing skill assistance affects play experience in a multiplayer first-person shooter game. In: Proceedings of the 2016 CHI Conference on Human Factors in Computing Systems (CHI '16). Association for Computing Machinery, New York, NY, USA, pp. 3462–3472 (2016). https://doi.org/10.1145/2858036.2858156
4. Vicencio-Moreira, R., Mandryk, R.L., Gutwin, C.: Now You Can Compete With Anyone: Balancing Players of Different Skill Levels in a First-Person Shooter Game. In Proceedings of the 33rd Annual ACM Conference on Human Factors in Computing Systems (CHI '15). Association for Computing Machinery, New York, pp. 2255–2264 (2015). https://doi.org/10.1145/2702123.2702242
5. Jansz, J., Tanis, M.: Appeal of playing online first person shooter games. Cyberpsychology Behav. **10**(1), 133–136 (2007)
6. STATESPACE. AimLab. Retrieved August 23, 2022 (2022). https://aimlab.g
7. Kou, Y., Gui, X.: Emotion Regulation in eSports Gaming: A Qualitative Study of League of Legends. Proc. ACM Hum.-Comput. Interact. 4, CSCW2, Article 158 (October 2020), 25 p. (2020). https://doi.org/10.1145/3415229
8. Zhou, S., Segawa, N.: Optimization of first-person shooter game control using heart rate sensor. In: Baalsrud Hauge, J., C. S. Cardoso, J., Roque, L., Gonzalez-Calero, P.A. (eds.) ICEC 2021. LNCS, vol. 13056, pp. 363–369. Springer, Cham (2021). https://doi.org/10.1007/978-3-030-89394-1_27
9. Zhou, S., Segawa, N.: Method for music game control using myoelectric sensors. In: Entertainment Computing–ICEC 2022: 21st IFIP TC 14 International Conference, ICEC 2022, Bremen, Germany, November 1–3, 2022, Proceedings. Cham: Springer International Publishing (2022)
10. Kim, H.-G., et al.: Stress and heart rate variability: a meta-analysis and review of the literature. Psychiatry Investigation **15**(3), 235 (2018)
11. PulseSensor. https://pulsesensor.com/. Accessed Aug 4 2023
12. Ursina Engine. https://www.ursinaengine.org/. Aaccessed 4 Aug 2023
13. Martin-Niedecken, Lisa, A., Schättin, A.: Let the body'n'brain games begin: toward innovative training approaches in esports athletes. Front. Psychol. **11**, 138 (2020)
14. Nagorsky, E., Wiemeyer, J.: The structure of performance and training in esports. PLoS ONE **15**(8), e0237584 (2020)

Serious Gameplay

Split Screen - Split Mind: An Innovative Format for Narrative Reflexive, and Pedagogical Games

Nicolas Szilas$^{(\boxtimes)}$ (iD), Jérôme Humbert, and Kim Le

TECFA - FPSE, Université de Genève, Villa Battelle (Bâtiment A) Route de Drize 7,
1227 Carouge, Switzerland
nicolas.szilas@unige.ch
https://tecfa.unige.ch

Abstract. Split screen is a cinematographic device in which the screen is divided into sub-sections representing different views. It is used only occasionally in films and narrative games, as it may be confusing and disrupts immersion. In this article, we propose to use split screen for learning purposes, and describe a fully implemented serious game based on the concept of simultaneous debriefing. The screen is divided into one part representing a character telling his story, and another part representing this told story, interaction occurring at both levels.

A qualitative evaluation showed that the game was not confusing for most users and that the split screen did change the in-game behavior and the vision of the story. However a minority of players reported that split screen improved their learning.

Keywords: Split Screen · Learning Games · Serious Games · Narrative Games

1 Exploration of Split Screen in Digital and Non Digital Media

1.1 Split Screen in Interactive Digital Storytelling

We are interested in narrative video games and their use for learning purposes. In the context of Interactive Digital Storytelling, this research aims at exploring the potential benefits of using the technique of split screen. This was originally a cinematographic technique that involved assembling several views into a single screen [10]. The screen is therefore split into those different views, for example to characters talking to each other on the phone. Split screen is not new and can be even tracked back as early as in 1903, in the movie "Life of an American Fireman" (see Fig. 1). The technique was used every now and then in film (e.g. the movie "The Thomas Crown" in 1968, the TV series "24" in 2001) and even became a standard way of delivering content in the digital world: screen split

© IFIP International Federation for Information Processing 2023
Published by Springer Nature Switzerland AG 2023
P. Ciancarini et al. (Eds.): ICEC 2023, LNCS 14455, pp. 83–95, 2023.
https://doi.org/10.1007/978-981-99-8248-6_7

into four quadrants in multi-player games, TV journal, management games with several windows, etc. Nevertheless, when it comes to telling a story, the dominant format is the single screen [19], including in games, while split screen tends to be reserved for experimental film [8].

The predominance of single screen narration is certainly related to the major perceptive characteristics of split screen: the human brain has difficulties to divide its attention between two stimuli presented at the same time [16], therefore the two (or more) views presented simultaneously might not be full perceived by the viewer or user, because each view may represent a different context. One hypothesis is that the users would be switching from one view to the other rather than perceiving them in parallel. While this certainly explains why split screen is used with parsimony in narrative media, this research aims at exploring the use of split in narrative games, and in particular in learning games. Indeed, we hypothesize that the multiplicity of options brought about by the interactivity of narrative games can be advantageously combined with another multiplicity, that of split-screen displays. To explore this possibility, a necessary step is to analyse the various dimensions that characterize the split screen, at the visual/perceptive (Sect. 1.2) and narrative (Sect. 1.3) levels.

Fig. 1. Split screen in the movie "Life of an American Fireman" (Edwin S. Porter, 1903)

1.2   Visual Characteristics of Split Screen

While the typical case of split screen involves the separation of the screen into two equal halves, many more configurations are possible. First, the number of screen parts (subscreens) can be greater than two. For example, in video games such as *Mario Kart* (Fig. 2) or *James Bond*, the screen is divided into four, allowing four player to play together. There are obvious limits in the number of subscreens, for readability reasons. Second, the spatial arrangement of different screens can vary greatly: regular or irregular division, orthogonal or diagonal divisions, rectilinear or curvilinear separations, etc. Also, the separation (border) may be more or less visible and graphically expressive, sometimes revealing a background.

Fig. 2. Mario Kart 8, multi-player game (Nitendo, 2024)

Because, as discussed above, split screen involves divided attention, some mechanisms may be added to guide the attention towards one subscreen in particular. Various visual effects are possible, such as highlighting the border, changing the coloration, the opacity, or increasing the size of the focused screen. Another approach to guide the viewer attention is to use audio. Typically, one of the subscreens would produce a dominant sound, and the gaze will be naturally attracted by the subscreen that correspond to the loud audio. This principle is used in the movie *Timecode* (Mike Giggis, 2000), entirely displayed on four quadrants. In addition, the sound spatialization could also help to guide the attention towards the corresponding subscreen, a technique largely used in 360 movies.

1.3   Narrative Analysis of Split Screen

Let us now analyze the split screen according to the narrative status of the content displayed in each subscreen. In a narrative context, when split screen is used to tell a story, the two (or more) subscreens correspond to two (or more) views on the fictional world. Depending on the relation between these views, the split screen get a different meaning and narrative potential.

In the case multiplayer video games (e.g. Mario Kart), as well as in some movies [21], the different subscreens represent the same place filmed from different viewpoints. In the classical case found in several cinematographic pieces, the different subscreens represent events happening in different places and at the same time, for example a telephone call between two characters. But many other forms of split screens exist. For example, in the example given above in the early movie *Life of a fireman* (Fig. 1), the inserted screen in the thought of the character, meaning that the two subscreens do no show a different view of the same world but two different worlds, the second one being imagined by a character in the first one. In this case, one of the world is embedded into the other. In a more recent movie, *500 Days of Summer*, for one specific scene, the screen is divided into two equal parts: the left one represents how the character wished a party would happen, while the right one represents what really happened, as shown in Fig. 3.

Fig. 3. Split screen in the movie "500 Days of Summer" (Marc Webb, 2009), showing he same scene in two distinct possible worlds

One could enumerate many different existing or imagined configurations, but all these cases could be more precisely theorized by referring to the Possible Worlds Theory, and in particular its applications in narratology [14,15]. This theory not only establishes that a fictional narrative constitutes a possible world that is more or less related to our real world but also distinguishes several types of possible worlds within a given narrative. Some possible worlds correspond to several expectations that the reader may produce, as described by U. Eco [5]. But possible worlds also include worlds that are told, thought, hoped, dreamt, etc. by characters. More importantly, the main characteristic of possible worlds is how they can be accessed from one to the other. This can be applied to split screens in interactive storytelling: a split screen is characterized by the relation between the worlds subscreens display: either the worlds are the same (and the subscreen may differ in viewpoint, place and time) or they are different, and what must be analyzed is the difference and accessibility between the displayed worlds.

Finally, an important characterization is where interactions takes place, that is in which subscreen(s). Depending on the relation between the worlds represented by the subscreens, such interaction can generate complex situations, for example when the subscreens represent different times.

2 Learning with Split Screen

The question raised by this article is the following: what type of split screen would be suited for a pedagogical narrative game? The games we are targeting are narrative games that involve taking decisions for a character, situated in a social environment [18]. This concerns fields as varied as nursing [4], family care, emergency care [12], police work [11], prevention of risky behaviour, or recruiting. At first sight, it may seem odd to use split screen for learning purposes. Games promote users' immersion, which is often claimed to be of great interest when games are used for learning [7]. But split screen is fundamentally anti-immersive: switching from one subscreen to the other requires to leave a first world and then to re-enter a second world. How, therefore, could split screen promote learning? However, the role of immersion in learning is also subject to debate. In learning games, as well as in learning simulations, only being engaged and immersed in an environment to practice some skills is not sufficient to promote learning, reflective practice remains central [6]. The debriefing phase, that follows the hand-on phase in order to reflect on it, appears to be an essential part in learning. Learning games need both to immerse the player into a rich learning environment and to provide comments on the players' actions and help them reflect on their actions. Therefore, split screen, as a device which both immerses and forces players to "un-immerse" may provide an original solution to promote learning with narrative games.

According to the previous section, the key design question is: what could be the relation between the two subscreens, that is between the two worlds they display? An initial proposition that stems directly from very nature of interactive storytelling consists in displaying two parallel worlds, both derived from the same world via a choice: in a choice situation (e.g. a dilemma), the player would see not only the consequence of his or her choice but also, simultaneously, what would have happened if the alternative option(s) had been selected. Although certainly interesting, this proposition was finally not retained, not because we tested it and/or found some limitations, but because another one appeared more promising.

The proposition that was chosen consists in implementing a "simultaneous debriefing", that is one subscreen is dedicated to the narrative worlds where the player practices some social skill, while the other is dedicated to comment/debrief regarding the first course of action. In the vast majority of cases, debriefing happens at the end of the practical experience, enabling the learner to go back to what he or she felt during the simulation and what he or she has learnt [6]. Simultaneous debriefing has been rarely implemented so far. A comparison between in-simulation and post-simulation debriefing showed that the latter had slightly better results [20]. Learners reported dissatisfaction when learning was frequently interrupted during the simulation by feedback, which was observed in other studies in serious games [17]. However, it is expected that split screen offers a far more fluid experience, interruption being integrated in a global narrative experience consisting of a character telling a story to another character.

More precisely, the two worlds are embedded as follows: in the first world, a main character, the player character, tells to another character, the listening/confidant character, what happened to him previously, these past events constituting the second world. The split screen displays on the one hand a dialogue between two characters, and on the other hand the events told by one of them. Regarding interaction, the player interacts in the second world, as in a usual narrative games, when he or she must makes decision for the main character. By commenting on the teller's actions, the listening character provides a feedback and encourages reflections on what the player did in the second world. In addition, the user can also interact with the confidant, for example to decide to tell the truth or no. We denote the first world, with the two characters, the *telling world*, while the second world, when action and decision takes place, the *told world*.

3   Design of a Reflective Game

3.1   Choice of a Topic

As a test-bed to experiment the concept of split screen, we have chosen the domain of gambling addiction. It is effectively a behavioral issue that is closely linked to everyday life and therefore is well suited to a narrative approach. In addition, it has been widely studied. In particular, the American Association of Psychology has established a list of 9 criteria that enable to diagnose such an addiction, 5 present criteria indicating pathological gambling [3]. These criteria helped us build the software.

3.2   The Story

The story is interactive and contains more than 200 dialog lines. The following description gives an overview of the main events and interactions. The story is in French. The story starts in an apartment setting (a kitchen), with the player's character talking to his best friend, Marianne, about what happened to him recently. The embedded story, told by the player character, starts in front of a bar, where the player character moves in and has several options, such as ordering a beer, playing slot machines, watching horse-racing games and betting, etc. Depending of his choices, he spends a variable amount of his initial money. But this money was for shopping groceries for his girl friend. He then goes to the shop, and if he has no money let, he has to either borrow money over the phone to a friend (if he accepts) or shoplift. Back home, he may or may not tell the truth to Carine. In all cases, he interacts regularly with Marianne, who reacts emotionally according to what she is told, evaluates/judges what she hears and offers advice. Note that in some situations, he may not tell the truth to Marianne.

3.3   Split Screen Design and Interactivity

As discussed above, several options are available to organise two subscreens. The design goal of this organisation is that it should reflect at best the relation between the two worlds. After various attempts, we chose to use the codes of comic strips and represent the told world as a speech bubble coming out from the characters in the telling world (see Fig. 4).

The proportion of the two parts was also an important interface design choice. Because most interaction occurs at the level of the embedded story (decision making regarding addictive behaviours), and also because this subscreen involves a rich environment (a bar, a shop, etc.,), it was logical to give more space to this subscreen. But if the telling subscreen was too small, it tended to become a sort of conversational agent commenting on user's actions, which was not the intended effect, as we wanted the user to feel that he is "traveling" in space and time between the two worlds. This constraint also guided us towards a non rectilinear separation between the subscreens, which would evoke too much windows in software.

Regarding attention guidance, we have opted to change opacity in order to guide attention of the player towards the subscreen where action takes place (Fig. 4). However, this guidance is not constraining: the greyed screen is still active and the user can manually change which screen is greyed.

Both subscreens are interactive. In the left subscreen (telling world), we have only dialogic interactions (choice between sentences to say) while in the right subscreen (told world), the user can also click on objects in the world to trigger a choice menu. Note that at a given time, interaction is possible only in one of the two subscreens.

3.4   Additional Features

Along with the core narrative interaction, three components have been implemented. First, a help sheet was made accessible from the main screen (button with a question mark in Fig. 4). Second, a history of dialogues has been added, which is classical in narrative games. Third, when the story is finished, a page indicates the addiction criteria and, according to the player's choices, whether

Fig. 4. Screenshot of the developed game, showing the organization of subscreens. The left part shows Marianne in a kitchen, talking to the player, while the right part shows the told world. The latter is greyed, because interaction occurs on the left part.

these criteria are met or not, informing the user on the severity of his or her gambling addiction. For doing that, several choices in the game are directly linked to those criteria.

3.5   Implementation

We are using for this game a classical graph-based approach, with conditional links. The structure however is not simple, especially regarding conditions. Some scenes are triggered according to some specific previous choices, to the number of repetitions of some choices (counter), or to the available money. Implementing such a logic is never straightforward when the structure's complexity exceeds a certain threshold. Therefore, the implementation took place in two stages. In the first stage, the story was implemented in *Twine*. *Twine* [2] is an easy to use software dedicated to branching interactive fiction, with a hypertext structure. Nevertheless, it also includes programming features to implement conditions and other improvements over simple hypertext stories.

The *Twine* version was intensively tested and tuned to improve the story's credibility and detect logical errors. Then, in a second stage, the game was implemented on *Construct 3*. *Construct 3* [1] is an authoring tool for 2D games, providing support for usual game and multimedia interaction, based on JavaScript for scripting.

The graphics of the games come from *freepik*, a website offering free images, and were reworked with *Adobe Photoshop* and *Illustrator* when necessary.

The game is available at the following address: https://tecfa.unige.ch/jeux/passe-incertain/.

4 Preliminary Evaluation

4.1 Material

An evaluation of the learning gain when playing with the game may seem the best approach to evaluate this work. However, we believe that such quantitative evaluation is premature at this stage, and that a more qualitative evaluation regarding the users' perception is necessary at first. Indeed, this is the first release of the game, and one needs to understand how it is perceived by users, regarding the design principles that were employed. More precisely, we want to answer to the four following questions, before tackling the learning efficiency issue:

- Does the division into two screens disrupt the user experience?
- How does the users understand the division?
- How users perceive the confidant character in the first world (Marianne in the scenario)?
- More precisely, does this character help their thinking and learning?

We expected that the use of split screen with the embedded story would be fluid, that the users would grasp the different temporalities of the subscreens, that they would perceive the confidant character as a pedagogical guide promoting reflection, and finally that they would find that this character both changed their thinking and improved their learning. Nevertheless, we were open to other interpretations of the narrative device, that would help us to better understand the role of split screen in the gaming and learning experience and help us improving the game. Therefore, we opted for a questionnaire with open questions (free text entry) that would not coerce too much users' answers. Finally, we also wanted to obtain free comments regarding the game, and added three questions regarding strengths, weaknesses and improvement suggestions.

This led to a questionnaire with 12 questions (translated from French to English for this article):

1. How did you find the screen layout?
2. Were you disturbed by the two-part screen layout? If so, why?
3. In your opinion, what is the relationship between the two parts of the screen?
4. In your opinion, what does dividing the screen into two parts bring to the gaming experience?
5. What role did Marianne play in your thinking?
6. Without Marianne, would your thinking have been the same?
7. Do you think Marianne helped you learn anything? If so, please specify.
8. On a scale of 0 to 10, was the experience mentally demanding?
9. Did splitting the screen into two parts require extra work? If so, why?

10. What were the strengths of your experience?
11. What were the weaknesses of your experience?
12. Do you have any suggestions for improvement?

These questions were designed specifically for this experiment, one of which—Question 8—being inspired by the work of Paas [13] regarding self-reporting of cognitive load.

4.2 Participants

Seven participants were recruited, within the network of the researchers, with no specific age constraints. The seven participants were selected on the basis of professional diversity, so that the results are not biased towards one specific population.

4.3 Protocol

The evaluation was performed at distance, the game itself being web-based.

The selected participants received instructions by e-mail, specifying that they had to play the game and possibly replay it if they wished. They were also informed of the help button in the game. They were asked to fill the online questionnaire after having finished testing the game.

4.4 Results

Here follows a summary of users' answers to the questionnaire:

– Question 1 (screen organization): All participants answered positively.
– Question 2 (possible disruption): Only one participant declared that he or she was confused. The answer to Question 2 was: "A bit, that was difficult to know which was the main screen. The fact that one part is shaded helps you understand where to look."
– Question 3 (relation between parts): four participants mentioned explicitly the time difference between the two parts.
– Question 4 (experience of the screen division): results were more mixed, with three positive comments, one negative comment and three neutral answers (descriptive). The negative comment mentioned confusion and information overload.
– Question 5: Marianne was perceived as a friend and helper, but one player reported being absorbed into the right part of the screen, and another was unsure about her influence ("Maybe she influenced me unconsciously").
– Question 6 (help from Marianne): six participants answered positively, they would not have played the same way without her.
– Question 7 (Influence of Marianne in terms of learning): results were clearly less positive. Four participants declared that they did not learn new things from Marianne, while three acknowledged some influence, for example: "She made me think about the fact that being honest is always a good thing".

– Question 8 and 9 (cognitive load): the mean score was 2.5 (out of 10). To the associated open question, they did not report any cognitive overload in 6 cases out of 7.

We will not report here the answers to the three last questions, which were mainly designed for improving future versions of the game.

4.5 Discussion

The first question raised by this research was the acceptability of the split screen. Answers to questions 1 and 2, as well as global positive comments regarding the design enable us to conclude that the proposed split screen design is well accepted by users, and is not disturbing (except for one user). Even for this user, the disturbance was moderate ("a bit"), and s/he acknowledged that the guidance was effective. One participant even answered to Question 4 (benefits of the split screen in terms of game experience): "It allows a more immersive game, in my opinion". This is surprising, given our discussion above regarding the "anti-immersive" nature of split screen. Immersion is of course a complex topic. We may suppose that this participant reports his immersion in the whole story, with both the scene in the kitchen with Marianne and the embedded scene, not just the latter one.

The division was also well understood by the participants, as a scene happening in the present (left subscreen), with a character telling his story happening in the past (right subscreen).

Participants recognized the role of the confidant (Marianne) in the experience, as well as the fact that she did influence their in-game behaviors. Three participants also mentioned the reflective nature of the experience (e.g. "the fact to be able to choose the answer makes the player think on his own personal life"). Nevertheless, they were less positive regarding her influence in terms of learning. Despite the fact that good conditions for learning were apparently gathered (interaction, reflection), this was not sufficient to facilitate learning for all users (at least the perception of learning). This will be investigated further in future research. Interestingly, an emerging theme was responsibility: "I felt accountable to Marianne", "I hesitate to tell her", "[without her] I would have kept on lying". This is definitely a dimension we want to explore.

5 Conclusion

We have proposed in this article an innovative way to approach non-technical/social skills learning with games, based on the cinematographic device of split screen. The narrative game was divided into a telling world and an embedded told world, with interaction occurring at both levels. The idea has been fully implemented in an online game, tested qualitatively by 7 participants. Our preliminary results showed that the split screen device, despite its complexity, was well accepted and understood. The game has interesting qualities, such as promoting reflection, in-game behavioral change and responsibility.

Regarding learning, results were less conclusive and additional evidence are needed. Following this preliminary evaluation, we plan to perform other evaluations, inspired from the Design-Based Research approach [22]: tuning the game according to previous iteration as well as proposing new hypotheses at each iteration, in a flexible way. For the next iteration in particular, we want to explore the role of responsibility in the proposed game, and how it may affect learning. This investigation may benefits from finding in pedagogical agents regarding the different roles such agents may take [9], but our case is more complex, because of the presence of agents in both the telling and told worlds. Progressively, we aim at writing a design guide dedicated to the type of split screen games introduced in this research.

References

1. Construct 3. https://www.construct.net/
2. Twine. https://twinery.org/
3. Crocq, M.A., Guelfi, J.D.: DSM-5: manuel diagnostique et statistique des troubles mentaux. Elsevier Masson, 5e éd edn (2015)
4. Petit dit Dariel, O.J., Raby, T., Ravaut, F., Rothan-Tondeur, M.: Developing the serious games potential in nursing education. Nurse Educ. Today https://doi.org/10.1016/j.nedt.2012.12.014
5. Eco, U.: Lector in fabula: Le rôle du lecteur ou la Coopération interprétative dans les textes narratifs. Grasset (1989)
6. Fanning, R.M., Gaba, D.M.: The role of debriefing in simulation-based learning. Simul. Healthcare J. Soc. Simul. Healthcare **2**(2), 115–25 (2007). https://doi.org/10.1097/SIH.0b013e3180315539
7. de Freitas, S., Liarokapis, F.: Serious games: a new paradigm for education? In: Ma, M., Oikonomou, A., Jain, L.C. (eds.) Serious Games and Edutainment Applications, pp. 9–23. Springer, London (2011). https://doi.org/10.1007/978-1-4471-2161-9_2
8. Hales, C.: Weird and wonderful: how experimental film narratives can inform interactive digital narratives. In: Bosser, A.-G., Millard, D.E., Hargood, C. (eds.) ICIDS 2020. LNCS, vol. 12497, pp. 149–163. Springer, Cham (2020). https://doi.org/10.1007/978-3-030-62516-0_14
9. Kim, Y., Baylor, A.L.: Research-based design of pedagogical agent roles: a review, progress, and recommendations. Int. J. Artif. Intell. Educ. **26**(1), 160–169 (2015). https://doi.org/10.1007/s40593-015-0055-y
10. Kumar, M., Gandhi, V., Ronfard, R., Gleicher, M.: Zooming on all actors: automatic focus+context split screen video generation. Comput. Graph. Forum **36**(2), 455–465 (2017). https://doi.org/10.1111/cgf.13140
11. Linssen, J., de Groot, T., Theune, M., Heylen, D.: LOITER-TB: thought bubbles that give feedback on virtual agents' experiences. In: Brinkman, W.-P., Broekens, J., Heylen, D. (eds.) IVA 2015. LNCS (LNAI), vol. 9238, pp. 283–286. Springer, Cham (2015). https://doi.org/10.1007/978-3-319-21996-7_30
12. Lourdeaux, D., et al.: VICTEAMS: a virtual environment to train medical team leaders to interact with virtual subordinates. In: Proceedings of the 19th ACM International Conference on Intelligent Virtual Agents, IVA 2019, pp. 241–243. Association for Computing Machinery (2019). https://doi.org/10.1145/3308532.3329418

13. Paas, F.G.W.C.: Training strategies for attaining transfer of problem-solving skill in statistics: a cognitive-load approach. J. Educ. Psychol. **84**, 429–434 (1992). https://doi.org/10.1037/0022-0663.84.4.429
14. Pavel, T.G.: "possible worlds" in literary semantics (1975). J. Aesthetics Art Criticism 34(2), 165–176 (1975). https://doi.org/10.2307/430073
15. Ryan, M.L.: Possible Worlds, Artificial Intelligence, and Narrative Theory. Indiana University Press (1991)
16. Spelke, E., Hirst, W., Neisser, U.: Skills of divided attention. Cognition **4**(3), 215–230 (1976). https://doi.org/10.1016/0010-0277(76)90018-4
17. Sutter Widmer, D., Szilas, N.: Un temps pour jouer, un temps pour écouter? In actes de la conférence. In: Environnements informatiques pour l'apprentissage humain - EIAH (2011)
18. Szilas, N.: Vers les simulations sociales pédagogiques, et au-delà: du réel au virtuel, du social au narratif. Raisons éducatives (21), 113–128 (2017). https://doi.org/10.3917/raised.021.0113
19. Talen, J.: "24": Split screen's big comeback (2002). https://www.salon.com/2002/05/14/24_split/
20. Van Heukelom, J.N., Begaz, T., Treat, R.: Comparison of postsimulation debriefing versus in-simulation debriefing in medical simulation. Simul. Healthcare J. Soc. Simul. Healthcare **5**(2), 91–97 (2010). https://doi.org/10.1097/SIH.0b013e3181be0d17
21. Villenave, B.: De la cicatrice Retour sur le split screen depalmien. Cahier Louis-Lumière **5**(1), 49–57 (2008). https://doi.org/10.3406/cllum.2008.913
22. Wang, F., Hannafin, M.J.: Design-based research and technology-enhanced learning environments. Educ. Technol. Res. Dev. **53**(4), 5–23 (2005). https://doi.org/10.1007/BF02504682

Accessibility Issues Within Serious Games in Engineering Education for Visual Impairment

Sundus Fatima[1]([⊠]) [iD] and Jannicke Baalsrud Hauge[1,2] [iD]

[1] BIBA- Bremer Institut Für Produktion Und Logistik GmbH, Hochschulring. 20, 28359 Bremen, Germany
fat@biba.uni-bremen.de
[2] KTH – Royal Institute of Technology, Kvarnbergagatan 12, Södertälje, Sweden

Abstract. In recent years, serious games have become more common in engineering education and vocational training as learning tools. Serious games often require active participation from learners, encouraging them to apply knowledge and skills in a practical context. They can simulate real-world scenarios, allowing students to practice decision-making, problem-solving, and critical thinking skills. Studies show that serious games have shown promising outcomes in improving engagement and learning outcomes. However, serious games are still not yet fully accessible to all learners. There is a need for more games to be designed and developed to accommodate the needs of individuals with impairments. By considering accessibility features, serious games can be made more inclusive and provide an equitable engaging experience for all learners. While progress has been made in improving accessibility, there are still issues in terms of accessibility features that need to be addressed to make serious games more accessible to diverse target groups' needs. Therefore, the focus of this paper is on discussing accessibility issues, examining and discussing the limitations of existing serious games in this context, as well as exploring guidelines to overcome these accessibility issues, which contribute to the development of more inclusive and effective engaging learning experiences for individuals with visual impairments mainly with the focus on colorblindness. To accomplish this, a systematic literature review (SLR) is performed to explore accessibility issues and limitations of existing serious games in this domain, and resulting guidelines are proposed based on the SLR findings. The paper is structured into five sections, beginning with the introduction, followed by the research methodology, findings, discussion, and guidelines, and ending with the conclusion.

Keywords: Serious Games · Visual Impairment · Engineering Education

1 Introduction

Serious games have gained popularity as an effective learning tool in engineering education and vocational training [1]. These games offer a dynamic and interactive learning experience that promotes active participation and engagement among learners [2]. One

P. Ciancarini et al. (Eds.): ICEC 2023, LNCS 14455, pp. 96–114, 2023.
https://doi.org/10.1007/978-981-99-8248-6_8

of the serious games' key strengths is its capacity to give learners real-world scenarios in which to apply their knowledge and skills [3]. Serious games may allow students to engage in hands-on learning and gain experience in decision-making, problem-solving, and critical thinking [4]. This experiential learning approach enhances their understanding of complex concepts and fosters the development of practical skills [2]. Overall, serious games have shown promising outcomes by offering engaging, interactive, and practical learning experiences that lead to improved learning outcomes [4]. Serious games, when designed with accessibility as a priority, can effectively cater to a wider range of students' preferences and requirements [16]. This is particularly important in serious games since the goal is often to deliver specific educational content [5]. When serious games are accessible, students with diverse impairments can engage [16].

"Accessibility for games can be defined as the ability to play a game despite limiting conditions. Limiting conditions can be temporary functional limitations or permanent impairments - such as blindness, deafness or reduced mobility" [6]. Accessibility of serious games refers to the design and implementation of features and considerations that ensure individuals with impairments can access and engage with the games [15]. However, it is important to acknowledge that these features have certain limitations and may not fully address the diverse needs of users with different types of visual impairments [11].

Visual impairment is a broad term that encompasses different types [17]. However, the focus of this paper is on "Color Blindness". Color blindness is a visual impairment in which individuals have difficulty distinguishing certain colors or perceiving them accurately [18]. There are different types and degrees of color blindness, including:

- Red-Green Color Blindness: This is the most common type of color blindness, where individuals have difficulty distinguishing between shades of red and green [18].
- Blue-Yellow Color Blindness: In this type, individuals have difficulty differentiating between shades of blue and yellow [18].
- Total Color Blindness: A rare form of color blindness, where individuals see the world in shades of gray [18].

When it comes to serious games, individuals with color blindness face specific accessibility challenges such as visual elements without accessibility features leading to understanding difficulties [13]. Games use much color coding to represent different elements, such as objects, characters, or interactive elements for individuals with color blindness distinguishing between colors or understanding color-coded information can be challenging or impossible which can result in confusion[14], and additionally, complex menus hinder navigation [15]. Furthermore, the lack of audio support also affects engagement [12]. Ensuring accessibility is crucial for inclusivity, overcoming challenges, and meeting legal requirements.

The importance of ensuring accessibility in serious games extends beyond inclusivity and providing access for individuals with various impairments; it encompasses legal obligations [7]. There exist legal frameworks and regulations that mandate digital content, including serious games, to be accessible to individuals with impairments. For instance, guidelines such as the Web Content Accessibility Guidelines (WCAG) [37], the Independent Game Developers Association (IGDA) Special Interest Group (SIG)

[35], and the Game Association Guidelines (GAG) [10]. By prioritizing accessibility, potential legal complications can be mitigated.

Accessible serious games allow diverse students, including those with impairments [16], to engage in inclusive learning. However, color blindness poses challenges [5] such as inappropriate color scheme selection for the content, lack of audio descriptions, and limited customizable setting options [6]. This incompatibility hinders their ability to fully engage in the learning experience. Therefore, there is a need to examine existing accessibility issues in this domain as it helps to examine the challenges allowing to identify areas that require improvement and effective solutions that can be developed. It also enables us to ensure compliance with accessibility standards and legal obligations. The need to address accessibility issues gives rise to the research question (**RQ**): Which accessibility issues within the serious games must be addressed which could improve the engagement factor for students with color blindness? In this context, "must be addressed" indicates the importance of identifying and resolving the accessibility issues within serious games. It indicates that addressing these issues is crucial for improving engagement for students with colorblindness within serious games.

The paper attempts to identify, examine and discuss the accessibility issues within serious games used in engineering education for colorblindness and to propose guidelines to overcome the examined accessibility issues.

2 Research Methodology

The systematic literature review (SLR) conducted in this research aims to address the research question regarding the accessibility issues in serious games in engineering education focusing on different types of color blindness. The methodology used follows a three-stage process proposed by Tranfield, Denyer, and Smart (2003), which includes planning review, conducting the review, and reporting and dissemination. The SLR process increases transparency, reduces bias, and establishes a strong foundation for conclusions. It advances knowledge in the field and fosters effective approaches and guidelines for improving serious game accessibility with specific impairments.

1. Planning The Review

This first stage concerns planning the review of the literature. To begin our research and conduct the review, we examined various databases, such as Scopus, Web of Science, Science Direct, and IEEE Xplore. The selection was based on our access to these databases. However, databases like ACM digital library were excluded from the research due to the lack of access.

The following three databases were selected:

- Scopus
- Web of Science
- IEEE Xplore

The above-mentioned databases were chosen because they contain sufficient publications in the areas of serious games, engineering education, and different impairments. At this stage, other databases were excluded due to limited resources on the topic. The literature search focused on "engineering" subject areas in English from 2013 to 2023. This ten-year timeframe allows for a comprehensive overview of previous research, an understanding of existing study limitations, and a recognition of technological advancements' impact. This approach enables a thorough understanding of accessibility issues in serious games and enhances engagement with colorblindness in engineering education, identifying gaps, opportunities, and areas for further exploration.

2. Conducting The Review.

To initiate the study it was needed to investigate the existence of accessibility issues within serious games for colorblindness in engineering education. To do so, a search query was created using the keywords: (1) games (2) accessibility (3) colorblindness, colorblind, visual-impairment, visual-impaired (3) engineering, manufacturing (4) and training, education.

The following string was used to make the search query in titles, abstracts, and keywords follow wild card rules:

- ("games*") AND ("accessibility*") AND ("colorblindness*" OR "colorblind*" OR "visual-impairment*" OR "visual-impaired*") AND ("engineering*" OR "manufacturing*") AND ("training" OR "education")

With the above-mentioned search query, it was difficult to find literature in the databases for that reason again some of the keywords like "colorblindness*" OR "colorblind*" were excluded to have an overview of the literature on the topic. Therefore, the updated search query was:

- ("games*") AND ("accessibility*") AND ("visual-impairment*" OR "visual-impaired*") AND ("engineering*" OR "manufacturing*") AND ("training" OR "education")

With the above-mentioned search query too, it was difficult to find literature in the databases for that reason again some of the keywords like "visual-impairment*" OR "visual-impaired*" were excluded to have an overview of the literature on the topic of accessibility.

Based on the initial analysis conducted, it has been observed that there is a limited amount of literature specifically addressing the topic of serious games and accessibility in the context of colorblindness specifically in engineering education. Furthermore, among the literature that does exist, the focus of accessibility within games tends to be on addressing different impairments. This involved examining the accessibility issues and evaluating the effectiveness of accessibility features in enhancing engagement for students with impairments. The finalized search query is:

- ("games*") AND ("accessibility*") AND ("engineering*" OR "manufacturing*") AND ("training" OR "education")

To mitigate potential bias in the selection process, using the above-mentioned search query the inclusion and exclusion criteria for the selection of articles are devised:

- List of Inclusion Criteria

- The abstracts included either all of these terms or at least two of the terms "serious games," "visual impairments," and "accessibility."
- The primary focus of the papers should be on visual impairment, specifically color blindness.
- The papers show research and studies primarily concentrating on the domain of serious games in engineering education.
- To ensure a certain level of quality, the papers were published in peer-reviewed journals or conference proceedings.

- List of Exclusion Criteria

  - Papers that predominantly emphasize other impairments will be excluded from consideration.
  - Publications that primarily focus on other technologies such as VR (Virtual Reality), MR (Mixed Reality), HCI (Human-Computer Interaction), and AI (Artificial Intelligence) will be excluded.
  - Articles that are not written in English will be excluded.

The final stage of the SLR is the reporting and dissemination of the results, which are presented in the next segment.

3. Reporting and Dissemination

Accessibility issues in serious games used in engineering education for colorblind during the last 10 years have been identified. A search query: ("games*") AND ("accessibility*") AND ("engineering*" OR "manufacturing*") AND ("training" OR "education") was created to analyze related literature in respective databases (Scopus, Web of Science and IEEE Xplore).

To have a detailed overview of the number of identified papers and relevant literature in each database, providing a detailed overview of the research and quality of relevant literature available in each source as shown in Fig. 1.

The final stage of the reporting and dissemination presented an overview of the number of identified articles individually for each database. A total of "25" papers were identified as relevant to our research from the respective databases which are presented in the next section.

3   Findings on Accessibility Issues in Serious Games

In this section, a total of "25" relevant papers that were identified from the respective databases for our research are presented (see Table 1). These papers were selected based on their relevance to the topic and their contribution to understanding and addressing accessibility issues in serious games.

The identified articles have been classified into five distinct categories (see Table 1) highlighting accessibility issues, utilizing a logical categorization approach that aligns with the research streams found in the existing literature.

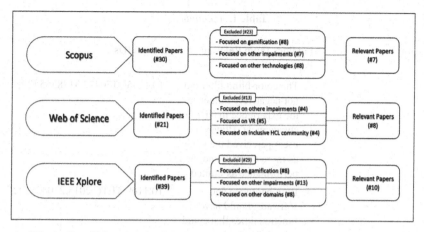

Fig. 1. Detailed overview of the number of identified papers in each database.

Table 1. Detailed findings from Systematic Literature Review (SLR)

Category	Findings From Relevant Papers	Papers IDs
A: Color	1. The use of color, along with complementary geometrical shapes and icons, is suitable for individuals with color blindness. However, identifying graphical elements in the background and colors becomes crucial, considering the type of colorblindness	10.1145/3290605.3300861 [21]
	2. Using whole-screen color filters is a common method for implementing color-blind accessibility. However, relying solely on color filters may not adequately address all challenges associated with colorblindness	10.1109/gem.2019.8811534 [11]

(continued)

Table 1. (*continued*)

Category	Findings From Relevant Papers	Papers IDs
	3. The color-blind filter did not negatively influence the experience in terms of engagement. However, users perceived the game as more difficult and their performance as limited	10.1145/3170427.3188555 [25]
	4. Both hardware and software should have functionalities that could provide access to users with functional diversity such as screen color adjustments, zooming, vibration options, etc	10.1109/TETC.2015.2504241 [28]
	5. Information provided in unstructured forms such as visual representation with different colors without alternative text descriptions or sound or inability to customize color will exclude those with this type of impairment	10.1109/SeGAH.2016.7586263 [29]
	6. It is difficult to navigate and search for icons, buttons, and the graphic display around it due to contrasting backgrounds and inappropriate color scheme selection, making navigation crucial for those with color blindness	10.1109/iceei47359.2019.8988791 [33]

(*continued*)

Table 1. (*continued*)

Category	Findings From Relevant Papers	Papers IDs
	7. Many serious games lack engagement factor since they do not benefit from visual enhancements such as color and contrast options and depend on audio feedback only, which is crucial for colorblindness or other severe visual impairments	10.1145/3411764.3445494 [36]
B: Sound/Audio	8. Development of a sound-based video game, and a haptic device, combining auditory feedback that helps color-blind players navigate and interact with the environment but could be crucial for different types of colorblindness	10.1093/iwc/iwac017 [20]
	9. Gaming environments for visually impaired users are dominated by audio games not specifically for colorblindness	10.1145/3242587.3242604 [24]
	10.Simple techniques such as captioning, changeable fonts, and sound can indeed make a significant difference in enhancing accessibility	10.1109/gem.2018.8516472 [34]
C: Interfaces	11. Approaches that involve particular interfaces and custom developments may lead to a lack of quality in the generated/adapted games and the segregation of diverse impaired players	10.1007/s10209–018-0628–2 [15]

(*continued*)

Table 1. (*continued*)

Category	Findings From Relevant Papers	Papers IDs
	12. Haptic feedback devices and audio interfaces describe visual content. These interfaces and related devices are effective in partially, but not completely, remediating the access barriers in accessibility	10.1177/0162643418759340 [22]
	13. Limited research specifically focuses on games accessible on interfaces for colorblind people	10.1109/gem.2018.8516457 [31]
D: Understanding Needs	14. Recognizing and acknowledging the needs of a diverse target group of people with different types, severities, and multiple impairments is crucial for creating accessible player experiences	10.1007/978–3-319–73356-2_10 [26]
	15. It is important that different colorblind individuals may have varying needs and preferences, so understanding diverse needs is challenging	10.23919/cisti49556.2020.9140904 [32]
	16. To make a game accessible it is important to use other non-visual modalities however, incorporating non-visual modalities is crucial for making games accessible	10.1109/fie.2014.7044493 [27]

(*continued*)

Table 1. (*continued*)

Category	Findings From Relevant Papers	Papers IDs
	17. Understanding the experiences of players in the game space is crucial for developing accessible player experiences focusing on engagement	10.1007/978–3-319–94277-3_40 [23]
	18. Accommodating all accessibility parameters in a design is crucial to ensure inclusivity for individuals with different types of needs depending on severities of colorblindness	10.1109/TAEE.2018.8476110 [30]
	19. Classifying the degree of impairment and identification of requirements is difficult in determining the specific accessibility parameters that need to be considered in game design	10.1007/s11042–022-11984–3 [38]
	20. Not all with colorblindness or other impairments have the same needs or face the same challenges, so understanding the specific impairments and their severity can help inform the design decisions	10.1145/3025453.3025518 [39]
	21. Color blindness should also be one of the considerations for game developers when they are creating and designing games	10.1016/j.procs.2021.01.070 [40]

(*continued*)

Table 1. (*continued*)

Category	Findings From Relevant Papers	Papers IDs
E: Recommendations on Accessibility	22. Recommendations listed by The Independent Game Developers Association (IGDA) Special Interest Group (SIG) on Game Accessibility proposes accessibility guidelines derived from a survey of "20" accessible games mainly for the specified impairments	10.1109/fie.2014.7044162 [35]
	23. Set of guidelines covering various aspects of accessibility for different types of visual impairments that a designer might use (GAG – Game Accessibility Guidelines)	10.1016/j.ijhcs.2019.06.010 [10]
	24. Web Content Accessibility Guidelines (WCAG) offer a wide range of guidelines	10.1109/iwsm-mensura.2016.032 [37]
	25. The standardized sets of proposed guidelines have a problem: they do not explain the accessibility problem the guideline is supposed to solve, making it difficult for a game developer to understand when and why the guideline can be applied	10.18517/ijaseit.10.3.10938 [41]

The section presents findings from relevant papers categorized into five sections: A) Color, B) Sound/Audio, C) Interfaces, D) Understanding Needs, and E) Recommendations on Accessibility. Each category highlights key insights on accessibility issues in serious games for colorblindness. The use of color, complemented by shapes and icons, proves suitable for colorblind players, but challenges vary depending on the type of colorblindness. Although whole-screen color filters are common, they may not fully address all issues. To cater to users with diverse needs, hardware, and software should provide functionalities like screen color adjustments. However, unstructured visual representations and inappropriate color schemes hinder navigation for colorblind individuals. Sound and haptic devices serve as helpful tools for color-blind players, enhancing their interaction with the gaming environment. While specific interfaces partially address accessibility barriers, customization for touchscreen gaming remains limited. Understanding the diverse needs and experiences of players plays a crucial role in creating inclusive gaming experiences. The table also highlights various guidelines and recommendations to enhance accessibility in serious games.

The section presented the SLR findings, examining accessibility issues and limitations of existing serious games in this domain. In the following section, the established categories from the SLR findings are discussed, offering insights into key findings related to accessibility issues in this context. Moreover, resulting guidelines are proposed based on the SLR findings.

4 Discussion and Guidelines

The section discusses established categories from SLR findings, offering insights on the accessibility issues and exploring guidelines.

4.1 Color

Color can present challenges for individuals with color blindness, but incorporating visual cues like geometrical shapes and icons can improve the usability and comprehension of graphical elements in games [21]. The combination of color, shapes, and icons without textual information and sound support in visual representation can pose challenges for players with color blindness. When games heavily rely on color differentiation without providing alternative text descriptions or customizable color options, individuals with color impairment may be excluded from fully participating in engaging experiences [29]. However, it's crucial to consider the specific type of color blindness when designing games, as different types affect color perception. Selecting easily distinguishable colors, shapes, and icons becomes more challenging when multiple impairments are combined. Additionally, ensuring appropriate contrast between foreground and background elements is important [36]. Adequate contrast helps individuals with color blindness discern graphical elements, even in complex color compositions in the background. By employing a combination of colors, shapes, and icons while considering contrast, games can provide accessible and engaging experiences for individuals with color blindness [33]. However, understanding their specific needs and limitations and incorporating suitable design strategies is key. Offering options to adjust contrast, brightness, and zooming in-game settings allows users with color blindness to customize visual settings for better visibility and differentiation. Alternative color schemes optimized for color vision deficiencies can also enhance contrast and differentiation [28]. By providing customization options, such as alternative color filters, color saturation adjustments, or additional visual indicators, games can improve accessibility for individuals with various types of color blindness [25]. Color filters may not address all challenges posed by different types of color blindness, including red-green, blue-yellow, and complete colorblindness [11].

Enhancing accessibility in serious games for individuals with color blindness requires the following important guidelines: These include ensuring sufficient color contrast between foreground and background elements, incorporating additional visual cues beyond color, offering alternative color schemes optimized for specific types of color blindness, and providing customizable color filters. By adhering to these guidelines, player experiences can be improved, allowing individuals with color blindness to engage more effectively.

4.2 Sound/Audio

The development of a sound-based video game accompanied by a haptic device that incorporates auditory feedback to assist color-blind players in navigating and interacting with the environment has shown promise in addressing accessibility for different types of color blindness. While audio support can provide an engaging experience, however addressing colorblindness requires additional considerations [20]. Gaming environments for visually impaired users have predominantly focused on audio games, there is a need for specific consideration of color blindness in game design to ensure inclusivity. Color-blindness affects the perception and differentiation of colors, making it challenging for individuals to distinguish between different color-coded elements in games. Therefore, relying solely on audio cues may not fully address the accessibility needs of color-blind individuals [24]. Therefore, by utilizing additional visual cues to convey important information or differentiate game elements. This allows colorblind people to rely on visual cues that are not dependent on color perception. In addition, text-based information alongside visual elements provides clear descriptions or explanations. Simple techniques such as captioning, changeable fonts, and adjustable sound can significantly enhance accessibility for individuals with color blindness, providing alternative ways to perceive and interact with game elements. This ensures that important details are communicated in a way that is accessible to individuals with colorblindness [34]. Overall, incorporating these techniques and design considerations holds great potential for creating a more inclusive gaming landscape, where individuals with color blindness can fully engage and enjoy the gameplay experience.

To enhance accessibility for colorblindness in serious games, several key considerations should be taken into account: Clear and distinct audio cues should be utilized, enabling colorblind players to differentiate between various game elements and events through auditory feedback alone. Audio cues become crucial for conveying color-dependent information, compensating for color perception difficulties. Incorporating audio cues with additional visual cues to indicate color-coded objects or changes in color gradients helps colorblind players understand and interact with the game environment effectively. Furthermore, integrating haptic feedback, such as vibrations or tactile cues, alongside audio feedback can enhance the player experience.

4.3 Interfaces

The discussion revolves around some important points concerning accessibility in gaming for students with colorblindness. Firstly, approaches that rely on specific interfaces and custom developments may inadvertently lead to a lack of quality in the generated or adapted games, potentially segregating diverse impaired players. This highlights the need for inclusive design practices that consider a wide range of impairments to ensure equal access for all individuals [15]. Secondly, the use of haptic feedback devices and audio interfaces to describe visual content in games has proven to be effective in partially addressing access barriers. However, it should be noted that these interfaces and related devices might not completely remediate all accessibility challenges, indicating the necessity for further research and improvements in this domain [22]. Lastly, there is a notable gap in research focusing specifically on games accessible through interfaces for colorblind individuals. This highlights the importance of exploring and developing accessible player experiences that cater to the unique needs of colorblind players, ensuring they can fully engage [31]. Overall, this discussion underscores the importance of inclusive design approaches, the potential of haptic feedback devices and audio interfaces, and the need for further research to address accessibility gaps in serious games for colorblind students. By addressing these points, more inclusive and accessible player experiences could be developed for a diverse range of players.

When aiming to improve accessibility for colorblindness in serious games, it is essential to consider key factors such as: To ensure inclusive and high-quality interfaces in serious games, relying solely on particular interfaces or custom developments should be avoided as that may segregate diverse impaired players. While haptic feedback devices and audio interfaces are effective in describing visual content, they partially address accessibility barriers for individuals with color blindness. Further research is needed, particularly in games accessible on interfaces for colorblind individuals. By adopting inclusive design practices, exploring improvements in existing interfaces, and considering unique needs, accessible interfaces could be developed that could enhance the player experience for students with colorblindness.

4.4 Understanding Needs

Understanding player needs is crucial for creating accessible player experiences, particularly for individuals with colorblindness [26]. Recognizing the diverse needs of this target group, which can vary based on the types, severities, and multiple impairments present, is essential [32]. However, understanding and accommodating these diverse needs can be challenging. To ensure accessibility, incorporating non-visual modalities in game design is vital, as relying solely on visual cues may exclude certain players [27]. Additionally, understanding the experiences of players within the game space is crucial for developing accessible and engaging player experiences [23]. Accommodating all accessibility parameters, considering the varying needs depending on the severity of colorblindness, is essential for ensuring inclusivity [30]. However, classifying the degree of impairment and identifying specific requirements can be difficult, posing challenges in determining the appropriate accessibility parameters [38]. Recognizing that not all individuals with colorblindness have the same needs or face the same challenges is important [39]. Color blindness should be a crucial consideration in the game design process [40]. The approach to focus more to address the specific needs of individuals with colorblindness can result in serious games being more engaging and inclusive.

To enhance accessibility for colorblindness in serious games, it is important to consider various key factors: Understanding and accommodating diverse needs in colorblindness and impairments include recognizing the varied needs based on types, severities, and multiple impairments present within the target group. Considering the varying needs based on colorblindness severity, in order to accommodate relevant accessibility parameters, it is crucial for inclusivity. There should be efforts made to determine appropriate accessibility parameters despite the challenges in classifying impairment degrees and identifying specific requirements and needs.

4.5   Recommendations on Accessibility

The Independent Game Developers Association (IGDA) suggests several guidelines for addressing colorblindness in serious games. These include using color-blind-friendly palettes that are distinguishable for individuals with different types of colorblindness, providing alternative visual cues such as icons or patterns to convey information, and offering customizable color options for players to adjust settings according to their needs [35]. The Game Accessibility Guidelines (GAG) recommend ensuring sufficient color contrast between foreground and background elements, using clear icons and text, and incorporating alternative visual cues [10]. The Web Content Accessibility Guidelines (WCAG) emphasize the importance of color contrast ratios, using color as an additional indicator rather than the sole means of conveying information, and offering customizable color settings [37]. The standardized sets of proposed guidelines face a problem: they lack explanations about the accessibility problem each guideline aims to address, which makes it challenging for game developers to comprehend when and why a particular guideline should be implemented [41].

This section discussed and proposed guidelines in key categories including A) Color, B) Sound/Audio, C) Interfaces, D) Understanding Needs, and E) Recommendations. Each category highlights key insights on accessibility issues in serious games for colorblindness. The incorporation of visual cues is a valuable approach to improving usability for colorblind players. By providing multiple visual indicators, players can rely on cues beyond color to interpret and differentiate game elements, reducing confusion caused by color-based information. However, it is critical to carefully select distinguishable colors and ensure sufficient contrast between foreground and background elements. While customizable in-game settings, such as color filters and alternative color schemes, offer flexibility for users to optimize their visibility, there may be challenges in finding the right balance between customization options and overwhelming users with choices. Moreover, the integration of sound and haptic feedback to assist color-blind players in interacting with the gaming environment is promising, but further research is needed to assess its effectiveness in addressing specific challenges posed by color blindness. Emphasizing inclusive interface design requires careful attention to individual needs. Understanding the unique needs of colorblind players and incorporating non-visual modalities in game design are vital steps toward improving accessibility. However, it is essential to strike a balance and ensure that the incorporation of non-visual modalities does not inadvertently exclude players who may rely on visual cues. The recommended guidelines from IGDA, GAG, and WCAG offer valuable insights, but it is crucial to critically assess their application in various serious gaming contexts and consider their limitations.

These findings and recommendations contribute significantly to the advancement of knowledge in serious game accessibility, but ongoing research and setting up some experiments are necessary to refine and expand these guidelines to ensure their efficacy in creating fully inclusive and engaging player experiences for color blindness.

5 Conclusion

Serious games have the potential to enhance active learning, decision-making, and problem-solving. However, addressing accessibility challenges is crucial to ensure inclusivity for those with colorblindness. Implementing design considerations such as color schemes, audio cues, interfaces and understating needs of the target group can enhance accessibility and engagement. By creating inclusive and engaging experiences, serious games can contribute to equitable learning opportunities for all students, irrespective of their abilities.

Although progress has been achieved, additional research is required to comprehensively address the diverse needs of individuals with color blindness. There are certain limitations to our research. There is a scarcity of literature specifically focusing on colorblindness in the context of serious games. Due to this reason, the selection process excluded numerous papers that were not directly relevant to the topic. The existing literature primarily emphasizes other visual impairments of different natures. Further research should prioritize the investigation of the specific challenges and needs related to colorblindness in the context of serious games to enhance our understanding of accessibility in this area.

In the next stage of our research, we will conduct experiments with a focus to address these accessibility challenges and assess the effectiveness of implementing these guidelines in improving the player experience for color blindness. To foster inclusivity and improve usability in serious games, it is essential to address a wide range of visual impairments and other disabilities; their design challenges, and limitations, all of which require thorough investigation.

Acknowledgments. This work has been funded by the project, INCLUDEME (No. 621547- EPP-1-2020-1-RO-EPPA3-IPI-SOC-IN) which is co-funded by the European Commission through the Erasmus+ program.

References

1. Bellotti, F., Kapralos, B., Lee, K., Moreno-Ger, P., Berta, R.: Assessment in and of serious games: an overview. In: Advances in Human-Computer Interaction, pp. 1–11 (2013). https://doi.org/10.1155/2013/136864

2. Anastasiadis, T., Lampropoulos, G., Siakas, K.: Digital game-based learning and serious games in Education. Int. J. Adv. Sci. Res. Eng. **4**, 139–144 (2018). https://doi.org/10.31695/IJASRE.2018.33016
3. Baptista, G., Oliveira, T.: Gamification and serious games: a literature meta-analysis and Integrative Model. Comput. Hum. Behav. **92**, 306–315 (2019). https://doi.org/10.1016/J.CHB.2018.11.030
4. Skrzypczyk, P., Linden, N.: Robustness of measurement, discrimination games, and accessible information. Phys. Rev. Lett. **122** (2019). https://doi.org/10.1103/PHYSREVLETT.122.140403
5. Jaramillo-Alcázar, A., Cortez-Silva, P., Galarza-Castillo, M., Luján-Mora, S.: A method to develop accessible online serious games for people with disabilities: a case study. Sustainability **12**, 9584 (2020). https://doi.org/10.3390/SU12229584
6. Lee, J.H., Park, C.: Factors influencing social game accessibility. e-Bus. Stud. **16**, 145–169 (2015). https://doi.org/10.15719/GEBA.16.3.201506.145
7. Martiniello, N., Eisenbarth, W., Lehane, C., Johnson, A., Wittich, W.: Exploring the use of smartphones and tablets among people with visual impairments: are mainstream devices replacing the use of traditional visual aids? Assist. Technol. **34**, 34–45 (2019). https://doi.org/10.1080/10400435.2019.1682084
8. Leuthold, S., Bargas-Avila, J.A., Opwis, K.: Beyond web content accessibility guidelines: design of Enhanced Text User Interfaces for blind internet users. Int. J. Hum Comput Stud. **66**, 257–270 (2008). https://doi.org/10.1016/J.IJHCS.2007.10.006
9. International Game Developer's Association - Game Access Special Interest Group (IGDA-SIG). https://igda-gasig.org/about-game-accessibility/guidelines/visual/. Accessed 29 May 2023
10. Cairns, P., Power, C., Barlet, M., Haynes, G.: Future design of accessibility in games: a design vocabulary. Int. J. Hum. Comput. Stud. **131**, 64–71 (2019). https://doi.org/10.1016/J.IJHCS.2019.06.010
11. Dela Torre, I., Khaliq, I.: A study on accessibility in games for the visually impaired. IEEE Games, Entertainment, Media Conference (GEM) (2019). https://doi.org/10.1109/gem.2019.8811534
12. Salvador-Ullauri, L., Jaramillo-Alcázar, A., Luján-Mora, S.: A serious game accessible to people with visual impairments. In: Proceedings of the 2017 9th International Conference on Education Technology and Computers (2017). https://doi.org/10.1145/3175536.3175576
13. López, J.M., Medina, N.M., de Lope, R.P.: Interaction in video games for people with impaired visual function. In: Proceedings of the XVII International Conference on Human Computer Interaction (2016). https://doi.org/10.1145/2998626.2998643
14. Brown, M., Anderson, S.L.: Designing for disability: evaluating the state of accessibility design in video games. Games Cult. **16**(6), 702–718 (2021). https://doi.org/10.1177/1555412020971500
15. Aguado-Delgado, J., Gutiérrez-Martínez, J.-M., Hilera, J.R., de-Marcos, L., Otón, S.: Accessibility in video games: a systematic review. Universal Access Inf. Soc. **19**, 169–193 (2018). https://doi.org/10.1007/s10209-018-0628-2
16. Bogdanova, G., Sabev, N., Noev, N.: Accessibility and some educational barriers for visually impaired users. In: INTED2019 Proceedings (2019). https://doi.org/10.21125/inted.2019.2333
17. Melthis, J., Brown, A., Tang, S., Hanneghan, M.: Using serious games to create awareness on visual impairments. In: International Conference on Developments of E-Systems Engineering (DeSE) (2015). https://doi.org/10.1109/dese.2015.65
18. Rathee, D., Mann, S.: Daltonizer: a CNN-based framework for monochromatic and dichromatic color-blindness. In: 4th International Conference on Artificial Intelligence and Speech Technology (AIST) (2022). https://doi.org/10.1109/aist55798.2022.10065004

19. Healthdirect Australia Colour blindness. https://www.healthdirect.gov.au/colour-blindness. Accessed 30 Mar 2023
20. Power, C., Cairns, P., Barlet, M., Haynes, G., Beeston, J., DeHaven, T.: Validation and prioritization of design options for accessible player experiences. Interact. Comput. **33**, 641–656 (2021). https://doi.org/10.1093/iwc/iwac017
21. da Rocha Tomé Filho, F., Mirza-Babaei, P., Kapralos, B., Moreira Mendonça Junior, G.: Let's play together. In: Proceedings of the CHI Conference on Human Factors in Computing Systems (2019). https://doi.org/10.1145/3290605.3300861
22. Scalise, K., et al.: Accommodations in digital interactive stem assessment tasks. J. Spec. Educ. Technol. **33**, 219–236 (2018). https://doi.org/10.1177/0162643418759340
23. Beeston, J., Power, C., Cairns, P., Barlet, M.: Accessible player experiences (APX): the players. In: Miesenberger, K., Kouroupetroglou, G. (eds.) ICCHP 2018. LNCS, vol. 10896, pp. 245–253. Springer, Cham (2018). https://doi.org/10.1007/978-3-319-94277-3_40
24. Schneider, O., et al.: Dualpanto. In: Proceedings of the 31st Annual ACM Symposium on User Interface Software and Technology (2018). https://doi.org/10.1145/3242587.3242604
25. Napoli, D., Chiasson, S.: Exploring the impact of colour-blindness on computer game performance. In: Extended Abstracts of the CHI Conference on Human Factors in Computing Systems (2018). https://doi.org/10.1145/3170427.3188555
26. Power, C., Cairns, P., Barlet, M.: Inclusion in the third wave: access to experience. In: Filimowicz, M., Tzankova, V. (eds.) New Directions in Third Wave Human-Computer Interaction: Volume 1 - Technologies. HIS, pp. 163–181. Springer, Cham (2018). https://doi.org/10.1007/978-3-319-73356-2_10
27. Ferreira, F., Cavaco, S.: Mathematics for all: a game-based learning environment for visually impaired students. In: IEEE Frontiers in Education Conference (FIE) Proceedings (2014). https://doi.org/10.1109/fie.2014.7044493
28. Callaghan, M., Savin-Baden, M., McShane, N., Eguiluz, A.G.: Mapping learning and game mechanics for serious games analysis in engineering education. IEEE Trans. Emerg. Top. Comput. **5**, 77–83 (2017). https://doi.org/10.1109/TETC.2015.2504241
29. Torres-Carazo, M.I., Rodriguez-Fortiz, M.J., Hurtado, M.V.: Analysis and review of apps and serious games on mobile devices intended for people with visual impairment. In: IEEE International Conference on Serious Games and Applications for Health (SeGAH) (2016). https://doi.org/10.1109/SeGAH.2016.7586263
30. Jaramillo-Alcazar, A., Guaita, C., Rosero, J.L., Lujan-Mora, S.: An approach to inclusive education in electronic engineering through serious games. In: XIII Technologies Applied to Electronics Teaching Conference (TAEE) (2018). https://doi.org/10.1109/taee.2018.8476110
31. De Biase, L.C.C., Correa, A.G.D., Dias, L., Lotto e, E.P., Lopes, R.D.: An accessible roller coaster simulator for touchscreen devices: an educational game for the visually impaired. In: IEEE Games, Entertainment, Media Conference (GEM) (2018). https://doi.org/10.1109/gem.2018.8516457
32. Garcez, L., Thiry, M., Fernandes, A.: Accessible features to support visually impaired people in game development: a systematic literature review of the last 15 years. In: 15th Iberian Conference on Information Systems and Technologies (CISTI) (2020). https://doi.org/10.23919/cisti49556.2020.9140904
33. Othman, N.I., Zin, N.A., Mohamed, H.: Accessibility requirements in serious games for low vision children. In: 2019 International Conference on Electrical Engineering and Informatics (ICEEI) (2019). https://doi.org/10.1109/iceei47359.2019.8988791
34. Correa, A.G., De Biase, L.C., Lotto, E.P., Lopes, R.D.: Development and usability evaluation of an configurable educational game for the visually impaired. In: IEEE Games, Entertainment, Media Conference (GEM) (2018). https://doi.org/10.1109/gem.2018.8516472

35. Scott, M., Ghinea, G., Hamilton, I.: Promoting inclusive design practice at the global game jam: a pilot evaluation. In: IEEE Frontiers in Education Conference (FIE) Proceedings (2014). https://doi.org/10.1109/fie.2014.7044162

36. Gonçalves, D., Rodrigues, A., Richardson, M.L., de Sousa, A.A., Proulx, M.J., Guerreiro, T.: Exploring asymmetric roles in mixed-ability gaming. In: Proceedings of the CHI Conference on Human Factors in Computing Systems (2021). https://doi.org/10.1145/3411764.3445494

37. Wille, K., Dumke, R.R., Wille, C.: Measuring the accessability based on web content accessibility guidelines. In: Joint Conference of the International Workshop on Software Measurement and the International Conference on Software Process and Product Measurement (IWSM-MENSURA) (2016). https://doi.org/10.1109/iwsm-mensura.2016.032

38. Sekhavat, Y.A., Azadehfar, M.R., Zarei, H., Roohi, S.: Sonification and interaction design in computer games for visually impaired individuals. Multimedia Tools Appl. **81**, 7847–7871 (2022). https://doi.org/10.1007/s11042-022-11984-3

39. Freeman, E., Wilson, G., Brewster, S., Baud-Bovy, G., Magnusson, C., Caltenco, H.: Audible beacons and wearables in schools. In: Proceedings of the CHI Conference on Human Factors in Computing Systems (2017). https://doi.org/10.1145/3025453.3025518

40. Reinaldo, I., Pulungan, N.S., Darmadi, H.: Prototyping "color in life" Edugame for dichromatic color blind awareness. Procedia Comput. Sci. **179**, 773–780 (2021). https://doi.org/10.1016/j.procs.2021.01.070

41. Flores-Garzón, E.P., Intriago-Echeverría, L.J., Jaramillo-Alcázar, A., Criollo-C, S., Luján-Mora, S.: Catch the thief: an approach to an accessible video game with unity. Int. J. Adv. Sci. Eng. Inf. Technol. **10**, 905 (2020). https://doi.org/10.18517/ijaseit.10.3.10938

Persuasive System Design for Climate Change Awareness

Ashfaq Adib$^{(\boxtimes)}$ ⓘ and Rita Orji ⓘ

Dalhousie University, Halifax, NS B3H 4R2, Canada
{ashfaq.adib,rita.orji}@dal.ca

Abstract. We have been experiencing warmer years than before especially during the last decade, which has raised concerns among researchers of all discipline about climate change. In our attempt to raise awareness and promote positive behavior change to mitigate climate change, we designed an intervention consisting of three design paradigms that are not commonly used together in the area of climate change: data visualization, interactive narrative, and persuasive system design. By conducting a user study with 100 participants, followed by interview of 20 participants, we found evidence showing that all the persuasive strategies implemented in our system were significantly persuasive. Moreover, our qualitative analysis provided insight on the effectiveness of the strategies, such as, *Customization, Simulation, Social Learning, Social Comparison* and *Cooperation* in increasing likeness towards the system, and motivating positive behavior change about climate change by providing a sense of togetherness among the participants. Based on our findings, we offer design recommendations for implementing persuasive strategies in such systems to increase their effectiveness.

Keywords: Climate Change · Interactive Narrative · Data Visualization · Persuasive System Design

1 Introduction

The abnormal warming of the climate we are experiencing since the last couple of decades is referred to as "global warming", which is the current ongoing trend in climate change. We are experiencing hotter temperatures each year, where 2020 was the warmest year in instrumental record (1.7°C global mean temperature increase) [12]. Although the majority of climate scientists (90–100%) agree that human activities are causing the recent global warming [8], many argue that climate change is a natural phenomenon [11]. Misinformation about climate change has created doubt about the phenomenon among the general public [20]. This emphasizes the importance of conveying correct information in an understandable way to raise awareness about climate change which is one of the objectives of our research. Moreover, since human activities play a major role in the warming of the climate, we also aim to promote positive behavior change to mitigate climate change.

ⓒ IFIP International Federation for Information Processing 2023
Published by Springer Nature Switzerland AG 2023
P. Ciancarini et al. (Eds.): ICEC 2023, LNCS 14455, pp. 115–129, 2023.
https://doi.org/10.1007/978-981-99-8248-6_9

We developed a persuasive intervention consisting of data visualizations, interactive narrative and persuasive strategies to raise awareness about climate change, a combined designed approach which to the best of our knowledge has not been explored in climate research. Then, we conducted a study with 100 participants, followed by an interview of 20 participants, and performed both quantitative and qualitative analysis on the collected data. Our data analysis reveal that our intervention was significantly persuasive, and we identified significant persuasive effect of certain strategies implemented in the system such as, *Customization, Simulation, Social Learning, Social Comparison* and *Cooperation* in promoting positive behavior change to mitigate climate change. Based on our findings, we share design recommendations that include: allow verification of displayed information, simulate outcome of climate change, provide customized experiences, and reinforce social presence for system designers aiming to mitigate issues such as, climate change.

2   Background

Data visualization is a powerful tool that helps visually detect patterns from complex structures, and in some cases can reveal information from data that cannot be observed in any other way [18]. It is desirable to convey messages regarding climate change using data visualizations that consists of spatio-temporal data [19]. Data visualization is widely used in climate research, and they have been employed in exploring various aspects of climate change such as, finding indicators and causes of the phenomenon [1,2,17,19,31], defining trends and building models to predict upcoming changes [27], or to establish the fact that climate change is real by providing evidence [16,26] which is also our purpose of using data visualizations in our intervention.

On the other hand, interactive narratives are story driven experiences where the reader or player makes decisions in the narrative that changes the direction of the story and its ending. Interactive narratives have a unique power to induce empathy on the users towards in-game content (e.g., characters and environment) [28]. This characteristic of interactive narratives can be harnessed to target issues that require people to feel responsible and act accordingly [30], such as climate change which is a global phenomenon that demands participation of individuals collectively due it being a collective-action problem [5]. Interactive narratives have been found to effectively elicit empathy on the participants towards in-game environment and raise awareness about ocean pollution [30,34]. We aim to develop a persuasive interactive narrative to raise awareness and promote positive behavior change to mitigate climate change.

3   Methodology

Based on our background research, we decided to design a web application that combines data visualizations, interactive narratives and persuasive strategies for climate change awareness. Participants accessed the web application via a computer web browser. In this section we describe the system design and its evaluation process.

3.1 System Design

The system starts with displaying visualizations of climate change data. We presented three screens with different data visualizations, with the goal to provide evidence about climate change and how humans are playing a role in accelerating the change. First, a choropleth map was displayed (Fig. 1) to the user which visualized data produced by NASA Goddard Institute for Space Studies (NASA-GISS) [13], showing how the world temperature has changed over the last 60 years (1961–2020). The next page showed data collected from National Oceanic and Atmospheric Administration (NOAA) [9], depicting a line chart showing possible correlation between the rise in global mean temperature, and emission of carbon-based gases, since carbon emission is considered as one of the leading causes of climate change [1,2,17,27,33]. The last data visualization screen shows how climate change related topics is becoming more popular in social media as people are becoming more conscious about this phenomenon. In this page, we display the number of posts on Twitter for the years 2006–2021 on topics: "climatechange", "globalwarming" and "climatecrisis", and we also showed recent posts on climate change from the platform collected using Twitter API [32]. All the visualizations were interactive, allowing participants to hover over data points to see details and zoom in-out for better exploration of visualized data.

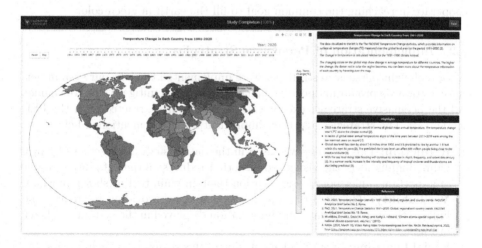

Fig. 1. Data visualization of world temperature change

The next part of the intervention is the interactive narrative, or story game where the participant drives the story by taking decisions that can impact the game's climate. First, the participant customizes the avatar which is reflected throughout the story. Then, different scenarios are presented, where the participant has to take actions that can positively, neutrally or negatively impact the climate of the in-game world. These scenarios were designed to reflect a regular life of an individual, and how our day-to-day actions affect the climate. There are a total of six different scenarios: the participant has to (1) find and turn off items that consume power in the house, (2) choose a daily mode of transportation (car/bus/bicycle), (3) decide on a policy to avoid or keep using disposable items in workplace, (4) decide to confront a stranger for littering the park, dispose the item him/herself, or do nothing, (5) decide to buy reusable bag, carry items by hand, or use plastic bag for grocery shopping and (6) recycle throw-away household items. The interaction in the game was performed via mouse clicks and type of interaction varied depending on the scenario e.g., participant could in first scenario click on a light bulb to turn off the light, or in sixth scenario drag and drop items on a recycle bin.

In each scenario, the participant is rewarded with points if he/she decides to perform a climate friendly action. Depending on the points collected by the participant, an ending (either positive or negative) is decided for the story and the future of the in-game world is displayed to the player. Screenshots of the positive ending for the story is provided in Fig. 2. At the end of the intervention, all participants and their collected points is shown in a scoreboard where participants can compare their performances with others. In this screen, an image of earth is also displayed which gets filled in green color as participants collect more points. This screen encourages participants to collect more points by playing the story game again if they have missed any points, and motivates them to cooperate in reaching the common goal to fill the earth in green color.

3.2   Implementation of Persuasive Strategies

A total of eight persuasive strategies were implemented to make our system persuasive towards promoting positive behavior change to mitigate climate change. All the persuasive strategies except *Customization* are extracted from the PSD model [23]. The strategies and their implementations are mentioned below.

1. **Reduction:** This strategy was used in the data visualization screens by providing highlights of the visualized data that reduces all the data into a couple of important bullet points and mention them in plain text as shown in Fig. 1.
2. **Verifiability:** This strategy was implemented by providing references and links to the visualized data and information displayed in the system, as shown in Fig. 1.
3. **Social Learning:** In our implementation of this strategy, we included a social feed from Twitter that consists of latest discussions on climate change from people across the world, which allowed participants to learn how others are engaging in climate friendly behaviors.
4. **Customization:** The customization strategy identified by Fogg [15], was implemented by allowing the participants to create and customize their own

character based on their liking, which is then reflected throughout the story game.

5. **Simulation:** We implemented the *Simulation* strategy by displaying illustrations of the future of the in-game climate in either a positive (Fig. 2) or negative manner. The simulations are drawn from the scenarios presented in the interactive story game, showing either a flourished environment in the future, or a community that has suffered from the consequences of a harsh climate.

6. **Social Comparison:** This strategy was implemented by showing a list of participants and the number of points they have collected by playing the story game. This list was displayed with a view to promote positive behavior change by helping the users reflect upon their own behavior by comparing with others.

7. **Cooperation:** We implemented this strategy by providing a mean for people to work together in reaching a common goal. Along with seeing the list of participants, participants saw an image of earth which would be filled in green color based on how many points all participants have collected. This encourages cooperation in reaching a common target goal by collecting points together to fill the earth in green color, indicating towards healing the climate.

8. **Self-monitoring:** This strategy was implemented by showing a screen where the player could see how their actions in each scenario of the game was rewarded with points, and where they may have missed points. By addressing their performance in the game, participants can both learn about their mistakes which helps them improve their pro-environmental behavior.

Fig. 2. Combined screenshots of visuals shown in the positive ending of the interactive story game

3.3   System Evaluation

To evaluate our developed system, we conducted a user study with 100 participants, followed by a one-on-one interview with 20 participants. Participants had
to be at least 18 years old, and have access to a computer device and the internet
to join the study. To capture the persuasive effect of the employed strategies in
mitigating climate change, we used the *Perceived Persuasiveness* scale adapted
from Drozd et al. [10] and Orji et al. [24] (e.g., "This feature influences me to
be aware of climate change."). The variable was measured with a 7-point Likert
scale, with the neutral value being four. This scale was used due to its wide use
and effectiveness in capturing the persuasiveness of a system [24].

The complete study was conducted online where recruitment notice was
shared via university email channels and social media posts. A link to the developed web application was provided in the notice. Participants went through intervention, and completed pre and post intervention questionnaires. They could
share their interest to join in an optional interview, and interested participants
were contacted by the lead researcher to conduct an online interview.

4   Results

In this section we present the results our analysis. First, we explored the effectiveness of the eight persuasive strategies that were applied in the system. This
is followed by the result of the analysis of qualitative data from the interview.
Most of the participants of the study were aged between 23–30 years (43%),
followed by 18–23 years (17%), 30–40 years (24%), 40–50 (9%), 50+ years (7%)
and undisclosed (1%). Among the participants, 54% were male while 46% were
female.

4.1   Effectiveness of the Persuasive Strategies

In addition to capturing the perceived persuasiveness of the eight implemented
persuasive strategies, we also captured the perceived persuasiveness of the overall
system, which led to a total of nine set of questions for the *Perceived Persuasiveness* scale. First, we performed descriptive statistical analysis on the collected
responses: results of which is provided in Table 1. All strategies reported higher
than neutral mean values. The highest mean was observed for the *Simulation*
strategy (M = 5.56), which is an indication of the effectiveness of illustrating
simulated outcome of the decisions taken by the participants in the interactive
story game, and how our individual actions can impact the climate. The *Reduction* and *Self-monitoring* strategies also received high mean values (M = 5.48
and 5.33), showing the effectiveness of providing highlights in textual format in
the data visualization screens, and allowing users to see how their decisions were
rewarded in the application. The persuasiveness of the overall system has the
second highest mean value (M = 5.53), suggesting that the system was overall
persuasive. The *Customization* strategy had the lowest mean (M = 4.52), but

it also has the highest standard deviation among the strategies (SD = 1.81), indicating that participants had most mixed perception of the persuasiveness of this strategy.

Next, we performed one-sample t-tests on the responses to the *Perceived Persuasiveness* scale to analyze whether the persuasive strategies are significantly effective. We can observe in Table 1, that all the persuasive strategies reported a *p-value* of less than 0.05, showing that the users found them to be effective with respect to their ability to motivate positive behavior change to mitigate climate change. Overall, the strategies are significantly above the neutral value with respect to their persuasiveness, showing that all the persuasive strategies were significantly persuasive.

Table 1. Descriptive statistics and one sample t-test of the perceived persuasiveness of the persuasive strategies

Persuasive Strategies	Mean	SD	t	p	df
Simulation	5.56	1.4	11.08	0.00	99
Reduction	5.48	1.16	12.80	0.00	99
Self-monitoring	5.33	1.42	9.36	0.00	99
Cooperation	5.17	1.66	7.08	0.00	99
Social Comparison	5.09	1.75	6.23	0.00	99
Social Learning	4.80	1.66	4.81	0.00	99
Verifiability	4.76	1.72	4.43	0.00	99
Customization	4.52	1.81	2.88	0.00	99
Overall System	5.53	1.31	11.65	0.00	99

4.2   Differences in the Effectiveness of Persuasive Strategies

To compare the persuasiveness of the strategies, we examined if the persuasiveness of the different persuasive strategies differed between each other. Each persuasive strategy is applied with different expected outcome as they differ in their implementation. Therefore, it is essential to compare the persuasiveness of the eight strategies to see if they are significantly different with respect to their effectiveness. To achieve this, we performed repeated measure ANOVA analysis on the persuasiveness of the eight strategies. The results of the RM-ANOVA shows that there is a significant main effect of strategy on persuasiveness ($F(5.407, 535.317) = 18.106$, $p < .001$).

Now, considering that the mean effect is significantly different for the persuasiveness of the strategies, we conducted a post-hoc pairwise comparison with Bonferroni correction to examine which strategies are significantly different, and plotted the resultant p values in a heatmap that is shown in Fig. 3. Observing Fig. 3, there are significant differences ($p < 0.05$) between most of the pairs of persuasive strategies. *Customization* was perceived as least persuasive among all strategies as can be seen in Table 1, and it is significantly different in persuasiveness from all the strategies except the *Verifiability* and *Social Learning* strategies. The *Verifiability* and *Social Learning* strategies also have second and third most lowest persuasiveness mean value as can be seen in Table 1. This along with the findings from the pairwise comparison test shows that *Customization, Verifiability* and *Social Learning* strategies were the least persuasive strategies with no significant difference in their perceived persuasiveness. Also, the strategies with high mean values of perceived persuasiveness i.e., *Reduction, Simulation* and *Self-monitoring* strategies do not have significant difference in their perceived persuasiveness (Fig. 3), showing that the strategies that are perceived as highly persuasive are not significantly different with respect to their persuasiveness. Overall, the strategy implementations were found to be significantly different in their effectiveness, and the pairwise comparisons between the strategies show that the strategies with the least persuasiveness score: *Customization, Verifiability*, and *Social Learning*, are similarly effective since they are not significantly different in their persuasiveness, the same applies for strategies which were found to be highly persuasive: *Reduction, Simulation* and *Self-monitoring*.

4.3   Qualitative Analysis

We conducted interviews to collect general feedback from participants. After conducting 20 interviews, we observed that enough themes could be generated from the feedback, thus, we concluded the interview process. Analysis of the qualitative data involved performing thematic analysis [7] on the interview responses, where we iteratively went through the comments and combined them to generate themes until no new themes could be generated to report new findings. We share the results from our thematic analysis below.

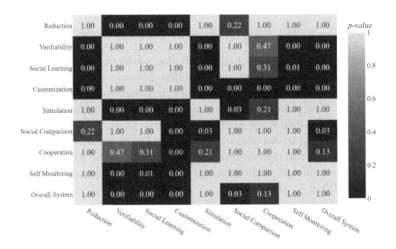

Fig. 3. Results of pairwise comparison between persuasive strategies

Verifying Sources of Information: We implemented the *Verifiability* strategy to reinforce the authenticity of the information displayed in our system. Participants noticed the strategy implementation and liked seeing that the system provided information from trusted sources which can be seen in the following comments:

P7: *I checked out the* ***references.***

P87: *I read the highlights, but I am not sure if I had read the bigger block of texts. Also, the* ***references showed that it is backed up by Nasa****, so they seem to be valid. They were really easy to read.*

P89: *The visualization is OK, and I liked the arrangement and* ***the text beside it.***

P96: ***The citations*** *at the bottom were really nice.*

The comments above show the importance of providing information from trusted sources and enabling users to verify the authenticity of information within a system.

Likeness Towards Customization: Participants appreciated being able to create their own avatar and how it was reflected throughout the story of the game, which can be observed in the following comments:

P7: *"I liked that* ***profession, city*** *(and) everything was linked."*

P8: *"At your workplace you could see what was happening, the* ***personalization*** *was well done and made me enjoy the game."*

P19: *"The (character)* ***name, company name*** *I can remember them, so it is really helpful for relating and feels good."*

P17: *"I really liked the* ***customization*** *of the character."*

Customization of the character also provided inclusion of diversity which was liked by participants. It allowed them to relate more to the story as can be seen in the following comment

P89: *"I liked where you* ***select body*** *and liked that it supported* ***diversity and inclusion.****"*

Although the *Customization* strategy had the lowest perceived persuasiveness score, the comments from the participants show that it helped increase likeness towards the system.

Effectiveness of Simulation: Many participants commented on the impact of seeing the simulated future of the game's environment, which was an implementation of the *Simulation* strategy to demonstrate the outcome of climate change. The simulation was effective in helping participants understand the consequences of their day-to-day actions on the climate, which can be observed in the following comments:

P8: *"I got the* ***bad ending****, that is when I realized in real life, I let things (household electronic items) turned on. I was very confident about myself, but it made me think more. Also, I had this attitude, "why should I care about recycling?". But after playing it, now I started thinking about* ***reconsidering my choices.****"*

P10: *"When the **system shows the amount of harm you can do** (by) maybe using your car or using more electricity, that made me think how we live our life right now."*

P87: *"It sticks with you like you **see the burning park** and (you would) think 'oh no!'."*

We showed both positive and negative simulation based on the decisions taken by the participant within the game, with a view to elicit either positive or negative emotion respectively. The following comments show that both types of simulation had the desired effect on the participants:

P8: *"I was pretty **happy with the outcome** and (it) made me feel really good."*

P86: *"When I saw the end, I really **felt bad**."*

P83: *"I really liked how you have added the **alternate situation**, how it would happen if I did not take care of my day-to-day life."*

P96: *"I liked to see the contrast where you see the **alternate ending**, that was the thing I liked the most."*

Success of the Social Elements: We applied three Social Support persuasive strategies in our system, all of which were mentioned by participants. Participants shared their keen observations on these implementations. The following comments show support for the success of *Social Learning* strategy:

P10: *"The Twitter part where **I could see posts**, that made me more aware about climate change."*

P19: *"The Twitter feed was interesting and after clicking it, I was gone into the rabbit hole. I went to **read the comments of Tweets** from there and it was interesting."*

P72: *"The Twitter data was showing **more people are focusing** on global warming."*

The *Cooperation* strategy was implemented as a motivating factor to participate together in tackling the climate change problem which requires collective effort, and provide a sense of togetherness among the participants. The following comments show that the implementation was able to achieve its target:

P7: *"Scoreboard: where the earth was healing, (it) was a hopeful thing seeing the earth filling in green. It basically said not all is lost (and) **we can help it, and gave me hope**."*

P8: *"Also, at the end, the goal was filling in, **it had the togetherness** in it which I really liked."*

P45: *"There is another key feature in the system, the scoreboard, that is my favorite part of the system... I would want to see more encouraging words like "**Let's Make the Earth Green**" in this screen."*

The *Social Comparison* strategy was implemented to help participants compare their performances and encourage lower performing participants to do better. The following comments show that the strategy was successful in doing so:

P87: *"Also, the scoreboard at the end, maybe you can find you are below average and **need to better**."*

P88: *When I saw my score, I felt I **would have done better**.*

5 Discussion

After analyzing the collected data, we were able extract findings to determine the persuasiveness of our system. In this section we reflect upon our findings and share our design recommendations.

5.1 Significant Persuasiveness of Strategies

Our results show that the persuasiveness of all the persuasive strategies implemented in our system were significantly effective as seen in Table 1. Ostrin et al. [25] stated that one of the main advantages of interactive narratives is their ability to enable the player empathize with the story elements. The highest rated strategy: *Simulation* (M = 5.56) was mentioned by participants to elicit both positive and negative emotion depending on the simulation they saw of the future climate, reflecting their empathy towards the story elements. This shows that the strategy implementation is well suited for interactive narratives. Orji et al. [24] also reported the effectiveness of *Simulation* strategy in their study on encouraging healthy eating, sharing that simulating outcomes can have significant motivational impact.

Our findings show that all the strategies from Social Support category of the PSD model [23] were significantly persuasive (Table 1), and were mentioned multiple times in the interviews to be one of the most liked features of the system. Climate problem demands participation of people all around the world to reverse the crisis, and people are social beings who rely on each other to improve their quality of life by solving problems together [3]. Considering that the social support strategies enabled participants to feel a sense of togetherness in tackling the climate problem was a positive outcome of the system. Moreover, strategies from the Social Support category are commonly found in interventions that address climate change related issue [4,6,14,21,29], which emphasizes the recommendation in implementing such strategies to raise awareness about climate change.

The *Customization* strategy had the lowest mean of perceived persuasiveness (Table 1). However, this strategy was repeatedly mentioned in the interviews as one of the most liked features of our system (Sect. 4.3), where participants enjoyed how their customized characters were reflected in the story game. This strategy implementation also gave sense of diversity and inclusion which made the system more relatable since it allowed players to tailor their avatar representations and appearances to reflect their ideal self. Nilsen et al. [22] designed a game for earthquake preparedness where players were allowed to choose different avatars, and they found no significant effect of avatar choice in increasing earthquake preparedness, but customization increased identification and similarity of the avatar. Comments from our participants also show increased relatedness and similarity with the avatar due to customization. Hence, although not being rated highly in perceived persuasiveness, considering that the customization strategy increased likeness and relatedness towards the system, these are desirable outcomes of the implementation of this strategy and it is considered beneficial for the system.

5.2   Exploring Different Implementations of Strategies

Implementation of the persuasive strategies in our system were effective as all the strategies were found as significantly persuasive (Table 1). However, other ways of implementations can be explored as improvements. Especially, considering the success of the *Social Comparison* and *Cooperation* strategies, implementing those strategies earlier in the intervention is desirable as many participants share their likeness for these implementations (Sect. 4.3). This can have a more positive impact as it was found to elicit hopefulness and togetherness among the participants. Moreover, *Simulation* strategy was rated the highest in perceived persuasiveness (Table 1), and in addition to our implementation of this strategy in the interactive narrative, we can show simulation of predicted data in the data visualization screens, such as showing expected world temperatures in future years. Predicting climate change data is an aspect of climate research [27], which can be used to simulate outcome of climate change in data visualizations. Exploring the effectiveness of such different implementations of persuasive strategies is desirable for our future work, since they have the potential of improving the persuasiveness of our system and may increase the level of awareness and promote more positive behavior change to mitigate climate change.

5.3   Design Recommendations

Our quantitative analysis shows significant persuasive effect of all the implemented strategies for climate change awareness. This indicates that our implemented strategies can be considered for systems that promote positive behavior change to mitigate climate change. Based on the findings from participant comments and considering the quantitative analysis findings, we offer the following design recommendations:

Access to Verification of Information: The *Verifiability* persuasive strategy helped participants verify the authenticity of the provided information in the system, and build their trust on the system. Since many misinformation exist regarding climate change [20], this strategy implementation is crucial for systems that aim to tackle the climate change problem and other related issues where misinformation is rampant such as issues like COVID-19.

Simulate Outcome: Through the implementation of the *Simulation* persuasive strategy, our system was able to elicit empathy among participants for the climate, and also helped them better realize the consequences of their actions and how their individual micro-activities may be contributing to climate change.

Since climate change is a complex issue with multiple spatio-temporal factors [19], understanding the outcome of climate is not an easy task, and simulating the outcome helps people get a better grasp of the severity of climate change problems and how our individual actions have an impact.

Provide Customization: The *Customization* persuasive strategy provided a sense of relatedness and similarity towards the story elements to the participants of the interactive narrative, which increased the likeness towards the system. Considering the characteristic of interactive narratives, where the player should feel in charge of the story, this strategy implementation played an important role in making the game more engaging. Thus, it is beneficial for system designers to incorporate customization to their system. It also gives a sense of diversity and inclusion which is desirable for system designers.

Reinforce Social Presence: All the Social Support persuasive strategies implemented in our system: (*Social Learning, Social Comparison* and *Cooperation*) were mentioned by participants as key features of the system that they liked. These features allowed the participants to feel connected, learn from others performing climate friendly behavior, improve their behavior by comparing with others participating in climate actions, and encourage them to mitigate climate change through cooperation. Considering that the nature of climate change problem requires collective effort, it is essential for system designers to create a social presence within the system to motivate them to become more aware of the phenomenon and promote positive behavior change to mitigate climate change.

6 Conclusion

Our system was significantly persuasive in promoting positive behavior change to mitigate climate change. We identified multiple design recommendations for future researchers aiming to develop interventions in mitigating issues such as, climate change. For future work, our system can be expanded to include data visualizations of other aspects of climate change such as, predicted temperatures of future climate, geographical changes due to rising sea level, and by adding more scenarios to the interactive narrative such as, impact of industrialization, individual shopping habits (buying biodegradable items), social gatherings (concerts, sport and games) on the climate that will further raise awareness about climate change among users of the system.

Acknowledgments. This research was undertaken, in part, thanks to funding from the Canada Research Chairs Program. We acknowledge the support of the Natural Sciences and Engineering Research Council of Canada (NSERC) through the Discovery Grant.

References

1. Andrysco, N., Benes, B., Gurney, K.: Interactive poster: visual analytic techniques for CO_2 emissions and concentrations in the united states. In: 2008 IEEE Symposium on Visual Analytics Science and Technology, pp. 173–174. IEEE (2008)
2. Andrysco, N., Gurney, K.R., Beneš, B., Corbin, K.: Visual exploration of the Vulcan CO_2 data. IEEE Comput. Graphics Appl. **29**(1), 6–11 (2008)
3. Bandura, A.: Social Foundations of Thought and Action. Prentice-Hall, Englewood Cliffs (1986)
4. Biggar, J., Middleton, C.: Broadband and network environmentalism: the case of one million acts of green. Telecommun. J. Austr. **60**, 1–15 (2010). https://doi.org/10.2104/tja10009
5. Chen, M.F.: Extending the theory of planned behavior model to explain people's energy savings and carbon reduction behavioral intentions to mitigate climate change in taiwan-moral obligation matters. J. Clean. Prod. **112**, 1746–1753 (2016)
6. Chin, A.: We are what we do-reflexive environmentalism in the risk society (2009)
7. Clarke, V., Braun, V., Hayfield, N.: Thematic analysis. In: Qualitative psychology: A Practical Guide to Research Methods, vol. 222(2015), p. 248 (2015)
8. Cook, J., et al.: Consensus on consensus: a synthesis of consensus estimates on human-caused global warming. Environ. Res. Lett. **11**(4), 048002 (2016)
9. Dlugokencky, E.: Trends in atmospheric methane. https://gml.noaa.gov. Accessed 30 May 2022
10. Drozd, F., Lehto, T., Oinas-Kukkonen, H.: Exploring perceived persuasiveness of a behavior change support system: a structural model. In: Bang, M., Ragnemalm, E.L. (eds.) PERSUASIVE 2012. LNCS, vol. 7284, pp. 157–168. Springer, Heidelberg (2012). https://doi.org/10.1007/978-3-642-31037-9_14
11. Elsasser, S.W., Dunlap, R.E.: Leading voices in the denier choir: conservative columnists' dismissal of global warming and denigration of climate science. Am. Behav. Sci. **57**(6), 754–776 (2013)
12. FAO: Temperature change statistics 1961–2020. Technical report. 19, FAO (2021)
13. FAO: Temperature change statistics 1961–2020: Global, regional and country trends. faostat analytical brief series no. 19. rome (2021)
14. Florença, B.: Is the world real? Or do most of us live in our own Truman show?. https://people.eng.unimelb.edu.au/vkostakos/courses/socialweb10F/projects/2010.dopplr.paper.pdf
15. Fogg, B.J.: Persuasive technology: using computers to change what we think and do. Ubiquity **2002**(December), 2 (2002)
16. Huang, X., Sathiaraj, D., Wang, L., Keim, B.: Deriving data-driven insights from climate extreme indices for the continental us. In: 2017 IEEE International Conference on Data Mining Workshops (ICDMW), pp. 303–312. IEEE (2017)
17. Kinakh, V., Bun, R., Danylo, O.: Geoinformation technology of analysis and visualization of spatial data on greenhouse gas emissions using google earth engine. In: 2017 12th International Scientific and Technical Conference on Computer Sciences and Information Technologies (CSIT), vol. 1, pp. 212–215. IEEE (2017)
18. Leban, G., Zupan, B., Vidmar, G., Bratko, I.: VizRank: data visualization guided by machine learning. Data Min. Knowl. Disc. **13**(2), 119–136 (2006)
19. Li, J., Zhang, K., Meng, Z.P.: Vismate: interactive visual analysis of station-based observation data on climate changes. In: 2014 IEEE Conference on Visual Analytics Science and Technology (VAST), pp. 133–142. IEEE (2014)

20. McCright, A.M., Charters, M., Dentzman, K., Dietz, T.: Examining the effectiveness of climate change frames in the face of a climate change denial counter-frame. Top. Cogn. Sci. **8**(1), 76–97 (2016)
21. Mun, M., et al.: Peir, the personal environmental impact report, as a platform for participatory sensing systems research. In: Proceedings of the 7th international conference on Mobile systems, applications, and services, pp. 55–68 (2009)
22. Nilsen, E., Safran, E., Drake, P., Sebok, B.: Playing a serious game for earthquake preparedness: Effects of resource richness and avatar choice. In: Extended Abstracts of the 2020 CHI Conference on Human Factors in Computing Systems, pp. 1–7. CHI EA 2020, Association for Computing Machinery, New York, NY, USA (2020). https://doi.org/10.1145/3334480.3383105
23. Oinas-Kukkonen, H., Harjumaa, M.: Persuasive systems design: key issues, process model, and system features. Commun. Assoc. Inf. Syst. **24**(1), 28 (2009)
24. Orji, R., Vassileva, J., Mandryk, R.L.: Modeling the efficacy of persuasive strategies for different gamer types in serious games for health. User Model. User-Adap. Inter. **24**(5), 453–498 (2014). https://doi.org/10.1007/s11257-014-9149-8
25. Ostrin, G., Frey, J., Cauchard, J.R.: Interactive narrative in virtual reality. In: Proceedings of the 17th International Conference on Mobile and Ubiquitous Multimedia, pp. 463–467 (2018)
26. Parvathy, K.R., McLain, M.L., Bijlani, K., Jayakrishnan, R., Bhavani, R.R.: Augmented reality simulation to visualize global warming and its consequences. In: Shetty, N.R., Prasad, N.H., Nalini, N. (eds.) Emerging Research in Computing, Information, Communication and Applications, pp. 69–78. Springer, New Delhi (2016). https://doi.org/10.1007/978-81-322-2553-9_7
27. Prejmerean, V., Ghiran, O., Frentiu, M., Cioban, V.: Decision support system for minimizing carbon footprint (impact on global warming). In: 2010 IEEE International Conference on Automation, Quality and Testing, Robotics (AQTR), vol. 3, pp. 1–5. IEEE (2010)
28. Ryan, M.L.: From narrative games to playable stories: Toward a poetics of interactive narrative. Storyworlds. J. Narrat. Stud. **1**, 43–59 (2009)
29. Takayama, C., Lehdonvirta, V., Shiraishi, M., Washio, Y., Kimura, H., Nakajima, T.: Ecoisland: a system for persuading users to reduce CO2 emissions. In: 2009 Software Technologies for Future Dependable Distributed Systems, pp. 59–63. IEEE (2009)
30. Thomas, A., et al.: Oceans we make: immersive VR storytelling. In: SIGGRAPH Asia 2018 Virtual & Augmented Reality. SA 2018, Association for Computing Machinery, New York, NY, USA (2018). https://doi.org/10.1145/3275495.3275513
31. Tominski, C., Donges, J.F., Nocke, T.: Information visualization in climate research. In: 2011 15th International Conference on Information Visualization, pp. 298–305. IEEE (2011)
32. Twitter, I.: Twitter API documentation. https://developer.twitter.com/en/docs/twitter-api. Accessed 10 Aug 2022
33. Varma, K., Linn, M.C.: Using interactive technology to support students' understanding of the greenhouse effect and global warming. J. Sci. Educ. Technol. **21**(4), 453–464 (2012)
34. Vasey, K., et al.: Water bodies: VR interactive narrative and gameplay for social impact. In: The 17th International Conference on Virtual-Reality Continuum and its Applications in Industry, pp. 1–2 (2019)

Reasoning of Intelligent Virtual Agents with Exceptional Behavior in Rare Scenarios

Alexander Lysek[1]([⊠]) [iD], Sven Seele[1], and Rainer Herpers[1,2,3] [iD]

[1] Institute of Visual Computing,
Bonn-Rhein-Sieg University of Applied Science, Sankt Augustin, Germany
lysek.alexander@gmail.com, rainer.herpers@h-brs.de
[2] Faculty of Computer Science, University of New Brunswick, Fredericton, Canada
[3] Department of Electrical Engineering and Computer Science, York University,
Toronto, Canada

Abstract. This paper presents a concept for *temporal reasoning*. Temporal reasoning enables non-player characters (NPCs) to infer new knowledge based on previously acquired information and apply it within their decision making process. The approach aims to enhances the credibility of NPC behavior by allowing them to make flawed decisions based on ambiguous or misleading information. As a proof of concept a pedestrian crossing scenario with occluded vision was realized and evaluated inside the FIVIS bicycle simulator system. It could be demonstrated that so far rare simulation scenarios such as traffic accidents could be simulated in a more plausible and nondeterministic nor randomized way. These scenarios only occur if certain conditions are met and even in these cases only if the decision making process has been influenced by incomplete, error prone or ambiguous input data, so that proper decisions were difficult to derive. That means our approach is able to model human failures and ambiguity in the decision making process.

Keywords: Serious Games · Games and Simulations for Learning · Traffic Simulations · Virtual Agents · Reasoning

1 Introduction

Believable behavior of non-player characters (NPCs), named agents in the following, is one major key aspect of creating realistic and immersive virtual worlds. Independent of the application in video games with entertainment purpose or serious games, believable behavior of intelligent virtual agents (IVAs) is neccessary in order to enhance the players immersion within virtual environments (VEs).

In video games, a reasoning component of agents is often realized as finite state machines (FSMs) or behavior trees (BTs). Both methods often lead to a predetermined and repetitive behavior of IVAs, which might have an impact on

© IFIP International Federation for Information Processing 2023
Published by Springer Nature Switzerland AG 2023
P. Ciancarini et al. (Eds.): ICEC 2023, LNCS 14455, pp. 130–138, 2023.
https://doi.org/10.1007/978-981-99-8248-6_10

the player's experience. The reasoning component is responsible for generating implicit knowledge based on perceived information of an agent's environment. Generated knowledge is then used within the decision making process to select an action neccessary to achieve an agent's goal.

Most often the agent's environment is observed only for a short or part of the current time instance and considered for the subsequent decision making process. The agent might immediately react to an event with a predefined action. Missunderstandings about an agent's intention in a given situation have to be implemented specifically for each case or may never occur since the behavior is deterministic. This deterministic behavior precludes the possibility that an agent will misjudge an observed event, which might lead to inadequate but credible actions.

In the real world such situations are the result of assumptions and assessments that are based on specific observations, knowledge and experiences of a human. These factors can simplify decision making, but can also lead to misunderstandings, wrong decisions and may lead to dangerous situations, which might be wanted in a realistic modelling scenario.

The foundation for this research paper was laid in the FIVIS project [5] to develop an immersive bicycle simulator. It enables cyclists to learn traffic rules in a safe environment and to participate in driver safety training. The simulator and its IVAs have been further improved through research conducted and supervised by Seele et al. [12].

In this contribution, a rule-based reasoning system is added to the IVAs perception and decision making system in order to achieve believable but in rare events flawed behavior. As a basis for the evaluation of the proposed reasoning system, the capabilities of virtual agents populating the FIVIS bicycle simulator were extended. IVAs represent vehicle drivers who drive along a road network inside a VE reacting to traffic events such as traffic lights, lane changes, and pedestrian crossings. Especially for the latter, a misinterpretation of pedestrian intentions can lead to dangerous encounters or traffic accidents between motorized agents and agents representing pedestrians in reality.

So far, it was not possible to model this behavioral uncertainty which however is wanted or even needed in realistic traffic scenarios. Until now it was either possible to model a rule-based perfect scenario which always avoids accidents or randomized the occurrence of accidents. This however, does not reflect the reality since in reality occurrence of an accident might often result from a misinterpretation of the context perceived by the human agent.

The focus of this research is on extending and evaluating driver intelligence to produce believable, but sometimes flawed behavior in agent-to-agent interactions in rare scenarios. A reasoning approach considering a longer period of time in the recent past has been developed and evaluated. It is able to allow the simulation of accidents only in rare situations in which the perceived information is considered as ambiguous, incomplete or missleading. The interpretation of this information results in a suboptimal decision (not to say disastrous one, which might cause an accident).

A crosswalk scenario was selected as base for the evaluation of the new approach. Parameters such as the agent's desired driving velocity, pedestrian movement behavior, and occluded traffic areas were simulated in selected traffic scenarios as a proof of concept.

2 Related Work

This work is related to research topics including synthetic perception, knowledge representation, reasoning, movement prediction, and decision making. The perception system for motorized agents within the FIVIS bicycle simulator is based on the perceptual cycle described by Goldstein and Brockmole [4]. Environmental stimuli are perceived via virtual sensors that represent the human sensory organs in a simplified manner [12]. Perceived stimuli are stored in a hierarchical memory module [12] following the approach of Peters and O'Sullivan [10], who applied the stage theory formulated by Atkinson and Shiffrin [1] to model the memory of a virtual human.

Pedestrian movement and hand signals are modeled using finite state machines (FSM). The motorized agent's decision making and action selection process is encoded inside a behavior tree (BT) [3,7] where action nodes represent driving strategies for traffic scenarios such as encountering traffic lights, performing lane changes or handling pedestrian crossings [12].

The knowledge base (KB) of agents in computer simulations often contains information that would normally be unavailable to a human in an identical situation because it is easily accessible and generating the same information per agent might be expensive at runtime. In order to keep computational costs low, a rule-based production system [2,11] was selected to allow individual knowledge generation for each agent.

In recent video games, increasingly sophisticated problem-solving algorithms such as Hierarchical Task Networks (HTNs) [6] or Goal Oriented Action Planning (GOAP) [9] have been applied to improve the intelligence of NPCs and present players with believable decision making skills. An HTN or GOAP use different approaches but solve a planning problem using similar data structures. Both approaches transform a start state into a goal state by the application of operators [9]. HTN and GOAP use the latest version of the agents perceived environmental data of the world state as the start state. A previously evaluated world state is generally not considered during the next planning cycle.

In simulated road traffic scenarios, movement data is crucial in order to predict and prevent accidents. Wakim et al. [13] deployed a discrete Markov chain model to predict the movement of a pedestrian based on previously observed and classified movement data. The movement data is then used to calculate the pedestrians trajectory in order to prevent car-to-pedestrian accidents.

3 Multi Choice Reasoning Concept

The underlying idea of the developed approach is to consider previously observed and inferred knowledge within the reasoning process of an agent to extend its knowledge base (KB). The extended KB is then used within the agent's decision making process. To achieve this, it is necessary to maintain knowledge for a certain amount of time by supplementing any perceivable entity with a history of inferred information about it. This means that an agent keeps a history of inferred knowledge about each entity he recently perceived. The accumulated knowledge of all entities of one time step can be seen as a single world state an agent is aware of.

As the inference engine, a rule-based production system was selected [2,11]. It generates implicit knowledge by executing rules which evaluate perceived environmental information in fixed time intervals. Each rule annotates a perceivable entity with *Tags*. A *Tag* represents a small piece of information combined with a confidence value that expresses how certain an agent is about the information. As a consequence, it is possible to include or discard *Tags* in subsequent rules or in decision making processes by evaluating confidence thresholds.

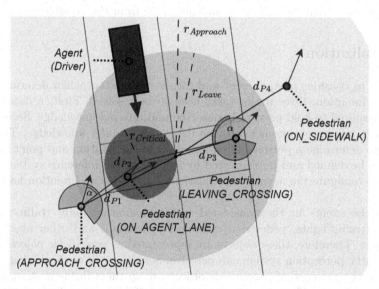

Fig. 1: Illustration of the modelling of the pedestrian intentions as phases $P_i(i = \{1...4\} = \{cyan, red, orange, blue\})$ when passing a pedestrian crossing (from left to right). Confidence values for each phase are calculated based on relative distances d_{Pi} and/or rotation values α towards the pedestrian crossing center or critical agent lane center (red).

For a motorized IVA to determine the intention of the next activity of a pedestrian at a pedestrian crossing, the pedestrian's distance and orientation are evaluated relatively to the closest crossing ahead. The possible intentions of a pedestrian at a pedestrian crossing are specified by the four states (*APPROACHING_CROSSING, ON_AGENT_LANE, LEAVING_CROSSING,*

ON_SIDEWALK) shown in Fig. 1. Each state represents a phase a pedestrian has to take when walking over a pedestrian crossing or staying on the sidewalk.

The prediction of the pedestrian's intention is further extended by considering his position and orientation one time step ahead in the future. The pedestrian's future position and orientation is calculated based on movement speed and angular speed values defined by the four movement states (*STAY, WALK, RUN, TURN*). First, the current movement state is selected by comparing the pedestrian's average movement speed and previously performed angular speed with the movement values for each state. The state which best matches the observed movement is selected and stored as a *Tag*.

A third order Markov chain is applied to predict the pedestrian's future movement state. The movement and angular speed values of the predicted movement state are evaluated to calculate the pedestrian's future position and orientation. To integrate ambiguity, alternative intentions are determined based on the predicted position and orientation. The system finally selects this inferred pedestrian intention with the highest confidence value from the possible ones.

4   Realization

In order to consider past, present and future information when determining a person's intention, three major tasks need to be resolved. First, a data structure is required to hold previously observed and inferred knowledge. Second, an extensible inference system has to be developed to infer knowledge. Third, a model to determine a person's intention at a certain position and point in time needs to be defined and implemented by leveraging the inference system. Last, a way to configure the agent's classification of a pedestrian intention had to be designed.

For the agents in the considered traffic simulation, only traffic-relevant objects (traffic lights, pedestrian crossings, pedestrians and other agents) are of interest. Therefore, these objects are represented as *perceivable objects* in the VE that the perception system can perceive. Sensors, such as the *Visual Sensor* sense for the presence of perceivable objects, wrap them inside a *stimulus* and store them in the *Short-term Sensory Storage* (STSS) for a limited time. As shown in Fig. 2, components such as the *Intelligent Driving Module* (IDM) can request stimuli and their perceivable object from *Short-term Memory* (STM) and evaluate them for decision making purposes.

An *ObservableState* was defined to store previously observed and inferred knowledge for a single inference step. *Tag* objects as mentioned in Chap. 3 represent inferred facts and are stored inside the *ObservableState* object. Combining multiple *ObservableState* objects into a sequence allows to retain previous knowledge. The sequence of states is held in the *PerceivableModel*, which is unique for each *perceivable object* in the agent's *PerceivableMemory*.

The annotation of an *ObservableState* with *Tags* is realized by the rule-based *Inference Engine*. In fixed time intervals a set of *TagRules* is evaluated and executed. Computational costs are minimized by executing a *TagRule* only when

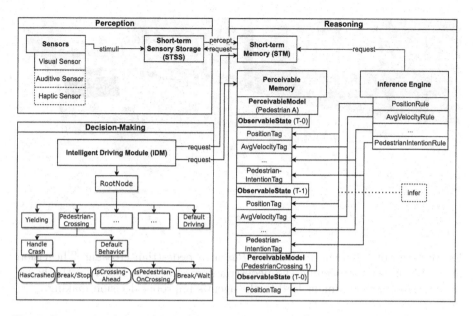

Fig. 2: Overview of the extended perception, reasoning and decision making modules of a motorized IVA inside the FIVIS bicycle simulator.

it is applicable, i.e., when the required knowledge is available in the agent's current knowledge base. *TagRules* request knowledge from the agent's memory, wrap newly inferred knowledge inside a *Tag* and attach it to the current *ObservedState* held inside the *PerceivableModel*.

For example the *AvgVelocityRule* requests the sequence of *PositionTags* of a perceivable object and calculates its average velocity based on the distance traveled and the time elapsed. In combination with the observed forward direction, a possible future position of a pedestrian can be predicted within the *Predict-PedestrianPositionRule*.

Finally, the *PedestrianIntentionRule* classifies each observed pedestrian based on its current position and orientation as well as predicted position and orientation relative to the closest predestrian crossing. For each possible intention a confidence value is calculated (see Fig. 1). The intention with the highest confidence value is stored as the current inferred intention for the observed pedestrian. A *PedestrianIntentionProfile* specifies confidence thresholds at which a pedestrian is considered to have the intention to cross the road.

5   Results

The extended reasoning approach of the FIVIS bicycle simulator with an inference system for virtual agents is evaluated on the basis of several traffic scenarios. The scenarios are modeled on observable behaviors of car drivers and pedestrians. Until now ten scenarios were developed and evaluated [8]. The scenario titled

Fig. 3: Setup of the scenario *Waiting Bus* at a pedestrian crossing. The vision of the black car approaching the pedestrian crossing is occluded by the house corner. The occlusion might lead to the agent's improper decision making.

Waiting Bus with occluded vision is presented in this contribution to demonstrate the combined perception, reasoning and action capabilities. Figure 3 shows the traffic situation in which a pedestrian wants to catch a bus waiting on the other side of the road. The agent represented as a black sports car accelerates from 0.00 m/s to 8.33 m/s. The house on the left road side obscures the agent's view of the pedestrian and thus prevents him from the early perception of the pedestrian. When the agent reaches the green area, the pedestrian starts crossing the pedestrian crossing with 3 m/s.

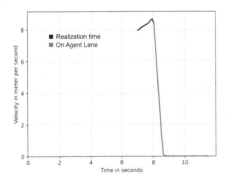

(a) The change in the agent's velocity over time.

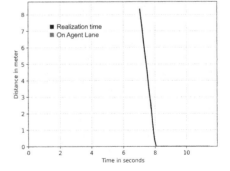

(b) The minimum distance between agent and pedestrian over time.

Fig. 4: Scenario *Waiting Bus* with occluded vision. At second 8 a critical situation was detected. Depending on the car's velocity and the driver's time to realize the pedestrian's intention to use the crossover, a traffic accident might occur.

Due to the occlusion of the pedestrian, the speed of the agent and the inference interval of one second, an unavoidable accident occurs in this scenario. After the initial perception of the pedestrian at second seven, the agent classifies the pedestrian as being in the critical area at second eight. Figure 4 demonstrates that the agent does not have enough time to stop the car to avoid the crash. In contrast, similar scenarios without occlusion allowed safe crossing of the pedestrian crossing [8]. This unavoidability might be further influenced by the character profile of the driver (e.g. reduced reaction time).

6 Conclusions and Discussions

This contribution presents a rule-based inference engine which can be applied to infer new knowledge based on previous information. Using a traffic simulation of motorized virtual agents and simple pedestrians interacting at a crosswalk, it was shown that the agents are able to infer possible intentions of a pedestrian. Instead of evaluating only the most current information about the traffic situation, past observations and model knowledge are incorporated into the decision making process by storing object-specific information over a short time period.

Rather than defining a separate path in a behavior tree for each decision an agent might make, this work is taking the approach of deriving as much general information as possible in the time domain before decision making. From a runtime perspective, this approach is only suitable for scenarios in which the virtual agents have to find solutions within a small problem space. Inference rules are only executed if their preconditions can be fulfilled by the information in the agent's memory hierarchy. However, grouping inference rules into categories could be advantageous, since the execution of a category would only takes place if the condition for the category is fulfilled.

It should be mentioned that the extension of the motorized virtual agent's reasoning and decision making is also possible exclusively through the extension of the memory hierarchy and the behavior tree. One goal of the rule-based inference system presented in this paper was to separate the inference of general information from decision making about the driver's driving strategies. The question arises in how far the additional temporal reasoning component is an improvement over an extended behavior tree.

The inference interval of one second corresponds approximately to the reaction time of a car driver. Thus, the behavior could be simulated realistically in comparison to previous nondeterministic behavior. By doing so it was possible to simulate rare scenarios like traffic accidents in a more realistic way. These scenarios only occur if certain conditions are met and even in these cases only if the decision making process has been influenced by incomplete, error prone or ambiguous input data.

To detach the static inference interval required for the discrete Markov chain, a timer based precondition could be defined. The condition would ensure that this rule is only executed in the required time interval.

Whether the extended knowledge base and inference system really leads to more realistic agent behavior and thus increased credibility need to be evaluated.

This aspect will be further investigated in a user study, including a comparison between the previous and the extended simulation approach.

References

1. Atkinson, R., Shiffrin, R.: Human memory: a proposed system and its control processes. In: Sternberg, R.J., Fiske, S.T., Foss, D.J. (eds.) Scientists Making a Difference, vol. 25, pp. 115–118. Cambridge University Press, Cambridge (2016)
2. Brachman, R.J., Levesque, H.J.: Knowledge Representation and Reasoning, 1st edn. Elsevier, Amsterdam (2004)
3. Collendanchise, M., Ögren, P.: Behavior Trees in Robotics and AI: An Introduction. Chapman & Hall/CRC Artificial Intelligence and Robotics, Taylor & Francis, Boca Raton (2018)
4. Goldstein, E.B., Brockmole, J.: Sensation and Perception: Cengage Learning. Cengage Learning, Boston (2016)
5. Herpers, R., et al.: FIVIS bicycle simulator - an immersive game platform for physical activities. In: Proceedings of the 2008 Conference on Future Play: Research, Play, Share, pp. 244–247 (2008)
6. Humphreys, T.: Exploring HTN planners through example. In: Game AI Pro 360: Guide to Architecture, pp. 103–122. CRC Press, Boca Raton (2019)
7. Isla, D.: Handling Complexity in the Halo 2 AI (2005). https://www.gamedeveloper.com/programming/gdc-2005-proceeding-handling-complexity-in-the-i-halo-2-i-ai. Accessed 13 June 2022
8. Lysek, A.: Introduction of a reasoning approach to enhance virtual agent perception capabilities. Master's thesis, Department of Computer Science, University of Applied Sciences Bonn-Rhein-Sieg (2023)
9. Neufeld, X., et al.: Building a planner: a survey of planning systems used in commercial video games. IEEE Trans. Games **11**(2), 91–108 (2019)
10. Peters, C., O'Sullivan, C.: Synthetic vision and memory for autonomous virtual humans. Comput. Graph. Forum **21**(4), 743–752 (2002)
11. Russell, S., Norvig, P.: Artificial Intelligence A Modern Approach, 4th edn. Pearson Education Inc, Upper Saddle River (2010)
12. Seele, S.: Attentive cognitive agents for real-time virtual environments. Ph.D. thesis, Universität Siegen (2023)
13. Wakim, C., Capperon, S., Oksman, J.: A Markovian model of pedestrian behavior. In: 2004 IEEE International Conference on Systems, Man and Cybernetics, vol. 4, pp. 4028–4033 (2004)

Game ON! a Gamified Approach to Household Food Waste Reduction

Francisco Vasconcelos[1] , Mara Dionísio[1,2]($\boxtimes$) , Sandra Câmara Olim[2,3] , and Pedro Campos[1,2,4]

[1] Universidade da Madeira, Funchal, Portugal
2044718@student.uma.pt, {mara.dionisio,pcampos}@staff.uma.pt
[2] ITI-LARSyS, IST, Universidade de Lisboa, Lisbon, Portugal
sandra.olim@iti.larsys.pt
[3] FCT, Universidade Nova de Lisboa, Lisbon, Portugal
[4] WoWSystems, Funchal, Portugal

Abstract. Food waste is an issue of high relevance to all countries around the globe. Many entities and governments work towards finding a solution to decrease or minimise the waste from its production to food consumption. Due to this impact, reducing food waste has also been implemented as a sub-goal of the United Nations Sustainable Development Goals. Several awareness campaigns have been developed to educate the population to be more mindful and responsible, most of these initiatives are focused on a general audience providing information about economic benefits for the customer and the well-being of the environment. In collaboration with the local Food Bank, we have identified that food waste reduction should be approached early on and that food waste awareness should not be introduced to children the same way as to adults. So new approaches should be developed to engage younger audiences with food waste reduction. Based on the potential that games have to engage children, this work proposes the design of a game targeting children ages eight to twelve years old to raise awareness about some of the best practices for food waste reduction in household consumers.

Keywords: Game Design · Concept Prototype · Wizard of Oz · Food waste reduction · children

1 Introduction

Food waste is referred to as the proportion of edible food that goes unconsumed [31], which includes materials for human consumption that are subsequently lost, degraded, discharged, or contaminated [12]. Due to its growing magnitude, complexity, and relevance food waste has attracted several initiatives [7,18] all in the hope that by 2030 food waste is going to be reduced by half [9]. According to Hebrok et al. [14] households are considered the major contributing factor to food waste. Household food waste refers to a portion of the overall food losses that occur due to consumers' choices, this includes actions like cooking

© IFIP International Federation for Information Processing 2023
Published by Springer Nature Switzerland AG 2023
P. Ciancarini et al. (Eds.): ICEC 2023, LNCS 14455, pp. 139–149, 2023.
https://doi.org/10.1007/978-981-99-8248-6_11

excessively large meals, purchasing excessive amounts of food, and neglecting to repurpose leftover food [2,5]. Scholars have highlighted the need for more empirical research at the household-level [11] in particular to study effective strategies to engage consumers in food waste reduction [15,30]. Current research shows that younger consumers are more likely to engage in food waste reduction than their older counterparts [1,15]. However, initiatives that can teach and motivate students and their relatives to have better food waste management need further exploration [21]. Hence, we see potential in designing a game for 9–12 years-old children about food waste reduction strategies. Previous research has shown that playful educational experiences and games have positive effects on a wide spectrum of children's cognitive skills development and facilitate the learning process [16]. A game about food waste can transmit children important life skills such as budgeting, resource management, creativity in using leftovers, and the value of sharing and donating food. By designing a game, we want to capture their attention and make learning about food waste a fun and memorable experience instead of associating food waste with negative emotions, as previous research shows to be very common among consumers [13]. Furthermore, this approach is aligned with the reality of the local context as this project is being developed in collaboration with the Local Food Bank.

This work contributes with the conceptual design and pilot evaluation of a game about food waste reduction strategies for children.

2   Related Work

2.1   Initiatives on Food Waste Awareness

Food waste is a critical problem in our days and accounts for a substantial quantity of wasted resources [24]. Therefore it is critical to find solutions that prevent and minimize food waste for our well-being and the sustainability of the environment [25]. Pinto et al. implemented an awareness campaign in the context of a University canteen by displaying simple posters with educative messages and conducting guerrilla actions during the busy lunch hour. The authors verified a reduction in plate waste and increased the recycling attitude of the canteen users (primarily students) [27]. In our search for material and initiatives to prevent food waste, we found several books that explain how to organise visits to the supermarket, organise food storage, and prepare dishes following good food waste practices [34]. In particular, we found a collection of four illustrated storybooks [17] targeted at children. Each book explores different aspects of food waste, with topics about organising the fridge and preventing food waste in various ways.

Other mediums used as inspiration for this research were food waste blogs [4], websites[1], social media pages [6] dedicated to finding solutions to this problem, books and lastly academic articles [1,28]. These sources were revealed to be very important to understand better the techniques and mediums currently used to raise awareness towards food waste reduction.

---

[1] https://www.bbcgoodfood.com/howto/guide/how-reduce-food-waste.

2.2   Serious Games About Food Waste Reduction

Serious games are designed with a primary purpose beyond mere entertainment. These games are powerful tools for education since through game-play children acquire content knowledge, enrich their experience, and are active participants in their learning process, social and cultural development and provide the opportunity for students to tackle real-world problems [3,8,26,29]. In this section, we present the related work on serious games for food waste reduction that have in mind younger audiences. The game "A família Consciência vai às compras" [23,32] targeting students with ages ranging from 8 to 12 years old, uses collaborative and cooperative mechanics within the gameplay, increasing the number of players. A study conducted for a period of three months showed positive responses regarding its effectiveness and children's engagement. "Feed the movement" is a gamified app [33] which aimed to target both children as well as their parents. This was achieved by having a character that is customisable with coins earned from the actions of the parents. The application presents a leaderboard that shows how other friends or relatives had their characters customised, with the intent to create some competitiveness among the users. The study involving children (9 to 13 years old), and their parents (32 to 48 years old) presented positive encouraging results in changing the parents' behaviour towards food management [33]. The central idea of the game "Tony Waste" [10], is to reduce food waste, by using an engaging character design. The player manages a pizza restaurant, if a mistake in the conception of a pizza is made, the player is penalized since it leads to food waste. "Upcycle" [20] is a game with a narrative plot around how food waste is affecting our world. The game develops around three core pillars: 1) Cooking: when helping people during the story, the user is given food spirits that allow the players to share new recipes. Following, the user can then cook in the game and in real life using a companion app; 2) Education: is achieved with the shared stories provided by the characters; 3) Community: players can help each other to make good decisions, by interacting through dialogues (leading to gather more food spirits) and having the world of the game less polluted. Overall, the described games [10,23,32] show the potential towards involving the youth in food waste reduction. Previous games have employed various strategies, including using memorable characters and their stories, to captivate children's attention. Game mechanics that use slice/cut, prepare meals, and storing food are reported as being engaging [32]. Additionally, game mechanics that foster collaborative environments between children and their parents are beneficial to support and reinforce positive behaviors related to food waste [23,32,33]. From the body of work, games that include repetitive actions help practice habits that can later be internalized and executed instinctively. While these works provide inspiration, further research is needed. Thus, we propose the design and development of a serious game as an artifact to assess its efficacy in educating children about the best practices for minimizing food waste.

3   Game Design

Our goal is to apply some food waste reduction strategies within the familiar setting of a kitchen. Games that are relevant by providing the information within the context of the user, in this case children, can help in the process of transferring skills that are useful beyond the game itself [22]. We decided to create a mobile game that appeals to children between the ages of 9 and 12, since most of the children in this age gap have access to mobile devices. The educational scope of this game is to focus on the following approaches for food waste reduction: 1) Proper food storage: How to organize the refrigerator/pantry to store food correctly, maintain its freshness, and prevent spoilage; 2) Leftover management: Re-purposing leftovers into new dishes; 3) Meal Planning: Plan meals in advance to avoid overbuying and ensure that all purchased ingredients are used efficiently. Hopefully, through gameplay children can apply these strategies, understand its relevance/application and eventually have the opportunity to share the game with other friends and relatives. To illustrate our game concept, an initial prototype of the game was developed with Figma[2] a platform used to develop prototypes in a fast and effective way.

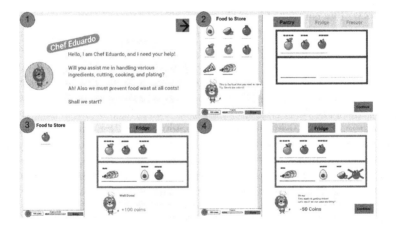

Fig. 1. Screenshots from the low-fidelity Figma prototype showcasing the gameplay. 1. Shows the introduction message from the main character, Chef Eduardo; 2. Screen showing the different sections of the game. On the left - the food to be stored is showcased. The colors presented below indicate the respective shelf to which each item belongs. The right side displays the pantry and the respective shelves. 3. Showcases Chef Eduardo and an example of the food stored properly. Above the food assets, the status indicator for its freshness is also displayed; 4. Shows an example of a food that was not stored properly.

---
[2] https://www.figma.com/.

Fig. 2. Further examples from the low-fidelity prototype gameplay; 1. Example of the gameplay of cutting to save the good parts of an apple; 2. Plating of the food to Chef Eduardo; 3. Customization Screen; 4. Summary of the day's performance, showing the XP points and coins gained.

3.1   Game Narrative and Mechanics

The game narrative revolves around a character named Eduardo, who is a lion and a cuisine chef responsible for overseeing the daily operations of a restaurant kitchen, ensuring that all food served meets the highest quality standards, as such he has to: 1) Plan the menu and design the plating presentation for each dish; 2) Coordinate kitchen staff, and assisting them as required; 3) Hire and train staff to prepare and cook all the menu items; 4) Stock ingredients and equipment, and placing orders as needed. In our game, the user plays as a chef's apprentice, and as the game develops, the user has a combination of education and on-the-job training by Chef Eduardo. The user learns how to prepare food and manage a professional kitchen. Eduardo's kitchen is special and has a motto: *"No food waste is allowed"*. Therefore the user has to learn the best practices to avoid food waste. The game goal is to develop a long-term engagement where new challenges and knowledge are given to the users each day, and users can learn about food waste reduction gradually over time. For example, the first day of gameplay starts with an "orientation day", which serves only as a tutorial for the game. The mechanics introduced in the game are meant to resemble real-life actions such as planning the menu, storing and managing the food, cooking, etc.; however, along these tasks, the users will be given concepts to avoid food waste (see Fig. 1). At the end of each day of work, the user performance in the kitchen is evaluated and rewarded with experience points accordingly. The experience points and coins will allow the user to acquire new tools for the kitchen and customize the avatar with accessories (see Fig. 2 - screen 3). The user is also responsible for organizing the food in the correct location by deciding whether to store the food in the fridge or pantry. Then by matching the color of the food with the color on the shelf, the user is given the opportunity to learn that it is essential to store food properly in the fridge to maintain its freshness, prevent spoilage, and ensure food safety (see Fig. 1 - screen 1,2). Another example of food waste reduction mechanisms is by having Chef Eduardo advise on how different fruits/vegetables might be spoiled or have a bruised or moldy area. However, it can still be salvaged by cutting off the affected portion before consuming the rest while the user prepares the food for the meals (see Fig. 2 - screen 1). As the game progresses, the challenges will increase as the food waste reduction tips that Chef Eduardo indicates. The game reward system has in consideration several factors: 1) The user's performance in storing the food; 2) if the recipes to be cooked were chosen based on the quantity needed 3) if the player had into consideration using food near the expiration date and 4) the food savings from chopping.

4   Preliminary Concept Evaluation

We designed and deployed in Figma an interactive low-fidelity prototype to evaluate the concept design of the game. The protocol assessment started with debriefing the experience, filling out questionnaires, and finally, answering a semi-structured interview. The interaction with the prototype included: 1) completing the tutorial; 2) playing the game; 3) using the character customization section of the game (purchasing some pants for the character and equipping him). Also, observational notes were taken while the participants interacted with the system. The questionnaire, using a Likert scale with a smiley-meter rating scale [19] asked questions to be rated from 1 (completely disagree) to 5 (completely agree), were used to gather usability information. The participants were also asked if they liked the game mechanics and the use of gamification elements like coins, experience points, kitchen upgrades, tools, and customisation of the character. Finally, the semi-structured interview with open-ended questions were: *What do you think was the game's final goal? Would you rather be rewarded with coins, points, or both? What is your overall experience with the game? Which activity within the game did you like most? What is your opinion about the main character? and finally, If you could change anything in the game, what would it be?* This initial evaluation was conducted in an informal setting with a group of six children between nine and thirteen years old. Our six participants (1 female and 5 males) were recruited through opportunistic sampling. Children were asked about their interest in participating, and their parents/guardians were contacted and informed of the study. Afterwards, the children and their parents were informed of the protocol and purpose of the research. Apart from the questionnaire and interview answers, no other personal data or pictures were taken.

4.1   Results from the Preliminary Concept Evaluation

Initial feedback from the observation of the participant's interaction with the prototype showed that the initial part of the game-play was clear and easy. Participants, aided by color cues, successfully organized the food items according to their appropriate positions within the refrigerator shelves. However, when it came to select other storage (e.g. selecting freezer or pantry) the process became confusing, leading participants to revisiting the tutorial for clarification. In the third part of the game, selecting the food from the storage to use in the meal preparation, only one participant did not realize they could select food that would be wasted. Most users liked the different mechanics of the game, except for one user that was indifferent regarding character customization. One user did not fully understand some game features, such as the upgrades and how to obtain experience. The top three favourite features from the game were: 1 - Recover the food from being wasted; 2 - Select the food for the meal and 3- Adding the food to cook (with the same amount of votes). Lastly, participants understood the different rewards systems coins (collected at each task) vs. experience (after storing, preparing a meal, and giving it to the chef to try). All participants except one understood everything correctly (see Table 1). Additionally, users were asked about their opinion of chef Eduardo (main character), and the answers were very similar, saying he was cool, funny, and cute. One participant said that Chef Eduardo was useful for guiding the user in the game. Also, the majority (4) of the participants agreed that the lion was appropriate, while (2) were hesitant. Finally, most participants (5) would like to be able to choose from a list of animals the appearance of the main character. The results of the semi-structured interview showcased that all the participants appreciated the mechanics and aesthetics of the main character, which was perceived as being "cute." The majority (5) of the users enjoyed the reward system (combination of coins and experience points), one preferred to have just coins as reward. Only two users noticed that the game goal was about awareness concerning "food waste." One user mentioned that it was about the customization of the chef, and one mentioned that it was about becoming a "good chef." Finally, regarding improvements to the game concept, most participants (5) answered to add more characters (to choose from and to customize).

Table 1. Questionnaire results

Question	Totally Disagree	Disagree	Disagree/Agree	Agree	Totally Agree
The tutorial was clear and easy to follow	0	0	1	1	4
Was it hard to organise the food in the correct place?	3	1	1	1	0
I enjoy saving wasted food	0	0	0	1	5
I liked to slice the food for the meal	0	0	1	3	2
I enjoyed having to cook the meal	0	0	0	3	3
I liked the confection of the food plate	0	0	0	4	2
I enjoyed getting my plate assessed by chef Eduardo	0	0	0	2	4
I understood how the different upgrades work	0	1	0	3	2
I liked to customise chef Eduardo with the clothes purchased	0	0	1	1	4
I understood how to get coins	0	0	0	3	3
I understood how to win experience to level up in the game	0	1	0	2	3

Fig. 3. Screenshots from current game prototype

5   Discussion and Future Work

This game prototype has allowed preliminary testing with the target audience. While the study was evaluated with a small sample, it was very valuable to gather feedback on usability, test game mechanics, and educational content. Overall, the game seems to be fun for the users and a good strategy to introduce the topic of food waste to children. The use of a character to guide the user in activities was well received. The gamification elements like customization, XP points, and coins were rewarding for the users. In terms of the level and game mechanics, participants felt compelled to try the different tasks. However, we also identified several aspects of the prototype that need improvements, namely: the tutorial should be clear; improve the feedback on the food storage placement (by adding visual cues of where the food should be stored); adding a button to facilitate the access to character customization; increase the items customisation offer and add further characters. Finally, we need to clearly convey the message of the game through its narrative and mechanics, since only two users noticed that the theme of the game was food waste reduction. We are incorporating the feedback of this preliminary study into the working prototype that is being designed and developed using Unreal Engine 5. This artifact will be used for a continued evaluation with the target audience (Fig. 3).

6   Conclusion

This work presents a serious game as a tool to engage children with food waste reduction strategies. Food waste is an ongoing problem in our society and children are at the center of the future solution to this problem as such we need to educate them about best practices to fight food waste in the household. Therefore, we presented a game prototype that leverages content that is familiar within the context of the child's household environment using gamification elements to sustain the child's engagement.

Acknowledgments. This research was funded by the Portuguese Recovery and Resilience Program (PRR), IAPMEI/ANI/FCT under Agenda C645022399-00000057 (eGamesLab), also supported by LARSyS-FCT Plurianual funding 2020-2023 (UIDB/50009/2020), and FCT Ph.D. Grant PD/BD/150286/2019.

References

1. Attiq, S., Danish Habib, M., Kaur, P., Junaid Shahid Hasni, M., Dhir, A.: Drivers of food waste reduction behaviour in the household context. Food Quality and Preference **94**, 104300 (2021). https://doi.org/10.1016/j.foodqual.2021.104300. https://www.sciencedirect.com/science/article/pii/S095032932100183X
2. Boulet, M., Hoek, A.C., Raven, R.: Towards a multi-level framework of household food waste and consumer behaviour: untangling spaghetti soup. Appetite **156**, 104856 (2021). https://doi.org/10.1016/j.appet.2020.104856.https://www.sciencedirect.com/science/article/pii/S0195666320301537
3. Calvo-Morata, A., Alonso-Fernández, C., Freire, M., Martínez-Ortiz, I., Fernández-Manjón, B.: Serious games to prevent and detect bullying and cyberbullying: a systematic serious games and literature review. Comput. Educ. **157**, 103958 (2020)
4. Cardenas, M., Joshi, S., Vergara, A.: Stopfoodwaste blog (2010). https://stopfoodwaste.org/
5. Cicatiello, C., Franco, S., Pancino, B., Blasi, E.: The value of food waste: an exploratory study on retailing. J. Retail. Consum. Serv. **30**, 96–104 (2016). https://doi.org/10.1016/j.jretconser.2016.01.004. https://www.sciencedirect.com/science/article/pii/S0969698916300078
6. o Desperdício, U.C.: Livro contra o desperdicio - receitas & dicas sustentáveis (2020). https://livrocontraodesperdicio.pt/
7. Dhir, A., Talwar, S., Kaur, P., Malibari, A.: Food waste in hospitality and food services: A systematic literature review and framework development approach. J. Clean. Prod. **270**, 122861 (2020). https://doi.org/10.1016/j.jclepro.2020.122861. https://www.sciencedirect.com/science/article/pii/S0959652620329061
8. Dwipayana, I., Sukajaya, I.: Delta's adventure: a constructivism-based serious game for the 1st grade of elementary school students on inequality concept. In: 2020 International Conference on Computer Engineering, Network, and Intelligent Multimedia (CENIM), pp. 127–131. IEEE (2020)
9. Edubirdie: Digging through school waste composition - edubirdie.com, May 2021. https://edubirdie.com/blog/school-waste-statistics
10. Ferreira, A., ao, D.B.: Tony waste: A serious game to fight food waste museum of ransom view project (2019). https://www.researchgate.net/publication/351736759
11. Filimonau, V., Matute, J., Kubal-Czerwińska, M., Krzesiwo, K., Mika, M.: The determinants of consumer engagement in restaurant food waste mitigation in Poland: an exploratory study. J. Clean. Prod. **247**, 119105 (2020). https://doi.org/10.1016/j.jclepro.2019.119105. https://www.sciencedirect.com/science/article/pii/S0959652619339757
12. Girotto, F., Alibardi, L., Cossu, R.: Food waste generation and industrial uses: A review. Waste Manage. **45**, 32–41 (2015) 10.1016/j.wasman.2015.06.008, https://www.sciencedirect.com/science/article/pii/S0956053X15004201
13. Graham-Rowe, E., Jessop, D.C., Sparks, P.: Identifying motivations and barriers to minimising household food waste. Resour. Conserv. Recycl. **84**, 15–23 (2014)
14. Hebrok, M., Heidenstrøm, N.: Contextualising food waste prevention - Decisive moments within everyday practices. J. Clean. Prod. **210**, 1435–1448 (2019). https://doi.org/10.1016/j.jclepro.2018.11.141. https://www.sciencedirect.com/science/article/pii/S0959652618335443
15. Heidari, A., Mirzaii, F., Rahnama, M., Alidoost, F.: A theoretical framework for explaining the determinants of food waste reduction in residential households: a case study of Mashhad. Iran. Environ. Sci. Pollution Res. **27**(7), 6774–

6784 (2020). https://doi.org/10.1007/s11356-019-06518-8. https://link.springer.com/10.1007/s11356-019-06518-8

16. Hosťovecký, M., Salgovic, I., Viragh, R.: Serious game in science education: How we can develop mathematical education, pp. 191–196, November 2018. https://doi.org/10.1109/ICETA.2018.8572158. Accessed 24 Jan 2023

17. Hugon, M., Gonçalves, A., Zambujal, I., ao de Sousa, R.G., Peixoto, J., Bakker, C., aes, A.M.M., Alçada, I., Nazareth, C.: Livros infantis de combate ao desperdício alimentar (5 2015), https://zerodesperdicio.pt/livros-infantis-combateaodesperdicioalimentar/

18. Issock Issock, P.B., Roberts-Lombard, M., Mpinganjira, M.: Understanding household waste separation in South Africa: an empirical study based on an extended theory of interpersonal behaviour. Manage. Environ. Quality Int. J. **31**(3), 530–547 (2020). https://doi.org/10.1108/MEQ-08-2019-0181. https://www.emerald.com/insight/content/doi/10.1108/MEQ-08-2019-0181/full/html

19. Kano, A., Horton, M., Read, J.C.: Thumbs-up scale and frequency of use scale for use in self reporting of children's computer experience. In: Proceedings of the 6th Nordic Conference on Human-Computer Interaction Extending Boundaries - NordiCHI '10, p. 699. ACM Press, Reykjavik, Iceland (2010). https://doi.org/10.1145/1868914.1869008. https://portal.acm.org/citation.cfm?doid=1868914.1869008

20. Kanonik, J., Boudreau, Z.: Upcycle: A Game About Food Waste. https://www.dandad.org/annual/2022/entry/newblood/4055/

21. Leal Filho, W., Lange Salvia, A., Davis, B., Will, M., Moggi, S.: Higher education and food waste: assessing current trends. Int. J. Sustainable Dev. World Ecology **28**(5), 440–450 (2021)

22. Lee, J.E.: Prospective elementary teachers' perceptions of real-life connections reflected in posing and evaluating story problems. J. Math. Teacher Educ. **15**, 429–452 (2012)

23. Linhares, E., Correia, M.: Reduzir o desperdício alimentar: aprender e sensibilizar através de um jogo online reduce food waste: learn and raise awareness through an online game 11 (2019). https://www.eduser.ipb.pt

24. Loss, F.F.: Waste and the right to adequate food: Making the connection. FAO: Rome, Italy 1 (2018)

25. Nations, U.: Objetivos de desenvolvimento sustentável - onu portugal (2015). https://unric.org/pt/objetivos-de-desenvolvimento-sustentavel/

26. Panagiotopoulou, L., et al.: Design of a serious game for children to raise awareness on plastic pollution and promoting pro-environmental behaviors. J. Comput. Inf. Sci. Eng. **21**(6) (2021)

27. Pinto, R.S., Pinto, R.M.D.S., Melo, F.F.S., Campos, S.S., Cordovil, C.M.d.S.: A simple awareness campaign to promote food waste reduction in a University canteen. Waste Manage. **76**, 28–38 (2018). https://doi.org/10.1016/j.wasman.2018.02.044. https://linkinghub.elsevier.com/retrieve/pii/S0956053X18301107

28. Russell, S.V., Young, C.W., Unsworth, K.L., Robinson, C.: Bringing habits and emotions into food waste behaviour. Resour. Conserv. Recycl. **125**, 107–114 (2017). https://doi.org/10.1016/j.resconrec.2017.06.007. https://linkinghub.elsevier.com/retrieve/pii/S092134491730160X

29. Sawyer, B.: Improving public policy through game-based learning and simulation (2002). https://www.wilsoncenter.org/publication/executive-summary-serious-games-improving-public-policy-through-game-based-learning-and. Accessed 06 Jan 2023

30. Schanes, K., Dobernig, K., Gözet, B.: Food waste matters - a systematic review of household food waste practices and their policy implications. J. Clean. Prod. **182**, 978–991 (2018). https://doi.org/10.1016/j.jclepro.2018.02.030. https://linkinghub. elsevier.com/retrieve/pii/S0959652618303366
31. Smith, T.A., Landry, C.E.: Household food waste and inefficiencies in food production. Am. J. Agr. Econ. **103**(1), 4–21 (2021). https://doi.org/10.1111/ajae.12145. https://onlinelibrary.wiley.com/doi/10.1111/ajae.12145
32. Sofia, M., Correia, M.: Sensibilizar para o desperdício alimentar: impacto de um jogo online em alunos do 1. ceb (2017)
33. Titiu, A.D.: Designing a gamified application to promote food waste awareness in household and further educate consumers on their food waste behavior (7 2019)
34. Trindade, B.: Desperdício Zero à Mesa com o Pingo Doce. Pingo Doce, 1 edn. (9 2020)

Acquiring and Assessing 21st Century Skills Through Game Development: A Case Study with an Escape Game Template

Chloé Vigneau[1,2]([⊠]) [iD], Stéphanie Mader[2] [iD], Catherine Rolland[1] [iD], and Axel Buendia[2] [iD]

[1] Chaire ScienceXGames (Ecole Polytechnique), Palaiseau, France
chloe.vigneau@polytechnique.edu
[2] CNAM, CEDRIC, Paris, France
stephanie.mader@lecnam.net

Abstract. In this study, we observe how a video game creation activity with an escape game template can enhance the acquisition of 21st century skills among high school students. In Game Development-Based Learning (GDBL), the use of customisable template eases the technical cost of entry, provides a structure to guide and motivate students as well as provides learning traces for the teachers. Through the modification of the template, students can engage in tasks directly related to 21st century skills while personalising the game. We present a study on 221 high school students with 10 voluntary teachers in France, analysing the students' engagement, and the complexity of skills assessment in this context.

Keywords: Game-Development-Based Learning · Template · Skills · Assessment

1 Introduction

In 2019, Andreas Schleicher, Director of the Education and Skills Directorate at the Organisation for Economic Co-operation and Development (OECD), commented: "*Education is no longer just about teaching students something; it is more about teaching them to develop a reliable compass and the navigation tools to find their own way in an increasingly complex, volatile and uncertain world*" [10]. To prepare the youth for the future, 21st century skills such as creativity and problem solving have been identified by Margarida Romero [13]. Game Development-Based Learning (GDBL) could be a solution to train those skills as many video game development tasks require the application of 21st century skills [3, 12]. However, video game development is a complex endeavor with many technical challenges, raising the cost of entry for students and teachers alike. Providing a template of a pre-coded game that already works may be an option to ease this cost of entry while maintaining the interest of the students for the activity. Through a case study, we evaluate whether video game creation with a template is a relevant approach to the acquisition of 21st century skills along with an observation of the complexity of skills assessment in this context. In this paper, we present our approach to

P. Ciancarini et al. (Eds.): ICEC 2023, LNCS 14455, pp. 150–158, 2023.
https://doi.org/10.1007/978-981-99-8248-6_12

template design for GDBL, the construction of the escape game template, and our study to evaluate our template with 221 students in 12 classrooms and 10 teachers in France. Finally, we discuss our findings and outline our future work.

2 Background

Voogt and Roblin [15] conducted a comparative analysis of international frameworks for 21st century skills to identify the most common skills shared among these frameworks: Collaboration, communication, ICT literacy and social skills. These skills cannot be taught the same way as curriculum knowledge, they require a constructivist approach where education is seen as the bridge between the individual and society, and students are invited to "learn by doing" as Dewey's theory suggests [4].

In GDBL, students learn by creating a videogame [1], either from scratch [7, 11] or with video game templates [14]. When students create their own videogame, they encounter many technical challenges, and the time they spend learning programming may come at the expense of developing other skills [11]. Video game templates allow to ease the technical complexity and have been used for the acquisition of 21st century skills in, among others, the Magical project [3] and the No One Left Behind project [12]. These experiences show pedagogical advantages of the use of such templates. The structuration around activities constrained by the template breaks down the creation of the game into a series of tasks providing students with specific goals, which guide students work and help them stay motivated [9], while providing clearer learning traces [8], helping the teachers' assessment of the learning outcomes. Indeed, in the context of GDBL, assessing a creative production such as a video game, and the learning outcome of the activity of video game creation are challenging for the teachers as they do not know which skills are used to execute which tasks in video game production. Moreover, while the game produced by students provide an indication of the skills mobilised, it is not sufficient to assess all the work that has been carried out. In fact, to complete a task in game development, a student goes through subtasks of various natures. According to Griffin's methodology [6], skills can be evaluated based on the subtasks that have been completed, using the learning traces collected through the digital environment [2, 5, 8]. For our study, we will compare the learning traces from three different sources: observation of the game, the teacher's assessment, and the student's self-assessment.

3 The Design of an Escape Game Template for GDBL

Our approach to design video game template for the acquisition of 21st century skills is to provide a functional game that students can modify, because the video game template objective is three-fold: (1) easing the technical challenges of video game creation through pre-coded features, (2) providing clear goals and tasks to guide the students' work and enhance their motivation, and (3) providing a structure and learning trace to facilitate the skills assessment for the teacher. To do so, we need a fine analyse of the work carried out by the students and skills applied during the activity. To delimit the analyse and prepare a first template, we focused on a game genre: the escape game. Escape games are well-known, easy to understand, split into puzzles, accessible to play, and provide a variety of tasks. We considered the usual production tasks of such games and split them into subtasks (see Table 1).

Table 1. Subtasks done by students to complete tasks in the video game template.

Tasks in video game template	Subtasks done by students
Custom character images (4 images)	Find images (preferably royalty free images) Upload image
Custom text (7 texts)	Write dialog
Custom variables (3 variables)	Change variable
Custom sounds (4 sounds)	Find sound (preferably royalty free sound) or record sound Upload sound
Custom other elements	Give credits

To connect the subtasks to the skills, we first had to adapt them to the French curriculum as our study is conducted in France: Understand and express themselves orally and in writing (Communication), Use digital tools to share and communicate (ICT literacy), Developing intellectual honesty (ICT literacy), Understand and respect common rules (Social skills), Organise individual and group work (Social skills). Creativity and Problem-solving remains the same in the French curriculum. To associate subtasks and skills, we designed a survey using a 5-point Likert scale to assess each potential association. We recruited a group of 12 experts, including teachers, educational engineers, and educational researchers, from the special digital working group mandated by the French Ministry of Education, to participate in the survey. As reported in Table 2, we kept the associations that achieved consensus among the experts (a mean value above 3.5, with a standard deviation below 1.5).

Finally, we created the resource necessary for a class session of 1 to 2 hours led by teachers without game development knowledge. We developed the escape game template in Construct3 an online game engine with a visual programming interface. The template is a 2D game of the escape game genre, a subgenre of the *point'n clic* games. The camera shows the game world from a 3rd person top isometric point-of-view (Fig. 1). The player's goal is to unlock the last door with a key found by solving 3 clue-based puzzles. First, the player must find the phone number of a character named Bj by talking to a resident of the village. Then, they have to call Bj to obtain a radio frequency. Finally, they discover an excerpt of the Mario video game music by listening to the radio. "Mario" is the code they must use to escape the village. Students can personalise every clue, text, and character. The aim is therefore to modify the game while keeping it functional. Teachers can draw on several sources for assessment: observation of the session, the games created. To facilitate the evaluation of the text written by the students, all texts are exported in a CSV file.

Table 2. Skills associated to subtasks with the mean value and standard deviation.

Skills	Subtask
Understand and express themselves orally and in writing	Write dialog (M: 4.8, SD: 0.37)
Develop creativity	Write dialog (M: 4;8, SD: 0.37) Recording / changing sound (M: 3.83, SD: 1.34) Modify variables (M: 3.58, SD: 1.38)
Solving problems	Find royalty free image (M: 3.8, SD: 0.79) Modify variable (M: 4.5, SD:0.80)
Use digital tools to share and communicate	Write dialog (M: 3.91, SD: 1.03) Upload sound in game (M: 3.58, SD: 1.49) Recording / changing sound (M: 4.08, SD: 0.9)
Developing intellectual honesty	Writing (M: 3.58, SD: 1.11) Find royalty free image (M: 4.75, SD: 0.43) Find royalty free sound (M: 4.75, SD: 0.43) Give image and sound credit (M: 4.75, SD: 0.43)
Understand and respect common rules	Find royalty free image (M: 3.66, SD: 1.24) Upload image in game (M: 3.6, SD: 1.46)
Organise individual and group work	Find royalty free image (M: 4.25, SD: 1.46)

Fig. 1. Template of the escape game developed on Construct3 game engine.

4   Method

The study took place over 4 months (November 2022 - February 2023) in 12 different classes from 10 different schools in France, involving 221 high school students (14 to 16 years old) and 10 voluntary teachers. Chloé Vigneau (first author of this paper) was present in the classroom to observe and ensure that the protocol was followed:

1. At least two weeks prior, the template, a tutorial on how to play the game and modify the template, and a link to a royalty-free images and sounds library, are provided to the teacher. Teachers are free to give these resources to their students or not.
2. At the start, each student receives a numbered USB that contains the template. The number is an identifier to associate a student with the game they have created in accordance with GDPR regulations[1]. The students play the game for 10 min, then they spend about 45–60 min searching for images and sounds on the internet, writing text, and customising the template.
3. At the end of the session, the students are asked to save their own game on the USB key and complete a survey, which serves as an initial learning trace. Teachers are asked to complete another survey, which serves as a second learning trace.
4. A few days after the experience, we play the games collected on the USB keys and analyse them to list the tasks that have been done in the game (boolean questions on text, sound, sound and variable changes). This data is the third learning trace.

5   Results

For this analysis, we define a game as functional when a player can play without any blocking bugs and we define a game as playable when it has no blocking bugs and when it allows a player to successfully complete the puzzle using the provided clues. With the template, 88% of the students were able to create a functional game, while 70% were able to create a playable game. In the game, they completed 0 to 4 tasks, with a mean at 1.9 tasks. Only 6 of the 186 games presented 0 task completed. The students self-reported in average 0 to 10 max subtasks, with a mean of 5.3 subtasks. Next, we compare the three learning traces to evaluate how they converge on skills applied during the activity.

5.1   Skills Assessment from Teachers' Point of View

In the survey, teachers assessed whether the skills have been trained using the following scale: not worked at all, insufficiently worked, sufficiently worked in relation to expectations, worked and developed. According to them, creativity, the use of digital tools, and problem-solving were always sufficiently worked (Fig. 2). While most of them found that Expression, Organisation and Respect rules were sufficiently worked the others found it insufficiently worked.

---

[1] GDPR defines the rights of individuals to their private data in Europe.

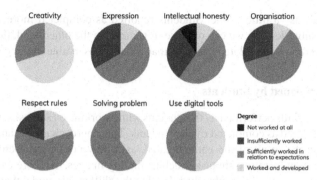

Fig. 2. Skills assessed by teachers.

5.2 Subtasks Performed According to Students

In the survey, students indicated the level of completion for each task using the following scale: not at all, a little, a lot, all done. The tasks related to pictures and writing are declared as the most completed (Fig. 3). They also indicated whether each subtask was new to them or not. New tasks were defined as those they had never done before. Three subtasks are considered new by most students: finding images (>80%), writing (>80%), and finding sounds (>70%).

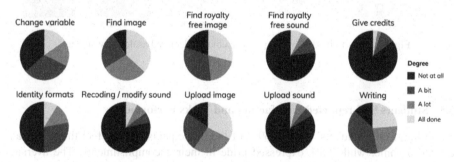

Fig. 3. Tasks performed according to students by degree in percent.

The two most frequently performed subtasks, finding images and writing, are new tasks for most students. The other subtasks declared as new, such as identifying format (60%), recording or modifying sound (60%), and giving credit (55%), were rarely done.

5.3 Tasks Completed Versus Self-reported Subtasks by Students

We analysed the 186 games to verify whether any text, image, sound, variables, or other elements had been modified. A task is considered as done when at least one element has been personalised. Images were the most customised (91% of the games), followed by text (66%), variables (23%), and finally sounds (10%). We compare the result with the tasks students reported as completed by taking into account the mean of the subtasks reported at least as "a little" done. Students reported as completed more writing and programming subtasks than we can observe in games. On the other hand, they reported doing less work on image-related subtasks than what is observable in the games.

5.4 Skills Performed by Students

To determine the skills performed by the students while working on subtasks, we consider the subtasks declared as completed by the students. This approach avoids an assessment solely based on the result of the game created, as it may not be representative of all the work done in preparatory subtasks such as finding images. To score each skill, we calculate the average of all the subtasks related to the skill in our model that the student indicated as at least "a little" completed (Fig. 4). Organisation, respect of rules, problem-solving, and expression being the most performed according to our model and students self-reporting on subtasks. We discuss below this discrepancy with the teacher's analysis.

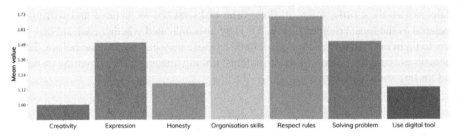

Fig. 4. Skills trained according to the subtasks declared as done by students.

5.5 Students Self-reported Satisfaction and Tasks Performed

According to the students' survey, 69% of the participants did not feel that they had created a game, while 58% expressed pride in their accomplishments. The average number of subtasks completed in relation to the sense of pride in the results shows that students who are proud of their achievements completed an average of 5.54 subtasks and 1.46 new subtasks. Those who were not proud completed 4.48 subtasks and 1.05 new subtasks. So, those who were proud of the result completed more subtasks overall and more subtasks that were new to them.

6   Discussions and Limitations

To analyse how learning happen and can be assessed in "learning by doing" activity, we compared the teachers' point of view, self-reported auto evaluation of the student and what has been done in the games. We noticed two main discrepancies.

First, subtasks self-reported by students and the tasks completed in the game were not equivalent. For example, 91% of the students had personalised the images in the game, but only 85% of students declared having done so. We analyse that students minimise the work done on tasks they already know such as image modification and overestimate their work on new tasks such as sound customisation and programming. An explanation may be that new tasks, requiring more learning, may have been tried, even some preparatory subtasks done, but without being completed in the template.

Second, the teachers' assessment of skills practiced and the skills mobilised by the subtasks declared as completed by the students converge on their evaluation of Organisation, Respect rules, Problem solving and Expression being practiced. However, all the teachers reported that Creativity and The use of digital tools were at least sufficiently worked while students reported few subtasks done related to those two skills. Plus, some teachers reported that Respect Rules, Organisation and Expression were insufficiently trained. We hypothesise that our model might not capture enough subtasks related to those skills and that providing the model to the teachers might help them to assess less obvious subtasks, tasks and skills. This last point emphasises the complexity of assessing such skills in this context and the importance of having a clear skills framework for this activity.

Finally, our template only provided learning trace on the text written, and a more comprehensive learning trace would be necessary to help teachers assess with more details the work carried out by their students.

7 Conclusion

Through this study on 221 high school students, we evaluated the use of an escape game template to train 21st century skills in a very short class session. The template was successful in providing a structure for the workshop, allowing 88% students to finish their project in a very short timeframe, and 70% of them with an entire playable game. We can confirm that the video game template is an effective method for motivating students to practice known subtasks and learn new subtasks. 96% percent of students who submitted their games have completed at least one task in the template, which is a very good result on students' engagement. A majority of students (58%) felt proud about the result. Moreover, we observed that they completed both known and new subtasks, showing that the video game template can be used in two ways: for the discovery and learning of new tasks and for the practice of tasks that are already known.

Compared to creating a video game "from scratch," using a template reduces the technical barriers to entry, provides a guide for game creation, motivates students, and facilitates progress tracking of their learning. However, even with three sources of learning traces, assessing the skills applied during the workshop is still challenging. We discovered two discrepancies by comparing the three sources. As a result, if our model splitting tasks into subtasks and linking subtasks to skills seems to capture well the tasks related to problem-solving, it was less precise on other skills showing the need for a finer grid. Our future work will reassess this model and deepen its level of details as well as reevaluate the connection found in discrepancy in this study. Providing an automated analyses of the tasks completed in the template would be a more comprehensive learning trace to help teachers figure out what students did during the activity.

Solidifying the model between tasks, subtasks and skills is an important step to provide teachers with clear instructions on assessment and extract finer learning traces.

As a next step, we will develop an easy to configure template so teachers can select in an interface which tasks they want their students to practice, and the template will adapt itself to the configuration. Indeed, we argue that, if teachers are more involved in the preparation of the video game template, they will have a better understanding of the tasks and subtasks required to complete the game and gain a better understanding of all the benefits of this Game Development-Based Learning activity. This configurable template, with a comprehensive learning trace of the tasks done, should help teachers prepare GDBL workshop on 21st century skills for their students and help them better assess their students' progress.

References

1. Bewer, N., Gladkaya, M.: Game development based approach for learning to program: a systematic literature review. In: Wirtschaftsinformatik 2022 Proceedings, vol. 3 (2022)
2. Boyer, A.: Quelques réflexions sur l'exploration des traces d'apprentissage, Distances et médiations des savoirs 27 (2019)
3. Dagnino, F., Earp, J., Ott, M.: Investigating the "MAGICAL" effects of game building on the development of 21st century skills (2012). https://doi.org/10.13140/2.1.3957.8564
4. Dewey, J.: Experience and Education. New York: Macmillan Company (1938)
5. Dimitracopoulou, A., Bruillard, E.: Enrichir les interfaces de forums par la visualisation d'analyses automatiques des interactions et du contenu. Sciences et Technologies de l'Information et de la Communication pour l'Éducation et la Formation 13 (2006). https://doi.org/10.3406/stice.2006.942
6. Griffin, P., Care, E., Wilson, M.: Assessment and Teaching of 21st Century Skills. Springer, Dordrecht (2018). https://doi.org/10.1007/978-94-017-9395-7
7. HolenkoDlab, M., Hoic-Bozic, N.: Effectiveness of game development-based learning for acquiring programming skills in lower secondary education in Croatia. Educ. Inf. Technol. **26**, 4433–4456 (2021)
8. Laflaquière, J., Prié, Y., Mille, A.: Des traces modélisées, un nouvel objet pédagogique? (2007)
9. Malone, T.: What Makes Things Fun to Learn? A Study of Intrinsically Motivating Computer Games. Pipeline. 6 (1981)
10. OECD Future of Education and Skills 2030, OECD Learning Compass 2030, A Series of Concept Notes
11. Pereira, E., Lopes, L.: Electronic game creation through scratch software: creative and collaborative learning fostering STEAM practices. Acta Scientiae **22**, 28–46 (2020). https://doi.org/10.17648/acta.scientiae.5535
12. Reynolds, R., Caperton, I.: Contrasts in student engagement, meaning-making, dislikes, and challenges in a discovery-based program of game design learning. Educ. Tech. Res. Dev. **59**, 267–289 (2015). https://doi.org/10.1007/s11423-011-9191-8
13. Romero, M., Lille, B., Patiño, A.: Usages créatifs du numérique pour l'apprentissage au XXIe siècle, Presse de l'Université du Québec (2017)
14. Spieler, B., et al.: Evaluation of Game Templates to support Programming Activities in Schools (2018)
15. Voogt, J., Pareja Roblin, N.: A comparative analysis of international frameworks for 21 st century competences: implications for national curriculum policies. J. Curriculum Stud. **44** (2012). https://doi.org/10.1080/00220272.2012.668938

Entertainment Methods and Tools

Semiotic Structuring in Movie Narrative Generation

Edirlei Soares de Lima[1]([⊠]) [ID], Marco A. Casanova[2] [ID], Bruno Feijó[2] [ID], and Antonio L. Furtado[2] [ID]

[1] Academy for Games and Media, Breda University of Applied Sciences, Breda, The Netherlands
soaresdelima.e@buas.nl
[2] Department of Informatics, PUC-Rio, R. Marquês de São Vicente 225, Rio de Janeiro, Brazil
{casanova,bfeijo,furtado}@inf.puc-rio.br

Abstract. In this paper we apply, in a novel way, our ongoing research work on the interactive composition of narratives based on *semiotic relations*. To the two basic components of interactive systems, namely, a software tool and a user interface, we add a third component – *AI agents*, understood as an upgraded rendition of software agents. Our semiotic relations approach considers four ways of composing new narratives from existing narratives. Along the horizontal syntagmatic axis one can form the new narrative by *combining* two or more previous narratives. Along the vertical paradigmatic axis, the new narrative may emerge as a similar version, which *imitates* the previous one in a different context. Along the depth meronymic axis, the hierarchic narrative levels, such as event and scene, are explored, allowing to *zoom in and out* in the composition process. Lastly, the antithetic consideration, rather than adding a dimension, aims at some form of *reversal*, through the adoption of opposite values. A fully operational prototype is described, with ChatGPT operating as the main AI agent component. To run the experiments, we concentrated on movie narratives.

Keywords: Interactive Story Composition · Semiotic Relations · Artificial Intelligence · Movie Narratives · Storyboards · Chatbots · ChatGPT

1 Introduction

In this work, we address the processes of analyzing and generating movie narratives, with the support of our proposed *semiotic relations*, previously introduced in the course of our Logtell[1] interactive storytelling project [13, 23, 29].

Our early work in the project, as formally described in [8], dealt mainly with interactive plan-based plot generation [8, 26–28] and dramatization [9, 25, 30, 31], wherein plots consisted of partially-ordered sequences of events. Our prototype tools, developed in logic programming notation, basically remained at what Mieke Bal [2] calls the *fabula*

---

[1] http://www.icad.puc-rio.br/~logtell/

© IFIP International Federation for Information Processing 2023
Published by Springer Nature Switzerland AG 2023
P. Ciancarini et al. (Eds.): ICEC 2023, LNCS 14455, pp. 161–175, 2023.
https://doi.org/10.1007/978-981-99-8248-6_13

layer, where a simple abstract account of *what* happens is presented, to be followed by the *story layer* indicating *how* what happens is told – i.e. how the author structures the narrative – and, lastly, by the *text layer* which materializes the narrative in some chosen medium (which could be animation, video, film, etc.).

On the one hand, our tools were generally well evaluated by the non-professional users who interacted with them, and were happy to see their decisions at branching points being taken into account so as to produce plots conforming to their taste [24], and noticed the curious unexpected solutions that the plan generator managed to find when given apparently impossible goals. On the other hand, by not trying to contemplate Mieke Bal's story layer, the plots invariably looked rather shallow, lacking the creative touch of talented professional authors.

We accordingly decided, while keeping user interaction, to extend our approach to the story layer, by composing the plots, still under the form of partially ordered sequences of events, by extracting them from narratives told by professionals. In an early attempt in this direction, we applied our previous work on semiotic relations to the analysis of folktale narratives, investigating how the innumerous *variants* of a folktale type might have emerged, and then proceeding to show how to automatically create new variants by the interactive application of the semiotic relations. One of our papers [29], based on the *Index* compiled by Aarne and Thompson [1], dealt in particular with the folktale type AT 333, to which pertains the *Little Red Riding Hood* story, reported in [39] to have appeared in no less than 56 variants in different regional and temporal contexts.

In the present paper, we propose to advance one fundamental step further in the application of semiotic relations to the process of interactive narrative analysis and generation by focusing on their natural language representation. We concentrate on movie narratives as the object of research, realizing that they are generally attractive to contemporary taste, inasmuch as their producers are compelled to strive for both critical acclaim and box office revenue.

Related works with stimulating results include a growing number of publications pertaining to the active research topic of *film semiotics*, a particularly influential contribution being Umberto Eco's characterization of what he calls 'cinematic code' [11]. Another important reference on the semiology of the cinema is the work by Christian Metz [32]. The relevance of scenes that function as leading *motifs* is confirmed by Folgert Karsdorp [21], who sees them as "the primary building blocks of stories". Our approach to achieve support to narrative generation is akin to *case-based reasoning* [22], in our case by looking at some 'virtual library' of popular movies to *search* for movies whose structure has certain characteristics and could then be *adapted* in order to compose new narrative structures. Previous attempts to employ case-based reasoning to narrative generation include, among others, the work reported by Pablo Gervás [16]. *Searching* through a library is a pattern-matching activity that, in principle, should not be too hard to implement if the library items are conveniently indexed. The subsequent *adaptation phase*, on the contrary, poses widely different sorts of unpredictable *blending* problems [12, 25] calling for human interaction, ideally combined with the development of heuristics that may promise some chance of success.

More importantly, what makes our proposal look viable is the fact that current efforts to cope with the difficulties of natural language understanding and generation are obtaining increasing success, thanks to technical novelties that allow to handle very large text repositories, such as *transformers* [20]. The GPT (Generative Pre-trained Transformer) model [33] has guided the production of the ChatGPT tool[2], which is now being tried for a variety of purposes. However, there are no in-depth references on ChatGPT for interactive plot generation for movie narratives, but simple examples in blogs and guidelines dealing with screenwriting exist. Among these applications, we find attractive the experiments by Gonsalves [17] to write screenplays, the practical guidelines for screenwriting by Carter [6], and the simple course materials of the University of New Hampshire [40]. None of those applications, nevertheless, have a robust foundation of movie semiotics that allows a more controlled use of the ChatGPT tool as we propose in the present paper.

The paper is organized as follows. Section 2 explains how our proposed semiotic relations support the structured analysis and generation of narratives. Section 3 applies the relations to the analysis of four popular movies, in an attempt to gain experience for the interactive generation process, which is the object of Sect. 4. Section 5 contains concluding remarks.

2 Semiotic Structuring

One major guideline of our Logtell interactive storytelling project is the *semiotic treatment* of both factual and narrative information, on the basis of four *semiotic relations* [13, 29].

The four relations – *syntagmatic, paradigmatic, meronymic, antithetic* – have been drawn from the so-called *four master tropes*, a topic of high interest in the area of *semiotic research* [7]. The word 'trope' comes from the Greek 'τροποσ' from 'τρεπειν', 'to turn', with the intended meaning that such rhetorical figures 'turn', i.e., alter the meaning of a word. Table 1 shows our four semiotic relations, together with their intuitive meaning, associated logical connectives, and corresponding tropes.

Table 1. Semiotic relations.

relation	meaning	operator	trope
syntagmatic	connectivity	and	metonymy
paradigmatic	similarity	or	metaphor
meronymic	hierarchy	part-of	synecdoche
antithetic	negation	not	irony

Present among the numerous rhetorical tropes compiled in Greco-Roman antiquity by Quintilian (c. 35-c. 100), these four tropes were later characterized as fundamental, first by Ramus (1515–72) and again by Vico (1668–1744) [7]. In modern times they

---

[2] https://openai.com/blog/chatgpt

were revived in Kenneth Burke's seminal study [5]. Their universality and completeness have been repeatedly emphasized, with the indication that they do constitute, according to Jonathan Culler, "a system, indeed *the* system, by which the mind comes to grasp the world conceptually in language" [10]. Applications to several topics have been reported, for instance, to worldviews and ideologies by the historian Hayden White [41] and, in our own work, to mathematical proof methods [15], to database conceptual modelling [13], and, more relevant to the present discussion, to digital interactive composition of story-plots [29].

With respect to the names we assigned to the proposed semiotic relations, the terms 'syntagmatic' and 'paradigmatic'[3] correspond to the two linguistic axes postulated by Saussure [36], who originally called the second axis 'associative'. His *horizontal* syntagmatic axis modelled sentences as aligned sequences of words connected in obedience to language syntax, whilst the *vertical* associative dimension offered alternative choices to be placed below some of the sentence components.

The now universally adopted renaming of 'associative' to 'paradigmatic' was promoted by Jakobson [19], who argued convincingly, while discussing aphasia disorders, that "the development of a discourse may take place along two different semantic lines: one topic may lead to another either through their *similarity* or through their *contiguity*. The metaphoric way would be the most appropriate term for the first case and the metonymic way for the second", in clear reference, respectively, to the paradigmatic and syntagmatic terminology.

In [42], wherein six types of *part-of* links are distinguished, one reads: "We will refer to relationships that can be expressed with the term 'part' in the above frames as 'meronymic' relations after the Greek 'meros' for part". About its associated trope, Burke affirms that "for synecdoche, we could substitute *representation*." [5]. In fact, breaking some signifying term into detail is an effective way to achieve its representation, whereas its identification should be possible by summarizing a detailed view. This zooming in / zooming out variation of granularity level suggests that meronymic relations introduce *depth* as a third dimension.

Lastly, the term 'antithetic' reflects the attribution of a *value scale* [7], either simply binary or graduated. No additional dimension is implied. According to Burke [5], the perspective induced by the associated irony trope refers to *dialectic*, which includes *antithesis* as a critical phase, expressing *negation*.

Section 3 contains examples of structured movie narrative analysis based on the four semiotic relations. The informally conducted analysis of four representative examples (which led us to examine long series of related narratives, not mentioned here to save space) furnished clues to formulate the verbal definitions of the semiotic relations, shown in Table 2 of Sect. 4.2, which guide the prototype in the generation of new movie narratives. At the close of the analysis, we verified the adequacy of each definition over the corresponding example in separate ChatGPT sessions.

As we proceed with analysis as a preliminary step to generation, we should have in mind Barthes's assertion that reusing other authors' work, in honest and imaginative fashion, is a culturally consecrated artistic practice, and that *intertextuality* can be

---

[3] Eco [11] and Metz [28] treat the syntagmatic and paradigmatic elements within a more general approach to the semiology of cinema, which lies beyond the scope of the present paper.

detected everywhere [3, p. 39]: "Any text is a new tissue of past citations ... the intertext is a general field of anonymous formulae whose origin can scarcely ever be located; of unconscious or automatic quotations, given without quotation marks".

3 Examples of Structured Movie Narrative Analysis

3.1 Syntagmatic Relation – Batman v Superman: Dawn of Justice

The narrative of *Batman v Superman: Dawn of Justice* (Warner Bros., 2016)operates the confluence of the life stories of the characters in the title, who premiered separately in the films *Batman* (Warner Bros., 1989) and *Superman* (Warner Bros., 1978), indicating a syntagmatic relation between the films. The two protagonists are *comics superheroes*, and their quest is to protect all citizens of the fictional town where they live, respectively named Gotham City and Metropolis, apparently modelled after New York. They are committed to fighting highly resourceful criminals, while often suffering opposition from the regular police and from conservative newspapers, given that they act in a vigilante extra-legal capacity.

The question is then why they behave as enemies, since they are engaged in the same kind of quest. It has been suggested [4] that the film could be interpreted thematically as an *allegory* about America's response to the 9/11 terrorist attack, in which case the opposition to Superman would be motivated by the fear that "an all-powerful alien" – referring not to the villain Zod but to Superman himself – "could destroy his adopted planet with ease". And yet Superman would be revived later in the interest of a common cause. Reconciled with Batman, he would join his repentant adversary, together with Wonder Woman, Aquaman, Cyborg and The Flash to form the *Justice League* (Warner Bros., 2017) to save the planet from an assault of catastrophic proportions. The Marvel Studios later embarked on the active production of superhero films[4] featuring, in particular, the *Avengers League*.

3.2 Paradigmatic Relation – *The Magnificent Seven*

The opening scene of *The Magnificent Seven* (United Artists, 1960)overtly announces that it is based on Akira Kurosawa's film *Seven Samurai* (Toho, 1954). First of all, the similarity between the American and the original Japanese narratives stems from their casting of solitary heroes – *gunmen* in the former, *ronin* in the latter – in both cases brought together for a minimally rewarded quest: to protect a poor defenseless farmer community against the repeated assaults of an army of bandits.

A ronin was a type of samurai who had no lord or master and, in some cases, had also severed all links with his family or clan [35]. Being unemployed, they were customarily poor, and thus not unwilling to accept the farmers' appeal simply in exchange of regular daily meals. On the other hand, as all types of samurai [37], they were hereditary members of noble families. Gunmen, too, moved independently most of the time, admired as folkloric figures by some, but execrated for their often-unlawful conduct by those who made efforts to raise the primitive farming settlements in the old American west to the

---

[4] https://editorial.rottentomatoes.com/guide/marvel-movies-in-order/

status of official political units. As opposed to the samurai, they were common people, with no pretense of nobility. The farmers begging for the help of the samurai are equally Japanese, whereas in the American retelling they come from a neighboring Mexican locality.

The intended narrative similarity is confirmed by a close correspondence, in terms of a number of *mappings*, between the characters and between the plot events. Each group of heroes has a leader, Kambei in the Japanese film, Chris in the American film, who accepts the calling and recruits his companions, one of which proves his superior fighting ability in a Japanese sword duel, mapped into a typical Old West gun showdown. A radical twist in the American version is the conflation of Katshushiro, the young apprentice of the leader, with the turbulent falsely pretending but brave and resourceful samurai, Kikuchiyo. The conflated character, the hot-blooded Chico, like Kikuchiyo, has a lot to do before overcoming the initial rejection of the group and, meanwhile, like Katshushiro, has a paternally opposed – but most touching – love case with a farmer girl.

3.3 Meronymic Relation – *The Sixth Sense*

The narrative of *The Sixth Sense* (Buena Vista Pictures, 1999)reconfigures the *type* of supernatural fantasy films, by applying an *Arthurian motif* inspired in Disney's *The Sword in the Stone* (Buena Vista Pictures, 1963).

One protagonist of *The Sixth Sense* is Cole Sear, a *psychic child*. The boy sees and hears dead people begging for his help to achieve some mission left unfinished. Another protagonist is the (dead) psychologist Malcolm Crowe, who, after a number of therapy sessions, counsels the boy to try to communicate with dead people and help them as they pleaded – and this counsel determines from then on Cole's heroic quest.

A symbol of his commitment to the quest is the scene the boy plays at a school theatrical performance, wherein the legendary Arthur's royal status is revealed by freeing the sword Excalibur from the rock that imprisoned it. The scene clearly reenacts the culminating event in Disney's *The Sword in the Stone*, creating a meronymic relation between both movies. An Arthurian scholar stressed how the boy then effectively assumed the figure of Arthur, who was reputed to generously attend the appeals of whoever came to his court, while Malcom the psychiatrist assumed a sort of sage Merlin figure: "a supernatural guide, it turns out, who helps Cole to understand the unique role he is called upon to play." [18].

3.4 Antithetic Relation – *The Shape of Water*

The narrative of *The Shape of Water* (Fox Searchlight Pictures, 2017) has been classified as a romantic fantasy, deliberately based but in radical opposition to the 1954 horror movie *Creature from the Black Lagoon* (Universal-International, 1954). The Mexican director of the former, Guillermo del Toro, who was also the producer and main author of the screenplay, provided, in an interview[5], an eloquent account of how the project

---

[5] https://www.latimes.com/entertainment/movies/la-et-mn-guillermo-del-toro-telluride-201
70905-htmlstory.html

developed. Watching, when he was 6 years old, *Creature from the Black Lagoon*, he thought "I hope they end up together."

The villain in the horror movie was definitely the creature, an amphibious humanoid found in the Amazon jungle, predestined to be killed by the hero, the scientist Dr. David Reed to save his girlfriend Kay Lawrence from the monster's clutches. In *The Shape of Water* romantic fantasy, the creature becomes the victim, and the villain would be the man who captured, kept for military purposes, and continuously tortured him: a coronel, called Richard Strickland. Most remarkably, the early victim, promoted to become the *hero* in the transgressive new movie (situated in the United States environment of 1962), was Elisa Esposito, a custodian at the secret government laboratory where the creature was kept. Found abandoned by the side of a river with wounds on her neck, she was mute, limited to communicate through signs. Her *quest* was to save the life and restore the freedom of the creature.

The quest seems to terminate in failure as she dies, but the creature's magic healing power not only revives her but also, when he touches the scars on her neck, they open to reveal gills like his. So, while the creature is introduced as a survival from the Devonian period, Elisa turns out to be a mutation with compatible traits. On a first sight, such narratives would seem affiliated to the *Beauty and the Beast* folktale, but there is a snag: the monster does not change into a prince, which would make him acceptable as a consort. In fact, a more closely related folktale might be evoked, *The Ugly Duckling*, since Elisa's birthmarks – the scars on her neck and her muteness – were a sign of her future felicitous metamorphoses, rather than marks of inferiority.

4 Semiotic Support for Movie Narrative Generation

The previous section analyzed the occurrence of semiotic relations in popular movies, which provided useful insights on how story writers can reuse ideas from existing movies. The possibility of using ChatGPT to identify semiotic relations in existing movies, combined with its writing capabilities, lead to the development of a novel system to support narrative generation, presented in the next subsections.

4.1 System Architecture

Figure 1 illustrates the architecture of the proposed movie narrative generation system, which comprises four main components: (1) the *Storywriter AI Agent*, which is responsible for writing story plots; (2) the *Illustrator AI Agent*, which is in charge of creating visual representations for the narrative scenes; (3) the *Plot Manager*, which controls the plot generation process by requesting story events and illustrations to the *Storywriter AI Agent* and *Illustrator AI Agent*, respectively; and (4) the *User Interface*, which provides a visual interface that allows users to compose and visualize new narratives in a storyboard format. In addition, a database (*Stories Database*) is used to store and retrieve all the narratives generated by the system.

The system is implemented in Python, PHP, and JavaScript, and relies on the knowledge of the AI agents to generate new stories using semiotic relations. The AI agents are integrated into the system through a plugin approach, which simplifies their replacement when new and more powerful models become available. In our current implementation, the *Storywriter AI Agent* is based on the ChatGPT model (GPT-3.5-turbo), which is accessed through the OpenAI API;[6] and the *Illustrator AI Agent* is based on the Stable Diffusion 2.1 model,[7] which is accessed through a REST API.

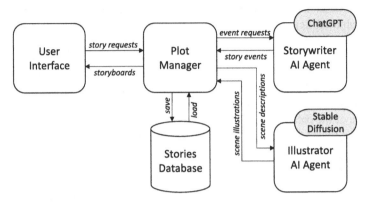

Fig. 1. Architecture of the movie narrative generation system.

4.2 Story Generation

The story generation process relies on the extensive movie knowledge of ChatGPT to create new stories using existing movie plots. Stories are generated according to a set of parameters that vary for each type of semiotic relation: the syntagmatic relation requires two *related movies*, M1 and M2 (creating a new story that combines both movies); the meronymic relation operates over a *related movie* M1 and a *scene description* S1 (creating a new story that details (zoom-in) the scene S1), and both paradigmatic and antithetic relations require only one *related movie* M1 (while the paradigmatic relation creates a story that is similar to M1, the antithetic relation generates a story that is the opposite of M1). Additionally, a *description of the protagonist* (PD) can be provided to guide the generated narrative.

Based on initial experiments conducted with ChatGPT to test its capacity to identify semiotic relations in existing movies, we designed a set of parameterized prompts that our system uses to instruct ChatGPT in the process of generating new stories using semiotic relations. Each prompt has three parts: (1) the definition of a semiotic relation; (2) a task description; and (3) a description of the output format. Table 2 presents the definitions and task descriptions created for each semiotic relation.

The description of the output format was designed to instruct ChatGPT to write the story in a format that can be interpreted by our system, which contains a description of the story event, a description of an image that illustrates the scene, and the title of the new story. The exact instructions provided to ChatGPT for the output format are:

---

[6] https://platform.openai.com/docs/api-reference.

[7] https://github.com/Stability-AI/stablediffusion.

"Always write just one line for the story, starting with 'EVENT:', followed by a second line starting with 'IMAGE:' containing a short description of an image that illustrates the narrative event. Also generate a new creative title for movie B and add it at the beginning of the response starting with 'TITLE:'.".

Table 2. Parameterized prompts designed to instruct ChatGPT on how to write new stories using semiotic relations and existing movie plots. The parameters are: <M1>- related movie 1; <M2>- related movie 2; <S1>- scene description; and <PD>- protagonist.

Relation		Prompt
Syntagmatic	Definition	The fictional protagonist in the plot of movie A is X. The fictional protagonist in the plot of movie C is Y. Movie A has a syntagmatic relation with movie C if X does not appear in C, Y does not appear in A, and there exists a movie B that features both X and Y
	Task	Considering this definition, write the first event for a new movie B considering that movie A is "<M1>" and movie C is "<M2>". The protagonist of movie B must be <PD>
Paradigmatic	Definition	Movie A has a paradigmatic relation with movie B if there is some similarity between their plots and their protagonists have similar objectives
	Task	Considering this definition, write the first event for a new movie B considering that movie A is "<M1>" (movie B must have a paradigmatic relation with movie A). The protagonist of movie B must be <PD>
Meronymic	Definition	There is a meronymic relation between two movies A and B if the plot of B is equivalent to a detailed narrative of a scene S taken from the plot of A
	Task	Letting A be the movie "<M1>", S be a scene taken from the plot of A where <S1>, and letting B be an imaginary new movie, please write the first event for the plot of B, so that there is a meronymic relation between A and B. The protagonist of movie B must be <PD>
Antithetic	Definition	Movie A has an antithetic relation with movie B if there is some similarity between their plots but the objective of the protagonist of movie A is the complete opposite of the objective of the protagonist of movie B
	Task	Considering this definition, write the first event for a new movie B considering that movie A is "<M1>" (movie B must have an antithetic relation with movie A). The protagonist of movie B must be <PD>

An important characteristic of the initial prompts is the fact that they instruct Chat-GPT to write only the first event of the story, which allows the system to generate narratives in a stepwise manner. This approach allows users to compose stories in an interactive manner, allowing them to decide when to regenerate certain events, continue, or finish the narrative. Whenever the user decides to continue the story, the system uses a specific prompt to instruct ChatGPT to generate the next event: *"Continue the story by generating another pair of lines (only 'EVENT' and 'IMAGE:')."*.

The general structure of the conversation between our system and ChatGPT is:

(1) **System:** SEMIOTIC RELATION DEFINITION + SEMIOTIC RELATION TASK + OUTPUT FORMAT
(2) **ChatGPT:** TITLE: *story title.* EVENT: *story event.* IMAGE: *scene description.*
(3) **System:** CONTINUE PROMPT
(4) **ChatGPT:** EVENT: *story event.* IMAGE: *scene description.*

where messages (3) and (4) are repeated until the user decides to end the story. An essential feature of ChatGPT used here and in all systems assisting screenwriters is that ChatGPT recognizes the context of the previous messages. Indeed, an exciting aspect of ChatGPT is its capacity to remember and work on earlier dialogs.

4.3 Image Generation

The process of generating images for the narrative events relies on the recent advancements on text-to-image machine learning models, such as DALL-E, Midjourney, and Stable Diffusion, which are capable of producing detailed images based on natural language descriptions. In our implementation, we use the Stable Diffusion 2.1 model [34].

The scene descriptions generated by ChatGPT play a fundamental role in the image generation process of our system. Providing them directly as input to the Stable Diffusion model would be enough to produce interesting results. However, to provide users with more control over the generated images, we included a parameter in our system that allows users to define the *style of the illustrations* (IS). This parameter is directly combined with the scene descriptions generated by ChatGPT to establish the prompt that is provided to the Stable Diffusion model: SCENE DESCRIPTION+IS.

In addition to the prompt, the system also ensures that the same *seed* is used for all images generated for the same narrative. The seed is used to initialize the model and can be used to produce similar images (the same seed and the same prompt always produce the same output image), which improves the coherence between the images generated for the same narrative.

4.4 User Interface

Users can access and interact with the system through our public webpage (http://www.icad.puc-rio.br/~logtell/semiotic-relations/). The user composes new stories by selecting a semiotic relation (action 1, Fig. 2) and provides the required parameters (action 2, Fig. 2). The field "Protagonist" is optional. The story generation process starts when the user presses the button "Generate Story" (action 3, Fig. 2), which leads to the story composition screen, where the user can see the title and the events of the story with a scene description and a visual illustration. In the example of Fig. 2, the user selected the antithetic relation, entered the movie "Guardians of the Galaxy", and generated a story called "The Annihilation of the Galaxy". After visualizing the first event, the user has two options: (1) regenerate the event by pressing the reload button on the right side of scene illustration, which will cause the system to produce another version of the event; or (2) continue the story by pressing the button "Continue", which will lead the system to generate the next event for the story. When the user decides to conclude the story, the button "Finish and Add to User Library" must be pressed, which will save the generated narrative in the current user's Library, wherein a few representative examples created by us are also kept. Such stories are available at the webpage, which can also be accessed by clicking in the link "View User Library".

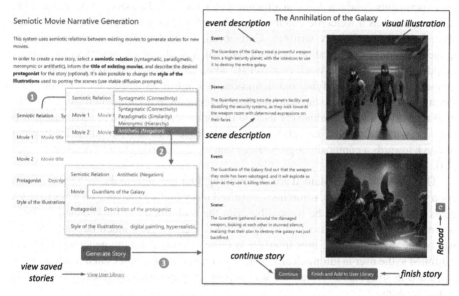

Fig. 2. User interface of the movie narrative generation system.

The complete description of the events generated for the story "The Annihilation of the Galaxy" is: *"The Guardians of the Galaxy steal a powerful weapon from a high-security planet, with the intention to use it to destroy the entire galaxy. / The Guardians of the Galaxy find out that the weapon they stole has been sabotaged, and it will explode as soon as they use it, killing them all. / The Guardians of the Galaxy, knowing that they have very little time before the weapon explodes, decide to fly directly towards the center of the galaxy to sacrifice themselves and destroy everything along with them. / The Guardians of the Galaxy finally reach the center of the galaxy, and the weapon explodes, destroying everything in a colossal explosion of light".* The complete storyboard version of this story available at: http://www.icad.puc-rio.br/~logtell/semiotic-relations/view. html?id=333. More examples of stories generated by our system are available at: http:// www.icad.puc-rio.br/~logtell/semiotic-relations/list.html.

5 Concluding Remarks

What we consider to be the main contribution of the present paper is the proposal and demonstration of a novel strategy for assisting different types of users, not necessarily professional writers, in the process of interactive story composition. As explained in the preceding sections, the strategy, based on our semiotic relations theory, comprises three components: a software tool, a user interface, and two AI-agents.

This third component, currently driven by ChatGPT, played from the start a fundamental role. The verbal definitions determining how semiotic relations instruct the prototype to react creatively to the user's prompts were first analyzed through guiding experiments conducted in consultation with ChatGPT. To users, an AI agent ought to be regarded as a welcome collaborator, like the traditional anonymous ghostwriter, invited to enhance literary writings. Collaboration, incidentally, is a normal practice in the movie industry, recalling in particular that specialized screenwriters are usually called to supplement the work of novelists when adapted screenplays are concerned. To ourselves, while specifying our definitions in English sentences, the AI agent gave the unique opportunity to start learning how to program in natural language, given that until recently we were exclusively used to reason in terms of logic programming. It is noteworthy that ChatGPT can also handle basic logic reasoning, which is leading our research towards a composite logic strategy that we are referring to as "metaverse logic" [14].

The results thus far obtained are encouraging. Our previous tools, using plan generation to compose the plots, sometimes surprised us by finding unexpected ways to reach goals that we believed to be impossible. But the multiplicity of unpredicted variants, obtained with the autonomous thinking of the AI agents, goes much beyond what we had before. Moreover, the user interface is quite informal, and the generated texts are exhibited to the user in idiomatically correct natural language. Since each resulting story is framed in storyboard format, the way is paved for approaching screenplay status in future versions.

Until now the prototype served mainly as a proof of concept and for gaining experience on how to more effectively explore the potentials of AI agents. Further research is needed to increase the degree of user interaction, as well as for measuring user satisfaction and using the responses to extend the functionality and improve the interface of the prototype. The set of definitions that, so to speak, parameterize the behavior of the prototype, may be extended and/or generalized to cover an increasing number of cases.

Future research may also be directed toward the different possible use of systems assisted by AI agents, along lines similar to those adopted in our project. One simple application is as a teaching resource to train language proficiency and also to develop literary skills. We chose to concentrate on movie narratives – which are known as habitual sources of games. Besides helping to create underlying stories for games and, in general, to serve as aides to screenwriters, an AI agent could play a part, perhaps as adversary to be defeated, but also as a Merlin-like mentor, offering wise advice to the human players.

Acknowledgements. We want to thank CNPq (National Council for Scientific and Technological Development) and FINEP (Funding Agency for Studies and Projects), which belong to the Ministry of Science, Technology, and Innovation of Brazil, for the financial support.

References

1. Aarne, A., Thompson, S.: The Types of the Folktale. Acad. Scientiarum Fennica (1961)
2. Bal, M.: Narratology: Introduction to the Theory of Narrative. University of Toronto Press, Toronto (2017)
3. Barthes, R.: Theory of the text. In: Young, J.C. (ed.) Untying the Text: A Post-Structuralist Reader, pp. 31–47. Routledge & Kegan Paul, Oxfordshire (1981)
4. Brody, R.: "Batman v Superman" Is Democrats vs. Republicans, The New Yorker, March 29, 2016. https://www.newyorker.com/culture/richard-brody/batman-v-superman-is-democr ats-vs-republicans. Accessed 16 May 2023
5. Burke, K.: A Grammar of Motives. University of California Press, Oakland (1969)
6. Carter, E. M.: ChatGPT for Screenwriters: An Easy-To-Follow Guide On How To Create A Screenplay Using Artificial Intelligence, Ethan Michael Carter (2023)
7. Chandler, D.: Semiotics: The Basics. Routledge, London (2002)
8. Ciarlini, A., Casanova, M.A., Furtado, A.L., Veloso, P.: Modeling interactive storytelling genres as application domains. J. Intell. Inf. Syst. **35**(3), 347–381 (2010). https://doi.org/10. 1007/s10844-009-0108-5
9. Ciarlini, A.E.M., Pozzer, C.T., Furtado, A.L., Feijo, B.: A logic-based tool for interactive generation and dramatization of stories. In: Proceedings of the 2005 ACM SIGCHI International Conference on Advances in Computer Entertainment Technology, pp. 133–140. ACM Press, New York (2005). https://doi.org/10.1145/1178477.1178495
10. Culler, J.: The Pursuit of Signs: Semiotics, Literature, Deconstruction. Routledge, Oxfordshire (1981)
11. Eco, U.: Articulations of the cinematic code. In: Nichols, B. (ed.) Movies and Methods, pp. 590–607. University of California Press, Oakland (1976)
12. Fauconnier, G., Turner, M.: Conceptual projection and middle spaces. Technical report 9401, University of California, San Diego (1994)
13. Furtado, A.L., Casanova, M.A., Barbosa, S.D.J.: A semiotic approach to conceptual modelling. In: Yu, E., Dobbie, G., Jarke, M., Purao, S. (eds.) ER 2014. LNCS, vol. 8824, pp. 1–12. Springer, Heidelberg (2014). https://doi.org/10.1007/978-3-319-12206-9_1
14. Furtado, A.L., Casanova, M.A., Lima, E.S.: Some Preliminary Steps Towards Metaverse Logic, arXiv:2307.05574 [cs.LO] (2023). https://doi.org/10.48550/arXiv.2307.05574
15. Furtado, A.L.: Semiotic Relations and Proof Methods. Monografias em Ciência da Computação n° 18/11. PUC-Rio, Rio de Janeiro (2011)
16. Gervás, P., Díaz-Agudo, B., Peinado, F., Hervás, R.: Story plot generation based on CBR. In: Macintosh, A., Ellis, R., Allen, T. (eds) Applications and Innovations in Intelligent Systems XII. SGAI 2004. Springer, London (2004). https://doi.org/10.1007/1-84628-103-2_3
17. Gonsalves, R. A.: Using ChatGPT as a creative writing partner, towards data science. https://towardsdatascience.com/using-chatgpt-as-a-creative-writing-partner-part-1-prose-dc9a9994d41f. Accessed 16 May 2023
18. Harty, K.J.: Looking for Arthur in all the wrong places: a note on M. night Shyamalan's "The Sixth Sense". Arthuriana **10**(4), 57–62 (2000)
19. Jakobson, R.: Two aspects of language and two types of aphasic disturbances. In: Jakobson, R., Halle, M. (eds.) Fundamentals of Language. Mouton, The Hague (1956)
20. Jurafsky, D., Martin, J.H.: Speech and Language Processing - An Introduction to Natural Language Processing, Computational Linguistics, and Speech Recognition. Third Edition Draft (2023)
21. Karsdorp, F., van Kranenburg, P., Meder, T., Trieschnigg, D., van den Bosch, A.: In search of an appropriate abstraction level for motif annotations. In: Proceedings of the Third Workshop on Computational Models of Narrative (2012)

22. Kolodner, J.: Case-Based Reasoning. Morgan Kaufmann, Burlington (2014)

23. Lima, E.S., Feijó, B., Casanova, M.A., Furtado, A.L.: Storytelling variants based on semiotic relations. Entertainment Comput. **17**, 31–44 (2016). https://doi.org/10.1016/j.entcom.2016.08.003

24. Lima, E.S., Feijó, B., Furtado, A.L.: Adaptive storytelling based on personality and preference modeling. Entertainment Comput. **34**, 100342 (2020). https://doi.org/10.1016/j.entcom.2020.100342

25. Lima, E.S., Feijó, B., Furtado, A.L., Barbosa, S.D.J., Pozzer, C.T., Ciarlini, A.E.M.: Non-branching interactive comics. In: Reidsma, D., Katayose, H., Nijholt, A. (eds.) ACE 2013. LNCS, vol. 8253, pp. 230–245. Springer, Cham (2013). https://doi.org/10.1007/978-3-319-03161-3_16

26. Lima, E.S., Feijó, B., Furtado, A.L.: Computational narrative blending based on planning. In: Baalsrud Hauge, J., C. S. Cardoso, J., Roque, L., Gonzalez-Calero, P.A. (eds.) ICEC 2021. LNCS, vol. 13056, pp. 289–303. Springer, Cham (2021). https://doi.org/10.1007/978-3-030-89394-1_22

27. Lima, E.S., Feijó, B., Furtado, A.L.: Hierarchical generation of dynamic and nondeterministic quests in games. In: Proceedings of the 11th Conference on Advances in Computer Entertainment Technology (ACE 2014), Article 24. ACM Press, New York (2014). https://doi.org/10.1145/2663806.2663833

28. Lima, E.S., Feijó, B., Furtado, A.L.: Managing the plot structure of character-based interactive narratives in games. Entertainment Comput. **47**, 100590 (2023). https://doi.org/10.1016/j.entcom.2023.100590

29. Lima, E.S., Feijó, B., Furtado, A.L.: Procedural generation of branching quests for games. Entertainment Comput. **43**, 100491 (2022). https://doi.org/10.1016/j.entcom.2022.100491

30. Lima, E.S., Feijó, B., Furtado, A.L.: Storytelling variants: the case of little red riding hood. In: Chorianopoulos, K., Divitini, M., Baalsrud Hauge, J., Jaccheri, L., Malaka, R. (eds.) ICEC 2015. LNCS, vol. 9353, pp. 286–300. Springer, Cham (2015). https://doi.org/10.1007/978-3-319-24589-8_22

31. Lima, E.S., Feijó, B., Furtado, A.L.: Video-based interactive storytelling using real-time video compositing techniques. Multimedia Tools Appl. **77**(2), 2333–2357 (2018). https://doi.org/10.1007/s11042-017-4423-5

32. Lima, E.S., Pozzer, C.T., d'Ornellas, M.C., Ciarlini, A.E.M., Feijó, B., Furtado, A.L.: Virtual Cinematography Director for Interactive Storytelling. In: Proceedings of the International Conference on Advances in Computer Entertainment Technology, pp. 263–270. ACM Press, New York (2009). https://doi.org/10.1145/1690388.1690432

33. Metz, C.: Language and Cinema. De Gruyter Mouton, Boston (1974). https://doi.org/10.1515/9783110816044

34. OpenAI: GPT-4 Technical Report. arXiv:2303.08774 (2023). [cs.CL] https://doi.org/10.48550/arXiv.2303.08774

35. Rombach, R., Blattmann, A., Lorenz, D., Esser, P., Ommer, B.: High-resolution image synthesis with latent diffusion models. In: 2022 IEEE/CVF Conference on Computer Vision and Pattern Recognition (CVPR), pp. 10674–10685. IEEE Press, New York (2022). https://doi.org/10.1109/CVPR52688.2022.01042

36. Rōnin, Encyclopædia Britannica. https://www.britannica.com/topic/ronin. Accessed 16 May 2023

37. Saussure, F.: Cours de Linguistique Générale. In: Bally, C., et al. (eds.). Payot, Paris (1995)

38. Samurai, Encyclopædia Britannica. https://www.britannica.com/topic/samurai. Accessed 16 May 2023

39. Silva, F.A.G., Furtado, A.L., Ciarlini, A.E.M., Pozzer, C.T., Feijó, B., Lima, E.S.: Information-gathering events in story plots. In: Herrlich, M., Malaka, R., Masuch, M. (eds.) ICEC 2012.

LNCS, vol. 7522, pp. 30–44. Springer, Heidelberg (2012). https://doi.org/10.1007/978-3-642-33542-6_3

40. Tehrani, J.J.: The phylogeny of little red riding hood. PLoS ONE **8**(11), e78871 (2013). https://doi.org/10.1371/journal.pone.0078871

41. University of New Hampshire: Getting the Most from ChatGPT, Teaching & Learning Resource Hub (2023). https://www.unh.edu/teaching-learning-resource-hub/resource/getting-most-chatgpt-march-2023. Accessed 10 May 2023

42. White, H.: Tropics in Discourse: Essays in Cultural Criticism. Johns Hopkins University Press, Baltimore (1978)

43. Winston, M.E., Chaffin, R., Herrmann, D.: A taxonomy of part-whole relations. Cogn. Sci. **11**(4), 417–444 (1987). https://doi.org/10.1207/s15516709cog1104_2

Girls vs. Men - The Prevalence of Gender-Biased Language in Popular YouTube Videos

Miriam-Linnea Hale$^{(\boxtimes)}$ and André Melzer

University of Luxembourg, 4365 Esch-Sur-Alzette, Luxembourg
miriam-linnea.hale@uni.lu

Abstract. Sexism does not only occur in overt hostile ways, but is often more subtle, such as gender biased language, which can be just as harmful. These subtler forms of sexism remain scarcely researched on social media, which is an important context of daily life especially for younger generations. The present content analysis examined 30 full transcripts of YouTube videos for evidence of online gender-biased and benevolent sexist language. The videos were selected in a survey ($N = 485$), where participants listed their favorite digital entertainment content creators. We focused on the two concepts androcentrism (i.e., the tendency to use more masculine than feminine terms) and paternalism using gendered infantilizing language (e.g., using "girl" when referring to a woman) that is prevalent in students' offline language (MacArthur et al., 2020). Our results are consistent with previous findings. We found significant indications for androcentric language. Masculine terms were used more often than feminine overall and especially when referring to mixed-gender groups. Results also showed some indicators of gendered infantilizing. The label "girl" was used in a higher proportion compared to other feminine labels than "boy" compared to other masculine labels. This form of paternalistic language is a subtle form of benevolent sexism. These findings indicate a need for more research on the effects of subtler forms of sexism, such as benevolent sexist language in social computing entertainment. It also stresses the importance of future research and interventions geared towards awareness of subtler forms of sexist language, both online and offline.

Keywords: Gender-Biased Language · Online-Sexism · Benevolent Sexism · Online entertainment · Youtube · Gender · Social Media Sexism · Gender Inequality · Sexist Language

1 Introduction

Sexism and sexist attitudes have been researched for many years [e.g. [1]]. Negative effects of sexism have been demonstrated in various areas of life, such as workplace inequalities [2], adolescent relationships [3], women's cognitive performance [4], and health [5], just to name a few. However, most research focuses on the hostile form of sexism (such as sexist slurs, or overt insults such as "women are horrible drivers"), which is societally better known and easier to recognize for both men and women [1,

© IFIP International Federation for Information Processing 2023
Published by Springer Nature Switzerland AG 2023
P. Ciancarini et al. (Eds.): ICEC 2023, LNCS 14455, pp. 176–186, 2023.
https://doi.org/10.1007/978-981-99-8248-6_14

6]. But sexism can also occur in more subtle ways, such as *benevolent sexism* (Glick & Fiske, 1996), but this is less researched. There is evidence of gender biased language in natural speech across different ages, and also in mediated contexts, such as books or television [7, 8]. However, there is little research on this topic in the context of language in social computing entertainment. Most existing studies focus on Twitter [e.g. 9–11]. The few studies that focus on YouTube, one of the largest social media platforms, primarily investigate language in comments on videos [e.g., 12]. Our study is the first that aims to analyze YouTube content itself, via video transcripts. Inspired by the findings of MacArthur and colleagues (2020), we focus on the two subtypes of gender biased language: paternalism as a component of benevolent sexism and androcentrism.

1.1 Theoretical Background

Language and Sexism. A large evidence base, spanning decades of research, suggests that gendered and sexist language can influence gender-related cognition, emotions and, ultimately, behavior [13–19]. Newer research investigating gendered language specifically finds that this subtle form of sexist language contributes to gender biased views by imposing binary categories and making gender salient [13]. Gendered language includes honorifics (e.g., Ma'am, Mr.), as well as nouns (e.g., boy, girl), job titles (e.g., policeman), and personal pronouns (e.g., she, her). It is often androcentric, meaning a majority of masculine labels is used [8].

While explicit sexist slurs fall within the definition of hostile sexism, gendered and androcentric language (i.e., using more male gendered labels than female) can be seen as a manifestation of the paternalistic and complementary gender differentiation aspects of *benevolent sexism*, a term coined by Glick and Fiske [20]. The three main components of benevolent sexism are (1) *protective paternalism*, according to which women should be valued and protected by men; (2) *complementary gender differentiation*, meaning women have a quality of purity that few men possess; and (3) *heterosexual intimacy*, suggesting that every man should have a woman he loves above all else [20]. Although this is also a form of sexism, it is often not socially categorized and sanctioned as such. It is less likely to be noticed than hostile sexism [e.g. 21, 9, 22, 23]. Some research even suggests that women perceive benevolent sexist attitudes in men as positive and approve of them [24]. This is especially problematic because negative effects of benevolent sexism can be just as serious as they are for hostile sexism and can effect areas such as women's sense of competence, cognitive performance, likelihood to pursue a career in STEM areas, or even victim-blaming in the case of sexual assault [e.g. 4, 25, 26]. Women and girls are more likely to be the recipients of both forms of sexism than men, and women can react with considerable negative emotions to both hostile and benevolent sexism. They are also more able to recognize both forms of sexism [6].

Using the everyday language of U.S. undergraduates, MacArthur and colleagues [8] analyzed sexist, gender-biased language patterns, namely androcentrism and benevolent sexism focusing on paternalism, specifically infantilizing (e.g., using *girl* when referring to an adult woman). They found evidence of gender infantilization, that is, "girl" was the term most often used for women, which was also used more often used in this way than "boy" for adult men. They also found evidence of students using masculine labels significantly more frequently than feminine labels. Given the high prevalence of sexist language in their sample, they call for more research in this area.

Sexism in Online Entertainment. Sexism does not only occur offline but is also very prevalent in online contexts, such as social media platforms. Social computing entertainment has become an important part of daily life for the younger generation, and YouTube is one of the largest platforms [27]. According to YouTube's own data, people around the world consume more than one billion hours of YouTube content every day [28], and YouTube was also the preferred platform of adolescents and young adults according to data from a recent Luxembourg study [29]. Hostile sexist hate speech is not the only form of sexism occurring online, less overt benevolent sexism also occurs in online spaces [9]. In the male dominated virtual entertainment space of YouTube, female content creators can receive more negative comments including sexism if they do not adhere to gender role norms [12]. In a quantitative content analysis of 500 video clips on YouTube and 1,000 comments, Döring and Mohseni [30] found that the women shown were objectified and sexualized twice as often as men. They also received five times more gendered hate comments than men did.

There are ongoing efforts to develop algorithms and systems that can better detect online hate speech against women [31]. Jahan and Oussalah [32] describe the process of generic automatic hate speech detection (including gender-based hate speech) in their systematic review in four steps. First the dataset is collected from a social media platform and prepared (removing noise, lemmatization, etc.). The second step consists of feature engineering, where specific features are extracted from the text, using a variety of extraction techniques (e.g., word embedding). The third step is model training. The output of this deep-learning model is either multi-class (distinguishing between different types of hate speech such as racism, sexism, or radicalization) or binary (hate speech vs. non-hate speech). In the final step the automatic model is evaluated on its performance (e.g., precision and accuracy). However, automatic systems for detecting online sexism have particular problems with more subtle forms of sexism, which is why researchers are currently working on improvements to machine learning in this area [33]. Methods, such as the ones described in Jahan and Oussalah's [32] systematic review rely heavily on variations of specific key words and phrases, which makes it less susceptible for benevolent sexism, which mainly uses common language and seemingly positive statements (e.g., "You're very smart for a girl!") and is significantly more context-dependent.

Given the prevalence of linguistic sexism online, our study uses a similar methodology to MacArthur and colleagues [8] and aims to examine their findings on androcentrism and infantilizing in everyday language in an online context using a corpus of YouTube video transcripts. Considering the difficulties of automatic detection of such subtle forms of sexism, we opted for a manually coded content analysis, which decreases the possible size of the dataset, but is essential for the accuracy of our analysis. Our hypothesis related to gender-biased and benevolent sexist language in the YouTube videos are the following:

Hypothesis 1: The transcripts are characterized by androcentric language, as indicated by a higher frequency of male than female labels.

Hypothesis 2: The transcripts will show infantilizing language, meaning the term "girl" is used more frequently than other labels when referring to women, and more frequently than the term "boy" is used for men.

2   Methods

2.1   Sample and Material

We asked $N = 485$ young persons in Luxembourg, aged between 15 and 35 ($M = 20.45$, $SD = 3.19$) to name their favorite social computing entertainment content creators ("influencers and social media channels"). Of the $N = 102$ most mentioned only those with a YouTube account were considered, and the most frequently viewed videos of that channel were added to our database. For comparability reasons, the videos had to be in English. Videos without sufficient amount of speech (e.g., cat videos, fail videos, workout videos) and music videos were excluded. Our final database included 30 videos from a broad range of topics such as beauty, celebrity, food, mental illness, comedy, and how to learn a language. Transcripts automatically generated by YouTube were added to the database and compared to the original videos by two research assistants for accuracy. The videos were exclusively videos from public channels with a large reach, the number of views ranging from 230,570 to 97,352,720. A full list of all videos with additional information can be found in the supplemental materials.

2.2   Coding

Using MAXQDA 2022 [34], several steps of automatic and manual coding were conducted.

Automatic Coding. Like the methodology used by MacArthur et al. [8], the following labels for women were coded: girl/gals, woman/women, lady/ladies, chick/s, sis/sister/s. After manual review the label madam was also added. For men the labels were: boy/s, man/men, gentleman/gentlemen, guy/s, dude/s, bro/brother/s. The label boyfriend was added after manual review. We examined whether any additional labels were used for non-cisgender persons, none were found.

Manual Coding. Targets were coded for all gendered labels according to whether they targeted a person or a non-person (e.g., expression or object) and according to target gender. Labels that were consistent with the target gender (e.g., "dude" referring to a man) were then also coded as "gender-congruent", and respectively labels that targeted a person or group of a different gender (e.g., "guys" addressing a group of women) were coded as "gender-incongruent". For the infantilizing analysis, the labels "girl" and "boy" were also coded for target age, meaning whether the target was an adult, a minor/child, or unspecified.

Statistical Analysis. To test both hypotheses, Chi-Square analyses and Fisher's exact test were conducted.

3 Results

All 30 transcripts were coded by two independent coders. Initial intercoder agreement was high at 90.80% across all codes. Unsure cases and disagreements were resolved through discussions including the first author. A total of $N = 321$ gendered labels were found, targeting persons and non-human targets (e.g., expressions or objects). Additionally, more explicit derogatory labels were identified and analyzed separately (see *Additional Findings*).

Androcentric Language. We hypothesized that androcentric language would be indicated by a higher frequency of male than female labels. Overall Chi-Square analysis showed significantly more male gendered labels ($n = 218$) than female ($n = 103$), $X^2(3) = 74.534, p < .000$. Cramer's V of 0.278 indicates a medium effect size supporting our hypothesis. Results from the contingency table across targets are shown in Table 1.

Table 1. Chi-Square Analysis Androcentrism Masculine vs. Feminine across Target Types

	Mascline Label n	χ^2	Feminine Label n	$\chi 2$
Gender-congruent	106	0.48	61	1.03
Gender-incongruent	1	0.09	1	0.20
Mixed-gender group	102	9.97	8	21.11
Non-human target	9	13.36	33	28.28

Note. See 2.2 for examples for different target types

Infantilizing Language. Our second hypothesis predicted that the transcripts would show infantilizing language, that is, the term "girl" is used more often than other labels when referring to women, and more often than the term "boy" is used for men.

As the absolute number of the label "girl" compared to the sum of other female labels was smaller but was still the most frequent female label alongside women/women ($n = 27$ each), we decided to calculate whether the ratio of using "girl" as a female label instead of other female labels was higher than "boy" compared to other male labels. Only labels targeting persons were used. A Chi Square test for a 2x2 contingency table was conducted. Due to the small sample of "boy" labels, Yates correction was used. The test was a significant, $X^2(1) = 59.272, p < .000$. Cramer's V of .458 indicates a strong effect indicating that "girl" ($n = 27$) was used at a higher ratio compared to other female labels ($n = 45$) than "boy" ($n = 6$) was used compared to other male labels ($n = 205$), supporting our second hypothesis. (For a full table of labels with frequencies and percentages see supplemental material.)

Due to the rare occurrence of the label "boy", Fisher's exact test was performed (2x2 adult/minor x girl/boy contingency table) to test whether "girl" was used more frequently in reference to adult women than boy was used in reference to adult men. Only labels targeting humans matching the target gender were used. The test was not significant. Though there were more instances of "girl" referring to an adult woman ($n = 21$) as opposed to a minor ($n = 5$), the number of instances for "boy" was only 6 in total, 5 referring to adults and only one instance when referring to a child. This makes it difficult to interpret the comparison in a meaningful way.

Additional Findings. During the manual coding process, we also found instances where hostile sexist slurs such as "bitch" and "pussy" were used ($n = 18$). As the main analyses focused on more subtle forms of bias through gendered language, rather than hate speech or overt sexism, it was decided to consider these cases separately, rather than grouping them together with the general female labels. In most cases, however, these terms were not used in a typically pejorative fashion. The most common term was "bitch" ($n = 14$). In $n = 12$ cases this term was not directed towards a woman as an insult but used in a LGBTQ + context either towards a man, a mixed gender group, or as a general exclamation, for example: "*I just love sugar! Bitch!*" (The secret world of Jeffree Star, Pos. 348). This does not qualify as reclamation, because it is not used in a positive manner by a woman (a member of the group that was traditionally targeted with this sexist slur). However, it is still not a negative, derogatory context. In this setting it should not be equated with a misogynistic sexist slur. In LGBTQ + media such as Queer Eye [35], RuPaul's Drag Race [36] or social media content by LGBTQ + creators, the use of female labels such as *Queen, Girl* and *Bitch* by LGBTQ + persons of all genders in a positive manner is rather common. So, this language in this specific context could be treated as a cultural linguistic phenomenon of a specific group or community, where gender norms and gendered language do not conform to the heteronormative societal traditions and standards and thus cannot be interpreted in the same way.

4 Discussion

MacArthur and colleagues [8] found evidence of gender bias and sexism in the everyday language of undergraduate students. The aim of our study was to examine the prevalence of this type of language in a social computing entertainment context. We analyzed transcripts from 30 popular YouTube videos with a variety of different topics for gender-biased language and benevolent sexism in the form of androcentrism (a bias shown by the use of more masculine gendered labels) and paternalism through infantilizing language (using the term "girl" when referring to adult women). Social media has become a virtual space of every-day communication and YouTube is the second most used platforms worldwide with over 2.5 billion users [27]. While there is a growing body of research on hostile sexism and gendered hate speech on social media [31], e.g. [37, 38], only little research exists on more subtle gender biases, such as benevolent sexism in social computing entertainment contexts. The few studies that look at benevolent sexism on YouTube focus on the language in user comments [e.g., 12]. To our knowledge, this is the first study looking specifically at gender biased and benevolent sexist language in YouTube videos themselves (via transcripts).

Our results showed a clear indication of androcentric language. Masculine labels were used more often over all (68% of gendered labels). This was especially true for mixed-gender groups. When referring to these groups, male gendered labels were used in 93% of the cases. This supports our hypothesis and is consistent with the findings of MacArthur et al. [8]. This kind of gender bias seems to be similarly prevalent in online language as in offline speech. Our findings related to paternalism were partially consistent with our hypothesis and showed a pattern of use of the term "girl" when referring to adult women. However, given the small number of cases ($n = 6$) in which "boy" was used in our sample, the gender comparison is difficult to interpret. These results mirror the previous offline results [8] but should be further corroborated with a larger database that provides better insight.

With regards to our additional findings, it is important to consider how language changes and develops, especially in social computing entertainment spaces. Context is important when interpreting language [39]. Many terms that were, and often still are, used in hate speech as derogatory slurs in misogynistic, homophobic, or racist etc. way, are used in a positive way by oppressed groups to reclaim those terms [40]. The LGBTQ + language contexts in our dataset in which the term "Bitch" was used in a neutral or positive manner are not the same but are nonetheless another example of context changing the meaning of terms. Many current studies use automated algorithms to code corpora of online data for language analysis. But these often do not account for such nuanced contexts and are thus prone to misinterpretations [33]. This underscores the importance of still conducting a manually coded content analysis as in this study.

Practical Implications. Language has an integral role in shaping cognition. Biased language both reflects learned biases, but also reinforces these cognitive biases and stereotypes. In a large-scale study [7] gender bias in language was found in the form of stereotypes consistently across corpora for different age groups in natural language as well as in mediated contexts (e.g., books, movies and TV). As social media has become an important daily context, with an estimated number of 3.96 billion users [27], our study makes an important contribution to the still small body of research in this context. Our results showed that benevolent sexism is prevalent not only offline, but also in online language. Paternalistic language, such as infantilizing is a form of benevolent sexism. Although it may be subtle, it is still harmful. It suggests that women are weaker, less capable or in need of (male) protection and contributes to existing gender biases and inequalities [18]. Given the abundant empirical evidence of the harm that benevolent sexist actions and cognitions can cause [e.g. 4, 25, 26], these findings should inform preventive and interventive policies and strategies. However, this is no easy feat when it comes to subtle forms of bias in online language. While automated algorithms and artificial intelligence are increasingly used to detect misogynistic hate speech and overt hostile sexism, they encounter difficulties in detecting more subtle forms of language bias, such as benevolent sexism [33].

Another difficulty is that while social media policies established by companies or countries can easily target and prohibit the use of certain offensive and discriminatory language, this approach does not work for benevolent sexism or other less overt forms of biased language. This form of sexist language can be harmful as well, but its nature is not captured by one term alone. It is highly contextual and works with terms such as "girl" or general male labels that are not harmful or negative in themselves but can be used in certain contexts or with unbalanced frequency. We recognize the difficulty this poses for policymakers and applied prevention and intervention. This calls for further research in this area, not only to determine overall online prevalence, but also to better understand the impact and find ways to effectively raise public awareness. Research suggests that having a more inclusive understanding of what constitutes sexist language is necessary for language to change [23]. Benevolent sexism is often not recognized as biased behavior or language [e.g. 21, 23], and it is also rated as significantly less sexist than hostile sexism on social media [41]. Language awareness and gendered bias has become an important issue not only in relation to men and women, but especially in relation to debates about inclusive language for gender minorities and is not only present in societal discourse, but has also sparked heated political debates [42]. This underscores the importance of a solid evidence base for gender-biased language in all its complexity and forms, not only in offline contexts, but especially online, as much of social and political discourse also takes place in social computing entertainment spaces. A larger scientific qualitative and quantitative evidence base could inform policies and preventative measures and provide a factual basis for discourse.

Limitations. This is a first qualitative study examining a limited number of 30 videos on a specific social media platform. While the videos selected for this analysis have a wide range, totaling over nine hundred million views, they are still not fully representative of all YouTube content or content on other platforms. Future studies should replicate our findings with other transcripts or aim to use a *Technology Equivalence Approach* [43], to compare effects across different platforms and in different mediated and non-mediated contexts.

Intersectionality is a term that describes the reality of persons whose identity encompasses more than one marginalized or oppressed group, such as a Black woman or a neurodivergent Indigenous person. It highlights the problem that in scientific discourse, the focus is usually on only one of these factors, disregarding the complexity of biases and discrimination, where these identities intersect [44]. This also applies to online sexism, as it can occur in combination with other forms of discrimination, such as agism and ableism [45] or racial discrimination [46], which this study did not account for.

Conclusion. This content analysis of subtle sexism and gendered language bias in YouTube content was the first investigation of paternalism and androcentrism in this social computing entertainment context. Our findings mirror previous research on young people's everyday language and show that sexist and biased language also occurs in everyday online life. Benevolent sexism may be subtle, but it is still harmful, and language has an important impact on cognitions and behavior. Research in this particular field is still scarce, so our study makes an important contribution to the evidence base. Our additional findings highlight the importance of qualitative studies such as this one, as manual coding can account for context of language that may be missed or wrongly interpreted by automated methods of language analysis, which operate mainly on frequency alone. Our findings stress the importance of more research, as well as more public awareness in the area of subtle sexist language in social media contexts.

References

1. Swim, J.K., Hyers, L.L.: Sexism. In: Handbook of prejudice, stereotyping, and discrimination, pp. 407–430. Psychology Press, New York, NY, US (2009)
2. Stamarski, C., Son Hing, L.: Gender inequalities in the workplace: the effects of organizational structures, processes, practices, and decision makers' sexism. Front. Psychol. 6 (2015)
3. Ramiro-Sánchez, T., Ramiro, M.T., Bermúdez, M.P., Buela-Casal, G.: Sexism in adolescent relationships: a systematic review. Psychosoc. Interv.. Interv. 27, 123–132 (2018). https://doi. org/10.5093/pi2018a19
4. Dardenne, B., Dumont, M., Bollier, T.: Insidious dangers of benevolent sexism: consequences for women's performance. J. Pers. Soc. Psychol. 93, 764–779 (2007). https://doi.org/10.1037/ 0022-3514.93.5.764
5. Homan, P.: Structural sexism and health in the united states: a new perspective on health inequality and the gender system. Am. Sociol. Rev.Sociol. Rev. 84, 486–516 (2019). https:// doi.org/10.1177/0003122419848723
6. Bosson, J.K., Vandello, J.A., Buckner, C.E.: The psychology of sex and gender. Sage Publications (2018)
7. Charlesworth, T.E.S., Yang, V., Mann, T.C., Kurdi, B., Banaji, M.R.: Gender stereotypes in natural language: word embeddings show robust consistency across child and adult language corpora of more than 65 million words. Psychol. Sci. 32, 218–240 (2021). https://doi.org/10. 1177/0956797620963619
8. MacArthur, H.J., Cundiff, J.L., Mehl, M.R.: Estimating the prevalence of gender-biased language in undergraduates' everyday speech. Sex Roles 82, 81–93 (2020). https://doi.org/10. 1007/s11199-019-01033-z
9. Jha, A., Mamidi, R.: When does a compliment become sexist? analysis and classification of ambivalent sexism using twitter data. In: Proceedings of the Second Workshop on NLP and Computational Social Science, pp. 7–16. Association for Computational Linguistics, Vancouver, Canada (2017). https://doi.org/10.18653/v1/W17-2902
10. Scotto di Carlo, G.: The velvet glove: Benevolent sexism in President Trump's tweets. Eur. J. Womens Stud. 28, 135050682091359 (2020). https://doi.org/10.1177/1350506820913599
11. Sharifirad, S., Matwin, S.: When a Tweet is Actually Sexist. A more Comprehensive Classification of Different Online Harassment Categories and The Challenges in NLP. http://arxiv. org/abs/1902.10584, (2019)
12. Döring, N., Mohseni, M.R.: Male dominance and sexism on YouTube: results of three content analyses. Fem. Media Stud. 19, 512–524 (2019). https://doi.org/10.1080/14680777.2018.146 7945
13. Bigler, R.S., Leaper, C.: Gendered language: psychological principles, evolving practices, and inclusive policies. Policy Insights Behav. Brain Sci.Behav. Brain Sci. 2, 187–194 (2015). https://doi.org/10.1177/2372732215600452
14. Chew, P.K., Kelley-Chew, L.K.: Subtly sexist language. Colum J Gend. L. 16, 643 (2007)
15. Collins, K.A., Clément, R.: Language and prejudice: direct and moderated effects. J. Lang. Soc. Psychol. 31, 376–396 (2012). https://doi.org/10.1177/0261927X12446611
16. Henley, N.M.: Molehill or mountain? What we know and don't know about sex bias in language. In: Gender and thought: Psychological perspectives, pp. 59–78. Springer (1989)
17. Leaper, C.: Gender similarities and differences in language. (2014)
18. Leaper, C., Bigler, R.S.: Gendered language and sexist thought. Monogr. Soc. Res. Child Dev.. Soc. Res. Child Dev. 69, 128–142 (2004). https://doi.org/10.1111/j.1540-5834.2004. 06901012.x
19. Stahlberg, D., Braun, F., Irmen, L., Sczesny, S.: Representation of the sexes in language. Soc. Commun., 163–187 (2007)

20. Glick, P., Fiske, S.T.: The ambivalent sexism inventory: differentiating hostile and benevolent sexism. J. Pers. Soc. Psychol. **70**, 491 (1996)
21. Hopkins-Doyle, A., Sutton, R.M., Douglas, K.M., Calogero, R.M.: Flattering to deceive: why people misunderstand benevolent sexism. J. Pers. Soc. Psychol. **116**, 167 (2019)
22. Barreto, M., Ellemers, N.: The burden of benevolent sexism: How it contributes to the maintenance of gender inequalities. Eur. J. Soc. Psychol. **35**, 633–642 (2005)
23. Swim, J.K., Mallett, R., Stangor, C.: Understanding subtle sexism: detection and use of sexist language. Sex Roles **51**, 117–128 (2004)
24. Bohner, G., Ahlborn, K., Steiner, R.: How sexy are sexist men? Women's perception of male response profiles in the Ambivalent Sexism Inventory. Sex Roles **62**, 568–582 (2010)
25. Kuchynka, S., et al.: Hostile and benevolent sexism and college women's STEM outcomes. Psychol. Women Q. **42**, 036168431774188 (2018). https://doi.org/10.1177/036168431774 1889
26. Viki, G.T., Abrams, D.: But she was unfaithful: benevolent sexism and reactions to rape victims who violate traditional gender role expectations. Sex Roles **47**, 289–293 (2002). https://doi. org/10.1023/A:1021342912248
27. Statista: Biggest social media platforms 2023. Satista (2023)
28. Goodrow, C.: You know what's cool? A billion hours. https://blog.youtube/news-and-events/ you-know-whats-cool-billion-hours/. Accessed 31 Mar 2022
29. Melzer, A., Hale, M.-L., Hall, M.: Abschlussbericht des Projekts #LETZSTEREOTYPE18— Geschlechterbezogene Rollen und Geschlechterstereotype bei Jugendlichen und jungen Erwachsenen in Luxemburg. University of Luxembourg, Ministry for Equality Between Women and Men (2019)
30. Döring, N., Mohseni, M.R.: Fail videos and related video comments on YouTube: a case of sexualization of women and gendered hate speech? Commun. Res. Rep.. Res. Rep. **36**, 254–264 (2019). https://doi.org/10.1080/08824096.2019.1634533
31. Frenda, S., Ghanem, B., Montes-y-Gómez, M., Rosso, P.: Online hate speech against women: automatic identification of misogyny and sexism on twitter. J. Intell. Fuzzy Syst. **36**, 4743–4752 (2019)
32. Jahan, M.S., Oussalah, M.: A systematic review of Hate Speech automatic detection using Natural Language Processing (2021). http://arxiv.org/abs/2106.00742,
33. Samory, M., Sen, I., Kohne, J., Floeck, F., Wagner, C.: "Call me sexist, but...": Revisiting Sexism Detection Using Psychological Scales and Adversarial Samples. ArXiv200412764 Cs. (2021)
34. VERBI Software: MAXQDA 2022. maxqda.com (2021)
35. Queer Eye: More than a Makeover. Netflix (2018)
36. RuPaul's Drag Race. MTV (2009)
37. Amaral, I., Simões, R.: Violence, misogyny, and racism: young adults' perceptions of online hate speech. Presented at the April 1 (2021)
38. Döring, N., Mohseni, M.R.: Gendered hate speech in YouTube and YouNow comments: Results of two content analyses. Stud. Commun. Media. **9**, 62–88 (2020). https://doi.org/10. 5771/2192-4007-2020-1-62
39. Roberts, C.: Context in dynamic interpretation. In: Horn, L.R., Ward, G. (eds.) The Handbook of Pragmatics, pp. 197–220. Blackwell Publishing Ltd., Oxford (2006). https://doi.org/10. 1002/9780470756959.ch9
40. Brontsema, R.: A Queer Revolution: Reconceptualizing the Debate Over Linguistic Recla-mation (2004). https://doi.org/10.25810/DKY3-ZQ57
41. Buie, H., Croft, A.: The Social Media Sexist Content (SMSC) database: a database of content and comments for research use. Collabra Psychol. **9**, 71341 (2023). https://doi.org/10.1525/ collabra.71341

42. Erdocia, I.: Language and culture wars: the far right's struggle against gender-neutral language. J. Lang. Polit. **21**, 847–866 (2022). https://doi.org/10.1075/jlp.21050.erd
43. Meier, A.: New media, new effects? Introducing the Technology Equivalence Approach (TEA). Presented at the 12th Biannual Conference of the Media Psychology Division of the German Psychological Society, Aachen, Germany (2021)
44. Crenshaw, K.: Mapping the margins: intersectionality, identity politics, and violence against women of color. Stanford Law Rev. **43**, 1241–1299 (1991). https://doi.org/10.2307/1229039
45. Park, C.S., Liu, Q., Kaye, B.K.: Analysis of Ageism, Sexism, and Ableism in User Comments on YouTube Videos About Climate Activist Greta Thunberg. Soc. Media Soc. **7**, 20563051211036060 (2021). https://doi.org/10.1177/20563051211036059
46. Hackworth, L.: Limitations of "just gender": The need for an intersectional reframing of online harassment discourse and research. Mediat. Misogyny Gend. Technol. Harass., 51–70 (2018)

i-Cube, an (In)tangible Interface for Multi-user Generative Art Creation

David, Siu-Wing Chung$^{(\boxtimes)}$ ⓘ, and Carlos Sena Caires ⓘ

University of Saint Joseph, Macau , Estrada Marginal da Ilha Verde, 14-17, Macau, China
{chung.siu.wing,carlos.caires}@usj.edu.mo

Abstract. Generative art is a highly innovative and dynamic art form that uses mathematical algorithms and computer programs to create intricate patterns, shapes, and designs. What sets it apart from traditional art forms is the level of interaction between people and the medium of creation, as most generative art requires collaboration between the artist, participants, and technology to produce visually engaging and thought-provoking outputs. This study aims to explore the use of intangible interfaces for human interaction and bring individuals to the diverse world of generative art. To achieve this, we developed the intangible cube (iCube), a wireless portable device that allows up to 20 people to interact with the same generative art using gesture and voice. Through collecting data from iCube, users' feedback will be integrated and visualized in real time. Rather than get a visually appealing result, this study focuses on how individuals interact with the device and create generative art through collaboration.

Keywords: User interface · tangible interface · generative art · human-computer interaction

1 Introduction

Generative art is a practice that has been evolving since the late 20th century, with examples of works created using generative ideas dating back much further. Coined by German philosopher Max Bense [1] in 1965, the term "generative aesthetics," now called "generative art," describes works based on an algorithmic code or a mathematical process that creates autonomous systems to produce art.

The forms of generative art have become more diverse with the development of technology. Most computer-generative art is static graphics generated by a drawing machine in the early stage. Georg Nees [2], a generative art pioneer, was the first to exhibit computer-generated drawings in Stuttgart in February 1965. His early works are drawn by flatbed plotters.

With advancements in computer technologies, artists and researchers are adopting the practice and pushing its limits. Examples of such practice and achievements can be seen on artworks produced by Vera Molnar, Manfred Mohr, Casey Reas, Marius Waltz among others. Today, generative art has become interactive and is a dynamic and

Published by Springer Nature Switzerland AG 2023
P. Ciancarini et al. (Eds.): ICEC 2023, LNCS 14455, pp. 187–192, 2023.
https://doi.org/10.1007/978-981-99-8248-6_15

innovative form of artistic expression. In the early 2010s, with the invention of the Leap Motion controller and Kinect sensor, human body movements and hand gestures in a three-dimensional space can be more accurate to identify. A lot of the artists integrated these kinds of sensors in their works. For example, Weiler et al. [3] made a generative art canvas for participants to dance and shake their bodies in front of a Kinect sensor to capture the dancer's pose and generate abstract art. Nathan Selikoff designed an experimental art app with leap motion called "Beautiful Chaos" to generate animating graphics [4].

Since many forms of generative art involve some level of interaction, the number of participants is restricted to a few people. We are curious about how individuals can leverage their creativity and unique perspectives to collaborate with others across various generative art contexts using a novel interface. Our goal is to explore the potential of intangible interfaces for collaborative art creation. This motivation has driven us to develop an interface that can support multiple users, has intangible characteristics, and can be easily set up for generative art.

2   (In)tangible Interface for Generative Art

Imagine that 20 people stand in front of a big screen and participate in generative art creation. Twenty pieces of generative art animate simultaneously, and all participants use different ways to interact with an interface to alter the art result. It could be a wonderful moment. To achieve this, we present the (in)tangible cube (iCube), a small portable device for generative art creation with distance and sound-sensing functions. It supports up to 20 users. The side length of the device is 50 mm, and the weight is 80 g. It's suitable for anyone holding it in one hand. The term "tangible" in this context refers to the physical interaction users can have with the iCube device, allowing them to touch and manipulate it. However, the iCube is also considered "intangible" because the outcomes of these physical interactions are displayed visually on screens that are not physically touched. This dual interaction process is what the concept of (In)tangible aims to convey.

2.1   Components and Functions

The iCube is comprised of a receiver and multiple transmitters, each containing an ESP32 C3 microcontroller that manages sensor readings and data transmission. The receiver is responsible for monitoring the connection status of all transmitters, collating all data into CSV format, and forwarding it to Processing for visual element generation. When a transmitter is connected, its LED will light up green (see Fig. 1). All transmitters are equipped with a VL53L01 ToF sensor to measure obstacle distance and a MAX4466 microphone amplifier to detect voice changes. We opted for these sensors as input modalities because they offer greater intuitiveness and expressiveness than conventional methods such as mouse and keyboard. Additionally, the sensors enable the incorporation of environmental data into creating dynamic visuals, leading to a more interactive and captivating experience.

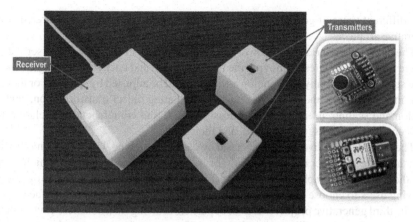

Fig. 1. (In)tangible Cube receiver (left), and transmitters (right)

2.2 Connectivity and Initial Testing

To enable connectivity between all transmitters and the receiver, we adopted a many-to-one approach, utilizing the ESP-NOW connectionless Wi-Fi communication protocol to synchronize all devices. According to the ESP-IDF Programming Guide [5], ESP-NOW can pair up to 20 devices. This low-power, low-latency wireless protocol allows for reliable and fast communication. We successfully conducted a connectivity test, connecting six transmitters up to 10 m away. Data was transmitted in real-time, without any noticeable latency, enabling users to interact with the generative art from a significant distance. This feature provides greater flexibility in device usage and encourages users to explore different physical spaces while engaging with generative art.

3 Experiment Setup and Progress

We divided the experiment into two stages to examine how individuals interact with generative art using the iCube and enhance our interface. In the first stage, we invited three university teachers to participate in a pilot study to observe how people use the interface across various visual contexts. Through face-to-face surveys, we received feedback about improving the interface, enhancing the user experience, and suggestions for playing methods. Participants indicated that instead of moving the cube forward and backward to modify attributes, they would prefer to shake it to see what will be happened. They also suggested that the cube's appearance could be more attractive. We will invite 20 art and design students to participate in a more extensive experiment in the second stage. We hope to obtain valuable feedback and insights from those 20 participants, which will aid in improving the iCube interface and enhancing the collaborative generative art creation experience.

3.1 First Stage - Pilot Study

For the first stage of our experiment, we arranged a computer and set up six iCubes in a room measuring 3m x 4m. We aimed to test whether users interacted differently with three different types of generative art visuals. To achieve this, we created three distinct generative art pieces.

The first generative artwork involved simple square stroke drawing. Users could change the size of squares by moving the iCube forward and backward to trigger the distance sensor. Additionally, the rotation attribute could be adjusted by speaking or making noise in front of the cube (see Fig. 2). By manipulating object transformation, such as rotation and scaling, users could effortlessly control and comprehend the relationship between visual changes, the interface, and their input.

The second generative artwork focused on cardioid drawing. Users could modify the angle attribute by either speaking loudly or moving their hands or body, which would alter the shape of the graphics (see Fig. 3). This functioned like a logic OR gate operation, allowing users to choose their preferred method of interacting with the interface.

The third generative project was a set of particle drawing. In a noiseless environment, the particles flowed steadily in one direction. However, when users made noise to the cube, it generated visual turbulence and modified the flowing speed based on distance sensing (see Fig. 4). This function required collaboration from all participants, with greater activity resulting in more distinct outcomes.

Fig. 2. Pilot study – six square drawing examples

3.2 Second Stage - Experiment

Scheduled for October 2023, more than 20 students with backgrounds in art and design will participate in a large-scale experiment involving numerous wireless devices. The main goal of the experiment is to gather valuable insights that will facilitate the improvement of the (In)tangible device, the iCube, as well as the quality of the visuals it produces. To achieve this objective, the experiment will focus on the following areas:

- User behavior: We will observe and analyze how users interact with the iCube, including how they move around the experimental space and respond to different visual

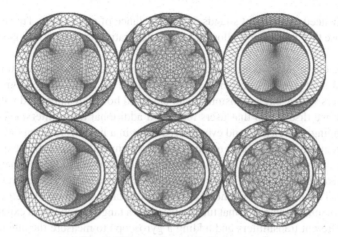

Fig. 3. Pilot study - cardioid drawing

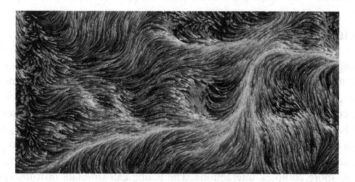

Fig. 4. Pilot study – particle flow

stimuli. This will provide valuable insights into user behavior and preferences that can be used to enhance the design and functionality of the devices.

- Device performance: The experiment will provide insights into the performance of the wireless devices. We will collect data on battery life, data transmission speed, and visual generation speed.
- User feedback: We will gather feedback from the users through surveys or interviews. This can provide valuable insights into user experience and satisfaction and suggestions for future improvements.

3.3 Discussion

In this project, we aimed to create a collaborative and immersive generative art experience by integrating distance and sound sensors into iCube and displaying the entire artwork on one screen. By doing so, individuals could collaborate, share ideas, and discover new interactive methods as a group. While users appeared to interact with their pieces in a specific area in the first and second generative artworks, the visual generation could also be influenced by ambient sounds and the distance of other users. This is precisely why we chose this approach; it allowed for a collaborative and immersive generative art experience.

Initially, our primary concern in this project was to minimize data transmission to achieve a swift response experience in generative art creation. To begin with, we provided users with a single transmitter and observed how they interacted with it. Upon observation, we discovered that users requested additional transmitters, experimented with rearranging the sensors, and even placed them in a linear formation on a table and triggered them sequentially. This resulted in a more engaging interaction experience.

As advised by the participants in the first experiment, users suggested that instead of viewing visual elements on the screen, this device can also be used to generate music or play games. This recalls our memory about the Reactable designed by Sergi Jordà [6], an interactive music controller that turns music into a tangible and visual experience. By grouping different transmitters and adding a gyroscope to measure the angular motion of iCube, our interface can achieve music generation function, which is also suitable for game applications. We will explore these kinds of applications in our next project.

4 Conclusion

The (In)tangible cube (iCube) encourages people to join together and co-create with generative art visual representations. By incorporating physical movement and environmental data, the device generates dynamic visuals that respond to the user's gestures and voice commands, resulting in a more interactive experience. We foresee that the iCube can be extended to support multi-user gaming experiences and music generation. Players can use physical gestures and voice commands to move game objects or trigger events in gaming. At the same time, the iCube's distance sensor can detect other players' presence for more complex interactions. The iCube can simulate instruments such as pianos, drums, and synthesizers for music generation, allowing users to trigger different sounds and manipulate parameters using specific gestures or voice commands. We look forward to seeing this device provide users with a unique and engaging experience in art, music, gaming, and other creative domains, and we are excited to see its potential applications continue to expand.

References

1. CompArt website. http://dada.compart-bremen.de/item/agent/209. Accessed 1 June 2023
2. CompArt website. http://dada.compart-bremen.de/item/agent/15. Accessed 0 June 2023
3. Weiler, J., Seshasayee, S.: Mushi: a generative art canvas for kinect based tracking. In: Proceedings of the 2016 Symposium on Spatial User Interaction (SUI '16), p. 171. Association for Computing Machinery, New York (2016)
4. Beautiful Chaos. https://www.nathanselikoff.com/works/beautiful-chaos
5. ESP-IDF Programming Guide. https://docs.espressif.com/projects/esp-idf/en/latest/esp32/api-reference/network/esp_now.html
6. Jordà, S.: The reactable: tangible and tabletop music performance. In: CHI '10 Extended Abstracts on Human Factors in Computing Systems (CHI EA '10), pp. 2989–2994. Association for Computing Machinery, New York (2010)

Content Design for Learning Support in Museum: Research on Exhibition Support System Using Tactile Senses

Yihang Dai[1]([✉]), Fusako Kusunoki[1], Makoto Kobayashi[2], and Shigenori Inagaki[3]

[1] Tama Art University, Hachioji, Tokyo, Japan
32247004@stdt.tamabi.ac.jp, {kusunoki,kusunoki}@tamabi.ac.jp,
koba@cs.k.tsukuba-tech.ac.jp
[2] Tsukuba University of Technology, Tsukuba, Ibaraki, Japan
[3] Rikkyo University, Toshima, Tokyo, Japan
inagakis@rikkyo.ac.jp

Abstract. In recent years, barrier-free accessibility, universal design, and social welfare support have been recognized as roadblocks for people with disabilities in their social inclusion. Moreover, the development of learning support and exhibition techniques for the visually impaired remains a long-term issue in research on barrier-free accessibility in European museums. This study focuses on the learning support for the visually impaired people in museums. We discussed the research till date. Moreover, we point out the shortcomings of current research, summarize previous surveys of existing museum facilities, and then propose a new universal design for learning support. To obtain an initial feedback and verification of the design, we conducted an evaluation experiment with the participation of children at the Museum of Nature and Human Activities, Hyogo. The results showed that the participants enjoyed learning about animals and had an unusual experience that incorporated tactile sensations. Future research will expand the scope of the test to include the visually impaired. This report outlines the design process of "ROUND ZOO" and the initial deliverable, "Content Design to Support Learning in Museums".

Keywords: Learning Support · Visually Impaired · Museum Exhibits · Touchable Exhibits · Tactile Sense

1 Introduction

Worldwide there are 43 million blind people and 295 million people with moderate to severe vision impairment [1]. They have shown interest in visiting museums despite their physiological defects [2]. However, surveys of barrier-free facilities in museums for the visually impaired, including those in Western countries such as London, Paris, Munich, and New York, show that only limited studies have focused on museum accessibility for the visually impaired, with several studies limited to single museums and few barrier-free

© IFIP International Federation for Information Processing 2023
Published by Springer Nature Switzerland AG 2023
P. Ciancarini et al. (Eds.): ICEC 2023, LNCS 14455, pp. 193–200, 2023.
https://doi.org/10.1007/978-981-99-8248-6_16

improvement measures [3]. Additionally, the design of exhibition aids for the visually impaired continues to face numerous difficulties. For example, visually impaired visitors cannot understand objects and information provided by museums, such as incomprehensible interpretive panels and identification tags. Lack of touchable elements, such as Braille and relief, prevents the visually impaired from experiencing museum exhibits [4]. This is in contrast to the "visually impaired-friendly museum development project" [5] we are currently advocating. It can be said that the most inaccessible things for the visually impaired is observation and appreciation in art galleries and museums. This is because, in many cases, exhibits are placed in glass cases, creating access barriers [6]. Moreover, the new coronavirus has made things more difficult for the visually impaired [7]. However, it was reported that, twenty years ago epidemics were not a further justification to provide fewer experiences for people with disabilities [8]. Therefore, it is necessary to consider issues related to the accessibility to visually impaired people in museums and their social inclusion [9]. Furthermore, the sense of touch can be used to promote understanding and enhance visitors' engagement with artworks even among the general public [10]. Therefore, the primary objective of this study was to create new exhibition techniques in museums specifically designed for visually impaired individuals. The emphasis was placed on incorporating elements such as "touch," "sound," and "being easy to understand." In order to address the challenge of effectively conveying information about museum exhibits to the visually impaired, we developed a unique device known as the "ROUND ZOO." This device allows users to experience tactile sensations associated with various animals, enabling them to interact with the exhibits. Moreover, the device also facilitates engagement by providing responses to a series of questions, thereby enhancing the understanding of museum exhibitions for visually impaired individuals. Through this innovative approach, we aim to overcome the communication barriers that exist and provide visually impaired individuals with a more immersive and inclusive museum experience.

2   Related Work

The proposed new universal design expands on the existing research mentioned below.

2.1   Current Status of Exhibition Support for the Visually Impaired in Museums

Worldwide, fewer museums are visually impaired friendly, and the public's perception of museums as "places for visual enjoyment and irrelevant to the visually impaired" has persisted for a long time [11]. Nevertheless, an increasing number of museums have special exhibits for the visually impaired including improvements in lighting, color contrast, tactile maps, Braille labels, enlarged texts, and accessible museum websites [12]. Moreover, less valuable exhibits that are not easily damaged or produced in large quantities, are increasingly being touched directly by visitors. However, many museums prohibit tourists from touching exhibits such as animal specimens owing to its long production time and high cost [13]. Hence, the inability to convey information about animals that are not commonly seen in daily life to the visually impaired is an issue.

2.2   Touchable Exhibits in Museums

What kind of museum would be best for the visually impaired? "Museums with exhibits that can be touched and observed by hand" are in demand by the visually impaired. Currently, 3D printing technology is being applied to museum exhibits [14] to create replicas of valuable exhibits, which visitors can touch and experience. Similarly, certain animal models can also be printed, allowing the visually impaired to touch and feel the external forms of animals [15]. However, as the 3D models only show the external form of the animals, it is not easy for the visually impaired to understand the feel and sound of the animals.

3   System Design, Structure and Concept

3.1   Animal Card

Background and Usage Scenarios. Currently, exhibition aids for the visually impaired are in the form of audio broadcasts and Braille, which prevent visitors from feeling the exhibits. Hence, there is a huge demand for "Museum of Tactile Experience" [16]. Therefore, in this study, we designed animal cards that can be experienced with a focus on themes such as "touch," "sound," and "being easy to understand". The method seeks to convey information to the visually impaired about the animals on display at the museum through corresponding animal cards that they can touch, hear, and read in Braille (Fig. 1).

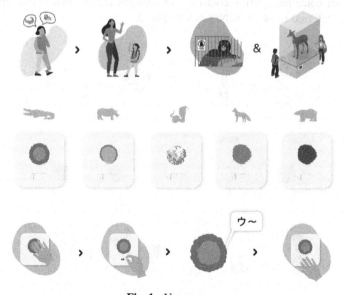

Fig. 1. Use scenes.

For the visually impaired, it can be difficult to recognize animals (crocodiles, snakes, etc.) that are not commonly seen in daily life. Even going to a museum doesn't help as there are almost no specimens that can be experienced. Therefore, in our proposed method, we let them experience these animal cards to provide a better understanding of the animals through the feeling of touch, sound and by providing an introduction about them without worrying about destroying the specimen.

Concept of the Work. Prototypes of five animal cards of animals rarely seen in everyday life were made. These included bears, crocodiles, rhinoceroses, foxes, and snakes (Fig. 2).

Fig. 2. Animal cards.

3.2 Round Zoo

Background and Usage Scenarios. We improved the function and experience of the prototypes by focusing on the feedback of the blind test. We replaced the mechanical switches with voice recognition controls and changed the original braille guide to an audio guide, referred to as "ROUND ZOO" (Fig. 3).

Fig. 3. Use scenes.

ROUND ZOO is for the visually impaired. Through audio guide and voice recognition technology, ROUND ZOO enables the visually impaired hear the sound of animals, play guessing games, solve problems encountered in the user test, and provide appropriate information about the corresponding animal. The background is the same as that described in 3.1, visually impaired people will experience ROUND ZOO, play animal quiz games, and better understand the information of corresponding animals by feeling it and hearing its sound.

About Tips. The quiz is designed to give participants a chance to learn about four aspects of animals: animal type, diet, habitat and physical abilities, by asking them to answer questions about their species, food, places they frequent and how they move. Below is a list of the types of quiz questions that were set. The options presented during the experience will vary based on each animal's ROUND ZOO (Table 1).

Table 1. Quiz question settings.

Number	Quiz	Choice	Investigate knowledge
1	Given hint was interesting?	①Birds ②Mammals ③Reptiles	Taxonomy knowledge
2	Where can you often meet them?	①In the soil ②In the sky ③In the river	Habitat knowledge
3	What kind of food do they like?	①Grass ②Meet ③Rice	Dietary knowledge
4	How do they move?	①Fly ②Crawl ③Walk	Knowledge of physical ability

Table 2. Questionnaire result

Questions	SA	A	N	D	SD
It was interesting to give hints	8	8	4	0	0
The quiz questions were easy to understand	10	8	2	0	0
The tips were easy to understand	14	4	2	0	0
Easy to understand how to play	13	5	1	1	0
It was interesting to think about the answer while touching the fur	13	5	1	1	0
More interesting than looking at specimens	11	5	3	1	0
It was fun to touch the fur	15	2	3	0	0
It was interesting to hear the sounds of animals	10	5	5	0	0

SA: Strongly agree, A: Agree, N: Neither agree nor disagree, D: Disagree, SD: Strongly disagree.

Voice Guidance and Voice Recognition. ROUND ZOO employed an audio guide instead of Braille to represent the clues. This not only avoids Braille errors, but is also easier for the visually impaired to understand. All quiz questions and options are read aloud, making it easier for the visually impaired and children who are not yet fully literate to understand the content. Additionally, voice guidance and voice recognition technology allows the visually impaired to answer the questions, and to hear the animal's sounds as well.

4   Workshop

4.1   Methodology

We conducted the workshop with 20 able-bodied elementary school students at the Museum of Human and Nature, Hyogo Prefecture. This research is aimed at designing products and services for the visually impaired. The current user testing was limited to able-bodied elementary school children to obtain the initial feedback and validation on basic functionality and user interface of the initial design phase. Their participation provided preliminary insights to improve and adjust the design in the next phase and also helped identify and resolve common problems and flaws in the early stages of a product or service. This workshop helped prepare the proposed method to be evaluated by the visually impaired to ensure that their needs are met to the fullest extent. The participants of the workshop were asked to experience "ROUND ZOO" as a hands-on user. Users experienced "ROUND ZOO" for about 10 min per session, and their reactions were observed and images were recorded based on their individual judgments. Finally, we asked them to fill out a questionnaire (Fig. 4).

Fig. 4. Experience photos.

4.2 Results

Through the workshop, we observed that the "ROUND ZOO" design generated learning activities for the children. Incorporating a quiz into it made it an interesting and effective learning method. We received many positive comments according to the post-workshop questionnaire result, such as "It was interesting to think about the answer while touching the fur" (Table 2).

5 Conclusion and Future Work

This work focused on designing a specimen viewing aid for museums, different from the traditional specimen exhibit. Initially, we designed animal cards with the fur and the sounds of corresponding animals. The audio could be played by sliding a switch. Next, we developed "ROUND ZOO" to enhance the experience of the visually impaired by encouraging the users to attempt quizzes with the help of audio clues while touching the fur. We hope that the experience of feeling the animals can cultivate their curiosity and desire to explore.

However, two limitations of this study should be considered. Firstly, the participant pool during the user testing phase was relatively small, which may have impacted the representativeness of the results. To ensure a more robust and reliable assessment of the effectiveness and usability of the designed specimen viewing aid, future studies should aim to include a larger and more diverse sample size. This would provide a broader range of perspectives and enhance the generalizability of the findings. Secondly, a limitation arises from the lack of direct feedback from visually impaired individuals during the design and testing stages. Collaborating directly with visually impaired individuals throughout the research process would offer valuable insights and enable the development of more tailored and effective solutions. By incorporating their feedback, the design of the specimen viewing aid could be refined to better meet the requirements of the target user group.

Addressing these limitations in future studies would contribute to a more comprehensive and inclusive approach, ensuring a broader representation of visually impaired individuals and enhancing the overall effectiveness and user experience of the specimen viewing aid in museum settings.

Acknowledgements. This work was supported by JSPS KAKENHI Grant. Number 22H00078, 22H01068. The evaluation experiment was supported by Museum of Nature and Human Activities, Hyogo.

References

1. IAPB homepage. https://www.iapb.org. Accessed 01 May 2023
2. Asakawa, S., Guerreiro, J., Ahmetovic, D., Kitani, K.M., Asakawa, C.: The present and future of museum accessibility for people with visual impairments. In: Proceedings of the 20th International ACM SIGACCESS Conference on Computers and Accessibility, pp. 382–384 (2018). https://doi.org/10.1145/3234695.3240997

3. Mesquita, S., Carneiro, M.J.: Accessibility of European museums to visitors with visual impairments. Disability Soc. **31**(3), 373–388 (2016). https://doi.org/10.1080/09687599.2016.1167671
4. Hinrichs, U., Schmidt, H., Carpendale, S.: EMDialog: Bringing information visualization into the museum. IEEE Trans. Visual Comput. Graph. **14**(6), 1181–1188 (2008). https://doi.org/10.1109/TVCG.2008.127
5. Asakawa, S., et al.: An independent and interactive museum experience for blind people. In: Proceedings of the 16th International Web for All Conference, pp. 1–9 (2019). https://doi.org/10.1145/3315002.3317557
6. Ginley, B.: Museums: a whole new world for visually impaired people. Disability Stud. Quart. **33**(3) (2013). https://doi.org/10.18061/DSQ.V33I3.3761
7. Cecilia, R.R.: COVID-19 Pandemic: threat or opportunity for blind and partially sighted museum visitors? J. Conservation Museum Stud. **19**(1) (2021). https://doi.org/10.5334/JCMS.200
8. Sandell, R.: Museums, society, inequality. 1st edn. Routledge, London (2002). https://doi.org/10.4324/9780203167380
9. Vaz, R.I.F.: Co-creating an integrative framework to enhance the museum experience of blind and visually impaired visitors. In Handbook of Research on Social Media Applications for the Tourism and Hospitality Sector, pp. 164–191 (2020). https://doi.org/10.4018/978-1-7998-1947-9.CH011
10. Christidou, D., Pierroux, P.: Art, touch and meaning making: an analysis of multisensory interpretation in the museum. Museum Manage. Curatorship **34**(1), 96–115 (2019). https://doi.org/10.1080/09647775.2018.1516561
11. Candlin, F.: Blindness, art and exclusion in museums and galleries. Int. J. Art Design Educ. **22**(1), 100–110 (2003). https://doi.org/10.1111/1468-5949.00343
12. Argyropoulos, V.S., Kanari, C.: Re-imagining the museum through "touch": Reflections of individuals with visual disability on their experience of museum-visiting in Greece. Alter **9**(2), 130–143 (2015). https://doi.org/10.1016/J.ALTER.2014.12.005
13. Candlin, F.: Don't touch! hands off! art, blindness and the conservation of expertise. Body Soc. **10**(1), 71–90 (2004). https://doi.org/10.1177/1357034X04041761
14. Wilson, P.F., Stott, J., Warnett, J.M., Attridge, A., Smith, M.P., Williams, M.A.: Evaluation of touchable 3d-printed replicas in museums. Curator: Museum J. **60**(4), 445–465 (2017). https://doi.org/10.1111/CURA.12244
15. du Plessis, A., Els, J., le Roux, S., Tshibalanganda, M., Pretorius, T.: Data for 3D printing enlarged museum specimens for the visually impaired. Gigabyte **2020**, 1–7 (2020). https://doi.org/10.46471/GIGABYTE.3
16. Pistofidis, P., et al.: Composing smart museum exhibit specifications for the visually impaired. J. Cult. Herit.Herit. **52**, 1 (2021). https://doi.org/10.1016/J.CULHER.2021.08.013

Extended Reality

Exploring the Influence of Collision Anxiety on Player Experience in XR Games

Patrizia Ring[(✉)] and Maic Masuch

University of Duisburg-Essen, Duisburg, Germany
{patrizia.ring,maic.masuch}@uni-due.de

Abstract. Extended Reality (XR) applications are becoming increasingly widespread due to technical advances, but also have their own challenges regarding the user's real-world orientation. Especially during virtual reality use at home, users are at risk of collisions with the environment due to restricted play space. Users might also experience discomfort due to this risk, even if no collisions occur. We propose a novel definition for the feeling of disorientation and fear of colliding with real objects in XR, called *Collision Anxiety* (CA). To measure the collision anxiety, we developed and tested a not yet validated questionnaire (Collision Anxiety Questionnaire) and used it to examine the influence of CA on immersion and general player experience. In three studies, a total of 149 participants played different variations of an augmented (AR) or virtual reality (VR) version of a game. Results suggest that while an AR game can provide a similar player experience compared to its VR equivalent, differences regarding CA exist.

Keywords: Virtual Reality · Augmented Reality · Collision Anxiety

1 AR and VR Technology

A significant development in the gaming industry is the rising market share of Virtual Reality (VR), Augmented Reality (AR), and Mixed Reality (MR)[1] applications. While hardware has been scarce and required technical knowledge in the past, VR and AR headsets are becoming less expensive and are marketed more toward consumers. Besides Meta's and Apple's latest advances, there is a rising number of different head-mounted displays (HMDs) available for consumers, such as the VIVE XR Elite or Sony's PlayStation VR 2[2].

With technological advances, the lines between AR and VR become more blurred [16]. For example, most AR technology is based on see-through VR, meaning that instead of augmenting the user's real view, a camera feed of the

---

[1] https://www.statista.com/topics/6072/extended-reality-xr, last visit: 19.05.2023.
[2] https://arinsider.co/2022/10/26/will-vr-revenue-exceed-28-billion-by-2026/, last visit: 25.05.2023.

P. Ciancarini et al. (Eds.): ICEC 2023, LNCS 14455, pp. 203–216, 2023.
https://doi.org/10.1007/978-981-99-8248-6_17

surroundings is augmented and displayed (e.g., the pass-through mode on Meta's Quest 2 virtual reality headset). Another example is the ambiguous meaning of the term AR. The term augmented reality can be used for smartphone applications that record and augment the environment, such as Pokémon Go (handheld AR), but also for head-worn AR hardware such, as the Microsoft HoloLense headset. One of the most common approaches for defining differences between different kinds of extended reality is the Milgram continuum [12], introducing the term mixed reality as including augmented reality and augmented virtuality. While Milgram coined the distinction between augmented and virtual reality as we use it today, another angle was taken by Skarbez et al. [16], arguing that virtual reality cannot be achieved unless "[...] all senses - exteroceptive and interoceptive - are fully overridden by computer-generated content." (p. 4). This means that true virtual reality would require both senses like vision or hearing (exteroceptive) but also perceptions regarding the internal state of the body (interoceptive) to be superseded by the virtual world. Hence, Skarabez et al. [16] argue to distinguish AR, MR (mixed reality), and VR in terms of immersion, coherence, and extent of world knowledge where what is commonly called VR still lies on the MR spectrum. A modern approach at a differentiation for the examples above being defined on the Milgram continuum was developed by Herur-Raman et al. [5], distinguishing between smartphone AR and high-end or pass-through AR, where the camera feed is augmented by the application. In the same manner, [5] also differentiates head-mounted displays between standalone or computer-tethered configurations and the tracking mode (external sensor tracking or HMD sensor tracking). Other distinctions can be made between stationary (standing or seated) and room-scale XR, where for the later movement in the real and virtual environment plays a crucial role. Finally, all these technologies are summarized under the term Extended Reality (XR).

1.1   Challenges in XR Gaming

To account for the hardware necessary for computational power, most VR games use a HMD that covers part of the user's face and either use input devices such as hand-held controllers or integrate hand-tracking for ease of control. The new generation of standalone HMDs, such as the Meta Quest or the Vive XR Elite offer a great range of movement, but while this minimizes distraction that comes with cable-bound HMDs, it also carries the risk of becoming disoriented and colliding with the environment. Especially room-scale games require an empty play area that is spacious enough to accommodate expansive movements, which is often not available when using XR at home. While most VR systems have some kind of border or chaperone in place (e.g., Meta's guardian) that alerts users if they get too close to obstacles or walls, calibrating the chaperone often means a trade-off between the limited space available and adequately safe distances from obstacles. Especially with fast arm movements as used in action-based games, there is the risk of collisions, resulting in injuries, damage to hardware or the hit objects. Even if no collisions occur, users might experience continuous discomfort while using VR due to this risk. This might cause players to focus on avoiding collisions instead of being immersed in the game.

One way to bypass those problems could be using AR instead of VR. While most current VR devices entirely cover the player's field of view and immerse the users in a virtual world, AR enables the users to see their surroundings in real-time, reducing the fear of disorientation and collisions. However, using AR instead of VR for gaming might influence the player experience. There is not much research yet, but especially with XR games in a setting that differs from the real world, AR might come with a loss of immersion and presence as real-life obstacles would mix with the surroundings of a fantasy world. While immersion refers to the technical sensory fidelity, presence refers to the user's subjective feeling of being in the virtual world [2]. As immersion is one of the main selling points of VR, simply switching to AR would not present a solution for all applications.

2   Collision Anxiety

When discussing the users' fear of colliding with the environment while using XR technology, we need a way to define and measure this feeling, as consistent collision anxiety might influence the player experience. Hence, it might be a key component for the design of games regarding gameplay such as player movements or calibration. Generally, different types of collisions are possible. Collisions can occur with natural room boundaries such as walls, with static obstacles such as furniture or with other people, for example other players in a shared play space or bystanders. While research regarding collision anxiety is very limited, collisions when using XR applications occur regularly, especially with the room boundaries or static objects [6]. Collision anxiety has not been consistently captured up until now and might be a confounding variable for other parts of the user experience. By measuring collision anxiety reliably, we might be able to differentiate it from other variables such as immersion and make more informed design decisions for XR applications. Hence, we propose the following general definition:

Definition 1. *The term collision anxiety (CA) refers to the feeling of discomfort and fear of colliding with or hitting the real-world environment while using an XR application.*

While reports of injuries sustained through XR usage are ample, empirical research on collision anxiety is very limited: To our knowledge, there is only one study with a focus on anxiety relief through gaming where CA is briefly mentioned and measured by a single question: Yang et al. [17] found that players who played the AR version of a game experienced less CA than players who played the VR version of the same game. However, the game that was used was rather static and did not require much movement within the room, minimizing the potential impact of collision anxiety. A paper by Boletsis and Cedergren [1] on locomotion techniques in VR has reported the participants' "fear of colliding with physical objects in real life", which was grouped under *psychophysical discomfort,* along with motion sickness. Here, fear of collision was deduced from participants' answers in semi-structured interviews. A work on obstacle avoidance used a self-developed questionnaire with five items asking about fear while walking and sense of distance to obstacles [7]. Finally, a four-item scale on fear as an emotional state has been used by Liu et al. [9] to assess discomfort in VR. Accordingly, it has been remarked that fear of collision needs further research [1].

Being able to directly measure CA will become increasingly more relevant in the future the more XR devices enable the user to move freely. Even if no collisions with the environment occur, the users might still experience CA. Even more so, collisions might only be avoided because the users are constraining themselves and playing carefully enough. Hence, the simple observation of whether a collision occurs is insufficient to measure collision anxiety. Furthermore, in order to make good design decisions, especially in XR gaming, there is the need to distinguish between the interaction of other variables (such as immersion) and CA. Hence, we developed a questionnaire to capture CA and tested it on a self-developed exergame with comparable AR and VR versions. To take a first step to differentiate CA from other factors, we conducted two more studies with a focus on the influence of the calibration method, human-computer trust, transition from AR to VR, and room size on collision anxiety.

2.1 Collision Anxiety Questionnaire

To measure the experienced CA we developed the Collision Anxiety Questionnaire (CAQ) with twelve items shown in Table 1. Due to the lack of existing theoretical work we created the items based on our own experiences and observations regarding the use of XR applications. The items are thematically divided into four subscales. The first subscale *physical collision* consists of a single item asking whether a collision has occurred during playing. The subscale *fear of collision* includes all items regarding the fear of hitting an object, getting injured, and being unaware of their own position within the real room. The third subscale *distraction* addresses to what extent the immersion is disrupted due to CA. For example, players may focus on not hitting real-world objects instead of getting involved within the game world. Furthermore, they may restrict their movements within the game world to avoid colliding with obstacles in the real world. The last subscale *disorientation* asked to what extent the players were aware of their own and surrounding objects positions during playing. All items are rated on a Likert scale ranging from "strongly disagree" (1) to "strongly agree" (5) with four items being reversed. The subscales are calculated by adding up the score within each subscale and diving it by the number of items in that subscale. The total score is calculated by adding the results of the subscales. A higher score (overall and on each subscale) indicates higher collision anxiety. The questionnaire is not yet validated. As a first insight, we conducted an exploratory factor analysis, which yielded two factors with eigenvalues exceeding 1 which accounted for 68.68 % of the total variance. Factor 1 is comprised of five items of the subscales fear of collision and distraction, factor 2 of two items of the subscale disorientation. Four items were dropped due to high side loadings, all other items have factor loadings between .909 to .596. After excluding the four items (as marked in Table 1) Cronbach's alpha shows acceptable to good values for both factors, .84 for factor 1 and .79 for factor 2. Cronbach's Alpha for the original scale used in the three studies showed at least acceptable values as well: Fear of collision scales between 0.88 to 0.90 between the three studies, distraction reaches values between 0.68 and 0.75, and disorientation reaches 0.75 to 0.84.

Table 1. The proposed Collision Anxiety Questionnaire (alpha CAQ). Items marked with an asterisk were excluded during the EFA.

Subscale	Item	Scale
Physical Collision	I collided with an object from the real environment during the use of the application	Yes/No
Fear of Collision	I was afraid of hitting an object in the real room	5-point Likert scale
	I was afraid of running into an object in real room	
	I was not afraid of getting hurt while playing.*	
	I felt uncomfortable because I did not know where objects were in the real room.*	
	I felt uncomfortable because I did not know where I was in the real room.*	
Distraction	I was focused on not colliding with objects in the real room	5-point Likert scale
	I could not engage with the virtual world because I had to pay attention to the real room	
	I moved through space during the game, as I would in a real room.*	
	I held back while playing to avoid a collision/(to avoid hurting myself)	
Disorientation	I knew at any time where I was in the real room	5-point Likert scale
	I knew at any time how far away I was from objects in the real room	

3 Study

To test the CAQ, the exergame *ExARcism* was developed using the game engine Unity and a Meta Quest 2. Exergames are a sub-genre of video games in which the player's body functions as an input device. They offer an increasingly relevant approach towards meeting people's need for at-home fitness activities by combining physical activity with a highly immersive gaming experience, increasing enjoyment and motivation [13].

3.1 *ExARcism* in AR and VR

Players play in first-person perspective inside a mansion haunted by ghosts. The game has two alternating phases completed twice: In the *Drumming Phase* (75 s), players have to use the Meta Quest 2 controller to hit one of four drums, that are hovering in different locations inside the room. To force players to move within the play area, they all activate and deactivate one after another at fixed times. In the *Ghost Hunting Phase* (90 s), the players have to capture the ghosts with the controllers and exorcise them by throwing them through a portal projected onto one of the walls. The players could only see the virtual environment in the VR version. In the AR version, players could see their surroundings through the *passthrough mode* of the Meta Quest 2 with relevant objects like the drums, portal, ghosts, and decorations projected into the monochrome camera feed. A grayscale-to-color mapping was used to make the game experience more aesthetically pleasing and create a similar environment compared to the VR version, as seen in Fig. 1. Furthermore, two slightly different versions of *ExARcism* were developed to enable a different focus for further studies.

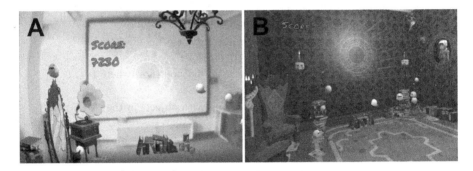

Fig. 1. A The AR game environment and **B** the VR game environment showing the portal during the *Ghost Hunting Phase*.

ExARcism Variation: Transition. In the first variation, all players started in AR mode, which then gradually, through two stages, switched to VR until the third stage consisted of the VR mode. In the transition, the walls as well as some decorative objects are gradually added with each phase. This variation offered two different game modes: In the automatic mode, the transition from AR to VR happened automatically after set time intervals. In the manual mode, players could manually activate the phase transition. The goal of this variation was to examine whether collision anxiety could be reduced by gradually introducing the VR environment to allow the user the opportunity to become accustomed to how much playspace is available.

ExARcism Variation: Calibration. The other variation mapped the game to a smaller room and implemented a new calibration system. The original game was mapped to a room of about $12\,m^2$, while the smaller room was only about $6\,m^2$. *ExARcism* has to be manually adjusted in the program code for the room to ensure the correct positioning of the drums, walls and decorative objects. A calibration by the player is not necessary. However, to examine how the calibration of an XR game might influence feelings of collision anxiety, a fake calibration for the player was implemented. The setup took place in the pass-through mode and consisted of placing virtual walls where the confines of the real world were. In the control condition with the simple calibration, players only had to press a button to align the game correctly to the room. This variation aimed to examine whether the calibration method influences the collision anxiety through the trust placed on the correct calibration of the play space.

3.2 1st Study: AR Versus VR

A total of 37 participants completed the study, mostly university students as reflected in the age demographics for this sample ($M = 24.87$, $SD = 3.00$) with more women ($N = 23$) than men. Most participants had prior experience with VR technology. Participants were randomly assigned to one of the experimental conditions and played either the AR ($N = 18$) or the VR version of the *ExARcism* game. Afterward, players were asked to fill out the CAQ as well as questionnaires regarding player experience [3] for delimitation from CA. In this study a 7-point Likert scale was used for the CAQ which was reduced to a 5-point scale for the two next studies since a 7-point scale seemed to be too nuanced.

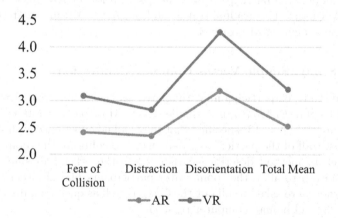

Fig. 2. A comparison between the AR and the VR version of *ExARcism* regarding the three relevant subscales and the total mean.

While there were no significant differences in the player experience, there was a significant difference between the AR and the VR players in collision anxiety. Differences became significant in the disorientation subscale ($t(35) = -2.163$, $p = .037$) as well as the overall collision anxiety score ($t(35) = -2.161$, $p = .038$). Tendencies towards higher collision anxiety when playing the VR version were given for all subscales as can be seen in Fig. 2.

3.3   2nd Study: Manual Versus Automatic Transition

In this study, 50 participants were randomly assigned to play one of two adapted versions of *ExARcism* using either manual ($N = 25$) or automatic transition from AR to VR mode. Again, most participants ($N = 36$) were women, and all but one participant were university students with an average age of $M = 21.98$ ($SD = 4.14$). In this group as well, the majority ($N = 45$) had experience with AR or VR applications. Players were asked to fill out the CAQ as well as questionnaires regarding player experience [3] and presence [14]. Finally, they were asked for their opinion about the phase transitions using qualitative questions.

No significant difference or tendencies in player experience between the manual and the automatic transition were found. However, there were tendencies towards higher collision anxiety throughout all subscales in the group with the automatic transition, but none of the tendencies became significant ($t(48) = 1.008$, $p = .319$ for the total score). There was no significant difference in presence between the automatic and manual transition. Furthermore, we asked participants for open feedback regarding the transition mechanic, the question being, "Any other feedback you'd like to give about the game mechanics with phase transitions in your own words?". The overall qualitative feedback was positive, with several participants stating that they were able to enjoy the game more and get more immersed in VR mode due to being able to get used to the play space in the AR mode. One participant even suggested a longer AR phase, especially for novice VR users. The gradual transition from AR to VR in two steps instead of one was also mentioned positively.

3.4   3rd Study: Simple Versus Complex Calibration

In the third study, 62 participants with an average age of 22.3 years ($SD = 5.50$) were asked to play *ExARcism* in a smaller room. Most participants were women ($N = 43$) and 21% ($N = 13$) specified that they had no experience with AR or VR applications. Half of the participants were asked to calibrate the room manually with the set-up method described earlier, while the other half simply had to press one button to align the room. After participants played either version of the game, they were asked to fill out the CAQ as well as questionnaires on player experience [3] and human-computer trust [4].

The group with the complex calibration generally reported a better player experience regarding curiosity, immersion and autonomy but without the differences becoming significant. However, there was a significant ($t(60) = -2.270$, $p = .027$) difference in collision anxiety in the subscale *fear of collision*. Tendencies towards a higher collision anxiety when using the simple calibration became visible through all subscales but did not yield significant results.

The human-computer trust scale [4] was used to measure trust regarding the use of the HMD before and after participants played the game. To examine how the experience with HMDs might influence user experience, collision anxiety, and trust regarding the HMD, we divided the sample into VR novices (measured as not having used an HMD beforehand) and more experienced users (having used an HMD at least several times). However, we did not find any significant differences between those two groups regarding player experience (subscales autonomy, immersion, and curiosity), human-computer trust, or collision anxiety.

Measured over all participants, the human-computer trust regarding the HMD was slightly ($d = .088$), but significantly higher after the VR game than before for both novices as well as experienced users ($t(61) = -2.731$, $p = .008$). When looking at the two different calibration methods, participants' pre- and post-use trust differed significantly for the complex calibration ($t(30) = -2.951$, $p = .006$), but not for the simple calibration ($t(30) = -0.670$, $p = .508$). To determine how the trust might influence the player experience, we calculated correlations between the relevant PXI subscales and the players' post-use trust. The sub scale immersion ($r = .451$, $p< .001$), and autonomy ($r = .340$, $p = .007$) both correlated significantly positive with the post-use trust.

3.5 Further Results

A comparison between all three studies shows that the overall collision anxiety was similar between the first and second studies, which took place in the same room ($12\,\mathrm{m}^2$). While there was no significant difference, the mean score of the CAQ was higher for the smaller room ($6\,\mathrm{m}^2$) as can be seen in Fig. 3. Regarding the player experience, there was a weak negative correlation between the PXI subscales curiosity and immersion and the distraction subscale of the CAQ ($r = -.234$, $p = .004$). With the given three samples of university students who mostly had some kind of experience with VR technology, no differences were found

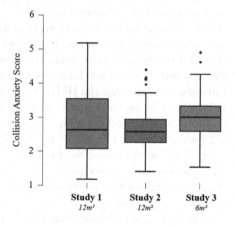

Fig. 3. A comparison between all three game variants regarding the total CAQ score.

between the VR novices and the experienced users in either player experience or collision anxiety.

4   Discussion

The goal of the present studies was to take a first step towards understanding and measuring feelings of discomfort due to fear of collisions while using XR applications. This phenomenon we defined as collision anxiety, might influence users' experience in XR directly or indirectly through influencing other variables such as immersion.

Even though the CAQ is not yet validated, exploratory factor analysis and Cronbach's alpha suggested that this first version of the questionnaire works well. Fear of collision and subsequent distraction seem to be one factor with the other factor being disorientation in the real room. This might suggest that collision anxiety is closely related to distraction, underlining the importance of identifying the influence of collision anxiety on player experience. By further developing the CAQ, we hope that the concept of collision anxiety will be further examined and more easily identified as a possible confounder variable. Moreover, the questionnaire might help the development of XR applications, especially as hardware becomes more readily available, autonomous, and flexible, increasing the potential risk of collisions.

Throughout the three studies, we found no significant differences between more experienced VR users and novices. However, experience levels varied greatly, and we only differentiated between participants with no experience at all and those who had used HMDs at least once before. Possible effects might have also been obscured through the large percentage of experienced users.

The calibration method seems to influence the overall player experience regarding curiosity, immersion, and autonomy, as well as the fear of collision. Hence, the calibration for VR applications might improve by not only focusing on a quick calibration method but rather one that gives the user a certain autonomy and the possibility to build trust by being in control of and understanding the method. Given that human-computer trust generally rose slightly in our third study after using the HMD, it seems as if players develop more trust in the XR technology as they use it. Mcknight et al. [10] use the definition of initial and knowledge-based trust by Lewicki and Bunker [8], with the later developing over time with the use of the specific technology. While the original work referred to interpersonal relationships, this approach might be fitting for pre- and post-use trust in technology. Since only very few slight collisions occurred during the studies the question remains open how a collision might influence the development of trust.

The first study showed that the overall player experience did not differ significantly between the AR and VR versions, suggesting that using AR in certain games can be a simple way to enable XR games in confined spaces without losing immersion. However, *ExARcism* has been developed specifically so that we had a game with very similar AR and VR versions and fitted to the room it was played in. As *ExARcism* took place in a haunted mansion, the real room fitted the theme close enough that it apparently did not break the immersion. Had we used a jungle or beach instead, the closed room would have probably had a larger impact on presence and immersion. Where using an AR version is not a good alternative, another way to help users avoid obstacles would also be to represent the real-life obstacle in the VR environment. An earlier work by Simeone et al. [15] introduces the concept of substitutional reality, where real-life objects are represented as theme-fitting virtual objects: In a medieval or sci-fi world a table either becomes a collection of crates or the control desk of a spaceship. A similar work with a focus on collision avoidance was done by

Liu et al. [9]. Here, obstacles in the virtual world were represented by theme-fitting obstacles in the virtual environment with good results. The negative correlation between curiosity and immersion and the CAQ subscale distraction suggests that the player experience might suffer from high collision anxiety. When the user is focused on not colliding with the environment, it might become more difficult to stay immersed in the game world. It follows that collision anxiety is a factor that should be considered, especially in VR games, since immersion is a big argument for using VR environments. The trust users place in the VR hardware also seems to play a role regarding immersion and autonomy. While the connection between collision anxiety and trust in the HMD is not clear yet, this suggests that the player experience in VR generally suffers from factors that pull the user out of the virtual world due to real-life constraints.

Insights gained from the qualitative questions in the second study were that, generally, the transition from AR to VR seemed to help with collision anxiety, spatial awareness, and orientation within the play space. The feedback suggests that while the VR mode is more immersive, AR enables users to orient themselves within the room. It is possible that the overlay of AR and the real room might enhance orientation once the VR phase starts because users can mentally map certain game objects to their place in the real room, improving spatial awareness. Our game took place in a single room of the mansion, hence players could use the transition from AR to VR to orient themselves as described above. If the game had taken place in several different virtual rooms or an open-world scenario (e.g., similar to Super Hot[3]), this would not have worked. Here, the transition from AR to VR would not have helped with spatial awareness. For games where players do not change the in-game location but still use large movements (e.g., Beat Sabre[4]) the use of a slow transition from AR to VR might, however, offer a good alternative for smaller spaces.

5   Conclusion

We conducted three studies with a self-developed AR and VR exergame to examine the influence of collision anxiety (defined as the fear of colliding with or hitting an object while using an XR application) in regards to player experience, differences in novices versus experienced users, calibration method and transition from AR to VR. Collision anxiety was measured with the Collision Anxiety Questionnaire, that is not yet validated, but seemed to perform well. We found that while no significant differences were found between users of different experience levels, collision anxiety seems to be influenced by the calibration method and influences in turn the player experience. Especially immersion seems to be a factor that correlates with collision anxiety.

---

[3] https://superhotgame.com, last visit: 26.05.2023.
[4] https://www.beatsaber.com, last visit: 26.05.2023.

5.1   Limitations

Most importantly, the CAQ is not yet validated and has little theoretical work to draw upon. The findings should also be interpreted with care as the effect size of significant results is often rather small. Some variables were only examined in one of the three studies, reducing the sample size in some results. As there is very little research up to date regarding collision anxiety, our research was mainly exploratory and should be seen as an impulse for further studies. Our game was developed with the clear intention of having very similar AR and VR versions for comparison, hence the game was made for AR use. Other applications will probably yield different results regarding the player experience in AR versus VR, for example scenarios that experience a larger disruption of immersion in AR through real-world objects, e.g., a jungle or medieval setting.

The CAQ has successfully been used for AR as well as VR, but might not make precise enough distinctions in some cases, e.g., if game designers need to know whether player experience is disrupted by the collision with virtual game objects. Generally, the CAQ focuses on collisions with real-world objects that can both be visible (in AR) or not visible (in VR) for the player. We do not specifically assess virtual collisions as they do not pose the risk of injuries. Hence, we suspect them to not cause the same worry and self-restraint in the player, but further research should be done on this assumption.

Regarding the AR and VR experience, differences between more experienced users were grouped together to enable clearer results, but levels of experience differed within the more experienced group. More homogeneous groups might yield clearer results. We used the human-computer trust scale [11] to measure the trust users placed in the HMD specifically. The questionnaire, while validated and developed for peoples' trust in hardware, did not fit the use case too well, so results might be skewed by participants' ambiguous answers. Adding to that, since presence was only queried in the second study as well as human-computer trust only in the third, the sample size on those two variables was smaller, making smaller effects more difficult to find.

5.2   Future Work

As we suspect different variables to influence collision anxiety and vice versa, the next step is the validation of the CAQ. An improved version is being developed with a new optional subscale for *interpersonal collisions*, meaning collisions with other real-world players or bystanders. With the extended and validated questionnaire, we aim to examine how a shared gaming experience and play space might influence collision anxiety in regard to player performance and experience. We also plan to examine the development of collision anxiety over time as well as after collisions occurred. Ultimately, our goal is to demarcate variables regarding player experience such as immersion from the influence of collision anxiety.

References

1. Boletsis, C., Cedergren, J.E.: Vr locomotion in the new era of virtual reality: an empirical comparison of prevalent techniques. Advances in Human-Computer Interaction 2019 (2019). https://doi.org/10.1155/2019/7420781

2. Bowman, D.A., McMahan, R.P.: Virtual reality: how much immersion is enough? Computer **40**(7), 36–43 (2007). https://doi.org/10.1109/MC.2007.257

3. Graf, L., Altmeyer, M., Emmerich, K., Herrlich, M., Krekhov, A., Spiel, K.: Development and validation of a German version of the player experience inventory (pxi). Mensch und Computer 2022 (2022). https://doi.org/10.1145/3543758.3543763

4. Gulati, S., Sousa, S., Lamas, D.: Design, development and evaluation of a human-computer trust scale. Behav. Inf. Technol. **38**(10), 1004–1015 (2019). https://doi.org/10.1080/0144929X.2019.1656779

5. Herur-Raman, A., Almeida, N.D., Greenleaf, W., Williams, D., Karshenas, A., Sherman, J.H.: Next-generation simulation-integrating extended reality technology into medical education. Front. Virtual Reality, 115 (2021). https://doi.org/10.3389/frvir.2021.693399

6. Jelonek, M.: Vrtoer: When virtual reality leads to accidents: a community on reddit as lens to insights about vr safety. In: Extended Abstracts of the 2023 CHI Conference on Human Factors in Computing Systems, pp. 1–6 (2023). https://doi.org/10.1145/3544549.3585783

7. Kanamori, K., Sakata, N., Tominaga, T., Hijikata, Y., Harada, K., Kiyokawa, K.: Obstacle avoidance method in real space for virtual reality immersion. In: 2018 IEEE International Symposium on Mixed and Augmented Reality (ISMAR), pp. 80–89 (2018). https://doi.org/10.1109/ISMAR.2018.00033

8. Lewicki, R.J., Bunker, B.B.: Developing and maintaining trust in work relationships. Trust Organizations Front. Theory Res. **114**, 139 (1996)

9. Liu, H., Wang, Z., Mazumdar, A., Mousas, C.: Virtual reality game level layout design for real environment constraints. Graph. Visual Comput. **4**, 200020 (2021). https://doi.org/10.1016/j.gvc.2021.200020

10. Mcknight, D.H., Carter, M., Thatcher, J.B., Clay, P.F.: Trust in a specific technology: an investigation of its components and measures. ACM Trans. Manage. Inf. Syst. (TMIS) **2**(2), 1–25 (2011)

11. Melo, M., Gonçalves, G., Vasconcelos-Raposo, J., Bessa, M.: How much presence is enough? qualitative scales for interpreting the igroup presence questionnaire score. IEEE Access **11**, 24675–24685 (2023). https://doi.org/10.1109/ACCESS.2023.3254892

12. Milgram, P., Kishino, F.: A taxonomy of mixed reality visual displays. IEICE Trans. Inf. Syst. **77**(12), 1321–1329 (1994)

13. Oh, Y., Yang, S.: Defining exergames & exergaming. Proc. Meaningful Play **2010**, 21–23 (2010)

14. Schubert, T., Friedmann, F., Regenbrecht, H.: The experience of presence: Factor analytic insights. Presence: Teleoperators Virtual Environ. textbf10(3), 266–281 (2001). https://doi.org/10.1162/105474601300343603

15. Simeone, A.L., Velloso, E., Gellersen, H.: Substitutional reality: Using the physical environment to design virtual reality experiences. Association for Computing Machinery, New York, NY, USA (2015). https://doi.org/10.1145/2702123.2702389

16. Skarbez, R., Smith, M., Whitton, M.C.: Revisiting milgram and kishino's reality-virtuality continuum. Front. Virtual Reality **2**, 647997 (2021). https://doi.org/10.3389/frvir.2021.647997
17. Yang, H., Li, J., Liu, J., Bian, Y., Liu, J.: Development of an indoor exergame based on moving-target hitting task for covid-19 epidemic: a comparison between ar and vr mode. IEEE Trans. Games **14**(3), 511–521 (2022). https://doi.org/10.1109/TG.2021.3118035

Mutually Imperceptible Skill Adjustment in VR for Making Hyakunin Isshu Karuta Inclusive

Ayaka Maruyama[✉] ⓘ and Kazutaka Kurihara ⓘ

Tsuda University, 2-1-1, Tsuda-Machi, Kodaira-Shi, Tokyo 187-8577, Japan
mm2383ma@gm.tsuda.ac.jp

Abstract. In this paper, we propose "Mutually imperceptible skill adjustment in VR" as a new method of skill adjustment to make multiplayer games inclusive. It is a skill adjustment in VR that is difficult for players to perceive each other's assistance. By carefully designing the assistance to minimize their impact on the opponents' environments, it is intended that the assistance will minimize their impact on the opponents' skill sets and allow skill adjustment without informing the opposing players. We prototyped a system that implements the mutually imperceptible skill adjustment in VR involving visual and auditory modalities to the game of Hyakunin Isshu Karuta, a popular traditional card game in Japan in which memory and quick reaction are important. Evaluation experiments showed that the visual assistance, one of the mutually imperceptible skill adjustments, was effective for novice players, and suggested that combining multiple assistance methods could bridge the skill gap between novice and experienced players.

Keywords: Virtual Reality · Multiplayer Game · Inclusiveness · Skill Adjustment · Hyakunin Isshu Karuta · Meta Quest2

1 Introduction

One important aspect of making multiplayer games inclusive is appropriate skill adjustment. In multiplayer games, it is common to adjust skills by introducing a handicap when one player has a clear advantage over the others. Skill adjustment makes it easier for players of different skill levels to have exciting and even games, which is expected to attract a wider variety of players and keep them motivated to continue playing the game.

However, the main existing methods of skill adjustments are starting from a scored state, significantly changing the rules, and imposing restrictions on the advantaged players. They do not allow the players to fully demonstrate their abilities. For instance, a skill adjustment that changes the original rules would force the players to use their bodies and strategies differently than usual, which could make play more difficult for players. In addition, skill adjustments that limit a stronger player's abilities will cause the players to remain aware of their handicap throughout the game. As a result, the opposing players may feel sorry for the stronger player, or the stronger player may feel obliged

P. Ciancarini et al. (Eds.): ICEC 2023, LNCS 14455, pp. 217–230, 2023.
https://doi.org/10.1007/978-981-99-8248-6_18

to match the other players and refrain from demonstrating his or her ability. If these physical and psychological effects make it difficult for players to demonstrate their true abilities, it becomes difficult for players to feel excitement. This would not be a good skill adjustment, even if the game were even.

It would be ideal if skill adjustments could be made that have little effect on the skill sets of the players and are difficult to even perceive. As a first step, we propose "mutually imperceptible skill adjustment in VR". This is a skill adjustment in VR that is difficult for players to perceive each other. Figure 1 illustrates this situation. By carefully designing the assistance to minimize their impact on the opponents' environments, it is intended that the assistance will minimize their impact on the opponents' skill sets and allow skill adjustment without the players being aware of it.

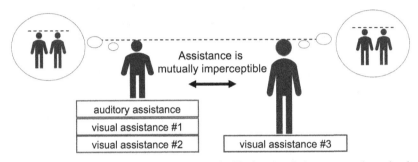

Fig. 1. Skill adjustment in VR. Players are under the illusion that their opponents have the similar level of skill as they do, while they receive different sets of skill assistance.

The subject multiplayer game of this paper is Hyakunin Isshu Karuta. The Hyakunin Isshu is a collection of classical wakas written by 100 poets. Waka is a traditional Japanese poetic form that expresses nature, seasons, human feelings and emotions in 31 letters. Hyakunin Isshu Karuta is a traditional and popular Japanese card game that uses a Hyakunin Isshu card deck. The game is played using cards with the second half of each poem written on them. Players touch the card corresponding to the poem read out by the reader as early as possible. The first player to touch a card gets that card, and the player who collects the most cards is the winner. Hyakunin Isshu Karuta is widely played in school classes, at home, and at tournaments in Japan. Some people play on a casual basis, while others play under a more competitive set of rules[1]. On the other hand, one of the disadvantages of this game is that the speed at which people take cards varies greatly depending on whether they have memorized the poems or are familiar with the action of taking cards. With these characteristics, we believe that more people can enjoy this game if appropriate skill adjustments are made.

The contributions of this paper are three-folded: 1) We proposed the concept of mutually imperceptible skill adjustment in VR multiplayer games; 2) We implemented a VR Hyakunin Isshu Karuta system with mutually imperceptible skill adjustment involving visual and auditory modalities; 3). We evaluated the effectiveness and performance of the

---

[1] https://m.youtube.com/watch?v=Sx2UqSxAPfk.

implemented mutually imperceptible skill adjustment through experiments with novice players and experienced players.

2   Hyakunin Isshu Karuta Game

2.1   Terms Used in Hyakunin Isshu Karuta and "Decisive Letters"

The Hyakunin Isshu consists of 100 poems. Each poem consists of 31 letters that form 5 fragments: each consisting of 5, 7, 5, 7, and 7 letters. A poem is divided into a first half and a second half. The first 5-7-5 is the first half and the following 7–7 is the second half. Only the second half of a poem is printed on each card.

In the Hyakunin Isshu Karuta (henceforth referred to as HIK), you can take the cards earlier if you remember the "decisive letters" of each poem. The decisive letters are the letters needed to determine which poem is being read out of the 100 poems. For instance, there are four poems start with "HA(は)", so if only the first letter "HA(は)" is read out, it is not yet clear which poem is being read out. However, if the first three letters "HA(は) RU(る) SU(す)" are read out, we can identify the poem being read out, since there is only one poem that begins with "HA(は) RU(る) SU(す)". In this case, "HA(は) RU(る) SU(す)" are decisive letters. The number of letters is roughly proportional to the duration of time required to read them out, as the Japanese script (Hiragana) is phonetic, with each letter representing a specific syllable. Therefore, the number of decisive letters is an important factor in identifying poem early. A poem with one decisive letter is called "1-letter decisive", a poem with two decisive letters is called "2-letter decisive", etc. The longest is a 6-letter decisive. Each poem is only read out once during the game, so each time a poem is read out, the number of possible poems to be read out next decreases, and the number of decisive letters in each poem changes.

2.2   Game Progression

This game can be played by two or more people. The game proceeds as follows. First, any number of cards from the 100 cards are randomly placed on the table or floor. The most commonly used card size is 7.3 cm × 5.2 cm, and each letter on the card is approximately 0.9 cm × 0.9 cm. When the game starts, the poems are randomly read out from the 100 cards. Each poem is read out in the order of the first half, followed by the second half. The first player to touch the card with the read out poem on it gets the card. The game ends when there are no more cards left on the table, and the player who has collected the most cards wins.

3   Related Work

3.1   Making Multiplayer Games Inclusive

Various methods have been considered to make multiplayer games inclusive. One is to change or create the rules of the game. YURU SPORTS [1] are such examples proposed by the World Yuru Sports Association and they can be enjoyed regardless of age, gender, athletic ability, or disability. Another way is to supplement skills by adding visual information. For instance, "Kimari-ji Karuta" [2] is a HIK card deck product with decisive letters physically printed on each card to help beginners. In sports, there are also examples of support for beginners by using information technologies to predict and visualize the trajectory of the ball [3] or the opponent's body motion [4]. Fujiwara et al. [5] discussed the use of color in an online multiplayer game to reduce the disadvantage of colorblind players. These studies have the same goal of making games more enjoyable for diverse people, but they differ from this study in that the supports for enjoyment affect all players in a game, whereas this study uses VR to provide these supports, which are less likely to interfere with the skills of other players.

An example of skill adjustment that does not affect player skills is the tug-of-war system by Maekawa et al. [6], which allows skill adjustment through the intervention of an outside force from the system. In this study, VR is introduced to enable these kinds of adjustments that are not even possible in reality, such as modification of the body or physical laws. Furthermore, it is expected that the difference in assistance between the players will be less perceptible, and the players' awareness will not be directed toward skill adjustment.

3.2 Training and Human Augmentation Using Mixed Reality

The use of Mixed Reality facilitates assistance with additional visual and auditory information, such as visual imagery of body use [7], providing feedback on the player's movements [8], and highlighting necessary information in the environment [9]. Furthermore, because VR allows users to change settings that cannot be changed in the real world, it is often used for training to master skills. For instance, forces such as gravity can be manipulated [10], time can be distorted [11], and speed perception can be misperceived [12]. These are intended to train for skill acquisition, which is a different goal from this study. However, we believe that the techniques used in these studies can be implemented in the future to temporarily reduce the skill gap between players.

Examples of using VR to augment the human body include Ogawa et al. [13] to change the length of the fingers and the Sun et al. [14] to change the length of the upper limb. Although these studies also have different objectives, utilizing these techniques to the extent that players do not feel uncomfortable is considered effective for temporary skill improvement.

3.3 Technology to Externally Control Body Movement

Technology to externally control body movements could be applied to skill adjustment in multiplayer games. This is because it can be expected for game players to temporarily perform the skills required for the game without training. There are several studies that use EMS to control the body. Ebisu et al. [15] is one of them. It enables beginners to play drums immediately. Although these systems differ from our study in that they target learning, incorporating the mechanisms used in these systems to enable even novices to quickly achieve ideal movements is a promising future prospect for our study.

3.4 Assistance in Playing HIK by Information Technology

Several methods have been proposed for assistance in HIK by IT. Kitagawa et al. [16] visualized players' movements in HIK games by posture estimation using PoseNet. Yamada et al. [17] measured time it takes to take a card in real games by attaching an acceleration sensor and an angular velocity sensor to the wrist. Others, such as Tomaru et al. [18], provide assistance in planning strategies before a game begins by visualizing the decisive letters. Some studies, such as Matsuda [19] and Takeda et al. [20], have shown acoustic differences up to the definite letter of each poem by analyzing the voice of the reader to assess the possibility of much faster poem identification. These studies are designed to help experienced players improve their skills in the real world, and their focuses are different from those of this study, which provides assistance in real time during a game using VR, regardless of whether the player is experienced or a novice. However, the results and implications of these studies may be useful in providing assistance as skill adjustment using VR, which is one of our future research directions.

Tokushima et al. [21] proposed a learning system for HIK that runs on a PC. This system allows users to learn the dynamic properties of decisive letters that change from moment to moment as the game progresses. The system is similar to the present study in that it visualizes dynamic changes in decisive letters, but the difference is that this study is a single player system for learning, whereas the present study uses the visualization for skill adjustment in a VR-based game.

4 System Implementation

4.1 System Overview

We prototyped a VR HIK game for two players with Unity. The system was designed to achieve that players who remember the poems and are not accustomed to take cards, and by players who do not remember the poems and often play HIK can enjoy the game together. In order to achieve this, some assistance for mutually imperceptible skill adjustment in VR were implemented.

For implementation, it is important to be able to obtain the correct coordinates and angles of the hands and to be able to change the visual and auditory information given to each player. We use the Meta Quest2 which has a resolution of 3,664 × 1,920 and a refresh rate of 90Hz. The Meta Quest2 was selected as the device that would satisfy these two requirements. HIK is a game that requires sensitive use of the hands and palms. One possible input option is to use the hand tracking feature of Meta Quest2. However, at the time of writing this paper, the hand tracking speed of Meta Quest2 was not fast enough to play HIK. Therefore, we created a 3D-printed attachment to attach the controller to the arm, while the Meta Quest2 controller was originally designed to be held in the hand. In the VR space, the hand object is displayed at the position of the Meta Quest2 controller, but through calibration, the actual hand position and the hand object position are adjusted to be the same. Figure 2 shows snapshots of the game and controller.

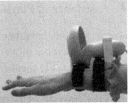

Fig. 2. Left: Snapshots of the game. Right: The controller attached to an arm.

4.2 Implementation of Mutually Imperceptible Skill Adjustment in VR

This system implements various features as the mutually imperceptible skill adjustment in VR, which deals with visual and auditory information. Visual information can be adjusted by displaying the decisive letters. This adjustment is reflected only on the vision of the assisted player and do not affect other player. There are two ways to display the decisive letters: one is to display decisive letter of the poem in a static manner, and the other is to display it dynamically, reflecting changes in the decisive letters during the game. In this paper, each display is referred to as "static decisive letter display" and "dynamic decisive letter display". Figure 3 shows how the display changes when dynamic decisive letter display is applied to the poem, which has 3 decisive letters "HA(は) RU(る) SU(す)". At first, the original decisive letters "HA(は) RU(る) SU(す)" were displayed, but as other poems were read out, the number of letters required to identify the poem decreased, and the decisive letters changed to "HA(は) RU(る)" and "HA(は)". Note that this method of overlapping characters is also used in "Kimari-ji Karuta" [2], and is not particularly strange. Figure 4 shows the game screens of the two players when the skill adjustment was applied. The left image shows the game screen of the player who used the dynamic decisive letter display as assistance, and the right image shows the game screen of the player who did not use the assistance.

Auditory information can be adjusted by changing the presence or absence of the cheering voice during the game, as well as by changing the timing of the poem reading out, as shown in Fig. 5. By listening to the poems earlier, the player can start looking for cards earlier and take them earlier. These is skill assistance that is difficult for the opponent to perceive because both players are using earphones. Similarly, the cheering voice assistance allows to affect the emotions of only one player, since the voice can only be heard by one player through the earphones.

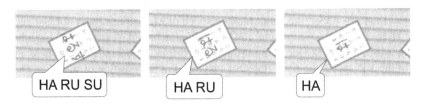

Fig. 3. The assisting letters change as a game proceeds.

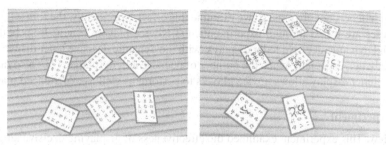

Fig. 4. Different perspectives between two players. Left: with displaying decisive letters. Right: without displaying decisive letters.

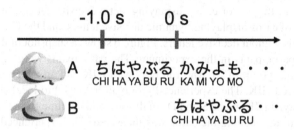

Fig. 5. The timing of the sound can be changed for each player.

5 Evaluation

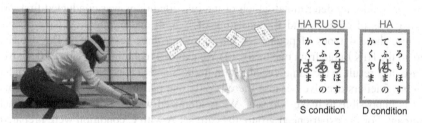

Fig. 6. Snapshots of the experiment. Left: in real world. Middle: in VR space. Right: S condition and D condition. Black texts represent second halves of the poems, while red texts represent the decisive letters. (Color figure online)

5.1 Hypotheses

We conducted an evaluation study to assess the effectiveness of the proposed skill adjustment methods. The main skill adjustment methods implemented in the prototype system presented in the previous section are the decisive letter display as a vision related assistance and adjustment the timing of the beginning of reading poem out as an auditory related assistance. The latter method of timing adjustment is relatively obvious in its effectiveness as skill assistance. On the other hand, the former method of displaying decisive letters is not obvious, so we examine this effect. Specifically, the following two hypotheses are tested through experiments. (1) Novice players benefit from both the static and dynamic decisive letter displays, with the dynamic decisive letter display performing better, especially when the number of decisive letters is large. (2) The dynamic decisive letter display allows novice players to perform as well as experienced players.

5.2 Experiment

Overview. This experiment examined the effectiveness of displaying decisive letters to novice players as skill assistance, and the difference between the two display methods. We also compared the performance of novice players with decisive letter display with that of experienced players without decisive letter display. In this experiment, the S condition refers to the use of cards displaying static decisive letters, the D condition refers to the use of cards displaying dynamic decisive letters, and the C condition refers to the use of cards without decisive letters. Figure 6 shows a snapshot of the experiment. There were 30 participants in the experiment. The participants were divided into two groups: a beginner group of 21 who rarely played HIK and an experienced group of 9 who often played HIK. The experienced group all belonged to local HIK clubs. The novice group played HIK on the S and D conditions, and the time from the beginning of reading poem out to touching the cards was measured. The experienced group played HIK under the C condition and measured the time as well.

Procedure. First, a questionnaire regarding HIK experience was administered, and then a series of card acquisition tasks were performed according to experience. Two conditions were used in the experiment for the novice group: the S condition and the D condition, and it was randomly determined which of the two conditions was conducted first. We used two sets of cards A and B, consisting of 2, 3, 4, and 6-letters decisive poems. We chose these 4 types of poems for the following three reasons. (1) The decisive letters in the HIK range from one to six. (2) We avoided including the 1-letter decisives because they result in the same visualization in the S and D conditions. (3) We avoided including 5-letters decisive because there is only one pair of 5-letters decisive poems, and it is impossible to make two sets. We randomized which set to use first for each participant. For the experienced group, the card set A with C condition were prepared. An experimental conductor read the instructions for the task flow, how the poems were read out, the meaning of the decisive letter display, and the game setup.

The assumed situation of the game in this task were as follows. The game was assumed to be in progress. Following the standard rules, poems that were not on the field were also read out. The poems already read out were assumed to 13 in card set A and 15 in card set B. There were 4 cards on the field. The original numbers of the decisive letters of the poems in the card sets were diverse. However, in this situation, players who had the enough knowledge of decisive letters could realize that all the 4 cards on the field dynamically became 1-letter decisive, i.e., you could identify a card to take just by listening to the first letter of the poem. The participants in the experienced group were able to take a card as soon as they listened the first letter of a poem, since they all had the knowledge.

Figure 6 shows how the novice participants were visually assisted in the S and D conditions. In the D condition, only one letter for each card was visible because all the cards dynamically became 1-letter decisive in this situation. Therefore, novice players could take a card as soon as they listened the first letter of a poem. In the S condition, the original decisive letters of each poem were displayed, independent of the situation. Therefore, novice players had to play without knowing how many letters they needed to listen to actually identify a card when a poem was read out.

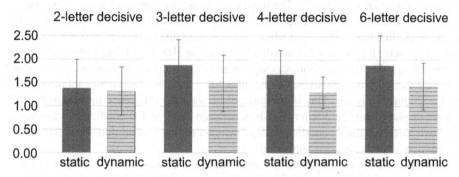

Fig. 7. Averages and ± standard deviations of time it takes to take a card. Blue: The novice group in the S condition. Orange: The novice group in the D condition. (Color figure online)

When participants touched an object in VR that mimics an audio player, the audio for reading a poem began to play. The reading was in the format specified in the rules of the All Japan Karuta Association. In this format, the second half of the previous poem was read out, and then the first half of the next poem was read out. In other words, you needed to listen to the first half of the poem and find the corresponding card on which the second half of the poem was written.

Results and Analysis. Figure 7 shows the average time and standard deviation to take a card in the S and D conditions for the novice group for each decisive letter category. Paired t-tests showed significant differences for the 3-, 4-, and 6-letter decisives ($p < 0.05$, and nonsignificant differences for the 2-letter decisives ($p = 0.812$). For the novice group, the overall average time in the D condition was 1.40 s with a standard deviation of 0.494, and for the experienced group, the average time in the C condition was 0.909

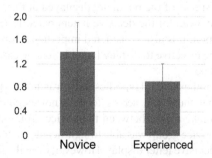

Fig. 8. Averages and ± standard deviations of time it takes to take a card. Left: novice group in condition D. Right: experienced group in condition C.

s with a standard deviation of 0.301 (Fig. 8). Note that obvious outliers were excluded from this analysis.

5.3 Discussion

First, we discuss hypothesis (1). The novice group did not remember most of the poem, but they were able to take the cards with the second half of the poem after listening only a part of the first half of the poem when the cards were displayed with decisive letters in the experiment. It indicates that a skill adjustment for HIK is possible with the decisive letter display. The D condition was significantly more effective than the S condition for 3-, 4-, and 6-letter decisives. On the other hand, there was no significant difference in the 2-letter decisives. This is presumably because the difference in the number of letters displayed for the 2-letter decisives between the S and D conditions was small, i.e., two letters for the S condition versus one letter for the D condition. From the above discussion, hypothesis (1) is supported.

In this experiment, we assumed a situation that all cards could be taken when the first letter was listened. It was an ideal situation in which the difference in the number of letters displayed in the D and S conditions was maximized and the difference in effectiveness was easily noticeable. However, this is still considered a realistic setting because this situation is often seen in many games when the number of cards remaining is small as the game progresses.

Note that in some cases, even with the 6-letter decisives, the D condition took longer than the S condition. Several participants commented that the more letters displayed, the more confident they could take the card, because they had more letters to compare with what they listened to identify the cards. For novice players who do not remember poems, it is presumed that they will hesitate to take cards when the number of letters displayed is small, since they can only use the display of a few decisive letters as a cue to identify the card. On the other hand, players who remember poems can be sure which poem is being read out by listening to the rest of the poem after the decisive letters.

To solve this problem, we propose the following new method of displaying decisive letters (Fig. 9). On the left is the S condition, in the middle is the D condition, and in the right is the new method: displaying the first six letters of a poem, highlighting its dynamic decisive letters. In this method, information about the decisive letters and information about the first half of the poem are displayed at the same time. We believe this allows the user to be aware of the decisive letters but still be able to take the card with confidence. In addition, it is also considered important to improve the legibility of the characters. It would be effective to display larger letters on cards placed at a distance to make them easier to read.

Next, we discuss hypothesis (2). Hypothesis (2) was not supported because it was subjectively observed that there still seems to be a non-negligible difference in the average times it takes to take a card between the novice group in D condition and the experienced group. The novice group was able to significantly reduce the time required to take a card by using the decisive letter display. However, even the assistance provided by the D condition, which has a stronger effect, did not fully compensate for the difference between novice players and experienced players. This may be due to other factors such

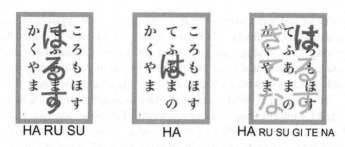

Fig. 9. Left: S-condition. Middle: D-condition. Right: proposed.

as differences in the speed of the physical action of taking a card, which is due to skill level. We believe that in addition to assistance in displaying the decisive letters, which can lead to significant time savings, other assistance could be provided to better adjust skills. For instance, the novice players may be able to close the skill gap by using the auditory assistance to begin listening to the poems earlier. If the average times for each player to take cards with various decisive letters are measured in advance and utilized, it may be possible to close the skill gap more accurately. Further study is needed on this respect. In addition, it would be necessary to investigate how effective and imperceptible the implemented adjustments are in actual game play by people with different levels of expertise.

6   Future Work

6.1   Application to Other Multiplayer Games

In order to achieve the mutually imperceptible skill adjustment in VR, it is important that skill adjustments have a small effect on the other players. This is because if the application of assistance has a side effect on the other players, it becomes difficult to set up assistance independently for each player. For instance, in table tennis, ball speed is one of the most important factors, and changing this for each player is effective as a technical adjustment. But if, for instance, the ball speed on the opponent's court is different from that on your own court, the players will easily perceive it, and furthermore, it will also be difficult to play because they will feel different from usual.

On the other hand, HIK using VR is a game in which the mutually imperceptible skill adjustment in VR can be realized relatively easily, because even though assistance is set unequally and asymmetrically for each player, each of them can only affect one of the players almost independently. By exploring other multiplayer games with similar characteristics to HIK, the findings of this study may be applied. By collecting such case studies, we hope to propose a design guideline for appropriate skill adjustments according to the characteristics of multiplayer games.

6.2   Skill Adjustments That are Imperceptible Even to the Adjusted Player

In this paper, we have discussed the imperceptible skill adjustment in VR mainly from the perspective of imperceptibility to the other players. However, if skills can be adjusted by altering visual or auditory information in a way that is imperceptible or less strange even to the adjusted player, this is an attractive option because it will reduce the feeling sorry for receiving the skill adjustment as well as the feeling of something strange. The auditory assistance implemented in our prototype, which changes the timing of the audio, is a type of skill adjustment with such characteristics. In visual assistance, for instance, adjusting the size of the card or hand in the VR space to an appropriate range may reduce the time required for unselfconsciously taking a card. This is because the task of taking a card in VR space can be modeled as a conventional pointing task in HCI, and thus task completion time reduction methods utilizing such as the implication of Fitts' law can be expected to apply.

6.3   Toward More Inclusive HIK

We intend to expand the range of assistance so that a diverse range of people can enjoy HIK games. In terms of accommodating disabilities, we believe that presenting auditory information such as reading out poems as visual information will make it possible to accommodate hearing impairments. Similarly, adjusting the colors in the VR space would be effective in assisting the visually challenged players. We also believe that it will be easier for international players to enjoy HIK games together by implementing multilingual support feature.

7   Conclusion

Toward making multiplayer games inclusive, we proposed the mutually imperceptible skill adjustment in VR, a skill adjustment that is difficult for players to perceive each other. We also prototyped a VR HIK system that implements the mutually imperceptible skill adjustment in VR to visual and auditory information. An evaluation experiment was conducted to verify whether the display of decisive letters, a type of visual information assistance, is effective for HIK novices and what would be a more effective display method. The results suggested that the decisive letter display can significantly reduce the time it takes novice players to take a card, and that the dynamic decisive display is more effective. Combining this with other assistance may enable novice players to perform at the similar level as experienced players. We would like to further investigate the imperceptible skill adjustment in VR assistance, and also consider making other multiplayer games more inclusive.

Acknowledgment. This research was partially supported by Exploratory IT Human Resources Project (MITOU Program) of Information-technology Promotion Agency, Japan (IPA) in 2023.

References

1. YURU SPORTS. https://yurusports.com/wp-content/uploads/2020/06/yurusports_english. pdf. Accessed 04 June 2023
2. Ohishi-Tengudo Corporation Homepage. https://www.tengudo.jp/100poems/competition/ 2528.html. Accessed 27 May 2023

3. Sato, K., Sano, Y., Otsuki, M., Oka, M., Kato, K.: Augmented recreational volleyball court: supporting the beginners' landing position prediction skill by providing peripheral visual feedback. In: Proceedings of the 10th Augmented Human International Conference 2019, pp. 1–9. Association for Computing Machinery, Reims, France (2019)

4. Wu, E., Koike, H.: FuturePose – mixed reality martial arts training using real-time 3D human pose forecasting with an RGB camera. In: 2019 IEEE Winter Conference on Applications of Computer Vision (WACV), pp. 1384–1392. IEEE, Waikoloa, HI, USA (2019)

5. Fujiwara, Y., Nakamura, S.: Testing a method of controlling online game advantage/disadvantage by color transformation considering color vision characteristics using Among us. In: Proceedings of Entertainment Computing Symposium, vol. 2022, pp. 120–128. IPSJ, Japan (2022). (in Japanese)

6. Maekawa, A., Kasahara, K., Saito, H., Uriu, D., Ganesh, G., Inami, M.: The tight game: implicit force intervention in interpersonal physical interactions on playing tug of war. In: SIGGRAPH '20 ACM SIGGRAPH 2020 Emerging Technologies, Article No.10, pp. 1–2. Association for Computing Machinery, New York, NY, USA (2020)

7. Suzuki, Y., Sakamoto, D., Ono, T., Suzuki.Y.: Gino.Aiki: MR software to support the mastery of aikido body movement. In: Proceedings of WISS2022. Japan Society for Software Science and Technology, Japan (2022). (in Japanese)

8. Masai, K., Kajiyama, T., Muramatsu, T., Sugimoto, M., Kimura, T.: Virtual reality sonification training system can improve a novice's forehand return of serve in tennis. In: 2022 IEEE International Symposium on Mixed and Augmented Reality Adjunct (ISMAR-Adjunct), pp. 845–849. IEEE, Singapore, Singapore (2022)

9. Wu, E., Piekenbrock, M., Nakumura, T., Koike, H.: SpinPong – virtual reality table tennis skill acquisition using visual, haptic and temporal cues. IEEE Trans. Visualization Comput. Graph., 2566–2576. IEEE (2021)

10. Adolf, J., Kán, P., Outram, B., Kaufmann, H., Doležal, J., Lhotská, L.: Juggling in VR: advantages of immersive virtual reality in juggling learning. In: 25th ACM Symposium on Virtual Reality Software and Technology (Parramatta, NSW, Australia) (VRST '19), pp. 1–5. Association for Computing Machinery, New York (2019)

11. Matsumoto, T., Wu, E., Koike, H.: Skiing, fast and slow: evaluation of time distortion for VR Ski training. In: Proceedings of the Augmented Humans International Conference 2022 (AHs '22), pp. 142–151. Association for Computing Machinery, New York (2022)

12. Löchtefeld, M., Krüger, A., Gellersen, H.: DeceptiBike: assessing the perception of speed deception in a virtual reality training bike system. In: Proceedings of the 9th Nordic Conference on Human-Computer Interaction (Gothenburg, Sweden) (NordiCHI '16). Article40, pp. 1–10. Association for Computing Machinery, NewYork (2016)

13. Ogawa, N., Ban, Y., Sakurai, S., Narumi, T., Tanikawa, T., Hirose, M.: Metamorphosis hand: dynamically transforming hands. In: Proceedings of the 7th Augmented Human International Conference, pp. 1–2. Association for Computing Machinery, New York (2016)

14. Sun, H., Shibata, F., Kimura, A.: Analysis of factors inducing upper limb elongation sensation in virtual reality. In: HCI IPSJ SIG Technical Reports, 2018.22, pp. 1–6. IPSJ, Tokyo Japan (2018). (in Japanese)

15. Ebisu, A., Hashizume, S., Suzuki, K., Ishii, A., Sakashita, M., Ochiai, Y.: Stimulated percussions: method to control human for learning music by using electrical muscle stimulation. In: Proceedings of the 8th Augmented Human International Conference (AH '17), Article 33, pp. 1–5. Association for Computing Machinery, New York (2017)

16. Kitagawa, R., Itoh, T.: In: Visualization of the motion of swiping Karuta. In: HCI IPSJ SIG Technical Reports, pp. 1–7. IPSJ, Tokyo Japan (2022)

17. Yamada, H., Murao, K., Terada, T., Tsukamoto, M.: Estimation method of the timing to take a card using wrist movement in Kyogi Karuta. In: Proceedings of Interaction 2015, pp. 969–971. IPSJ, Tokyo, Japan (2015)

18. Tomaru, Y., Fujioka, Y., Yasumoto, M., Hada, H., Ohta, T.: Interactive content for arranging competitive karuta cards. In: Proceedings of the 75th National Convention of IPSJ, pp. 255–256. IPSJ, Tokyo, Japan (2013). (in Japanese)
19. Matsuda, T.: Statistical Analysis of Decisive Letters in Competitive Karuta. In: Japanese journal of applied statistics 49.1, pp. 1–11. Japanese Society of Applied Statistics, Japan (2020). (in Japanese)
20. Takeda, S., Hasegawa, Y., Tsukui, T., Kiryu, S.: Psycho-acoustical measurement of timings of target-card recognition by Hyakunin-Isshu Karuta-Game Players and Estimation of Acoustic Cues. In: IEICE technical report, vol. 114, pp.141–146. IEICE, Japan (2015)
21. Tokushima, C., Soga, M.: Development of a simulation support system for changing decision character during playing Japanese poem card game. In: Proceedings of the 32nd Annual Conference of the Japanese Society for Artificial Intelligence, The Japanese Society for Artificial Intelligence, Tokyo, Japan (2018)

Design of Collaborative Learning Experience with AR–AR Collaboration Game for Children at Museum

Kihiro Tokuno[1(✉)], Ryohei Egusa[2], Fusako Kusunoki[1], and Shigenori Inagaki[3]

[1] Tama Art University, Hachioji, Tokyo, Japan
32247007@stdt.tamabi.ac.jp, kusunoki@tamabi.ac.jp
[2] Chiba University of Commerce, Ichikawa, Chiba, Japan
egusa@cuc.ac.jp
[3] Rikkyo University, Toshima, Tokyo, Japan
inagakis@rikkyo.ac.jp

Abstract. We are currently developing an AR–AR collaboration game to support children's learning in museums. This system provides an AR–AR collaboration experience between multiple mobile PC devices for a collaborative exhibition viewing experience through joint physical actions in the game. A prototype of an exploration game for one person using physical actions that can be played on a mobile PC device has been developed as the first stage of our project. We evaluated the operability of the physical actions and the appropriateness of the gameplay style for child visitors in a preliminary experiment. On this basis, we developed an AR–AR collaboration game that can be played by two people using joint physical actions. This paper describes the preliminary experiments, evaluation results, and current system.

Keywords: Augmented Reality · AR–AR Collaboration · Gamification

1 Introduction

Informal learning, such as that in museums, is learning that takes place according to the learner's interests and choices [5], and is important for children's development. It includes hands-on activities such as exploring, touching, listening, watching, physically moving, and disassembling and reassembling objects freely following the children's interests and curiosity [3]. Furthermore, physical activities have been shown to yield higher learning outcomes than non-physical learning [18]. However, as opposed to traditional classrooms [1], such experiences are difficult to provide in schools. Therefore, museums play an important role as a venue for children's growth in the public space.

Social interaction is important to encourage children to learn among one another. Children's learning in a museum takes place in a social context. Visitors use one another for information, shared beliefs, and meaning construction [7]. It has been shown that the facilitation of in-group conversations significantly enhances user learning in the museum

© IFIP International Federation for Information Processing 2023
Published by Springer Nature Switzerland AG 2023
P. Ciancarini et al. (Eds.): ICEC 2023, LNCS 14455, pp. 231–240, 2023.
https://doi.org/10.1007/978-981-99-8248-6_19

experience [10]. Therefore, in addition to the learning support between the exhibition and visitor, further learning effects can be expected by providing learning support among visitors in the form of informal learning.

A system that combines augmented reality (AR) technology and cooperation can be developed to promote social interaction on mobile terminals. The system will support children's learning in museums by making exhibition observation in social groups more attractive. Collaboration has been discussed as a means of increasing engagement in immersive content, including AR [16]. Joint action can be viewed as any form of social interaction in which two or more individuals orchestrate their actions in space and through time, resulting in a change to their learning environment [14]. Hence, joint action is an element of collaborative activities. In this paper, we present a cooperative learning system based on AR–AR collaboration using several different mobile terminals.

2   Related Work

2.1   Digital Technology Supporting Museums

The proliferation of mobile PC devices in recent years has made it possible for anyone to access digital information with ease. The development of mobile PC devices has optimized AR technology for gaming [13]. Unlike virtual reality, AR does not fully separate the user from the real environment, but rather, combines virtual elements into a three-dimensional physical reality.

AR technology can support learning experiences in museums. Following the concept of object-centered learning, children's learning from their interactions with displayed exhibits is a characteristic feature of museum education [12]. AR can visualize information in the form of literal overlays on physical exhibits. In fact, AR can visualize historical events relating to a place, the situation in the past, and even the future situation [2]. The addition of digital information to exhibits that are difficult to understand using AR technology can improve the effectiveness of learning in museums [11]. Thus, a learning support system that combines AR and gamification is a valuable method in the context of learning in a museum.

2.2   AR as a Tool for Socialization

ICT technology, particularly through the use of mobile PC devices, is a powerful tool for enhancing individual experiences in museums. However, designing mobile-based cultural experiences that effectively facilitate the visitor–exhibit and visitor–visitor interactions is a challenging task [10].

The AR mobile experience, which is based on a single screen per person holding a mobile PC device with both hands and positioning it over the exhibition, suppresses opportunities for natural social interactions among visitors. Therefore, we propose the support of learning in a social group by making the AR experience collaborative among visitors through wireless connections among multiple mobile PC devices, and by integrating physical joint actions that visitors must perform while holding their mobile PC devices during the game.

3 Approach

We are developing a system to support children's collaborative learning using mobile PC devices and AR technology to provide support for observing exhibitions in the context of informal learning in a museum as a public space. As the first stage of the project, we have developed a prototype of a one-player game that integrates physical actions by tilting the tablet and enables exploration through the exhibit, and evaluated it in a preliminary experiment. Based on the results, we designed and implemented a prototype of a two-player AR–AR collaboration game.

In this paper, we first describe the design and validation of the game format and gesture interaction. Subsequently, we outline the design process of an AR–AR collaboration game for two or more mobile PC tablets.

4 Preliminary Experiment

We conducted a workshop to evaluate the validity of the tablet tilt control and gameplay style. We developed and implemented the tablet tilt control as a physical action that can be performed while the user holds the device. We evaluated the tablet tilt control based on the results of a questionnaire that was collected from a workshop for one person in front of a museum exhibit. We designed the system without adding AR and wireless connection functions in the preliminary experiments to assess the validity of the tilt control.

4.1 Context

Geological formations are one type of exhibit that require AR and gamification to motivate visitors. It is difficult for children to engage with exhibits based on their appearance alone because the background and history of the exhibits are also important [8]. However, many geological contents are inherently unobservable owing to the scale of time and space, and observation is extremely complicated and difficult for children to understand [17]. Although museums have also established creative panels, as illustrated in Fig. 1, it is quite unlikely that children will acquire such information simply by looking at the geological exhibits.

Fig. 1. Left: Geo-layer in Fukuoka City Museum. Middle: Dolphin bones possibly used for ritual ceremony. Right: Dog bone presumably eaten and thrown away by Fukuoka natives.

4.2 Physical Action Interaction Design

It is important to provide an experience that is not unfamiliar to the user when considering physical interactions for AR experiences. The tilting of a smartphone device has not been examined extensively despite the fact that it is an action that is often observed in daily life [6]. Given the nature of the AR mobile experience, which is generally performed by holding the device with both hands and holding it up to the display, the interaction of touching the screen would require the user to perform an unnatural movement. Therefore, in this preliminary experiment, we adopted the tablet tilt control as a physical action as shown in Fig. 2, and we evaluated its validity and the implementation area.

Fig. 2. Left: Tilt control. Middle: All artifacts are simplified and placed according to the geo-layer exhibit. Right: Using tilt interaction to control the character.

4.3 Exploration Game Design

Imagination is an essential part of children's learning behavior [4]. In particular, imaginative play is important for children's development [19]. Children's imagination is critical for their understanding of exhibits that are described by abstract concepts such as geological layers. Therefore, we selected a gameplay that allows children to explore freely in a manner that stimulates their imagination.

As illustrated in Fig. 3, the game was designed in the form of an exploration game in which a light-emitting character navigates through the gloomy world of geological layers using the tablet tilt control. The player starts at the lowest level of the layer and climbs up to the next stage to clear the game successfully. The locations of the artifacts on the layer and digital objects that are displayed in the world stage correspond to one another, and the player can visualize the contents of the layer as he or she progresses through the game.

Fig. 3. Screen captures of game play. The glowing green character in the middle must move through digitalized geo-layers. A: Burning fields of a war scene. B: Bowls and dishes. C: Bones thrown away.

4.4 Experiment

Participants

We recruited visitors of Fukuoka city visitors. Informed consent was obtained from the participants and their parents before the study took place. The children were informed in advance of the experiment and the data collection process, and their participation in the study was completely voluntary. The children had the option of stopping the experiment or withdrawing their consent for data collection at their own will.

Twenty-four students (17 boys and 7 girls), ranging from the first grade of elementary school to the second grade of high school, participated in the workshop. The participants were visitors to the Fukuoka City Museum. The experience of each participant was approximately 20 min. As shown in Fig. 4, the data from the questionnaire survey were collected from the participants immediately following the experience.

Fig. 4. Left: Game screen from experiment. Middle: Visitor participant playing the game. Right: Visitor answering the questionnaire.

Results of Preliminary Experiment. The results of the questionnaire are presented in Fig. 5. The results demonstrate that positive responses were dominant in all except two items. As positive responses were significantly favored for the questions "Was the game fun?" with 95.8%, "Was the game easy to understand?" with 95.8%, "Would you like to play more?" with 95.8%, and "Did you feel a sense of accomplishment?" with 95.8%, we believe that the exploration game using the tilt control was enjoyable and comfortable for the participants. The responses to the question "Does your body feel tired?" was also positive with 87.5%, indicating that the participants did not feel fatigue from the tablet tilt control, regardless of the experience time of approximately 20 min; therefore, little discomfort was experienced with the tablet tilt control.

The questions for which no significant difference was observed were "Does your mind feel tired?" with 58.3% and "Was the character easy to control?" with 62.5%. Both are considered to be owing to the complexity of the game, which requires precise movement and manipulation of the character, although the tablet tilt control itself was simple. Considering that the participants felt that the exploration experience was entertaining, we believe that the process of exploration should be made simpler and more intuitive. Therefore, the gameplay itself was modified to a simpler and more intuitive form of interaction, while the exploratory game format and tablet tilt control were incorporated into the AR–AR collaboration game.

Conclusions of Preliminary Experiment. In this preliminary experiment, we evaluated the validity of the tablet tilting control, the method of its incorporation into the game, and the gameplay style. The questionnaire results demonstrated that the simple physical

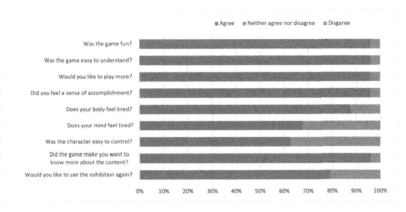

Fig. 5. Questionnaire results from preliminary experiment.

control for tilting the mobile device was effective and not stressful for the users. The exploration style of the gameplay was also found to be effective, but too much precision in terms of control increases the burden on the user.

5   Design Exploration

5.1   Overview

We developed an AR–AR collaboration game based on our preliminary experiments. The results showed that although the exploration experience itself and tablet tilt control were favored, simpler gameplay was required. Therefore, we made significant modifications to the core framework of the game, while retaining the main concept of searching for hidden objects by illuminating the darkness, to create a more direct intuitive exploration experience. The gameplay concept is depicted in Fig. 6 and a flowchart of the designed gameplay is presented in Fig. 7.

Fig. 6.   Process of AR collaboration game.

5.2   AR–AR Collaboration User Interface Design

The sharing of interests supports collaborative learning. It is important to create visitor–exhibit interactions as well as visitor–visitor interactions. Grinter et al. facilitated the collaboration of visitors by allowing visitors to eavesdrop on the audio guides of others

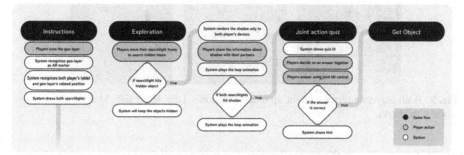

Fig. 7. System flow of AR collaboration game.

[9]. Sung et al. demonstrated that sharing the gaze direction can promote cooperation [15]. It is preferable to visualize and share the points of interest to which visitors pay attention to induce interaction. Hence, in this game, the aim is to share the attention of interest through AR–AR collaboration with wireless connections. For this purpose, we designed and implemented the searchlight user interface (UI) shown in Fig. 8, which is inspired by the act of searching for a hidden object by illuminating the darkness with light.

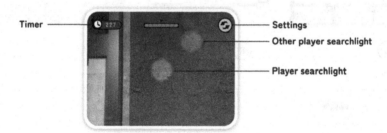

Fig. 8. User interface of AR collaboration game. The green light is the player's searchlight and the red light is the other player's searchlight.

5.3 Exploration Design

The contents of the geological layer exhibition are not directly visualized by AR, but are represented as shadows that are projected by the AR searchlight, as illustrated in Fig. 9. Both visitors need to understand the movement of the shadows and to shine a searchlight on the shadows to catch the shadows. The shadows were selected from a total of 11 artifacts presented by experts, and a total of 6 shadows were selected as important to exhibit the story.

5.4 Quiz UI Design

For this situation, which provides an opportunity to acquire knowledge directly, we used a simple three-choice quiz. The quiz must be answered by two participants simultaneously

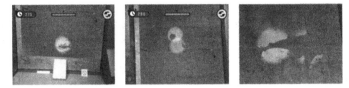

Fig. 9. Both players attempt to light up hidden shadows. Left: River fish. Middle: Clam shells. Right: Sea sharks.

tilting their devices in the same direction to promote collaborative actions. Both users tilt the device to the left to answer the left question, both users tilt the device to the front to answer the middle question, and both users tilt the device to the right to answer the right question. As indicated in Fig. 10, after the acquisition effect is displayed for correct answers, the description of the object is displayed.

Fig. 10. Quiz UI of AR collaboration game. A: Quiz UI. B: Transition when answered. C: Transition when answered correctly. D, E: Correct answer animation. F: Information of the discovered object.

6   Conclusions and Future Work

We developed an AR–AR collaboration game with the aim of supporting collaborative learning in a museum. We described the current limitations of visitor–visitor experience design owing to the restraints of physical actions in mobile experiences. From the results of a preliminary experiment that was conducted with visitors to examine the physical actions in mobile PC device experiences, we concluded that the tilt control of the tablet is adequate, but a more intuitive and simpler gameplay style would be appropriate. Based on the results, we designed a searchlight UI for an AR–AR collaborative game and developed a prototype that uses the tilt control as a joint action in a quiz-answering scenario. We designed the UI expression to share the attention of visitors, and further modified the game to be intuitive and easy to control in an exploratory manner.

In future studies, it will be necessary to evaluate the effectiveness of the developed game. Therefore, we will examine the appropriateness of the AR–AR UI design for encouraging cooperation among visitors, using a questionnaire for the affective aspect and an eye-tracking system for the objective aspect.

Acknowledgements. This work was supported by JSPS KAKENHI (Grant Numbers 22H00078 and 22H01068). The evaluation experiment was supported by The Fukuoka City Museum and Museum of Nature and Human Activities, Hyogo.

References

1. Andre, L., Durksen, T., Volman, M.L.: Museums as avenues of learning for children: a decade of research. Learn. Environ. Res. **20**, 47–76 (2017). https://doi.org/10.1007/s10984-016-9222-9
2. Azuma, R., Baillot, Y., Behringer, R., Feiner, S., Julier, S., MacIntyre, B.: Recent advances in augmented reality. IEEE Comput. Graphics Appl. **21**(6), 34–47 (2001). https://doi.org/10.1109/38.963459
3. Behrendt, M., Franklin, T.: A review of research on school field trips and their value in education. Int. J. Environ. Sci. Educ. **9**, 235–245 (2014). https://doi.org/10.12973/ijese.2014.213a
4. Caiman, C., Lundegård, I.: Young children's imagination in science education and education for sustainability. Cult. Sci. Edu. **13**, 687–705 (2018). https://doi.org/10.1007/s11422-017-9811-7
5. Callanan, M., Cervantes, C., Loomis, M.: Informal learning. WIREs Cogn. Sci. **2**(6), 646–655 (2011). https://doi.org/10.1002/wcs.143
6. Chang, Y., L'Yi, S., Koh, K., Seo, J.: Understanding users' touch behavior on large mobile touch-screens and assisted targeting by tilting gesture. In: Proceedings of the 33rd Annual ACM Conference on Human Factors in Computing Systems (CHI 2015), pp. 1499–1508. Association for Computing Machinery, New York, NY, USA (2015). https://doi.org/10.1145/2702123.2702425
7. Falk, J.: The director's cut: toward an improved understanding of learning from museums. Sci. Educ. **88**(S1), S83–S96 (2004). https://doi.org/10.1002/sce.20014
8. Van Gerven, D., Land-Zandstra, A., Damsma, W.: Authenticity matters: children look beyond appearances in their appreciation of museum objects. Int. J. Sci. Educ. Part B **8**(4), 325–339 (2018). https://doi.org/10.1080/21548455.2018.1497218
9. Grinter, R.E., Aoki, M.P., Szymanski, H.M., Thornton, D.J., Woodruff, A., Hurst, A.: Revisiting the visit: understanding how technology can shape the museum visit. In: Proceedings of the 2002 ACM Conference on Computer Supported Cooperative Work (CSCW 2002), pp. 146–155. Association for Computing Machinery, New York, NY, USA (2002). https://doi.org/10.1145/587078.587100
10. Katifori, A., et al.: Cultivating mobile-mediated social interaction in the museum: towards group-based digital storytelling experiences. In: Annual Conference of Museums and the Web (MW 2016), Los Angeles, CA, USA (2016)
11. Moorhouse, N., tom Dieck, M.C., Jung, T.: An experiential view to children learning in museums with augmented reality. Mus. Manag. Curatorship **34**(4), 402–418 (2019). https://doi.org/10.1080/09647775.2019.1578991

12. Paris, S.G.: Perspectives on Object-Centered Learning. Museums. 1st edn. Routledge (2002). https://www.routledge.com/Perspectives-on-Object-Centered-Learning-in-Museums/Paris/p/book/9780805839272
13. Queiroz, A.C.M., Tori, R., Nascimento, A.M., Leme, M.I.D.S.: Augmented and virtual reality in education: the role of Brazilian research groups. In: 20th Symposium on Virtual and Augmented Reality (SVR), pp. 170–175, Foz do Iguacu, Brazil (2018). https://doi.org/10.1109/SVR.2018.00034
14. Sebanz, N., Bekkering, H., Knoblich, G.: Joint action: bodies and minds moving together. Trends Cogn. Sci. 10(2), 70–76 (2006). https://doi.org/10.1016/j.tics.2005.12.009
15. Sung, G., Feng, T., Schneider, B.: Learn more and instructors track better with real-time gaze sharing. Proc. ACM Hum. Comput. Interact. 5(CSCW1), 1–23 (2021). Article 134. https://doi.org/10.1145/3449208
16. Tan, J.T.C., Mizuchi, Y., Hagiwara, Y., Inamura, T.: Representation of embodied collaboration behaviors in cyber-physical human-robot interaction with immersive user interfaces. In: Companion of the 2018 ACM/IEEE International Conference on Human-Robot Interaction, pp. 251–252. Association for Computing Machinery, New York, NY, USA (2018). https://doi.org/10.1145/3173386.3176993
17. Trend, R.: An investigation into understanding of geological time among 10- and 11-year old children. Int. J. Sci. Educ. 20(8), 973–988 (1998). https://doi.org/10.1080/0950069980200805
18. Vazou, V., Pesce, C., Lakes, K., Smiley-Oyen., A.: More than one road leads to Rome: a narrative review and meta-analysis of physical activity intervention effects on cognition in youth. Int. J. Sport Exerc. Psychol. 17(2), 153–178 (2019). https://doi.org/10.1080/1612197X.2016.1223423
19. Whitebread, D., et al.: The role of play in children's development: a review of the evidence (research summary). The LEGO Foundation, DK (2017). https://doi.org/10.13140/RG.2.2.18500.73606

Unity-VRlines: Towards a Modular eXtended Reality Unity Flight Simulator

Giuseppe Di Maria[1], Lorenzo Stacchio[2], and Gustavo Marfia[3]

[1] University of Bologna, Department of Computer Science and Engineering,
Bologna, Italy
giuseppe.dimaria2@studio.unibo.it
[2] University of Bologna, Department for Life Quality Studies, Bologna, Italy
lorenzo.stacchio2@unibo.it
[3] University of Bologna, Department of the Arts, Bologna, Italy
gustavo.marfia@unibo.it

Abstract. Computer-aided flight simulation systems (CAFSS) make it possible to simulate flying an airplane using software and hardware. These simulations range from simple programs to intricate, full-motion simulators that often integrate physical feedback and visual clues to create realistic and affordable entertainment and pilot training. Nowadays, eXtended Reality (XR) paradigms have been integrated in CAFSS, to increase the immersiveness and realism of the experience, demonstrating positive cognitive learning effects in training procedures. However, no extensive results for simulator effectiveness are available to this date, considering the reach of such systems is limited by the costly hardware and unavailability of open-source software. For this reason, we here introduce Unity-VRlines, an open-source modular virtual reality flight simulator baseline, based on the Unity game engine and the SteamVR SDK, that can be deployed in any compatible VR device. The system components and software architecture enables developers to add new flight control instructions, alter aircraft parts, and change the surrounding environment.

Keywords: eXtended Reality · Flight simulator · Open source

1 Introduction

Computer-aided flight simulation systems (CAFSS) refers to the set of technologies that allows one to emulate the experience of flying an aircraft using software/hardware-based simulation to replicate the actions, environment, and dynamics of piloting an actual plane. Flight simulations range from entry-level programs to complex, full-motion simulators, often adopted for low-cost pilot training in the aviation industry. These simulations can also include visual and audio cues, as well as physical feedback, to create a realistic environment that

Maria Di, G and Stacchio, L—These authors should be considered as joint first authors.

© IFIP International Federation for Information Processing 2023
Published by Springer Nature Switzerland AG 2023
P. Ciancarini et al. (Eds.): ICEC 2023, LNCS 14455, pp. 241–250, 2023.
https://doi.org/10.1007/978-981-99-8248-6_20

mimics the sensations of flying [1,2,16,23]. This means that the simulator must incorporate various equations and models related to aircraft performance, such as how the aircraft flies, how the flight controls respond, and how the aircraft reacts to external factors like gravity, air density, turbulence, damping, and so on. By including these elements, the simulator can provide a realistic experience that closely mirrors actual flight conditions.

In this context, one of the disruptive technologies which are nowadays employed to increase realism and the immersiveness of the experience is eXtended Reality (XR) [7]. In particular, the gaming and training industry has been using XR to empower CAFSS, mostly in commercial sectors, with an emphasis on Virtual Reality (VR) [7]. The injection of VR paradigms in CAFSS, resulted in positive cognitive learning outcomes, paving the way to VR extensions in education and training [4,7,14,21]. Virtual Reality Flight Simulation Systems (VRFSS) become a new and important tool for companies since they may help reduce costs, save implementation time, and improve accessibility to training contexts [7].

Despite this interest, the limited hardware and the lack of open-source software have hindered the ability to carry out extended analyses of the effectiveness of such simulators [7]. Indeed, the most relevant works published in literature take advantage of already existing commercial solutions to implement flight simulators, either providing low-quality graphics or not using realistic 3D environments in the simulation [7,16,18,22]. Moreover, existing CAFSS are hard to extend, not providing a modular approach for the environment and its dynamics (e.g., simulate a particular training situation) [7].

For these reasons, we introduce Unity-VRlines[1][2], a modular VRFSS based on the Unity game engine and the SteamVR SDK, that can be experienced using any compatible VR device (e.g., HTC-Vive, Meta Oculus Quest). Different from similar works, Unity-VRlines provides an immersive open-source experience for both flight simulations and plane cockpit control which also includes the chance to easily adapt a novel 3D aircraft model and surrounding environment. In particular, developers can easily add new flight control commands, customize the aircraft components, integrate different training scenarios (e.g., resource shortage), and change the surrounding environment. In our implementation, we provide a VR command mapping for the HTC VIVE, but it could also be easily deployed on different VR headsets (e.g., Varjo XR-3, Meta Oculus Quest 2).

2   Related Works

Some works in the literature designed and implemented flight simulators, but just a few have exploited virtual reality technologies to provide an immersive experience [7,9,12,18,22].

Authors of [22] introduced a VRFSS for mobile devices (i.e., android smartphones) exploiting the Unity game Engine and adopting a Samsung Galaxy Gear

---

[1] The source code is available at *https://github.com/giuseppdimaria/Unity-VRlines*.

[2] A video demo of the experience is available at *https://youtu.be/YtbWemils_s*.

VR for stereoscopic rendering and a gamepad to control the movement direction of the aircraft. They defined the 3D aircraft model and a fixed 3D environment, also providing a system to compute the equations of motion, involving the individuation of aerodynamic coefficients used to calculate aerodynamic forces and moments and to obtain body frame linear velocities and rates. Despite this cheap alternative to classical VRFSS, the provided experience does not take full advantage of VR interactions and adopts low-quality 3D models, with a consequent limitation of realism. In addition, both the aircraft and the environment are fixed and no modular approach is provided for their customization.

Aerofly FS 4 [12] provides a more dynamic commercial alternative, exposing a realistic VR experience with 21 highly detailed aircraft and interactive 3D cockpits integrated with state-of-the-art real-time flight physics with dynamic computations for airfoil lift, drag, and moment based on flap, slat and spoiler positions, propeller wash, ground effect, and wing down-wash. The system includes more than 1,200 custom-modeled airports and high-resolution aerial images. Finally, they furnish VR support for both Oculus Rift and HTC VIVE controllers. The realism provided by the system is consistent with state-of-the-art products, however, the system is not open-source and, to the best of our knowledge, appears not extensible.

Authors of [18] provided instead an implementation of a collaborative VRFSS including a virtual/physical cockpit connected to commercially available flight simulation software. They implemented several systems to interact with the cockpit such as fully virtual collision detection, a haptic-based one, and interactive hardware elements. In particular, they tested a fully-virtual system by subjecting users to a system management task completion trial while flying the aircraft. The reported completion results demonstrate the effectiveness of the system. However, the introduced system relies on a professional and commercial flight simulator making the 3D environment hardly customizable.

On a similar line, Loft Dynamics introduced the first VRFSS systems approved by The European Union Aviation Safety Agency [9,10]. This VRFSS implements a mixed reality experience for Varjo Aero with a 6DoF Motion System where a user can freely fly a professional plane over different landscapes and weather scenarios. The authors also provided a full replica of the physical cockpit and chair, superimposed with virtual elements in the user's view thanks to their Pose Training System. The user interacts with physical elements while manipulating their virtual counterparts. This aspect, along with chair motion and seat fidelity, increases the level of training realism. However, the system is not free and not open-source.

Finally, to the best of our knowledge, this is the first work designed and implemented as a Unity-based VRFSS exploiting only freeware and open-source tools.

3   System Architecture and Implementation

Unity-VRlines is a VRFSS developed with the Unity Game Engine and SteamVR SDK. The SteamVR SDK allows for defining immersive virtual experience by providing out-of-the-box tracking and interaction systems for all the VR head-sets that support it (e.g., Varjo XR-3, HTC VIVE, Oculus Quest). Unity-VRlines interactions rely completely on the SteamVR SDK. The virtual experience con-sists of a client-only application: the entire experience is contained and executed on the client device (i.e., desktop computer).

Unity-VRlines exploits out-of-the-box libraries to define and manage both the Aircraft flight logic and the surrounding environment. Figure 1 depicts an abstraction of the system architecture and all its components. In practice, the Unity Game renders the aircraft along with its flight simulation logic and inter-action components along with a custom 3D environment. The latter is built on top of several freeware/open-source tools (detail can be found in Sect. 3.1).

The user interactions can be easily adapted with Steam VR-compatible head-sets. In our case, we adopted an HTC VIVE headset as hardware interface [3].

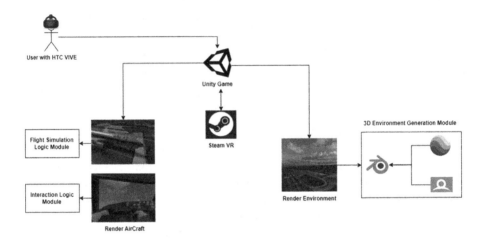

Fig. 1. Unity-VRlines System Architecture

3.1   Aircraft and Environment

For both the Aircraft and the Cockpit, we select an existing aircraft template from the Jet Strike [6] package of the Element3D (E3D) plugin of Adobe After Effects [5,20]. E3D allows to design and create high-quality 3D models, also starting from already existing ones. In the selected 3D model, the cockpit was also included. We then customized and exported the 3D model in a format compatible with Unity (i.e., obj). Figure 2 depicts the 3D model of the Aircraft and the inner cockpit in the Unity Editor.

To guarantee a realistic immersive experience, not only the aircraft but also the surrounding environment should consist in high-quality 3D models that resemble reality. To reach such a result, we exploit RenderDoc to capture the 3D

Fig. 2. 3D model of the Aircraft and Cockpit.

view of the Bologna airport provided by Google Earth [8]. The model was then adapted with Blender, to generate both the mesh and the texture to correctly render the model in the Unity simulation. Figure 3 depicts the final environment. This approach is modular by construction: changing the scenario, means using RenderDoc in a different area and following the aforementioned Blender pipeline.

Fig. 3. 3D environment of the Bologna Airport.

3.2   Flight Physics

As aforementioned, the Unity experience allows interaction with the aircraft with the SteamVR SDK and provides a simple yet functional flight physics management system, to provide the user with an as realistic as possible simulation. To understand how to model a consistent flight physics simulation, we need to correctly define the structure of a plane which mainly consists of three components: the fuselage, wings, and tail.

Each part of the aircraft has its own specific function in thrust generation, stability, maneuverability, and drag reduction. For this reason, it is important to analyze the aerodynamic characteristics of each part of the aircraft and how these combine to achieve the desired flight behavior.

To model these components in Unity, we defined custom RigidBodies per each to let them be included in the calculation made by the Unity Physics Engine [17].

In particular, the Drag and Angular Drag fields are set to zero, as these control the air resistance on the rigid body of the aircraft and the rotation resistance of the aircraft respectively, which are customized in our implementation.

The Aircraft Physics component then applies the aerodynamic forces and thrust to the RigidBodies by exposing a field for the thrust force and a list of Aircraft Surfaces. The total force and moment are calculated as the sum of the actions of the individual Aereo Surfaces, thus the separate parts of the aircraft. These Aereo Surfaces represent the surfaces of the aircraft that interact with the air, such as the wings and tail. Figure 4 depicts the different Aereo Surfaces of the aircraft.

Fig. 4. Aircraft Mesh and corresponding Aereo Surfaces.

Each individual Aereo Surfaces are represented by blue rectangles on the aircraft mesh and provide a custom component that contains the aerodynamic parameters that follow: (a) The lift slope refers to the slope angle of the lift coefficient in a low angle of attack mode. It describes how the lift coefficient changes with respect to the angle of attack; (b) Skin friction determines the amount of drag generated by the surface due to friction. It accounts for the drag created by the surface in addition to the drag caused by the lift; (c) The zero lift angle of attack, on the other hand, is the angle at which the surface creates zero lift. At this particular angle, the lift generated by the surface is neutralized; (d) The stall angle high/low signifies the angles of attack at which the stall begins. The stall occurs when the airflow over the surface becomes separated and results in a sudden loss of lift; (e) The chord represents the average length of the surface from its leading edge to its trailing edge. It is an essential parameter in determining the aerodynamic characteristics of the surface; (f) The flap fraction indicates the extent to which the surface can be moved as a control surface. In our implementation, it is shown as an orange region in the Unity Editor, and it allows control over the aerodynamic forces acting on the surface; (g) The span refers to the length of the surface from one end to the other. It provides an indication of the overall size of the surface; (h) Lastly, the aspect ratio is the ratio of the span to the chord. It can be automatically calculated using the chord and span values, or set manually for surfaces that are part of a longer structure.

The third component is the Aircraft Controller, which interacts with the Aircraft Physics and the Aereo Surfaces to apply the input controls. Moreover, additional custom colliders were defined in order to exploit physical phenomena like friction fields for wheels to implement the braking, used in landing, exploiting the already existing Unity physics engine.

All of these components provide a modular aspect: changing an aircraft model means adapting all the objects and the parameters described above to have a working system. Our implementation is mostly based on the guidelines provided in [13] and the baseline furnished by [19]. As a final detail, we do not simulate turbulence.

3.3 Flight Simulation

The Flight Simulation involves the user continuously interacting with available commands to control the plane. As mentioned earlier, all user interactions with the immersive environment rely on the SteamVR SDK. The SteamVR provides an out-of-the-box interaction system.

In particular, the Player asset offers a basic configuration to create a VR experience. It includes various elements, such as a controller for the hands, a camera for the player's point of view, and a component to manage the player's tracking. SteamVR also furnishes logical components to define teleporting points around the virtual world and interaction between the player and objects exploiting hand controllers. In our experience, all the user's interactions are codified using inputs from the hand controllers.

When the simulations start, the user finds himself in the plane cockpit. He can explore taking advantage of the 6DoF tracking provided by the SteamVR tracking system. When the user decides to start the flight, she/he must use the associated command to start increasing the velocity by simulating a "thrust" to counteract the initially set drag. Each usage corresponds to an increase in the velocity rate of 10 km/h. When the velocity approaches 40 km/h, based on our Aero Surfaces positioning and aerodynamics parameters chosen, the generated lift allows to take-off of the aircraft. After the aircraft takes off, the user can easily turn the aircraft by using the commands associated to modify the value of the yaw, pitch, and roll-axis using the controller pad. The user is supported in this process with a live and dynamic tutorial that guides the user in the aircraft departure (Fig. 5).

Whenever the user decides to land, s/he decreases the thrust value in order to reach a velocity that could avoid the plane to crash when touching the ground. Approaching the ground, the plane wheels will collide with it and the user will be able to pull the brakes. At any moment of the simulation, the user could switch between the first-person camera view and an external view of the plane, which is set according to the player's position. Figure 6 depicts the user's view while flying the plane from the first-person perspective and the external camera.

Fig. 5. Unity-VRlines Flight Simulation: tutorial for guiding the user in the aircraft departure.

Fig. 6. Unity-VRlines Flight Simulation: view from the cockpit and with an external camera.

When the user decides to land, he starts bracketing the aircraft and turns the plane towards the ground. Approaching the ground, the aircraft wheels come out, allowing the plane to stop. In this particular step, and also during the departure, we provide a simple animation for opening and closing the aircraft wheel bogie.

4   Conclusions and Future Works

In this work, we introduced Unity-VRlines, a modular flight simulator for Unity. Our simulator provides a basic parametrized physical flight simulation system along with a modular approach for generating a 3D environment and adapting all the AereoSurfaces for different aircraft 3D models. Differently from existing works in the literature, Unity-VRlines is built to easily customize both the environment and the Aircraft and provides a base code for extending the immersive experience in different contexts (e.g., simulate incidents, supply shortage). For future works, we plan to: (a) create the virtual counterparts of all the functionalities provided in a real cockpit; (b) provide basic real-life training scenarios; (c) improve the modularity of Unity-VRlines by including a procedural approach for environment generation; (d) predict the aerodynamical parameters of all the components based on the aircraft structure. Concerning (a) we plan to integrate a Real Sim Gear [11] hardware interface and haptic gloves (such as Manus VR [15]) to integrate novel aircraft control and increase the realism. For (b) instead, we aim at defining environmental scenarios for training situations such as supply shortages, rescue missions, and severe weather. Finally, to evaluate the efficacy of our immersive experience and also to get new insights for the development of future immersive training systems, we will design and conduct a user study with a diverse set of participants.

References

1. Baarspul, M.: A review of flight simulation techniques. Prog. Aerosp. Sci. **27**(1), 1–120 (1990)
2. Bell, H.H., Waag, W.L.: Evaluating the effectiveness of flight simulators for training combat skills: a review. Int. J. Aviat. Psychol. **8**(3), 223–242 (1998)
3. Borges, M., Symington, A., Coltin, B., Smith, T., Ventura, R.: HTC Vive: analysis and accuracy improvement. In: 2018 IEEE/RSJ International Conference on Intelligent Robots and Systems (IROS), pp. 2610–2615. IEEE (2018)
4. Cai, Y., van Joolingen, W., Walker, Z. (eds.): VR, Simulations and Serious Games for Education. GMSE, Springer, Singapore (2019). https://doi.org/10.1007/978-981-13-2844-2
5. Copilot, V.: Element 3D. https://www.videocopilot.net/products/element2/ (2022)
6. Copilot, V.: Jet Strike package. https://www.videocopilot.net/products/3d/jetstrike/ (2023)
7. Cross, J.I., Boag-Hodgson, C., Ryley, T., Mavin, T., Potter, L.E.: Using extended reality in flight simulators: a literature review. IEEE Trans. Vis. Comput. Graph. **29**(9), 3961–3975 (2022)
8. Doc, R.: Render Doc. https://renderdoc.org/ (2014)
9. Dynamics, L.: Virtual Reality (VR) based Flight Simulation Training Device. https://www.loftdynamics.com/news/detail-1/spotlight-may-2023/ (2023)
10. EASA: EASA approves the first Virtual Reality (VR) based Flight Simulation Training Device. https://www.easa.europa.eu/en/newsroom-and-events/press-releases/easa-approves-first-virtual-reality-vr-based-flight-simulation (2023)
11. Gear, R.S.: Real Sim Gear: For Pilots By Pilots. Master avionics controls before you get in the air. https://realsimgear.com/ (2022)
12. IPACS: Aerofly FS 4 Flight Simulator. https://store.steampowered.com/app/1995890/Aerofly_FS_4_Flight_Simulator/ (2022)
13. Khan, W., Nahon, M.: Real-time modeling of agile fixed-wing UAV aerodynamics. In: 2015 International Conference on Unmanned Aircraft Systems (ICUAS), pp. 1188–1195. IEEE (2015)
14. Laamarti, F., Eid, M., Saddik, A.E.: An overview of serious games. Int. J. Comput. Games Technol. **2014**, 11–11 (2014)
15. Manus: Manus Haptic XR. https://www.manus-meta.com/vr-gloves (2022)
16. Microsoft: Flight Simulator 40th Anniversary Deluxe Edition. https://www.flightsimulator.com/ (2022)
17. Nvidia: PhysX SDK. https://developer.nvidia.com/physx-sdk (2004)
18. Oberhauser, M., Dreyer, D.: A virtual reality flight simulator for human factors engineering. Cogn. Technol. Work **19**, 263–277 (2017)
19. Pensionerov, I.: Aircraft-Physics. https://github.com/gasgiant/Aircraft-Physics/tree/master (2020)
20. Reader, A.: Adobe After Effects. https://t.ly/LJK3 (2015)

21. Sfakaki, A., Apostolakis, K.C., Ntoa, S., Margetis, G., Stephanidis, C.: RAVEN: A VR prototype for the training of aviation technicians. In: 2022 IEEE International Symposium on Mixed and Augmented Reality Adjunct (ISMAR-Adjunct), pp. 913–914. IEEE (2022)
22. Valentino, K., Christian, K., Joelianto, E.: Virtual reality flight simulator. Internet Working Indonesia J. **9**(1), 21–25 (2017)
23. Zeyada, Y., Hess, R.A.: Computer-aided assessment of flight simulator fidelity. J. Aircr. **40**(1), 173–180 (2003)

Augmented Adventures: Using Different Perspectives to Design Novel Tabletop Game Experiences with Augmented Reality

Kaj Coolen, Jeppe Groen, Hao-Xuan Lu, Niels Winkelman,
and Erik D. van der Spek(✉) ⓘD

Eindhoven University of Technology, Groene Loper 3, 5612AE Eindhoven, The Netherlands
{k.j.c.coolen,j.j.groen,h.lu3,n.winkelman}@student.tue.nl,
e.d.vanderspek@tue.nl

Abstract. The proliferation of smartphones and accelerating development of Augmented Reality tools have made it possible to both research and deploy new gameplay interaction paradigms for gaming at a relatively low cost. Here we explore the design space of using Augmented Reality in Tabletop gaming. A research through design approach is followed, where 80 novel gameplay ideas have been brainstormed and subsequently categorized. From this, we found that Augmented Reality can be used to provide interesting perspectives on a game, with especially a second-person perspective opening up new avenues for having interesting gameplay experiences. We subsequently developed this second person perspective into a design exemplar called Eye of the Cyclops, a collaborative adventure game where the smartphone provides the perspective of the main antagonist. Subsequent playtests show that the game led to a significantly higher immersion, audiovisual appeal, curiosity, and meaning compared with benchmark games, even though some clear limitations remain.

Keywords: Augmented Reality · Tabletop Games · Games · Tangible Interaction · Second Person Perspective

1 Introduction

Tabletop games have already existed for centuries, but the design of new games by the industry seems to follow an iterative pattern, where new games are based off successful previous games, albeit with punctuated equilibria leading to new trends [1]. Different research endeavors found roughly 185 existing game structures, mechanics and interactions [1–3]. For most of their history, tabletop games have been confined to static, physical props, such as boards, characters, dice, cards, etc. As multimedia technologies advance and becomes cheaper however, the opportunity to create novel game mechanics

Supplementary Information The online version contains supplementary material available at https://doi.org/10.1007/978-981-99-8248-6_21.

© IFIP International Federation for Information Processing 2023
Published by Springer Nature Switzerland AG 2023
P. Ciancarini et al. (Eds.): ICEC 2023, LNCS 14455, pp. 251–260, 2023.
https://doi.org/10.1007/978-981-99-8248-6_21

and interactions arises. In the past, technologies such as VHS/DVD, electronic game boards [4] and digital screens as game boards [5, 6] have been introduced into tabletop games, usually to enhance interactivity and immersion [4, 5]. Recently, precipitated by the proliferation of smartphones and more advanced free toolkits, it's possible to include Augmented Reality (AR) into tabletop games as well.

Some early examples of AR in commercial tabletop games are Eye of Judgment and Wonderbook: Book of Spells by Sony Interactive Entertainment [7, 8]. In both cases, the player lays out tangible objects that are scanned by a camera, and the configuration of the physical objects controls gameplay on the screen. In these cases, the screen is a TV screen or PC monitor, but similar setups have been used in research with head mounted visors [9] and mobile phones [10]. These are more 'traditional' mixed reality games, where the tabletop layout is used as input for the gameplay on the screen. Already some research has been done on how to design these mixed-reality games to creating engaging gameplay, for instance by using tangible interaction and diegetic feedback [11], and creating compelling fantasies [12]. By introducing augmented reality, the designers can turn the tabletop game into something more of a videogame, by utilizing the dynamic audiovisual possibilities of screen-based games. The downside to this approach is that, while it might make the game more visually appealing, it does not always necessarily enhance the gameplay of the tabletop game itself. Wetzel et al. criticized Eye of Judgment for this in 2008, and came up with a number of guidelines for good AR game design [13]. However, ten years later Kosa and Spronck found that tabletop game players were still unenthused about the potential of AR for their hobby, because AR tabletop games felt like poor imitations of videogames to them [14]. Having most of the game play out on a screen is inimical to the qualities of a tabletop game.

While we think there is still a lot of merit to this approach for other reasons, for the purpose of this paper we therefore focus on the opposite direction: how can Augmented Reality meaningfully improve the gameplay experience of the tabletop game itself? In addition, technology has changed since some of the earlier pioneering work in AR games. Most notably the advent of smartphones with AR capabilities, which makes it feasible to have low-cost solutions for commercial applications (in the opposite direction, something like Tilt Five [15] provides exciting new possibilities, but requires serious investment for more casual tabletop game players, consequently we decided to limit our scope to smartphone interactions).

2   Process and Categorization

For this research we followed an informal Research-through-Design approach, starting with a literature review and then following up with a brainstorm session by 4 of the authors, leading to the generation of 80 new game ideas where Augmented Reality could plausibly enhance the experience. These were then reflected on, categorized, and the ideas with the most potential developed further. It should be noted that the results of this process should not be seen as authoritative or exhaustive. Rather, the purpose of the research is to find interesting new avenues for the use of AR in tabletop games, which can provide designers with tried and tested new gameplay mechanics, as well as help chart the design space of AR tabletop games.

From the literature review and the reflection on the brainstormed concepts, two things became apparent. First, AR usually enhanced the game experience by providing one or more of the following benefits: a) The ability to bring videogame mechanics into a board game (e.g. interactivity, customization, stats), b) added audiovisual appeal (or juiciness [16], c) streamlining (e.g. offloading complex mechanics, dice rolls and Non Player Character (NPC) behavior to the smartphone), and d) providing different perspectives of the game board. Since a) and b) were already mentioned in previous research and could lead to tabletop games being poor facsimiles of videogames, and c) is more supportive than innovative, we focused on d) as a way of framing our concepts and teasing out new ideas for novel gameplay experiences.

We subsequently propose a framework for categorizing perspectives in games, consisting of a first-, second-, third- and fourth-person perspective. This framework is particularly useful when designing AR games that are character-based, in a sense that different perspectives can be had on a game configuration. It can help designers frame and understand the value of their current game designs as well as iterate on existing ideas. This framework attempts to combine multiple dimensions like whose eyes you are looking through, whom you are controlling and how many characters are involved.

2.1 First, Third, Second and Fourth-Person Perspective

The **first-person perspective** means that the player both looks through the eyes of a character and controls the character. In video games, the player is generally the most immersed in this perspective compared to the third-person perspective [17]. The controls share a strong connection with the events on the screen. Players feel ownership over the character [17]. In AR games, the AR device camera is the eye(s) of the character. A well-known AR first-person example is Pokémon GO [18], where you control and look through the eyes of a Pokémon trainer.

The **third-person perspective** means that the player controls a character but looks at them from an external perspective. The player can see more than what they would see through the eyes of the character. However, players tend to be less immersed than in the first-person perspective [17]. The third person perspective is common in classical board games, e.g. Monopoly, Cluedo and Game of the Goose. It can be found in some video games where the external camera often follows the player in an 'over-the-shoulder' way. For example, adventure exploration games benefit from this extended view because you can explore better. Interestingly, not a lot of mobile AR games use this perspective. This might be because the over-the-shoulder perspective is not possible due to the player controlling the position of the camera. Some Tilt5 AR games feature this perspective.

The **second-person perspective** means that the player can look through the eyes of a character that is not the protagonist. The player might have their own different character(s) that they control, and looking through the eyes of the other character could provide a different perspective of the game they are playing. The second-person perspective character might fulfill many types of roles like a friend, competitor, neutral or enemy. Few videogames feature this perspective because of its impracticalities in the context of a video game. One exception is the racing game 'Driver: San Francisco' [19]. In one level, you see and control the car that you are driving from the perspective of the car that is chasing you. In serious games, the second person perspective seems to be a good fit to stimulate empathy [20] As far as the authors are aware, no AR games feature this perspective yet.

The **fourth-person perspective** means that the player controls multiple characters at the same time and therefore looks at them from an external perspective. The controls are often less directly paired to the actions and more general. Many tabletop games like Ludo, Risk, chess and Warhammer 40,000 feature this perspective. Within tabletop games, the lines between third- and fourth-person perspective are thin, as the only difference is the number of characters controlled while the top-down view stays the same. In video games, the fourth person perspective can be found in many strategy games. Some Tilt5 AR games follow this perspective.

Some games **feature multiple perspectives at the same time**. For example, tabletop war games like Warhammer 40,000 [21] primarily play in a fourth-person perspective as the player controls an army, but occasionally requires the players to briefly switch perspective to determine line of sight from one's own character (first person) and characters from the opposing army (second person).

3   Novel AR Tabletop Gameplay Ideas

Since this research produced over 80 different ideas – with numerous different themes and varying levels of detail – we only present a selection of concepts that exemplify how the different perspectives can lead to interesting new gameplay experiences in AR tabletop games. For more detailed explanations of the game ideas, we refer to the supplementary material.

Fig. 1. Maze Explorers   **Fig. 2.** The Heist

Maze Explorers – 1st Person

The game is played on a playing board with a labelled grid (e.g. A1 – H8), and utilizes one phone and an accompanying phone stand. The maze itself can only be seen through the phone using AR and can be moved through the maze by moving the phone over the board. The goal of the game is for the players to find the maze's exit by moving as a group (the phone) through the maze (turn-based), but they also have individual objectives. With the maze being completely virtual, its layout and number of hidden items can be randomized/customized almost infinitely. By having players take turns looking through the viewport to observe the maze they can determine, what information they want to share with the rest, all while planning out how to reach their personal objectives (Fig. 1).

The Heist – 1ˢᵗ/4ᵗʰ Person

Players choose a role: mapper, hacker, thief or security, and are given tools to play this role. The main goal of the robbers is to retrieve the money from the vault within a given timeframe, with the security's goal being to stall them long enough for the alarm to go off, making them lose the game. Different roles can have different perspectives, i.e. top-down 4ᵗʰ person (mapper), and 1ˢᵗ person for the thief and security, opening up new ways of collaboration and competition in an AR tabletop space (Fig. 2).

Fig. 3. Hide from Seeker   **Fig. 4.** Moth Mania

Hide from Seeker – 2nd/3rd Person

This tabletop game concept has a board layout of a grid-based route with a start and finish that the players must move along, but with several small walls that are placed alongside the route. The first player to reach the end wins, but the catch is that they must do so without getting spotted by the enemy. The latter is a phone that is mounted to a circular track around the board, on which it is able to move around using a small motor (Fig. 3).

Moth Mania – 1ˢᵗ/3ʳᵈ Person

The players find themselves in a cave, where it is their goal to find, collect and secure as many moths as they can. Each player uses their phone as a pawn, through which they can see their character's view, holding a flashlight that illuminates the cave in front of them. Once a player spots a moth with their flashlight, it will linger in the light. At that point, the player must guide the moth to their starting point to secure it (Fig. 4).

4 Researching a Second-Person Perspective in Tabletop Games

4.1 First Iteration: Dragon Game

Some of the most interesting mechanics to arise from the above games were combined into a single design exemplar. From the Maze Explorers game, the phone as a pawn that moves across the playing board was used. From the Moth Mania game, the ability of the screen to reveal 'hidden' objects was considered interesting and multiple roles were included from the Heist games. Most importantly however, the second person perspective of the Hide from Seeker game was considered the most novel and unexplored contribution of AR to tabletop games. This mimics design research in Virtual Reality experiences that also found the second person perspective to be a unique contribution of game technologies to traditional media [22]. In our case using a second person perspective of a single enemy also solved the more practical problem that multiple people having to take turns to look at a small screen creates a lot of inconvenience.

The game that emerged was initially called the 'Dragon Game', in which four players need to find treasure in a cave while avoiding being caught by a dragon. The players do not know beforehand whether a treasure chest is good or bad and looking through the camera on the phone's screen- the eyes of the dragon- reveals if the chest is a treasure or a trap. The game ends when one player has a certain number of treasures. Players control their own pawn, and the phone represents a dragon that acts as an enemy that also moves around the board, creating a second-person perspective experience.

After internal playtest and reflection, the Dragon game showed potential with its unique approach of using the phone as a pawn on the board rather than using it just as a viewport. However, the Dragon game also demonstrated some flaws in its mechanics. Because the relationship between players is competitive, the limited angles at which the phone screen could be seen by all players worked against the benefits that the revealing mechanic should have. In a competitive nature, this concept simply did not work well. Therefore, a new version was designed that was played collaboratively.

4.2 Final Design: Eye of the Cyclops

In the Eye of the Cyclops, up to four players must work together to find buried treasure in ancient ruins that are guarded by a cyclops. The cyclops is represented by the phone in the holder. Only the cyclops knows where the treasure is, but the players can cast spells to look through the eye of the cyclops—the AR camera—to see where the treasure is hidden. This game again uses the second person perspective. We refer to the Electronic Supplementary Material for the full instruction manual (Fig. 5).

Fig. 5. Eye of Cyclops

The game is turn-based, and to win the players must find six treasures and bring them safely back to the starting area. The players have three collective lives, a life is removed if a player gets caught by the cyclops. When no lives are left, the players lose the game. A player starts their turn by rolling the die. The number they roll determines how many action points they can spend during that turn. These actions can be either moving their pawn, picking up treasure, casting the vision spell to reveal treasure through the AR camera, or performing a role-specific action. There are four different player roles with different abilities. These are: the Necromancer who can summon a decoy; the archer who can distract the cyclops with a burning arrow; the Voodoo Master who can move other players; and the Wizard who can place a magic barrier on the board. After each player's turn, the cyclops moves on the board. If it sees a player, it will chase it (Figs. 6 and 7).

Fig. 6. The cyclops reveals a treasure, fights a player or sees the player teleport to another location

Fig. 7. The cyclops reveals a hidden treasure chest on the board

4.3 Playtest

Two playtests were conducted with the Eye of the Cyclops prototype. Both tests had four participants. The participants were asked to play the game for one hour, and fill in a questionnaire about their experience. The Player Experience Inventory scale (PXI) [23] was used, as well as the social presence module from the Gameful Experience Questionnaire (GAMEFULQUEST, here abbreviated as GQ) [24]. Furthermore, observations were made about decisions the players took and thoughts the players expressed.

After the first user test, the rules of the game were adapted in a second iteration to improve the experience based on the results. The board was shortened from 12×12 to 11×11, attacking was simplified and the movement of the cyclops was taken over by a player to make sure that it did not bump into walls as much. This showed the need for AR to streamline the process, as was mentioned in Sect. 2. The interactions need to be as simple as possible, as was also mentioned in [13], however streamlining might irk some players that demand clarity of rules [14].

4.3.1 Results

Although there were only a few participants, with each playtest consisting of a single player group, tentatively some conclusions can be drawn from the PXI and GQ questionnaires. Most of the scores improved from the first to the second iteration, but only

Mastery $t(6) = -2.751, p = 0.033, d = 0.54$ and Audiovisual Appeal $t(6) = -2.573, p = 0.042, d = 0.78$, improved significantly, both in favor of the second iteration.

The Player Experience Inventory has a dataset of other games to benchmark one's game with (https://playerexperienceinventory.org/bdata). In our case the closest analogue would be board games. One-sample T-tests with the player experience of our game compared with the benchmark mean scores as the test value, show that Eye of the Cyclops scores significantly better than the benchmark group on Meaning $t(3) = 4.998$, $p = 0.015$, Curiosity $t(3) = 6.784, p = 0.007$, Immersion $t(3) = 6.168, p = 0.009$, and Audiovisual Appeal $t(3) = 5.330, p = 0.013$. Both the mean scores for Immersion (M = 2.07) and Audiovisual Appeal (M = 2.75) in fact are higher than for all the board games in the database (highest values 2.0 and 2.67 respectively). In comparison with the only other AR game in the benchmark, Pokemon Go, Eye of the Cyclops scores significantly higher on Curiosity $t(3) = 11.484, p = 0.001$, Immersion $t(3) = 4.663, p = 0.019$, and Audiovisual Appeal $t(3) = 6.330, p = 0.008$. All other comparisons are non-significant. The GQ did not improve between iterations and does not have benchmark data, so it is unclear how social presence during this game compares with similar games.

5 Discussion and Conclusion

Based on observations from two tests, the second-person perspective offers users a fresh and captivating gameplay experience, fostering meaning, curiosity, mastery and audiovisual appeal, as well as excitement about the Cyclops' actions. Participants e.g. expressed "I feel a lot of tension now" and "Where is it going now?". Overall, "Switching Perspectives" as a game mechanism generates heightened tension in character-based games, as users continually shift between 3rd and 2nd-person perspectives.

For curiosity, there are likely multiple game mechanics that were conducive to this higher rating. By adopting the second-person perspective (Cyclops), users gain visibility of the Cyclops' imminent actions and can wonder what that means for their own character's actions. In addition, the hidden treasures that get revealed through the AR lens themselves likely add quite a bit to a continuous feeling of curiosity. For Audiovisual Appeal it was likely the visualizations of the battle mechanics, and juiciness in terms of particle effects, that the AR added over traditional tabletop games. The higher score for Meaning is more difficult to conclusively link to a certain game mechanic, but could possibly be explained by the second person perspective stimulating a more empathetic connection between Cyclops and player [20].

Throughout, we used a grid-based system to try to anchor the tabletop game experience to that of a traditional board game, however the 360° view offered by the AR sometimes made this combination feel awkward and unintuitive. It would be interesting to see if the experience works better in a free movement style tabletop games.

We created a framework and a design exemplar that can help AR game designers ideate, categorize, and explain AR games, and to create AR tabletop games where AR is used as a meaningful mechanic instead of a novelty gimmick. It would also be interesting to see how this framework would inspire other types of games like videogames, non-augmented tabletop games and even physical games like tag and hide and seek.

References

1. Reiber, F.: Major Developments in the Evolution of Tabletop Game Design. In: 2021 IEEE Conference on Games (CoG), pp. 1–8. IEEE (2021)
2. BoardGameGeek. http://www.boardgamegeek.com
3. Engelstein, G., Shalev, I.: Building Blocks of Tabletop Game Design: An Encyclopedia of Mechanisms. CRC Press (2022)
4. Booth, P.: Board, game, and media: interactive board games as multimedia convergence. Convergence 22(6), 647–660 (2016)
5. Bakker, S., Vorstenbosch, D., Van Den Hoven, E., Hollemans, G., Bergman, T.: Weather-gods: tangible interaction in a digital tabletop game. In: Proceedings of the 1st International Conference on Tangible and Embedded Interaction, pp. 151–152 (2007)
6. Park, J.W.: Hybrid monopoly: a multimedia board game that supports bidirectional communication between a mobile device and a physical game set. Multimedia Tools Appl. 76(16), 17385–17401 (2017)
7. Sony Computer Entertainment. Eye of Judgment (2007)
8. Sony Computer Entertainment. Wonderbook: Book of Spells (2012)
9. Nilsen, T., Looser, J.: Tankwar-tabletop war gaming in augmented reality. In: 2nd International Workshop on Pervasive Gaming Applications, PerGames, vol. 5 (2005)
10. Rizov, T., Đokić, J., Tasevski, M.: Design of a board game with augmented reality. FME Trans. 47(2), 253–257 (2019)
11. Li, J., Van der Spek, E.D., Hu, J., Feijs, L.: Turning your book into a game: improving motivation through tangible interaction and diegetic feedback in an AR mathematics game for children. In: Proceedings of the Annual Symposium on Computer-Human Interaction in Play, pp. 73–85 (2019)
12. Zuo, T., Birk, M.V., van der Spek, E.D., Hu, J.: The mediating effect of fantasy on engagement in an AR game for learning. Entertainment Comput. 42, 100480 (2022)
13. Richard, W., McCall, R., Braun, A-K., Broll, W.: Guidelines for designing augmented reality games. In: Proceedings of the 2008 Conference on Future Play: Research, Play, Share (Future Play 2008), pp. 173–180. Association for Computing Machinery, New York, NY, USA (2008). https://doi.org/10.1145/1496984.1497013
14. Kosa, M., Spronck, P.: What tabletop players think about augmented tabletop games: a content analysis. In: Proceedings of the 13th International Conference on the Foundations of Digital Games, pp. 1–8 (2018)
15. Tilt Five. http://www.tiltfive.com
16. Hicks, K., Dickinson, P., Holopainen, J., Gerling, K.: Good game feel: an empirically grounded framework for juicy design. In: Proceedings of DiGRA 2018 (2018)
17. Denisova, A., Cairns, P.: First person vs. third person perspective in digital games: do player preferences affect immersion? In: Proceedings of the 33rd Annual ACM Conference on Human Factors in Computing Systems (CHI 2015), pp. 145–148. Association for Computing Machinery, New York, NY, USA (2015). https://doi.org/10.1145/2702123.2702256
18. Niantic, Inc. Pokemon Go (2016)
19. Ubisoft Reflections. Driver: San-Francisco (2011)
20. Kors, M.J., et al.: The curious case of the transdiegetic cow, or a mission to foster other-oriented empathy through virtual reality. In: Proceedings of the 2020 CHI Conference on Human Factors in Computing Systems, pp. 1–13 (2020)
21. Games Workshop. Warhammer 40,000 (1987)
22. Kors, M.J., Van der Spek, E.D., Ferri, G., Schouten, B.A.: You; the observer, partaker or victim. delineating three perspectives to empathic engagement in persuasive games using immersive technologies. In: Proceedings of the 2018 Annual Symposium on Computer-Human Interaction in Play Companion Extended Abstracts, pp. 493–501 (2018)

23. Abeele, V.V., Spiel, K., Nacke, L., Johnson, D., Gerling, K.: Development and validation of the player experience inventory: a scale to measure player experiences at the level of functional and psychosocial consequences. Int. J. Hum Comput. Stud. **135**, 102370 (2020)
24. Högberg, J., Hamari, J., Wästlund, E.: Gameful experience questionnaire (GAME-FULQUEST): an instrument for measuring the perceived gamefulness of system use. User Model. User-Adap. Inter. **29**(3), 619–660 (2019)

Game Design

Visualising Game Engine Subsystem Coupling Patterns

Gabriel C. Ullmann[1]([✉])(iD), Yann-Gaël Guéhéneuc[1](iD), Fabio Petrillo[2](iD),
Nicolas Anquetil[3](iD), and Cristiano Politowski[2](iD)

[1] Concordia University, Montreal, QC, Canada
g_cavalh@live.concordia.ca, yann-gael.gueheneuc@concordia.ca
[2] École de Technologie Supérieure, Montreal, QC, Canada
{fabio.petrillo,cristiano.politowski}@etsmtl.ca
[3] Univ. Lille, CNRS, Inria, Centrale Lille, UMR 9189 - CRIStAL, Lille, France
nicolas.anquetil@inria.fr

Abstract. Game engines support video game development by providing functionalities such as graphics rendering or input/output device management. However, their architectures are often overlooked, which hinders their integration and extension. In this paper, we use an approach for architecture recovery to create architectural models for 10 open-source game engines. We use these models to answer the following questions: Which subsystems more often couple with one another? Do game engines share subsystem coupling patterns? We observe that the Low-Level Renderer, Platform Independence Layer and Resource Manager are frequently coupled to the game engine Core. By identifying the most frequent coupling patterns, we describe an emergent game engine architecture and discuss how it can be used by practitioners to improve system understanding and maintainability.

Keywords: Game Engines · Coupling · Game Engine Architecture

1 Introduction

Game engines are tools made to support video game development. From the perspective of Software Engineering, game engines are systems composed of subsystems, each providing functionalities essential for any video game, such as 2D/3D graphics rendering or input/output device management. However, the versatility of game engines also makes them architecturally complex and often difficult to understand. The lack of architecture understanding hinders software integration and extension, which is important in the context of plugin-extendable game engines such as Unreal, Unity and Godot. Therefore, studying game engine architecture is necessary: "[a] prerequisite for integration and extension is the comprehension of the software. To understand the architecture, we should identify the architectural patterns involved and how they are coupled." [1].

In this paper, we apply the approach for game engine architecture recovery described in our previous paper [11] to 10 popular open-source game engines. By

© IFIP International Federation for Information Processing 2023
Published by Springer Nature Switzerland AG 2023
P. Ciancarini et al. (Eds.): ICEC 2023, LNCS 14455, pp. 263–274, 2023.
https://doi.org/10.1007/978-981-99-8248-6_22

following this approach, we obtain *include* graphs tagged by subsystem, which we call architectural models for the sake of simplicity, for each game engine.

By studying these models' nodes and relationships, we answer the following research questions:

- **RQ1**: Which subsystems more often couple with one another?
- **RQ2**: Do game engines share subsystem coupling patterns?

The remainder of the paper is organized as follows: Sect. 2 presents related work on game engine architecture and architectural recovery. Section 3 describes our game engine architecture recovery approach. Section 4 shows the architectural models resulting from applying our approach and Sect. 5 discusses lessons learned from frequent coupling patterns. Section 6 presents threats to validity and Sect. 7 concludes with future work.

2   Related Work

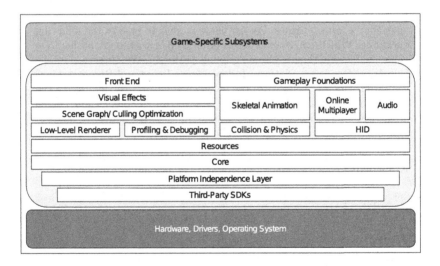

Fig. 1. Runtime Engine Architecture, adapted from Gregory [5, p. 33].

Few studies focused solely on game engine architecture and those that did focused on describing a specific game engine in detail. For example, Jaeyong and Changhyeon [7] explain the scripting and networking subsystems of a game engine for MUDs[1]. Bishop et al. [3] describe the NetImmerse engine. Both authors represent subsystems and their relationships in diagrams. However, they do not discuss why these relationships exist, how often they appear or whether they are representative of all game engine architectures.

---

[1] Multi-User Dungeon, a text-based precursor of MMORPG games.

Gregory [5] proposed a "Runtime Game Engine Architecture" (Fig. 1), which describes common subsystems, their responsibilities, and some of their relationships. While also not focused on subsystem relationships, this is, to the best of our knowledge, the most comprehensive game engine architecture. Therefore we use it as a reference architecture in the following, as we explain further in Subsect. 3.2.

Guided by a reference architecture, we apply an architecture recovery approach. Architecture recovery is concerned with the extraction of architectural descriptions from a system implementation [4]. Researchers have applied it to systems such as the Apache Web server [6], the Android OS and Apache Hadoop [8] as a way to improve understanding and maintainability.

Game engine developers can also reap the benefits of architecture recovery for their systems. For example, the information obtained through architecture recovery can be "used in the process of identifying suitable improvements and enhancements to a specific engine and have supported implementing these in an appropriate manner" [9]. This potential for assisting software architectural improvement is the main reason why we chose to apply architectural recovery to game engines in this work.

3   Approach

We now explain the six-step approach we proposed in a previous work [11], summarized in Fig. 2 and used in this paper in a slightly modified version. Steps 1 to 3 are performed manually. Steps 4 to 6 are largely automated with Smalltalk and Python code, which is available on GitHub.[2]

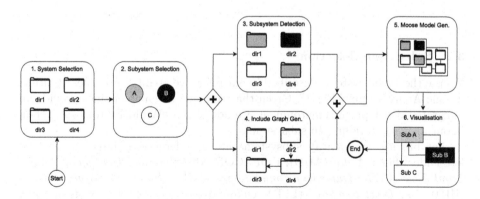

Fig. 2. Steps of our architecture recovery approach.

---

[2] https://github.com/gamedev-studies/game-engine-analyser.

3.1   System Selection

We searched for the term "game engine" on GitHub and then selected all repositories showing C++ as the predominant programming language, given its relevance to game engine development [10]. This initial selection consisted of 20 game engine repositories. We then removed from the selection all non-general-purpose game engines. For example, we did not select the engine *minetest*[3] because it is limited to creating games in the style of Minecraft. Finally, we sorted the remaining repositories by the sum of their GitHub forks and stars (as of May 2022) in descending order. We selected the top 10 in this list, as shown in Table 1.

Table 1. Overview of the selected GitHub repositories.

Repository	Branch	Commit	Forks + Stars	Files (.h, .cpp)
UnrealEngine	v4	90f6542cf7	64100	66390
godot	3.4	f9ac000d5d	59200	5603
cocos2d-x	v4	90f6542cf7	23300	1601
o3de	development	21ab0506da	6400	7278
Urho3d	master	feb0d90190	4956	4312
gamePlay3d	master	4de92c4c6f	4900	688
panda3D	master	2208cc8bff	4100	5344
olcPixelGameEngine	master	02dac30d50	3963	81
Piccolo	main	b4166dbcba	3892	1572
FlaxEngine	master	7b041bbaa5	3613	2134

3.2   Subsystem Selection

We use the 15 subsystems described in our reference architecture, the "Runtime Engine Architecture" (Fig. 1). Given that commercial game engines provide an integrated development environment, we added the "World Editor" subsystem in our analysis, totalling 16 subsystems.

For brevity, we identify subsystems in the reference architecture with 3-letter identifiers: *Audio* (AUD), *Core* (COR), *Profiling and Debugging* (DEB), *Front End* (FES), *Gameplay Foundations* (GMP), *Human Interface Devices* (HID), *Low-Level Renderer* (LLR), *Online Multiplayer* (OMP), *Collision and Physics* (PHY), *Platform Independence Layer* (PLA), *Resources* (RES), *Third-party SDKs* (SDK), *Scene graph/culling optimizations* (SGC), *Skeletal Animation* (SKA), *Visual Effects* (VFX), *World Editor* (EDI).

---

[3] https://github.com/minetest/minetest.

3.3 Subsystem Detection

In this step, we clustered all folders in each repository into the selected subsystems. When deciding which folders belong to a subsystem, we considered four pieces of information from each folder: its name, contents, documentation, and source code. We show an example of this decision process in Table 2.

Table 2. Subsystem detection example for Cocos2d-x.

Can we determine the subsystem of /cocos/editor-support/spine by:	
1) Folder name?	No, the name *spine* does not match or relate to the reference architecture
2) Parent folder name?	No, the folder *editor-support* might be related to EDI, but we need more data to confirm
3) Documentation?	**Yes**, according to docs: "Skeletal animation assets in Creator are exported from Spine"[a]
4) Source code?	No code analysis needed, subsystem detected on step 3.
Conclusion	*Skeletal Animation* (SKA)

[a]https://docs.cocos.com/creator/manual/en/asset/spine.html

3.4 Include Graph Generation

In parallel to detecting subsystems, we generated an *include* graph of each game engine using a two-pass algorithm. In the first pass, our analyser reads every source code file composing the game engine, collects all includes and outputs an *include* graph in the DOT graph description language. In the output DOT file, each row is an *include* relationship described as follows: */home/engine/source.cpp -> /home/engine/target.h*. The analyser attempts to resolve each relative *include* path into an absolute path. If the resolution fails, the analyser writes the path to another file called *engine-includes-unr.csv*.

In the original implementation of the approach [11], we read and resolved each of the unresolved *include* paths manually. However, repeating this operation for thousands of paths is time-consuming and error-prone. Therefore, we automated this step by adding a second pass to our analyser. In this pass, it loads *engine-includes-unr.csv*, iterates over each of its paths, and splits them by their folder delimiters. Then it searches for each part of the path, starting with the file name and moving towards the repository root folder. It repeats this search until it finds a match. Finally, the resolved absolute path is appended to the DOT file.

Some *include* paths inevitably remain unresolved because they refer to system or OS-specific libraries (e.g., *stdio.h*, *windows.h*) which do not belong to the game engine. In Cocos2d-x, all third-party dependencies are located in a separate repository. However, these paths do not contain code written by game engine developers, so their absence is not detrimental to the consistency of our architectural models.

3.5   Moose Model Generation

In this step, we merge the data collected in step 3 (the CSV file containing the detected subsystems) and step 4 (the DOT file containing the *include* graph) for each game engine. We build on Moose 10^4, a platform for software analysis implemented in Pharo[5], a Smalltalk development environment. By importing the files into Moose, we create a Moose model, which is our architectural model.

3.6   Architectural Model Visualisation

Finally, we use Moose's "Architectural map" visualisation, which displays all subsystems and their relationships, to visualise each of the 10 selected game engines. By compiling the information from all generated "Architectural maps", we created a heatmap which we will show and explain in Subsect. 4.2. We also used Gephi[6], a graph analysis software, to compute metrics such as in-degree and betweenness centrality, which are the main point of discussion in Subsect. 4.1. We chose to use Gephi instead of Moose in this case because Moose does not come with graph analysis tools out of the box.

4   Results

Figure 3 shows the architectural models of Godot and Unreal Engine. The high number of relationships and subsystems shows that both game engines are highly coupled and follow the reference architecture. In Godot, the most coupled subsystem is *Scene graph/culling optimizations* (SGC) because it centralizes files with diverse functionalities in its */scene/3d* folder, such as *camera.h* for *Low-Level Renderer* (LLR) and *physics_body.h* for *Collision and Physics* (PHY). In contrast, in Unreal's */Engine/Source/Runtime* folder, we observe LLR and PHY are divided in several distinct subfolders (e.g. *PhysicsCore, Renderer*).

While the "Architectural map" provides us with an overview of coupling in a given game engine, its density makes interpretation hard, especially because we want to understand how two or more subsystems are coupled. In the following subsections, we answer our RQs and explain how subsystem coupling can be identified and understood with the use of graph analysis and a coupling heatmap.

4.1   RQ1 - Which Subsystems More Often Couple with One Another?

We computed the in-degree for each subsystem of each game engine. Next, we computed the averages and sorted them in descending order. As we can observe in Fig. 4, the top-five subsystems in average in-degree are: *Core* (COR), *Low-Level Renderer* (LLR), *Resources* (RES), *World Editor* (EDI) and, tied in 5th place, *Front End* (FES) and *Platform Independence Layer* (PLA).

---

[4] https://github.com/moosetechnology.

[5] https://pharo.org/.

[6] https://gephi.org/.

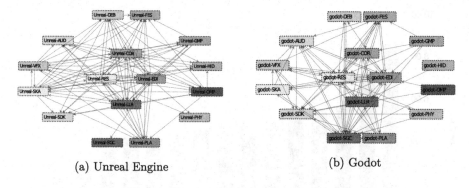

(a) Unreal Engine   (b) Godot

Fig. 3. Game engine architectural models generated with Moose 10.

The subsystems in the top-five act as a foundation for game engines because most of the other subsystems depend on them to implement their functionalities. Two subsystems in this list are graphics-related: *Low-Level Renderer* (LLR) and *Front End* (FES). We expected it because video games depend on visuals.

Same as the in-degree, we computed the average betweenness centrality, shown in Fig. 5. This metric represents the extent to which a node lies in the path of others [2]. It helps us understand whether a highly coupled subsystem is an isolated occurrence, or if it consistently plays a central role within its respective system. Figure 5 shows that the top-five systems with the highest average betweenness centrality are: *Core* (COR), *Resources* (RES), *World Editor* (EDI), *Low-Level Renderer* (LLR) and *Platform Independence Layer* (PLA). For this reason, we decided to draw the top four subsystems in the centre of the architectural maps shown in Fig. 3.

We observe that all subsystems with high in-degree also have high centrality, being *Front End* (FES) the only exception. While subsystems frequently depend on FES, we observe FES often depends only on *Core* (COR) and *Low-Level Renderer* (LLR) and therefore does not play the role of intermediate or "gatekeeper" between groups of subsystems. We further discuss subsystem "gatekeeping" observed in the COR subsystem in Subsect. 4.2.

4.2   RQ2 - Do Game Engines Share Subsystem Coupling Patterns?

To answer this question, we created a heatmap which shows aggregated coupling counts from all architectural models (Fig. 6). For example, if we take the first line from the top, we can observe the *Audio* (AUD) subsystem includes files from itself in eight game engines, and it includes files from COR in six game engines. We show the most frequent coupling pairs from the heatmap in Table 3.

While we applied our approach to 10 game engines, no square shows the value 10 in the heatmap's central diagonal. This happens because olcPixelGameEngine is fully decoupled. As an educational game engine, each of its subsystems was written in a single .h file, which is meant to be included by developers to their

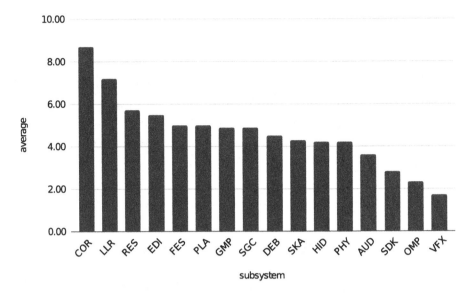

Fig. 4. Average subsystem in-degree.

own .cpp file. Also, not all subsystems were detected in all game engines, and therefore not all self-include nine times.

Table 3. The most frequent subsystem coupling pairs.

Pair	Count	Pair	Count	Pair	Count
GMP -> COR	9	FES -> COR	7	EDI -> FES	6
COR -> LLR	7	LLR -> COR	7	GMP -> FES	6
COR -> PLA	7	SKA -> COR	7	PLA -> COR	6
COR -> RES	7	AUD -> COR	6	RES -> COR	6

While the analysis of in-degree and betweenness centrality highlights which subsystems are fundamental, the heatmap shows how they work together. *Core* (COR) is the subsystem that most frequently includes others, and also the most frequently included. It is often reciprocally related to *Resources* (RES) and *Platform Independence Layer* (PLA), reflecting a "gatekeeper" role described in the reference architecture: when loading or saving game assets, RES uses PLA to interface with the OS and hardware such as the hard disk. We will further explore these frequent relationships in Sect. 5.

5   Discussion

By compiling the game engine coupling pattern information from Table 3 we observe a new architecture emerge. In Fig. 7, we placed in the centre of the

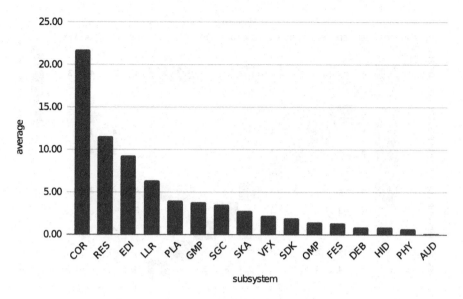

Fig. 5. Average subsystem betweenness centrality.

model the subsystems with the highest betweenness centrality, forming an inner core (dark red). Next, we placed other subsystems which appear in Table 3 in the outer core (light red). Finally, we placed the subsystems which do not appear in Table 3 in the outer core's periphery (white). All relationships shown in the diagram are among the most frequent, as shown in Table 3 and Fig. 6. When there was a tie (e.g. two pairs had the same frequency), we chose the coupling pair with the highest sum of betweenness centrality.

In this emergent architecture, we observe the *Low-Level Renderer* (LLR) often inter-depends on *Core* (COR), which it uses to access functionality in the *Platform Compatibility Layer* (PLA) and the *Resources* (RES) subsystem. In Fig. 1, we can observe these subsystems are also placed close to each other in the reference architecture.

While not part of the inner core, the *Front End* (FES) subsystem plays an important role. It is often included by the *World Editor* (EDI) and *Gameplay Foundations* (GMP), which are both visual interfaces between the user and the game engine. Because it manages UI elements which emit events and trigger actions throughout the system, *Front End* (FES) often depends on the event/messaging system in *Core* (COR).

More practically, the information provided by the architectural models and coupling patterns can be used by practitioners as follows:

- **Learning**: architectural model visualisations provide a friendly way for novice game engine developers to understand this kind of system and start developing their own subsystems or plugins.
- **Refactoring**: game engine developers can refactor their code more safely by visualising how changes to a subsystem could impact the whole game engine.

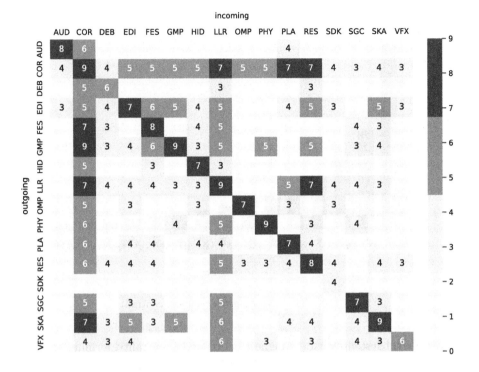

Fig. 6. Subsystem coupling heatmap showing aggregated coupling counts.

- **Anomaly Detection**: a subsystem coupling heatmap can help game engine developers to find unusual or unexpected coupling patterns, and then improve the source code as necessary.
- **Reference Extraction**: game engine architects seeking to design a new engine can extract architectural models from similar systems and use them as references. This is useful both for large companies and small indie developers who develop tailor-made solutions, e.g. for performance.

6   Threats to Validity

First, the selected game engines may not be representative of all open-source game engines and the entire video game industry. Similarly, Gregory [5] is our reference architecture and we are aware other architectures exist, as explained in Sect. 2, even though not as detailed. Moreover, we acknowledge some modern game engine features, such as AR and VR support, were not present in the subsystem selection because they are not described in the reference architecture.

Subsystem detection was performed manually by the first author only, which may bias the detection process. To mitigate this issue, we intend to assign multiple people to work in this step and later combine the results by consensus. We

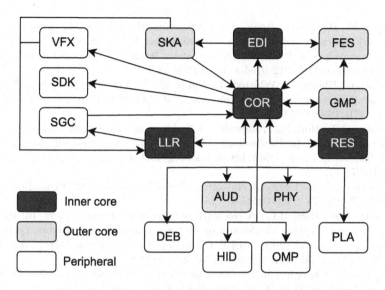

Fig. 7. Our emergent open-source game engine architecture.

are also aware that our approach is dependent on the behaviour and metrics provided by Moose and Gephi, and changing them could also change the results and therefore our perception of these game engine architectures.

7 Conclusion

In this paper, we show that by generating and studying game engine architectural models, game engine developers can identify which subsystems are the centre-pieces of their system and therefore give them proper maintenance. Additionally, by understanding frequent coupling patterns, game engine architects can take better decisions when extending existing game engines or creating custom-made solutions for a specific kind of video game or interactive experience.

In future work, we will apply our approach to a wider variety of game engines and subsystems. We will also conduct experiments with developers to determine to which extent the visualisations produced by our approach can help improve system understanding and maintainability. Finally, we intend to explore automated approaches to architecture recovery and other software quality metrics, such as cohesion and complexity.

Acknowledgement. The authors were partially supported by the NSERC Discovery Grant and Canada Research Chairs programs.

References

1. Agrahari, V., Chimalakonda, S.: What's inside unreal engine? - A curious gaze! In: 14th Innovations in Software Engineering Conference, Bhubaneswar, Odisha India, pp. 1–5. ACM (2021). https://doi.org/10.1145/3452383.3452404

2. Badar, K., Hite, J.M., Badir, Y.F.: Examining the relationship of co-authorship network centrality and gender on academic research performance: the case of chemistry researchers in Pakistan. Scientometrics **94**(2), 755–775 (2013). https://doi.org/10.1007/s11192-012-0764-z. ISSN 0138-9130

3. Bishop, L., Eberly, D., Whitted, T., Finch, M., Shantz, M.: Designing a PC game engine. IEEE Comput. Graph. Appl. **18**(1), 46–53 (1998). https://doi.org/10.1109/38.637270. ISSN 02721716

4. Bowman, I.T., Holt, R.C., Brewster, N.V.: Linux as a case study: its extracted software architecture. In: Proceedings of ICSE 1999, Los Angeles, California, USA, pp. 555–563. ACM Press (1999). https://doi.org/10.1145/302405.302691. ISBN 978-1-58113-074-4

5. Gregory, J.: Game Engine Architecture. Taylor & Francis, CRC Press, Boca Raton (2018). ISBN 978-1-138-03545-4

6. Hassan, A.E., Holt, R.C.: A reference architecture for web servers. In: Proceedings Seventh Working Conference on Reverse Engineering, Brisbane, QLD, Australia, pp. 150–159 (2000). IEEE Computer Society (2000). https://doi.org/10.1109/WCRE.2000.891462. ISBN 978-0-7695-0881-8

7. Jaeyong, P., Changhyeon, P.: Development of a multiuser and multimedia game engine based on TCP/IP. In: 1997 IEEE Pacific Rim Conference on Communications, Computers and Signal Processing, PACRIM, 1987–1997, vol. 1, Victoria, BC, Canada, pp. 101–104. IEEE (1997). https://doi.org/10.1109/PACRIM.1997.619911. ISBN 978-0-7803-3905-7

8. Link, D., Behnamghader, P., Moazeni, R., Boehm, B.: The value of software architecture recovery for maintenance. In: Proceedings of the 12th Innovations on Software Engineering Conference (formerly known as India Software Engineering Conference), Pune, India, pp. 1–10. ACM (2019). https://doi.org/10.1145/3299771.3299787. ISBN 978-1-4503-6215-3

9. Munro, J., Boldyreff, C., Capiluppi, A.: Architectural studies of games engines - the quake series. In: 2009 International IEEE Consumer Electronics Society's Games Innovations Conference, London, UK, pp. 246–255. IEEE (2009). https://doi.org/10.1109/ICEGIC.2009.5293600. ISBN 978-1-4244-4459-5

10. Politowski, C., Petrillo, F., Montandon, J.E., Valente, M.T., Guéhéneuc, Y.: Are game engines software frameworks? A three-perspective study. J. Syst. Softw. **171**, 110846 (2021). https://doi.org/10.1016/j.jss.2020.110846

11. Ullmann, G.C., Guéhéneuc, Y., Petrillo, F., Anquetil, N., Politowski, C.: An exploratory approach for game engine architecture recovery. In: 7th International ICSE Workshop on Games and Software Engineering (2023)

Enhancing Stockfish: A Chess Engine Tailored for Training Human Players

Andrea Manzo[1] and Paolo Ciancarini[2]

[1] AlphaChess srl., Muggia, Italy
[2] DISI - University of Bologna, Bologna, Italy
paolo.ciancarini@unibo.it

Abstract. Stockfish is a highly popular open-source chess engine known for its exceptional strength. The recent integration of a neural network called NNUE has significantly improved Stockfish's playing ability. However, the neural network lacks the capability to explain the reasoning behind its moves. This poses a challenge for human players who seek moves that align with their playing style.

The objective of this paper is to describe some modifications to Stockfish, making the engine more suitable for training human players of all skill levels. We have refactored the move search and evaluation algorithms to selectively analyze potential continuations, incorporating dynamic evaluations based on the specific nature of the position and the player's training abilities. The engine remains strength is still very high, in some situations even better than the original. We evaluate and discuss the outcomes of these enhancements.

1 Introduction

Working on a chess engine like Stockfish is challenging for several reasons. One of the main challenges is how to enhance its highly optimized and efficient algorithm that can quickly evaluate positions and make decisions. Any enhancement requires a deep understanding of chess strategy and tactics, as well as the ability to implement these ideas in code.

There is a large community of people interested in discussing and working on this topic, modifying Stockfish and developing new versions almost daily. They constantly update and test the engine based on new research and discoveries in the fields of chess and machine learning. This requires a strong commitment to staying current with the latest developments and being willing to continuously modify and test the progress of the engine.

Overall, modifying a chess program like Stockfish is a fascinating and rewarding endeavor that requires a combination of chess knowledge and software engineering expertise.

For years, chess engines have had a stable architecture based on the evaluation of alternative moves according to positional factors inspired by established chess strategy concepts. Recently, applying deep learning techniques has replaced the conventional evaluation [3]. The use of a neural network greatly increases the

P. Ciancarini et al. (Eds.): ICEC 2023, LNCS 14455, pp. 275–289, 2023.
https://doi.org/10.1007/978-981-99-8248-6_23

quality of analysis [12]. However, abandoning conventional evaluation functions, and replacing them with neural models obtained by machine learning, makes the use of a chess engine more arduous for training human players, because it is difficult to explain the "meaning" of the moves suggested by the engine. Hence, an interesting research goal consists in combining a conventional evaluation with the techniques able to exploit neural networks aiming at offering functions useful for training human players [11].

In this paper we show how we modify Stockfish to obtain a program that is still a strong player but also a flexible trainer, customizable according to the needs of the users. We have followed two ways. The first way consists of exploiting a formal theory of chess strategy, introduced and developed by the physicist Alexander Shashin in [18]. We use this theory to classify chess positions, to dynamically modify the evaluation function and drive the search in different modalities. The second way consists of introducing a reinforcement learning component able to improve from actual play. We exploit a stateful concept of *experience*, which increases the effectiveness of both the evaluation and the search. We combined these two approaches in the new enhanced version of Stockfish that we name ShashChess. All the software used and experimental data gathered throughout this research are publicly available[1].

This paper has the following structure:

Section 2 presents our motivations. Section 3 briefly describes the state of the art of chess engines, focusing on the recent successes of machine learning. Section 4 is the core of this paper: we describe the improvements we introduced in Stockfish to improve both its playing strength (in particular, exploiting Shashin's theory of chess strategy combined with reinforced learning) and its flexibility and usability by players of all types and levels. Section 5 outlines our testing strategy and evaluates the results we obtained with Stockfish enhanced with Shashin's theory and reinforced learning. Section 6 draws our conclusions and lists some open research issues.

2 Motivation

The Stockfish chess engine (current version 16), is an open source program written in C++. Its search component is based on alpha-beta pruning with iterative deepening.

Until version 11, the evaluation function was a long polynomial including several terms rating chess concepts like material, mobility, king safety, etc. [22]. Any addition or modification of the weights of the terms included in the evaluation function need tests over a large number of games. The tests are performed on a distributed platform called FishTest to play thousands of games between different versions of the program at two different time controls: first a very short time control (initially 5 s per game plus 0.1 s per move) is used, then if the first phase has positive results a longer time control (initially 10 s per game plus 0.1 s per

---

[1] https://github.com/amchess/ShashChess.

move) is used. After these extensive test games if the results are positive the new version is accepted. This approach is necessary because enhancing Stockfish faces the *oracle problem*: if the chess engine plays better than any potential tester, how can a tester claim that a certain evaluation is wrong or that a suggested move is not the best one [13]?

In 2020 a new component called *Efficiently Updatable Neural Network* (NNUE in short) was introduced in Stockfish version 12. The NNUE is a particular type of neural network trained to predict the output of the conventional evaluation function, saving time and enhancing the search depth [9]. It was developed to have the benefit of machine learning without needing a GPU. The idea was first applied to Japanese chess Shogi [14], then was applied to chess; Stockfish clearly improved its performance when NNUE was introduced. The NNUE evaluation is so strong even with short evaluation times that is likely that in the next version the classic evaluation function will be dropped from the source code.

Stockfish has a number of well-known limitations in terms of usability for the human player:

- in handicap mode Stockfish makes mistakes randomly on purpose in greater numbers as the target Elo rating decreases. This is of little use to human players; an handicap mode tailored on the human to train would be much better;
- the score given to moves or positions is often not aligned with the Informant symbols: this creates to humans interpretation problems on the engine output;
- machine learning techniques were applied to the scoring function, but not to the search algorithm;
- search includes several sophisticated selectivity techniques (in particular, the pruning): while these techniques make Stockfish very strong in matches, especially at short times, they also weaken it in solving unbalanced positions that we call *chaotic* [11]. Chaotic positions are very useful for strong human players who want to play unexplored opening variants. It is possible to remedy this weakness by manually disabling some of the selectivity techniques (in particular, Late Move Reductions (LMR) and the null move), to improve the resolving ability. This approach is inflexible, however, because it is weak in actual game play;

Strong human players like grand masters need support not only to find good new opening moves: these moves must be understandable and playable, meaning that they should be adequate to the knowledge and playing style of the player. We exploit Stockfish to build repertories of positions tailored for a specific human player, who has to meet some specific human opponents in a forthcoming match or tournament, either over the board or even by correspondence.

3   Related Works

The component which evaluates a chess position is a polynomial usually including several terms measuring each some specialized domain knowledge. For instance, *King safeness* is a term included in most evaluation functions. The weight of such term among others (for instance, *control of the center of the board* or *mobility* or *quality of the pawn structure*) has to be carefully tuned.

In [7] a method was introduced to modify the evaluation function of a chess engine according to the style of play of human players (the paper made experiments with Kasparov and Kramnik styles). The authors used temporal difference learning for tuning the weights of the terms of the evaluation function.

Reinforcement learning is dynamically learning how to best give weights with a trial and error method to maximize the outcome [21]. Instead *deep reinforcement learning* is learning from existing knowledge and applying it to a new data set [15].

Reinforcement learning applied to Chess has been studied in several papers. KnightCap [2] was the first program to use fruitfully reinforcement learning playing over the Internet Chess Club. The use of a regression network to learn non-linear combinations of the individual values of pieces was later used in [8], again playing against grand masters but with results less convincing than those obtained by KnightCap.

Deep learning uses neural networks to evaluate chess positions, decide which game tree branches to search, and order moves. In 2016, DeepChess obtained a grandmaster-level performance using a learning method incorporating two deep neural networks, trained using a combination of unsupervised pre-training and supervised training [3]. The unsupervised training extracts high level features from a given chess position, and the supervised training learns to compare two chess positions to select the more favorable one. In order to use this approach inside a chess program, a novel version of alpha-beta is used that does not require bounds.

At the end of year 2017, the DeepMind team published [19] a generalized AlphaZero algorithm, combining Deep learning with Monte-Carlo Tree Search. AlphaZero achieved superhuman performance learning chess starting from scratch in four hours and convincingly defeated Stockfish 8. The impact of Go playing engines on human play has been studied in [5], showing how the performance of professional Go players has changed since the advent of AlphaGo.

4   Method

We now outline and discuss a number of improvements we explored modifying Stockfish; our goal is to achieve greater flexibility using Stockfish as a coach for humans.

- modifying Stockfish evaluation function: our goal is to improve the understandability of moves and positions suggested by the chess engine maintaining a high playing strength both in matches and in solving complex positions;
- application of reinforced learning techniques (both standard and q-learning): our goal is to exploit machine learning in search, not only in the evaluation of positions;

– customization of the thinking system of the engine, exploiting a configurable handicap mode and avoiding an handicap based on random errors.

4.1 Modifying the Evaluation Function

Alexander Alexandrovich Shashin is a physicist and a chess trainer. He introduced a theory which models chess as a complex system described by the following factors [18]:

a the *material*, corresponding to a concept similar to mass;
b the *relative mobility* of White and Black pieces, corresponding to a concept similar to kinetic energy;
c the "*safety*" of the deployment structure of White and Black, respectively;
d a first spatial factor consisting of the so-called "*packaging density*", corresponding to a concept of density;
e a second spatial factor consisting of the so-called "*expansion factor*", corresponding to a concept of potential energy.

These factors are inspired by classic evaluation functions and can be used to estimate if a chess position requires attack, defense, or strategic thinking.

In fact, based on these five factors, three playing modalities are introduced (we use for each modality the name of a world champion):

– Tal, or the modality of the attack;
– Capablanca, or the modality of the strategy;
– Petrosian, or the modality of defence.

There are also two boundary modalities (called Tal-Capablanca and Capablanca-Petrosian, respectively), referred to as "chaos zones," in which Shashin suggests to follow the principle, borrowed from thermodynamics, of the so-called line of least resistance, i.e., try the most aggressive approach first and then the other, more cautious one.

Some positions are "chaotic", as safety is so difficult to assess that one could apply any of the modalities. These are the most interesting ones for human players. Shashin wrote that his method is useful for both humans and programs, but gave no hint on its implementation.

Starting from a large database of grand master games, we coded a filtering program that selects only the games that led to positions with "unclear" evaluation (chaotic). It was interesting to note that a chaotic position can be obtained in few moves from the initial position. An example is the well-known Leningrad system of Dutch defence: **1 d4 f5 2 ♗g5 h6 3 ♗h4 g5.**

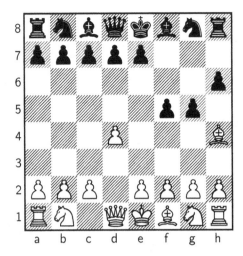

The resulting position is classified as chaotic (Tal-Capablanca modality). In fact, even for strong engines, it is extremely difficult to figure out what is the right course of action in this position: a cautious, Capablanca-type one opting for Bg3 or the more aggressive, Tal-type one playing moves like e3 or e4?

Initially, we planned to replace the evaluation function in Stockfish using directly Shashin's formulae. This approach soon proved unsuccessful: Shashin's safety is too complex to be calculated in a way that is even remotely comparable in efficiency to that of the original Stockfish.

Therefore we reasoned backwards: given a position to be classified according to Shashin, we started from the score provided statically by Stockfish; then we iterate search and after each iteration we substitute the value computed by a thread to its preceding score.

Table 1 shows how we associate a numeric evaluation, an Informant symbol, and a Shashin type. We calibrated the scores having as a reference the initial position, to which we assigned a conventional score of 15cp (*cp* stands for *centipawn*, namely 1/100 of the conventional value of a pawn).

We remark that these scores have an approximation of 10cp, because if two moves have a score differing by max this value, they can be considered equivalent. Due to a parameter called *contempt* (the estimated superiority/inferiority of the program over its opponent) and imperfect scaling, the score provided by Stockfish is not consistently aligned with the Informant symbols. We have therefore "normalized" the scale as follows (seen from White player's perspective):

- a Capablanca position has a score between -0.25 and 0.25; in Informant terms the position is either equal (=), or unclear (∞);
- a Tal position has a score > 0.25, so it is at least $\pm$ or even $\pm$ or +−;
- a Petrosian position has a score < -0.25, so it is at least $\mp$ or even $\mp$ or −+.

The basic idea is to rate a position analyzing it by three parallel threads executing each one of the three modalities (Tal, Capablanca, and Petrosian). Simplifying as much as possible, the result is that two parameters are associated

Table 1. Informant symbols and their evaluation range in centipawns

Range	Symbol	Position type
≤ -140	−+	high Petrosian/defensive decisive advantage
[-140,-75)	∓	medium Petrosian/defensive
[-75,-25)	∓	low Petrosian/defensive
[-35,-15]	∞	unclear Capablanca/Petrosian
[-15,15]	=	Capablanca/strategic/quiescent
[15,35]	∞	unclear Capablanca/Tal
(25,75]	±	low Tal/attacking
(75,140]	±	medium Tal/attacking
> 140	+−	high Tal/attacking decisive advantage

with a position: (*int shashinValue*; *int shashinPositionKey*). The first parameter can take only three values (CAPABLANCA, PETROSIAN, or TAL). The second corresponds to the Zolbrist key of the evaluated position. This key is needed because, at certain points in the search algorithm such as in null moves, it is expected to "pass the move" and the last position must be kept track of. Such values can be initialized by the user; if the user does not take action, the Capablanca modality is initially assumed and a static evaluation is performed to determine, via the score obtained, the position type.

This classification is used both to set the weights and elements of the classical evaluation function and to guide the search algorithm in its various steps.

In this way, the engine becomes more flexible because both the evaluation and the search dynamically adapt to the type of position. For example, dynamic elements such as King's security carry more weight for non-quiescent positions (Tal or Petrosian modalities). Similarly, in search, selectivity techniques such as null moves are effective more on quiescent positions (Capablanca type). Other engines, such as the commercial Komodo, have an option to disable them, but in doing so, the engine loses in match strength because there are many more quiescent positions. In contrast, ShashChess does this only when needed. Our tests show that the modified engine has greater playing strength in a match with long time control; it also solves many more critical testing positions. Depending on the nature of the position, the algorithm adapts dynamically its evaluation function. The goal is to store incrementally more and more complex positions, with their evaluation and depth of exploration, while maintaining the same or even higher playing strength. In fact, it is known that many selectivity techniques work very well at short times, but fail on more complicated positions.

An inflexible approach consists in disabling the selectivity, but in this way we lose game power. Adopting Shashin's theory we are succeeding and the engine, on decent machines, works very well even in blitz games.

In summary: we initialize a root position's rating by classifying its "zone" (Tal, Capablanca or Petrosian, or a borderline zone). This is to "bootstrap" the engine if we already know the position's rating. Then, we calculate a new rating for such a position going deeper in the game tree and finally updating its value. Based on it, we drive both a modified classical evaluation and the search.

ShashChess[2] is the program obtained exploiting Shashin's theory in Stockfish. Basically it executes specific code for each modality, be it Tal, Capablanca, or Petrosian. For example, in the case of a highly tactical position, we do not execute the null move and we explore deeper the game tree in the Late Move Reductions selectivity parts. We found that Stockfish patches - which are released quite often, almost daily - can be easily modified to include this specific code.

4.2   Exploiting Reinforcement Learning

Another important idea is to apply reinforcement learning techniques to Stockfish's search function rather than to its evaluation function, starting from the MTD(f) (Memory-enhanced Test Driver: the alphabeta with memory) algorithm [16]. This has the goal to avoid a run on expensive hardware as required by AlphaZero or Leela. The reinforcement learning search technique we employ was introduced by Kelly Kinyama of the Fishcooking group, that is the Stockfish engine community.

Since human grand masters memorize positional evaluations since when they begin to learn to play chess, why cannot chess engines be allowed to do the same? We therefore designed BrainLearn[3], another Stockfish derivative that, like the original, runs on inexpensive computers and phones. In fact its reinforcement learning algorithm can be plugged into any game playing program. We extended the Forward Sparse Sampling Search (FSSS) Algorithm in the minimax framework [23]. In order to address the practical issues of its implementation, in the rest of this section we will refer to our FSSS algorithm implementation as a reinforcement learning algorithm.

The problem with the original implementation, as in [23], is that it requires a lot of computation and many samples of the same state for several numbers of moves. Our implementation does not sample the states. We collect the samples differently: while the program is playing, it collects the positions evaluated in an *experience file*. The information in each record in this file is shown in Table 2.

The Zobrist key is a position's identifier. This structure needs only 24 bytes and is saved whenever the engine finishes thinking. The samples are stored in memory as an *"experience file"*, conceptually similar to the Stockfish transposition table. This file is stored permanently and will be reloaded when the engine starts a new game. If a position is found in the file, we use the information to make pruning decisions. In this way, we eliminate the computational requirements for FSSS to collect the samples. As the number of games increases, also the samples increase.

We call this "standard learning" because it is based on a single score for each position; it is similar to *transfer learning* [17,20]. The experience files computed

---

[2] https://gitlab.com/amchess/shashchess.

[3] https://gitlab.com/amchess/brainlearn.

Table 2. Structure of the experience file: the main difference with respect to an opening library is the storage of the minimax score and the depth the move was calculated

Type	Field	size	Meaning
uint64_t	Key	8 bytes	The position's Zobrist key
Int	Move	4 bytes	The move made for this position
Int	Score	4 bytes	The minimax score of the move
Int	Depth	4 bytes	The depth the move was calculated
Padding		4 bytes	

in this way can easily be merged. Essentially, if we have two samples/entries with the same position and move, we store the one with the greater depth. The experience file can be navigated as an opening book enriched with the depth information.

4.3   Customization of the Engine

Given an arbitrary position, usually a chess player is not interested in the absolutely best move, that is a quite abstract concept, but in the most effective one coherent with his/her thinking system or playing level. Moreover, some players are interested in sub-optimal moves which however can pose specific difficulties to specific opponents.

Traditionally, the handicap mode in chess is implemented as the engine playing some random errors, eg. it plays weaker moves at lower Elo rating settings. This randomized "fault injection" is not really useful for training human players. We implemented a customized handicap system based on the Elo rating.

The work [4] correlates the Elo rating with an engine search depth. We derived from this paper a specific handicap depth range to each playing category, as shown in Table 3.

Table 3. Handicap depth range as a function of the player category

Elo range	Playing level	Handicap depth range
[0,1999]	Beginner (B)	[1,6]
(1999, 2199]	Intermediate (I)	(7,9]
(2199, 2399]	Advanced (A)	10
(2199, 2850]	Expert (E)	(11,20]

Then we defined for each playing category a set of suitable positional factors, distinguishing static/long term and dynamic/short term. An expert human coach can correlate ShashChess classical evaluation's positional factors with ideas understandable by his/her human trainees, depending on the particular player's thinking system. The most common, logical and pedagogically useful are those based on simple ideas like material count, mobility in space and time, king safety, pawn structure, piece development, possess of the initiative. Fig. 1 shows how the handicap mode impacts the evaluation function according to the selected playing level.

Positional factors				Player Level			
Human		Shashchess		B	I	A	E
Static	Dynamic	Static	Dynamic				
Quantitative material eval	Threats	Material	Threats	x	x	x	x
			Space	x	x	x	x
	Mobility (relative legal moves number): space and time		Mobility	x	x	x	x
	King safety (both sides)		King safety	x	x	x	x
Pawn's structure	Passed pawns	Pawns	Passed pawns	x	x	x	
Pieces positions and mobility related to pawns structure and passed pawns		Pieces positions and mobility related to pawns structure and passed pawns		x	x	x	
	Initiative (position's dynamics)		Winnable			x	x
Qualitative material eval		Imbalances					x

Fig. 1. Configuring ShashChess according to the strength of a human player

5 Evaluation

The playing strength of a chess engine, that is its rating measured in Elo points, can be assessed through various methods. One approach is to engage in *match play* against humans or other programs whose ratings are known. Alternatively, *suites of complex positions* can be collected and used to evaluate how effectively the engine solves them [6].

It is important to note that the evaluation function of any chess engine, including the refined version obtained through NNUE, remains a heuristic and is far from perfect. Similarly, the search process is not flawless, as selectivity techniques can yield imperfect results. Consequently, a chess engine that performs well in match play is not necessarily equally proficient at solving particularly challenging positions.

To ensure the quality and strength of each new official Stockfish distribution, extensive testing is conducted using Fishtest. This involves playing thousands of games at both short and long time controls to confirm that the new version surpasses its predecessors in terms of playing strength.

In this project we are not interested in developing a stronger Stockfish version. In fact, usually we do not use Fishtest to test a new version of ShashChess. Instead, ShashChess is tested against standard Stockfish as follows:

- (LTC 25/10): 10 games with reversed colors on the 10 most common center types in opening theory;
- on a battery of hard positions classified according to Shashin and using LTC 25/10.

We verified the reproducibility of the results obtained.

ShashChess gives its best at non-bullet times (at least blitz on a decent machine), since, at each iteration, it has to rate a position and this improves the quality of analysis, but it also has a high computational cost.

In Table 4 we show some results we obtained with different types of evaluation.

Table 4. Results of some experiments: LTC means Long Time Control, usually 25/10

Player	opponent	type of test	result
ShashChess	Stockfish 15	LTC, 40 games complex positions	+5=33−2
ShashChess	Stockfish 15	test suite 318 pos	solved 207-187
BrainLearn	Stockfish 11	bullet, 1000 games	+108=694−70
ShashChess	Brainlearn	blitz, test suite 80 pos	+4 =80 −4
ShashChess+RL	Leela 0.22	LTC, 20 games	+4 =13 −3

The table shows that ShashChess is at least as strong as Stockfish. This is confirmed by several independent testers[4].

The evaluation of ShashChess in handicap mode is performed choosing specific positions, and in particular, their type. The idea is to identify several positions with different characteristics to train the engine in different situations and also determine the modality most suitable for that kind of position. A reviewer of a preliminary version of this paper suggested to test the ability of ShashChess to guess different moves in a same position according to the Elo settings, thus simulating different humans with different chess strength. We used the 40 positions contained in [1], and got a good overall 47% score.

Finally, the evaluation of Brainlearn is more conventional, performed by playing several games against Stockfish.

---

[4] See for instance: https://ccrl.chessdom.com/ccrl/4040/rating_list_all.html,
http://fastgm.de/60-0.60.html,
https://sites.google.com/site/computerschess/scct-cs-1-3600-elo?pli=1.

5.1 Training Humans

We have received positive feedback from strong human players (here undisclosed for privacy reasons) who use ShashChess for their training, whether it be over-the-board or correspondence games.

This is our approach: we request the human player to provide his/her games, which will be utilized to construct an experience file. This experience file, referred to as the *avatar*, is then given to ShashChess to develop a new opening repertoire and a chess profile specific to the human player. To construct the repertoire, ShashChess engages in hundreds of games, separately exploring white and black lines. The human player profile consists of a list of attributes defined by a human trainer, including Elo rating, repertoire quality (large/small, varied, forcing/quiet), attacker/defender tendencies, preferred center types, and positional characteristics (pawn structure, king's position, bishop pair), as well as strategic, tactical, and endgame skills.

If the human player is aware of his/her next opponent, an avatar for the opponent can also be created to contribute to the preparation for the next game. ShashChess is then used to play experimental games, helping to determine the opening to use against the opponent and allowing for the exploration of potential novelties.

ShashChess employs the classification of chess positions, as discussed in Sect. 4.1, within a test suite. This enables us to identify a "style" or "personality" associated with the player, which influences the move selection when there are multiple good moves for a given position. Some evaluated positions can be found in the ShashChess repository [10], along with the games and test suites.

On the other hand, BrainLearn is employed to play another set of games, aiming to discover potential opening novelties by leveraging the NNUE approach. However, caution must be exercised when interpreting the results, as it can be challenging to fully appreciate or understand the moves and lines suggested by the program.

6 Conclusions and Further Work

We have summarized our work, which involves modifying Stockfish to support the training of human players. To achieve this, we have developed a program called ShashChess, which is not only strong like Stockfish but also flexible enough to be useful in various ways.

ShashChess is based on a theory of chess strategy that helps classify positions and provides suitable plans to human players based on their level of play. These plans can be customized to meet the specific needs of players, such as training for a tournament where the opponents are known in advance. Building experience files using the games of a particular player to explore their strengths and weaknesses, and combining it with an opponent's experience file, allows us to find opening lines and novelties that are effective against that opponent. The moves suggested by Shashchess are more easily understandable through the handicap mode, which aims to mimic the thinking process of the player.

When organizing training sessions for humans, we utilize ShashChess instead of BrainLearn. ShashChess is focused on the human-understandable theory of chess strategy, while BrainLearn combines reinforcement learning and q-learning and utilizes the NNUE component of Stockfish during the search process. Both programs are derivatives of Stockfish, as depicted in Fig. 2.

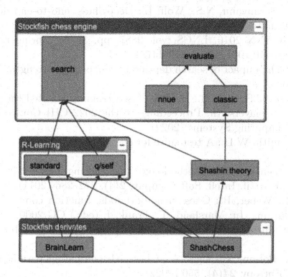

Fig. 2. Stockfish employs two evaluations, primarily relying on NNUE, while the classic evaluation is used upon user demand or in specific positions. ShashChess modifies the "evaluate" module, whereas BrainLearn modifies the search process by altering the basic search algorithm of Stockfish, performing additional sub-steps as necessary.

We employ a combination of both programs to conduct experiments and generate specialized opening books and experience files tailored for the training of human players, even at the world championship level.

Another use case for ShashChess involves analyzing collections of games, such as Fischer's *"My 60 Memorable Games"*, and ranking them by complexity based on Shashin's theory. This ranking system proves useful for both authors and readers. Additionally, we have plans to perform an extensive analysis on all 500 ECO codes using ShashChess, employing both conventional search and q-learning techniques. Subsequently, we will merge all the results into a single experience file and utilize the games to generate a new opening tree, which we expect to be rich in theoretical novelties. This systematic approach will not only help us redefine the theory of the opening phase of the game but also enable us to offer customized experience files to specific players based on their playing style and thinking process.

Acknowledgments. We thank Augusto Caruso and Kelly Kinyama for fruitful discussions on some topics dealt with in this paper. We also ack the support of CN-HPC under PNRR.

References

1. Adams, M., Hurtado, P.: Think like a Super-GM. Quality Chess (2022)
2. Baxter, J., Tridgell, A., Weaver, L.: KnightCap: a chess program that learns by combining td () with minimax search. In: Proceeding 15th International Conference on Machine Learning, pp. 28–36 (1997)
3. David, O.E., Netanyahu, N.S., Wolf, L.: DeepChess: end-to-end deep neural network for automatic learning in chess. In: Villa, A.E.P., Masulli, P., Pons Rivero, A.J. (eds.) ICANN 2016. LNCS, vol. 9887, pp. 88–96. Springer, Cham (2016). https://doi.org/10.1007/978-3-319-44781-0_11
4. Ferreira, D.: The impact of search depth on chess playing strength. ICGA J. **36**(2), 67–80 (2013)
5. Kang, J., Yoon, J.S., Lee, B.: How AI-based training affected the performance of professional go players. In: Proceedings of the 2022 CHI Conference on Human Factors in Computing Systems (2022)
6. Lang, K.J., Smith, W.D.: A test suite for chess programs. ICGA J. **16**(3), 152–161 (1993)
7. Levene, M., Fener, T.: A methodology for learning players' styles from game records. Int. J. Artif. Intell. Soft Comput. **2**(4), 272–286 (2011)
8. Levinson, R., Weber, R.: Chess neighborhoods, function combination, and reinforcement learning. In: Marsland, T., Frank, I. (eds.) CG 2000. LNCS, vol. 2063, pp. 133–150. Springer, Heidelberg (2001). https://doi.org/10.1007/3-540-45579-5_9
9. Maharaj, S., Polson, N., Turk, A.: Chess AI: competing paradigms for machine intelligence. Entropy **24**(4), 550 (2022)
10. Manzo, A.: ShashChess repository. https://github.com/amchess/ShashChess (2023)
11. Manzo, A., Caruso, A.: The Computer Chess World - How to make the most of chess software. AlphaChess (2021)
12. McIlroy-Young, R., Sen, S., Kleinberg, J., Anderson, A.: Aligning superhuman AI with human behavior: chess as a model system. In: Proceedings 26th ACM SIGKDD International Conference on Knowledge Discovery & Data Mining, pp. 1677–1687 (2020)
13. Méndez, M., Benito-Parejo, M., Ibias, A., Núñez, M.: Metamorphic testing of chess engines. Inf. Softw. Technol. 107263 (2023)
14. Nasu, Y.: Efficiently updatable Neural-network-based evaluation functions for computer Shogi. The 28th World Comput. Shogi Championship Appeal Doc. **185** (2018)
15. Plaat, A.: Conclusion. In: Learning to Play, pp. 233–254. Springer, Cham (2020). https://doi.org/10.1007/978-3-030-59238-7_8
16. Plaat, A., Schaeffer, J., Pijls, W., De Bruin, A.: Best-first fixed-depth minimax algorithms. Artif. Intell. **87**(1–2), 255–293 (1996)
17. Scherzer, T., Scherzer, L., Tjaden, D.: Learning in Bebe. In: Computers, Chess, and Cognition, pp. 197–216. Springer (1990). https://doi.org/10.1007/978-1-4613-9080-0_12
18. Shashin, A.: Best Play The Best Method for Discovering the Strongest Move. Mongoose Press, Swindon (2013)
19. Silver, D., et al.: A general reinforcement learning algorithm that masters Chess, Shogi, and go through self-play. Science **362**(6419), 1140–1144 (2018)

20. Slate, D.J.: A chess program that uses its transposition table to learn from experience. ICGA J. **10**(2), 59–71 (1987)
21. Sutton, R.S., Barto, A.G., et al.: Reinforcement learning. J. Cogn. Neurosci. **11**(1), 126–134 (1999)
22. Various-authors: stockfish evaluation guide. https://hxim.github.io/Stockfish-Evaluation-Guide/ (2020)
23. Weinstein, A., Littman, M.L., Goschin, S.: Rollout-based game-tree search outprunes traditional alpha-beta. In: Proceedings European Workshop on Reinforcement Learning, pp. 155–166. PMLR (2012)

Combating Computer Vision-Based Aim Assist Tools in Competitive Online Games

Mathias Babin and Michael Katchabaw[✉]

Department of Computer Science, University of Western Ontario,
London, ON, Canada
katchab@csd.uwo.ca

Abstract. This work presents a novel approach to the application of adversarial attacks to the domain of video games, specifically, the exploitation of computer vision-based aim assist tools in the first-person shooter genre. As one of the greatest issues plaguing modern shooters, aim assist (also referred to as aimbots) greatly increase the speed and accuracy of cheating players, giving them an unfair advantage over their competitors. The latest versions of these aim assisting tools make use of object detection models such as YOLO (You Only Look Once); fortunately, these models are vulnerable to attack via small perturbations to their input space which results in the misclassification of objects. The purpose of this work is to formulate an attack on a black-box object detection model which can be feasibly implemented in a commercial game environment. What makes our solution unique is the generation of attack images in the form of in-game objects rendered by the game engine itself, instead of a set of screenshots or from a generic differentiable renderer. Results show that our approach is capable of generating adversarial examples which can fool an object detection model in a black-box environment, as well as recreating the game's original textures such that these perturbations go unnoticed by players.

Keywords: procedural content generation · adversarial attacks · aim assist

1 Introduction

The modern day cheaters of today's video games employ a diverse and evermore sophisticated set of strategies to obtain an unfair advantage over their opponents. Arguably, there is no genre of game plagued by cheaters more than that of the first-person shooter (FPS), with the most popular form of cheating being that of aim assisting tools referred to as *aimbots*. Traditionally, aimbots have been implemented by modifying the game's locally installed client to detect the exact positions of enemy players and aim accordingly. While it is possible for anti-cheat solutions to detect many of these illegal modifications, it has also been proposed

© IFIP International Federation for Information Processing 2023
Published by Springer Nature Switzerland AG 2023
P. Ciancarini et al. (Eds.): ICEC 2023, LNCS 14455, pp. 290–305, 2023.
https://doi.org/10.1007/978-981-99-8248-6_24

that in the environment of cloud-based games cheating will become much more difficult due to the elimination of game clients being hosted on player's machines [13–15]. However, in an attempt to circumvent both client-side anti-cheat systems and prepare for a cloud-based future, cheaters have began developing aim assist tools which rely upon recent advancements made in computer vision (CV), specifically AI-based object detection models [21]. The advantage to this new style of aimbot is that it is nearly impossible to distinguish it from a highly skilled player as both rely on interpreting the screen to aim accordingly.

Fortunately, it has been well established in other domains that the CV models used to develop these aim assist systems are often vulnerable to adversarial attacks (AA) which aim to compromise these model's ability to classify objects correctly through the addition of subtle perturbations made to the victim's input space [1]. As such, the goal of this work is to replicate the success AA have found in disrupting these models and apply it to the domain of video games, specifically, through the generation of attacks which can successfully thwart a CV-based aimbot. What makes this problem challenging is that there are two main factors that we must keep in mind while devising our solution outside of the implicit requirement to minimize any visual impact our perturbations have on our source material. The first of these requirements assumes that we will never have direct access to the model we are attacking; a constraint which significantly reduces the number of possible algorithms we have at our disposal. The second requirement is that our solution must minimize its computational cost once it is deployed into the game we are attempting to defend: video games can have frame rates that run upwards of 120 frames per second, which is 5 times higher than that of standard film. This makes most games extremely resource intensive to run and if we wish our solution to be commercially viable, we must find a solution which minimizes our impact on system performance.

The solution this work ultimately arrives to is a strategy capable of generating game textures which fool a CV-based aimbot into misclassifying inanimate game objects as players with the goal of confusing it to aim at them instead of actual players; with this in mind, we also explore the possibility of minimizing the CV model's ability to classify the player itself, effectively rendering it invisible to the aimbot. This is significant as CV-based aimbots pose a major problem for many game developers, a problem which will only intensify in the coming years. Currently there are no available solutions to this problem that we are aware of, and as such, this work could stand to benefit game developers and their millions of players.

The remaining sections of this paper outline not only how we arrive to this solution, but also provides an overview of important terms and existing works in Sect. 2, further details on the technical aspect of our approach are discussed in Sect. 3, with results presented in Sect. 4. Finally, we outline the future works of this research in Sect. 5 where we discuss not only improvements that can be made to its implementation but also call for the further investigation into claims and assumptions made throughout the course of this work.

2 Background

Before introducing some related works in the field, we will first briefly summarize some important concepts related to this work including what precisely constitutes an aim assist/aimbots within the context of competitive FPS games, as well as some relevant distinctions that exist between the types of AA we may want to consider for our own solution.

2.1 Aim Assist/Aimbots

Throughout the history of the FPS game genre, players have engaged in competitive online play against one another. It was inevitable that some players would turn to cheating to gain a competitive edge over their opponents, and amongst the myriad of strategies cheaters employ, perhaps the most pervasive is that of aim assisting tools, later dubbed *aimbots* by the community.

A traditional approach to implementing an aimbot would involve modifying the game's client to provide the aimbot with the game's world space position of all enemy players, to which the system would rapidly move the cheater's cursor to the corresponding part of the screen containing an enemy player; however, as anti-cheat systems become more sophisticated, would-be cheaters are having an increasingly hard time accessing the relevant information from the game's client, or when doing so are flagged and immediately banned. Unfortunately, advancements in object detection systems such as YOLO (You Only Look Once, [2]) or SSD (Single Shot MultiBox Detector, [3]), have led to a new generation of aimbots that do not require access to the game's client in any fashion, as these models can identify enemy players simply by looking at the game's output to the screen.

2.2 Adversarial Attacks

AAs [1] are a method of disrupting machine learning-based object detection models by modifying an image to contain subtle perturbations such that these models misclassify objects; these perturbed images being an instance of an adversarial example (AE). Depending on whether or not we have access to the target model, we can classify it as either a white-box, black-box, or grey-box attack.

White-Box Attacks. White-box attacks assume we have full access to the model we are attacking, and as such, can use gradient data to optimize the perturbations we are applying to our AE. [1] introduces a white-box attack called the Fast Gradient Sign Method (FGSM), which optimizes its AE image x' using the sign of the gradient obtain from input image x to model $F(X)$. FGSM's objective function is as follows:

$$x' = x - \epsilon * sign(\nabla loss_{F,t}(x)) \tag{1}$$

Here, the hyperparameter ϵ controls how much the image x is altered when forming its perturbed counterpart x'. FGSM's approach to generating a successful AEs x' relies on tuning ϵ such that perturbations are visible enough to disrupt the target model, but not so obvious that they can easily be discerned by humans.

Another white-box approach to generating adversarial examples is called a Carlini and Wagner (CW) attack [5]. This approach involves two main components: 1) a portion of the update function which concerns itself with generating examples that maximize the misclassification rate of the target model, and 2) a component which attempts to minimize the distance between the attack image x' and its source image x, i.e. we construct AEs by minimizing $d(x, x')$ such that $F(x') = t'$ for the chosen target class t' [6].

In a later work, the authors of [7] build on the CW attack method by introducing the concept of Expectation Over Transformation (EOT) which modifies the CW objective function to account for changes in position, rotation, and lighting of a 3D object being perturbed. The major contribution of this work was to find the expected value for both of CW's components across all transformations T in an attempt to make the model more robust:

$$\operatorname*{argmin}_{x}(\underset{t \sim T}{\mathbb{E}}[log P(y_t | t(x'))] - \lambda * \underset{t \sim T}{\mathbb{E}}[d(t(x'), t(x))])) \qquad (2)$$

Like FGSM's hyperparameter ϵ, this EOT objective function contains a hyperparameter λ which controls the strength of the image reconstruction portion found in the latter half of the formula.

Black-Box Attacks. Black-box attacks assume that we do not have access to the model we are attacking; however, we can assume that we can query the target model for results. The major difference between this style of attack and white-box methods is that we cannot rely on any updates that require a gradient signal. It is often the case that black-box methods will rely on a CW style objective function, with optimization being performed via a genetic algorithm or evolutionary strategy [8].

Grey-Box Attacks. Like black-box, grey-box attacks assume we do not have access to the target model we are attacking, however, they do assume that we are able to create our own local model that approximates its performance. From here, white-box solutions can be implemented using the substituted model and any resulting AEs x' can be applied to the target model due to the property of transferability [9].

Evolutionary Strategies. As a popular form of black-box optimization method, evolutionary strategies (ES) behave much like a genetic algorithm, as ES rely on a set of randomly mutated copies of some source material and updates towards a solution that maximizes a user-defined objective function

$f(w)$; however, unlike a genetic algorithm, this ES does not have a crossover function to produce new children, but rather simply applies random noise to the original. Much like a hill climbing algorithm, the ES' update rule steps proportionally towards children that $f(w)$ scored highly and away from those that scored poorly, resulting in a method that estimates the gradient of the expected reward returned from $f(w)$.

2.3   Related Works

Anti-Cheat in FPS Games. [10] presents a classifier which identifies if a player's game has been altered to contain additional elements which highlight the positions of enemy players on their screen. In this scenario, the classifier must be integrated into the game so it can be running on the cheater's machine, however, this also makes their classifier vulnerable to the cheater's own AAs. To test their model's robustness, they subject their classifier to AEs generated via a number of strategies including FGSM. An important distinction between this work and our own is that we are not aiming to identify whether or not a player is in fact cheating, but rather actively prevent them from doing so in the first place. Another important distinction is the type of cheating that is being discussed in both works. While we are interested in automated aim assisting tools, this work focuses on the problem of identifying cheaters whose in-game visuals have been enhanced to better inform them on where other player's are hiding, but not necessarily on increasing their ability to aim at them.

Adversarial Attacks on Game Playing Agents. [4] applies FGSM to generate attacks on the state space of reinforcement learning (RL) agents. While not entirely the same scenario, this work does overlap with the problem we are attempting to solve as both aim to hinder the performance of a game playing agent. Here, an FGSM attack is applied to the entire screen space the RL agent receives as input in an attempt to make the agent misclassify which action should be taken given the current state of the game environment.

Adversarial Attacks on YOLO. [22] presents the application of EOT to the task of attacking a YOLO object detection model, specifically in an attempt to hide a human subject from being classified. Their approach involves manually masking out the human in each image and allowing EOT to reconstruct the masked part of the image to that of the original person in a manner which is not recognizable to the object detector. One key area in which our work will differ from this one's is that we will not mask portions of the screen for reconstruction as we can instead attack the texture space of our game; in a sense, attacking texture space functions like a perfectly fit mask as our perturbations will only applied to our target object's mesh and nothing else in the game scene. The second major difference is that we would like to receive our attack images directly from our game engine's render pipeline, as we would like to generate a generalized solution which is tolerant to any changes in our game's dynamic elements such as lighting, shadow, particle effects, moving objects, etc.

3D Adversarial Attacks. [11] applies FGSM attacks to 3D objects. Like in the previous work, attacks are performed on the model under various changes to rotation and lighting with the difference being that attacks are applied to the object's texture space instead of the screen space of a final render; this means that for FGSM optimization to take place, the gradient signal must run backwards through a differentiable renderer which converts an object's mesh X and texture T into an attack image Y via the following:

$$Y = r(X(T), \rho, \theta, \phi) \tag{3}$$

Here, the parameters ρ, and θ control the objects rotation along two axis while parameter ϕ controls light intensity. As previously stated, our solution will be using renders directly from our game engine's rendering pipeline in lieu of a differentiable one like this. Our reason for this decision rests on the assumption that images rendered using a game engine will outperform those from a generic differentiable 3D renderer, as results directly from the engine contain scene specific lighting, shadows, particle effects, post-processing effects, and dynamic objects. In Sect. 5, the closing discussion of this work, we will present some preliminary thoughts and evidence for why we suspect this assumption to be true, as well as lead a discussion on how this topic can be further explored in future works.

3   Methods

This section will serve to not only outline the core technical details of our proposed solution, but also provide some rationale as to why each decision was made. We will begin by providing an overview of our entire proposed solution before discussing in detail each of its components in the following subsections.

3.1   Proposed Solution

While the general problem this work is attempting to solve is the disruption of aim assisting tools in FPS games; the specific scenario we are aiming to develop a solution for assumes the position of that of a game development studio attempting to protect their online FPS game from cheaters armed with CV-based aimbots. What this scenario entails is that we have access to our own game's source-code but not the object detection models being used by the cheating players. As such, the first step in developing a solution will be to build our own basic FPS game using the *Unity* game engine [18] such that we will have access to the game's source code and render pipeline; just as any game studio would. Next, we will train an object detection model to serve as a cheating aimbot using labelled screenshots collected from our game. It is important to note that in a real-world scenario, we cannot assume that we will have access to this model directly such that we can make use of white-box methods, but rather, as in a black-box approach, we would be able to query it for results. Finally, we will attempt to build adversarially textured objects which confuse the aimbot into targeting them over actual players.

Fig. 1. A render of our game's player using both the regular rendering pipeline as well as a custom pass used for testing occlusions in a window found in the top left-hand corner of the leftmost image. The rightmost image provides an example of an annotated screenshot captured by our automated annotation system. (Color figure online)

3.2   Data Collection

Because we have developed our own game, there will be no existing datasets available to train our own object detection model. Fortunately, because we have access to the game's source code, the task of collecting and labeling data can be completed automatically. Inside the game, we can place virtual trackers on the player's head and torso or any other parts we would like labelled. From here, we can simply convert these trackers from world space positions to screen space coordinates and record them as a label's bounding box. For the collection of data we simply play the game for an indeterminate amount of time, recording both screenshots taken from the game itself as well as the label's bounding box coordinates. The only issue that remains is to filter out any images where the player is occluded by other objects such as walls. There are any number of ways this could be implemented, for this work, we choose to simply discard any images where the player's trackers are not at least 50% visible. As shown in Fig. 1, the implementation of an occlusion check involves creating a second custom rendering pass that reduces the game's visuals to a low resolution map of the environment. This custom pass renders all environmental objects as black, the player's head tracker as blue, and their body tracker as pink. Next, if either tracker is occluded by any object, that portion of the model is rendered as a different colour: red for the head tracker, and yellow for the body tracker. Finally, we simply calculate the ratio of blue to red pixels for the head, and pink to yellow pixels for the body to determine what percentage is visible and discard any screenshots where these ratios are not above 50%. The leftmost image of Fig. 1 shows a player character rendered in our game environment, with a window displaying the custom rendering pass of the same scene in the top left-hand corner. The rightmost image of the same Figure provides an example of an annotated image captured by our system.

3.3   Object Detection

For our object detection model we use an implementation of YOLOv5 [12]. We choose YOLO over other object detection models such as SSD, because of the model's widespread popularity; however, future works should include testing multiple object detection models.

We train our YOLO model on over 10,000 annotated images gathered from our game. As a test of transferability, we also test a YOLOv5 model pretrained on the COCO dataset [19] on the same test dataset to see if our game's player model would be classified as a *person*. Results presented in Sect. 4 show that while a generic pretrained YOLOv5 model performs above our expectations, in order to implement a successful aimbot one must train on a dataset specific to the game they are attempting to cheat as character models will likely not be transferable between many games—save perhaps some military shooters where character models and environments are relatively similar to one another.

3.4 Optimization Strategy

As stated in previous sections, this work assumes that we do not have access to the aimbot's CV model, eliminating the possibility of white-box approaches for the generation of our AEs, leaving only black and grey-box methods. The issue that arises with using grey-box methods is that if we wish to use our game engine to render our attack textures instead of using a differentiable renderer, we still cannot rely on any white-box methods to run on our local substitute model as our game engine's rendering pipeline is non-differentiable. From this process of elimination, we can conclude that we will be relying on black-box methods for developing our attacks, specifically, we will be implementing an evolutionary strategy [8] to generate our attack textures in a manner similar to the work presented in [20].

The objective function $f(w)$ we will be using, follows an approach similar to that of CW, where we are attempting to maximize the misclassification rate of the object detection model $F(x)$ when supplied with an in-game render Y containing our attack texture t'. This objective function simultaneously aims to minimize the distance between its source texture t and its perturbed attack texture t', with a hyperparameter λ to control the strength of this reconstruction portion of the function. Our objective function $f(w)$ can be written as follows:

$$f(w) = P(y|F(Y)) - \lambda * MSE(t', t) \tag{4}$$

3.5 Image Reconstruction

As stated in the previous subsection, we can decompose our objective function into two components, and as a result, we can formulate two separate tasks to test whether our black-box optimization strategy will work independently before recombining them into a single function. First, we will look at the task of image reconstruction, which will require the latter half of our objective function: $-\lambda * MSE(t', t)$.

For this task, we simply begin with random noise w with the same dimensionality as our source texture t. We then apply the ES with the objective function $f(w)$ defined as $-1 * MSE(w', t)$: the mean squared error between the current

Fig. 2. 16 test image results obtained from our trained YOLOv5 model (right), and 16 results from a pre-trained YOLOv5 model trained on the COCO dataset (left).

child texture w' and the target texture t. At each iteration of the algorithm, a small amount of noise is applied to w to produce children w', each of which are tested for fitness using $f(w)$. Finally, an update is applied to the original noisy texture w towards the children which most closely resemble the texture t and away from those that do not based on the results obtained from $f(w)$; by the end of this process, we obtain a noisy texture w which is nearly identical to our target t.

3.6 Misclassification

Optimizing a texture to maximize the misclassification rate of our YOLO model is extremely similar to the process outlined in the previous subsection, with the only major difference being the objective function $f(w)$ which now returns a value proportional to the confidence that the in-game render Y contains a player $P(y|F(Y))$; specifically, we are interested in the sum of the confidence of all bounding boxes in the set B returned by YOLO that are labelled as either a head, or a body.

For us to be able to obtain these confidence values, we need a method for converting our child attack texture w' into a screenshot using our game engine. First, we Base64 encode the image and send it to a special version of our game which is listening for incoming messages; next, the game loads the texture onto a 3D mesh, in our case a garbage bin model, and sends back a base64 encoded screenshot of the game window to our ES to load and evaluate. Finally, it should be noted that one advantage to formulating the system in this manner is that we can easily parallelize training across many devices locally or remotely if needed.

4   Results

This section provides the results for three key areas of our work including the performance of our custom trained YOLOv5 model as well as a general pretrained model, from our image reconstruction and misclassification tasks, and finally, from our combined objective function which achieves both misclassification and near perfect image reconstruction.

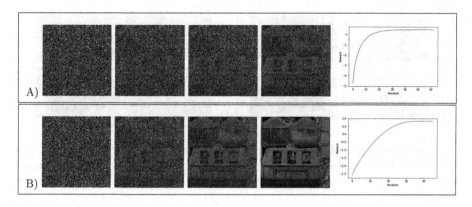

Fig. 3. A visualization of two experiments for image reconstruction. A) displays results for an *npop* of 100, while B) does so for an *npop* of 3000. Plots provide the respective reward received from the objective function $-\lambda * MSE(x', x)$. Note that the iterations displayed on the x-axis were recorded every 25 iterations and the reward on the y-axis as been standardized.

4.1 Object Detection

We begin by presenting the results from training our YOLOv5 model on our dataset of over 10,000 annotated screenshots gathered from the automated process outlined in Subsect. 3.2. This model achieved 99% accuracy across our test set of over 1,000 images. The left-most grid of 16 images of Fig. 2 presents examples of labelled results from this model. It is important to note that nearly all of the images not classified correctly were due to an error in our labelling process which only accounts for environmental objects occluding the target but not the player's own weapon. With this correction made, we believe that the model would score a near 100% accuracy. One such example of this can be seen in the second row and column of Fig. 2.

We also ran our model on a pretrained generic YOLOv5 classifier trained on the COCO dataset, which notably does not contain any video game examples. The right-most 4×4 grid of Fig. 2 presents examples of labelled images from this model. For our purposes, we will treat a correct classification as any character which is labelled as a *person*. Results from this experiment that of the 80 possible classes, this model achieved an accuracy of 46%, a result much higher than we had anticipated; nevertheless, this degree of accuracy is still too low for implementing a reliable aimbot, but it does reinforce our initial claim that if a cheater wishes to implement one for a specific game they will need to first label a substantial amount of data themselves.

4.2 Image Reconstruction

Recall the decomposition of our objective function (Eq. 4) into two separate tasks: image reconstruction, and misclassification. Results regarding the image

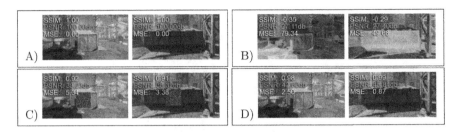

Fig. 4. SSIM, PSNR, and MSE values for both sides of our object: Row A), the original screenshots (100% similarity to itself); row B), an inverted version of the base image from A); row C), our noise patches before evolution; and row D), our noise patches after evolution.

reconstruction portion of our solution are presented in Fig. 3. Both rows A)/C) of Fig. 3 provide a visualization of the evolutionary process of our initial noise sample w towards our original texture x over the course of 1000 iterations. The plots B)/D) at the end of each row presents the reward (objective function $-\lambda * MSE(x', x)$) over time as our ES arrives to its final solution. What is of note is the *npop* hyperparameter which denotes the population size used by the ES; after multiple experiments, it was found that sufficient results were only obtainable using an *npop* of at least 1500 with marginal improvements as *npop* is increased. It is also important to address the trade-off that exists between time and *npop*, as evolving a texture with a population size of 3000 will certainly take longer than one using a size of 100. For this work, we mostly ignore the time penalty incurred by increasing *npop* as the primary focus is the quality of the resulting output texture. Row A) of Fig. 3 shows results for an *npop* of 100, while the row C) shows results for an *npop* of 3000. For the purpose of reproducibility, each experiment used a learning rate α and a noise standard deviation σ of 0.01.

As a means of evaluation, Fig. 4 reports the values obtained from several image quality metrics: SSIM, PSNR, and MSE. As seen in row A), we compare each image against a base screenshot containing the object wrapped in its original unperturbed texture. The subsequent rows of this figure report these values for an inverted version of the base, the noise patches before evolution, and our patches following evolution. We provide rows B) and C) as a baseline to help contextualize the values reported in D) and find that the values closest to the ideal scores of row A) are those of our evolved patches in row D).

4.3   Misclassification

For our second task, we aim to simply maximize the misclassification rate of our YOLO model without any concern given towards how the resulting texture appears. In general, there are two ways to approach this problem, you can either generate noise that modifies the entire texture as seen in image A) of Fig. 5, or you can attack only a small part of it as seen in the noisy patch of Fig. 6. The only advantage to the second approach wherein we are evolving a single

Fig. 5. A) A perturbed texture optimized for misclassifications. B) A test render displaying misclassification rates. C) A plot providing the reward received from our misclassification objective function.

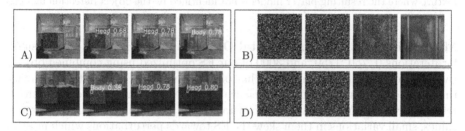

Fig. 6. Row A) Object classification results for iteration 0, 750, 1750, and 3000 of our ES optimized using combined objective function 5, with corresponding noise patches provided in row B). Similar results for another side of the same object are provided in rows C) and D).

patch as opposed to an entire texture, is that training times can be reduced significantly due to the fact that once image reconstruction is reintroduced in our combined objective function, the size of parameter *npop* would need to be scaled up accordingly; recall the effects of *npop*'s size in Fig. 3 where an *npop* of 100 was too low to successfully reconstruct the entire texture, instead requiring a value of over 3000. Figure 5 provides the final texture file A) as well as its accompanying in-game render B) as well as plots C) of their respective rewards over time.

4.4   Combining Image Reconstruction and Misclassification

With results from Subsects. 4.2 and 4.3 providing evidence that these tasks can be performed in isolation, we now attempt to evolve a set of noise patches on our texture which follow our original objective function 4; that is an objective function which aims to both maximize the confidence in classification of our non-player object to that of a target player, as well as towards its original unperturbed state such that it resembles the original texture as closely as possible. We will also provide some preliminary results for the misclassification of target players themselves, that is, we will be attempting to mask them from the object detection model altogether.

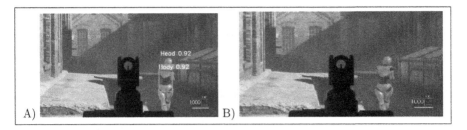

Fig. 7. A) the result of our object detection model on a statically posed player object with a combined confidence of 1.84 (0.92 for both head and body). B) A perturbed texture where the resulting player model is not identified by the object detection model.

Maximizing Static Environmental Objects. Images in Fig. 6 show results for iterations 0, 750, 1750, and 3000 of our ES optimized using combined objective function 5, which is similar to that of Eq. 4, however, we find that training times are significantly reduced when we clip the combined confidence values returned from our YOLO model by constant C. Without clipping the confidence values, small variations in them skew the ES towards perturbations which mostly optimize towards misclassification, but mostly ignore reconstruction scores. We believe this phenomenon is caused by the fact that the variance in confidence values is much greater than that of the reconstruction scores, and clipping above a certain threshold is a way of removing this variance in one of our components altogether. During training it was observed that the ES algorithm would first evolve a noise patch to meet this clipping threshold C (1.5 in our experiments) before beginning to solve the image reconstruction task near the halfway point of a training run.

$$f(w) = \begin{cases} C, \text{if } P(y|F(Y)) \geq C \\ P(y|F(Y)), \text{otherwise} \end{cases} - MSE(t', t) \qquad (5)$$

Minimizing Target Players. While much of this work has focused on the misclassification of static environmental objects with the goal of confusing aimbots on who their true targets are, a more direct approach would be to simply make players not be able to be seen in the first place. The issue that arises with this strategy is that players are dynamic objects and thus would require a more robust AE which can support the various actions and positions these characters find themselves in. While we also suggest this as a topic for future investigation, we do provide some promising preliminary results in Fig. 7. The first image of this figure contains a statically posed player model similar to that of one of our test images found in Fig. 2. With an unperturbed texture this frame yields a combined confidence score of 1.84; however, in the following image, we see how a perturbed texture was evolved to produce a character which does not get classified at all, i.e. its confidence for both its head and body are 0.0. To achieve this we simply minimize the misclassification value of objective function 4 as oppose to maximizing it, and unlike in the previous experiments where clipping was applied, these results can be achieved by leveraging that fact that minimization has an inherent floor of 0.0 instead.

5   Conclusion

5.1   Future Works

As raised in each of the previous sections, there remains many topics and points of improvement for future work, the most significant is a more thorough investigation into the evolution of textures for dynamic objects such as players. While this work provided one such example in Fig. 7 as a proof of concept, for this to prove viable in a commercial setting would require the resulting perturbed texture to camouflage the character model from any angle and position in its animation. This could be achieved via a method similar to EOT wherein changes in position, rotation, and lighting of the character should be accounted for during texture optimization.

In terms of possible improvements to system performance, there exists a substantial bottleneck between the communication of our ES and our game engine. Currently our ES used for generating our AE requires the transmission of perturbed textures to our game engine for rendering before they are transmitted back for evaluation; ideally, this could take place within the game engine itself. The solution to this problem depends on whether we can compile our YOLO model using the Open Neural Network Exchange (ONNX) [16] standard and execute it from within our game, to which there appears to be libraries currently available to do so [17]. We expect this singular change could improve real-world training times immensely, which in turn, could help make processes like those described above more feasible in a real-world setting.

Another important aspect for future work should include an investigation into our claims that our generated noise patches are indeed imperceptible to players. While we firmly maintain this to be the case, a formal study should be conducted such that these claims can be fully substantiated.

The last major area of future research should explore the effects of transferability, specifically, in the case where textures are generated using a greybox method and a differentiable render before being placed in a game environment which contains different lighting, shadows, post-processing effects, particle effects, and dynamic objects. For the purposes of this work, we rest on the assumption that this approach cannot outperform frames rendered directly from the game itself; however, what does warrant investigation is whether or not the difference between these game-rendered textures substantially outperform those produced using a differentiable render enough to warrant choosing one over the other.

5.2 Summary

Throughout this work, we have presented the first steps in developing a novel approach to the generation of AEs which target malicious players in FPS games by attacking the black-box object detection models that give them an unfair advantage over their opponents. We have shown that it is not only possible to evolve textures to fool their aimbots into misclassifying static environmental objects, but we have done so in a manner which makes them retain their original appearance.

A significant aspect of this work that is not only unique to the medium of video games but is integral to the long-term success of our solution is the ability to quickly generate large annotated datasets without the need to manually label each image individually. Currently, one way to counter AEs is to train directly on them, thus in the inevitable race to stay ahead of these new models, it is critical that developers be able to generate new AEs faster than the cheaters can train their models to counter them. In order for a cheater to train on the textures we produce, they must manually label thousands of images by hand as they do not have access to the game's source code and thus cannot take advantage of the automatic data collection system outlined in Sect. 3.2. This means that the process for developers to evolve new textures is guaranteed to out pace the cheaters' attempts to retrain their aim assisting models. This approach excludes the possibility that game developers can evolve a set of textures, only deploying a small subset of them at any given time. This means even if new models are trained to detect some objects, new textures can easily be loaded that the cheaters' updated models have never encountered before.

References

1. Goodfellow, I., Shlens, J., Szegedy, C.: Explaining and harnessing adversarial examples. In: ICLR 2015 International Conference On Learning Representations (2015)
2. Redmon, J., Divvala, S., Girshick, R., Farhadi, A.: You only look once: unified, real-time object detection. In: 2016 IEEE Conference On Computer Vision And Pattern Recognition (CVPR), pp. 779–788 (2016)
3. Liu, W., et al.: SSD: single shot multibox detector. In: Leibe, B., Matas, J., Sebe, N., Welling, M. (eds.) ECCV 2016. LNCS, vol. 9905, pp. 21–37. Springer, Cham (2016). https://doi.org/10.1007/978-3-319-46448-0_2
4. Huang, S., Papernot, N., Goodfellow, I., Duan, Y., Abbeel, P.: Adversarial attacks on neural network policies. ArXiv Preprint ArXiv:1702.02284 (2017)
5. Carlini, N., Wagner, D. Towards evaluating the robustness of neural networks. In: 2017 IEEE Symposium on Security and Privacy (SP), pp. 39–57 (2017)
6. Carlini, N., Katz, G., Barrett, C., Dill, D.: Provably minimally-distorted adversarial examples. ArXiv Preprint ArXiv:1709.10207 (2017)
7. Athalye, A., Engstrom, L., Ilyas, A., Kwok, K.: Synthesizing robust adversarial examples. In: International Conference on Machine Learning, pp. 284–293 (2018)
8. Salimans, T., Ho, J., Chen, X., Sutskever, I.: Evolution strategies as a scalable alternative to reinforcement learning. ArXiv Preprint ArXiv:1703.03864 (2017)

9. Papernot, N., McDaniel, P., Goodfellow, I.: Transferability in machine learning: from phenomena to black-box attacks using adversarial samples. ArXiv Preprint ArXiv:1605.07277 (2016)
10. Jonnalagadda, A., Frosio, I., Schneider, S., McGuire, M., Kim, J.: Robust Vision-Based Cheat Detection in Competitive Gaming. Proc. ACM Comput. Graphics Interact. Tech. **4**, 1–18 (2021)
11. Yao, P., So, A., Chen, T., Ji, H.: On multiview robustness of 3D adversarial attacks. Practice and Experience In Advanced Research Computing, pp. 372–378 (2020)
12. Ultralytics YOLOv5. (2021), https://github.com/ultralytics/yolov5
13. Quigley, K.: Reduce Cheating and Hacking up to 90% with Cyrex GST (2020), https://cyrextech.net/cyrex-gst-cloud-service-stops-90-of-hackers-and-cheaters/
14. Pinto, S.: Cloud-Based Gaming: A Game Changer For Security? (2021), https://blog.anybrain.gg/cloud-based-gaming-a-game-changer-for-security-70dd0f831869
15. Chronicle, D.: New cloud-based solution launched to counter cheating in eSports (2019), https://www.deccanchronicle.com/technology/in-other-news/280919/new-cloud-based-solution-launched-to-counter-cheating-in-esports.html
16. Foundation, T.: Open Neural Network Exchange (2019), https://onnx.ai/
17. Software, U.: Unity Package Manuals: Introduction to Barracuda (2020), https://docs.unity3d.com/Packages/com.unity.barracuda@1.0/manual/index.html
18. Software, Unity Real0Time Development Platform (2023), https://unity.com
19. Lin, T., et al.: Microsoft COCO: common objects in context. In: European Conference On Computer Vision, pp. 740–755 (2014)
20. Qiu, H., Custode, L., Iacca, G.: Black-box adversarial attacks using evolution strategies. In: Proceedings of The Genetic and Evolutionary Computation Conference Companion, pp. 1827–1833 (2021)
21. Cunha, P.: Pine (2021), https://github.com/petercunha/Pine
22. Jonnalagadda, A., Frosio, I., Schneider, S., McGuire, M., Kim, J.: Building towards invisible cloak: robust physical adversarial attack on yolo object detector. In: 2018 9th IEEE Annual Ubiquitous Computing, Electronics & Mobile Communication Conference (UEMCON), pp. 368–374 (2018)

Research on the Gameplay Evolution Based on Warcraft 3 Mod Platform

Xing Sun$^{(\boxtimes)}$ ⓘ and Hongbo Lin ⓘ

Tsinghua Shenzhen International Graduate School, Nanshan District, Shenzhen 518055, China
sunxking@sz.tsinghua.edu.cn, linhb21@mails.tsinghua.edu.cn

Abstract. With the ongoing and rapid growth of the game industry, numerous gameplays of varying popularity and duration have emerged. This study explores gameplay development and evolution by analyzing mod gameplay evolution using the Warcraft 3 map editor. We examined the 10 most popular map sequences on the Warcraft 3 mod platform, analyzing gameplay characteristics in trending maps and iterative trends of successful gameplays. The results revealed that most downloads centered on a few trending map sequences, with varying downloads within the same sequences. New gameplays faced player preference pressure, prompting constant evolution to cater to players. Finally, gameplay evolution was observed through experiments, confirming the feasibility of using evolutionary design in gameplay design.

Keywords: Game mechanics/Gameplay · Mod · Evolution · Warcraft 3 · MOBA · Battle Royale

1 Introduction

1.1 Development of Gameplay

Since the release of video games, different game genres had been popular; and new game genres emerge constantly. Some game genres have enjoyed continued popularity worldwide for years, while others are gradually phased out. Examples include the decline of RTS games in the market and the rise of MOBA games. According to Adams et al., video game genres are defined by gameplay [1]. Therefore, we hold that the development of game genres essentially is the evolution of gameplay. This study aims to explore the influencing factors for gameplay evolution.

Gee et al. defined video games as a unique real-virtual story produces a new form of performance art coproduced by players and game designers [2]. Players and game designers connect through multimode human-computer interaction. Uncertainty exists in creating popular games accepted by players. Nowadays, designers innovate existing gameplays rather than inventing new genres from scratch, leading to new gameplay genres through constant accumulation. The evolution of different gameplay mods developed from a single game is an ideal research object.

© IFIP International Federation for Information Processing 2023
Published by Springer Nature Switzerland AG 2023
P. Ciancarini et al. (Eds.): ICEC 2023, LNCS 14455, pp. 306–314, 2023.
https://doi.org/10.1007/978-981-99-8248-6_25

1.2 Game Mod

Game mod, i.e., Modification, refers to the modification program spontaneously made by players for a video game [3]. With its increasing influence on the game industry, a great number of studies have been carried out by the academic circle. Some studies focused on the development form of mod. Nieborg once carried out a specialized study on the *mode total conversion mod team* [4]. Sotamaa proposed to select excellent works and developers through mod competition [5]. Some studies analyzed players' motivations for choosing mods. Identified the influencing factors behind their motivations through the analytical investigation on users of mods of the Skyrim [6]. Dey identified the characteristics of popular mods by analyzing the data of two sequences from The Elder Scrolls and the Dragon Age on Nexus [7]. Additionally, some studies attempted to apply mod to teaching [8].

For game developers, gameplay mods are a huge treasure trove of creativity. In recent years, mods are prevalent in many popular game creativities. However, currently there is a lack of research on the gameplay evolution during the development of mods for individual games in the academic circle.

1.3 Mods on Warcraft 3 Map Editor

Warcraft 3 released by Blizzard Entertainment in 2002, was one of the most popular RTS games in the world. As of 2004, its sales had already reached 4.4 million copies [9]. The game offered a map editor enabling players to create custom gameplays (mods). Map authors had creative freedom to develop unique gameplays using terrain editing, scripts, and more. Mod gameplay based on Warcraft 3 map editor had uniform image performance, fast iteration, and no advertisement marketing. These mods attract players with gameplay purely and control of artistic effects and business models, making it an ideal platform for gameplay research.

In this paper, various mods based on Warcraft 3 were used as research objects to explore the characteristics of different gameplays in the process of development and evolution, with a view to discovering an evolutionary rule of a gameplay.

2 Methods

2.1 Data Collection

We gathered data from several major Warcraft III mapping sites on the game's player-made maps and plotted Google Trends.

Through the Google trend chart, we found that Epic War was significantly more popular than other websites, and there was no other meaning for this keyword, so we chose Epic War as the data collection site.

Google Trends data on Warcraft 3 and Epic War indicates a smooth decline in Warcraft 3's search volume since 2004, while Epic War's search volume has steadily risen since its launch in 2005, surpassing Warcraft 3's volume in November 2008. This shift highlights Warcraft 3's transformation from a game to a diverse game platform, with the most popular gameplay being various mods developed by enthusiasts.

We downloaded 285,691 pieces of public map information from Epic War website as of October 2020 and selected the following fields for analysis: Name, Author, Submit time and Downloads. After data collection, the popularity of this version of map was indicated by its downloads. According to this, we got the 10 most downloaded map sequences, which are: *DotA, Map Tong Hop, Legend of Dragon, DDay: Judgement, Thien Kiem, Fight of Characters, Pokémon Defense, Bleach Vs One Piece, X Hero Siege* and *Footmen.*

2.2 Data Processing

To observe the proportion of the downloads of maps with different popularity, the download accumulation curve (Fig. 1.A) was plotted. In this figure, the abscissa is the number of maps, ranked from most to least downloaded, while the ordinate is the proportion of total downloads. It can be seen from the figure that the top 5% of maps with the highest downloads on the EpicWar website contributed to 70% of the total map downloads.

Meanwhile, the top 10 high-influence sequence maps were also sorted. The number of maps of these sequences accounted for about 4% of the total number of maps. The downloads of these maps accounted for about 35.2% of the total map downloads.

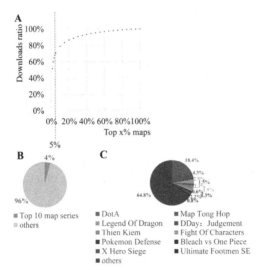

Fig. 1. Graphs and pie charts of the number of maps and downloads of mods on EpicWar. A. The top 5% of maps accounted for 70% of total downloads. B. Top 10 map sequences accounted for 4% of the total number of maps. C. Top 10 map sequences accounted for 35.2% of total downloads

Besides, the top 10 high-influence sequence maps with the highest downloads were obtained from the Epic War website for trial, and compared them to the regular gameplay of War3. The core experience of gameplays of Warcraft 3 is about collection, production and combat. We analyzed the gameplay rules that make up these core experiences, and based on these rules we compared the gameplay differences between different mods.

Next, the downloads, upload time, author name and other data on DotA and other popular map gameplay sequences were collected, plotted and compared (Fig. 2).

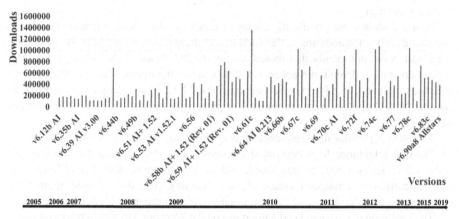

Fig. 2. Changes in Downloads of Various Versions of DotA Sequence

We found that downloads of mods for different versions of the Dota sequence varied greatly. The highest number of downloads is concentrated in a few specific versions, while most other versions have few downloads.

We also performed data analysis on the other 9 sequences of mods and obtained similar results.

3   Results

3.1   Main Features of Popular Map Gameplays

The analysis of popular map gameplays on the Warcraft 3 mod platform revealed the following observations:

1. New gameplays often reduce resource types and change collection methods to primarily killing enemies or wild monsters.
2. Many new gameplays have fewer building and combat unit types, and some eliminate construction or combat unit production altogether.
3. Combat in new gameplays may involve single unit control or require no unit operation, with item synthesis introduced in 9 new gameplays.

These head mods significantly differ from the regular combat gameplay of War3. Figure 1 shows players' uneven distribution among gameplays, with popular maps having the majority of downloads, indicating concentrated player preferences.

3.2   Iterative Trend of Successful Gameplay Map

As of October 2020, the highest downloaded sequences in Warcraft 3 Mod maps recorded 76,100,358 downloads, comprising 18.4% of all map downloads.

Actually, DotA did not evolve linearly and had a number of evolutionary directions for various gameplay genres. Many authors modified and developed simultaneously, resulting in multiple DotA branches. Finally, DotA Allstars branch became the most popular gameplay.

Figure 2 shows the popularity trends of DotA Allstars, with average downloads increasing early on, stabilizing in the middle, and slightly decreasing later. However, the downloads were not evenly distributed among the 269 maps of the subsequence. The highest downloaded version reached 1,372,805, while the lowest was just 586. Among 268 maps analyzed, 48.88% experienced a rise, and 51.12% saw a drop from the previous version. Not all updates were recognized by players, as only about half of the changes were accepted.

The other 9 popular mod sequences have similar downloads to DotA.

Players' reluctance to accept most changes leads them to stick to familiar versions, while new versions go unnoticed, making players more skilled in old versions. Consequently, new changes increase players' learning cost, discouraging them from experiencing new versions, and they eventually settle on the most recognized version.

The evolution of classical head gameplays on the Warcraft 3 platform isn't a one-stop process; they gradually form after multiple updates and iterations by different authors, modifying or adding new gameplay. Not every iteration gain popularity, and maps failing to be accepted will be eliminated (Fig. 3).

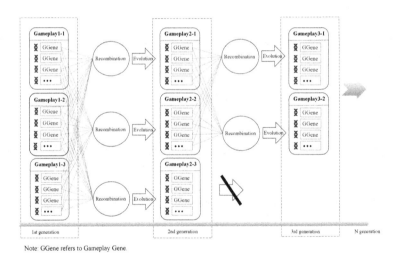

Note: GGene refers to Gameplay Gene.

Fig. 3. Evolution Process of Gameplay

4 Discussion

4.1 From RTS to MOBA

RTS games are a strategy game subclass where participants engage in real-time resource collection, base construction, army development, and unit control. The ultimate objective is to destroy the enemy's base [10].

Warcraft and StarCraft series are typical RTS games with dual experience: tactical real-time unit operation and strategic thinking. Such experience is fascinating, but it is a little too difficult to operate, for example, the APMs of professional players is over 400 [11]. Obviously, RTS games have a high threshold. Demands for fast-paced and accessible games have led to the decline of the RTS category.

On the contrary, the MOBA category is a sudden rise among gamers. In such games, each player controls a role with a series of unique abilities that can be constantly improved during the game and contribute to the overall strategy of the team [12].

MOBA integrates role-playing, action elements, and directly influenced by RTS games. DotA, a representative MOBA, originated from Warcraft 3's map editor as a mod by Eul in 2002. Afterwards, it has had multiple authors and has experienced several version update and iteration [13]. It's been more than 18 years since the DotA mod appeared, and MOBA games are dominating major gaming markets around the world.

Warcraft 3 Map Editor creates diverse mod gameplays. Players experience a new genre born from game's original essential changes. Designers innovate gameplay, exploring different directions. Constantly emerging new gameplays may differ significantly from the initial version.

4.2 Development and Evolution of Gameplay

In 2019, a scholar proposed that computerized algorithm showed characteristics similar to those of biological evolution [14]. In game design, the study on evolution is also an important field. Dominic Arsenault proposed the idea of game classification, evolution and fusion [15]. Andrew et al. proposed a framework for the evolution of game consumption [16] and explained the evolution of game consumption and its difference from traditional media forms. Cameron Browne developed an automatic game generation system named LUDI. LUDI used a design approach similar to that of biological evolution [17].

The mod gameplay evolution on Warcraft 3 platform shows similarities to biological evolution. Designers create various new gameplays through changes and integrations, which undergo player selection. Over time, some sequences survive and evolve due to subtle mutation and recombination. The entire sequence's gameplay undergoes significant change, akin to biological evolution's slow transformation.

We summarized gameplay evolution: players' random selection causes changes and survival of favored gameplays. The cyclic process generates more gameplays, with new head gameplays emerging. Similar to biological evolution's Matthew effect, favored gameplays gain popularity, attracting map makers to improve them efficiently. Players tend to download popular maps their friends play, explaining the attention popular map sequences receive from most users on Warcraft 3 platform.

4.3 Evolution of Battle Royale

In order to further explore the range of application of the evolution laws, the Battle Royale categories that have been very popular in recent years. BR gameplay can be traced back to the DayZ, a mod of the Armed Assault 2 [18]. Afterwards, Phenomenal

BR games like PUBG gained global popularity. More BR games, like Call of Duty: Warzone and Apex Legends, continue to emerge and win players' favor.

The evolution of BR gameplay from DayZ to PUBG follows similar patterns to those seen on the Warcraft 3 mod platform. DayZ, born from Armed Assault 2's authentic environment and powerful task editor, gained acceptance and survived environmental selection, passing down its gameplay genes. H1Z1: King of the Kill's optimized gun-handling expanded the player base. PUBG's explosive popularity attracted more players through the Matthew Effect.

It was observed that the investment in commercial game R&D has been increasing, e.g., 'Cyberpunk 2077' cost over $121million [19]. However, gameplays are randomly selected, increasing development risk. Developers opt for a conservative strategy, making small mutations on recognized gameplays. To improve success rates of innovative games, developers must evolve in multiple directions and accept player feedback to find the most popular gameplay. A low-cost rapid development mode can be chosen, experimenting on existing mod platforms before formal development. This aligns with evolution laws observed from Warcraft 3 mod and other platforms. By continually evolving and adapting, developers increase the likelihood of creating successful and popular gameplays that resonate with players.

4.4 Practices of Gameplay Evolution and Design

Whether gameplay evolution theory can assist in game design? We designed a group of experiments to explore its feasibility.

Experimental design: First of all, an initial gameplay was designed. It is a simple card battle mini-game (hereinafter referred to as the OPG) and supports two players against each other. Players can select role cards with different skills to play against other players to defeat the opposing character after several rounds of skill game.

30 subjects were invited to participate in each experiment. Two experiments were carried out. A total of 60 subjects were recruited. The subjects are masters studying for a master's degree in game design major in universities and have certain game design experience and planning and writing abilities. 30 subjects were divided into 5 groups (n = 6). They were required to write a one-page plan as a group within 15 min. In the first round, they were required to design based on the OPG gameplay, after which the most popular gameplay was selected by voting by the 30 subjects (voting for their own group was not allowed). The second round began after the voting. In this round, all groups are required to further design a gameplay based on the gameplay selected by voting in the first round for 15 min, after which the most popular gameplay was selected by voting again. Finally, in the third round, all groups were required to finally design a gameplay based on the gameplay selected by voting in the second round for 15 min. At the end of the third round, the most popular gameplay was also selected by voting.

Experimental results: According to the experimental results, the gameplay that finally survived was significantly different from the original OPG gameplay.

First experiment: selected gameplay combined Monopoly rule, integrated quadratic elements popular in East Asian market, expanded gacha, EDU, home systems, evolving into rich content game with perfect gameplay loop.

Second experiment: surviving gameplay changed 1v1 PVP to multiplayer PvP, combining popular BR elements, introducing level design and random card drawing, evolving into tense and exciting BR game genre.

Meanwhile, One-page selected by voting each time was written by different groups; no group's One-page was selected twice.

Experimental conclusions:

1. Evolution-assisted game design has potential. In a 30-person environment, basic gameplay evolved into multiple new gameplays quickly.
2. Combining basic gameplay with others created diversified game elements and mechanisms through designers' competition.
3. Designers added popular elements for more votes, showing gameplay evolution's sensitivity to the game environment.
4. The most popular gameplay selection was highly random.

5 Conclusions and Future Works

In this study, we analyzed Warcraft 3 mod platform gameplay maps to analyze gameplays evolution under player selection pressure. Data, including upload time, downloads, and more, were collected from the Object of Study website. Similar maps were grouped as sequences, analyzing features to identify popular ones. Preliminary results showed significant user attention. We discussed changes in DotA and other gameplay downloads, explaining why DotA replaced regular Warcraft 3 gameplay to create MOBA. Our interpretation suggested gameplays follow laws akin to biological evolution within the gaming environment. We validated it by explaining Battle Royale gameplays evolution beyond Warcraft 3 platform, obtaining expected results.

This study has some limitations: the evolution logic of only Warcraft 3 mod and Battle Royale was explored; and the evolution of more gameplays has not been analyzed. It will be the focus of the further work. Meanwhile, we hope to further perfect evolution design method through subsequent research to better assist in game design.

References

1. Adams, E.: The Designer's Notebook: Sorting Out the Genre Muddle. Gamasutra (2009). https://www.gamedeveloper.com/design/the-designer-s-notebook-sorting-out-the-genre-muddle
2. Gee, J.P.: Why game studies now? Video games: a new art form. Games Cult. 1(1), 58–61 (2006)
3. Poor, N.: Computer game modders' motivations and sense of community: a mixed-methods approach. New Media Soc. 16(8), 1249–1267 (2014)
4. Nieborg, D.B., Van Der Graaf, S.: The mod industries? The industrial logic of non-market game production. Eur. J. Cult. Stud 11(2), 177–195 %@ 1367–5494 (2008)
5. Sotamaa, O.: Have fun working with our product!: Critical perspectives on computer game mod competitions. Citeseer (2005)
6. Hirvonen, E.: Improving the game with user generated content: an overview of Skyrim mod users (2017)
7. Dey, T., et al.: Analysis of popularity of game mods: a case study (2016)

8. El-Nasr, M.S., Smith, B.K.: Learning through game modding. Comput. Entertainment (CIE) **4**(1), 7-es %@ 1544–3574 (2006)

9. Bramwell, T.: WarCraft III tops 1 m sales in Europe (2004). https://www.eurogamer.net/art icles/news050104War 3

10. Ayangbekun, O.J., Akinde, I.O.: Development of a real-time strategy game. Asian J. Comput. Inf. Syst. **2**(4) (2014)

11. Lewis, J., et al.: A corpus analysis of strategy video game play in starcraft: brood war. In: Proceedings of the Annual Meeting of the Cognitive Science Society (2011)

12. Cannizzo, A., Ramírez, E.: ToWards procedural map and character generation for the MOBA game genre. Ingeniería y Ciencia **11**(22), 95–119 (2015)

13. Tan, D.N.: Owning the world's biggest ESport: intellectual property and DOTA. Harv. JL Tech. **31**, 965 (2017)

14. Rahwan, I., et al.: Machine behaviour. Nature **568**(7753), 477–486 %@ 1476–4687 (2019)

15. Arsenault, D.: Video game genre, evolution and innovation. Eludamos. J. Comput. Game Cult. **3**(2), 149–176 (2009)

16. Kuo, A., et al.: From super mario to Skyrim: a framework for the evolution of video game consumption. J. Consum. Behav. **16**(2), 101–120 (2017)

17. Browne, C., Maire, F.: Evolutionary game design. IEEE Trans. Comput. Intell. AI Games **2**(1), 1–16 (2010)

18. Schmeink, L.: DayZ: fan-modification for the video GameArmA II [video game]. SFRAReview: 18 (2013)

19. Trock, D.: How much did it cost to make cyberpunk 2077? (2020). https://gamerjournalist. com/how-much-did-it-cost-to-make-cyberpunk-2077/

A SandBox to Sandbox: A Tangible Terrain Generator for Prototyping Game Worlds

Sebastian Schwarz[1], Benedikt Strasser[1], Michael Lankes[2], and Martin Kocur[2(✉)]

[1] University of Regensburg, Regensburg, Germany
{sebastian.schwarz,benedikt.strasser}@stud.uni-regensburg.de
[2] University of Applied Sciences Upper Austria, Hagenberg, Austria
{michael.lankes,martin.kocur}@fh-hagenberg.at

Abstract. Designing the game world is foundational for creating games. However, existing software solutions for creating game worlds such as terrain generators often require a significant amount of time and experience to be mastered. Particularly for beginners, this poses a challenge and slows down the progress in development. To address this issue, we propose a tangible terrain generator named *SandBox* composed of a small sandbox enabling users to create a terrain landscape using sand. Leveraging the engaging and familiar activity of playing in a sandbox and creating simple models, we hypothesize that SandBox offers easy-to-learn and intuitive landscape creation for games. We evaluated SandBox in a study with eight participants and compared it to a common terrain builder using the 3D-modeling software Blender. Qualitative insights indicate that SandBox was well-received. Neither usability nor task completion time was significantly different. We discuss the use of our tangible terrain generator and propose further features for future work.

Keywords: Landscape Generator · Terrain Generator · Haptic Interface · Game Worlds

1 Introduction

Designing the game world is a fundamental part of the game design process. One popular way of creating game worlds are terrain generators. They allow to manually create landscapes and natural looking terrains with a consistent but still random appearance. Level designers frequently generate terrains to create two or three-dimensional maps and game worlds. *Minecraft* [24], for example, uses different terrains involving different kind of biomes, e.g. jungles, deserts, or oceans. Terrains with highly-detailed appearances and large land areas are also typically used in commercial open-world games such as *Skyrim* [1] or *Elden Ring* [6]. While AI approaches support landscape creation [5], designers and researchers typically generate terrains manually by hand, using complex digital

© IFIP International Federation for Information Processing 2023
Published by Springer Nature Switzerland AG 2023
P. Ciancarini et al. (Eds.): ICEC 2023, LNCS 14455, pp. 315–325, 2023.
https://doi.org/10.1007/978-981-99-8248-6_26

tool sets and techniques to create the virtual environment. Brushes, for example, are used to sculpt and modify the geometry of landscapes. Consequently, creating terrains is not trivial and necessitates a significant amount of time and expertise to be mastered [29]. Particularly for beginners, this poses a challenge as the complexity of such tools causes a high barrier of entry and can also be detrimental for the created outcome, resulting in a less engaging experience [2,16].

The concept of tangible user interfaces (TUIs) aims to transfer digital tools into the physical world to enable a natural and intuitive interaction [12,28]. As TUIs leverage users' innate ability of interacting with real-world objects, users can employ familiar physical actions to control and manipulate digital content [12]. SandScape [11], for example, uses physical sand to enable computational simulations. Users can manipulate the form of a landscape using sand and see topological analysis projected onto the sand. While there are many more examples for TUIs [28], there is empirical evidence that tangible interaction can increase productivity [3] and produce engaging experiences [7,9]. Hence, leveraging tangible interaction to facilitate terrain generation for games could reduce the complexity of the process and increase engagement.

In this paper, we present a tangible and intuitive interface that allows for physical landscape prototyping. Inspired by Ishii [11], the interface employs a sandbox—we call our prototype SandBox—filled with physical sand and a depth camera that detects the height of the sand model. In a study with 8 non-experts, we demonstrate that our prototype offers an intuitive experience allowing to manipulate and sculpt physical terrains. As the prototype is a work-in-progress, we discuss potential implications and further features.

2   Related Work

Our research builds on existing knowledge concerning TUIs and landscape creation, as well as how the sense of touch can affect user experience.

2.1   Tangible Landscape Creation

Tangible prototypes engage people's sense of touch in landscape design [10]. Haptic interfaces and tangible prototypes allow users to interact with physical models of landscapes. Harmon et al. conducted a study on tangible landscape prototyping, finding that it enables rapid iterative design, quantitative testing, and effective design tool for landscape architects [10].

Tateosian et al. [30] developed a tangible geospatial modelling visualization system for terrain data . Users can interact with and modify the topography, receiving feedback on the impact of changes. The system facilitates initial design decisions, GIS simulations, and design improvement based on feedback. Mitasova et al. [23] focused on tangible geospatial modelling environments, achieving similar results in 3D landscaping.

Tato et al. [31] explored rapid prototyping in 3D printing, finding that virtual simulations can provide a similar user experience to architectural scale models .

Piper et al. [26] built a system for real-time computational analysis of landscape models. Users can change the topography of a clay model while a laser scanner captures the changes in real-time. The system offers various tested scenarios and benefits.

2.2 Increasing Engagement Through Haptics

The importance of haptics has been extensively researched ranging from the role of touch in language teaching and learning [8,22], as well as prior research investigating the interpersonal side of touch [19,22].

Haptic perception plays a significant role in shaping emotional and cognitive responses, functioning as a language [8]. The sensitivity of the skin enables touch to convey information about materials, objects, and textures, which designers should consider [21,25]. Therefore adding haptic feedback to static prototypes can create a more immersive experience [2].

In this vein, MacLean [21] provides an overview of benefits of haptic perception. Khan et al. [17] review methods for evaluating haptic systems and identify the need for further development of use case independent evaluation methods. Enabling haptic perception in virtual reality, for example, can also create a natural and intuitive experience while being immersed in a virtual environment (e.g., [13–15,18,20,27]).

2.3 Summary

Literature explores the use of TUIs in landscape design, highlighting their effectiveness as a design tool. Haptic perception shapes emotional and cognitive responses and communicates material information. Consequently, tangible terrain generation could provide an engaging and intuitive experience for creating game worlds.

3 Method

To investigate how SandBox affects terrain generation and how well users can interact with it, we compared our prototype with a common terrain generator using Blender[1] in a formative evaluation.

3.1 Development of the Prototype

To allow a natural and playful experience while creating game worlds, we developed SandBox—a $39 \times 28 \times 14$ cm box filled with play sand, with an Intel RealSense D435 depth camera placed above it. Unity version 2021.3.14f1 with a processing pipeline was used to capture and edit depth images. Filters were applied to remove holes and smooth values. Height thresholds were set, and the

---

[1] https://www.blender.org/.

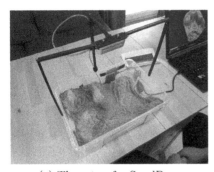   

(a) The setup for SandBox   (b) The UI of Blender

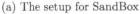

Fig. 1. Both systems were set up together

image was cropped and further smoothed by applying Laplacian filtering. Afterwards, the depth image was converted into a mesh, that mirrors the surface of the SandBox. A laptop with a 17-inch display and external mouse was used. Blender version 3.4.1 ran on the laptop, with a flat, 360×480 polygon plane object matching the SandBox's aspect ratio. Unnecessary screen elements were removed in the sculpting workspace (Fig. 1).

Current Limitations. Since the interaction possibilities in SandBox at the stage of our current work-in-progress are limited (e.g. no colour or other surface can be added), we also had to adjust the functionality of Blender. We removed all tools that are not related to object creation (e.g. scaling, inversion, rotation). We tried to create an equal level of possibilities between the two systems to conduct a formative evaluation to gain initial feedback for our approach.

3.2   Study Design

We conducted a formative evaluation to compare our prototype with a common terrain generator in Blender. We used a within-subjects design with the one independent variable TERRAIN GENERATOR with the levels *SandBox* and *Blender*.

3.3   Measures

User experience was assessed qualitatively during tasks via thinking-aloud and post-experience interviews. Participants could provide feedback verbally and in written form. A questionnaire was provided for participants who preferred not to answer verbally.

Quantitative measures were taken to further evaluate SandBox. The User Experience Questionnaire (UEQ+) [32] was used, measuring eleven scales including Efficiency, Perspicuity, Dependability, Novelty, Haptics, Adaptability, Usefulness, Intuitive Use, and Clarity. Task completion time was recorded with participants able to stop at their discretion.

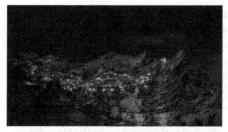 

(a) Image A depicting a mountain city at night

(b) Image B depicting a hilly landscape at daytime

Fig. 2. Image A and Image B were used in our study

3.4 Tasks

We used two different images by the same artist to inspire participants during terrain generation. Both depict a landscape, which should be a reference for the participants. Participants were asked to freely create a terrain based on the two images. To minimize learning effects and foster engagement, we used two different images with a similar topology. We alternated the images per system so that each participants were first presented one of both images while using either SandBox or Blender and then the second image with the next system. The images are shown in Fig. 2.

3.5 Participants

We recruited 8 participants from the university. They were compensated with points for their study course. As we focused on novices, only non-expert users were eligible to partake in the study. Participants' ages ranged from 22 to 29 years ($M = 25.4, SD = 2.45$) with two identifying as female and six as male. The participants ranked their experience in 3D modelling and their own creativity via a seven point Likert scale. While one participant had a little experience in 3D modelling, seven participants were inexperienced users ($M = 2.38, SD = 1.19$). The participants ranked themselves as creative in their self-assessment ($M = 4.5, SD = 1.24$).

3.6 Procedure

Participants signed an informed consent form after learning about the study's aims, process, and implications. They followed four steps for their participation, starting with providing basic demographic information and indicating their knowledge of 3D terrain building. Participants received a scripted explanation of the tools and task. The experimenter answered their questions if they had any. Each participant was presented with one of two images and given 20 min. An informal pre-test showed that 20 min was enough to interact with the system using the image as the reference terrain. They were encouraged to think aloud during the task. Participants completed the UEQ+ after each condition and participated in a post-experience interview for qualitative feedback. The total duration of the experiment ranged from 45 to 60 min.

4   Results

We conducted an analysis of the collected qualitative and quantitative data.

4.1   Qualitative Analysis

We evaluated the participants' feedback to gather insights for further improvement and impressions through think-aloud and a post-experience questionnaire. We analysed and then summarized the feedback into three categories: SandBox, Blender, and Post-Interview.

SandBox. Several key points emerged for SandBox. Participants found that the sand in the SandBox tool needed to be wet in order to stick together and create a stable structure. Additionally, fine details were difficult to model, and natural structures were easier to build than human-made ones (i.e. mountains vs. houses). Participants appreciated that details were not overly emphasized and could be smoothed out during post-processing. However, some found that the sand would collapse in on itself, limiting the height and complexity of the model. Overall, participants found the SandBox to be intuitive and relaxing to use, but suggested additional tools and features such as colouring options and more visual indicators for height and slope.

Blender. For Blender, participants found the tool to be more complex and difficult to use than the SandBox. They found it necessary to rely heavily on reference images and to adjust the brush size for height adjustments. Some also found the tool to be limiting in terms of pin shape and the difficulty in creating flat surfaces. However, participants appreciated the ability to work more precisely and create more complex structures, although this required more experience and practice. Suggestions for improvement included adding height indicators and more informative visual cues for the brush tool.

Post-Interview Feedback. Finally, within the post-interview feedback, participants compared the two tools directly. They found the SandBox to be faster and more intuitive, but also more imprecise and limited in terms of height and complexity. Some participants also found that the sand in the SandBox was too dry, making it difficult to create stable structures. On the other hand, they found the Blender to be more complex and time-consuming but provided more control and precision in creating models. They also noted that the use of reference images was more necessary in Blender than in SandBox.

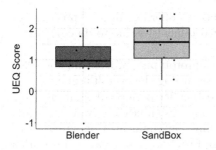 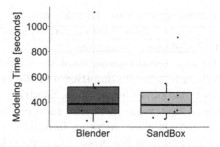

Fig. 3. Comparison in the average UEQ+ score of the investigated systems

Fig. 4. Comparison in the average interaction time of the investigated systems

4.2 Quantitative Analysis

We calculated average total score for the UEQ+ based on each single dimension. Statistical analyses were performed using the *Wilcoxon* signed-rank test due to the non-normal distribution of data. These initial analyses provide insights into participant performance and experience with our prototype.

User Experience. Each participant's UEQ+ score was first determined, and for each system the scores were aggregated in a total score. We conducted a *Wilcoxon* signed test with $p = 0.05$ to compare the systems' UEQ+ scores. The test indicated no significant difference between the scores for the SandBox and Blender ($V = 6, p = 0.1094$). Figure 3 shows the average total UEQ+ score.

Task Completion Time. We first computed participants' overall time used for each system and determined the mean. A *Wilcoxon* test indicated no significant difference for $p = 0.05$ between time spend on the tasks in SandBox and Blender ($V = 23, p = 0.5469$). Figure 4 depicts the mean task completion time per condition.

5 Discussion

The presented study investigates the effects of SandBox on prototyping in landscape design for game designers. Results suggest that SandBox did not provide a significant modelling time benefit compared to Blender (Sect. 4.2). Furthermore, participants did not perceive SandBox's usability significantly better than Blender's (Sect. 4.2).

The primary drawback of SandBox was identified as its material properties and associated modelling problem. However, participants praised its commendable attributes of high intuitiveness and efficiency. As indicated by qualitative data, participants perceived the time passing quicker while using SandBox. However, this could not be confirmed quantitatively by the task completion time.break In contrast, Blender was described as offering superior precision in modelling, but some participants encountered difficulties due to its complexity and required time to master it.

Overall, results suggest that the landscape prototyping process did not differ significantly between SandBox and Blender regarding the overall usability.

In terms of modelling time, SandBox and Blender performed similarly. This suggests that while SandBox may not provide a significant advantage, users can achieve similar outcomes in a 3D modelling environment. Combining these findings, SandBox is a promising approach for future work to create game worlds and terrains in a natural and intuitive way.

6 Future Work

Future work could improve on this prototype by including modelling tools, e.g., tools used in building sand castles to be more precise while modelling, different materials, like modelling sand and clay, and markers to virtually insert objects, like trees and characters, or environmental effects like rain and snow (e.g., [10]). This could address the participants' need for sculpting tools, which is in line with Evans et al. [4] showing that designers were not able to sculpt form through touch and produce acceptable results. In addition, satisfaction with modelling in the two systems should be further addressed, as we could show that modelling in the SandBox produces acceptable UEQ+ scores. This could be attributed to its intuitive interaction experience.

7 Conclusion

In this paper, we presented a tangible terrain generator using physical sand to create an intuitive and engaging experience while creating terrains for game worlds. A formative evaluation comparing our prototype with a common terrain generator using Blender showed first insights into users' performance and experience. Overall, our prototype was well-received. Our study suggests that our prototype could be promising as a terrain generating tool for prototyping game worlds. SandBox is planned to be extended with more features in future work.

References

1. Bethesda Game Studios: Skyrim. Game [PC, PS4] (2017). bethesda Game Studios, Rockville, USA
2. Camburn, B., et al.: Design prototyping methods: state of the art in strategies, techniques, and guidelines. Des. Sci. 3, e13 (2017). https://doi.org/10.1017/dsj.2017.10
3. Catala, A., Jaen, J., Martinez-Villaronga, A.A., Mocholi, J.A.: AGORAS: exploring creative learning on tangible user interfaces. In: 2011 IEEE 35th Annual Computer Software and Applications Conference, pp. 326–335 (2011). https://doi.org/10.1109/COMPSAC.2011.50

4. Evans, M., Wallace, D., Cheshire, D., Sener, B.: An evaluation of haptic feedback modelling during industrial design practice. Des. Stud. **26**(5), 487–508 (2005). https://doi.org/10.1016/j.destud.2004.10.002, https://www.sciencedirect.com/science/article/pii/S0142694X04000717

5. Frade, M., de Vega, F.F., Cotta, C.: Breeding terrains with genetic terrain programming: the evolution of terrain generators. Int. J. Comput. Games Technol. **2009**, 125714:1–125714:13 (2009). https://doi.org/10.1155/2009/125714

6. FromSoftware Inc.: Elden ring. Game [PC, PS, Xbox] (2017), fromSoftware Inc., Toky, Japan

7. Gallud, J.A., Tesoriero, R., Lozano, M.D., Penichet, V.M.R., Fardoun, H.M.: The use of tangible user interfaces in K12 education settings: a systematic mapping study. IEEE Access **10**, 24824–24842 (2022). https://doi.org/10.1109/ACCESS.2022.3154794

8. Gumtau, S.: Tactile semiotics: the meanings of touch explored with low-tech prototypes. In: First Joint Eurohaptics Conference and Symposium on Haptic Interfaces for Virtual Environment and Teleoperator Systems. World Haptics Conference, pp. 651–652 (2005). https://doi.org/10.1109/WHC.2005.124

9. Ha, T., et al.: ARtalet: tangible user interface based immersive augmented reality authoring tool for digilog book. In: 2010 International Symposium on Ubiquitous Virtual Reality, pp. 40–43 (2010). https://doi.org/10.1109/ISUVR.2010.20

10. Harmon, B., Petrasova, A., Petras, V., Mitasova, H., Meentemeyer, R.: Tangible topographic modeling for landscape architects. Int. J. Architectural Comput. **16**, 4–21 (2018). https://doi.org/10.1177/1478077117749959

11. Ishii, H.: The tangible user interface and its evolution. Commun. ACM **51**(6), 32–36 (2008). https://doi.org/10.1145/1349026.1349034

12. Ishii, H., Ullmer, B.: Tangible bits: towards seamless interfaces between people, bits and atoms. In: Proceedings of the ACM SIGCHI Conference on Human Factors in Computing Systems, pp. 234–241. CHI 1997, Association for Computing Machinery, New York, NY, USA (1997). https://doi.org/10.1145/258549.258715

13. Kalus, A., Kocur, M., Henze, N.: Towards inducing weight perception in virtual reality through a liquid-based haptic controller. In: Workshop on Visuo-Haptic Interaction, AVI 2022, pp. 1–5 (2022). https://epub.uni-regensburg.de/53628/

14. Kalus, A., Kocur, M., Henze, N., Bogon, J., Schwind, V.: How to induce a physical and virtual rubber hand illusion. In: Proceedings of Mensch Und Computer 2022, pp. 580–583. MuC 2022, Association for Computing Machinery, New York, NY, USA (2022). https://doi.org/10.1145/3543758.3547512

15. Kalus, A., Kocur, M., Klein, J., Mayer, M., Henze, N.: PumpVR: rendering the weight of objects and avatars through liquid mass transfer in virtual reality. In: Proceedings of the 2023 CHI Conference on Human Factors in Computing Systems. CHI 2023, Association for Computing Machinery, New York, NY, USA (2023). https://doi.org/10.1145/3544548.3581172

16. Kaplan, K.: Complex application design: A 5-layer framework (2020). https://www.nngroup.com/articles/complex-application-design-framework/ summary: Various contexts of complexity should be considered by UX designers and researchers designing complex applications, including complexities of integration, information, intention, environment, and institution

17. Khan, M., Sulaiman, S., Said, A.M., Tahir, M.: Usability studies in haptic systems. In: 2011 International Conference on Information and Communication Technologies, pp. 1–5 (2011), https://doi.org/10.1109/ICICT.2011.5983569

18. Kocur, M., Habler, F., Schwind, V., Woźniak, P.W., Wolff, C., Henze, N.: Physiological and perceptual responses to athletic avatars while cycling in virtual reality. In: Proceedings of the 2021 CHI Conference on Human Factors in Computing Systems. CHI 2021, Association for Computing Machinery, New York, NY, USA (2021). https://doi.org/10.1145/3411764.3445160

19. Kocur, M., Kalus, A., Bogon, J., Henze, N., Wolff, C., Schwind, V.: The rubber hand illusion in virtual reality and the real world - comparable but different. In: Proceedings of the 28th ACM Symposium on Virtual Reality Software and Technology. VRST 2022, Association for Computing Machinery, New York, NY, USA (2022). https://doi.org/10.1145/3562939.3565614

20. Kocur, M., Kloss, M., Schwind, V., Wolff, C., Henze, N.: Flexing muscles in virtual reality: effects of avatars' muscular appearance on physical performance. In: Proceedings of the Annual Symposium on Computer-Human Interaction in Play, pp. 193–205. CHI PLAY 2020, Association for Computing Machinery, New York, NY, USA (2020). https://doi.org/10.1145/3410404.3414261

21. MacLean, K.: Designing with haptic feedback. In: Proceedings 2000 ICRA. In: Millennium Conference. IEEE International Conference on Robotics and Automation. Symposia Proceedings (Cat. No.00CH37065). vol. 1, pp. 783–788 (2000). https://doi.org/10.1109/ROBOT.2000.844146

22. McIntyre, S., et al.: Language of social touch is intuitive and quantifiable. Psychol. Sci. **33**(9), 1477–1494 (2022). https://doi.org/10.1177/09567976211059801

23. Mitasova, H., Mitas, L., Ratti, C., Ishii, H., Alonso, J., Harmon, R.: Real-time landscape model interaction using a tangible geospatial modeling environment. IEEE Comput. Graphics Appl. **26**(4), 55–63 (2006). https://doi.org/10.1109/MCG.2006.87

24. Persson, M., Bergensten, J.: Minecraft. Game [Windows, macOS, Linux] (2011). mojang Studios, Stockholm, Sweden

25. Petrelli, D., Dulake, N., Marshall, M., Willox, M., Caparrelli, F., Goldberg, R.: Prototyping tangibles: exploring form and interaction. In: Proceedings of the 8th International Conference on Tangible, Embedded and Embodied Interaction, pp. 41–48 (2014)

26. Piper, B., Ratti, C., Ishii, H.: Illuminating clay: a 3-D tangible interface for landscape analysis. In: Proceedings of the SIGCHI Conference on Human Factors in Computing Systems, pp. 355–362. CHI 2002, Association for Computing Machinery, New York, NY, USA (2002). https://doi.org/10.1145/503376.503439

27. Schuhbauer, P., et al.: Hover loop: a new approach to locomotion in virtual reality. In: Extended Abstracts of the Annual Symposium on Computer-Human Interaction in Play Companion Extended Abstracts, pp. 111–116. CHI PLAY 2019 Extended Abstracts, Association for Computing Machinery, New York, NY, USA (2019). https://doi.org/10.1145/3341215.3356984

28. Shaer, O., Hornecker, E.: Tangible user interfaces: past, present, and future directions. Found. Trends® Hum. -Comput. Interact. **3**(1–2), 4–137 (2010). https://doi.org/10.1561/1100000026

29. Smelik, R.M., Tutenel, T., de Kraker, K.J., Bidarra, R.: Declarative terrain modeling for military training games. Int. J. Comput. Games Technol. **2010**, 360458 (2010). https://doi.org/10.1155/2010/360458

30. Tateosian, L., Mitasova, H., Harmon, B., Fogleman, B., Weaver, K., Harmon, R.: TanGeoMS: tangible geospatial modeling system. IEEE Trans. Visual Comput. Graph. **16**(6), 1605–1612 (2010)

31. Tato, M., Papanikolaou, P., Papagiannakis, G.: From Real to Virtual Rapid Architectural Prototyping. In: Ioannides, M., Fritsch, D., Leissner, J., Davies, R., Remondino, F., Caffo, R. (eds.) EuroMed 2012. LNCS, vol. 7616, pp. 505–512. Springer, Heidelberg (2012). https://doi.org/10.1007/978-3-642-34234-9_52
32. Thomaschewski, J., Hinderks, A., Schrepp, M.: Welcher ux-fragebogen passt zu meinem produkt? (2018). https://doi.org/10.18420/muc2018-up-0150

Interactive Entertainment

Empirical Studies on the Conditions of Achieving Interactive Mindfulness Through Virtual Reality Single User Experience in Macao

Sandra Olga Ka Man Ng[✉] and Carlos Sena Caires

University of Saint Joseph, Macau, Estrada Marginal da Ilha Verde, 14-17, Macau, China
{sandra.ng,carlos.caires}@usj.edu.mo

Abstract. Virtual reality, a computer-generated 3D environment, allows one to navigate and possibly interact, resulting in real-time simulation of one or more of the user's five senses (Gutierrez et al., 2008; Vince, 2004). Virtual tours and places have swiftly become popular in education, professional training, arts, exhibitions, and medication and rehabilitation. The empirical studies derived from the PhD thesis research aim to identify the conditions for Macao's single-user experience to achieve mindfulness in virtual reality through immersion and interactivity.

The writers describe three spectrums on the levels of immersion, interactivity, and mindfulness-based on multiple definitions. For the empirical study, immersion and interaction are controlled experiment constants. As an international city in Southern China, we suggest four Macao experiment settings, addressing spiritual memory, historical memory, aesthetic appreciation, and idea meditation, collect qualitative and quantitative survey data. The collected data are analysed to improve virtual reality conditions for local mindfulness.

Keywords: Single user experience · virtual reality · immersion · interactivity · mindfulness

1 Introduction and Literature Review

This first chapter discusses definitions of virtual reality and immersion, highlighting the transformative nature of virtual environments and the importance of immersion for creating a sense of presence. It also explores interactivity in virtual reality, emphasising user engagement and control levels. Additionally, it distinguishes between meditation and mindfulness, proposing different virtual environments to help individuals achieve mindfulness.

There are definitions of virtual reality and immersion out in the field. To name a few: Mazuryk & Gervautz suggest that a virtual environment can transform the surrounding into another dimension with objects that are non-accessible in reality or do not even exist [1]; Sutherland and Sensorama insisted on the notion of immersion with the coverage of as much as possible to all human senses [2]; being immersed allows us to feel like

© IFIP International Federation for Information Processing 2023
Published by Springer Nature Switzerland AG 2023
P. Ciancarini et al. (Eds.): ICEC 2023, LNCS 14455, pp. 329–334, 2023.
https://doi.org/10.1007/978-981-99-8248-6_27

"being in" the virtual environment, which makes it the crucial criterion no matter the theory by Saeed et al. [3] and Mortara & Catalano [4].

In the empirical studies here, also based on the combination of literature review and according to the Cambridge Dictionary, we take that virtual reality as "a set of images and sounds (an environment), produced by a computer, that can be seen and heard using a computer that seems to represent a place or a situation (a three-dimensional virtual environment) that a person can take part in (interact with) without going anywhere or talking to anyone.". The variables controlling the immersion level include output hardware (sight and hearing) and input hardware (interaction and response). These variables affect the level of immersion and limit the user's interaction inside a virtual experience. That said, we summarise a spectrum (Fig. 1) for immersion, dividing it into three levels: the non-immersive, a computer desktop experience through the screen (Window to the Virtual World); the semi-immersive, a hybrid system based on a non-immersive system augmented with additional input such as gloves or other tangible sensors; and the Immersive, usually with a Head-Mounted Display that immerses the user in a visual environment and adds sound and hand interactions (through controllers or not).

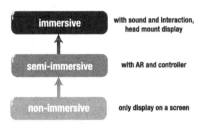

Fig. 1. The immersion spectrum with its three levels.

Despite the various definition of interactivity by Stromer-Galley [5], Jonasson [6], Steuer [7], Bretz & Schmidbauer [8], and Rafaeli [9], it is generally defined as the interaction between humans and computers. Considering real-time interactivity (or not) in virtual reality environments requires different development, as does navigation control. We, therefore, propose the spectrum for interactivity (Fig. 2) as the following: The lowest level of interactivity is when the user is immersed in virtual reality with digital technology with only simple navigation and passive perception of information. As the level of interactivity increases, navigation introduces more flexibility, like different movements to wander in virtual reality at the same time. The user, instead of being fed with information, has more authority in choosing where to go and what to explore.

Meditation, a form of mental training [10], serves as a tool for psychotherapy or to advance oneself in spirituality, self-understanding, and self-regulation [11]. It is seen to be an effective way to reduce stress. Yet, meditation is a practice while mindfulness is a qualitative state of mind with different statuses (see Fig. 3) [12] with many ways to achieve mindfulness, meditation being one of them. Mindfulness is non-judgemental, focusses on the present moment. One can achieve through different activities, which can vary among individuals, namely going on a walk, creating a journal, using a mindfulness app, etc.

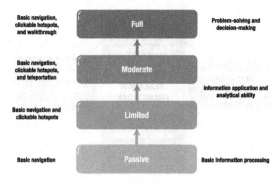

Fig. 2. The spectrum for interactivity in VR with its four levels

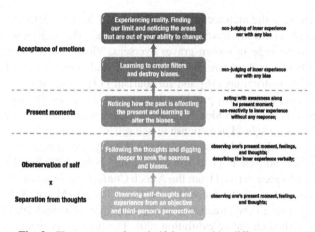

Fig. 3. The spectrum for mindfulness and its different status

We understand that mindfulness aims to have one focussing on the present moment. Still, the actual goal of this state of mind is to be able to reflect on the self, understand the cause of certain feelings and experiences, change biases and emotions, and define the uncontrollable aspects. Therefore, considering the many ways to achieve mindfulness, we propose different virtual environments to the interviewees and seek the most efficient condition for helping the achievement of mindfulness [13, 14, 15].

2 Experiment Settings

Four experiment settings are virtually constructed targeting four different approaches, they are, "spiritual memory" for the Chapel of St. Michael, "Historical memory" for the Old Macao Household, "aesthetic appreciation" for the ARTeFACTo 2022 Macao Virtual Exhibition, and "meditation through concepts" for the Seven Chakras Meditation Dome (Fig. 4).

Fig. 4. The conceptualisation of the four different experiment settings

The first setting is the architecture of the Chapel of St. Michael in Macao. During COVID-19, people could not travel in and out of Macao. This setting was inspired by and dedicated to the urge to mourn graves overseas. Virtual grave mourning is not a new topic worldwide, as there have been different virtual graveyards in other countries against geographic restrictions [16] and for tourism [17]. Nonetheless, it is relatively new in Macao. This setting [18] provides the opportunity to see the reaction from the community towards this novel idea. The second experiment takes the apartment of a traditional Chinese household in response to one self's connection to their childhood in Macao. Instead of finding public spaces around the city, we focus more on childhood memories in a local household [19]. The third setting is the ARTeFACTo 2022 Macao International Conference derived from the Artech Conference, organised by the Faculty of Arts and Humanities of the University of Saint Joseph (Macau S.A.R, China) in November 2022. Due to the situation and the lockdown of Covid-19, the organising committee established an online exhibition [20]. The final experiment setting is about meditation and is based on the seven main chakras in the human body, using their respective colours and sound frequencies in building void virtual environments. The idea is to immerse one into a void environment. By asking about the current emotion or feeling on the "home" page, guiding the viewer to the colour with the sound of the crystal singing bowl associated with the corresponding chakra [21].

3   The Quantitative and Qualitative Survey

For a fair and controlled experiment, only Meta Quest 2 is used as the hardware as we can keep the level of immersion at its highest (see Fig. 1). Also, all four experiment settings have hotspots for teleportation and media information disseminated. Thus, the level of interactivity is kept at "moderate" (see Fig. 2). These levels are the controlled variables for the experiment. The measuring variables for the single-user experience are set around the level of mindfulness and the user's sense of engagement, satisfaction, difficulties in operation, first impression, user interface and personal affection towards his/her experiences in those virtual worlds. We target the public from Macao between 15 to 64 years old. The experiment started by circulating advertising posters in the city with a QR code leading to the registration form. The experience period from 15

May until 21 June 2023 targeted 107 surveys (with a confidence level of 90% and a margin of error of 8%). During the application process, applicants needed to fill out personal information with their contacts and background, which contact information is confidential and only used for organising the experiment. This process allowed us to understand the demographic background and trends in Macao.

The complete single-user experience was set up in a study room on the University of Saint Joseph campus in Ilha Verde, Macao, China. Only the author and the participant were in the room for each time slot. This helped to facilitate mindfulness by keeping the space private and quiet. Each survey took approximately 40 to 60 min. The Meta Quest 2 was cast onto a laptop for real-time screen casting for easier guidance and the author's observation of user behaviours. A printed background and introduction of the research and the settings was provided. To maintain personal hygiene, the foam buffer on Quest for the eye area was replaced with leather and was cleansed per usage. Disposable fabric to be placed in between the face and the Quest was also provided if needed or for people who wear makeup. The participant first listened to the explanation of the research background. Then, four settings were shown in random order. While each setting was being prepared, the participant would read the scenario's background and fill out the survey for the experience of the previous setting.

4 Conclusion

These empirical studies aim to seek the conditions for achieving interactive mindfulness for the population of Macao. The findings shed light on virtual environments' effectiveness in facilitating these experiences and would be presented during the conference. Technology and innovation are supposed to and can benefit mankind if used properly, or else they can also be destructive. Social media and virtual meeting apps are developed at a fast pace to provide convenience to us. However, the downside is that people seem less communicative and expressive in face-to-face communication. The concern is that one may be too addicted and rely on virtual reality to avoid reality; one may feel too safe in the old times to avoid new impacts from inevitable daily challenges; one may enjoy interacting with the device too much to remember how to interact with people. Paying attention to society's mental health is not only to get rid of negativity but also to use this recent technology to facilitate better communication among individuals as we are, as humans, supposed to be gregarious.

References

1. Mazuryk, T., Gervautz, M.: History, applications, technology and future. Virtual Reality **72** (1996)
2. Sutherland, I.:. The ultimate display (1965)
3. Saeed, A., Foaud, L., Fattouh, L.: Environments and system types of virtual reality technology in STEM: a survey. Int. J. Adv. Comput. Sci. Appl. **8**(6) (2017)
4. Mortara, M., Catalano, C. E.: 3D virtual environments as effective learning contexts for cultural heritage. Italian J. Educ. Technol. IJET-ONLINE FIRST (2018)
5. Stromer-Galley, J.: Interactivity-as-product and interactivity-as-process. Inf. Soc. **20**(5), 391–394 (2004)

6. Jonasson, D. (ed.): Instruction Design for Microcomputing Software. 1st edn. Routledge, New York (1988)
7. Steuer, J.: Defining virtual reality: dimensions determining telepresence. J. Commun. **42**(4), 73–93 (1992)
8. Bretz, R., Schmidbauer, M.: Media for Interactive Communication. Sage Publications (1983)
9. Rafaeli, S.: Interactivity: from new media to communication. Sage Ann. Rev. Commun. Res. (1988)
10. Tang, Y.-Y., Hölzel, B.K., Posner, M.I.: The neuroscience of mindfulness meditation. Nat. Rev. Neurosci. **16**(4), 213–225 (2015)
11. Sedlmeier, P., et al.: The psychological effects of meditation: a meta-analysis. Psychol. Bull. **138**(6), 1139–1171 (2012)
12. Schultz, J.: 5 Differences Between Mindfulness and Meditation. PositivePsychology.Com (2022). https://positivepsychology.com/differences-between-mindfulness-meditation/. Accessed 30 Apr 2023
13. Failla, C., et al.: Mediating mindfulness-based interventions with virtual reality in non-clinical populations: the state-of-the-art. Healthcare **10**(7), 1220 (2022)
14. Arpaia, P., D'Errico, G., De Paolis, L.T., Moccaldi, N., Nuccetelli, F.: A narrative review of mindfulness-based interventions using virtual reality. Mindfulness, 1–16 (2021)
15. Damen, K.H.B., van der Spek, E.D.: Virtual reality as e-mental health to support starting with mindfulness-based cognitive therapy. In: Clua, E., Roque, L., Lugmayr, A., Tuomi, P. (eds.) Entertainment Computing – ICEC 2018, pp. 241–247. Springer, Cham (2018). https://doi.org/10.1007/978-3-319-99426-0_24
16. Häkkilä, J., et al.: Visiting a virtual graveyard: designing virtual reality cultural heritage experiences. In: Proceedings of the 18th International Conference on Mobile and Ubiquitous Multimedia, pp. 1–4 (2019)
17. Virtual Rosewood Cemetery – Rosewood Heritage & VR Project. https://www.virtualrosewood.com/virtual-rosewood-cemetery/. Accessed 16 Jan 2023
18. Chapel of St. Michael. Kuula (n.d.). https://kuula.co/share/NvC7f/collection/7qvJz?logo=0&info=1&fs=1&vr=0&sd=1&thumbs=1. Accessed 5 Jan 2023
19. Old Macao Household. Kuula (n.d.). https://kuula.co/share/NWsyf/collection/792M9?logo=0&info=1&fs=1&vr=0&sd=1&thumbs=1. Accessed 5 Jan 2023
20. ARTeFACTo2022Macao—Virtual Exhibition. Kuula (n.d.). https://kuula.co/share/N2CZx/collection/79DjN?logo=0&info=1&fs=1&vr=0&sd=1&thumbs=1. Accessed 29 Dec 2022
21. Seven Chakras Meditation Dome. Kuula (n.d.). https://kuula.co/share/5Nl46/collection/7F8b9?logo=0&info=1&fs=1&vr=1&sd=1&thumbs=1. Accessed 20 Apr 2023

Gameplay Audio Description: *Death of Internet* as a Pilot Study

María Eugenia Larreina-Morales[1]([⊠]) [iD], Allan Di Rosa[2,3] [iD], and Jérôme Dupire[2,3] [iD]

[1] Universitat Autònoma de Barcelona, Bellaterra, Spain
mariaeugenia.larreina@uab.cat
[2] Conservatoire National des Arts et Métiers, Paris, France
allan@capgame.fr, jerome.dupire@lecnam.net
[3] CapGame, Paris, France

Abstract. Audio description (AD), an accessibility service that narrates visual elements for persons with visual disabilities, is starting to be implemented into video game trailers and cutscenes. However, its potential to improve accessibility in real-time gameplay has yet to be fully explored. In their final project of a Master's degree, a team of game design, development, and art students at Cnam-Enjmin University in France rose to the challenge and created *Death of Internet*, a PC video game with gameplay AD. This paper presents the process of AD implementation, from the writing of the script to its integration with other accessibility features, namely text-to-speech and navigation from one point of interest to the next. Although user testing is required, this pilot study highlights the game-changing possibilities of AD for players with and without sight, industry, and training of future professionals.

Keywords: Accessibility · Audio Description · Video Game · Visual Disability

1 Introduction

More than three billion people around the globe regularly play video games [1]. But when it comes to players with disabilities, who account for 16% of the world population [2], the numbers are less rosy. According to Westin and al. [3], playing a game is "the voluntary attempt to overcome unnecessary obstacles," whereas game accessibility is "to remove unnecessary barriers for people with disabilities, within the limitations of game rules." Although interest in accessibility within the game industry has increased significantly in the past five years, there is still a lot of work to do to make mainstream video games accessible for everyone.

Video games are primarily based on visual stimuli, which pose accessibility barriers for players who are blind or have low vision. As a result, their ability to complete the interaction may be hindered, as well as their chance to progress in the game [4]. Traditionally, players with visual disabilities resort to playing with someone else's assistance, thus compromising autonomy, or to limiting their experience to audio games, whose

P. Ciancarini et al. (Eds.): ICEC 2023, LNCS 14455, pp. 335–340, 2023.
https://doi.org/10.1007/978-981-99-8248-6_28

interactions are based on sound instead of visuals. More recently, assistive technology may be available in video games, such as text-to-speech (TTS), screen magnifiers, and built-in accessibility features that modify the mechanics of the game, like difficulty customization, assisted gameplay, or bypassing quests.

Audio description (AD) is an accessibility service that narrates visual elements for persons who cannot access the visual channel, particularly those without or with limited sight. It provides essential information about settings, characters, and actions in the silent pauses between the soundtrack of the source material, namely dialogue, sound effects, and music. In 2020, it was implemented in Ubisoft's game trailers and, in 2022, in the cutscenes of Naught Dog's *The Last of Us Part I*. However, its potential for real-time gameplay is still largely untapped.

This was the starting point for *Death of Internet*, one of the first games ever to implement gameplay AD. It was developed by eleven students at Cnam-Enjmin (*École nationale du jeu et des médias interactifs numériques*) in France as their final project for the Master's degree in Video Games & Interactive Media. The authors of this paper were involved in the development as AD researcher, UX designer, and supervisor. Here, we present the state of the art of AD in video games, *Death of Internet* and its accessibility features for players with visual disabilities, and future work regarding gameplay AD.

2 State of the Art

The use of AD is widespread in film, television, museums, opera, and theater. However, it has only just started making its way into video games. Players with visual disabilities have expressed their interest in this accessibility service, as shown in a 2022 survey by RNIB [5]. They request descriptive narrations about scenarios, characters, and actions to be combined with audio and haptic cues, such as TTS, surround sound, and controller vibration.

First efforts to integrate AD into video games have focused on non-interactive media, namely game trailers and cutscenes. In this case, AD follows the same conventions as in film, particularly regarding the time constraints and the interplay between different soundtrack elements. However, interactivity poses new challenges: how can AD address the non-linearity that results from player agency? What are the linguistic challenges of describing fast-paced events or characters customized by players? What about the technical challenges of implementing AD through the game engine? To answer these questions, it is important to keep in mind that gameplay AD may not be enough of a solution on its own, but instead another feature that adds to TTS, audio cues, and haptic feedback. The main challenge here is to determine which feature is more suitable for each interaction [6].

In 2022, three games started tackling these issues by integrating AD into gameplay: Bridge Multimedia's *Cyberchase: Duck Dash*, CowCat Games' *Brok the InvestiGator*, and Soft Leaf Studios' *Stories of Blossom*. The three are slow-paced, narrative games, meaning that there is enough time for AD to describe settings, characters, and points of interest (POI). *Duck Dash* combines AD with TTS for the randomly generated events in the game, while *Brok* and *Stories of Blossom* pause the action while AD is playing. In *Duck Dash* and *Stories of Blossom*, AD is voiced by the game's characters, adding to the immersive experience. In turn, *Brok*'s AD is read by a synthetic voice. In all three, AD is only available in English, meaning that there are still linguistic barriers for some players. In fact, localization into different languages should cover both the game and its accessibility features. Simultaneously, in 2022, *Death of Internet* was developed in an educational context aiming to identify the challenges and potential of gameplay AD for players with and without sight. These are presented hereafter.

3 Death of Internet

Your childhood friend, Nova, is dead. No trace of her in reality. However, while mourning in her apartment, you receive a message from her. Fall down the rabbit hole and lose yourself in the meanders of her intimacy through reality and the internet. Dive into her troubles and loneliness to perhaps understand what led to her death. But is she really dead?

These are the opening words of *Death of Internet* (*DOI*), a single-player, first-person, point-and-click PC game. The player controls Diane, a young woman searching for her friend, Nova, who has recently disappeared. The story takes place in a retro futuristic world that blends colorful nostalgia with a cold thriller, creating a unique and unsettling atmosphere. The game was developed in Unreal Engine 5 by a team of eleven students: three graphic designers, two programmers, two game designers, two sound designers, an UX designer, and a project manager.

All interactions are based on handling objects. There is no Head-Up Display, although a cursor appears on screen when the player is close to an object they can interact with. There are only two inputs: the left button on the mouse to interact with an object; and the scroll to rotate it. Both inputs may be remapped on the keyboard, along with the following accessibility features: independent volume settings, customizable screen resolutions and cursor color, full and windowed mode, X and Y axis inversion, sensitivity adjustment, subtitles for character dialogues and settings for font size, color, background opacity, and speaker name, deactivation of screen flash effects, and a "Blind Mode" for players with visual disabilities, detailed in the next section.

4 Playing without Sight

Death of Internet poses three main interaction constraints for players with visual disabilities: navigation (i.e., handling the free camera to explore the scenario), selection (i.e., handling the mouse cursor to interact with the visuals), and comprehension of visual elements. To tackle them, three features were combined, all under the Blind Mode setting: POI navigation, TTS, and AD.

POI navigation allows the player to move from one narratively relevant point of interest to the next through a fixed position camera. TTS is a narration of all texts in the game, including UI and in-game written content, and voiced by a male synthetic voice. AD is a description of the scenario, points of interest and events in first-person, from the point of view of Diane and voiced by its female actress.

In the Blind Mode, inputs are restricted to moving and interacting with the POIs. AD and TTS are automatically launched when the player arrives at a scenario, interacts with an object, triggers a game event, or selects a UI element. At any moment, the player can provide a "Move" input, moving to the next or the previous POI.

Let's take Fig. 1 as an example. When the player with the Blind Mode activated enters the room, the AD plays with Diane's voice: "The capsule is round, bathed by a warm, orange light. The walls are metallic, but the space is cozy. It is full of colorful pillows piling up on the floor. There are two holograms showing blog posts, one page of a notebook laying on a pillow, and one small post-it note glued to the wall on the right." Here, the POIs are the two holograms, the notebook page, and the post-it note. When the player interacts with the notebook page, the AD narrates: "On an orange pillow, there is a notebook page of Nova's handwriting. She used a black pen. Maybe they are from her diary. But why would she tear out the pages? Let's read what it says." Then, the TTS reads out the words written by Nova: "It's difficult for me to look at someone in the eyes."

The TTS posed a programming challenge. While AD was added as an additional voice line, TTS was directly integrated through Unreal. This means that TTS settings are taken from the player's PC configuration. As a result, TTS speed could not be predicted so, to ensure that there is silence before launching the next voice line, an AD or TTS line is always preceded by an empty TTS.

Fig. 1. A point of interest: the entry of a capsule

5   Conclusions and Future Work

Death of Internet is one of the first-ever attempts at implementing AD into gameplay. The interdisciplinary approach that joined the efforts of each specialty of the development team with an AD researcher proved to be successful in creating a new gaming experience, called the Blind Mode. Although it is specifically addressed to players with visual disabilities, it may also be enjoyed by people who are looking for a challenge or a different experience of the same game.

While the UX designer was the main person responsible for the AD in *Death of Internet*, every team member's work was impacted by its implementation. For example, the project manager prioritized AD in the production process, which aided its rapid implementation. After the completion of the project, the graphic artist raised an interesting possibility: she realized that she could have been involved in AD scriptwriting, because she could provide insight about the characters and scenarios she had designed. This shows that accessibility is cross-disciplinary and concerns all members of the development team in sometimes unforeseen ways.

Future work includes conducting playtests with players with and without visual disabilities to assess the usability of the Blind Mode and the AD. Likewise, different versions of AD could be created and compared, such as first and third-person AD, and voiced by a human or a synthetic voice. The impact of this feature on gameplay could also be studied through reception research. Moreover, more training and education are also needed beyond UX designers and programmers. Joint seminars between development teams, accessibility providers (such as audio describers) and users could set the ground for a common language to create quality accessibility from the design stage of the game.

Finally, this pilot study has highlighted that AD provides game-changing possibilities for players, industry, and training of future professionals in a cross-disciplinary manner. The rapid development of the game, in just three months, shows that accessibility is not difficult or costly to implement if done from the start of the design process. As the game designer in an informal interview conducting at the end of the project, "if students can implement AD in a game, everyone can. With accessibility, we have everything to gain."

6 Technical Requirements

The optimal playing experience for *Death of Internet* is to use a laptop with headphones. No internet connection is required.

Acknowledgments. This research is part of the Researching Audio Description: Translation, Delivery and New Scenarios Project, supported by the Spanish Ministerio de Ciencia, Innovación y Universidades, the Spanish Agencia Estatal de Innovación, and the European Regional Development Fund [PGC2018-096566-B-I00 (MCIU/AEI/FEDER, UE)]. María Eugenia Larreina-Morales is part of the TransMedia Catalonia research group, funded by Secretaria d'Universitats i Recerca del Departament d'Empresa i Coneixement de la Generalitat de Catalunya, under the SGR funding scheme (Ref. Code 2021SGR00077), and she has been awarded a PhD grant from the Catalan Government (2021FI_B1 00049) to carry out this research.

References

1. Statista, Number of gamers worldwide in 2021 by region https://www.statista.com/statistics/293304/number-video-gamers/. Accessed 26 Apr 2023
2. World Health Organization. https://www.who.int/news-room/fact-sheets/detail/disability-and-health. Accessed 26 Apr 2023
3. Westin, T., Ku, J.J., Dupire, J., Hamilton, I.: Game accessibility guidelines and WCAG 2.0 – a gap analysis. In: Miesenberger, K., Kouroupetroglou, G. (eds.) Computers Helping People with Special Needs. LNCS, vol. 10896, pp. 270–279. Springer, Cham (2018). https://doi.org/10.1007/978-3-319-94277-3_43

4. Yuan, B., Folmer, E., Harris, F.C.: Game accessibility: a survey. Univ. Access Inf. Soc. **10**(1), 1–19 (2011). https://doi.org/10.1007/s10209-010-0189-5
5. Accessible Gaming Research Report. https://media.rnib.org.uk/documents/RNIB_Accessible_ Gaming_Report_2022.pdf. Accessed 26 Apr 2023
6. Mangiron, C., Zhang, X.: Video games and audio description. In: Taylor, C., Perego, E. (eds.) The Routledge Handbook of Audio Description. Routledge, London (2022)

A Serious Video Game on Cybersecurity

Giorgia Bassi$^{(\boxtimes)}$ (iD), Stefania Fabbri$^{(\boxtimes)}$ (iD), and Anna Vaccarelli$^{(\boxtimes)}$ (iD)

Institute of Informatics and Telematics of the National Research Council, via G. Moruzzi, 56124 Pisa, Italy
{giorgia.bassi,stefania.fabbri,anna.vaccarelli}@iit.cnr.it

Abstract. The present paper deals with the videogame "Nabbovaldo and the Cyber Blackmail", designed, developed and promoted by the Ludoteca del Registro.it, the educational section of Registro.it, the registry of Italian internet domains that works within the Institute for Informatics and Telematics of the National Research Council (CNR). The videogame is aimed at children aged 11–13 to improve their knowledge related to the use of digital resources, and encourage the adoption of good cybersecurity practices. The paper describes its objectives, contents and methods for using it in the classroom.

Keywords: serious game · game for learning · cybersecurity education

1 Ludoteca del Registro.it

Ludoteca is the educational section of Registro.it. The registry of Italian internet domains - that works within the CNR Institute for Informatics and Telematics (CNR-IIT). Since 2011, the staff of Ludoteca has met more than 16,000 students, all over Italy and beyond. This project (freely offered to the schools involved), supported by the Italian Authority for Children and Adolescents, promotes the internet culture across educational establishments of all types and at all levels and aims to encourage a more aware and safer use of the Internet among young people. All the learning tools and contents provided in the school labs are certified and assessed by CNR-IIT researchers.

The potential offered by the Internet are at the core of the project but, in recent years, it has also focused on cybersecurity topics.

2 Edutainment Tools for Digital Education

All the activities proposed by the Ludoteca project are based on the union between play and learning, in order to always keep the attention and interest of children and young people alive. Games and videogames are charming and engaging for children, teens, and adults as well. Therefore, they are easily welcome as a learning tool, both in school and professional environments. In the latter case, they are generally called "serious games".

Nowadays, edutainment mostly uses games promoting players' "problem solving" skills and use of creativity to face the challenges and threats posed by the game.

P. Ciancarini et al. (Eds.): ICEC 2023, LNCS 14455, pp. 341–345, 2023.
https://doi.org/10.1007/978-981-99-8248-6_29

Even the field of cybersecurity education can therefore benefit from the use of edutainment and serious games, declined in various forms depending on the category of the learner.

As an example, in the Italian context, we can mention Interland (https://beinternetaw esome.withgoogle.com/it_it/interland), provided by Google's programme "Vivi Internet al meglio", in cooperation with Telefono Azzurro. It provides game-based training sections on digital education (non-hostile communication, content reliability) without though a specific focus on cybersecurity issues (i.e. malware or cyber attacks). Another interesting example is "Cybercity Chronicles" (https://www.sicurezzanazionale.gov.it/ sisr.nsf/cybercity-chronicles.html), released in 2019, and commissioned by the Department of Security Intelligence (DIS), dealing with cybersecurity topics, but with a sci-fi scenario that makes it not very adherent to the daily experiences of children's online life. Within the academic research context, we can mention "CyberCraft" developed by the engineering students of Politecnico di Torino and "CyberVR", created by DIAG (University of Rome), designed for corporate training and therefore for an adult target.

Internationally, we point out CyberCIEGE, (https://nps.edu/web/c3o/cyberciege) sponsored by the US Navy and used by government agencies and universities; Spoofy (http://www.spoofy.fi), developed in Finland in 2019 and launched in Estonia in 2021,

entirely aimed at children and including different worlds that go through different scenarios that kids encounter: internet communication, bullying, passwords, internet purchases, spam, device safety, and so much more.

Also considering the state of the art of game-based initiatives and video games on cybersecurity, Ludoteca staff decided to design and develop a serious game aimed at middle school students.

3 The Videogame "Nabbovaldo and the Cyber Blackmail"

The videogame "Nabbovaldo and the Cyber Blackmail" (in Italian: "Nabbovaldo e il ricatto dal cyberspazio") is a video game designed, developed and promoted by the Ludoteca del Registro.it.

It is aimed at children aged 11–13 to improve their knowledge related to the use of digital resources, and encourage the adoption of good practice. It is a single-player game that can be used both in the classroom, as a supplement for the teacher's lectures, and by kids on their own as a self-consistent game.

The main character is Nabbovaldo, a young inhabitant of Internetopoli, the city of the Internet, passionate about the online world but naive (as the name "nabbo" tells, the Italian translation of "noob") and not very aware of the possible risks.

The videogame deals with these cybersecurity issues: malware, phishing, online scams, hackers, cyberattacks, dark web, troll, haters, fake news. The setting is Internetopoli, a city in which landscapes and characters feature the complexity of the Internet world.

In this videogame, Nabbovaldo faces, as the title tells, a specific cyber-attack, that is ransomware. To advance in this challenge and win the game, he will have to perform a series of actions and to go through several minigames. The videogame also features new characters who help Nabbovaldo in his quest and have a functional role in the game.

The game has a hybrid structure: players can either follow a fixed path, or move freely along the map, talk to characters and play the mini-games in any order.

During the gameplay, the player constantly moves across the sections of the fictional city of Internetopoli, and is involved with Nabbovaldo in dialogues with a number of other characters. When moving across the Settings (both inside and outside) the player can use a Map to know Nabbo's localization. The players are involved in exciting scenarios that change according to the challenges to overcome, all of which are divided into levels. They can move freely around the map, talk to the characters, and solve the minigames in the order they prefer, but the game's plot revolves around four main chapters, plus an epilogue in which the player can only perform a final dialogue. The game also features a section called Nabbopedia, which is a small dictionary collecting definitions of the technical terms on cybersecurity (i.e. malware, phishing, trojan horse, firewall, spamming). The player can access this dictionary at any time. The game progress can be saved, so that players opening the game at subsequent times can start off where they left. At the end of the game the player is ranked according to the number of likes collected during the game.

3.1 Design and Implementation

Before designing the videogame, a feasibility study was implemented. The type of game chosen for the study was a graphic adventure with multiple-choice dialogues, alternated with puzzle and/or arcade-style minigames, for a total duration of about 1 h of continuous gameplay.

The feasibility study led to the creation of a Game Design Document (GDD), including all the elements required to develop the videogame: the subject of the plot and concept of the game, design and technical description of the graphics adventure mechanics, including interactions with the environment and dialogues. After the GDD was completed, the actual development of the game was entrusted to a specialized video game developer company, Grifo Multimedia.

About the development, in order to be able to deploy on multiple platforms, the Unity3D engine/framework was used, which allows cross-platform game development.

Furthermore, the C# language was used which is the most common language in Unity3D: it runs much faster during the development and has several useful features over the alternative of other languages supported by the engine.

The implementation of the video game was carried out in different stages. First minigames were created, to test their performances, then, the Internetopoli scenario was designed and finally dialogues and interactive elements.

3.2 Labs in Schools: How to Use the Videogame

The learning activities based on the videogame took place in the 2021/22 and 2022/23 school years, involving a total of 45 middle school classes. The training was designed by adopting educational models typical of the "flipped classroom", a method which increases student engagement and learning by making them learn the educational contents autonomously at home and by deepening the topics and discussing them in class. While this model is particularly suitable for young people, also considering their familiarity with videogames, it was necessary to plan training activities for teachers.

During these two school years the staff of the Ludoteca del Registro.it supported the teachers for the entire duration of the project, with the aim of passing on all the knowledge relating to the game and its contents, but above all the teaching methods for proposing it in the classroom. These are the phases in which the classrooms activity was divided:

- preliminary meeting with teachers on videogame; delivery of support teaching materials and insights relating to the project;
- classroom lab conducted by the staff of the Ludoteca, in collaboration with teachers, concerning the first chapter of the video game;
- game experience independently, at home, by students
- in-depth video game lab by teachers, always supported by the staff of the Ludoteca as regards the first chapter of the video game;
- creation of resources by the class on the project topics;
- project evaluation.

The classroom activity, carried out by the teachers, was supported by the use of two Guides, one for students, another for teachers, both provided and explained by the Ludoteca staff. The project evaluation, in the sense of effectiveness in cognitive and educational objectives, was carried out thanks to the collaboration with the University of Florence (Department of Education, Languages, Interculture, Literature and Psychology). The evaluation, which took place through ex ante and ex post questionnaires pro-posed to students, highlighted a general positive change in terms of knowledge related to IT security and a more aware attitude towards possible risks online. The sample consisted of 270 students (mean age $= 12.66$, SD $= .70$) of four schools in Tuscany participating n the project. 38% of the sample is female, while 3% prefer not to specify sex. The sample is well balanced, with 53% of participants attending the third year of middle school and 47% attending the second one. 96% of the respondents are of Italian nationality. The results were analyzed by comparing the level of incoming knowledge (ex-ante) with that of outgoing knowledge (ex-post). Any differences related to gender, age, and effective use of videogame were checked.

The knowledge that improves the most concerns technical aspects of the Net, such as: "I know what spyware is", "I know what ransomware is", "I know what a denial of service attack is". The video game was rated by the kids as user-friendly, with an easy to understand game mechanism and operation, and with original graphics. Playing was interesting, as well as delving into the themes presented in the game paths, and the mini-games were considered fun.

4 Future Developments

In the 2023–2024 school year, the video game will still be the main tool of the Ludoteca laboratories on cybersecurity and the next activities will be dedicated to encouraging schools to use it with the support of specially created guides for teachers and students.

The video game will also be at the center of the "Super Cyber Kids" European project, funded by the Erasmus + programme, which aims to create teaching tools and methodologies to teach cyber security at school. The objective of the project, in collaboration with six European partners, is to provide young kids in the early years of secondary school (10–13 years old) with appropriate skills and knowledge for the safe use of digital media. To this purpose, we will design, develop and test a comprehensive educational ecosystem on cybersecurity-related skills. The programme will include a wide range of materials in various digital formats to anchor the topic of cybersecurity in the classroom, and will be addressed both to the kids in the age bracket 10 to 13 and to their teachers.

A game-based learning platform will be created, also accessible via mobile apps, which will use the typical mechanics of gamification (missions, scores, levels, rankings, immediate feedback, badges, etc.) to make the learning experience more effective and engaging for the target audience. "Nabbovaldo and the cyber blackmail", translated and localized in all project languages, will be part of the platform which will also contain recommendations and guidelines for teachers to help them use the learning materials available in the learning ecosystem.

References

1. Smahel, D., et al.: Survey results from 19 coun- tries. EU Kids Online (2020). https://doi.org/10.21953/lse.47fdeqj01ofo(2020)
2. Coenraad, M., Pellicone, A., Ketelhut, D.J., Cukier, M., Plane, J., Weintrop, D.: Experiencing cybersecurity one game at a time: a systematic review of cybersecurity digital games. Simul. Gaming. **51**(5), 586–611 (2020). https://doi.org/10.1177/1046878120933312
3. Finkelhor, D., Walsh, K., Jones, L., Mitchell, K., Collier, A.: Youth internet safety education: aligning programs with the evidence base. Trauma Violence Abuse. **22**(5), 1233–1247 (2021). https://doi.org/10.1177/1524838020916257
4. Connolly, T.M., Boyle, E.A., MacArthur, E., Hainey, T., Boyle, J.M.: A system- atic literature review of empirical evidence on computer games and serious games. Comput. Educ. **59**(2), 661–686 (2012). https://doi.org/10.1016/j.compedu.2012.03.004
5. Clark, D.B., Tanner-Smith, E.E., Killingsworth, S.S.: Digital games, design, and learning: a systematic review and meta-analysis. Rev. Educ. Res. **86**(1), 79–122 (2016). https://doi.org/10.3102/0034654315582065
6. Ranieri, M.: Linee di ricerca emergenti nell'educational technology. Form@ re-Open J. per la formazione rete. **15**(3), 67–83 (2015)

Robotic Choreography Creation Through Symbolic AI Techniques

Allegra De Filippo[✉] and Michela Milano

DISI, University of Bologna, Bologna, Italy
allegra.defilippo@unibo.it

Abstract. Symbolic Artificial Intelligence (AI) techniques in robotic choreography contribute to the broader field of human-robot interaction and address the main limitations of learning approaches in terms of computational requirements. A general symbolic approach leveraging dance sequence rules and constraints can (1) reduce computational effort and (2) allow the possibility to easily insert aesthetic and musical constraints. In this direction, this paper presents a preliminary approach based on symbolic AI techniques that is able to plan a robotic choreography based on a general problem description and music input. The algorithm is adaptable using different symbolic AI techniques, and by considering different user requirements. For the demonstration phase, a challenge in a Master course on AI was organized, with resulting choreographies available in a public repository. The possibility to easily insert aesthetic constraints also allows to a more intuitive and expressive communication between humans and robots. This has implications not only in the field of entertainment but also in different areas like healthcare and education.

Keywords: Robotic Choreography · Symbolic AI · Dance Automation

1 Introduction

In the context of robotic choreography creation, the recent developments in the field of deep learning [3,11], with a massive use of large end-to-end neural architectures, usually come with several drawbacks, such as a low degree of user control, a lack of global structure, and the inherent impossibility of online generation due to their high computational costs and specific hardware requirements.

For these reasons, we propose a general approach for robotic choreography creation based on symbolic AI techniques, exploiting the fact that the creation of dance sequences typically follows a set of common rules and/or constraints, with the aim of drastically reducing the computational requirements of learning approaches. From a more general perspective, symbolic AI, in the context of robotic choreography, enables the representation of abstract concepts related to movement, timing, coordination, and aesthetics, by encoding these symbolic representations to create coherent and expressive dance sequences [7].

© IFIP International Federation for Information Processing 2023
Published by Springer Nature Switzerland AG 2023
P. Ciancarini et al. (Eds.): ICEC 2023, LNCS 14455, pp. 346–351, 2023.
https://doi.org/10.1007/978-981-99-8248-6_30

The process of robotic choreography creation through symbolic AI typically begins with capturing movements in motion data that can be processed and analyzed using symbolic AI techniques. This involves extracting meaningful features and patterns from the data, identifying key poses or movements, and representing them symbolically. For example, a specific dance move could be represented by a symbolic sequence of basic movements as building blocks to create new choreography. Algorithms can generate variations of existing movements or combine different sequences to form original routines [1]. By incorporating rules and constraints defined by the choreographer or AI designer, the system can ensure coherence, rhythm, and style in the generated choreography.

Robotic choreography created through symbolic AI has numerous applications. It can be used for entertainment purposes, such as live performances or exhibitions [4,5]. Additionally, it can serve as a tool for choreographers and dancers to explore new possibilities in movement generation, expand their creativity, and collaborate with robotic systems as dance partners. The development of symbolic AI techniques for robotic choreography creation contributes to the broader field of human-robot interaction [10]. It opens doors for more intuitive and expressive communication between humans and robots, enabling robots to understand and mimic human gestures and movements more effectively. This has implications not only in the field of entertainment but also in areas like healthcare, rehabilitation, and education.

In this paper, we propose a preliminary approach able to plan a choreography (sequence of positions) given a problem description, and based on a music track given as input. The choreography creation algorithm is set as a black-box procedure which could be replaced by one of the three main symbolic AI techniques (i.e., Planning, Search Algorithm, Constraints), provided that the same constraints are respected. In particular, we proposed this creation setting in the context of a Master course on Fundamentals of Artificial Intelligence[1] by organizing a challenge among our students. All the choreographies are available at the public repository mentioned in the following sections.

2   Proposed Approach

2.1   Focus on Planning Problem Description

Planning algorithms play a crucial role in designing and orchestrating robotic choreographies. Classical AI planning algorithms, such as STRIPS (Stanford Research Institute Problem Solver) [2], can be utilized to generate high-level choreographic plans from symbolic representations [6]. These algorithms consider various constraints, such as the capabilities of the robots, physical limitations, aesthetics, and storytelling aspects [8,9].

During the planning process, the algorithms must satisfied, based on the symbolic representations of dance movements and music, the synchronization

---

[1] https://corsi.unibo.it/2cycle/artificial-intelligence.

requirements to generate a sequence of actions for the robots to perform. Symbolic representations also enable choreographers to express their creative ideas in a structured manner. Starting from this idea, in Fig. 1, we can observe the macro phases of our proposed approach. We define: (1) an initial problem description based on initial/final positions, a set of movements and music track features; (2) the choreography generation phase based on the symbolic AI algorithm that must satisfied the rules and constraints that can be defined by a choreographer or an AI designer; (3) the last phase of synchronization and execution of the robotic choreography. Based on the description of the initial and final states of the planning, it is possible to insert constraints on time duration, movement incompatibilities, music. The planning algorithms can then generate a choreographic plan that satisfies these constraints and rules while maintaining a cohesive performance. Once a high-level choreographic plan is generated, execution and synchronization algorithms come into play. This enables the translation of the planned dance movements into robot-specific instructions.

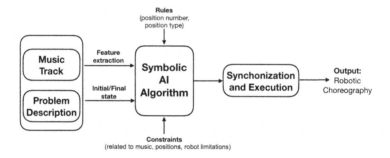

Fig. 1. Approach schema

2.2   Domain and Constraints Definition Phase

The problem description is given with an initial and final state description in Natural Language. Moreover a repository of robot positions[2] is created with mandatory and intermediate positions already implemented for the NAO robot (e.g., sit position, stand position, ...).

The constraints to be satisfied for the position sequence are the following: (1) the choreography must start with the represented initial position and must end in the represented final state; (2) the total duration of the choreography must be fixed; (3) each choreography must contain at least one repetition of each mandatory position; (4) to move from a mandatory position to another, it is possible to use positions from the available set of intermediate positions; (5) each choreography must contain at least one repetition of 5 of the intermediate

---

[2] https://github.com/ProjectsAI/RoboticChoreography.

positions provided; (6) the sequence of positions must avoid possible incompatibilities between two consecutive positions. The choreographies implemented are based on three main symbolic AI techniques: Planning, Search Algorithm, and Constraints.

2.3   Choreography Creation Phase

After the problem definition phase, the algorithm considers rules like dance-music synchronization and position patterns, finally creates a position sequence for a robot that satisfies the required constraints. During the first analysis, design choices can be carried out, similarly to how a choreographer would make choices to respect constraints in human choreography. The problem definition also defines some parameters and their values in order to be taken into account for the constraint satisfaction and design choices. These choices involve these parameters: (1) the music track's features (e.g., amplitude), which are used to establish different intervals associated with various music-related moments; (2) the type of a move, which is defined according to factors including the robot's ability to move fluidly and the execution time of the movement; (3) a value which quantifies the effectiveness of a particular move based on the transition time from the previous move. Smaller transition times are associated with higher values. The optimal solution is the sequence of moves for which all the constraints of the problem and the aesthetic constraints mentioned earlier are satisfied. *The creation can be thought of as a black-box procedure which could be replaced by any other algorithm, provided that the same constraints are respected.*

2.4   Choreography Demonstration Phase

We tested our approach on a case study based on choreographies for a NAO robot[3]. Based on the common setting of constraints and positions to be satisfied by the AI algorithm, we implement and perform all the choreographies with a simulated NAO robot, using the graphical tool Choregraphe. For the demonstration phase, a competition for the creation of robotic choreographies has been held within a course of Fundamentals of AI for the Master Degree of Artificial Intelligence. One of the fundamental aspects of this competition aims at contributing to reconstruct the creation processes adopted by artists in the field of performing arts, thus providing the user with new methodological perspectives.

The problem description is given to the students with an initial and final state description, a repository of robot positions, and constraints to respect, in order to left them sufficient degrees of freedom to involve creativity in their final artistic output. All the details of the used techniques for each choreography can be found at the repository mentioned above.

---

[3] https://www.aldebaran.com/en/nao.

3 Conclusion and Future Directions

In conclusion, robotic choreography creation through symbolic AI represents a captivating blend of artistry and technology. By leveraging symbolic representations and computational algorithms, it enables the generation of intricate and aesthetically pleasing dance sequences for robotic systems. This interdisciplinary field holds promise for advancing the capabilities of robots, enhancing human-robot interaction, and pushing the boundaries of artistic expression. We claim that this research area can particularly benefit from AI when humans are kept in the loop in the creative process.

We plan to explore several research directions. The natural follow-up of this work is to perform analysis to subjectively evaluate the generated choreography, an approach commonly adopted in the evaluation of AI-assisted creations. In particular, this can be done by recruiting participants willing to assess the quality of the artistic outputs, ideally including both artists and AI experts. The evaluation of the performances will then be conducted with the help of a human audience unaware of the choreography creation processes, and using a shared evaluation scheme. Furthermore, starting from this evaluation phase, we can aim at discovering correlations between certain features of a choreography and its success among a human audience. The final purpose is twofold, since we would like both to explore new creative paths where humans ideas can be broadened by the use of AI software and to foster awareness about which aspects of a choreography correlate with a major impact on the audience.

References

1. Barbaresi, M., Bernagozzi, S., Roli, A.: Robot choreographies: artificial evolution between novelty and similarity. In: AIRO@ AI* IA, pp. 17–21 (2020)
2. Bylander, T.: The computational complexity of propositional strips planning. Artif. Intell. **69**(1–2), 165–204 (1994)
3. Crnkovic-Friis, L., Crnkovic-Friis, L.: Generative choreography using deep learning. arXiv preprint arXiv:1605.06921 (2016)
4. De Filippo, A., Giuliani, L., Mancini, E., Borghesi, A., Mello, P., Milano, M.: Towards symbiotic creativity: a methodological approach to compare human and AI robotic dance creations. In: Proceedings of the Thirty-Second International Conference on International Joint Conferences on Artificial Intelligence (2023)
5. De Filippo, A., Mello, P., Milano, M.: Do you like dancing robots? AI can tell you why. In: PAIS 2022. IOS Press (2022). https://doi.org/10.3233/faia220064
6. Karpas, E., Magazzeni, D.: Automated planning for robotics. Annu. Rev. Control Robot. Auton. Syst. **3**, 417–439 (2020)
7. Laumond, J.P., Abe, N.: Dance Notations and Robot Motion. Springer, Cham (2016). https://doi.org/10.1007/978-3-319-25739-6
8. Norvig, P.R., Intelligence, S.A.: A modern approach. Prentice Hall, Upper Saddle River (2002)
9. Rani, M., Nayak, R., Vyas, O.P.: An ontology-based adaptive personalized e-learning system, assisted by software agents on cloud storage. Knowl.-Based Syst. **90**, 33–48 (2015)

10. Thörn, O., Knudsen, P., Saffiotti, A.: Human-robot artistic co-creation: a study in improvised robot dance. In: 2020 29th IEEE International Conference on Robot and Human Interactive Communication (RO-MAN), pp. 845–850. IEEE (2020)
11. Zhang, S.: Recent advances in the application of deep learning to choreography. In: 2020 International Conference on Computing and Data Science (CDS), pp. 88–91. IEEE (2020)

HabitAR: Motivating Outdoor Walk with Animal-Watching Activities

Mengyan Guo[1]([⊠]), Alec Kouwenberg[1], Alexandra van Dijk[1], Niels Horrevoets[1], Nikki Koonings[1], Jun Hu[1], and Steven Vos[1,2]

[1] Eindhoven University of Technology, 5612 AZ Eindhoven, The Netherlands
m.guo@tue.nl
[2] Fontys University of Applied Sciences, Eindhoven, The Netherlands

Abstract. Outdoor exercise has been indicated to have physical and mental benefits over indoor exercise and tends to take place in more engaging and attractive settings. Increasing motivation is a critical factor in behavior change. We envision that the interaction between users' walking data and components of their walking environment can be a potential method to motivate physical activity and offer novel opportunities. In this study, we introduce HabitAR, a blog-community-based application connecting the walk experience with the animal watching activities that provide different routes in which the types of animals that can be watched are proportional to walking distance. Following the research-through-design approach, we explored how this concept works on users' motivation by building an emotional connection between users and animals with social blogging. We present the results of the pilot study and the insights gained from this study.

Keywords: Interactive System · Physical Activity · Interaction Design

1 Introduction

Physical inactive has become a serious public health issue globally, which can be prevented by motivating people to exercise regularly. Moreover, growing evidence indicates that outdoor physical activity (PA) has considerable benefits for physical and mental health than indoor physical activity [4, 16]. Indeed, a steady stream of interactive technologies has been developed to enhance users' exercise experience. However, most of them are designed to track PA data and reflect on performance through a quantitative presentation, such as charts and graphs, which are reported to potentially harm motivation [12]. And common motivating strategies used by these apps are rewards in terms of points and virtual badges or competitions by ranking on the leaderboard based on PA data, of which these kinds of fun are not enough to keep users using over two weeks and maintain behavior change [14].

To motivate people to exercise more sustainably, we propose a new approach from the perspectives of human-computer interaction and human-environment interaction, linking peoples' movement with the interesting elements in their walking environment

Published by Springer Nature Switzerland AG 2023
P. Ciancarini et al. (Eds.): ICEC 2023, LNCS 14455, pp. 352–359, 2023.
https://doi.org/10.1007/978-981-99-8248-6_31

as rewards to strengthen the emotional and social value. Specifically, we developed Habit AR, a community-based platform, using animal-watching activities on the walking route as stimuli to motivate people to walk out and walk longer. In this preliminary study, following the research-through-design method, we explore the impact of this approach on users' motivation to walk outside. Beyond the implications of encouraging outdoor walking with an AR-based animal-watching app, we believe our findings could serve as a novel lens for extending the digital intervention to a more public and environmental context.

2 Related Work

In the HCI domain, flora and fauna metaphors have been used to represent PA data. To engage people in tracking and reflecting on their fitness data, many researchers explore the effect of mapping fitness data into the growth of flora and fauna on users' motivation. For example, Consolvo et al. designed a background-screen-based glanceable display of a mobile phone in which butterflies indicate goal attainments; flowers mean activity variety [5]. The development of virtual pets also has been used to map individuals' [17] and groups' [10] daily exercise progress toward their goals. For instance, Fitbit Pet [17] turns users' step counts into treats to feed a virtual pet. Lin et al. developed Fish'n'steps, a computing game mapping users' walk steps to the growth and emotional state of a virtual fish pet in a shared fish tank [10]. Most participants developed a certain emotional attachment to their virtual pet, which provided extra motivation. Their results from a 14-week study reported that this fun and engaging method could generate sustainable behavior change, although the initial fascination with the game subsided after a few weeks. Beyond virtual metaphors, Botros et al. designed Go & Grow, a living plant physically visualizing users' PA by watering it according to owners' walking steps [3]. This study suggested that living visualization results in a strong commitment to maintaining healthy behavior.

These trends show that a non-literal, aesthetic representation of physical activities and goal attainment through virtual and physical metaphors can improve awareness and lead to behavior change. Flora and fauna could create multiple emotional and social connections with users, such as responsible, curiosity, and concern, which can trigger implicit motives for PA. Our work is to extend this trend to a more public and physical context by connecting walk distance with the types of animals in their walking environments. We aim to explore how people's attachment to the animal can be an engaging motivator for behavior change. Additionally, it is suggested that users can be more involved in PA by engaging in activities that enhance social value or finding social support from (online) communities [19]. Building on this, we focus on applying elements like collaboration and reward to strengthen the social and positive impact.

3 HabitAR System

We created the HabitAR system (Fig. 1), a community-based platform to motivate walking, which is consisted of a mobile application (bottom right of Fig. 1) and public displays mounted on wooden poles (right of Fig. 1) in the outdoor environment. The HabitAR system features animals in users' walking environment as motivators to encourage walking, providing different routes with the function of navigation and blog (personal walk data-driven blog). The public displays are situated outdoors where people walk and can find animals, such as parks, with an interface offering different routes accessible to anyone passing by to attract more people to participate. The types of animals that may be encountered on the route are proportional to the length of the route. Users can choose or customize their route on the public displays and scan the popup QR code to log in and start their journey. After a route is created, users will see question marks on the maps that show the expected area of a certain animal (these are generated by the blog post by others in the community). Then they can start walking along the route navigated on their phone. When they spot the animal, they can start watching it, use this app to take a picture of it and add a blog post. After uploading a blog about a specific animal, the user can unlock all blogs about that specific animal and stay updated about it as a reward. It means that users, who upload pictures, maintain this blog and therefore create a bond with the animals in their walking environment. However, after seeing three new blogs, the blog will automatically lock and cannot be read. If they want to know the latest situation of that animal, they need to walk back to this area and upload a new picture of it to contribute to the community.

Initial design steps involved extracting the design concept from brainstorming and concept sketching. Then a low-fidelity prototype was made to test this concept further. Figure 2 shows examples of such artefacts. Following the gathered insight, we improved our concept. Then HabitAR was developed using FlutterFlow and attached to a Firebase database which stores the users' information, photos and blogs. Next, APIs were created in the Google Cloud platform to realize a safe connection between the app and the databases (for Android, IOS and Web). Lobe.ai was used to test the functioning animal detection system with machine learning, which worked well in our test of distinguishing two different stuffed animals with similar features, shown in the top right of Fig. 2. It was not integrated into the demonstrator app but is part of the final concept.

Fig. 1. The HabitAR system components overview (top left), App interface (bottom left), and the public displays in the wild (right).

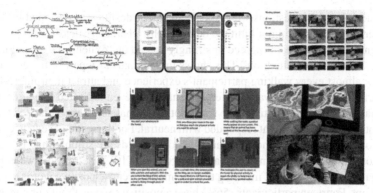

Fig. 2. Examples of design artefacts, including the outcome of a brainstorm (top left), sketches (bottom left), mockup app (top middle), storyboards (bottom middle), the result of Lobe.ai test (top right), prototypes (bottom right).

4 Pilot Study

We conducted a pilot study, deploying mixed methods to collect quantitative data through a questionnaire and more in-depth qualitative data through user experience tests and a semi-structured interview afterward. Through the pilot study, we aimed to explore if a system with features like HabitAR could motivate people by creating a valuable bond with people and the environment's component to have more physical activity.

4.1 Questionnaire

An online questionnaire was used with a storyboard explaining the concept of HabitAR for evaluation and to find design opportunities, which consisted of 11 questions focused on the effect of motivation and general walking experience. As HabitAR is a system including a digital app and public display in the public space, anyone has access to participate. Participants were recruited online by publishing the questionnaire online through social media. Completion of the questionnaire was anonymous and voluntary,

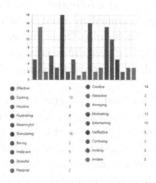

Fig. 3. Result of sentence completion on the HabitAR concept

and no demographic questions were asked. Since our design was designed to motivate the general public, we did not limit the demographic characteristics.

Twenty-four participants agreed or strongly agreed on "When I see an animal while walking, it attracts my attention" This shows that animals as a part of the environment influence almost every walking participant's experience and attract their interest. However, participants were motivated differently; namely, seven indicated that after spotting an animal, they were not motivated to spot another animal, ten were motivated by this to spot another animal, and eight responded with neutral. For the result of sentence completion (shown in Fig. 3), the most frequently chosen words are stimulating (16), creative (14), motivating (13), exciting (13), and entertaining (10). The ratio between positive and negative terms was 17:5, meaning that the majority chose positive words to describe the concept. Fourteen participants (56%) have a positive feeling about our concept, and nine (36%) are neutral. Two participants (P12 and P21) had negative feelings about our concept. These two participants also chose only negative words (boring, frustrating, ineffective, irrelevant, annoying) in the previous question. This outcome, combined with the ratio of positive and negative terms, showed that people are overall optimistic about the playfulness and motivating effect of HabitAR.

The concept features that had the most potential and motivating effect were: creating your route, seeing where other people had spotted something on your route and the disappearance of other users' posts that became visible again when you performed physical activity. In addition, three participants indicated that they would like an option to spot other things instead of animals (P6, P16 and P21). It is because their interest was in a different area. P6 stated, "When people love animals, they will probably like it (HabitAR)." Regarding motivation, 10 participants (40%) indicated that HabitAR would motivate them to walk outside more often. Seven participants (28%) are neutral. Eight participants (32%) stated that HabitAR was unlikely to motivate them. But six of them indicated that some features of the concept, like spotting things, taking pictures, uploading and disappearing posts, were motivating and stimulating. Two participants did not like to be on their phones while walking (P7 and P12).

4.2 User Test

To further get more in-depth feedback on the experience with the application and its usability, an in-the-wild user test and a following semi-structured interview was conducted. Five participants were recruited by word of mouth for the user test on our university campus, aged 19 to 23 years old). During the preliminary testing, we, following the Wizard of Oz method [21], placed different types of stuffed animals on terrains according to the routes users chose to represent real animals to control the same setting for different users.

In general, all participants reported the experience of walking with HabitAR as fun. The features of the app that the participants considered the most useful correspond to the answers from the questionnaire, namely being able to create their own route and seeing where other people have spotted something. In addition, the ability to create, upload and read posts from other users was also mentioned. Features that the participants would add in the future are being able to add comments under the posts of others (P2, P4 and P5). According to the participants, other things that could be added to the concepts were fun facts or more information about the animal found. Furthermore, participants prefer filtering what they want to find on the route so that they can adjust their route accordingly (P1 and P3). P3 explained that his interests were in mammals, which he wanted to spot, rather than birds, which he disliked. It made a big difference in his motivation when using HabitAR, which shows that personal differences greatly influence the concept's effectiveness.

However, four participants (P1, P3, P4 and P5) indicated that HabitAR could motivate them to walk more and they would choose a longer route if they saw on the app that another user had spotted something a little further on. For them, building a connection with the animals through a shared blog is a motivating aspect. "What I like the most about using this app is reading the blog posts of others, and what they write about the other animals." (P4) and "With the shared blog, you have engagement with the animals and learn about them." (P1). Based on quotes like "What is the challenge?" (P5) and "I liked the scavenger hunt element" (P3), it seems like the other participants experience it more as a game and therefore see it as motivating rather than wanting to maintain their connection with the animals.

5 Conclusion

This paper presents HabitAR, a system designed to motivate outdoor walking with the connection between walkers and animals. Its feasibility was empirically demonstrated through preliminary user studies. Both our survey and interview showed that HabitAR has a motivating effect on encouraging people to walk outdoors with a fun experience. The degree of motivating effectiveness depended on personal factors such as the value the individual attaches to the interest, which seemed to work better on users who were more interested in animals. It provides insight that customized applications with personal interests can be considered to stimulate people's intrinsic motivation when designing PA interventions. It also suggests providing interactivity regarding the elements of the physical walking space, which may engage people to walk outdoors and result in long-term behavior change, but lack relevant research and design practice [1].

Habit AR Video https://surfdrive.surf.nl/files/index.php/s/OSIvGlBLybXpfRP.

Acknowledgments. This research is part of the Motivating Environments for Vitality and Sports Project. The first author of this paper is partially supported by China Scholarship Council (CSC).

References

1. Aldenaini, N., Alqahtani, F., Orji, R., Sampalli, S.: Trends in persuasive technologies for physical activity and sedentary behavior: a systematic review. Front. Artif. Intell. **3**, 7 (2020). https://doi.org/10.3389/frai.2020.00007
2. Baranowski, T., Lyons, E.J.: Scoping review of pokémon go: comprehensive assessment of augmented reality for physical activity change. Games Health J. **9**(2), 71–84 (2020). https://doi.org/10.1089/g4h.2019.0034

3. Botros, F., Perin, C., Aseniero, B.A., Carpendale, S.: Go and grow: mapping personal data to a living plant. In: Proceedings of the International Working Conference on Advanced Visual Interfaces, pp. 112–119 (2016).https://doi.org/10.1145/2909132.2909267

4. Bowler, D.E., Buyung-Ali, L.M., Knight, T.M., Pullin, A.S.: A systematic review of evidence for the added benefits to health of exposure to natural environments. BMC Public Health 10(1), 456 (2010). https://doi.org/10.1186/1471-2458-10-456

5. Consolvo, S., et al.: Activity sensing in the wild: a field trial of ubifit garden. In: Proceeding of the Twenty-Sixth Annual CHI Conference on Human Factors in Computing Systems - CHI 2008, pp. 1797–1806 (2008). https://doi.org/10.1145/1357054.1357335

6. Deci, E.L., Ryan, R.M.: Intrinsic Motivation and Self-Determination in Human Behavior. Springer, US (2013). https://books.google.nl/books?id=M3CpBgAAQBAJ

7. Deterding, S., Dixon, D., Khaled, R., Nacke, L.: From game design elements to gamefulness: defining "gamification", pp. 9–15 (2011). https://doi.org/10.1145/2181037.2181040

8. Hamari, J., Koivisto, J.: "Working out for likes": an empirical study on social influence in exercise gamification. Comput. Hum. Behav. 50, 333–347 (2015). https://doi.org/10.1016/j.chb.2015.04.018

9. Erin Lee, H., Cho, J.: What motivates users to continue using diet and fitness apps? Application of the uses and gratifications approach. Health Commun. 32(12), 1445–1453 (2017). https://doi.org/10.1080/10410236.2016.1167998

10. Lin, J.J., Mamykina, L., Lindtner, S., Delajoux, G., Strub, H.B.: Fish'n'Steps: encouraging physical activity with an interactive computer game. In: Dourish, P., Friday, A. (eds.) UbiComp 2006: Ubiquitous Computing. LNCS, vol. 4206, pp. 261–278. Springer, Heidelberg (2006). https://doi.org/10.1007/11853565_16

11. Mandigo, J.L., Holt, N.L.: Putting theory into practice: how cognitive evaluation theory can help us motivate children in physical activity environments. J. Phys. Educ. Recreat. Dance 71(1), 44–49 (2000). https://doi.org/10.1080/07303084.2000.10605984

12. Murnane, E.L., et al.: Designing ambient narrative-based interfaces to reflect and motivate physical activity. In: Proceedings of the 2020 CHI Conference on Human Factors in Computing Systems, pp. 1–14 (2020). https://doi.org/10.1145/3313831.3376478

13. Ryan, R.M., Deci, E.L.: Self-determination theory and the facilitation of intrinsic motivation, social development, and well-being. Am. Psychol. 55(1), 68–78 (2000). https://doi.org/10.1037/0003-066X.55.1.68

14. Stragier, J., Abeele, M.V., Mechant, P., De Marez, L.: Understanding persistence in the use of online fitness communities: comparing novice and experienced users. Comput. Hum. Behav. 64, 34–42 (2016). https://doi.org/10.1016/j.chb.2016.06.013

15. Teixeira, P.J., Carraça, E.V., Markland, D., Silva, M.N., Ryan, R.M.: Exercise, physical activity, and self-determination theory: a systematic review. Int. J. Behav. Nutr. Phys. Act. 9, 78 (2012). https://doi.org/10.1186/1479-5868-9-78

16. Thompson Coon, J., Boddy, K., Stein, K., Whear, R., Barton, J., Depledge, M.H.: Does participating in physical activity in outdoor natural environments have a greater effect on physical and mental wellbeing than physical activity indoors? A systematic review. Environ. Sci. Technol. 45(5), 1761–1772 (2011). https://doi.org/10.1021/es102947t

17. Tong, X., Gromala, D., Shaw, C., Jin, W.: Encouraging physical activity with a game-based mobile application: FitPet. In: 2015 IEEE Games Entertainment Media Conference (GEM), pp. 1–2 (2015). https://doi.org/10.1109/GEM.2015.7377251

18. Toscos, T., Consolvo, S., McDonald, D.W.: Barriers to physical activity: a study of self-revelation in an online community. J. Med. Syst. 35(5), 1225–1242 (2011). https://doi.org/10.1007/s10916-011-9721-2

19. Rungting, T., Hsieh, P., Feng, W.: Walking for fun or for "likes"? The impacts of different gamification orientations of fitness apps on consumers' physical activities. Sport Manage. Rev. 22(5), 682–693 (2019). https://doi.org/10.1016/j.smr.2018.10.005

20. Zuckerman, O., Gal-Oz, A.: Deconstructing gamification: evaluating the effectiveness of continuous measurement, virtual rewards, and social comparison for promoting physical activity. Pers. Ubiquit. Comput. **18**(7), 1705–1719 (2014). https://doi.org/10.1007/s00779-014-0783-2
21. What is Wizard of Oz prototyping? - Definition from WhatIs.com. SearchCIO (2022). https://www.techtarget.com/searchcio/definition/Wizard-of-Oz-prototyping. Accessed 18 Aug 2022

Mystery in the Ecological Park: An Interactive Narrative to Promote Interaction with Biodiversity

André Freitas[1]([envelope]) [ORCID], Francisco Fernandes[1] [ORCID], Mara Dionísio[1,2] [ORCID], and Sandra Olim[2,3] [ORCID]

[1] Universidade da Madeira, Funchal, Portugal
{2048019,2056219}@student.uma.pt, mara.dionisio@staff.uma.pt
[2] ITI-LARSyS, IST, Universidade de Lisboa, Lisbon, Portugal
sandra.olim@iti.larsys.pt
[3] FCT, Universidade Nova de Lisboa, Lisbon, Portugal

Abstract. In a world of increasing environmental degradation, there is an urgency to promote care for nature. UNESCO advocates that by 2025 the integration of environmental education is an essential element in all countries, to actively contribute towards the well-being of the planet and adopt sustainable lifestyles. One way to combine both these goals is to promote engagement in nature-based experiences as these have been widely associated with notable positive outcomes for both individuals and the planet. In this context we propose, a Nature-themed interactive narrative called: Mystery in the Ecological Park. The location-based narrative incorporates educational content about biodiversity threats weaved in the narrative that inspires a sense of mystery and adventure. The aim of this work is to increase awareness to the impact that animal abandonment has in fragile ecosystems.

Keywords: Biodiversity · Interactive Narratives · Visual Novel · Location-based · Human-Nature Interaction · Informal learning · Mobile Application

1 Introduction

Recent studies have emphasized the vital role of education in fostering knowledge about biodiversity [1]. It is crucial to inspire children to appreciate and safeguard endemic species and local wildlife. Furthermore, experiences in which children are in contact with natural environments increases their empathy and concerns for nature [2,6,7]. However, there is a decrease in the number of children engaging with nature, raising concerns that those who are deprive of such encounters may not fully appreciate and value it [9]. And while the allure of screens, gadgets, and virtual experiences can sometimes overshadow the appeal of the natural world, it is essential to strike a balance and find ways to integrate technology with nature related experiences rather than viewing them as

P. Ciancarini et al. (Eds.): ICEC 2023, LNCS 14455, pp. 360–364, 2023.
https://doi.org/10.1007/978-981-99-8248-6_32

mutually exclusive. As such, we developed, *"Mystery in the Ecological Park"*, a location-based interactive narrative experience designed for preadolescents (9 to 12 year old children), with the aim to showcase the beauty of the Ecological Park situated in Funchal, Madeira, while drawing attention to the biodiversity threats that it is currently facing. The narrative aims to increase awareness to the impact that animal abandonment has in fragile ecosystems. The abandonment of pets in the wilderness, in particular cats, leads to the endangerment of the local biodiversity putting birds and lizards at risk as the domestic cats hunt them to survive. Previous research has showed the potential of interactive narratives (IN) to support the conservation of biodiversity [3,4,8] as they can create a more enjoyable and interactive environment for learning [5]. Aiming to leverage this potential, we have designed a mystery-fun story-plot and dialogues with characters representing local species, that encourage participants to explore points of interest within the Park and gather clues to solve an enigma, while learning about biodiversity.

2   Mystery in the Ecological Park (MEP)

Mystery in the Ecological Park (MEP) is a location-based narrative driven experience, targeting children/preteens with ages between 9 to 12 years old. The experience leverages the persuasive power of narratives with the interactive capabilities of a smartphone to provide and showcase the beauty of the ecological park while inspiring curiosity and desire to experience nature at firsthand. MEP was developed with the intention of persuading preadolescents to explore the Park while also indulging in an interactive story. The experience divides the narrative into several locations where the user will meet many different characters and their take on the issue at hand. Upon arriving to the ecological park, the experience begins with a small introduction to the story, where the player is introduced to the main characters, the quest and the User Interface (UI) located in the map *(see Fig. 1 - number 1)*. Drawing inspiration from the concept of "Geocaching"[1] and "Pokemon Go"[2], this experience entails users walking along distinct pathways aided by a map interface in search of QR Codes. Upon scanning these QR Codes, users are introduced to mini-episodes each featuring a novel character *(see Fig. 1 - number 3)*. Within these mini-episodes, the player can freely respond to the dialogues prompts (two options), leading to a change in the character's reaction, but not to the story plot. During these encounters, important information will be highlighted and underlined in red, to give more emphasis. Afterwards, this information is stored in the virtual notebook provided by the application *(see Fig. 1 - number 2)*. Through engaging with all the characters and gathering their version of the events and clues, the player participates in a court hearing with all the species to figure out who really committed the crime *(see Fig. 1 - number 5)*. Finally, after discovering the culprit of the crime, a conclusive sequence begins, where all the characters interact one last time with

---

[1] https://education.nationalgeographic.org/resource/geocaching/.

[2] https://pokemongolive.com.

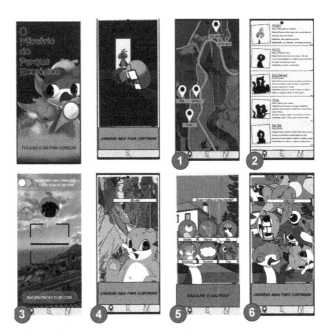

Fig. 1. Mystery in the Ecological Park - Game Flow

the player, saying their farewells and goodbyes, while also congratulating them for figuring out who really did it *(see Fig. 1 - number 6)*.

The experience was developed for android mobile devices using the Unity Engine[3], using ARCore and Indkle SDKs[4] to implement branching narrative structures. We used a cartoon art style to visually attract our target audience. The characters were thoughtfully stylised to seem cute and approachable, while concurrently highlighting their distinct personalities and unique mannerisms.

2.1 Narrative Design

Our narrative was constructed to allow for non-linear exploration, education on the many species, and as a warning against pet abandonment due to them endangering other species and unbalancing the ecosystem.

The narrative starts by introducing Avisa, a Zino's petrel, who will be our guide in the park. Avisa finds her husband Azul, another petrel, seemingly dead. Upon looking at the body Avisa finds bite marks on his wing, leading her to believe that this was a murder, and that potentially one of her friends did it. Avisa asks the players for help in solving the crime. The player then is given the role of detective, and with a digital map and notebook in hand, must now find and interrogate the many suspects and witnesses around the park, these being

---

[3] https://unity.com/pt.
[4] https://developers.google.com/ar?hl=pt-br.

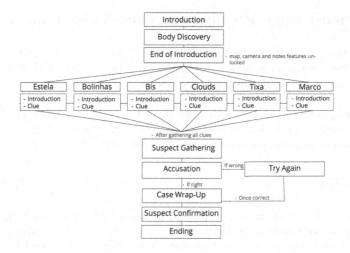

Fig. 2. Mystery in the Ecological Park - Narrative Flow

Marco the Bat, Tixa the Lizard, Estela the Star Mushroom, Bis the Madeira Firecrest, Bolinhas the Cat and clouds. Speaking with all characters is necessary to begin the game's final act, but players are given the freedom to speak with whoever in whichever order they please *(see Fig. 2)*, differentiating the experience between players. Furthermore, this will not only impart clues to the player, but also facts about their own species. Once all species have been discovered and interrogated the player is instructed to walk to a specific spot where the final trial/accusation takes part. Then the player can choose who they believe to be culprit based on the gathered clues. In the closing narrative scene the player discovers that due to the cause of death, the location, the time and even its own body, Bolinhas the cat is the culprit. Finally, in a plot twist, Azul turns out to be alive and explains that he was only unconscious due to fear and panic after being chased and attacked by Bolinhas. Bolinhas clarifies that he was only trying to survive and ate wild animals because his owner abandoned him in the park. All the other creatures forgive him and promise to help in the future.

3   Conclusion and Future Work

The application was created to attract potential users to visit the Funchal's Ecological Park, and raise awareness to biodiversity threat that causes the endangerment of many bird, lizard and other species. In future iterations, we will explore AR features as to facilitate the process of finding the different scenarios of the maps using *Geolocation*. Finally, we wish to explore how collaborative features could make this experience a lot more memorable and enjoyable.

4 Demonstration Requirements and Video Link

The mobile devices required for demonstration will be provided by the authors. To facilitate the demo, a table with access to a power plug and wall space to place the QR Code would be necessary. Video

Acknowledgments. This research was funded by the following FCT Grants: PD/BD/150286/2019 and EXPL/ART-DAQ/1444/2021: Sense and Sensibility in Interactivity: Connecting children and teenagers to nature through the design of sensory.

References

1. Børresen, S.T., Ulimboka, R., Nyahongo, J., Ranke, P.S., Skjaervø, G.R., Røskaft, E.: The role of education in biodiversity conservation: can knowledge and understanding alter locals' views and attitudes towards ecosystem services? Environ. Educ. Res. **29**(1), 148–163 (2023)
2. Chawla, L., Derr, V.: The development of conservation behaviors in childhood and youth (2012)
3. Dionisio, M., Bala, P., Nisi, V., Nunes, N.: Fragments of laura: incorporating mobile virtual reality in location aware mobile storytelling experiences. In: Proceedings of the 16th International Conference on Mobile and Ubiquitous Multimedia, pp. 165–176 (2017)
4. Ferreira, M.J., Paradeda, R.B., Oliveira, R., Nisi, V., Paiva, A.: Using storytelling to teach children biodiversity. In: Vosmeer, M., Holloway-Attaway, L. (eds.) ICIDS 2022. LNCS, vol. 13762, pp. 3–27. Springer, Cham (2022). https://doi.org/10.1007/978-3-031-22298-6_1
5. Kawas, S., Kuhn, N.S., Tari, M., Hiniker, A., Davis, K.: "Otter this world": can a mobile application promote children's connectedness to nature? In: Proceedings of the Interaction Design and Children Conference, London, United Kingdom, pp. 444–457. ACM (2020). https://doi.org/10.1145/3392063.3394434. https://dl.acm.org/doi/10.1145/3392063.3394434
6. Lumber, R., Richardson, M., Sheffield, D.: Beyond knowing nature: contact, emotion, compassion, meaning, and beauty are pathways to nature connection. PLoS ONE **12**(5), e0177186 (2017)
7. Mathers, B., Brymer, E.: The power of a profound experience with nature: living with meaning. Front. Psychol. **13**, 764224 (2022). https://doi.org/10.3389/fpsyg.2022.764224. https://www.frontiersin.org/articles/10.3389/fpsyg.2022.764224/full
8. Prandi, C., Nisi, V., Loureiro, P., Nunes, N.J.: Storytelling and remote-sensing playful interventions to foster biodiversity awareness. Int. J. Arts Technol. **12**(1), 39–59 (2020)
9. Vella, K., Dema, T., Soro, A., Brereton, M.: Fostering children's stewardship of local nature through game co-design. In: 33rd Australian Conference on Human-Computer Interaction, Melbourne, VIC, Australia, pp. 38–50. ACM (2021). https://doi.org/10.1145/3520495.3522702. https://dl.acm.org/doi/10.1145/3520495.3522702

SEC-GAME: A Minigame Collection for Cyber Security Awareness

Nicola Del Giudice$^{(\boxtimes)}$ ⓘ, Fausto Marcantoni, Alessandro Marcelletti ⓘ, and Francesco Moschella

University of Camerino, Camerino 62032, Italy
{nicola.delgiudice,fausto.marcantoni,alessand.marcelletti}@unicam.it,
francesco.moschella@studenti.unicam.it

Abstract. Cybersecurity awareness is a fundamental aspect of cyber-attack prevention and web threats. Every day, end users are attacked by hackers through malwares, phishing techniques and vulnerability exploitation. However, current teaching approaches are not effective for non-expert people, that have difficulties understanding such topics using traditional lectures. For this reason, in this work, we present Sec-Game, a collection of minigames aiming to raise cybersecurity awareness. Our game combines gamification techniques and game design theories, taking advantage of both approaches to provide complete mechanics and learning principles. To demonstrate the feasibility of the approach, we provide a prototypical implementation of Sec-Game which evaluation was conducted with practitioners.

Keywords: Cybersecurity · Cybersecurity Awareness · Gamification · Game-Based Learning

1 Introduction

Cybersecurity awareness is becoming a crucial topic for helping the prevention of web threats. Daily, every kind of person is the potential subject of cyber attacks such as malware, phishing, social engineering and vulnerability exploitation [1,4,14]. Indeed, it is very common to encounter such threats when using emails or online applications. Over the years, these attacks are becoming more frequent, due to the growing number of vulnerabilities and the complexity of modern techniques. In the first semester of 2022, more than a thousand meaningful cyberattacks have been detected globally. According to the CLUSIT report[1], the Italian Association for Cybersecurity, 1,141 major attacks have been registered, on an average of 190 monthly offences. In addition, the pandemic [2] and the Russian-Ukrainian [6] conflict are stressing this tendency, requiring new forms of prevention and defence. For this reason, increasing awareness about cybersecurity concepts can help to mitigate exploitation and attacks at every

---

[1] Available at https://clusit.it/rapporto-clusit/.

© IFIP International Federation for Information Processing 2023
Published by Springer Nature Switzerland AG 2023
P. Ciancarini et al. (Eds.): ICEC 2023, LNCS 14455, pp. 365–370, 2023.
https://doi.org/10.1007/978-981-99-8248-6_33

level. However, due to the heterogeneous range of people involved, it is complicated to provide effective teaching activities about these challenging arguments [11]. Similarly, the training through seminars and laboratories usually is not fully perceived due to the complexity of the argument [12]. Among the novel emerging approaches [3,7–10], a prominent alternative considers games as learning strategies can be more effective in improving the knowledge of cybersecurity concepts like basic attacks and their effect on the users.

In this work, we propose an approach based on a collection of minigames named Sec-Game. This approach aims at improving awareness by giving the user a set of games related to cybersecurity principles that represent everyday situations. It is also possible to help people understand how a type of attack is conducted and how to prevent it through games. Sec-Game combines gamification techniques and game design theory, taking advantage of both of them to provide complete mechanics and learning principles. To demonstrate the feasibility of the approach we implemented a prototype of Sec-Game. This was also tested on a group of practitioners, measuring the satisfaction of the proposed teaching strategy.

The rest of the paper is structured as follows. In Sect. 2, we describe the Sec-Game learning principles and the included minigames. The implementation and validation of Sec-Game are then reported in Sect. 3, while in Sect. 4 we give concluding remarks and future development.

2   Sec-Game Design

In this section, we point out the design of Sec-Game methodology and the adopted solutions to transmit cybersecurity concepts to users[2]. The game has been developed using the Unity 2D Real-Time Engine, v. 2021.3, based on C# programming language and WebGL as a building system.

2.1   Learning Principles

Sec-Game considers several learning principles derived from [5]. Active learning is encouraged through contexts that mimic real-world problems. Recreating everyday life, people can understand the importance of cybersecurity, and they can realise if some of their attitude towards the Internet is correct. In this way, Sec-Game proposes an approach that lets learners rethink their knowledge of the world. Also, a score is used to provide a rewarding mechanism through the "Achievement" principle, signalling the learner's ongoing progress.

2.2   Minigames Description

We provide here a detailed description of the different minigames implemented in the Sec-Game approach. In particular, Sec-Game is composed of five minigames[3]

---

[2] The build is available in the Docker file here.

[3] The figure representing the minigames gameplay flow is available here.

chosen according to the most famous cyberattacks targeting inexperienced users reported in the CLUSIT document previously mentioned. Players can start their session and choose a specific minigame from the available ones. Once they conclude it, they can play the next one, explore the world or end their session. This enhances player freedom by creating a fully player-driven story [13].

The Sec-Game environment resembles common places like a small park or the town's local pub. This shows how potential attacks can frequently happen to people. The prototypically implemented minigames and the related cybersecurity principles are shown in Fig. 1.

Secure Password. The first minigame has the objective of teaching how a proper password can be created. Indeed, a lot of people still do not care enough about basic security precautions making their devices and online accounts vulnerable. The minigame is structured as a snake-like game where the player has to capture different random characters without crashing (Fig. 1e). To handle the overall score of the user, the game increases the points for each correct pick.

Brute Force. The second minigame is based on the brute force concept. The player has to try different combinations in order to unlock a smartphone (Fig. 1a). For each sequence, the game will show if a number is correct or in the wrong order. For each invalid sequence, the game decreases points from the overall score, while in case of success, it increases it. With this game, the user gains awareness of how brute force attacks work.

Caesar's Code. The third minigame aims at teaching some cryptographic aspects and the gameplay is based on Caesar's code encryption technique. The player has to detect the content of a message coded according to the related algorithm (Fig. 1b). Each letter is shifted accordingly to a number that is chosen randomly. The player can attempt many times to find the correct decryption key. The score of this game is based on how many tries the user does.

Emails Phishing. The fourth minigame is related to phishing attacks. The game consists of an email inbox view in which some emails appear (Fig. 1d). The user has to select if the mail seems real or not. To mimic a phishing attack, each one can contain for example strange sender accounts or malicious links. After some attempts, the user becomes aware of the common practices of phishing emails. During the game, each email gives the player a positive or negative score.

Malware Protection. The last game represents how a user can contrast malwares. The gameplay is similar to *Space Invaders* and it presents malwares attacking the player's computer, requiring firewalls and antiviruses for defence (Fig. 1c). Here, we aim to provide an example of how the user can simply use a common typology of software to prevent the diffusion of malwares. The overall score is modified only after the losing or the winning of the game.

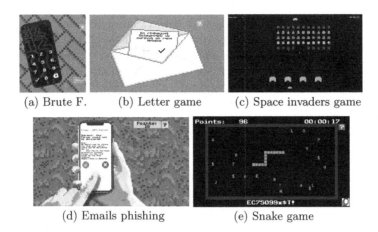

(a) Brute F.   (b) Letter game   (c) Space invaders game

(d) Emails phishing   (e) Snake game

Fig. 1. Sec-Game minigames interface

3 Experiments

In this section, we discuss the conducted experiments involving student practitioners with Sec-Game. Notice, our game is at a prototypical version and, during this phase, we only aim at measuring the overall experience and satisfaction of the users. These results[4] will be used to improve the implemented minigames and the related cybersecurity principles.

The evaluation session was conducted on 23rd January 2023 with a group of around 50 students of 2nd year of high school without cybersecurity expertise. For technical reasons, the students were split into two major groups working alternatively. For each major group, smaller teams of 4–5 individuals were created by combining students with different competencies and interests. This division permits to have a heterogeneous user experience and the resulting feedback. Each small group had to complete all available minigames and compete against the others to reach the highest score. We noticed that the first big group was more interested in playing Sec-Game, demonstrating a major fierceness while completing the minigames and trying to reach a higher score. The second one, instead, showed less engagement than the others and proceeded to complete the games without caring about competition and score. In both cases, each group found effortlessly and played all the available minigames. We administered a survey where we asked about the general satisfaction with the game, especially what the candidates found more or less appealing. Indeed, for this brief session, we asked only which was (i) the most-liked game, (ii) the hardest one, and (iii) the easiest one. The results of the survey showed that the most liked games correspond to Letter and Space Invaders. The Phone and Snake minigames were instead the less liked ones. The Brute force one was considered the most difficult game among the available ones. On the contrary, the Letter minigame

---

[4] The results are available at the following link, in the "survey results" folder.

has been considered the easiest one. The resulting feedback confirms the initial expectations of some minigames on which further implementation is needed.

4   Conclusions

Cybersecurity awareness is becoming a crucial strategy to contrast and prevent attacks that are affecting more people every day. New learning techniques are required, especially those using game design and gamification principles which are gaining success. In this paper, we proposed Sec-Game, a novel approach to improve cybersecurity awareness through playable minigames, where each one represents a cybersecurity principle. In the future, we will add new minigames representing more cybersecurity concepts. From the evaluation and awareness point of view, we plan to propose our tool to more candidates and schools. We would like to do further experiments, with different contexts and with other practitioners.

5   Gameplay

A full gameplay video is available at the following link in the folder "gameplay video". The video presents the login process and shows the minigames.

6   Requirements

The technical requirements to play the game are minimal. The optimal gameplay experience would be using a Chrome web browser on a desktop computer with a mouse and keyboard or a laptop. It is necessary for the computer and the browser to support at least WebGL 3.0. The WebGL Compatibility can be verified at the following link: https://get.webgl.org/. Also, a strong internet bandwidth may lower waiting times while entering levels or moving between game zones.

There are no specific physical or space requirements, eventually playing the game in a calm and non-chaotic room may improve the overall user experience.

References

1. Blackwood-Brown, C., Levy, Y., D'Arcy, J.: Cybersecurity awareness and skills of senior citizens: a motivation perspective. J. Comput. Inf. Syst. 61(3), 195–206 (2021)
2. Bozzetti, M., Olivieri, L., Spoto, F.: Cybersecurity Impacts of the Covid-19 Pandemic in Italy. In: Armando, A., Colajanni, M. (eds.) Proceedings of the Italian Conference on Cybersecurity. CEUR Workshop Proceedings, vol. 2940, pp. 145–155. CEUR-WS.org (2021)
3. Coenraad, M., Pellicone, A., Ketelhut, D.J., Cukier, M., Plane, J., Weintrop, D.: Experiencing cybersecurity one game at a time: a systematic review of cybersecurity digital games. Simulat. Gaming 51(5), 586–611 (2020)

4. Desolda, G., Ferro, L.S., Marrella, A., Catarci, T., Costabile, M.F.: Human factors in phishing attacks: a systematic literature review. ACM Comput. Surv. **54**(8), 1–35 (2021)

5. Gee, J.P.: What video games have to teach us about learning and literacy. Comput. Entertain. **1**(1), 20–20 (2003)

6. Guchua, A., Zedelashvili, T., Giorgadze, G.: Geopolitics of the Russia-Ukraine War and Russian cyber attacks on Ukraine-Georgia and expected threats. Ukrainian Policymaker **10**, 26–36 (2022)

7. Hajny, J., Ricci, S., Piesarskas, E., Sikora, M.: Cybersecurity curricula designer. In: Reinhardt, D., Müller, T. (eds.) ARES 2021: The 16th International Conference on Availability, Reliability and Security, Vienna, 17–20 August 2021, pp. 144:1–144:7. ACM (2021)

8. Hajny, J., Sikora, M., Grammatopoulos, A.V., Franco, F.D.: Adding European cybersecurity skills framework into curricula designer. In: The 17th International Conference on Availability, Reliability and Security, pp. 82:1–82:6. ACM (2022)

9. Hendrix, M., Al-Sherbaz, A., Victoria, B.: Game based cyber security training: are serious games suitable for cyber security training? Int. J. Serious Games **3**(1), 53–61 (2016)

10. Jin, G., Tu, M., Kim, T., Heffron, J., White, J.: Game based cybersecurity training for high school students. In: Barnes, T., Garcia, D.D., Hawthorne, E.K., Pérez-Quiñones, M.A. (eds.) Proceedings of the 49th Technical Symposium on Computer Science Education, pp. 68–73. ACM (2018)

11. Khan, M.A., Merabet, A., Alkaabi, S., Sayed, H.E.: Game-based learning platform to enhance cybersecurity education. Educ. Inf. Technol. **27**(4), 5153–5177 (2022)

12. Lallie, H., Sinclair, J.E., Joy, M., Janicke, H., Price, B., Howley, R.: Pedagogic Challenges in Teaching Cyber Security - A UK Perspective. arXiv preprint arXiv:2212.06584 (2022)

13. Lebowitz, J., Klug, C.: Interactive Storytelling for Video Games: Proven Writing Techniques for Role Playing Games. First Person Shooters, and More. Routledge, Online Games (2012)

14. Maan, P., Sharma, M.: Social engineering: a partial technical attack. Int. J. Comput. Sci. Issues **9**(2), 557–559 (2012)

Student Game Competition

Designing a VR-Simulation Module to Support Marine Pollution Control Training

João Silva[1]([⊠]) [iD], Jorge C. S. Cardoso[2]([⊠]) [iD], Luís Pereira[2] [iD], and Licínio Roque[2] [iD]

[1] University of Coimbra, DEI, Coimbra, Portugal
`joaopedro@student.dei.uc.pt`
[2] University of Coimbra, CISUC, DEI, Coimbra, Portugal
`jorgecardoso@dei.uc.pt`

Abstract. To become able to respond quickly and effectively to oil spills, the teams in charge of marine pollution control must undertake regular training sessions to preserve and expand the proficiency of its members for the job. However, conducting such training can become quite expensive and time consuming when practiced on real vessels. With that in mind, the goal of the MPCS (Marine Pollution Control Simulator) project is to create a simulator that can serve as a safer and more affordable alternative to conduct those training sessions. This paper presents the progress that has been made on a VR-based navigation and on-board equipment manipulation module for the MPCS project. The main contribution of the work is the exploration of the design space enabling shared VR-based operation, with insights on the challenges placed for coordinated actions such as realistic VR-based interfaces for placing oil spill containment measures and piloting two or more boats to contain and divert the spill to a collection point.

Keywords: simulation · virtual reality · oil spill containment · marine pollution control

1 Introduction

Simulators have proven to be a very useful tool for training in high-risk professions, such as navigation, aviation, or medical care [1]. They enable students and professionals to train in a safe environment where expensive hardware, software systems or even lives will not be at risk. The use of simulators gives practitioners the freedom to fail and observe the direct consequences of inappropriate actions, an aspect that has a huge impact on education, since many of the most memorable lessons are the ones where we learn from our own mistakes. Simulation-based training also allows practitioners to prepare for very rare situations that would be impossible to train in real life, such as evacuating a sinking ship.

With the goal of bringing the benefits of simulation-based training to the area of marine pollution control, the MPCS project is focusing on the development of a cloud-based platform that can serve as an environment for teaching, training, and evaluation

P. Ciancarini et al. (Eds.): ICEC 2023, LNCS 14455, pp. 373–379, 2023.
https://doi.org/10.1007/978-981-99-8248-6_34

of MPC (Marine Pollution control) operations. Through this simulator, we aim to create virtual scenarios that can be used to develop/refine individual and collective skills geared towards the spill containment process. To enable the coordinated readiness, the simulations must take place in multi-user environments, where each participant will assume one of a set of possible roles of professionals involved in marine pollution control (command and control, communications, navigation, operation of specialized equipment such as barriers, skimmers, pumps, and containers). Inside those environments, users should be able to interact with the equipment around them, the spill, and with each other, to meet the desired training exercise goals.

For economic purposes, most operational coordination actions in the MPCS project target easily accessible 2D interfaces for PC/Tablets. However, as an exploratory extension, we are currently developing a VR-based simulation module to enable cooperative action for training specific maritime operations such as deploying oil containment barriers. In this paper, we describe the architecture, functionality, and insights into the design space, while developing this module. A demo of the current version can be seen at https:// www.youtube.com/watch?v=rgNUfuFCmQY.

2   Marine Pollution Control

Oil and other Hydrocarbons (HC) are substances that have a low density compared to water, so when released into the ocean, they tend to float to its surface [2]. If no containment method is applied, the spilled HCs may quickly spread over the surface of the sea, usually making the contaminated area increasingly larger as time passes, or create a heavy emulsion mixed with salt water, possibly reaching sensitive coastal areas where cleaning becomes increasingly difficult. To facilitate the collection process and prevent further damage to the environment, specialized teams use containment booms to stop the spill from spreading.

Containment booms are floating barriers that are usually deployed and towed by two boats with the goal of forming a "J", "U", or "V" shape, as we can see in Fig. 1. Each boom configuration has its own advantages and disadvantages, but the process always involves skilled and coordinated steering of the vessels against the wind and current to trap the HC as it moves in the opposite direction [3] while simultaneously deploying the trapping and recovery equipment.

Once the spill is contained, the pollutant substance can be collected from the ocean surface by a dedicated vessel (such as in V configuration) or through a skimmer deployed by either a third boat (U configuration) or one of the vessels towing the barrier J configuration).

3   MPCS VR Module

The MPCS VR Module is the component of the MPCS project responsible for providing a multiplayer VR experience that allows for a game-based approach enabling users to practice essential coordinated steps that compose the marine pollution control operations at sea. More specifically, the process of placing the oil spill containment barriers and piloting two or more boats (by two or more users,) while carrying equipment and other operators, to contain and divert the contamination area to a collection point. The module is still in its early stages and is being prototyped with Unreal Engine 5 and tested on Meta Quest 2.

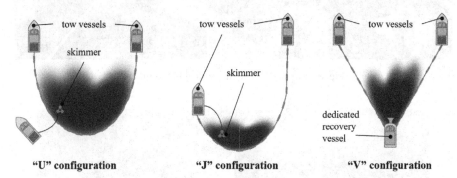

"U" configuration   "J" configuration   "V" configuration

Fig. 1. Boom configurations.

3.1 Functionality and Interactions

Player Movement. During the VR experience, each participant is represented by an avatar that moves through the scenario by teleportation or by replication of the user's movement in the real world (see Fig. 2). By moving the right joystick, users can control the teleport mechanism: pushing the joystick generates a teleport pointer; releasing it teleports the user.

Hand Gestures. Each avatar has two virtual hands that match the controllers' position relative to the VR headset (see Fig. 2). By pressing a combination of buttons, users can perform different hand gestures – touching the A/X or B/Y buttons closes the thumb; pressing the trigger button closes the index finger; pressing the grip button closes the remaining fingers. These two virtual hands mediate most of the interactions between the participants and the virtual world. Through grip gestures, users can grab and rotate the steering wheel to adjust the boat's direction or grab and push/pull the throttle handles to control the left and right engines (see Fig. 3).

Fig. 2. Teleport mechanism and VR hands.

Fig. 3. Interaction with the virtual environment.

Fig. 4. Environment configuration.

Equipment Operation. Besides steering the boat, users will also be able to grab and handle different pieces of equipment to perform the steps that compose the boom deployment into the ocean. In the first phase of the deployment, users will need to connect one of the barrier's ends to the second tow vessel. For that, the ones inside the first boat must attach the tow line to a buoy and then place it into the ocean. Once the buoy is close to the second vessel, the other group of participants must grab it, detach the tow line, and then connect it to the back of the boat. After that, the second phase of the deployment will involve turning on the air compressor to start inflating the booms and rotating the reel to unroll them.

2D Interfaces. Regarding menus and other 2D interfaces, users can use a pointer in the shape of a ray to point and select different buttons, as we can see in Fig. 3 (right).

Reconfigurable Environmental Conditions. Lastly, the training environments inside the VR module will be reconfigurable, providing a wide range of parameters that can control the ocean state, time of the day, the spill initial shape and size, available boom length, and weather conditions involving fog density, wind and rain (see Fig. 4).

3.2 Physics Simulation

Having training environments capable of simulating real-world physics with enough accuracy is a factor that has a significant impact on the users' immersion and how easily they can bring the developed skills to a real-life context. When using game engines, such aspects as force application, collisions, and gravity are usually pre-implemented, and although configuring them may require some time, it's generally more advantageous than implementing everything from scratch. Oceans and fluid simulations, however, represent a bigger challenge, since most of the time we have to come up with our own solutions.

Ocean Simulation. The water system implemented for the VR module follows the simulation approach described in [4]. In that approach, the water surface is represented by a geometric plane with multiple vertices that has its shape deformed by a vertex shader running on the GPU. Based on the current position of each vertex, the shader performs a series of mathematical operations responsible for moving or updating those vertices and thus producing the undulations on the water surface. To compute the movement, the vertex shader sums the outputs of multiple periodic waves, all of them describing ocean waves with distinct directions, shapes, sizes, and velocities.

Oil Spill Simulation. The simulation of oil spills involved using the Ray Marching [5] algorithm to render the oil particles that compose the fluid. Ray Marching is a class of rendering algorithms very similar to Ray Tracing, where each frame is obtained by tracing multiple rays that start from the camera and pass through each point of a grid representing the final image. If any of those rays intersects an object, the corresponding pixel is then assigned with the color of the intersected surface.

What differs Ray Marching from Ray Tracing is the way objects are represented in the scene and the way intersections are detected. Instead of using 3D meshes, Ray Marching defines their objects through Signed Distance Functions (SDF) [6]. The reason for representing objects through SDFs rather than using other conventional methods is because SDFs can be combined to form new objects with very complex geometries. Client-Server Architecture.

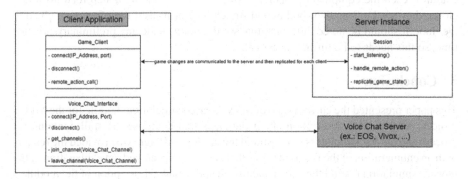

Fig. 5. VR Module's Architecture.

The VR module uses the tools and libraries readily available in Unreal Engine 5 [7] to set up a client-server model where each player uses a client application to connect and communicate with a server hosting one or multiple sessions of the VR game. During the VR experience, the server replicates information about the game state to each client, telling them where the objects, players and other entities should be in the scenario, how they should behave, and what values different variables should have. Each client then uses this information to simulate a very close approximation of what is happening on the server. So, despite the game being visually presented to the players through the client application, the server is the one who keeps the coordinated game state, which means that the simulation state is in fact being managed on the server. In addition to the existing server and client application there will also be a third-party component responsible for handling a voice communication channel between players (see Fig. 5).

4 Preliminary Evaluation

After we finished implementing the ocean physics and the necessary features to steer the boat, we carried out an informal testing session with a group of high school students who never experienced virtual reality. The goal of that testing session was to find potential problems in the implemented mechanisms and make a preliminary evaluation of the VR module's usability.

By observing the students' behavior while testing the module, we noticed that none of them seemed to have problems maneuvering the boat. In general, all of them quickly deduced what they would need to do to rotate the steering wheel or push/pull the throttle handles. To our surprise, the main source of problems was in fact the avatar's movement through the scenario. We noticed that some of the students had difficulties aiming at the spot they wanted to teleport to; sometimes, having to perform several attempts until they manage to get to the right place. This may have been due to the fact that the virtual space inside the boat is small, making it harder to use the teleport controls.

Besides the problems with the teleport mechanism, another issue related to the navigation was the fact that many students constantly forgot that they could move through the virtual scenario by simply moving in the real world. A lot of the times, when they couldn't reach the equipment properly, instead of simply taking a step forward to get closer, they tried to lean their bodies and stretch their arms as if their feet were glued to the floor. It should be noted, however, that we did not provide any preliminary practice time, so this needs to be further investigated.

5 Conclusion

This paper presented the current state of the VR-based simulation module for the MPCS project. After a brief description about the steps that compose the spill containment process and the VR simulators that inspired the module's design, we provided the readers with an enumeration of the functionalities that are being developed, an explanation of the physics simulation behind the ocean and the oil spills, and a description of the module's architecture.

With the preliminary evaluation of the module's usability, we concluded that the teleport mechanism used for the avatar's navigation was the main source of problems. In the future we may have to come up with different approaches for the teleport pointer or for the avatar's navigation in general.

References

1. Beaubien, J., Baker, D.: The use of simulation for training teamwork skills in health care: how low can you go? BMJ Qual. Saf. **13**, 51–56 (2004). https://doi.org/10.1136/qshc.2004.009845
2. Zdrazil, T.: How does an oil containment boom work? https://www.absorbentsonline.com/spill-containment-blog/how-does-an-oil-containment-boom-work/. Accessed 04 Oct 2022
3. SEAPRO: Booming operations. https://www.seapro.org/pdf_docs/Booming%20and%20Anchoring.pdf. Accessed 09 Oct 2022
4. Fernando, R.: GPU Gems: Programming Techniques, Tips, and Tricks for Realtime Graphics, vol. 590. Addison-Wesley (2004)
5. Jamie W.: Ray marching and signed distance functions. https://jamie-wong.com/2016/07/15/ray-marching-signed-distance-functions/. Accessed 06 Dec 2022
6. Wikipedia contributors: Signed distance function. https://en.wikipedia.org/wiki/Signed_distance_function. Accessed 06 Dec 2022
7. Unreal Engine Documentation: Networking Overview. https://docs.unrealengine.com/5.0/en-US/networking-overview-for-unreal-engine/. Accessed 22 Feb 2022

ECO-QUEST: An Educational Game Designed to Impart Knowledge About Ecological Practices and Selective Waste Management

Déborah Fernandes de Araujo[1]([envelope]), Thiago Porcino[2], Luciane Carvalho Jasmin de Deus[1], and Venício Siqueira Filho[1]

[1] University Center of Volta Redonda - UniFOA, Volta Redonda, Brazil
deefaraujo@gmail.com

[2] TecGraf Institute - Pontifical Catholic University of Rio de Janeiro - PUC-Rio, Rio de Janeiro, Brazil
https://www.puc-rio.br
https://www.unifoa.edu.br

Abstract. This study delves into the role of gamification in bolstering environmental education, particularly with regard to addressing the challenges associated with solid waste management. The research proposes the development of an educational game as a pedagogical tool for educators, with the objective of facilitating meaningful and impactful learning experiences within the school community. Through an interactive and playful approach, the game seeks to sensitize students to the intrinsic importance of selective waste collection and recycling, thereby fostering environmental awareness and promoting behavioral changes. The game's design adheres to the Game Design Document (GDD) methodology, while the project's requirements are defined employing the Startup Business Model Canvas methodology. In summary, the overarching aim of this research is to seamlessly integrate environmental education into schools by harnessing the potential of digital technology to foster sustainability in a manner that is both engaging and effective.

Keywords: Gamification · Environmental Education · Solid Waste Management · Educational Game · Sustainability

1 Introduction

Environmental destruction actions are tied to crucial consequences not only to the ecosystems but also to humans health and economic sectors, including tourism, and energy production [10]. On the other hand, serious games can not only significantly contribute to teaching but can also teach important lessons related to social life, including environmental education behaviors [2].

© IFIP International Federation for Information Processing 2023
Published by Springer Nature Switzerland AG 2023
P. Ciancarini et al. (Eds.): ICEC 2023, LNCS 14455, pp. 380–385, 2023.
https://doi.org/10.1007/978-981-99-8248-6_35

When individuals take on the persona of a digital avatar within an imaginary realm and engage in tasks like tidying up a bustling plaza, constructing a metropolis, or navigating intricate choices regarding city management or military strategy, they effortlessly assimilate the information presented to them within the game [4].

For this reason, this projects aims to propose a serious game that explores environmental education content with the entertainment provide by digital games. Moreover, we proposed a serious and educational game centered around selective waste collection. With the increasing emphasis on environmental awareness, this game focus on provide a playful, engaging, and educative experience about responsible environmental practices.

2   Motivation

The advent of the digital era has ushered in a novel paradigm for education and learning, wherein digital games have emerged as a potent instrument for facilitating learning experiences by offering an enticing amalgamation of enjoyment and instruction. The specific focus of this research endeavor lies in harnessing the potential of these games to augment awareness and comprehension of environmental issues, with particular emphasis on the significance of waste collection and recycling.

Within an increasingly sustainability-oriented society, effective waste management has acquired a pressing imperative. In this context, fostering awareness and imparting education pertaining to appropriate waste disposal and recycling practices assumes critical importance. However, engendering engagement and motivation, particularly among children, to actively learn and take tangible action regarding these issues poses a formidable challenge.

We believe that the insights garnered from this study will not only contribute to an enhanced understanding of the utility of educational games, but also facilitate the development of more efficacious and captivating educational games in the future.

3   Related Work

The field of serious games for environmental education has witnessed substantial growth in recent years, with numerous studies delving into various aspects within this domain [1,3,5,8,10]. In this section, we shall explore two relevant works that bear significance to our own game, ECO-QUEST, and elucidate how our work distinguishes itself.

The first work under consideration is titled "A Serious Game for Environmental Awareness of Students in the Amazon Region" [9]. This game was designed with the objective of instilling environmental consciousness among children attending schools situated in the islands of the Pará state, known for being inhabited by river dolphin species. The game aims to depict the boto as an indigenous creature of the Amazon biome, thereby debunking the negative mythological connotations associated with it and subsequently fostering the conservation of Amazon river dolphin species.

The second work [6] investigates the cultivation of essential professional skills for sustainability in university students through the use of serious games. The focal game revolves around empowering students to make informed decisions encompassing economic, social, and environmental considerations in order to effectively govern a defined territory.

Both aforementioned works share similarities with our proposition in the sense that they too are serious games targeted at promoting sustainability. They require players to navigate decision-making processes that harmonize economic, social, and environmental factors. Both games strive to educate players about sustainability and the imperative nature of making choices that benefit the environment. Moreover, in our work, we propose a straightforward and concise game that incorporates a narrative feature capable of engaging players.

In summary, the aim of this study is to utilize the developed game as a research tool to evaluate the effectiveness of educational games in promoting environmental education and instilling sustainable practices in children and adolescents. The primary objective is to assess the impact of the game on environmental knowledge acquisition, the development of ecological attitudes, and the initiation of responsible actions related to selective waste management.

4 Development

The development of the ECO-QUEST game followed the guidelines of the game development life cycle (GDLC) proposed by Ramadan et al. [7], encompassing the stages of Initiation (or Game Design), Pre-production, Production, Testing, and Release. The Unreal Engine was utilized as the development platform for the game.

During the Initiation phase, the principles of design thinking were employed (such as desk research and prototyping), and a preliminary survey was conducted to ascertain the needs and preferences of the target audience. This stage involved defining the educational objectives, formulating the game concept, and determining crucial components such as narrative, mechanics, and learning resources.

In the Game Design phase (see Fig. 1), the game was designed as an educational adventure game, incorporating exploration mechanics and environmental challenge-solving elements. Players assume the role of a character tasked with navigating a meticulously crafted virtual world and engaging with various environmental elements. Through dialogues with non-playable characters (NPCs) and the collection of information from scattered items within the game environment, players acquire knowledge about pertinent environmental issues, such as the significance of recycling and the conservation of natural resources.

The game's challenges are carefully designed to mirror real-life situations, drawing inspiration from successful residential recycling programs. In these programs, residents are encouraged to use separate bins for different recyclable

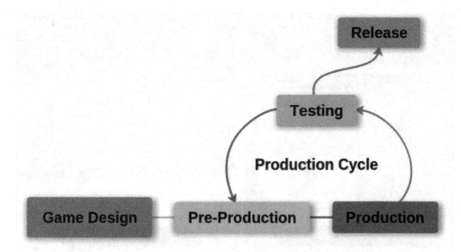

Fig. 1. Development Workflow of ECO-QUEST Game

materials like paper, plastic, glass, and metal. Similarly, in the game, players are presented with scenarios that require them to sort and manage waste efficiently, just like in a residential recycling setup. By putting players in charge of decision-making and devising solutions to environmental problems, the game fosters critical reflection and cultivates problem-solving skills. The complete workflow of the development process is illustrated in Fig. 1.

5   Gameplay

The gameplay structure is organized into discrete matches, comprising three successive waves, each having a fixed duration of 60 s. With each advancing wave, the game's intensity escalates, accompanied by an augmented volume of waste items to be collected. Consequently, players are required to demonstrate adept navigation skills as they diligently explore the game environment, purposefully seeking out items for collection while adroitly evading obstacles that impede their progress. A central aspect of the gameplay experience entails the acquisition of various waste types, such as paper, plastic, metal, glass, and organic matter, each necessitating appropriate disposal within the corresponding designated collection bin. The successful adherence to this waste categorization scheme directly influences the player's overall score, serving as a quantifiable metric of their performance and competency within the game's context.

Furthermore, ECO-QUEST offers the option of gameplay in either a single-player mode or a multiplayer mode (as depicted in Fig. 2). In both modes, the central goal is to engage in a competition against a countdown timer while diligently collecting and properly disposing of a wide variety of items.

Additionally, the game contains a reward and progression system to further enhance player engagement. As players diligently collect waste and successfully

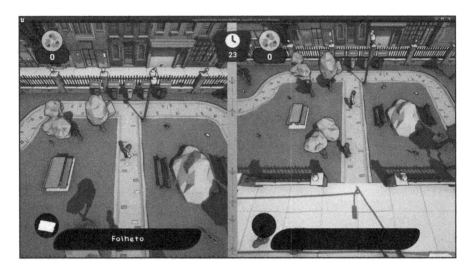

Fig. 2. Multiplayer gameplay.

overcome challenges, they are duly rewarded with points, thereby fostering a sense of accomplishment and advancement.

6   Conclusion

In this study, we introduce an educational game designed to impart knowledge about ecological practices and selective waste management. The game's distinctive feature lies in its implementation of item collection mechanics, which are carefully crafted to provide an enjoyable and challenging experience for players while concurrently serving as pedagogical tools to educate them about the intrinsic significance of selective waste collection. Additionally, the developed game offers a multiplayer mode, allowing real-time competition among players.

In conclusion, we firmly believe that ECO-QUEST holds the potential to inspire other designers and developers within the gaming industry to create similarly immersive and educational games. Such initiatives have the capacity to make substantial contributions to environmental education and elevate awareness regarding the critical importance of waste management practices.

References

1. Aguiar Castillo, L., Rufo Torres, J., De Saa Pérez, P., Pérez Jiménez, R.: How to encourage recycling behaviour? The case of WasteApp: a gamified mobile application. Sustainability (Switzerland) **10**, 1544 (2018)
2. Breuer, J., Bente, G.: Why so serious? On the relation of serious games and learning. J. Comput. Game Cult. **4**, 7–24 (2010)

3. Garcia, M.B.: Trash attack: a 2D action puzzle video game to promote environmental awareness and waste segregation behavior. Int. J. Simul. Syst. Sci. Technol. **20** (2019)
4. Gee, J.P.: Video games, learning, and "content". In: Games: Purpose and Potential in Education, pp. 43–53 (2009)
5. Nunes, E.P., Luz, A.R., Lemos, E.M., Maciel, C., dos Anjos, A.M., Borges, L.C., Nunes, C.: Mobile serious game proposal for environmental awareness of children. In: 2016 IEEE Frontiers in Education Conference (FIE). pp. 1–8. IEEE (2016)
6. Peãa Miguel, N., Lage, J.C., Galindez, A.M.: Assessment of the development of professional skills in university students: sustainability and serious games. Sustainability **12**(3), 1014 (2020)
7. Ramadan, R., Widyani, Y.: Game development life cycle guidelines. In: 2013 International Conference on Advanced Computer Science and Information Systems (ICACSIS), pp. 95–100. IEEE (2013)
8. Satria, E., Fitriani, L., Muhsin, Y., Tresnawati, D.: Development of educational games for learning waste management. IOP Conf. Ser. Mater. Sci. Eng. **1098**, 032064 (2021). IOP Publishing
9. Sobrinho, F.A., et al.: Jogo do boto: Serious game para sensibilização ambiental de estudantes da região amazônica. In: Anais do XXIII SBGames, pp. 415–424. Sociedade Brasileira de Computação (2015)
10. Varela-Candamio, L., Novo-Corti, I., García-Álvarez, M.T.: The importance of environmental education in the determinants of green behavior: a meta-analysis approach. J. Clean. Prod. **170**, 1565–1578 (2018)

Workshops

Towards Sustainable Serious Games

Barbara Göbl[1]([✉]) [iD], Jannicke Baalsrud Hauge[2,3] [iD], Ioana A. Stefan[4],
and Heinrich Söbke[5,6] [iD]

[1] Centre for Teacher Education, University of Vienna, 1090 Vienna, Austria
barbara.goebl@univie.ac.at
[2] BIBA – Bremer Institut für Produktion und Logistik GmbH, 28359 Bremen, Germany
baa@biba.uni-bremen.de
[3] KTH-Royal Institute of Technology, 15181 Södertälje, Sweden
jmbh@kth.se
[4] ATS, Targoviste, Romania
ioana.stefan@ats.com.ro
[5] Hochschule Weserbergland, 31875 Hameln, Germany
soebke@hsw-hameln.de
[6] Bauhaus-Institute for Infrastructure Solutions (b.is), Bauhaus-Universität Weimar, 99423
Weimar, Germany
heinrich.soebke@uni-weimar.de

Abstract. This paper introduces the concept of sustainable serious games and
discusses selected issues regarding sustainability with respect to the serious game
life cycle. We take a closer look at game aging and maintenance, particularly in
the context of educational serious games. We outline what aspects play into game
aging and argue for the need to consider these aspects earlier in the design process.
In line with the goal to outline sustainable practices in the field of serious games,
we further look into the reuse of artefacts, as well as repurposing of serious games
as means to create long-term value.

Keywords: Game Aging · Game Maintenance · Serious Games · Game
Repurposing · Game Component Reuse

1 Introduction

Serious games and their associated potentials and challenges are a widely debated topic
in academia. The term serious games (SG) summarizes games that look beyond a mere
entertainment purpose and introduce additional "characterizing goals" [1]. These characterizing goals may take up various forms, such as incorporating exercise [2], advertising certain products or services [3], or supporting educational or learning goals [4, 5].
This work focuses on the latter and discusses selected issues in the context of creating
sustainable SGs for education.

Numerous works underline the potentials of educational SGs, ranging from their
positive impact on learning outcomes and motivation [6–8], to providing safe and efficient means for training [9], and facilitating self-determined learning and exploration
[10]. Nevertheless, the literature also highlights a number of challenges. Generally, the

Published by Springer Nature Switzerland AG 2023
P. Ciancarini et al. (Eds.): ICEC 2023, LNCS 14455, pp. 389–396, 2023.
https://doi.org/10.1007/978-981-99-8248-6_36

intricacies of game design – and for SGs in particular, the need to integrate domain and game design expertise – and technically complex implementation processes lead to resource- and time-intensive development processes [11, 12]. Thus, efficient and sustainable design approaches are crucial. Existing works introduce several tools, methods, and frameworks to support and streamline the various stages in SG development. These works provide recommendations, formalizations and/or guidelines for several stages in the serious game development process, from design [13, 14], operation, i.e., the didactic scenarios [15–17], to corresponding evaluation [18, 19]. Notably, so far post-production has received little attention [29], specifically the topics of SG maintenance and game aging [30]. Further, while SGs have been studied as an effective educational tool for learning about sustainability [20–22], to our knowledge, there is little research that explicitly addresses sustainability of SGs.

Sustainability is a fundamental concept for the development of a global society in alignment with the natural boundaries of the planet [23, 24]. The United Nations capture a comprehensive understanding of sustainability in their 17 main (and 169 sub-) Sustainable Development Goals (SDGs) [25]. Notably, operationalizing sustainability, or the SDGs, remains a major challenge [26]. A prevailing, general definition of sustainability builds on three pillars comprising economic, social, and environmental (or ecological) factors or 'goals' [27]. Table 1 outlines potentially relevant factors in the context of SGs and maps them to these three pillars. Further, both product- (the game) and process-related aspects (the life cycle) [28] can be differentiated. Accordingly, we perceive the SG life cycle model and its stages (ideation, design, implementation, evaluation, operation, and maintenance [30]) as a normative model for the evaluation of SGs regarding their sustainability.

Previous work highlights that many SG projects are research-oriented prototypes, or proof-of-concepts, that are developed, evaluated with users, and analyzed by researchers within limited time frames (e.g., due to limited project funding) [31]. We acknowledge that in these contexts, maintenance and longevity may not always be a priority issue. However, fostering sustainable SG development may help to alleviate the short lifetime of educational SGs and provide a strong argument to foster further research and development in this field.

2 Sustainable Serious Games

As outlined above, numerous works focus on the earlier stages and there is still little research on SG maintenance and their potential further evolution beyond their initial implementation and their intended application setting. SG development is often a dynamic and iterative process, rather than a linear one. The interdependence between these stages underlines the need for early consideration of maintenance and further evolution of a SG and its components. To further the goal of sustainable serious games, we outline the issue of serious game aging below, and discuss the reuse of educational SGs and their components. Additionally, we discuss SG repurposing as a potential means towards sustainable SG design.

Table 1. Factors Potentially Impacting Sustainability of SGs

Pillar	Potential Factors
Economic	Efficient development of SGs may be achieved, for example, by a long life cycle (cf. Sect. 2.1 Serious Game Aging) as well as by reduced development efforts (cf. Sect. 2.2 Reuse and Repurposing)
Social	Social factors of SGs concern, among other things, the acceptance and engagement by players as well as the achievement of the intended effects, e.g., learning outcomes
Environmental	The environmental factors of SGs include, for example, the energy required for providing a SG on a website, or the energy consumption of playing a SG. Further resources, such as the need for sophisticated hardware, e.g., graphics cards, might reduce the environmental sustainability of SGs

2.1 Serious Game Aging

Generally, the concept of software aging refers to both internal and external factors. Internal factors refer to increasing difficulties to maintain software, while external factors refer to the users' perspective and how software's usability decreases with time [32]. Similarly, game aging refers to the continuously decreasing capacity of the game software to meet external requirements on the software [31]. Games are certainly also subject to internal factors of aging, but external factors may even prove more important in the case of SGs [31]. For example, SGs need to factor in players' aesthetic demands, advances in domain knowledge, and the impact of changing didactic and play settings [15, 31].

Accordingly, serious game aging maybe categorized into different aspects regarding Technology, Domain Knowledge and User Experience [31]. In addition, educational games and their application are strongly impacted by the play environment and involved actors (e.g. with regard to socio-cultural aspects, changing didactic or curricular demands, or availability of trained teachers and game facilitators [15, 33, 34]). These factors are summarized in Table 1. As mentioned, the game as such may reach its end-of-life stage due to the different categories of game aging (Table 2) quite fast, but many components might not be that time-critical. The next section therefore discusses how re-use and repurposing can contribute to extending the lifetime of the individual artefacts.

2.2 Reuse and Repurposing

Additional measures may be taken to facilitate the design process and reduce resource costs, such as the reuse or repurposing of games, their building blocks, and related artefacts. Repurposing may refer to a number of practices and "includes updating, changing, enriching serious games to reflect new functionalities, amending to different pedagogies, technologies, representations, cultures, contexts and learners." [35, p. 37]. Generally, repurposing refers to applying an SG in a new context [35], while reuse may refer to the repeated use of SGs, specific game components, or artefacts from the development or evaluation process [35, 36].

Table 2. Categories of Serious Game Aging (in extension of [31])

Category	Example
Technology	hardware and software necessary to run a game evolves, for example new game consoles enter the market or the operating system evolves further
Domain Knowledge	learning objectives or knowledge evolve so that they are no longer covered by the game
User Experience	user interfaces and user habits evolve so that the game appears outdated and thus the motivation to play decreases
Play Environments	Educational settings, competencies of facilitators, teachers and players, or didactic principles change so that previous application scenarios or instructions are no longer suitable

Software reuse and the design for reusability may improve productivity, quality and optimize the development schedule [37] – advantages that SG developers or practitioners may build on as well. In line with this notion, previous works identify reuse and repurposing of game-based and gamified learning concepts and artefacts as a promising means for resource-efficient development [38, 39], but also find that these approaches are hardly practiced in the research community so far [37].

It is worth noting that reuse and repurposing of SGs comes with additional hurdles. SGs and their building blocks and associated artefacts need to be scrutinized properly before reuse or adaptation for different contexts, as these games are often tailored to specific learning goals, target groups and/or application scenarios [15]. However, there are several items that may lend themselves well to these practices: ranging from specific in-game assets such as graphics or audio to project plans, architecture design, tools for evaluation, or test cases [39].

Similar to the above outlined categories of game aging and what external factors impact the applicability of the game, the approach in repurposing and reuse are impacted by external demands on the SG, posed by technological, knowledge- or user specific, as well as environment-related aspects and accompanying demands. Reuse and repurposing are both facilitated by deeper understanding of underlying pedagogical, technical, and game design aspects and the context and user group they are applied in.

3   Discussion

The complex nature of SGs and their costly development process calls for further research on how to facilitate and foster sustainable SG design practices. SGs' impact and longevity is deeply dependent on situational, individual or even technical factors [31, 35]. The above outlined concept of serious game aging summarizes some of these challenges, while reuse and repurposing are outlined as means to foster efficient, sustainable SG design and development.

Sustainable SG design may certainly benefit from formalized design practices, adherence to technical and educational standards, or standardized documentation. Several efforts have been made so far to facilitate development, such as SG design and analysis frameworks [13, 40], the use of game engines and asset stores, or metadata formats [41]. However, the large growth of the SG community in recent years has led to fragmentation, which in turn has created additional hurdles for reuse and harmonizing development efforts [37].

Notably, while game aging seems like an issue that is situated towards the later stages of the SG lifecycle [30], SG developers, researchers and designers need to pave the way early on to address related technical, usability, learning or socio-cultural aspects. Additionally, as often argued in SG development [1], several perspectives need to be considered regarding SGs' complexities and input from additional stakeholders such as learners, trainers, or teachers, needs to be heeded. Thus, this work emphasizes the need for and value of establishing sustainable practices for SG development and provides a theoretical foundation to facilitate these efforts.

4 Conclusion

The paper contextualizes sustainability of serious games (SGs). We outline various concepts and factors, such as SG aging and reuse and their components, as well as repurposing, that impact sustainability of SGs. We argue that the focus on the early life cycle stages of serious game design may undermine sustainability efforts in SG development. Further, we argue that the SG development and research community needs to explore new ways to create sustainable, interdisciplinary practices along the stages of the SG life cycle.

Acknowledgements. This work has been partly funded by INCLUDEME (No. 621547-EPP-1-2020-1-RO-EPPA3-IPI-SOC-IN) co-funded by the European Commission through the Erasmus+ program and the work also acknowledges the projects DigiLab4U (Nos. 16DHB2112/3), AuCity 2 and AuCity 3 (Nos. 16DHB2131 and 16DHB2204) by German Federal Ministry of Education and Research (BMBF). The presented work represents the authors' view.

References

1. Dörner, R., Göbel, S., Effelsberg, W., Wiemeyer, J.: Introduction. In: Dörner, R., Göbel, S., Effelsberg, W., Wiemeyer, J. (eds.) Serious Games, pp. 1–34. Springer, Cham (2016). https://doi.org/10.1007/978-3-319-40612-1_1
2. Göbel, S., Hardy, S., Wendel, V., Mehm, F., Steinmetz, R.: Serious games for health: personalized exergames. In: Proceedings of the 18th ACM International Conference on Multimedia, pp. 1663–1666. ACM, Firenze, Italy, October 2010. https://doi.org/10.1145/1873951.1874316
3. Cauberghe, V., De Pelsmacker, P.: Advergames. J. Advert. **39**(1), 5–18 (2010). https://doi.org/10.2753/JOA0091-3367390101
4. Kayali, F., et al.: A case study of a learning game about the internet. In: Göbel, S., Wiemeyer, J. (eds.) Games for Training, Education, Health and Sports. LNCS, vol. 8395, pp. 47–58. Springer, Cham (2014). https://doi.org/10.1007/978-3-319-05972-3_6

5. Baalsrud Hauge, J., Bellotti, F., Nadolski, R., Berta, R., Carvalho, M.B.: Deploying serious games for management in higher education: lessons learned and good practices. EAI Endorsed Trans. Game-Based Learn. 1(3), e4 (2014). https://doi.org/10.4108/sg.1.3.e4

6. de Freitas, S.: Are games effective learning tools? A review of educational games. J. Educ. Technol. Soc. 21(2), 74–84 (2018)

7. Westera, W.: Why and how serious games can become far more effective: accommodating productive learning experiences, learner motivation and the monitoring of learning gains. J. Educ. Technol. Soc. 22(1), 59–69 (2019)

8. Connolly, T.M., Boyle, E.A., MacArthur, E., Hainey, T., Boyle, J.M.: A systematic literature review of empirical evidence on computer games and serious games. Comput. Educ. 59(2), 661–686 (2012). https://doi.org/10.1016/j.compedu.2012.03.004

9. Kazar, G., Comu, S.: Effectiveness of serious games for safety training: a mixed method study. J. Constr. Eng. Manag. 147(8), 04021091 (2021). https://doi.org/10.1061/(ASCE)CO.1943-7862.0002119

10. Clark, D.B., Tanner-Smith, E.E., Killingsworth, S.S.: Digital games, design, and learning: a systematic review and meta-analysis. Rev. Educ. Res. 86(1), 79–122 (2016). https://doi.org/10.3102/0034654315582065

11. Carmosino, I., Bellotti, F., Berta, R., De Gloria, A., Secco, N.: A game engine plug-in for efficient development of investigation mechanics in serious games. Entertain. Comput. 19, 1–11 (2017). https://doi.org/10.1016/j.entcom.2016.11.002

12. Baalsrud Hauge, J., et al.: Business models for Serious Games developers - transition from a product centric to a service centric approach. Int. J. Serious Games 1(1), (2014). https://doi.org/10.17083/ijsg.v1i1.10

13. Carvalho, M.B., et al.: An activity theory-based model for serious games analysis and conceptual design. Comput. Educ. 87, 166–181 (2015). https://doi.org/10.1016/j.compedu.2015.03.023

14. Arnab, S., et al.: Mapping learning and game mechanics for serious games analysis. Br. J. Educ. Technol. 46(2), 391–411 (2015). https://doi.org/10.1111/bjet.12113

15. Göbl, B., Hristova, D., Jovicic, S., Hlavacs, H.: Serious game design for and with adolescents: empirically based implications for purposeful games. In: Fang, X. (ed.) HCI in Games. LNCS, vol. 12211, pp. 398–410. Springer, Cham (2020). https://doi.org/10.1007/978-3-030-50164-8_29

16. Tang, S., Hanneghan, M., El-Rhalibi, A.: Pedagogy elements, components and structures for serious games authoring environment. Presented at the 5ht International Game Design and Technology Workshop, Liverpool, UK, 2007, pp. 25–34 (2007)

17. Slootmaker, A.: EMERGO: A Generic Platform for Authoring and Playing Scenario-Based Serious Games. Open Universiteit, Heerlen (2018)

18. Calderón, A., Ruiz, M.: A systematic literature review on serious games evaluation: an application to software project management. Comput. Educ. 87, 396–422 (2015). https://doi.org/10.1016/j.compedu.2015.07.011

19. Fu, F.-L., Su, R.-C., Yu, S.-C.: EGameFlow: a scale to measure learners' enjoyment of e-learning games. Comput. Educ. 52(1), 101–112 (2009). https://doi.org/10.1016/j.compedu.2008.07.004

20. Gheorghe, A.F., Stefan, I.A., Stefan, A., Baalsrud Hauge, J., Soebke, H.: Serious games for modelling sustainability skills and competencies. In: 15th International Conference on Virtual Learning (ICVL31), University of Bucharest, Faculty of Mathematics and Computer Science, 31 October 2020, pp. 424–431. Bucharest University Press, Romania (2020)

21. Speelman, E.N., Rodela, R., Doddema, M., Ligtenberg, A.: Serious gaming as a tool to facilitate inclusive business; a review of untapped potential. Curr. Opin. Environ. Sustain. 41, 31–37 (2019). https://doi.org/10.1016/j.cosust.2019.09.010

22. Bjørner, T.: How can a serious game be designed to provide engagement with and awareness of the plastic crisis as part of UN's SDGs. In: GoodIT 2021 - Proceedings 2021 Conference on Information Technology for Social Good, pp. 157–162 (2021). https://doi.org/10.1145/3462203.3475887

23. Meadows, D.H., Meadows, D.L., Randers, J., Behrens, W.W.: The limits to growth. In: Conca, K., Dabelko, G.D. (eds.) Green Planet Blues, 5th Editio, pp. 25–29. Routledge (2018)

24. Rockström, J., Steffen, W., Noone, K.: Planetary boundaries: exploring the safe operating space for humanity. Ecol. Soc. 14(2) (2009)

25. United Nations: The 17 Goals | Sustainable Development. Sustainable Development (2015). https://sdgs.un.org/goals. Accessed 14 Dec 2022

26. Sachs, J.D., Schmidt-Traub, G., Mazzucato, M., Messner, D., Nakicenovic, N., Rockström, J.: Six transformations to achieve the sustainable development goals. Nat. Sustain. 2(9), 805–814 (2019). https://doi.org/10.1038/s41893-019-0352-9

27. Purvis, B., Mao, Y., Robinson, D.: Three pillars of sustainability: in search of conceptual origins. Sustain. Sci. 14(3), 681–695 (2019). https://doi.org/10.1007/s11625-018-0627-5

28. Chiu, M.C., Chu, C.H.: Review of sustainable product design from life cycle perspectives. Int. J. Precis. Eng. Manuf. 13(7), 1259–1272 (2012). https://doi.org/10.1007/s12541-012-0169-1

29. Aleem, S., Capretz, L.F., Ahmed, F.: Game development software engineering process life cycle: a systematic review. J. Softw. Eng. Res. Dev. 4(1), 6 (2016). https://doi.org/10.1186/s40411-016-0032-7

30. Baalsrud Hauge, J., Söbke, H., Duin, H., Stefan, I.A., Göbl, B.: Current opportunities and challenges of digital game-based learning. In: Göbl, B., van der Spek, E., Baalsrud Hauge, J., McCall, R. (eds.) Entertainment Computing – ICEC 2022. LNCS, vol. 13477, pp. 443–450. Springer, Cham (2022). https://doi.org/10.1007/978-3-031-20212-4_38

31. Söbke, H., Harder, R., Planck-Wiedenbeck, U.: Two decades of traffic system education using the simulation game MOBILITY. In: Göbel, S., et al. (eds.) Serious Games, pp. 43–53. Springer, Cham (2018). https://doi.org/10.1007/978-3-030-02762-9_6

32. Parnas, D.L.: Software aging. In: ICSE 1994: Proceedings of the 16th International Conference on Software Engineering, pp. 279–287. IEEE (1994)

33. Fernández-Manjón, B., Moreno-Ger, P., Martinez-Ortiz, I., Freire, M.: Challenges of serious games. EAI Endorsed Trans. Game-Based Learn. 2(6), 150611 (2015). https://doi.org/10.4108/eai.5-11-2015.150611

34. Baalsrud Hauge, J., et al.: Current competencies of game facilitators and their potential optimization in higher education: multimethod study. JMIR Ser. Games 9(2), e25481 (2021). https://doi.org/10.2196/25481

35. Protopsaltis, A., et al.: Scenario-based serious games repurposing. In: Proceedings of the 29th ACM International Conference on Design of Communication, pp. 37–44. ACM, Pisa, Italy, October 2011. https://doi.org/10.1145/2038476.2038484

36. Meyer, M., Hildebrandt, T., Rensing, C., Steinmetz, R.: Requirements and an Architecture for a Multimedia Content Re-purposing Framework. In: Nejdl, W., Tochtermann, K. (eds.) Innovative Approaches for Learning and Knowledge Sharing. LNCS, vol. 4227, pp. 500–505. Springer, Heidelberg (2006). https://doi.org/10.1007/11876663_43

37. Stefan, I.A., Warmelink, H.J.G., Arnab, S., Dagnino, F., Lo, J., Mooney, J.: Accessibility, reusability and interoperability in the European serious game community. Presented at the eLSE 2013, Bucharest, RO, pp. 55–60, April 2013. https://doi.org/10.12753/2066-026X-13-116

38. Baalsrud Hauge, J., Stefan, I.: Improving learning outcome by re-using and modifying gamified lessons paths. In: Ma, M., Fletcher, B., Göbel, S., Baalsrud Hauge, J., Marsh, T. (eds.) Serious Games. LNCS, vol. 12434, pp. 150–163. Springer, Cham (2020). https://doi.org/10.1007/978-3-030-61814-8_12

39. Stefan, I.A., Lim, T., Baalsrud Hauge, J., Wendrich, R., Gabriela, N., Bellotti, F.: Strategies and tools to enable reuse in serious games ecosystems and beyond. Presented at the The 10th International Scientific Conference eLearning and Software for Education, Bucharest (2014)

40. Amory, A.: Game object model version II: a theoretical framework for educational game development. Educ. Technol. Res. Dev. **55**(1), 51–77 (2007). https://doi.org/10.1007/s11423-006-9001-x

41. DIN SPEC 91380:2018-06, Serious Games Metadata Format, Beuth Verlag GmbH. https://doi.org/10.31030/2853739

Challenges for XR Experiences
in Industry 4.0: A Preliminary Study

Thiago Malheiros Porcino[1]([✉]) and Esteban Clua[2]

[1] Pontifical Catholic University of Rio de Janeiro - PUC-Rio, Rio de Janeiro, Brazil
tmalheiros@tecgraf.puc-rio.br
[2] Federal Fluminense University - UFF, Niteroi, Brazil
esteban@ic.uff.br
http://www.puc-rio.br, http://www.ic.uff.br

Abstract. This research paper presents an initial investigation into the multifaceted challenges pertaining to Extended Reality (XR) experiences within the context of Industry 4.0. With the progressive evolution of immersive technologies, their integration into various Industry 4.0 applications exhibits promising prospects for augmenting productivity and fostering innovation across diverse sectors, including but not limited to healthcare, military, and entertainment. Nevertheless, the complete realization of XR's transformative potential within the industrial realm is beset by a range of obstacles that hinder its seamless adoption and effective implementation. Additionally, this study undertakes the identification and comprehensive analysis of the primary challenges encountered in the context of Industry 4.0. Its findings serve as a foundational resource for researchers and professionals within the industry, facilitating deeper insights and avenues for further investigation.

Keywords: virtual reality · extended reality · training · industry 4.0 · immersive environments

1 Introduction

XR (Extended Reality), including VR (Virtual Reality), and AR (Augmented Reality) technologies offers a versatile platform to create, integrate, and refine various simulated environments within a computer-based framework. As a visualization tool within the context of Industry 4.0, XR presents promising prospects for revolutionizing simulation and training and processes in different areas such as. However, to fulfill its potential as a visualization component in Industry 4.0, VR must address specific challenges and adhere to stringent requirements.

For achieve immersive experiences in XR, AR, or VR, its common the use of Head-worn displays (HWDs). HWDs constitute a class of technological devices designed to facilitate immersive experiences within the realm of mixed reality or virtual reality. Comprising electronic displays and lenses affixed over the user's head and directed towards the eyes, HWDs have found extensive utility across

© IFIP International Federation for Information Processing 2023
Published by Springer Nature Switzerland AG 2023
P. Ciancarini et al. (Eds.): ICEC 2023, LNCS 14455, pp. 397–402, 2023.
https://doi.org/10.1007/978-981-99-8248-6_37

diverse domains. Examples of these domains include military applications [13], educational settings [1], therapeutic interventions [3], as well as medical practices [2, 8].

Moreover, applications employing Head-Worn Devices (HWDs) possess the capacity to offer novel avenues for investigating, monitoring, and making data-driven decisions. Specifically, the integration of Spatial Context, Interactive Data Exploration, and Collaborative Decision-making within a simulated Extended Reality (XR) environment can significantly augment Industry 4.0 applications. This paper proposes a discussion among different approaches involving immersive technologies such as augmented, extended, mixed and virtual reality systems and their challenges.

2   Related Work

In Oil&Gas field, Porcino et al. [12] developed a 3D visualization system intended to enhance the monitoring and analysis process in drilling operations. This system incorporates two distinct usability forms: non-virtual reality (non-VR) and virtual reality (VR) interfaces. Data from diverse sources is integrated into a unified cloud-based database, which serves as the primary data source for our application. This data is then utilized to generate a comprehensive 3D visualization of the drilling well and the Bottom Hole Assembly (BHA), illustrated in Fig. 1.

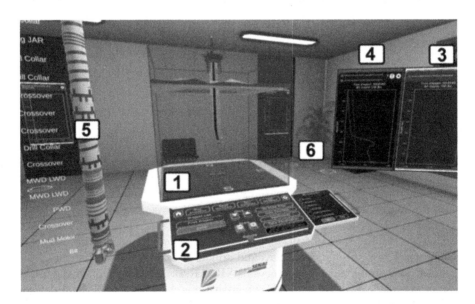

Fig. 1. The figure illustrates a comprehensive Virtual Reality (VR) Environment specifically designed for the Oil & Gas industry, featuring various integral components [12].

Additionally, the system enables the plotting of historical and real-time variable data, which can be effectively monitored and associated with custom alarms. Moreover, the application facilitates the visualization of diagnostics information generated by artificial intelligence (AI). To implement the application, they employed the Unity 3D development platform, leveraging SteamVR compatibility to ensure seamless integration with various head-mounted display (HMD) devices such as HTC Vive and Oculus Rift when operating in VR mode. While these VR systems offer highly immersive experiences, it is worth noting that some users have reported discomfort symptoms, including nausea, sickness, headaches, and other related issues. According with authors they addressed some of these issues implementing some strategies to avoid cybersickness, such as teleportation and mesh optimization, to maintain a stable frame rate during the interactions.

Besides, focused on Military domain and XR context, researchers [11], presented an architecture that effectively integrates XR head-worn display with a physical tabletop display to facilitate decision-making processes in naval organizations, specifically focusing on monitoring vessels' roles. The architecture allows for seamless collaboration among multiple users, supporting the use of both immersive devices (e.g., HoloLens) and non-immersive devices such as tablets or smartphones. The authors adeptly integrated pre-existing data and visualization methodologies, including a visual query language complemented by touch-based and Augmented Reality (AR) gestures. The resulting prototype is visually depicted in Fig. 2, encapsulating their innovative efforts.

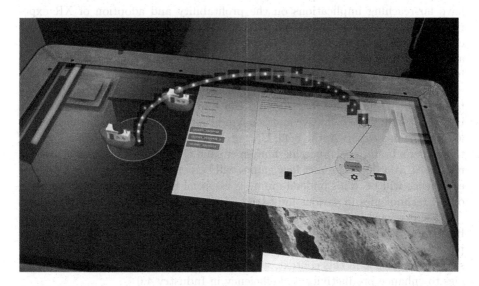

Fig. 2. The prototype, as developed by [11] in accordance with their proposed architecture, embodies an integration between HoloLens and a tabletop display, thereby establishing a collaborative Extended Reality experience among users dedicated to the analysis of maritime routes.

In a recent work by [10] authors presented a framework tailored for the XR environment, aiming to enhance autonomous navigation and obstacle detection capabilities in marine sailing vessels. The proposed framework establishes a robust foundation for effectively perceiving marine objects essential for vessel navigation and obstacle avoidance, leveraging image processing as the primary method. A diverse range of methodologies is explored to extract pertinent features, including waterline, terrain, and other vessels, enabling the system to gain comprehensive situational awareness.

3   Main Challenges

Althrough, XR can create a new way of training in different fields of industry 4.0. There are some challenges that need to be addressed for a real consolidation of this plataform in order to have robust solutions in each field. In Clua et al. [4] work, they highlighted some of these challenges, such as Cybersickness (CS), user experience and design guidelines.

Regarding to CS, its demands particular attention due to its widespread adoption and its frequent association with prolonged exposure to Head-Mounted Displays (HMDs). Notably, more than 60% of usability issues with HMDs are significantly linked to discomfort [7]. The adverse effects of CS are among the most persistent symptoms, encompassing general discomfort, headaches, stomach awareness, nausea, vomiting, sweating, fatigue, drowsiness, disorientation, and apathy [5]. These symptoms significantly influence the user experience and have far-reaching implications on the profitability and adoption of XR experiences for industry 4.0. Designing intuitive and natural user interfaces that enable seamless interaction with XR environments remains a challenge. HCI aspects, such as reducing motion sickness and optimizing user comfort, need to be addressed.

In the context of Industry 4.0 and the development of Extended Reality (XR) technologies, a prominent focus lies on User Experience (UX) and its critical role in understanding the cognitive and behavioral aspects of users. As highlighted by [6], a renowned expert in the field, UX entails a comprehensive understanding of the gamer's brain, encompassing human capabilities, limitations, and emotional responses, in order to predict how games will be perceived and how engaging the experience will be. This understanding is essential for the successful integration of XR technologies in various industrial applications.

In this regard, we firmly believe that leveraging insights from cognitive and behavioral psychology can provide tangible and practical guidelines for anticipating and resolving design challenges in the XR domain. By acknowledging the significance of UX in this context, we can harness the potential of XR technologies to enhance productivity and efficiency in Industry 4.0.

To achieve this goal, it is imperative to explore and employ various Human-Computer Interaction (HCI) techniques. Techniques such as user interviews, surveys, usability heuristics, and the analysis of physiological signals play a crucial role in gaining deeper insights into user behavior and preferences when interacting with XR environments. Moreover, the application of methods like Wizard of

Oz [9] can facilitate the evaluation and validation of the entire UX in XR, thereby ensuring a seamless integration of these technologies into industrial workflows.

By embracing a multidisciplinary approach that combines insights from cognitive and behavioral psychology with HCI methodologies, we can effectively address design challenges and optimize the user experience in XR applications for Industry 4.0. This interdisciplinary effort is vital for unlocking the full potential of XR technologies and ensuring their successful adoption in various industrial settings.

Another challenge is that XR applications require advanced hardware and software components, such as high-resolution displays, sensors, tracking systems, and powerful computing capabilities. Integrating these technologies seamlessly and efficiently can be challenging. Additionally, the initial investment in XR hardware and software can be substantial. For widespread adoption in Industry 4.0, cost-effective solutions must be developed.

4   Conclusion and Next Steps

In this study, we have elucidated several challenges associated with the widespread adoption of XR (Extended Reality) experiences within the context of Industry 4.0. By addressing these issues, developers have the opportunity to create a more potent XR environment that aligns seamlessly with the specific objectives of industries, such as training, monitoring, or simulation.

Furthermore, it is important to acknowledge that this research has potential areas for improvement, prompting us to embark on a forthcoming systematic review. This review will delve deeper into the challenges and novel approaches pertaining to the convergence of Industry 4.0 and XR technologies. This endeavor aims to contribute to the advancement of knowledge and understanding in this domain.

Nonetheless, this preliminary work can serve as a valuable starting point for XR developers seeking to implement immersive training environments across diverse sectors within Industry 4.0.

References

1. Ahir, K., Govani, K., Gajera, R., Shah, M.: Application on virtual reality for enhanced education learning, military training and sports. Augmented Human Research 5(1), 7 (2020)
2. Ali, S.M., Aich, S., Athar, A., Kim, H.C.: Medical education, training and treatment using xr in healthcare. In: 2023 25th International Conference on Advanced Communication Technology (ICACT). pp. 388–393. IEEE (2023)
3. Carrión, M., Santorum, M., Benavides, J., Aguilar, J., Ortiz, Y.: Developing a virtual reality serious game to recreational therapy using iplus methodology. In: 2019 International Conference on Virtual Reality and Visualization (ICVRV). pp. 133–137. IEEE (2019)

4. Clua, E.W.G., et al.: Challenges for XR in games. In: dos Santos, R.P., Hounsell, M.d.S. (eds.) Grand Research Challenges in Games and Entertainment Computing in Brazil - GranDGamesBR 2020–2030: First Forum, GranDGamesBR 2020, Recife, 7–10 November 2020, and Second Forum, GranDGamesBR 2021, Gramado, 18–21 October 2021, Revised Selected Papers, pp. 159–186. Springer, Cham (2023). https://doi.org/10.1007/978-3-031-27639-2_8

5. Dennison, M.S., D'Zmura, M.: Cybersickness without the wobble: experimental results speak against postural instability theory. Appl. Ergon. **58**, 215–223 (2017)

6. Hodent, C.: The Gamer's Brain: How Neuroscience and UX Can Impact Video Game Design. CRC Press (2017). https://books.google.com.br/books?id=JzyhDwAAQBAJ

7. Kolasinski, E.M.: Simulator sickness in virtual environments. Tech. rep, DTIC Document (1995)

8. Kühnapfel, U., Cakmak, H.K., Maaß, H.: Endoscopic surgery training using virtual reality and deformable tissue simulation. Comput. Graph. **24**(5), 671–682 (2000)

9. de Oliveira, E., et al.: FPVRGame: deep learning for hand pose recognition in real-time using Low-End HMD. In: van der Spek, E., Göbel, S., Do, E.Y.-L., Clua, E., Baalsrud Hauge, J. (eds.) ICEC-JCSG 2019. LNCS, vol. 11863, pp. 70–84. Springer, Cham (2019). https://doi.org/10.1007/978-3-030-34644-7_6

10. PD, A.A., Chandrasekharan, G.P., Clua, E.W.G., Preux, P., Vasconcellos, E.C., Gonçalves, L.M.G.: Vision of the seas: open visual perception framework for autonomous sailing vessels. In: 2023 30th International Conference on Systems, Signals and Image Processing (IWSSIP), pp. 1–5. IEEE (2023)

11. Porcino, T., Ghaeinian, S.A., Franz, J., Malloch, J., Reilly, D.: Design of an extended reality collaboration architecture for mixed immersive and multi-surface interaction. In: Göbl, B., van der Spek, E., Baalsrud Hauge, J., McCall, R. (eds.) Entertainment Computing – ICEC 2022: 21st IFIP TC 14 International Conference, ICEC 2022, Bremen, 1–3 November 2022, Proceedings, pp. 112–122. Springer, Cham (2022). https://doi.org/10.1007/978-3-031-20212-4_9

12. Porcino, T.M., et al.: A real-time approach to improve drilling decision-making process using virtual reality visualization. In: 2021 IEEE Conference on Virtual Reality and 3d User Interfaces Abstracts and Workshops (VRW), pp. 755–756. IEEE (2021)

13. Rizzo, A., et al.: Virtual reality goes to war: a brief review of the future of military behavioral healthcare. J. Clin. Psychol. Med. Settings **18**(2), 176–187 (2011)

Aesthetics and Empowerment

Mengru Xue[1,2(✉)] ⓘ, Cheng Yao[1,2] ⓘ, Jun Hu[3] ⓘ, Yuqi Hu[1,2] ⓘ, and Hui Lyu[1,2] ⓘ

[1] Zhejiang University, Ningbo, 1 Xuefu Road, Ningbo, China
{mengruxue,yaoch,yuqihu,lvhui}@zju.edu.cn
[2] Zhejiang University, 866 Yuhangtang, Hangzhou, China
[3] Eindhoven University of Technology, 5612 AZ Eindhoven, The Netherlands
j.hu@tue.nl

Abstract. Aesthetics in design are known to be empowering in terms of various perspectives in one's life. This paper aims to discuss innovative approaches, methodologies, and technologies that can further enhance the role of aesthetics in empowering individuals in the digital age. By delving into the relationship between aesthetics and empowerment, we seek to foster discussions and collaborations among researchers, practitioners, designers, artists, and industry professionals. It is worth building up a platform for sharing insights, exchanging ideas, and exploring new and emerging trends in this exciting area.

Keywords: Aesthetics · Empowerment

1 Introduction

Aesthetics refer to the appreciation, understanding, and evaluation of beauty, art, and sensory experiences [9]. In design, aesthetics relate to the visual and sensory elements of an object, space, or artwork that evoke emotional responses and perceptions of harmony, balance, and pleasure [10]. In human-computer interaction, aesthetics play a crucial role in user experience. It encompasses the visual design [11], interface layout, and interaction patterns that enhance user engagement and satisfaction [2]. Aesthetics can also expand to other senses, such as sound, touch, and smell, creating immersive and engaging experiences. In summary, aesthetics can significantly impact how users perceive and interact with technologies, as well as their overall well-being and empowerment.

2 Aesthetics for Empowerment

The origins of empowerment can be traced back to the civil rights movement, particularly in regard to the struggles for overcoming domination in women's rights and minority rights [7]. Individuals can be empowered when they obtain skills or abilities that enable

---

An event of the IFIP TC14 working group Art and Entertainment (https://ifiptc14.org/?pag eid=901).

© IFIP International Federation for Information Processing 2023
Published by Springer Nature Switzerland AG 2023
P. Ciancarini et al. (Eds.): ICEC 2023, LNCS 14455, pp. 403–406, 2023.
https://doi.org/10.1007/978-981-99-8248-6_38

them to act independently, thereby leading to success in their professional and personal lives. Empowerment encompasses notions of power, agency, autonomy, and the enabling conditions necessary for individuals and communities to assert themselves, overcome challenges, and strive for a better future [1].

Aesthetics and empowerment intersect in a transformative manner, highlighting the potential for aesthetic design interventions to contribute to individual or social empowerment. Aesthetics play a crucial role in providing individuals with a sense of autonomy and self-actualization to achieve one's potential. The drive for autonomy and self-actualization is a key factor in the design of various technologies, both during the design process and in the design outcomes. Technologies facilitate users by empowering them to reach their full potential and take control of their lives in many perspectives, such as behavior change, education, and health management. Aesthetics is empowering and allows individuals or communities to develop skills and capacities, which enable them to thrive and make meaningful contributions to their lives and society.

3 Case Research and Call to Action

There is a growing interest in understanding immeasurable aesthetic parameters such as sensory experiences and their impacts on satisfaction in urban development and the social environment. Integrating aesthetics into urban planning can significantly empower and enhance the overall quality of cities and communities. Beyond the visual appeal, aesthetics can influence urban spaces' functionality and livability [12]. Rsearchers investigated designerly ways to trigger behavior change for healthier lifestyles, with solutions contributing to both physical and mental vitality and healthy living, relying on aesthetics of interaction principles and the use of data and connectivity as creative materials [6, 13, 17–21]. In the healthcare domain, researchers explored how an aesthetic atmosphere design of a birth environment affects the experiences of new fathers. They found that the aesthetic birthing room design can empower the fathers to take more active support in the birth process [8]. In the workplace scenario, previous research showcases how arts-based learning interventions have the ability to initiate both individual and collective processes of change [14]. Research in education discovered aesthetics within educational spaces had been noticed to influence learning and teaching positively [3].

The above cases reveal how aesthetic approaches used in various contexts are well suited to trigger actions from the present situation toward a promising outcome. The "non-measurable" aesthetics brought discussions in the field. Böhme argues that aesthetics should not focus on the assessment of art [4]. However, some claimed that many obvious elements (e.g., context, interpretations, cultural conventions) highlighted the existing barriers to generalizing and applying successful aesthetics to other relevant scenarios. Several approaches can tackle the difficulties in terms of operationalizing aesthetics to empower people. For instance, using qualitative research methods [5] to explore users' experiences to fully capture the nuances and complexities of aesthetic factors that are hard to quantify. Researchers can explore ways to engage the involvement of users in the aesthetic factors that matter to them in the design process. A comprehensive understanding of contextual factors (e.g., culture, social norms) that affect users' aesthetic preferences can provide insights that are relevant in the specific con text [16].

Considering the emotional and experiential aspects that aesthetics can empower people, techniques such as affective computing [15] can assist designers in capturing and incorporating the emotional and experiential dimensions of aesthetics. We value embracing subjectivity, cultural diversity, and the complex nature of aesthetics and encourage insights sharing and discussions addressing this exciting area.

To effectively implement prior approaches and fully leverage the value that aesthetics bring to empowerment, future research can further explore the relationship between aesthetics and empowerment in HCI. Enriching the cases of aesthetics and empowerment in practice, and examining where the aesthetics can and where they cannot empower. It is worth identifying potential research directions, methodologies, and design strategies for future investigations, and sharing knowledge on generalizing the aesthetics to empower other scenarios.

4 Summary

Aesthetics refer to the appreciation, understanding, and evaluation of beauty, art, and sensory experiences [9]. In design, aesthetics relate to the visual and sensory elements of an object, space, or artwork that evoke emotional responses and perceptions of harmony, balance, and pleasure [10]. In human-computer interaction, aesthetics play a crucial role in user experience. It encompasses the visual design [11], interface layout, and interaction patterns that enhance user engagement and satisfaction [2]. Aesthetics can also expand to other senses, such as sound, touch, and smell, creating immersive and engaging experiences. In summary, aesthetics can significantly impact how users perceive and interact with technologies, as well as their overall well-being and empowerment.

Acknowledgement. This is an event of the IFIP TC14 working group Art and Entertainment, organized by researchers from Ningbo Research Institute, Zhejiang University, Ningbo; School of Software Technology, Zhejiang University; Department of Industrial Design, Eindhoven University of Technology. We would like to express great thanks to our sponsors: Ningbo Research Institute, Zhejiang University, Ningbo; China Institute of Eco-design Industry; Computer Aided Product Innovation and Design Engineering Center (Ministry of Education); World Eco-Design Conference (WEDC).

References

1. Adams, R.: Social work and empowerment (2003)
2. Ahmed, S.U., Al Mahmud, A., Bergaust, K.: Aesthetics in human-computer interaction: views and reviews. In: Jacko, J.A. (ed.) HCI 2009. LNCS, vol. 5610, pp. 559–568. Springer, Heidelberg (2009). https://doi.org/10.1007/978-3-642-02574-7_63
3. Barton, G.: The importance of aesthetics in educational spaces and relationships. In: Barton, G. (ed.) Aesthetic Literacies in School and Work: New Pathways for Education, pp. 69–81. Springer, Cham (2023). https://doi.org/10.1007/978-981-19-7750-3_6
4. Böhme, G.: Atmosphere as the fundamental concept of a new aesthetics. Thesis Eleven **36**(1), 113–126 (1993)
5. Breel, A.: Audience agency in participatory performance: a methodology for examiningaesthetic experience. Participations J. Audience Reception Stud. **12**(1), 368–387 (2015)

6. Chen, Y., Lin, Y., Wang, J., Liu, L., Yao, C., Ying, F.: Ipanda: a playful hybrid product for facilitating children's wildlife conservation education. In: Extended Abstracts of the 2019 CHI Conference on Human Factors in Computing Systems, pp. 1–6 (2019)
7. Crawford, V.L., Rouse, J.A., Woods, B.: Women in the civil rights movement: trailblazers and torchbearers, 1941–1965, vol. 16. Indiana University Press (1993)
8. Folmann, B.: Room for transition by aesthetic empowerment?, atmospheres andsensory experiences of a new hospital birth environment. In: Proceedings of the 4th International Congress on Ambiances, Alloaesthesia: Senses, Inventions, Worlds, vol. 1, pp. pp–126. RÅLeseau International Ambiances (2020)
9. Goldman, A.: The aesthetic. In: The Routledge Companion to Aesthetics, pp. 275–286. Routledge (2005)
10. Hekkert, P., Leder, H.: Product aesthetics. In: Product Experience, pp. 259–285 (2008)
11. Jahanian, A.: Quantifying Aesthetics of Visual Design Applied to Automatic Design. Springer, Cham (2016). https://doi.org/10.1007/978-3-319-31486-0
12. Lee, D.: "Anybody can do it": aesthetic empowerment, urban citizenship, and the naturalization of indonesian graffiti and street art. City Soc. 25(3), 304–327 (2013)
13. Liu, X., et al.: The artwork generating system of escher-like positive andnegative pattern evolution. In: ACM SIGGRAPH 2017 Posters, pp. 1–2 (2017)
14. Meltzer, C.: What matters? Empowering non-artists to use arts-based learning. Organizational Aesthetics 11(1), 94–115 (2022)
15. Picard, R.W.: Affective Computing. MIT Press, Cambridge (2000)
16. Seo, K.K., Lee, S., Chung, B.D.: Effects of perceived usability and aesthetics on emotional responses in different contexts of use. Int. J. Hum.-Comput. Interact. 32(6), 445–459 (2016)
17. Toeters, M., Feijs, L., van Loenhout, D., Tieleman, C., Virtala, N., Jaakson, G.K.:Algorithmic fashion aesthetics: Mandelbrot. In: Proceedings of the 2019 ACM International Symposium on Wearable Computers, pp. 322–328 (2019)
18. Wang, R., Hu, J.: Design for connecting people through digital artworks with personal information. In: Göbl, B., van der Spek, E., Baalsrud Hauge, J., McCall, R. (eds.) Entertainment Computing–ICEC 2022, pp. 386–397. Springer, Cham (2022). https://doi.org/10.1007/978-3-031-20212-4_32
19. Xue, M., Liang, R.H., Hu, J., Yu, B., Feijs, L.: Understanding how group workersreflect on organizational stress with a shared, anonymous heart rate variability data visualization. In: CHI Conference on Human Factors in Computing Systems Extended Abstracts, pp. 1–7 (2022)
20. Xue, M., Yao, C., Hu, J., Hu, Y., Lyu, H.: Digital arts and health. In: Göbl, B., van der Spek, E., Baalsrud Hauge, J., McCall, R. (eds.) Entertainment Computing–ICEC 2022, pp. 436–442. Springer, Cham (2022). https://doi.org/10.1007/978-3-031-20212-4_37
21. Yu, B., Hu, J., Funk, M., Feijs, L.: Delight: biofeedback through ambient light for stress intervention and relaxation assistance. Pers. Ubiquit. Comput. 22(4), 787–805 (2018)

Workshop: Aesthetics and Empowerment

Research and Practice of Hierarchical Painting-Based Digital Design Method

Weiqiang Ying[1(✉)] 🆔, Lingyan Zhang[1], Shijian Luo[1], Cheng Yao[1], and Fangtian Ying[2]

[1] Zhejiang University, 866 Yuhangtang, Hangzhou, China
{11921165,Zhangly,luosj,yaoch}@zju.edu.cn
[2] Macau University of Science and Technology, Macau 999078, China
130678488190163.com

Abstract. As digital systems and information become an important part of people's daily lives and social relationships, new insights into how technology interacts with traditional painting practices are crucial in education. To study how digital painting can be promoted in education in the future, we combine virtual digital painting with traditional painting in an educational environment to explore innovative experiences of new forms of painting, supporting new attempts in art education and inspiring people's enthusiasm for art. We attempted to combine three interactive methods: 1) painting robot technology for creating texture, 2) computer software for generating painting styles, and 3) UV printing for producing colors. 20 students from an art collage participated in our user study. Through this approach, we created a new painting experience, triggering discussions on how technology can support existing painting practices. The discussions revealed that participants hoped to use technology-assisted methods to handle the levels of their paintings, involving human-machine collaboration in the creative process, and to enhance their understanding of traditional painting's use of color, texture, and layers. Most participants expressed interest in integrating digital art into reality. The results of this study can serve as considerations for guiding future painting education initiatives.

Keywords: Painting Style · Layered Texture · Human-Machine Collaboration

1 Introduction

The use of digital image processing in computer art and digital entertainment has great potential. It allows for the transformation of digital works into realistic painting effects and the addition of textures, promoting collaborative creation between humans and machines [7]. The production of hierarchical texture

Supported by Computer Aided Product Innovation Design Engineering Center, Ministry of Education.

Published by Springer Nature Switzerland AG 2023
P. Ciancarini et al. (Eds.): ICEC 2023, LNCS 14455, pp. 409–417, 2023.
https://doi.org/10.1007/978-981-99-8248-6_39

involves combining machine-generated texture forms with printing to create new effects. This paper focuses on the creative experience and the use of tangible computational media to physically represent hierarchical textures [1]. The concept of painting hierarchy involves creating a painting style with variations in thickness and color, and exploring how digital painting can be presented in a printed form. However, with the increasing influence of interactive technologies and systems [12,17], it is important to study how digital technology can be integrated into painting creation [14], specifically in relation to hierarchical texture. To further explore these ideas, the authors have developed a system with three functionalities to inspire participants in manipulating their digital textures [6,14] and hierarchies to create new forms of painting expression (Fig. 1).

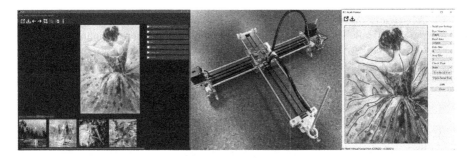

Fig. 1. Screenshots of our three working prototype systems

In our study, we introduced three systems to participants to explore their behaviors and perspectives on digital painting. These systems included painting effect generation software, drawing texture path generation software, and painting robots. The participants were asked to select photos, create digital paintings using these systems, and print them out. We then conducted qualitative interviews to discuss their experiences and interactions with the technologies. In the following sections, we will explain related work, describe the design and implementation of these technologies, and discuss the painting method employed in the study.

2   Methodology

First of all, it is important to understand how digital materials shape the texture of layers and make practices effective in certain situations [9,11,16]. This includes a detailed explanation of the design and implementation of three interactive systems that enable participants to engage with digital and real-life artwork. Furthermore, the text elaborates on three opportunities for advancement in this field [4,8,15]. We aim to bridge the gap between digital artwork and traditional paintings by creating layered textures in digital art. While computer programs and UV printing can produce realistic paintings, there is still a noticeable difference in the portrayal of textures compared to actual paintings. To address this, we have developed software tools that allow users to generate paths, convert painting styles, and design their own paths within a computer drawing program. By using a painting robot, users can create the texture of the image. The final step involves printing the image using a colored printer, overlaying the colors with the texture to create a unique visual effect (Fig. 2).

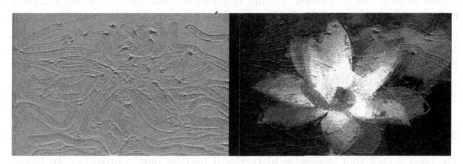

Fig. 2. The effect picture of the painting

The importance of understanding how digital materials shape the texture of layers in artworks. It discusses the design and implementation of three interactive systems that enable participants to engage with digital and real-life artwork. The text also mentions opportunities for advancement in this field. The aim is to bridge the gap between digital artwork and traditional paintings by creating layered textures in digital art [10, 13, 19]. The text further explains how software tools and a painting robot can be used to generate paths and textures in digital art, and how printing techniques can create unique visual effects [13]. The research explores the use of hierarchy in digital painting systems and incorporates real-world objects. The texture model consists of a hierarchical texture path generation system and a painting robot. The text mentions the conversion of digital photos into different painting styles and the generation of hierarchical texture paths. The aim of the new interactive system is to effectively utilize real-world objects in digital painting. The text also mentions the concept of layers in painting creation and how it influenced the design of interactive devices and systems. The texture model includes a layered texture path generation system and a painting robot. The text concludes by mentioning the implementation of the digital painting function and the transformation of texture paths into output models (Fig. 3).

Fig. 3. Show the effects of layering and printing

2.1 Paint Texture Layering Tool

Our goal is to design a process that involves interacting with participants to explore their perceptions of the texture of digital paintings. We will focus on the theme of digital painting texture, which involves creating explorations of how digital objects are generated, finding inspiration from the real world to study images related to texture, understanding how the process of texture occurs, and exploring their meanings. The three tools we have created are called style transfer software, texture path generation system, and painting robot (Fig. 1). Each tool is designed to address specific aspects that may arise when exploring the texture of digital paintings, providing a means to reexamine perception, beliefs, and experiences [3,18,19]. We will describe each tool below.

2.2 Hierarchical Texture Path Generation

We need a tool that generates hierarchical texture paths, providing an image texture generation experience [2,5,17]. The tool should incorporate contour map and stroke trend path map generation, and should be adjustable on a texture generation software platforms (Fig. 4). Additionally, we need a PC application for converting images into path images, and an application based on a painting robot for assisting painters in interacting with virtual and physical content.

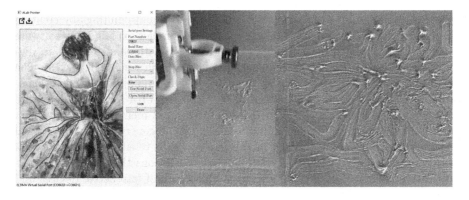

Fig. 4. Path generation software interface

Unlike traditional layered texture, it is replaced by an automated painting robot in creating layered texture. Throughout this process, the interaction between human and technology is achieved through a collaborative approach, resulting in a layered digital artwork. The creation process ignites the creative passion within individuals and showcases the diversity of painting.

We have created three functional tools for this project. Their development focuses on generating digital paintings, aiming to enable participants to explore the potential ways of digital painting and ignite their passion for creative expression through digital art. To organize and plan the creation of digital paintings, we will explore methods for generating textures and examine the hierarchy and texture of digital paintings. We use a painting machine to imitate the process of creating textures with a paintbrush, generating layered textures on the canvas. We collaborate with the computer to complete the process of creating layered textures, designing and constructing hierarchical textures and other paths. Finally, we use a painting robot to draw out the layered textures. In the end, we print the resulting image using a UV printer. The completed creations can be seen in Fig. 5.

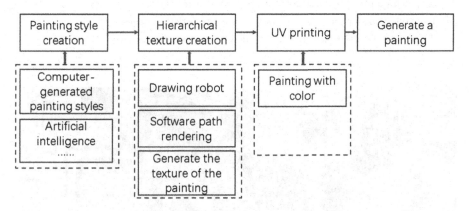

Fig. 5. Creative effect flow

3   Evaluation

Twenty art students from an art college participated in this study, as shown in Table 1. Participants were recruited through emails and social media advertisements disseminated by the research team, inviting art college students to take part in a study investigating artists' attitudes and experiences towards digital painting.

The semi-structured qualitative research method was used to conduct interviews with 20 students (n = 20, SD = 1.9), including 15 females and 5 males, in order to understand their personalized experiences. Thematic analysis revealed a series of facilitating factors and obstacles that were consistent with our initial challenges. The students demonstrated several different approaches in designing their styles and creating paintings (Fig. 6).

These approaches included:

- Individual groups (n = 1) adopting a method of creating a batch of style images using style transfer and then applying texture effects.
- Groups of three (n = 3) taking a similar approach but also aiming to produce unique painting styles.
- Groups of two (n = 2) deciding on texture effects corresponding to each painting.
- Groups of four (n = 4) deciding on capturing their own photographs and applying corresponding styles and texture effects (Table 1).

The same set of tests will be repeated by different people as a combination test, and a total of 20 people will complete the test.

Table 1. Free creation.

ID	Style picture making and experiment with texture styles	Member number
1	A very methodical way to make paintings	4
2	For each painting, make the corresponding texture effect	2
3	Use style transfer and texture effects to create artistic images	1
4	Took a similar approach, but also added a unique painting style	3

Fig. 6. User study photos and the outcomes

4   Results

We analyzed student participation levels in artwork creation and texture production across different group sizes. Larger groups (3 or 4 students) were able to divide tasks and collaborate, saving time and allowing for improvement. In pairs, students tested layering textures and made changes through dialogue. Trios worked together to discuss styles, build style maps, and exchange feelings. Smaller groups (1 or 2 students) found it challenging to complete everything on time. However, one student still found enjoyment in producing and showcasing style paintings.

As shown in the Fig. 7. In the first screening step, we excluded 539 images based on clarity. Due to copyright issues, the collected images were only used for internal communication and research. In the second screening step, we evaluated the accessibility of the images and received input from professional art teachers, resulting in the exclusion of 703 images. In the final step, we applied exclusion and inclusion criteria, excluding images with cultural bias and those that did not meet the criteria. We excluded studies measuring unintended effects. We also excluded images with unclear usage in the scene, resulting in the selection

Fig. 7. Style making process

of 8 images for content analysis. Participants in the tests were divided into two categories: Research 1 used predefined images for painting, while Research 2 allowed participants to use their own images for painting.

During our study, we collected both qualitative and quantitative data to address our research questions. Our analysis of the quantitative data revealed a lack of enthusiasm among students to actively create pictures, and their performance in producing artwork was average. However, in the free creation phase, we observed that students enjoyed the challenge of creating artwork they liked. As they gained more experience, their artistic skills improved. We also found that increased efficiency enhanced students' creativity and imagination, leading to remarkable painting experiences. Additionally, their mindset became more positive and relaxed throughout the study.

In the post-study survey, nearly all students (except one) reported that converting their pictures into stylized images was easy. The majority of students believed that incorporating digital art into their lives was beneficial. When asked about their enjoyment of creating digital paintings that interact with physical reality, the ratings were consistent, with most students finding the devices easy to use. Students expressed satisfaction with using digital painting to create their own style with real textures, emphasizing the freedom and fun involved in integrating different elements and the ease of engaging in these activities.

This experience also teaches us that people prefer virtual worlds to have relevant connections to reality. We need to establish communication between the virtual digital world and the real world. With our design guidelines, we can create a layered texture in artwork, allowing students to engage in artistic style creation and texture reproduction, ultimately showcasing more confidence in their paintings and sparking greater creativity.

5 Conclusion

This article introduces an innovative experience in the field of education by combining digital painting with traditional painting, blending digitization with authenticity to support new attempts in art education and inspire passion for the arts. Additionally, aiming for the desired painting effects, we propose a method of creating painting styles and texture paths through computer algorithms and utilizing painting robots. This allows artists to design and incorporate their own textures into their artwork, merging virtual content with reality to create a unique painting experience. We believe that this provides a more direct and unique opportunity to engage in digital painting and showcase the power of digital art through platforms such as artificial intelligence painting and painting robots. With our design guidelines, we aim to reduce barriers to entry in painting style design, creation, and digital art, and promote the future dissemination of digital painting in education. The focus of this research is to explore the practical and educational value of texture at the digital painting level. Through interviews and design surveys, we have initiated discussions on how technology influences the texture at the digital painting level. Our findings begin to elucidate the inheritance and value of texture in digital painting education, representing a vast space for future work.

Acknowledgements. This research was supported by the Fundamental Research Funds for the Central Universities (Grant No. 226-2023-00086), Research Center of Computer Aided Product Innovation Design, Ministry of Education, National Natural Science Foundation of China (Grant No. 52075478), and National Social Science Foundation of China (Grant No. 21AZD056).

References

1. Ashikhmin, M.V.: Synthesizing natural textures. In: Interactive 3D Graphics and Games (2001)
2. Ashikhmin, M.V.: Fast texture transfer. IEEE Comput. Graph. Appl. **23**(4), 38–43 (2003)
3. Buchón-Moragues, F., Bravo, J.M., Ferri, M., Redondo, J., Sánchez-Pérez, J.V.: Application of structured light system technique for authentication of wooden panel paintings. Sensors **16**(6), 881 (2016). https://doi.org/10.3390/s16060881, https://www.mdpi.com/1424-8220/16/6/881
4. Cabral, B., Leedom, L.C.: Imaging vector fields using line integral convolution. In: Proceedings of the 20st Annual Conference on Computer Graphics and Interactive Techniques, SIGGRAPH 1993, pp. 263–270 (1993)
5. Chu, N., Tai, C.L.: An efficient brush model for physically-based 3D painting. In: 10th Pacific Conference on Computer Graphics and Applications, Proceedings (2003)
6. Dana, K.J., Nayar, S.K.: Histogram model for 3D textures. In: Computer Vision and Pattern Recognition (1998)
7. Dellermann, D., Calma, A., Lipusch, N., Weber, T., Ebel, P.: The future of Human-AI collaboration: a taxonomy of design knowledge for hybrid intelligence systems. arXiv - CS - Human-Computer Interaction (2019)
8. Hutchinson, H., Bederson, B.B., Druin, A., Plaisant, C., Westerlund, B.: Technology probes: inspiring design for and with families. In: Human Factors in Computing Systems (2003)

9. Lanitis, A.A., Taylor, C.J., Cootes, T.F.: Towards automatic simulation of ageing effects on face images. In: IEEE International Conference on Automatic Face & Gesture Recognition (2001)

10. Maiden, N., Lockerbie, J., Zachos, K., Wolf, A., Brown, A.: Designing new digital tools to augment human creative thinking at work: an application in elite sports coaching. Expert Syst. **40**(3), e13194 (2023). https://doi.org/10.1111/exsy.13194, https://onlinelibrary.wiley.com/doi/abs/10.1111/exsy.13194

11. Mao, X., Nagasaka, Y., Yamamoto, S., Imamiya, A.: Automatic generation of pencil drawings using line integral convolution. In: The Society for Art and Science, pp. 147–159 (2002)

12. Nilsson, L.: Textile influence : exploring the relationship between textiles and products in the design process. DiVA - Academic Archive Online (2015)

13. Orth, D., Thurgood, C., Hoven, E.V.D.: Designing meaningful products in the digital age: how users value their technological possessions. ACM Trans. Comput.-Hum. Interact. **26**(5), 1–28 (2019). https://doi.org/10.1145/3341980

14. Robles, E., Wiberg, M.: Texturing the "material turn" in interaction design. In: Proceedings of the 4th International Conference on Tangible and Embedded Interaction 2010, Cambridge, MA, USA, 24–27 January 2010 (2010)

15. Tholander, J., Normark, M., Rossitto, C.: Understanding agency in interaction design materials. In: Human Factors in Computing Systems (2012)

16. Vallgrda, A., Boer, L., Tsaknaki, V., Svanaes, D.: Material programming: a new interaction design practice. In: ACM Conference Companion Publication on Designing Interactive Systems (2016)

17. Wang, B., Wang, W., Yang, H., Sun, J.: Efficient example-based painting and synthesis of 2D directional texture. IEEE Trans. Visual Comput. Graphics **10**(3), 266–277 (2004). https://doi.org/10.1109/TVCG.2004.1272726

18. Wang, C.M., Tseng, S.M.: Design and assessment of an interactive role-play system for learning and sustaining traditional glove puppetry by digital technology. Appl. Sci. **13**(8), 5206 (2023). https://doi.org/10.3390/app13085206, https://www.mdpi.com/2076-3417/13/8/5206

19. Wu, Y.: Application of digital painting technology in the creation of an oil painting containing graphene. Adv. Mater. Sci. Eng. **2022**, 7611500 (2022). https://doi.org/10.1155/2022/7611500

Research on the Influence of Object Recognition Based on Intelligent Algorithm on Staff's Anxiety

Lingyan Zhang[1] ⓘ, Cheng Yao[1](✉), Lanqing Huang[1], Weiqiang Ying[1],
and Fangtian Ying[2]

[1] Zhejiang University, Hangzhou, China
{Zhlingyan,yaoch,11921165}@zju.edu.cn
[2] Macau University of Science and Technology, Macau 999078, China

Abstract. This study aims to investigate the influence of object recognition based on intelligent algorithms on staff's anxiety levels in professional settings. Anxiety was measured through self-report questionnaires and physiological indicators, while object recognition performance was evaluated based on the accuracy and speed of intelligent algorithm-based systems. The study provides insight into the potential impact of technology on mental health and offers suggestions for optimizing the implementation of intelligent algorithms in the workplace.

Keywords: object recognition · intelligent algorithms · staff's anxiety · artificial intelligence · mental health

1 Introduction

Anxiety, as a common psychological emotion of human beings, often occurs when individuals are facing greater unknown risks. Because when human beings face unknown risks, if the individual's loss assessment value of the unknown risks exceeds the level they can accept, they will have a sense of powerlessness and inexplicable fear, resulting in anxiety [1]. In terms of clinical manifestations, patients with mental anxiety often have depression, depression, slow thinking, panic disorders, such as feelings of dying, loss of control, mental breakdown and other symptoms, as well as somatic symptoms of panic attacks, such as shivering, rapid heartbeat, asthma, etc., followed by generalized anxiety disorder, which is clinically divided into mental anxiety, somatic anxiety Motor restlessness symptoms of nerves and muscles [2, 3]. For people with anxiety, regulating their negative emotions and enlightening their thinking play an important role in the treatment of anxiety disorders. However, most adults have limited ability to regulate their own emotions and thinking. When facing great pressure and risks in work and life, they are prone to psychological imbalance and suffer from serious psychological anxiety [4]. Therefore, the use of auxiliary tools and methods to reduce the psychological pressure brought by work may also have a positive effect on the mental health of employees.

The rapid advancements in artificial intelligence (AI) have significantly impacted various industries and fields, including computer vision and object recognition. Computer vision systems rely on intelligent algorithms, such as deep learning models and convolutional neural networks (CNNs), to identify and classify objects in digital images or videos. These models have been instrumental in achieving state-of-the-art results in object recognition, significantly surpassing traditional machine learning methods.

One such groundbreaking work is by Krizhevsky, who introduced the deep CNN architecture known as AlexNet [5]. This network achieved remarkable performance on the ImageNet Large Scale Visual Recognition Challenge (ILSVRC), a benchmark dataset for object recognition. Their work shifted the research focus to deep learning, primarily utilizing CNNs for object recognition tasks. Consequently, many deep learning models, including VGG, Inception, and ResNet, have been developed and further advanced the field.

While the application of intelligent algorithms for object recognition has brought numerous benefits, such as higher accuracy and faster processing, it is essential to consider the possible implications on employees who interact with these technologies in their daily work. The introduction of AI and automation has raised concerns over job security, quality, and potential skill obsolescence [6, 7]. a common emotional response to such concerns, can negatively impact work performance and overall well-being [8–10].

Several studies have investigated factors contributing to anxiety in the workplace, such as job insecurity and work overload [11, 12]. However, limited research has explored the psychological impact of AI-powered technologies, like intelligent algorithms for object recognition, on staff members' mental health. Understanding the relationship between these technologies and staff anxiety is crucial for designing interventions, policies, and support systems that promote employees' mental well-being [13–15].

This exploratory study aims to investigate the impact of object recognition using intelligent algorithms on staff anxiety levels in professional settings. By examining the potential psychological consequences of technology adoption, we strive to provide insights and recommendations for optimizing technology implementation in workplaces while mitigating mental health concerns.

2 Subjects and Methods

To explore the impact of using the security inspection item identification system based on intelligent algorithm on the work anxiety of security personnel. In this study, the research team purchased a piece of data about the work of security personnel from data dealers. Specifically, the data includes the work anxiety level data of security inspection staff using the security inspection item identification system based on different intelligent algorithms in the past three years [11, 16]. The anxiety level is measured by the self rating of security inspection staff, and the score is 10 points. The higher the score, the higher the anxiety level. When the score is higher than 4 points, 6 points and 8 points, it is considered that security inspection staff suffer from mild, moderate and severe work anxiety respectively.

Let the job anxiety score of the security personnel be denoted by A, and the intelligent score of the security inspection item identification system be denoted by B. Then, we can represent the correlation coefficient between A and B as r.After cleaning the data set, we perform correlation analysis using different regression methods. Let the best fit line obtained from the linear regression be $Y = aX + b$, where a is the slope and b is the intercept. Similarly, let the best fit curve obtained from polynomial regression, power regression and exponential regression be $Y = a_0 + a_1X + a_2X^2 + \ldots + a_nX^n$, $Y = aX^b$ and $Y = ae^{(bx)}$ respectively.

The correlation significance level is taken as 0.05, which means that the probability of obtaining a correlation coefficient as extreme as r under the null hypothesis (that there is no real correlation between A and B) is less than 5%.

The strength of the correlation between A and B can be evaluated based on the absolute value of r. If $|r| < 0.2$, there is no correlation. If $0.2 \leq |r| < 0.4$, there is a weak correlation. If $0.4 \leq |r| < 0.6$, there is a medium correlation. If $0.6 \leq |r| < 0.8$, there is a strong correlation. If $0.8 \leq |r| \leq 1.0$, there is a very strong correlation.

3   Participants and Grouping

A total of 100 employees from various industries participated in this study, assigned to either a control group (without exposure to intelligent algorithm-based object recognition tasks) or an experimental group (with exposure). Both groups completed self-report questionnaires assessing anxiety levels and demographic information. Participants in the experimental group performed tasks using intelligent algorithm-based object recognition systems, and their anxiety levels were measured pre- and post-task.

4   Task and System Design

An AI-based object recognition task was designed to reflect practical use cases in the participants' industries. The task utilized state-of-the-art deep learning models, such as a pre-trained CNN, to identify and classify objects in images or videos. To evaluate the impact of using such systems, the experimental group participants were asked to perform the object recognition task using the AI-powered system, whereas the control group performed a similar task without AI assistance.

5   Data Collection

A pre-test and post-test design was employed for data collection. Before the task, all participants filled out a self-report questionnaire assessing demographic information, job characteristics, and anxiety levels.

The anxiety assessment might include established measures such as the State-Trait Anxiety Inventory (STAI) or the Generalized Anxiety Disorder 7-item (GAD-7) scale.

The widely used self-report questionnaire, the State-Trait Anxiety Inventory (STAI), measures anxiety levels through two subscales - the State Anxiety Scale (S-Anxiety) and the Trait Anxiety Scale (T-Anxiety). Each subscale has 20 items which respondents rate on a 4-point Likert scale. The S-Anxiety subscale assesses current anxiety levels, while

T-Anxiety evaluates predisposition to anxiety. Scores range from 20 to 80 with higher scores indicating greater anxiety and can be compared to normative data.

Similarly, the Generalized Anxiety Disorder 7-Item Scale (GAD-7) [17] is self-reported and designed to screen and measure anxiety severity; it has seven 4-point Likert scale items which score from 0 to 21. Researchers can use these tools to assess the impact of interventions on anxiety levels through pre- and post-test scores, using appropriate statistical analyses to identify significant differences between groups.

Physiological indicators of anxiety, such as heart rate variability and cortisol levels, were also collected using wearable devices or non-invasive methods. These data provided quantitative measures of stress response before and after the tasks.

6 Task Performance Measurement

The performance of the experimental group participants in the object recognition task was measured in terms of accuracy, speed, and efficiency. The AI system's performance was compared with the control group's manual performance to assess the effectiveness of the intelligent algorithms in object recognition tasks.

7 Post-task Assessment

After completing the tasks, participants in both groups completed a post-test self-report questionnaire to re-assess their anxiety levels. Additionally, physiological indicators were measured again to capture any changes in stress response due to the tasks.

8 Data Analysis

In this study, we aimed to examine how implementing object recognition technology based on intelligent algorithms impacts staff anxiety. We compared pre- and post-test anxiety measures and physiological indicators both within and between groups to analyze the effects. Our research builds upon prior studies in this area that have explored the impact of AI technology on employee psychological well-being.

For example, previous research has shown that AI may negatively affect the work-life balance of employees, leading to burnout and psychological distress. Holmes et al. [18] found that AI technology affected the work-life balance of employees, causing psychological distress and burnout. Similarly, Qamar et al. [19] found that the introduction of AI resulted in an increase in workload for employees, leading to job dissatisfaction and emotional exhaustion.

However, other studies have found that AI can enhance employees' psychological well-being and job performance. For instance, Choi and Lim [20] found that the use of AI-based chatbots in the workplace reduced employee stress and improved their job satisfaction. Additionally, Loureiro et al. [21] found that AI increased employees' job autonomy and task identity, leading to higher job satisfaction and psychological well-being.

These studies highlight the need for a balanced approach to the integration of AI in the workplace, taking into account its potential implications for the psychological well-being of employees. We used multivariate analysis techniques, including ANOVA and regression, to account for potential confounding factors and identify predictors of anxiety in the experimental group. The relationship between task performance and anxiety levels was also examined to identify potential predictors of anxiety in the experimental group.

By employing a robust methodology grounded in artificial intelligence research and psychological assessment, this study investigates the impact of object recognition using intelligent algorithms on staff anxiety levels and provides valuable insights for optimizing technology implementation in professional settings. Table 1 was used to rank the items based on their correlation with the remainder of the items. The rankings were used to create two-, four-, six-, eight-, and ten-item forms of the STAI, with equal numbers of anxiety-present and anxiety-absent items. The correlation coefficients between scores on these short forms and the full-length STAI were very high: $r = .97$ for the 10 items; $r = .96$ for the eight items; $r = .91$ for the six items; $r = .90$ for the four items; and $r = .89$ for the two items.

Table 1. The item-remainder correlations refer to the Pearson correlation coefficients between each item and the total score of the remaining items on the STAI.

Item no.	Adjective	r	Item no.	Adjective	r
1	calm	0.86	11	self-confident	0.65
2	secure	0.81	12	nervous	0.57
3	tense	0.77	13	jittery	0.63
4	regretful	0.52	14	high-strung	0.65
5	at ease	0.81	15	relaxed	0.86
6	upset	0.68	16	contend	0.84
7	misfortunes	0.66	17	worried	0.73
8	rested	0.57	18	over-excited	0.48
9	anxious	0.64	19	joyful	0.55
10	comfortable	0.73	20	pleasant	0.78

Note. The italics show the top three items with the highest level of anxiety present and absent

9   Results

Preliminary analyses showed a significant increase in anxiety levels for participants in the experimental group compared to the control group. The increase in anxiety was associated with lower confidence in task performance and concerns about job security.

The correlation analysis between the job anxiety score of security personnel and the intelligent score of security inspection item identification system is carried out, and Fig. 1 is obtained.

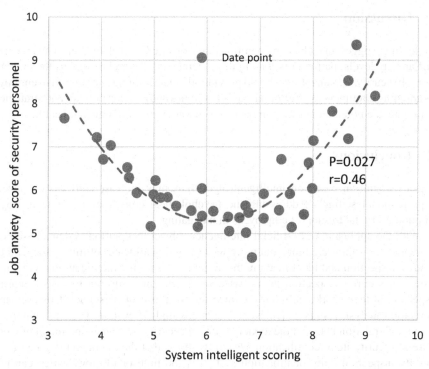

Fig. 1. Correlation Analysis between job anxiety score of security personnel and intelligent degree score of security inspection item identification system

It can be seen from Fig. 1 that the output p value of the correlation significance test between the two indicators is 0.027, which is less than the significance level of 0.05. It is considered that there is a polynomial function correlation, and the correlation coefficient r is 0.46, indicating that the correlation degree between the two indicators is medium correlation. When the intelligent degree score of the security inspection article identification system is low, the security inspection personnel's work anxiety degree score is high. With the improvement of the intelligent degree of the intelligent algorithm used by the system, the security inspection personnel's work anxiety score shows a downward trend. When the intelligent degree score of the system is about 6.5, the security inspection personnel's anxiety score is the lowest as a whole, and then the anxiety score data gradually increases. Consulting the front-line management personnel in the transportation industry, it is found that this is because the security inspection item identification system can alleviate the anxiety and helplessness of employees due to the repetition of work to a certain extent. However, when the system is so intelligent that employees think that the system may rob their jobs, employees will have anxiety about being replaced by intelligent systems.

10 Discussion

Our findings suggest that object recognition based on intelligent algorithms may increase staff anxiety levels, particularly among those perceiving the technology as threatening their job security. Organizations should provide adequate training and support to employees adopting intelligent algorithm-based technologies and develop policies and strategies to mitigate the potential negative impact of technology on staff's mental health.

11 Conclusions

Object recognition based on intelligent algorithms may increase staff anxiety levels in professional settings. Addressing the psychological consequences of technology adoption is crucial to support employees in navigating.

With the application of artificial intelligence, object recognition systems based on intelligent algorithms are more and more widely used in all walks of life. In the field of security inspection and identification, the system that uses the intelligent identification system of security inspection items based on intelligent algorithm to assist security inspectors in their work can greatly reduce the workload of personnel. However, the correlation analysis results of a relevant data in this study show that. There is a binomial medium correlation between the anxiety score of security personnel and the intelligent score of security item identification system. It shows that the intelligent degree of the security inspection item identification system is too high or too low, which can not alleviate the work anxiety of the security inspection staff. Only when the intelligent degree of the system is moderate, the security inspection staff will reduce the workload and do not have to worry about being robbed of their work by artificial intelligence to alleviate their anxiety.

Acknowledgements. This research was supported by the Fundamental Research Funds for the Central Universities (Grant No. 226-2023-00086), Research Center of Computer Aided Product Innovation Design, Ministry of Education, National Natural Science Foundation of China (Grant No. 52075478), and National Social Science Foundation of China (Grant No. 21AZD056).

References

1. Kwon, M., et al.: When humans aren't optimal: robots that collaborate with risk-aware humans. In: 2020 15th ACM/IEEE International Conference on Human-Robot Interaction (HRI), pp. 43–52 (2020)
2. Pavlichenko, A.: Clinical staging in panic disorder and agoraphobia. Eur. Psychiatry 33(S1), S326–S326 (2016)
3. Raju, N.N., Naga Pavan Kumar, K.S.V.R., Nihal, G.: Clinical practice guidelines for assessment and management of anxiety and panic disorders in emergency setting. Indian J. Psychiatry 65(2), 181–185 (2023)
4. Gehrt, T.B., et al.: Encoding and retrieval biases for health-related scenes in patients with severe health anxiety*. Memory 27(7–8), 1–12 (2019)

5. Krizhevsky, A., Sutskever, I., Hinton, G.: ImageNet classification with deep convolutional neural networks. In: Advances in Neural Information Processing Systems, vol. 25, no. 2 (2012)

6. West, J.C.: The second machine age: work, progress, and prosperity in a time of brilliant technologies. Psychiatry **78**(4), 380–383 (2015)

7. Majzlíková, E., Vitáloš, M.: Potential risk of automation for jobs in slovakia: a district- and industry-level analysis. East. Eur. Econ. **60**(5), 452–478 (2022)

8. Autor, D.H.: Why are there still so many jobs? The history and future of workplace automation. J. Econ. Perspect. **29**(3), 3–30 (2015)

9. Bambra, C.L.: Clear winners and losers are created by age only NHS resource allocation. BMJ Br. Med. J. **344**, e3593 (2012)

10. Edmondson, A.C., Lei, Z.: Psychological safety: the history, renaissance, and future of an interpersonal construct. Annu. Rev. Organ. Psych. Organ. Behav. **1**(1), 23–43 (2014)

11. Ayalp, G.G., Özdemir, N.: Relationship between test anxiety and learning styles of architecture undergraduates. Creat. Educ. 364–375 (2016)

12. Schlese, M., Schramm, F.: Tracing the relationship between job insecurity, individual expectations and the satisfaction of German workers (1994)

13. Ridley, M., et al.: Poverty, depression, and anxiety: causal evidence and mechanisms. Science **370**(6522), eaay0214 (2020)

14. Nawrocka, S., et al.: A person-centered approach to job insecurity: is there a reciprocal relationship between the quantitative and qualitative dimensions of job insecurity? Int. J. Environ. Res. Public Health **20**(7), 5280 (2023)

15. Probst, T.M.: Countering the negative effects of job insecurity through participative decision making: lessons from the demand-control model. J. Occup. Health Psychol. **10**(4), 320–329 (2005)

16. Foubert, J.: Book review: Jukka Vuori, Roland Blonk and Richard H Price (eds), sustainable working lives: managing work transitions and health throughout the life course. Work Employ. Soc. **31**(4), 715–717 (2017)

17. Demartini, J., Patel, G., Fancher, T.: Generalized anxiety disorder. Ann. Internal Med. **170**(7), ITC49–ITC64 (2019)

18. Holmes, E.G., et al.: Taking care of our own: a multispecialty study of resident and program director perspectives on contributors to burnout and potential interventions. Acad. Psychiatry **41**(2), 159–166 (2017)

19. Qamar, Y., et al.: When technology meets people: the interplay of artificial intelligence and human resource management. J. Enterp. Inf. Manag. **34**(5), 1339–1370 (2021)

20. Choi, S.B., Lim, M.S.: Effects of social and technology overload on psychological well-being in young South Korean adults: the mediatory role of social network service addiction. Comput. Hum. Behav. **61**, 245–254 (2016)

21. Loureiro, S.M.C., Guerreiro, J., Tussyadiah, I.: Artificial intelligence in business: State of the art and future research agenda. J. Bus. Res. **129**, 911–926 (2021)

Theatre of Tomorrow - A Virtual Exhibition and Performing Arts Platform Created by Digital Game Technology

Zhen Wu[(⊠)] [iD]

Beijing Dance Academy, No.1, Wanshousi Road, Haidian District, Beijing, China
wuzhen@bda.edu.cn

Abstract. In recent years, the rapid development of gaming technology has made it possible to apply it to exhibitions and performances. *Theater of Tomorrow* is a virtual exhibition and performance platform integrating artificial intelligence, digital games, and performing arts. The platform provides an exhibition space that breaks the limits of time, space, interactive communication, and theatrical experience. Through the internet, the platform has the function of playing both exhibition and performance arts. It is also a social media where professionals can have a specific virtual community to create performing arts and learn from each other. In addition, this platform can display the Intangible Cultural Heritage, preserving the traditional performing arts. *Theater of Tomorrow* has significant social value, especially during the epidemic. Of course, it has some things that could be improved, such as visual effects limited by the accuracy of the model and the need for more weight and fluidity in the movements of the digital dancers. Nowadays, physical performances are re-emerging, but virtual online platforms are relevant and valuable as a powerful complement to offline versions, which continue to improve with technology development.

Keywords: Digital Game Technology · Performing Arts · Exhibition

1 Introduction

In the past half-century, the digital game industry has been thriving with the support of technologies. Nowadays, digital game technology is widely used in cultural tourism, industrial automation, healthcare, education, etc. For example, Since 2021, American singer Travis Scott, Lady Gaga, and French singer Aya Nakamura have all tried to perform as digital humans in Fortnite's Soundwave concert series, interacting with players through online performances (a special edition of the Unreal Editor for Fortnite was released to facilitate developers' development of the metaverse platform) [1]. The epidemic has substantially affected the physical performing arts and exhibitions in the last few years. The virtual online performance platform's interactive, social, and immersive characters have made it a supplementary solution to traditional theater. Some artists and institutions have also started to work with game developers to explore and create new digital online performance platforms.

P. Ciancarini et al. (Eds.): ICEC 2023, LNCS 14455, pp. 426–437, 2023.
https://doi.org/10.1007/978-981-99-8248-6_41

2   Background

The COVID-19 pandemic has impacted traditional theater hugely in the past few years. The bare revenue of the box office has been pushing more and more theaters to shut down permanently. The international tour for the shows is facing more complex problems. As a result, more and more virtual exhibitions and online performing arts platforms are being created. However, most are just live steam shows without any interactive activity, much less than inviting the audience to participate in the event as the performers. Therefore scholars, artists, and scientists worldwide are keen to explore the new trend of exhibition and performing arts venues to replace the traditional galleries, museums, and theaters in the pandemic era. The MetaLab at Harvard initiated *The Manifesto for the Future Stage,* which points out among the stages that most powerfully shape contemporary life are those associated with the ubiquity of networks and networked devices, the many ways in which they are reshaping the contours of human experience and interaction [2] Whether for performers or audiences, the resulting halo of data streams and algorithms that now surround, inform, and emanate from every human act demands an expanded notion of live performance: what we call liveness plus online performance platforms with standard video-conferencing and TV apps such as Zoom, Skype, VooV Meeting have been developed [3]. The first Digital International Festival for Dance Academies (IFDA) with screenings and interactive student forums is the 2022 Hong Kong International Dance Festival, where we witnessed how creative minds explore dance and technology via the internet. The digital platform used by IFDA has its limitation, which could not demonstrate the whole movement and space. On the screen, the dance looks like a 2D collage art. The interactive and immersive virtual online exhibition platform combines digital game technology with motion capture technology to participate in the virtual theater performance through digital humans. This cyber show is just a breakthrough for the new era of digital theater.

Today, digital games technology, exhibition, and performing arts platforms have impacted each other much more profoundly and further toward a more virtualized system trend. Some artists and institutions have cooperated with game developers to explore and create digital online exhibitions and performing arts platforms, such as Swiss Choreographer Giles Jobin's *La Comédie Virtuelle-Live Show*[1] (Real-time multiuser performance in VR) in 2020. The live show is a real-time dance piece. The five performers are geographically distant, physically separated by thousands of kilometers but gathered in a virtual space with the audience, remotely connected from where they are. The work plays on presence and absence, the notion of reality, simultaneity, and community. In 2021, dancers from Shanghai, Paris, and Geneva were invited to work together on *La Comédie virtuelle* with motion capture equipment to choreograph the dance work, which the audience downloaded, installed the software, and watched the show. They interacted with an app developed with Unity, see Fig. 1(a). After the epidemic, the director presented the work *Cosmogony*, a performance in combination of online and offline, with the audience sitting in the theatre or at home (at the Sundance Film Festival 2023 and the Théâtre National de la Danse in Paris).

---

[1] https://www.gillesjobin.com/cr%C3%A9ation/comedie-virtuelle-live-show/.

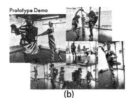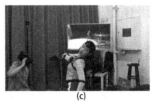

(a)   (b)   (c)

Fig. 1. Digital online performance platforms: (a) *La Comédie virtuelle* by Giles Jobin. (b) *DAZZLE* by Gibson/Martelli. (c) The prototype of *Theater of Tomorrow* by Zhen Wu.

As a global digital village, virtual space reduces the distance between bodies to create a meaningful and dynamic common area, as shown in Fig. 1(b). British duo artists Gibson / Martelli's piece *DAZZLE Ball 2020* reimagines the 1919 Chelsea Arts Club. *DAZZL Ball*[2] is a next-generation immersive performance in mixed reality (see Fig. 1b). These two pieces are pioneer projects of the virtual performing arts. They were both created in the era of the pandemic but challenged the difficulties faced by traditional performing arts. The new virtual platforms have developed the social media character through digital game technology. In the virtual venue, performers from different regions can co-create art pieces presented by digital virtual avatars on the virtual stage in the Internet cloud. In developing the motion capture module, the Animation Retargeting technology transfers the motion capture data to the digital figure. The audiences can also wander among their interactive devices. The integrated creating and entertaining tool has significant economic, social, and aesthetic values.

Theatre of Tomorrow (TOT) is a virtual exhibition and performing arts platform created by the author through digital game engine technologies. *TOT* doesn't exist in the physical world. This innovative virtual theater challenges the limitations of the interaction between the visual-Audio senses and the in-person experience. The exhibition is hosted by the network online. Through digital technology, the size of the virtual performer can be freely scaled up or down in the three-dimension space. Through virtual reality technology, the audience's perspective can be positioned anywhere in the virtual area, bringing different visual experiences to the audience [4]. They would have a very intense and authentic immersive experience (see Fig. 1c, Fig. 2a).

(a)   (b)   (c)

Fig. 2. The prototype of *TOT* and 3D scan technology: (a) The prototype of *TOT*. (b)(c) 3D scanning technology helped scan models of Mr. Solanyagi and his costumes and props.

---

[2] https://gibsonmartelli.com/dazzleball2020creativexr/.

3 Development of the Next Generation of the Virtual Exhibition and Performing Arts Platform

3.1 *Theatre of Tomorrow* has Both Social Media and Immersive Experiences

Theatre of Tomorrow combines motion capture with digital games to create a virtual reality immersive theater. It provides a virtual version of the choreography and performance platform for drama, dance, acrobatics, and other performing arts. It also functions as a museum exhibition, so worldwide audiences can attend the show online through smartphones, computers, VR glasses, and other devices. *Theatre of Tomorrow* adopts the architectural design concept of the China National Theater, The Classical Gardens of Suzhou, the water stage of the Bregenz Festival House, and the Shakespeare's Globe in the UK. In addition, it is an immersive multi-party interactive performing arts platform. The audience can participate in platform events on any device, computer, tablet, VR glasses, or smartphone through the Internet. Like a real-life theatre, *Theatre of Tomorrow* provides an immersive venue for audiences, each with a specific character incarnation, who gather to visit the museum and theatre, interact, and watch real-time performances together. The virtual digital performance at *Theatre of Tomorrow* involves dancers, performers, and engineers worldwide. And the programs can also be movies, concerts, gallery shows, or even performing arts played by AI (Artificial Intelligence). It has exciting interactive functions. During the pandemic, *Theatre of Tomorrow* has reshaped into a traditional exhibition and performing arts platform, showing a trend for displaying and serving arts platforms.

3.2 How the Next Generation of the Exhibition and Performing Arts Platform Could Be

Theatre of Tomorrow provides a multi-media platform for the show. It breaks the limitations of space and time, getting creators from different geographic locations to work together in a virtual community with virtual characters to complete the art projects for the virtual stage. Meanwhile, the creation will be permanently preserved as digital assets in the cloud Server or hard drive. Post-productions represent these archived art projects in different art forms, such as games, animation, and movies. *Theatre of Tomorrow* exhibits the Tibetan Reba Dance[3] *Snow* as a representative of the Chinese national intangible cultural heritage. In July 2021, Mr. Solang Yaci, the inheritor of Tibetan intangible culture, was invited to perform in the motion capture laboratory. The optical motion capture systems collect, sample, analyze, and archive his performance data. 3D scanning technology helped scan models of Mr. Solanyagi and his costumes and props. Afterward, the software creates digital dancers according to Tibetan dance and cultural characteristics in specific scenarios. The system would get as close as possible to represent actual performance (see Fig. 2b, 2c).

---

[3] https://www.mysterioustibet.com/tibetan-reba-dance-reba-dance-of-dengqen-county-in-qamdo.html. In recent years, the rapid development of gaming technology has made it possible to apply it to exhibitions and performances.

Theatre of Tomorrow is a virtual reality immersive system that collects Data and information meanwhile represents the outcome through game engine technologies. Compared to Laban movement analysis[4], this way visually archives the dance movement [5]. To help the audience enjoy the experience in the virtual theater even when there is no online performance, the developer builds the virtual stage according to the architectural structure of the actual theater. It has seats, side screens, sky curtains, booms, adjustable orchestra pools, and professional digital stage lights that can follow the performers' dance. To achieve a more realistic theater experience, a control room for lighting and sound has also been set up. The computer in this control room operates the program of the performance (see Fig. 3).

Fig. 3. Solang Yaci and his digitized body in *TOT*: (a) Virtual **Tibetan** dancer. (b) Optical mocap system collecting data from Solang Yaci. (c) Solang Yasi's digitized body is dancing in *TOT*.

Theatre of Tomorrow is also a social media platform where professionals can have a specific virtual community to create performing arts together and learn from each other. It is a virtual theater, an online museum, a learning space, and a public social space [6]. Audiences can choose and customize their characters or roles to make friends with similar interests and topics. The participator can interact with the web camera in real-time as an audience or performer, like a modern dancer, ballet dancer, Kunqu Opera actor, or cartoon character (see Fig. 4). The participator can upload photos they like on third-party platforms such as Character Creator or Readyplayer and customize the digital human avatar.

Fig. 4. (a) The audience is watching the show in *TOT* through Avatar. (b) The participator interacted with the web camera in real-time as an audience in *TOT*. (c) Digital Dancers Group.

The education of performing arts in the next-generation virtual performance platform: In the virtual space of *Theatre of Tomorrow*, students can follow teachers through

---

[4] https://en.wikipedia.org/wiki/laban_movement_analysis.

interactive devices to learn performances and even co-create art pieces. The system provides students a virtual theater stage environment to excite their learning interests. There are many different performing spaces inside *Theatre of Tomorrow,* a cyberpunk style of surrealist performance space, or stage in the kind of an ancient Chinese canal town. Students can learn how to program the interactive function through VR/AR facilities to create immersive experiences for the audience.

Fig. 5. (a), (b) The conception of a virtual exhibition and performing arts platform. (c) bone link formed by four bones mapping to the pose formed by two bones.

3.3   Develop a Game Engine to Capture Performance Data Through Different Motion Capture Technologies to Represent Digital Humans in Real Time

How to create a new space for the immersive performance? How to connect between the natural world and the virtual venue? To achieve these goals, the virtual online performance platform must integrate the performing data of different motion capture devices with the game engines and represent the digital figures in real time. It integrates digital game technology, motion capture systems, and remote collaboration tools. The platform will sync the movement of the digital figures with their original performers from different physical locations, developing game engine plug-ins based on the chain mapping principle.

3.3.1   Develop Game Engine Plug-Ins Based on the Chain Mapping Principle

With the development of technology in recent years, motion capture technology has been extensively developed. And there are many kinds of motion capture: Inertial Motion Capture[5], Optical Motion Capture[6] (passive and active), Marker-less motion capture[7], Marker-based motion tracking using Microsoft Kinect[8], etc. [6]. The cost of hardware has been reduced hugely. The development of digital game technology makes the motion capture process a one-click operation. Meanwhile, the system generates a real-time rendering. Then the audience could edit and download the captured data and rendered file.

---

[5] https://ps.is.mpg.de/pages/inertial-motion-capture.

[6] http://physbam.stanford.edu/cs448x/old/Optical_Motion_Capture_Guide.html.

[7] https://www.mo-sys.com/what-is-motion-capture-and-how-does-it-work/.

[8] https://www.sciencedirect.com/science/article/pii/S2405896318332828.

To process different data types, convert them into the same format, and locate the position in the virtual space remotely and accurately so that digital humans would not mess up, performing harmonically (can accurately present *pas de deux* or *pas de trois* in ballet). This requires using the technology of remote locating and other collaborative technologies to enable each digital performer of the different physical participators to have an accurate position to achieve synchronization. Motion capture represents the digital human's performance on the virtual stage through the Chain Mapping Principle.

Figure 5(c) above shows a bone link formed by four bones mapping to the pose formed by two bones. So how do you align the end bones? First, calculate the vector from the start bone to the end bone of the bone chain, such as A1 to B1. Then normalize these two vectors and determine the minimum rotation of turning B1 to A1. This rotation is demonstrated in quaternions, describing an axis perpendicular to both vectors plus a rotation angle Theta value. This quaternion calculation process can be obtained using the dot product, cross product, half angle orthonormal formula, and double hook orthonormal procedure of vectors, avoiding the expensive trigonometric function calculation process. The recipe below shows a simple calculation process. It can be seen that it uses vector calculation to optimize efficiency. as shown in Fig. 6.

$$a \cdot b = |a||b| \cos(\theta),$$
$$a \times b = |a||b| \sin(\theta)n,$$
$$Cosine(\theta/2) = (1 + cos\theta)/2,$$
$$sin(2\theta) = 2sin(\theta)cos(\theta),$$

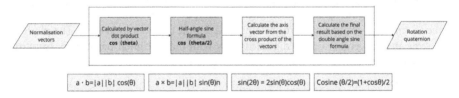

Fig. 6. Vector calculation to optimize efficiency.

Many software is developed to connect different types of motion capture system APIs (the acronym for Application Programming Interface)[9]. After the data collection, the software converts the information into standard formats, such as FBX, which can be transmitted to the remote end users through the server see Fig. 7(a), 7(b). The audience can access the virtual exhibition at home through a capture device such as Kinect or an inertial motion capture system such as Neuron. In the professional laboratories, the participators can even use the higher precise optical motion capture devices, such as Vicon[10], OptiTrack[11], CHINGMU[12], etc., to perform in the virtual platform. Participants

---

[9] https://www.mulesoft.com/resources/api/what-is-an-api.

[10] https://www.vicon.com/.

[11] https://optitrack.com/.

[12] http://www.chingmu.com/.

are often invited to co-create a work of art, which they perform alongside professional dancers. The system can represent the end users from different geographic regions using motion capture equipment in the same virtual stage space and then accurately sync the performance. By drawing the same size chessboard with the white tape on the moving capture sites in different regions, then making the actors wear motion capture equipment to perform in the chessboard, the camera of motion capture can be calibrated and positioned according to the chessboard. This method works appropriately for professional performance teams. Participants can adjust their positions through the keyboard (WASD key) and Xbox game /VR controllers. Participants that are physically from different regions but using the same motion capture technology will have more precise locational fusion in the virtual performing platform.

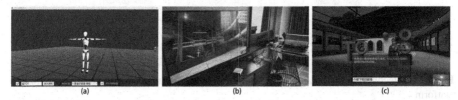

Fig. 7. Plug-ins and AI NPC in *TOT:* (a)(b) Plug-ins developed to connect Neurons and *TOT.* (c) AI NPC can answer the question from the audience.

3.3.2 The Gaming Function in the Next-Generation Virtual Exhibition and Performing Arts Platform

At this virtual venue, the dancers communicate with the audience in an immersive way, providing direct feedback to adjust their creations simultaneously. The audience wears HMD (Head Mounted Display)[13]; by setting up virtual figures in the system, they can feel the Augmented Reality in the virtual world. For example, a live venue dancer wearing motion capture equipment, making him or herself become Avatar[14], the dancer could respond to the participator's feedback in real-time, extending the motion capture touch beyond the virtual space. The live virtual reality performance integrates dancers and their avatars with the audience. The multi-characters online collaboration creates an art piece jointly, improving aesthetics and promoting sharing, especially in the pandemic era.

The system organizes and then analyzes the pre-captured motion data using motion capture technology. Combining traditional and contemporary art, the virtual platform demonstrates the dance arts' evolution. The preset default digital dancers can have different styles to choose from, such as a Reba dancer, the inheritor of Tibetan intangible culture, or a modern choreographer. By introducing new and better motion capture technologies, audiences can learn and create dance pieces in the virtual world (see Fig. 8).

---

[13] https://en.wikipedia.org/wiki/Head-mounted_display.

[14] https://en.wikipedia.org/wiki/Avatar_(computing).

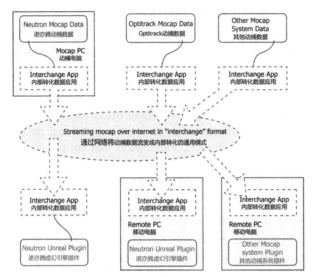

Fig. 8. The technology roadmap for the next-generation virtual exhibition and performing arts platform

3.4   AIGC Technology Allows NPC Digital Humans to Take on Roles Such as Teachers and Guides

In addition, the NPC (non-player character) in the *Theater of Tomorrow* is connected to ChatGPT by API. Using artificial intelligence technology, the dialogue of digital humans is self-generated with only essential information input. A role can be assigned to an NPC, a guide, a teacher… etc. The audience enters questions, and the AI NPC introduces related knowledge; see Fig. 7(c).

4   The Virtual Platform is a Complement to the Physical Venues

The virtual activities could only partially replace the physical theater performance. The virtual platform does have imperfect sides. The interactive digital game technology has the limitation of the number of the vertex/edge/face in the engineering model (including both characters and scene models). Therefore, the motion capture technology can only partially represent all the performers' subtle body movements and expressions. Thus, the system recreates the actual performance captured through the participants' computer cameras in the virtual space and keeps the participants and their digital humans synchronized harmonically. Unlike the Low poly digital human facial expression, the audience can now see the actual image and status of the other party, which is more like a video call in a virtual space. In *Theatre of Tomorrow*, the participants use computer cameras to capture their performance. All the data from different participants are assembled on the central server through the Internet. The virtual system platform would represent the performance remotely on the video monitors on the wall of the rehearsal room through advanced telecommunication technology in virtual space. Through the wall monitors, you can also see the Time Zone and the name of the different locations where the performers are. The dance of the digital human and the live video in the virtual display complement each other, making up for the stiff feeling of the digitally created actions.

According to the type of performance, there are several modules in the *Theatre of Tomorrow*: The Chinese Garden Theater, which introduced the architectural styles of Suzhou Museum(an I. M. Pei Masterwork), is planned to be a stage for Chinese Opera. The Music and Fashion Show venues are a stage for concerts and fashion shows. The International Theater is a modern architecture designed for traditional dance performance, drama, and opera. The Drama Theater, which has the design concept of Shakespeare's Globe, is the venue for the classical Shakespeare plays. The Contemporary Dance Theater is mainly used as a dance rehearsal place.

The narrow but long aisle at the entrance is designed to be the Art Museum. It exhibits fine arts, installations, and other visual arts. Because the space of *Theatre of Tomorrow* is vast, the audience can quickly reach the specific venue by setting the jump function on the map: pressing the spacebar, a map will appear, and moving the mouse to select the performance space. You can achieve fast jumping, as shown in Fig. 9 (a). Of course, there is also a transmission gate on each floor, which can be transmitted to different bases so the audience can avoid losing companions. Again, the online interactive function also limits the vertex/edge/face number in the engineering model, the lighting animation, and the rendering function. The combination of motion capture and dance also has some things that could be improved; for example, using motion capture technology to make avatar dance lacks a sense of weight and flow [7]. Therefore the final visual effect will be flawed. With the progress of science and technology, these problems will eventually be solved.

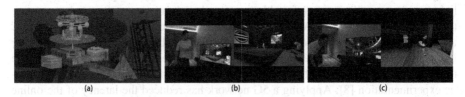

(a)   (b)   (c)

Fig. 9. Set the jump function on the map.

The system is currently used for distance education in secondary school dance education. In April 2023, in an experiment with the dance troupe of the Second Affiliated High School of Beijing Normal University, we used the system to test two groups of students (30 in total, divided into two identical groups according to same age and gender) for a period of 30 days (see Fig. 9b, 9c). A Chinese translation of a scale developed by Goodenow in 1993, the Psychological Sense of School Membership scale (PSSM, Goodenow, 1993)[15], was used. The experimental flow is shown below in Fig. 10. In the experiment, the independent variable was whether or not to use *TOT* for instruction; the dependent variable was students' sense of belonging to the teaching institution. Sense of belonging was measured in three dimensions: Caring relations, Acceptance, and Rejection, measured through different scale questions.

---

[15] https://files.eric.ed.gov/fulltext/ED622156.pdf/.

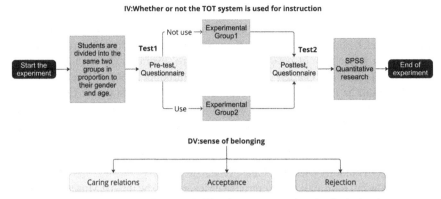

Fig. 10. The experimental flow

The results show that the system effectively enhances students' interest in performing and their sense of belonging to the school. Many people, including professional dancers and art enthusiasts, will use it.

5 The Future of the Virtual Exhibition and Performing Arts Platform

Digital gaming technology and the performing arts are becoming more and more closely integrated. With the development of virtual reality technology, VR glasses have become lighter, cheaper, and more comfortable to wear; the advancement of spatial computing technology (represented by Apple-vision-pro) and the development and use of AIGC technology, the enhancement of game technology has enabled audiences to have a better immersive experience; Digital humans will become more realistic and more accessible to be created, as a new form of self-representation will have been fertile ground for artistic experimentation [8]; Applying a 5G network has reduced the latency of the online performance interaction; Motion capture technology is becoming more mature, the cost is becoming more reasonable, and the accuracy of capture is becoming higher, which will make the integration of digital game technology and performing arts play an increasingly crucial role in the expression and creation of digital artworks. Dancers, audiences, educators, and learners will increasingly meet in virtual exhibitions and performing arts platforms such as *Theater of Tomorrow*, which will become a new trend in art creation [9].

Acknowledgments. Many thanks to Beijing Normal University Future Fund, No. 03800-111122113, which supports the development of *Theater of Tomorrow*.

References

1. Unreal Homepage. https://www.unrealengine.com/en-US/spotlights/unreal-engine-5-helps-aya-nakamura-stun-music-fans-in-the-fortnite-soundwave-series

2. FutureStage Homepage. https://mlml.io/p/futurestage/
3. Zylinska, J.: The Future of Media, 2nd edn. Goldsmiths Press, London (2022)
4. Strutt, D., Cisneros, R.: Virtual relationships: the dancer and the avatar. Virtual Models **7**(1–2), 61–81 (2021)
5. Salter, C.: Entangled: Technology and the Transformation of Performance, pp. 266–274. The MIT Press, London (2010)
6. Lu, L.: 3D virtual worlds as art media and exhibition arenas: students' responses and challenges in contemporary art education. Stud. Art Educ. **54**(3), 232–245 (2013)
7. Masura, N.: Digital Theatre: The Making and Meaning of Live Mediated Performance, US &UK 1990–2020, pp. 277–285. Palgrave Macmillan, Switzerland (2020)
8. Paul, C.: Digital Art. 3rd edn, pp. 250–259. Thames & Hudson World of Art, London (2015)
9. Rospigliosi, A.: Metaverse or Simulacra? Roblox, Minecraft, Meta, and the turn to virtual reality for education, socialization, and work. Interact. Learn. Environ. **30**(1), 1–3 (2022)

Reminder Bag: Designing Smart Bag for New Parents

Md Farhad Hossain and Mengru Xue$^{(\boxtimes)}$ 🄳

Ningbo Research Institute, Zhejiang University, Ningbo, China
mengruxue@zju.edu.cn

Abstract. Taking care of a newborn requires a lot of concentration on the part of the parent, who has to remember a lot of different things. It is challenging for new parents to remember and pack every item needed when bringing the baby out the door. In this paper, we present a reminder bag design that utilizes a pressure sensor to give a lighting alert when anything is missing from the bag. We carried out a pilot user study with 12 participants (9 mothers and 3 fathers) and a formal user study with 13 participants (8 fathers and 5 mothers) to understand their experiences with this reminder bag through interviews. According to the findings, the lighting feedback reminder works as an eye-catcher for parents to ensure they have packed all of the items needed for their babies outside trip, which can help them with stress reduction and practicality. This work transfers the focus from newborns to new parents in order to enable them to adapt to the new role with less burden. We discuss design implications and design guidelines for designing reminder systems to facilitate new parents' daily lives.

Keywords: Smart Bag · Reminder System · Pressure Sensor · New Parents

1 Introduction

Parents have to work hard to take care of their babies because inappropriate activities and practices that aren't right for babies can hurt them [19, 27]. Becoming a parent is sometimes recognized as one of the most challenging experiences in a person's lifetime [6]. Parents need a lot of focus and a good memory to take care of a new baby because they have to remember so many different things [1, 14]. In order to do so, they must pay close attention to the needs of the baby at all times. Whenever they go on a trip with their baby, they need to ensure that they remember to bring all of the items that are necessary for the baby.

There are several instances in which they consistently fail to remember to carry essential items, and the bags don't do a very good job of letting them know when something is missing from the pack. Consider the diaper bag as an example. This bag keeps clean diapers, wipes, a changing pad, lotion, hand sanitizer, finger foods, chew toys, a change of clothes, and much more all in the same place. While the bag keeps all the items together, it makes it difficult for mothers to remember if a critical item, such as sanitizing wipes, is missing, and this can lead to a rather embarrassing and stressful moment [16, 17]. As a result, they have to put up with the situation and the inconvenience brought.

In this paper, we present a smart bag design for a reminder that uses modular pressure sensors to provide lighting feedback when any items are missing from the bag. The feedback indicates that there is something that should have been in the bag but is not there. The bag uses a modular pressure sensor that is easily removable. Parents can customize the number of pockets used. And they can tag their commonly used items on the front of each pocket.

We carried out a pilot user study with 12 participants (9 mothers and 3 fathers) and a formal user study with 13 participants (8 fathers and 5 mothers) to understand their experiences with this smart bag through interviews. The vast majority of the parents who took part in the research were enthusiastic about the idea of a smart reminder bag, as evidenced by qualitative data analysis. However, a few of the users pointed out that the bag we utilized was tiny, which made it a little bit difficult for them to package everything. They also offered creative ideas regarding how the concept could be improved. Finally, we address the design insights of creating reminder systems as well as the design criteria for designing such systems in order to make new parents' everyday lives easier.

2 Related Work

Improper baby product procedures and activities may harm babies, making it a challenging task for parents. To keep track of a wide variety of specific things, parents require a lot of attention and a good memory [2]. The forgetting of objects is an everyday problem [13, 18]. As a result, it is necessary to constantly remind them to make their lives easier.

According to the findings of a number of studies, there are a variety of different approaches that are referred to as "reminders" that families take in order to successfully juggle the competing demands of their jobs, their families, their homes, and their participation in enrichment activities [12, 15, 26]. It's like a spell checker that helps a youngster spell better or an activity pack that helps them build routines. However, there is no specific concept of a reminder that is able to remind the user.

Scholars at Simon Fraser developed the Lady Bag, a series of concepts for lady's handbags that use LEDs [26]. Such as the Torch Bag, one use of the bag is for self-expression. Their designs also showed the usage of an RFID system, which meant that the LEDs would be able to function in order to communicate with one another when an item was missing. However, using an RFID system does come with a few limitations [21]. RFID comes at the cost of an increasing number of possible security and privacy threats and attacks [14]. Particularly, RFID tags are usually larger than bar-code labels, and tags are application-specific because most tags are attached to the inside of the back cover. Also, tags may cause interference with each other when placed within 1/8 of an inch of each other [14].

Additionally, there are several other studies that provide a conceptual reminder for various sites [9, 11, 24, 26]. These investigations are likewise making use of the method of reminder. Based on what older people said they wanted and needed, studies show some of the needs and wants of older users for a multi-modal reminder system.

The findings of past research have led to the discovery of a variety of distinct reminder concepts, each of which may be applied using a range of alternative methods. Following an investigation into the benefits and drawbacks of several reminder systems, it was found that the majority of the systems do not seem to have a well-defined reminder that is able to bring something to the user's attention in a dependable manner. Also, there are currently no adequate reminders available to help new parents remember to carry vital necessities for their newborns.

3   Reminder Bag

The objective of this project is to design a smart reminder bag aimed at alleviating the burden of forgetfulness for new parents, ensuring they carry all necessary supplies for their baby and enhancing their overall experience. The rest of this section describes the system design and the implementation of the smart bag reminder prototype in detail.

3.1   System Design

The system consists of a pressure sensor module which gives a lighting alarm when the pressure sensor receives the pressure. In this paper, we design a reminding system in the context of bringing a newborn outdoors. Under the above conditions, we thought it was important that the reminder system be portable and give feedback in real time. Moreover, due to the limitations of RFID, a pressure sensor should be implemented. For the reasons stated above, our research team believes that "bag" is an ambient and excellent media to embed the reminder system. It is the most context-relevant product since it is direct and has sufficient space for inserting sensors unobtrusively.

There have been a number of projects in which the concept of the smart bag reminder has been used [12, 16]. In a similar vein, we were intrigued by the smart bag reminder concept. Following an investigation into the advantages and disadvantages of a number of different reminder systems, we came up with the concept of a reminder bag system that consists of a pressure sensor module [4] that gives a lighting alarm when the pressure sensor receives the pressure. This light alarm serves as a prompt reminder for new mothers whenever they forget to pack something, and the system is designed to be portable and easy to use.

The system remind the user in a speedy manner at the appropriate time without the need for any extra programs. Existing reminder methods [5, 13, 22, 25], such as using a variety of programs, may be able to support the reminder process. However, this may occasionally cause users to experience technical difficulties while using the application. A pressure sensor module was used in the development of reminder bag so that we could provide immediate and generalized reminder input. We decided to utilize a LED light that can be rapidly glanced at to increase users' awareness of the reminder signal. There is a number of additional studies that together provide a conceptual recall for various areas [8, 10, 23]. We thought that this sort of reminder could prove to be beneficial to users.

3.2 Implementation

The research utilized a baby essentials bag as the main platform. It featured six pockets (four interior, two exterior) as depicted in Fig. 1(a, c).

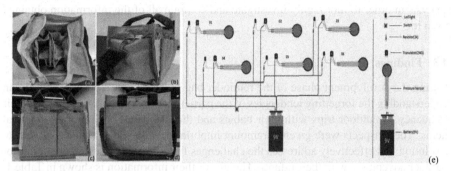

Fig. 1. (a, b, c, d) The design of reminder bag and (e) The technical implementation of reminder bag.

4 Pilot User Study

The purpose of the pilot user research was to acquire a deeper understanding of the challenges that are encountered by mothers in their everyday lives and their visions with a reminder bag concept.

4.1 Procedure

Due to the pandemic policy, we conducted a pilot user study online and recruited 12 users (9 mothers and 3 fathers) from different countries using the linear snowball sampling technique via social media. All the participants signed the consent form to participate in this interview. We begin by investigating the behaviors of parents and how often they take their babies outdoors. We inquire about the challenges they face while packaging for such trips, the frequency of their outdoor excursions with the baby, and their tendencies regarding forgetting essential items. By gathering this comprehensive data, we aim to gain valuable insights into the patterns and pain points that new parents encounter during these outings.

After that, we conducted a video demonstration of our reminder bag system. During the demonstration, we highlighted how this system could potentially serve as a solution to assist them in remembering the essential items they often forget to pack when taking their baby outdoors. We then sought valuable feedback from the participants to share their observations regarding the bag's advantages, limitations, and suggestions for further enhancement. By gathering their input, we aimed to gain valuable insights to refine and optimize the reminder bag, ensuring it meets the specific needs and preferences of parents and ultimately providing a more effective and user-friendly solution for their outdoor activities.

4.2 Data Collection and Analysis

While we were conducting the interviews, we recorded the whole process under their consent so that we could later use them to compile qualitative data analysis. The data obtained from the interview questions was subjected to an approach known as thematic analysis in order to thoroughly investigate and compile all of the information obtained from it.

4.3 Findings

During the development phase of the reminder bag, our research focused primarily on understanding the forgetting tendencies of the participants, particularly concerning their frequency of outdoor trips with their babies and the likelihood of forgetting essential items. These aspects were given paramount importance in the design process to create a solution that effectively addresses the challenges faced by parents when preparing for outdoor adventures with their infants. The gist of their information is shown in Table 1.

Table 1. Behaviors of participants, including forgetting behaviors and the habit of taking outdoor trips with their babies.

Participants	Nationality	Habit of taking baby outdoor	Forgetting behaviors
P1	Bangladesh	Usually	Never
P2	Bangladesh	Rarely	Frequently
P3	Bangladesh	Sometimes	Frequently
P4	United Kingdom	Often	Occasionally
P5	Bangladesh	Rarely	Frequently
P6	Bangladesh	Sometimes	Occasionally
P7	Bangladesh	Usually	Occasionally
P8	Bangladesh	Often	Occasionally
P9	Bangladesh	Rarely	Frequently
P10	Saudi Arabia	Sometimes	Frequently
P11	Bangladesh	Usually	Occasionally
P12	Bangladesh	Usually	Frequently

Benefit of the Reminder Bag. The emergence of innovative design concepts has engendered novel avenues for enhancing user experience and productivity. The reminder bag, an inventive concept that seamlessly integrates functionality and aesthetics, has been meticulously investigated in this research. Our study seeks to unravel the inherent potential of the reminder bag in capturing attention and serving as an effective memory aid.

Through a comprehensive user-centric study, we delved into the intricate dynamics of the reminder bag's impact on user behavior. A diverse group of participants, each with unique memory-related tendencies, engaged in the study. The participants showed different extent of forgetfulness in their daily life (frequent forgetters, occasional forgetters, and non-forgetters).

Attention-Captivating Design: The configuration of the reminder bag emerged as a pivotal factor influencing its efficacy as a reminder. Participants expressed an affinity for the reminder bag's design, highlighting its ability to effortlessly attract attention. Their language was replete with positivity, underlining the integration of the reminder feature into the bag's design. This convergence of form and function resonated well with users, setting the reminder bag apart.

Favorable Reception Among Frequent Forgetters: Participants identified as frequent forgetters (P2, P3, P5, P9, P10, and P12) showed a heightened receptiveness to the reminder bag. The design's straightforwardness garnered favorable commendation, with users acknowledging its simplicity in aiding their memory. Their enthusiastic response to the prototype underscores the reminder bag's potential to address a persistent challenge.

Accessibility for Various User Groups: Participants who occasionally experienced forgetfulness (P4, P6, P7, P8, and P11) acknowledged the reminder bag's potential to serve diverse user segments. These participants recognized the concept's applicability beyond tech-savvy individuals, envisioning its utility for parents who might not be accustomed to app-based reminders. Their endorsements emphasize the inclusive nature of the reminder bag's design.

Attention Enhancement for Non-forgetters: Even among participants who seldom forgot items (P1), the reminder bag's allure as an attention enhancer was noted. While he didn't face forgetfulness challenges frequently, he acknowledged the potential benefits of the reminder bag in augmenting vigilance and mindfulness. This dynamic showcases the cross-functional versatility of the design.

Our research illuminates the multifaceted advantages of the reminder bag design concept. Its capacity to seamlessly blend aesthetics with functionality resonates strongly with users of diverse memory inclinations. The reminder bag possesses the potential to alleviate forgetfulness-related woes while simultaneously offering an aesthetic and accessible solution to a wider user spectrum. Through a strategic convergence of design and user psychology, the reminder bag epitomizes the harmonious synergy between aesthetics and utility in contemporary product innovation.

Design Challenges. Research on the reminder bag's design confirmed the initial idea and revealed key challenges to address in the next iteration. During the process of our user research, the vast majority of users commented that "more electrical wire, which can cause technical issues". Additionally, some users (P6 and P7) felt the bag's size was too small, suggesting a larger size might be more practical in their daily use. Another participant (P8) recommended incorporating a sound alarm along with the light, to make the design more unique.

5 Formal User Study

The pilot study was conducted using an online interview due to the pandemic situation. However, to gain a comprehensive understanding of the users' demands, we deemed it necessary to conduct an offline field study. A formal user study was carried out to thoroughly assess the user experience with our prototype design.

5.1 Procedure

We went to a nearby children's park, where parents often brought their newborns to socialize and have fun. We found one mother to participate at the park, and using linear snowball sampling, we recruited a total of 13 participants (8 fathers and 5 mothers), who were the baby's primary carer.

Fig. 2. During the user study, (a) interviewing the mother, (b) showing her the bag and letting her try it out, (c) ask the mother packaging items using our reminder bag, and (d) carrying her baby with our reminder bag design.

All participants provided written informed consent. Our goal was to gain insights into their daily lives and interactions with a reminder bag designed for parents. In the initial phase of our research, we conducted interviews to explore the hobbies and behaviors of participants when taking their babies outdoors. This step provided valuable insights into their current practices and challenges faced during packing for such outings. Then, we presented the participants with the design of our reminder bag and allowed them to engage in a practical exercise of packing the bag (Fig. 2). This hands-on approach allowed us to observe their interactions with the bag and gain feedback on its usability and effectiveness. In the final stage, we conducted follow-up interviews with the participants, seeking their opinions on the reminder bag's design. We also encouraged them to share their suggestions for improvements and identify any potential drawbacks they noticed during the practical exercise.

5.2 Data Collection and Analyses

The data gathered from the participants' responses to the questions was meticulously recorded. We transcribed all the data using a methodical approach known as thematic analysis to comprehensively investigate and synthesize the information obtained.

5.3 Findings

In the course of our investigation, participants provided us with compelling insights into their engagement with the task we offered. Among the thirteen participants, an appreciable nine displayed proficiency in correctly discerning the bag's role as a mnemonic aide. Their accounts conveyed that the ambient illumination, triggered during the act of packing, became a focal point that captured their attention. As they methodically filled the bag's compartments, this luminous input served as a beacon, guiding them to the areas awaiting items.

The consequence of this light-guided approach was manifestly evident in the expeditiousness with which the packing process unfolded. Notably, the participant designated as P3 demonstrated exceptional efficiency, culminating in the shortest completion time. Reflecting upon this phenomenon, P8 voiced, "while packing, my attention was solely on the illumination within those compartments where light was visible. Subsequently, I noticed that I had neglected to position an object within those spaces, despite having already sealed them." Mirroring this sentiment, (P5) emerged as another rapid achiever, articulating, "during the packaging undertaking, my focus shifted between the empty and occupied compartments. The interaction of light served as an instinctive mentor, unveiling the pockets that demanded attention by means of illumination, a visual hint for my diligent behavior."

Notwithstanding the commendable success of the aforementioned participants, a subset including P2, P4, P7, and P9 grappled with a precise grasp of the device's intended function. In their perception, the nightly packing ritual assumed a distinct dimension wherein the light-mediated feedback was construed as a facilitator, enhancing visibility into the bag's contents. However, upon probing whether this luminous feedback could potentially serve as a mnemonic device, a paradigm shift transpired. This cohort collectively recognized the innovative light-based reminder, foreseeing its utility as an enhancer of attentiveness and an aide-memoire, forestalling the inadvertent omission of items during the packing endeavor.

In the broader context of their lives, the participants offered poignant insights. The exigencies of attending to infants necessitate the carriage of an assortment of paraphernalia. Here, the illuminated reminder emerges as an invaluable ally, augmenting vigilance and mitigating forgetfulness a sentiment poignantly captured by (P11): "the light feedback appears as heightened attentiveness. It introduces us to a novel packaging method that prevents objects from being accidentally excluded." Echoing this sentiment, P12 astutely noted, "considering the variety of memory aids available in everyday life, this specific form of integrating mild feedback with no unnecessary uses is both innovative and intriguing."

The participants' responses evinced a palpable satisfaction stemming from the notion of light-mediated feedback. Their discourse, infused with optimism and affirmation, served to substantiate the design's underlying concept. Concurrently, the exercise unearthed areas for refinement. Predominantly, participants identified the luminosity deficiency of the light as an impediment. Furthermore, the external wiring configuration incurred unintended implications for addressing technical anomalies an aspect meriting focused resolution.

Our empirical exploration delved into the profundities of participants' engagement with the proposed concept. Their narratives not only validated the efficacy of light-guided reminders but also illuminated nuances warranting further refinement. Through their eloquent articulation, the participants illuminated the path towards enhancing our design, underscoring the intricate interplay between aesthetics, utility, and technical implementation.

However, there were also valuable suggestions and considerations for improvement, particularly related to personalization, durability, aesthetics, and pricing. Participants recommended adding adjustable compartments or customizable reminder labels for personal preferences and needs. They also suggested increasing the bag's size and using durable, easy-to-clean materials for longevity and usability. Integrating the bag with a mobile app for real time updates and personalized packing suggestions was proposed by some. Additionally, using eco-friendly materials aligned with environmentally conscious parenting trends was emphasized.

6 Discussion

In the bustling milieu of parenting, the role of caregivers has evolved to encompass a myriad of tasks beyond child care. This research addresses the need to aid parents in managing their complex responsibilities by introducing a novel concept of the reminder bag. In a world teeming with various bag types and parental requirements, the integration of customizable modular sensing technology emerges as a pivotal solution. By catering to a range of bag styles and facilitating the incorporation of multiple pockets, the design imbues adaptability and relevance to individual parenting scenarios.

Flexibility and Modular Sensing: Central to this study is the notion of flexibility and modularity, which underpin the reminder bag's transformative capabilities. The bag's design, encompassing six pockets in the current iteration, serves as a foundational model, fostering the idea that pockets can be tailored to fit specific parenting needs. The number and arrangement of pockets are not predefined. They can be fine-tuned according to the carer's requirements. This malleability of design is rooted in the essence of modular sensing, allowing for seamless transitions between various bag configurations and ensuring the technology's applicability across a spectrum of caregiving situations.

User Survey and Versatility: A comprehensive user survey was conducted to gauge the potential of the reminder bag beyond its initial scope. Participants from diverse backgrounds highlighted the universality of the concept, echoing its adaptability not only for parents but also for students, office workers, and individuals from various walks of life. The results underscored the reminder bag's capacity to serve as an intelligent reminder system, fostering efficient organization and planning. The study's findings illuminate the bag's potential to transcend caregiving, presenting an aesthetic embodiment of functional versatility.

Transitioning Attention and Nurturing Preparedness: In the context of parenting, the prevailing discourse often centers on infant care. However, this research redirects attention towards parents themselves, acknowledging the myriad challenges they face in tandem with child-rearing responsibilities. The reminder bag emerges as a catalyst for preparedness, recognizing that caregivers are juggling multiple roles. Through its strategic reminder system, the bag eases the cognitive load on parents, streamlining their packing routines and enhancing their readiness for daily excursions. The Bag's capacity to intelligently prompt caregivers to pack essential items elevates its significance as an embodiment of thoughtful assistance.

In a dynamic world where caregiving transcends conventional boundaries, the reminder bag encapsulates the synergy of flexible design and modular sensing, revolutionizing parental support. This research establishes a foundation for future endeavors, inviting further exploration into personalized assistance and adaptive technologies that harmonize with the evolving demands of modern parenting. As we shift our gaze from infants to parents, the reminder bag stands as a testament to the fusion of aesthetics, functionality, and transformative design.

7 Future Work and Conclusion

Following the experiment, the feedback provided by the participants served as a catalyst for us to contemplate the potential for elevating the aesthetics of the reminder bag prototype. This contemplation arose as we entered the subsequent iteration of the design process. Our objective is to enable users to cultivate an emotional connection while employing the reminder bag within the milieu of their real-life experiences. As we progress to the subsequent phase of this research endeavor, our primary focus is to comprehensively grasp the outcomes of the user study. This will be achieved by refining the design and implementation of the prototype, drawing inspiration from the novel insights that have emerged from this research exploration.

This paper delves into the development of a reminding system designed to accompany parents when taking their newborns outdoors. The central aim of this work is to shift the attention from the infants to the new parents, facilitating their seamless transition into parenthood by alleviating some of the associated challenges. Through our discourse, we delve into the implications and guidelines surrounding the design of reminder systems, aimed at enhancing the daily lives of these new parents.

References

1. Abdul Razak, F.H., Sulo, R., Wan Adnan, W.A.: Elderly mental model of reminder system. In: Proceedings of the 10th Asia Pacific Conference on Computer Human Interaction, August 2012, pp. 193–200 (2012)
2. Brewer, R.N., Morris, M.R., Lindley, S.E.: How to remember what to remember: exploring possibilities for digital reminder systems. Proc. ACM Interact. Mob. Wearable Ubiquit. Technol. 1(3), 1–20 (2017)
3. Barclay, L., Everitt, L., Rogan, F., Schmied, V., Wyllie, A.: Becoming a mother an analysis of women's experience of early motherhood. J. Adv. Nurs. 25(4), 719–728 (1997)
4. Beech, S., Geelhoed, E., Murphy, R., Parker, J., Sellen, A., Shaw, K.: Lifestyles of working parents: Implications and opportunities for new technologies. HP Tech report HPL-2003-88 (R.1) (2004)

5. Fikry, M.: Requirements analysis for reminder system in daily activity recognition dementia: Phd forum abstract. In: Proceedings of the 18th Conference on Embedded Networked Sensor Systems, November 2020, pp. 815–816 (2020)
6. Gibson, L., Hanson, V.L.: Digital motherhood: how does technology help new mothers? In: Proceedings of the SIGCHI Conference on Human Factors in Computing Systems, April 2013, pp. 313–322 (2013)
7. Groß-Vogt, K.: The drinking reminder: prototype of a smart jar. In: Proceedings of the 15th International Conference on Audio Mostly, September 2020, pp. 257–260 (2020)
8. Harjuniemi, E., Häkkilä, J.: Smart handbag for remembering keys. In Proceedings of the 22nd International Academic Mindtrek Conference, October 2018, pp. 244–247 (2018)
9. Hansson, R., Ljungstrand, P.: The reminder bracelet: subtle notification cues for mobile devices. In: Extended Abstracts on Human Factors in Computing Systems, CHI 2000, April 2000, pp. 323–324 (2000)
10. Kim, S.W., Kim, M.C., Park, S.H., Jin, Y.K., Choi, W.S.: Gate reminder: a design case of a smart reminder. In: Proceedings of the 5th conference on Designing interactive systems: processes, practices, methods, and techniques, August 2004, pp. 81–90 (2004)
11. LadyBag Project. http://www.ladybag.official.ws/
12. Lee, M.K., Davidoff, S., Zimmerman, J., Dey, A.K.: Smart bag: managing home and raising children. In: Proceedings of the 2007 Conference on Designing Pleasurable Products and Interfaces, August 2007, pp. 434–437 (2007)
13. McGee-Lennon, M. R., Wolters, M.K., Brewster, S.: User-centred multimodal reminders for assistive living. In: Proceedings of the SIGCHI Conference on Human Factors in Computing Systems, May 2011, pp. 2105–2114 (2011)
14. Marquardt, N., Taylor, A.S., Villar, N., Greenberg, S.: Rethinking RFID: awareness and control for interaction with RFID systems. In: Proceedings of the SIGCHI Conference on Human Factors in Computing Systems, April 2010, pp. 2307–2316 (2010)
15. Nanda, G., Cable, A., Bove, V.M., Ho, M., Hoang, H.: bYOB [Build Your Own Bag] a computationally-enhanced modular textile system. In: Proceedings of the 3rd International Conference on Mobile and Ubiquitous Multimedia, October 2004, pp. 1–4 (2004)
16. Park, S.Y., Zimmerman, J.: Investigating the opportunity for a smart activity bag. In: Proceedings of the SIGCHI Conference on Human Factors in Computing Systems, April 2010, pp. 2543–2552 (2010)
17. Petre, M., et al.: The interactive punching bag. In: CHI'12 Extended Abstracts on Human Factors in Computing Systems, pp. 1469–1470 (2012)
18. Reschke, D., Böhmer, M., Sorg, M.: Tactifloor: design and evaluation of vibration signals for doorway reminder systems. In: Proceedings of the 16th International Conference on Mobile and Ubiquitous Multimedia, November 2017, pp. 449–455 (2017)
19. Roy, S., Bhattacharya, U.: Smart Mom: an architecture to monitor children at home. In: Proceedings of the Third International Symposium on Women in Computing and Informatics, August 2015, pp. 614–623 (2015)
20. Stawarz, K., Cox, A.L., Blandford, A.: Don't forget your pill! Designing effective medication reminder apps that support users' daily routines. In: Proceedings of the SIGCHI Conference on Human Factors in Computing Systems, April 2014, pp. 2269–2278 (2014)
21. Sheth, D.S., Singh, S., Mathur, P.S., Vydeki, D.: Smart laptop bag with machine learning for activity recognition. In: 2018 Tenth International Conference on Advanced Computing (ICoAC), December 2018, pp. 164–171. IEEE (2018)
22. Uhlig, M., Rieß, H., Klein, P.: Reminder objects in the connected home of the future and beyond. Technologies 6(1), 1 (2017)
23. Williamson, J.R., McGee-Lennon, M., Freeman, E., Brewster, S.: Designing a smartpen reminder system for older adults. In: CHI'13 Extended Abstracts on Human Factors in Computing Systems, pp. 73–78 (2013)

24. Williamson, J.R., McGee-Lennon, M., Brewster, S.: Designing multimodal reminders for the home: pairing content with presentation. In: Proceedings of the 14th ACM international conference on Multimodal interaction, October 2012, pp. 445–448 (2012)
25. Warnock, D.: The application of multiple modalities for improved home care reminders. In: CHI'12 Extended Abstracts on Human Factors in Computing Systems, pp. 951–954 (2012)
26. Zimmerman, J.: Designing for the self: making products that help people become the person they desire to be. In: Proceedings of the SIGCHI Conference on Human Factors in Computing Systems, April 2009, pp. 395–404 (2009)
27. Zhang, L., Liu, L., Ying, W., Huang, M., Yao, C., Ying, F.: ModHera: a modular kit for parents to take care babies. In: Interaction Design and Children, June 2021, pp. 547–551 (2021)

A Study on the Emotional Responses to Visual Art

Zhenyu Liu[1(✉)], Cheng Yao[1], Qiurui Wang[2], and Fangtian Ying[3]

[1] College of Computer Science and Technology, Zhejiang University, Hangzhou, China
{liuzhenyu0713,yaoch}@zju.edu.cn
[2] Department of Industrial Design, Eindhoven University of Technology, Eindhoven,
The Netherlands
q.wang1@tue.nl
[3] School of Industrial Design, Hubei University of Technology, Wuhan, China

Abstract. We experimented with examining how Visual Art affects people's emotional responses to images. Participants viewed 27 images from our art image database, which were either static or dynamic. We aimed to gather subjective data through self-reports and physiological measures like skin conductance and heart rate to assess emotional responses. The results showed that dynamic pictures significantly increased arousal, incredibly when the image was already arousing. Both self-report measures and skin conductance data supported these findings. Additionally, dynamic picture motion elicited more heart-rate deceleration, indicating greater attention toward highly arousing images. However, the influence of dynamic pictures on affective valence was only evident in self-report measures. Images with motion were rated as more positive if they were positive, to begin with, and more damaging if they were negative. These findings have important implications for understanding the impact of dynamic pictures on emotional responses and can be applied to fields such as psychology, marketing, and media studies. Further research is needed to delve deeper into the underlying mechanisms of these effects.

Keywords: Visual art · Emotional responses · Physiological data

1 Experiment Design

This study utilized a dual within-subject design to investigate the impact of dynamic images on emotional responses. The design consisted of two components: a 2 (dynamic) X 3 (positive, neutral, and negative valence) design and a 2 (dynamic) X 3 (low, medium, and high arousal) design. To establish the categorical emotion variables, the images were sorted based on participants' self-reported ratings for each dimension.

Each participant was required to view 27 different images twice: once in a static format and once in a dynamic format. Simultaneous physiological data collection was conducted during both viewings. After each of the 54 image presentations, participants rate their emotional response to the previously viewed image (see Fig. 1).

© IFIP International Federation for Information Processing 2023
Published by Springer Nature Switzerland AG 2023
P. Ciancarini et al. (Eds.): ICEC 2023, LNCS 14455, pp. 450–460, 2023.
https://doi.org/10.1007/978-981-99-8248-6_43

Eighteen undergraduate students from Zhejiang University participated in this study. The participants represented four majors: Computer Science, Art, Psychology, and Industrial Design. Of the 18 participants, eight were male and ten were female, with a mean age of 20.6 years.

Fig. 1. Some images used for the experiment.

2   Stimuli

The stimuli utilized in this study consisted of 27 diverse images obtained from our art image database. These images were carefully selected to encompass various emotional experiences, measured by valence and arousal ratings. Both valence and arousal are significant emotional dimensions examined in this study [5]. Each stimulus was presented for 6 s during the experiment, appearing as either a dynamic or static version of the same image. The static version of each image consisted of a single frame that accurately represented the full-motion clip. All images, including instructions for the rating task, were stored on a disc. This disc was connected to a computer for a smooth presentation of the stimuli [3].

The sequence and duration of the stimuli were controlled by a program that managed the order and timing of stimulus presentation. To ensure fairness and avoid any potential bias, the order in which participants viewed the dynamic or static versions of the pictures was counterbalanced across different orders [15].

3 Measurement

3.1 Skin Conductance

Skin conductance responses were measured using a Coulbourn Model S21-22 constant voltage skin conductance coupler. The coupler maintained a constant voltage of 0.5V and had a time constant of 5 s. Before recording, the palm of the nonpreferred hand was cleaned with distilled water to ensure accurate readings. Beckman Standard Ag/AgCl electrodes with a diameter of 0.5 cm were placed on the thenar and hypothenar eminence of the palm. Johnson & Johnson KY Jelly was applied as an electrolyte to ensure proper conductivity [13].

3.2 Heart Rate

Heart-rate data was collected by attaching a Grass photoplethysmograph transducer (Model PPS) to the participant's right ear lobe. This transducer accurately measured and recorded the participant's heart-rate readings throughout the experiment [4]. The signal from the photocell was routed into a Grass Model 7P1 Low-Level DC Preamplifier and Model 7D Driver Amplifier. From there, the signal was transmitted to a Grass Model 7P4 Cardiotachometer. The cardio tachometer converted the interpulse intervals into heart rate measurements, expressed in beats per minute (BPM). This process allowed for accurate and precise tracking of participants' heart rates throughout the experiment [18].

3.3 Self-report

The Hamilton Depression Scale (HAMD) and the Autism Treatment Assessment Scale (ATAS) were used. The indicators covered by the HAMD are self-care, language, motor, communication, and sensory abilities.

The data were analysed using SPSS software. The measurement data were expressed as ($x \pm s$) and t-test for comparison between groups. The difference was considered statistically significant at $P < 0.05$. 18 participants were requested to rate each image's level of interest on a continuous line. For each image, the 18 participants were asked to rate the level of interest on a continuous line. This line was labeled with the descriptors "boring" and "interesting," and participants marked their rating accordingly. Additionally, participants rated the valence of each image using a nine-point Self-Assessment Manikin (SAM) scale [6]. To assess the level of arousal evoked by each image, participants utilized a visual scale consisting of five graphics representing a gender-neutral human figure (manikin) with varying levels of visceral agitation [12]. The graphics ranged from a calm and relaxed figure to an intensely agitated figure. Participants indicated their level of arousal by marking on or in between the graphics, reflecting the extent of visceral agitation experienced in response to each image.

4 Procedure

After a brief introduction about the stimuli, rating task, and recording techniques, 18 participants were asked to provide informed consent by signing a form. Next, skin conductance electrodes were attached to their non-dominant hands. They were then guided to a comfortable room with an armchair placed approximately 1.4 m away from the Monitor. The ear attachment of the photoplethysmograph was checked to ensure the quality of physiological recordings. Subsequently, complete instructions were given to the participants, and they were provided with two neutral practice trials.

Before commencing the experiment, several conditions were ensured. Firstly, it was confirmed that the participants clearly understood the instructions and had accurately completed the practice trials. Additionally, the quality of the physiological recordings was verified to be free from interference or disturbances. The experiment consisted of a total of 54 trials, which were controlled by two laboratory computers. The first computer, a 486 PC, initiated each trial and collected the physiological data. The second computer, a Macintosh, was responsible for controlling the disc player. At the beginning of each trial, a signal was transmitted from the PC to the Macintosh through a simple serial connection. The Macintosh then proceeded to display one of the 27 images, either in a still or moving form, for six seconds. After the clip concluded, the viewing screen turned dark for one second, followed by a four-second presentation of instructions for rating the image on three scales - valence, arousal, and interest [16]. Participants were given clear instructions to rate the image promptly and to divert their attention back to the screen before the subsequent image was displayed. The duration of the rating period varied randomly between 17 and 27 s. The collection of physiological data initiated two seconds before the presentation of the image and persisted for a duration of 10 s.

At the midpoint of the experiment, the experimenter returned to the viewing room to grant the participants a brief break. During this break, the experimenter ensured that the participants were on the correct page of the rating booklet. Once the experiment ended, the participants were verbally debriefed and provided with a concise written explanation of the experiment, accompanied by pertinent citations [14]. Each participant's involvement in the entire experiment lasted less than an hour.

5 Data Analysis

The initial data analysis stage consisted of computing each image's average valence and arousal ratings, regardless of whether they were still or moving. The valence means were then arranged from the most positive to the least positive, and the set of 27 images was divided into three categories: 9 positive, 9 neutral, and 9 negative images. Likewise, the arousal means were ranked from lowest to highest, and the images were categorized into three groups based on arousal level: 9 low-, medium-, and high-arousal images, irrespective of their static or dynamic nature.

The heart rate and skin conductance data were categorized based on valence and arousal categories. All dependent measures were then subjected to a repeated-measures analysis of variance (ANOVA). The within-subject variables included image category (valence or arousal) and motion. To represent the category variable, orthogonal trends were employed. The linear trend $(1, 0, -1)$ captured the contrast between positive and negative valence or low and high arousal. On the other hand, the quadratic trend $(1, -2, 1)$ represented the contrast between the middle category and the two extremes.

In addition to analyzing trends related to image categories and movements, the heart rate analysis also considered changes in heart rate over time. This analysis examined orthogonal trends across the fifteen half-second data points [10].

6 Results

6.1 Heart Rate

Upon the onset of the image stimuli, the heart rate response exhibited a predominant deceleration pattern. Shortly after the stimuli were presented, the heart rate started to decrease and remained below the baseline throughout the recording period. Figure 2 presents heart rate per half-second as a function of image valence (left-hand panel), image arousal (center panel), and image motion (right-hand panel). The significant linear trend across the presentation period $(F(1,16) = 16.90, p < .001)$ accounted for 70% of the relevant variance. Heart-rate change was significantly related to both emotion properties of the stimuli (i.e., valence and arousal). Participants experienced larger decelerations in response to negative images than to positive images $(F(1,16) = 8.52, p < .01)$, and both high- and low-arousal images elicited more deceleration than medium arousal images $(F(1,16) = 7.62, p < .05)$.

The effects of motion on heart-rate response were intricate. As depicted in the right-hand panel of Fig. 2, motion had a gradually unfolding impact on heart rate over time (Motion X Half-second $F(14,224) = 3.39, p < .01$). The differentiation between heart-rate responses to still and moving images was most pronounced as the image progressed. More specifically, the heart rate continued to decrease steadily throughout the presentation period when participants were exposed to images with motion. However, when viewing still images, the heart rate remained relatively stable without significant changes [2]. The statistical interactions (Motion with the linear and quadratic components of the half-second variable) provided weak evidence of significance ($Flin(1,16 = 3.30, p < .10$; $FqUacj(1,16) = 4.09, p < .10$). Moreover, no interactions were found between motion and valence or arousal, indicating that the effects of motion and emotion on heart rate are independent.

6.2 Skin Conductance

In line with our hypothesis, the intensity of the skin conductance response was found to be positively correlated with the arousal levels of the image stimuli. The results showed that high-arousal images induced the greatest SCRs, which was confirmed by ANOVA ($Flin(1,16) = 31.49, p < .001$; $Fquad(1,16) = 19.22, p < .001$). Our hypothesis regarding the influence of image motion on skin conductance activity was also supported, as it was found to impact the level of skin conductance response significantly. Similar to the arousal self-report, motion resulted in overall larger SCRs ($F(1,16) = 12.83, p < .01$). However, this effect was more evident when images were in the high-arousal category (Motion X Arousal $Flin(1,16) = 8.78, p < .01$). No significant interaction was observed between the magnitude of skin conductance response (SCR) and image valence.

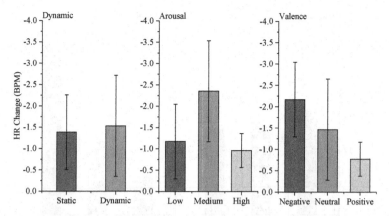

Fig. 2. Emotion Category and Dynamic Effects on Heart Rate (inbeats perminute).

6.3 Self-Assessment Manikin (SAM) Ratings

Figure 3 illustrates the valence and arousal ratings for both still and moving images. The analysis revealed a significant effect of motion on arousal ratings, with moving images being perceived as more arousing compared to still images $(F(1,17) = 33.98$, p $< .001)$. The impact of motion on arousal ratings was evident across all levels of arousal; however, it had a stronger influence on high-arousal images specifically (Motion X Arousal $F_{quacj}(1,17) = 5.43$, p $< .05)$. Moreover, although moving images were rated more positively than still images $(F(1,17) = 15.29$, p $< .01)$, motion amplified the subjective valence difference between positive and negative images. More specifically, the presence of motion in negative images led to more negative perceptions, whereas the inclusion of motion in positive images resulted in more positive perceptions (Motion X Valence $F_{lin}(1,17) = 22.59$, p $< .001)$ [9].

The statistical analysis indicated that there was not complete independence between valence and arousal for the image set. High-arousal images received more negative valence ratings, while neutral and positive images were rated differently. As commonly observed, neutral valence images were perceived as less arousing than positively or negatively valenced images. Both of these effects were found to be statistically significant $(F(2,34) = 27.27$, p $< .001$ and $F(2,34) = 6.63$, p $< .01$, respectively).

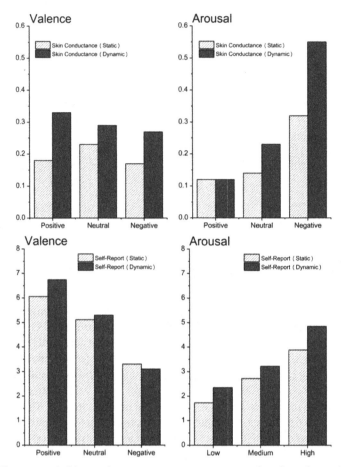

Fig. 3. Self-report and skin conductance response means as a function of emotion category (Valence and Arousal) and presentation mode (Static and Dynamic).

7 Discussion

The study's findings provide empirical support for the influence of dynamic pictures on emotional responses to images. Additionally, the results reveal that motion, as a formal variable in image presentation, specifically impacts emotional responses to picture content. It enhances viewer arousal, while its effect on emotion's positive/negative aspects is more limited.

7.1 Valence

With the impact on emotional valence, the study suggests that dynamic pictures did not alter the pleasant or unpleasant nature of emotional reactions to images. Unlike the arousal aspect, the two measures used to assess valence did not consistently produce the same results. As indicated by the SAM ratings, the participants' affective judgments showed an overall increase in the positivity of responses to the moving images. However, the interaction between dynamic visuals and the valence dimension (i.e., dynamic negative images elicited more negative ratings than static images, while positive images received higher positive ratings) suggests that dynamic visuals enhanced subjective evaluations of emotional quality, possibly influencing arousal levels [7]. Simply put, dynamic visuals intensify the negativity of reactions to negative images and the positivity of reactions to positive images, as these images typically evoke more vital arousal levels. However, the heart rate data did not observe this kind of interaction.

The analysis of heart rate yielded complex findings. Consistent with previous research, heart rate responded to the emotional valence of the images, with negative images eliciting a more extended deceleration period than positive images. However, whether the images were dynamic or static, the relationship between heart rate and valence remained unaffected. While participants' subjective reports of emotional experience (SAM valence) were amplified for dynamic stimuli, this interactive effect of dynamic visuals was not evident in the heart rate response to valence. Instead, the impact of dynamic visuals on heart rate response was more generalized, with dynamic images inducing more deceleration than static images, regardless of the arousal or valence content of the images [19]. Additionally, this effect intensified as the images were presented. The lack of correlation between dynamic visuals and emotional dimensions in the heart rate data indicates that emotional factors may not primarily drive the impact of dynamic visuals on heart rate [17]. The deceleration pattern of heart rate observed in this study resembles the changes in heart rate associated with attention shifts. The distinction in heart rate response between static and dynamic images towards the end of the viewing period indicates the ability of dynamic visuals to capture and sustain the viewer's attention. Therefore, the initial deceleration period suggests that static and dynamic images effectively capture the participant's attention. However, the presence of motion in the images enhances the maintenance of this attentional focus.

7.2 Arousal

Based on the study data, it is evident that dynamic pictures evoke higher arousal levels, as expected than static pictures. This effect remains consistent across various types of content, regardless of whether the pictures are positive or negative. We also discovered that skin conductance is an additional measure related to autonomous arousal. Both self-report and physiological data exhibited the same pattern of results. The alignment between arousal ratings and skin conductance measures is noteworthy, suggesting that the results are unlikely to be coincidental or erroneous. Of particular significance, the data reveals that dynamic picture motion had a notable interaction with the emotional content of the images. Specifically, dynamic visuals substantially augmented arousal responses when the images depicted the most emotionally stimulating events [11]. This interaction was observable in the introspective self-report data and the automatic skin conductance responses, indicating that this synergistic effect was evident across different aspects of emotional experience [8].

8 Conclusion

Based on the findings of this study, several observations can be made regarding the psychological significance of dynamic pictures. Firstly, dynamic visuals appear to heighten the arousal level experienced by individuals when viewing images on a television screen. However, they do not significantly alter emotional responses' hedonic quality (valence). Secondly, motion tends to enhance arousal in both physiological and subjective facets of emotional experience. Thirdly, the data suggests that picture motion can capture and maintain attention and influence certain aspects of emotional responses.

The study's findings also hold practical implications. For multimedia producers concerned about the expenses associated with incorporating video clips or creating animations in their products, the results suggest that the investment may be justified, especially if the objective is to enhance the excitement. This study's conclusions align with the intuitions and current practices of video and computer game designers, further validating their approaches. Additionally, filmmakers and video directors may find empirical support for their visual sensibilities, given the main finding of the study that dynamic pictures increase arousal [1]. Nonetheless, the interaction effect observed in this study (where more significant increases in arousal were observed for more arousing images) suggests that the relationship between motion and arousal is multifaceted, and its impact on viewers' excitement depends on the specific image being displayed. This type of relationship provides visual media producers with a range of possibilities to achieve the desired emotional impact by strategically combining motion and potentially different types of dynamic visuals with various images.

In addition to the observations above, several suggestions can be proposed for future research on the effects of picture motion. Given the remaining uncertainty regarding the impact of motion on the valence dimension of emotional responses, particularly in the physiological domain, it would be beneficial to employ more sensitive measures of image valence, such as facial electromyographic (EMG) activity, to explore subtle effects. Furthermore, other measures such as electroencephalography (EEG) and memory tests could provide insights into how motion influences cortical arousal and other cognitive processes. The intriguing relationship between motion and heart rate deceleration warrants further investigation in an expanded version of the present study.

Acknowledgments. This research was supported by the Fundamental Research Funds for the Central Universities (Grant No. 226-2023-00086), Research Center of Computer Aided Product Innovation Design, Ministry of Education, National Natural Science Foundation of China (Grant No. 52075478), and National Social Science Foundation of China (Grant No. 21AZD056).

References

1. Cohen, J.L., Johnson, J.L. (eds.): Video and Filmmaking as Psychotherapy: Research and Practice. Routledge, New York (2015)
2. Day, T.N., Mazefsky, C.A., Wetherby, A.M.: Characterizing difficulties with emotion regulation in toddlers with autism spectrum disorder. Res. Autism Spectrum Disord. **96**, 101992 (2022). https://doi.org/10.1016/j.rasd.2022.101992

3. Edmonds, E.: The art of interaction. Digit. Creativity **21**, 257–264 (2010). https://doi.org/10.1080/14626268.2010.556347

4. Ettehadi, O., Jones, L., Hartman, K.: Heart waves: a heart rate feedback system using water sounds. In: Proceedings of the Fourteenth International Conference on Tangible, Embedded, and Embodied Interaction, pp. 527–532. ACM, Sydney, NSW, Australia (2020). https://doi.org/10.1145/3374920.3374982

5. Giannakakis, G., Grigoriadis, D., Giannakaki, K., Simantiraki, O., Roniotis, A., Tsiknakis, M.: Review on psychological stress detection using biosignals. IEEE Trans. Affective Comput. **13**, 440–460 (2022). https://doi.org/10.1109/TAFFC.2019.2927337

6. Jo, H., Rodiek, S., Fujii, E., Miyazaki, Y., Park, B.-J., Ann, S.-W.: Physiological and psychological response to floral scent. horts **48**, 82–88 (2013). https://doi.org/10.21273/HORTSCI.48.1.82

7. (Poonkhin) Khut, G.: Designing biofeedback artworks for relaxation. In: Proceedings of the 2016 CHI Conference Extended Abstracts on Human Factors in Computing Systems, pp. 3859–3862. ACM, San Jose, California, USA (2016). https://doi.org/10.1145/2851581.2891089

8. Leong, T.W., Gaye, L., Tanaka, A., Taylor, R., Wright, P.C.: The user in flux: bringing HCI and digital arts together to interrogate shifting roles in interactive media. In: CHI 2011 Extended Abstracts on Human Factors in Computing Systems, pp. 45–48. ACM, Vancouver, BC, Canada (2011). https://doi.org/10.1145/1979742.1979571

9. Rathod, P., George, K., Shinde, N.: Bio-signal based emotion detection device. In: 2016 IEEE 13th International Conference on Wearable and Implantable Body Sensor Networks (BSN), pp. 105–108. IEEE, San Francisco, CA, USA (2016). https://doi.org/10.1109/bsn.2016.7516241

10. Silvia, P.J.: Emotional responses to art: from collation and arousal to cognition and emotion. Rev. Gen. Psychol. **9**, 342–357 (2005). https://doi.org/10.1037/1089-2680.9.4.342

11. Wang, Q., Liu, Z., Hu, J.: Effects of color tone of dynamic digital art on emotion arousal. In: Göbl, B., van der Spek, E., Baalsrud Hauge, J., McCall, R. (eds.) Entertainment Computing – ICEC 2022, pp. 363–371. Springer, Cham (2022). https://doi.org/10.1007/978-3-031-20212-4_30

12. Wang, R., Hu, J.: Design for connecting people through digital artworks with personal information. In: Göbl, B., van der Spek, E., Baalsrud Hauge, J., and McCall, R. (eds.) Entertainment Computing – ICEC 2022, pp. 386–397. Springer, Cham (2022). https://doi.org/10.1007/978-3-031-20212-4_32

13. West, V.L., Borland, D., Hammond, W.E.: Innovative information visualization of electronic health record data: a systematic review. J. Am. Med. Inform. Assoc. **22**, 330–339 (2015). https://doi.org/10.1136/amiajnl-2014-002955

14. Wijasena, H.Z., Ferdiana, R., Wibirama, S.: A survey of emotion recognition using physiological signal in wearable devices. In: 2021 International Conference on Artificial Intelligence and Mechatronics Systems (AIMS), pp. 1–6. IEEE, Bandung, Indonesia (2021). https://doi.org/10.1109/AIMS52415.2021.9466092

15. Wu, D.T.Y., et al.: Evaluating visual analytics for health informatics applications: a systematic review from the American Medical Informatics Association Visual Analytics Working Group Task Force on Evaluation. J. Am. Med. Inform. Assoc. **26**, 314–323 (2019). https://doi.org/10.1093/jamia/ocy190

16. Yao, C., Li, B., Ying, F., Zhang, T., Zhao, Y.: VisHair: a wearable fashion hair lighting interaction system. In: Streitz, N., Konomi, S. (eds.) Distributed, Ambient and Pervasive Interactions: Understanding Humans, pp. 146–155. Springer, Cham (2018). https://doi.org/10.1007/978-3-319-91125-0_12

17. Yu, B., Funk, M., Hu, J., Wang, Q., Feijs, L.: Biofeedback for everyday stress management: a systematic review. Front. ICT. **5**, 23 (2018). https://doi.org/10.3389/fict.2018.00023

18. Yu, B., Arents, R., Hu, J., Funk, M., Feijs, L.: Heart calligraphy: an abstract portrait inside the body. In: Proceedings of the TEI 2016: Tenth International Conference on Tangible, Embedded, and Embodied Interaction, pp. 675–680. ACM, Eindhoven, Netherlands (2016). https://doi.org/10.1145/2839462.2856341

19. Yu, B., Funk, M., Hu, J., Feijs, L.: StressTree: a metaphorical visualization for biofeedback-assisted stress management. In: Proceedings of the 2017 Conference on Designing Interactive Systems, pp. 333–337. ACM, Edinburgh, United Kingdom (2017). https://doi.org/10.1145/3064663.3064729

Calm Digital Artwork for Connectedness: A Case Study

Qiurui Wang[1]($\boxtimes$), Luc Streithorst[1], Caihong He[2], Loe Feijs[1], and Jun Hu[1]

[1] Department of Industrial Design, Eindhoven University of Technology, Eindhoven, Netherlands
wwqrr@126.com, l.j.streithorst@student.tue.nl, {l.m.g.feijs, j.hue}@tue.nl
[2] Guangzhou Wanqu Cooperative Institute of Design, Guangzhou, Guangdong, China
hch01prime@163.com

Abstract. Connectedness is increasingly recognized as an important aspect of life and wellbeing. The technology-driven solutions aimed at fostering connectedness can also introduce negative pressure or influence when too much precise and real-time information is involved. There are also growing concerns regarding information security and privacy associated with these solutions. This study aims to address these challenges by proposing a novel approach that combines the principles of calm technology with the expressivity of Mondrian style digital artwork to create connectedness between loved ones apart. Using a co-constructing story approach, we conducted a user study involving five participant groups to stimulate their imaginations and visions. The results showed that combining wearable data with Mondrian style artwork can provide a unique and meaningful way to strengthen emotional bonds among distant loved ones. This study provides a fresh perspective on connectedness, suggesting a novel engaging solution. Future research could explore wider applications of this approach and further refine the user experience and practical implementation.

Keywords: Calm Technology · Connectedness · Digital Artwork

1 Introduction

Connectedness, the feeling of belonging and emotional closeness in relationships, is a fundamental aspect of human well-being and social functioning [1]. Researchers have reported several different forms of connectedness, including connectedness to the self; connectedness to others, including the social network of family, friends, colleagues, and other social groups; and connectedness to a larger meaning or purpose in life [2]. Studies have consistently shown that individuals with higher levels of connectedness experience lower levels of stress, depression, and anxiety [3]. Moreover, strong social connections have been associated with improved immune system functioning and a reduced risk of mortality [4].

Technology-driven solutions have emerged to facilitate connectedness, enabling people to transcend geographical boundaries and forge closer relationships [5]. Visual-based studies such as the Carenet Display [6], Aurama [7], Daily Activities Diarist [8] and MarkerClock [9] rely on the contextual information for supporting connectedness. For individuals who do not require health monitoring, the design approach that involves exposing precise and specific data may actually have some negative effects. However, an excessive reliance on digital communication platforms and the constant availability of real-time information can lead to superficiality, information overload, heightened stress, and diminished well-being [10, 11]. This can strain family relationships, disrupt privacy, and create pressure to respond immediately, causing stress and misunderstandings [12].

In relationships and interactions, connectedness can be strengthened through the expression and recognition of implicit emotions [13]. These emotions add depth and meaning, allowing individuals to connect on a deeper level beyond explicit communication. To strike a balance between leveraging technology for connectedness and addressing potential drawbacks, this study proposes a unique approach. It combines the principles of calm technology [14] with the expressive power of Mondrian style digital artwork [15]. The abstract compositions of Mondrian, such as "Broadway Boogie Woogie," represent the lively and energetic atmosphere of New York [16]. Our study uses gathered data on a person's activities to create artwork.

2   Related Work

2.1   Calm Technology and its Application in Design

The principles of calm technology aim to create a harmonious relationship between humans and technology by reducing cognitive load, providing ambient feedback, and respecting users' attention and focus [17]. One of the key principles of calm technology is to prioritize the display of information in a non-intrusive manner. Calm technology principles have found applications in various domains, including wearable devices, smart homes, and ambient displays [18]. Wearable devices leverage calm technology to provide users with relevant health and activity information without disrupting their daily routines. Smart homes equipped with ambient displays and context-aware devices use calm technology to create a harmonious living environment that adapts to users' needs and preferences.

2.2   Understanding Mondrian Art and its Potential for Expressing Connectedness

Mondrian's artwork, known for its geometric abstraction and use of primary colors, its adaptable style has been applied in fashion, architecture, digital design, and generative art, reflecting its lasting impact [19]. Utilizing Mondrian's artwork, particularly his Broadway Boogie Woogie (BBW) (see Fig. 1), can evoke emotions and create a visual language that transcends cultural and linguistic boundaries, allowing individuals to connect and relate to the artwork on a deeper level [20]. The BBW, with its vibrant colors, dynamic rhythm, and energetic patterns, represents the pulsating vitality and dynamism of human interactions [21]. Incorporating the aesthetic principles of BBW

into design by using wearable technology, offers the potential to create visually captivating experiences that resonate with individuals, evoke emotions, and strengthen the
sense of connectedness.

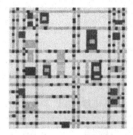

Fig. 1. Broadway Boogie Woogie (BBW), Piet Mondrian 1943

3   Design and Implementation

3.1   Design Concept of Artify

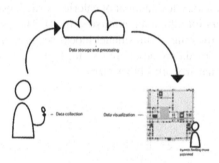

Fig. 2. Concept structure of Artify system

Artify system (see Fig. 2) aims to connect users by means of artistic data visualization,
which consists of data collection, data storage and processing, and data visualization.
Data is collected by wearable which could track the step, calorie and heartrate, which
could be tracked by current health products. Asynchronously collected data is then
processed for generating artwork visualization. This program is written in the Processing
environment, based on Java. To strike a balance between the artwork's aesthetic effect
and the meaningful representation of activity data, we have incorporated rules based on
Mondrian's BBW artwork principles, such as creating little blocks inside the lines and
not overlapping blocks or lines, to maintain similar visual effect to the original.

3.2   Data Mapping in Processing

Amount of Steps. The number of steps taken by an individual influences the composition of the artwork, specifically the number of bars and small squares. The relationship

between the two is intertwined, with approximately 20–25 small squares corresponding to the desired number of bars. The original artwork displays the maximum of 20 lines, which is equivalent to a person walking up to 15000 steps a day. However, to maintain visual recognition and aesthetic appeal, the minimum number of lines is set at 6 (see Fig. 3).

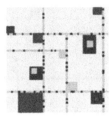

Fig. 3. Example of minimum lines (6) displayed

Amount of Calories. Recommended calorie ranges [22] for men (2000–3000) and women (1600–2400) are used as a basis for calculating the number of calories burned per hour. The calories burned are divided into three levels: low, medium, and high. A single layer block represents a low amount of calories burned, two layers for a medium amount, and three layers for a high amount (see Fig. 4). The size of the blocks varies randomly within a specific range, with smaller blocks representing lower calorie levels and larger blocks accommodating nested blocks for higher calorie levels. The range is determined by the original artwork's block sizes.

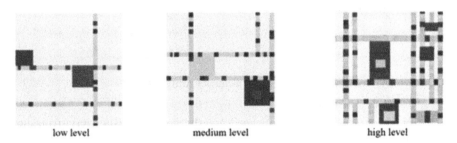

low level   medium level   high level

Fig. 4. Example of level of calories

Heart Rate. Heart rate would be mapped to the dynamic part of the little blocks. Have the little blocks move in place, pulsing based on the average heart rate per day. The little blocks on the yellow lines would be stationary and would enlarge and get smaller in a pulsating manner.

3.3 Integration of Calm Technology Principles

Prioritize the Display of Information in a Non-Intrusive Manner. This means that notifications and alerts should be designed to be subtle and unobtrusive, minimizing disruptions to the user's focus and flow. So we use wristband information to stay connected, and display one day activity asynchronously through Mondrian style artwork, so the receiver will not be overwhelmed by constant interruptions.

Design for the Periphery. In the context of connectedness systems, this means presenting information and interactions in a peripheral or secondary manner, rather than demanding constant attention. In our study, we involve using ambient photo frame to convey information without requiring direct and continuous user interaction.

Consider the User's Cognitive Load and Mental Well-Being. Excessive cognitive load, such as dealing with an overwhelming amount of information or complex interactions, can lead to user frustration and reduced engagement. Our study minimizes cognitive load, receivers can better focus on and maintain meaningful connections with their loved ones, without being overwhelmed by excessive or precise information that may cause worry or anxiety.

3.4 Incorporation of Mondrian-Inspired Elements to Express Connectedness

In terms of design principles, this artwork embodies several important principles of Mondrian's art. Firstly, it exhibits balance, as the lines and shapes within the composition are distributed and balanced, with no single element dominating the visual weight, resulting in an overall sense of harmony. Secondly, it demonstrates boldness, with Mondrian's use of vibrant and saturated colors, as well as precise lines and shapes, showcasing his courage and determination in visual expression. Lastly, it incorporates white space, creating visual space and balance, allowing other elements to stand out and command attention.

4 Methodology

The co-constructing story [23] is a participatory design technique to elicit users' in-depth feedback and suggestions about the design concept. Artify is a system which aims to connect users by means of artistic data visualization. In this study, Artify was presented as a probe to evoke users' contextualized visions based on their experiences. We have created a storyboard that presents Artify as an open design concept, rather than a completed prototype, to stimulate users' imagination and vision.

4.1 Participants

A total of 10 participants (5 pairs of parents and children) were selected as participants for the study, aged from 20 to 60 years old(parents M = 49.8, SD = 4.83; children M = 22.2, SD = 1.74). The inclusion criteria for participant selection were based on the relationship between the participants (parent-child) and their willingness to participate in the study. The snowball sampling [24] technique was employed for participant recruitment. This study was approved by the local Ethical Review Board (ERB). To avoid causing unwanted feelings, users are informed in the consent form that they can stop participating at any time. They can revoke their permission to use their data under any circumstances.

4.2   Co-constructing Stories

Sensitization Phase. *"Jim has been living with his parents for a long time now and this was of course not always easy or fun, but overall it was a good time. Jim recently moved out of his parents' house to live on his own while studying in a different city. While he enjoys the freedom, he also misses certain aspects of living with his parents. His parents, on the other hand, miss him greatly and frequently reach out to him through text messages and calls during the week. Although sometimes inconvenient, Jim understands that their messages come from a place of love and concern."*

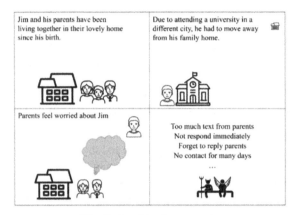

Fig. 5.   Sensitization scenario

In the sensitization phase, we started with a fictional story through sketch(see Fig. 5) to introduce a couple of scenarios in order to evoke participant's past experiences on connectedness. As a result of this dialogue, stories revealing past experiences were elicited that enriched our understanding of the current context of interaction between the parents and the child.

Fig. 6.   Visioned context

Elaboration Phase.   In the elaboration phase, we introduced Artify in a visioned con-text(see Fig. 6) and illustrated the concept. Then we explained how the Artify system worked and how Jim and his parents interacted with it. After the story ended, we asked the participants to illustrate suggestions about the Artify design to elicit their positive and negative feedback. At last, they were asked to fill out a questionnaire with 5 points Likert scales (ranging from −2 to 2), the questionnaire is developed independently for connectedness(unobtrusiveness, minimal disruption and calm), calm technology(more connected, easily contact, emotion enhancement, understand lives of others) and user experience(enjoyable, customized, positive impact, relaxed) for liking-the overall impression of the concept. The whole session lasted about forty minutes and was audio recorded.

Analysis. We transcribed the interview recordings that covered the whole storytelling session. In total, there were 530-min of data from all the participants; each in-depth interview lasted for approximately one hour. We conducted the thematic analysis method to identify user's contexts, expectations, as well as attitudes on the usage of visualization design. These aspects formed our main analytic interests.

5 Results

5.1 Calm Technology and Connectedness

Figure 7 shows the average score of Calm Technology, Connectedness and User Experience for Liking score of the different concepts. Several participants mentioned that using the technology made them feel more connected to others. It allows users to stay in touch over any distance, offering some personal implicit representation of the loved one through activity data. One participant even envisioned a collective artwork as a symbol of their family's unity. They believed that having a shared piece of art will allow them to bond with siblings and strengthen their family bonds. They also expressed a desire for works of art to incorporate data reflecting mood and emotion. They believed this would lead to a deeper understanding of each individual's emotional state and facilitate more meaningful dialogue and support among family members. By avoiding an over-reliance on precise data and prioritizing emotional communication and interaction, participants believed that calm technology could foster genuine connection without compromising privacy or causing discomfort.

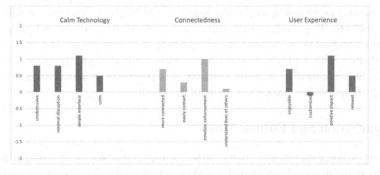

Fig. 7. Mean score of calm technology, connectedness and user experience of 10 participants.

5.2 Mondrian-Inspired Digital Artwork

The participants expressed keen interest in the Artify system, envisioning it as a platform for fostering connectedness within families. They desired a shared artwork representing the family unit, with personalized sections for each family member. The visually appealing Mondrian art style was seen as suitable for prominent display in living environments, serving as a central piece for family connection and conversation. Privacy concerns were emphasized, with participants emphasizing the need to respect personal boundaries and avoid surveillance. Additionally, some participants wanted the freedom to customize their own digital works beyond the constraints of Mondrian's style.

6   Discussion and Limitations

6.1   Discussion

Artify system offers a unique and innovative way to foster personal and family connections. Where traditional approaches typically rely on communication platforms, social media or messaging apps to facilitate connection, Artify leverages art and data visualization to create a more engaging and meaningful experience. A notable strength of Artify is its ability to bridge the gap between technique and aesthetics. While other technology-driven approaches may focus primarily on function and information exchange, the Artify system emphasizes visual appeal and artistic expression. By incorporating personal data into visually pleasing artwork, the system adds an aesthetic dimension that enhances users' emotional connection and engagement.

Furthermore, Artify provides a balance between privacy and connection. Participants expressed the importance of privacy and did not want the system to be intrusive or overly revealing. The system solves this problem, allowing individual artwork for each person or family member, enabling individualized performance while promoting a sense of togetherness through shared visual elements.

6.2   Limitations

The small sample sizes used in the user study may limit the generalizability of the findings. It is important to include a larger and more diverse pool of participants to gain a comprehensive understanding of user experiences and preferences related to connectivity and digital arts. This study mainly relies on hypothetical scenarios and participants' perceptions and preferences rather than real-world implementations. The lack of testing and evaluation with deployment in the real context can lead to unanticipated challenges or limitations not identified in the research. It is crucial to conduct practical trials to verify the functionality and effectiveness of the system.

7   Conclusion and Future Work

The study explored the integration of calm technology principles with Mondrian-inspired elements in the design of an artwork based on activity data. The findings contribute to: 1) understand how technology can be used to facilitate connection to address the limitations of traditional communication methods; 2) Designers and researchers can develop interventions that promote meaningful and balanced connectedness while addressing privacy concerns and avoiding information overload.

Future research directions could focus on gaining insights into how individuals perceive the meaning of data visualizations and integrating these interpretations within interconnected contexts are crucial steps to elevate the efficacy and influence of Artify. The artwork could find application in healthcare settings, creating visually stimulating and calming environments that promote well-being and connectedness. Future research and practical applications could further explore the impact of such artwork on individuals' well-being and expand its utilization in various contexts.

References

1. Lee, R.M., Robbins, S.B.: Measuring belongingness: the social connectedness and the social assurance scales. J. Couns. Psychol. **42**(2), 232 (1995)
2. Townsend, K.C., McWhirter, B.T.: Connectedness: a review of the literature with implications for counseling, assessment, and research. J. Couns. Dev. **83**(2), 191–201 (2005)
3. Holt-Lunstad, J., Smith, T.B., Layton, J.B.: Social relationships and mortality risk: a meta-analytic review. PLoS Med. **7**(7), e1000316 (2010)
4. Uchino, B.N.: Social support and health: a review of physiological processes potentially underlying links to disease outcomes. J. Behav. Med. **29**, 377–387 (2006)
5. Coyne, S.M., Padilla-Walker, L.M., Howard, E.: Emerging in a digital world: a decade review of media use, effects, and gratifications in emerging adulthood. Emerg. Adulthood **1**(2), 125–137 (2013)
6. Consolvo, S., Roessler, P., Shelton, B.E.: The carenet display: lessons learned from an in home evaluation of an ambient display. In: Davies, N., Mynatt, E.D., Siio, I. (eds.) UbiComp 2004. LNCS, vol. 3205, pp. 1–17. Springer, Heidelberg (2004). https://doi.org/10.1007/978-3-540-30119-6_1
7. Dadlani, P., Sinitsyn, A., Fontijn, W., Markopoulos, P.: Aurama: caregiver awareness for living independently with an augmented picture frame display. AI Soc. **25**, 233–245 (2010)
8. Metaxas, G., Metin, B., Schneider, J., Markopoulos, P., Ruyter, B.: Daily activities diarist: supporting aging in place with semantically enriched narratives. In: Baranauskas, C., Palanque, P., Abascal, J., Barbosa, S.D.J. (eds.) INTERACT 2007. LNCS, vol. 4663, pp. 390–403. Springer, Heidelberg (2007). https://doi.org/10.1007/978-3-540-74800-7_34
9. Riche, Y., Mackay, W.: Markerclock: A communicating augmented clock for elderly. In: Baranauskas, C., Palanque, P., Abascal, J., Barbosa, S.D.J. (eds.) INTERACT 2007. LNCS, vol. 4663, pp. 408–411. Springer, Heidelberg (2007). https://doi.org/10.1007/978-3-540-74800-7_36
10. Burke, M., Marlow, C., Lento, T.: Social network activity and social well-being. In: Proceedings of the SIGCHI Conference on Human Factors in Computing Systems, pp. 1909–1912 (2010)
11. Hertlein, K.M., Ancheta, K.: Advantages and disadvantages of technology in relationships: Findings from an open-ended survey. Qual. Report **19**(11), 1–11 (2014)
12. Przybylski, A.K., Weinstein, N.: Can you connect with me now? how the presence of mobile communication technology influences face-to-face conversation quality. J. Soc. Pers. Relat. **30**(3), 237–246 (2013)
13. Mota, S., IJsselstein, W., Markopoulos, P.: Challenges for enhancing social connectedness at home
14. Weiser, M., Brown, J.S.: Designing calm technology. PowerGrid J. **1**(1), 75–85 (1996)

15. Feijs, L.: Divisions of the plane by computer: another way of looking at mondrian's nonfigurative compositions. Leonardo **37**(3), 217–222 (2004)
16. Haddon, L.: Social exclusion and information and communication technologies: Lessons from studies of single parents and the young elderly. New Media Soc. **2**(4), 387–406 (2000)
17. Case, A.: Calm technology: principles and patterns for non-intrusive design." O'Reilly Media, Inc." (2015)
18. Tugui, A.: Calm technologies in a multimedia world (2004)
19. Blotkamp, C.: Mondrian: The art of destruction. Reaktion Books (2001)
20. Deicher, S.: Piet Mondrian, 1872–1944: Structures in Space. Taschen (1999)
21. Feijs, L.: From mathematics to aesthetics: towards the design of smart products, systems and services (2021)
22. DeSalvo, K.B., Olson, R., Casavale, K.O.: Dietary guidelines for americans. Jama **315**(5), 457–458 (2016)
23. Buskermolen, D.O., Terken, J.: Co-constructing stories: a participatory design technique to elicit in-depth user feedback and suggestions about design concepts. In: Proceedings of the 12th Participatory Design Conference: Exploratory Papers, Workshop Descriptions, Industry Cases-Volume 2, pp. 33–36 (2012)
24. Sedgwick, P.: Snowball sampling. Bmj 347 (2013)

DataVisage: A Card-Based Design Workshop to Support Design Ideation on Data Physicalization

Xiaoyu Zhang⬤, Dongjun Han⬤, Yihan Dong⬤, and Xipei Ren^(✉)⬤

School of Design and Arts, Beijing Institute of Technology, Beijing, China
x.ren@bit.edu.cn

Abstract. As a rapidly booming research field, data physicalization has received significant explorations in recent decades. While previous studies have considered various aspects of creating physical artifacts, there is still a lack of structured method for guiding designers to generate design ideations. In this paper, we propose a card-based design workshop that takes proactive health as a starting point to design physicalizations, aiming at promoting users' self-reflection. Building upon prior researches and our thoughts, we propose design strategies and develop cards and toolkits to bridge designers' thinking processes and workshop process, thereby maximizing the effectiveness. The workshop was implemented and validated within a graduate-level design course. Qualitative and quantitative results demonstrated the effectiveness of the workshop in optimizing group work and structuring the design process. The workshop also contributes to the creation of quick, aesthetic, and practically applicable physical prototypes.

Keywords: Data Physicalization · Physical Visualization · Proactive Health · HCI · Workshop

1 Introduction

With the development of digital fabrication [1], tangible computing [2] and TUI [3], data physicalization has become an emerging research field in the past decades [4]. Compared to data visualization, data physicalization demonstrates greater potential for human-data interaction, such as increasing emotional connections [5], improving data accessibility [4] and enhancing sensory modalities [6]. The physical nature of materials allows physicalizations to be easily explored and interacted with in physical space, and the close contact with human and material promotes reflection on the data [7]. Data physicalization has been increasingly explored in proactive health, where it is used for recording and changing self-behavior [8].

In the theoretical framework of physicalization, some studies tried to summarize and consolidate the design frameworks of data physicalization through case studies and literature review. For instance, Bae et al. [9] suggested describing and analyzing data physicalization from three aspects: context, structure, and interactions, with a focus on

© IFIP International Federation for Information Processing 2023
Published by Springer Nature Switzerland AG 2023
P. Ciancarini et al. (Eds.): ICEC 2023, LNCS 14455, pp. 471–483, 2023.
https://doi.org/10.1007/978-981-99-8248-6_45

establishing a dialogue between users and artifacts. Khot and colleagues [8] categorized four categories of representing physical activity: mapping, outcome, material, and process. Additionally, previous researches have emphasized the benefits of creating data physicalization from different perspectives. For example, Hull and Willett [10] based on the architectural scale models and discussed the support for contextualized design and rapid iterative data physicalization exploration through the construction of physical artifacts. Offenhuber and Telhan [11] started from a semiotic perspective, and highlighted the importance of the correspondence between materials and data for users rapidly capturing visual content. From the user's perspective, the aesthetics and attractiveness of artifacts are critical considerations. For instance, Forlizzi and Battarbee [12] indicated that aesthetics must align with user needs.

In the area of data visualization techniques, rhetorical techniques as one of the mapping approaches are considered to be more attractive and capable of fostering user empathy [13]. Some cases of data physicalization tend to employ the metaphor of animals and plants to enhance the understanding of data and promote self-reflection. In proactive health area, for instance, Yu et al. [14] visualized individual heart rate variability data as flowers through mechanical movement, where the size and shape of the printed flowers on paper reflect the user's health status. Stusak and colleagues [15] transformed running data into 3D-printed sculptures in the shape of human bodies, using the sculpture's state to represent the physical activity. Additionally, the simplification techniques could help focus user attention and reduce information overload [16]. For example, Sauvé et al. [17] employed simplified and abstract data sculptures to depict the relationship between food data and carbon emissions. Sauvé et al. [18] suggested that simplifying the representation of spatial and physical data can improve data interpretability and optimize perception of physical space. Moreover, additional means such as storytelling [7], personalization [19] also possess the ability to increase user insights by invoking self-experience and triggering reflection.

However, although there have been many designs and studies using data physicalization to express personal information, there is no unified and clear design guideline for helping designers in creating health data physicalizations [4]. Therefore, we expect to propose a design methodology for supporting designers in constructing data physicalization. Card-based workshops, as a widely accepted method for exploring design approaches, can effectively combine design strategies with design practice. In this paper, based on a comprehensive consideration of physicalization strategies, we propose a card-based design workshop as a support for the design ideations of data physicalization. The contribution of this study includes the following three aspects: (1) We proposed a design method for the design ideation of data physicalization, and collected insights and usage experiences of this method from participants. (2) We explored ways to integrate personal health data physicalization into daily life. (3) Provide insights for future data physicalization in the field of proactive health.

2 The Design of the Ideation Cards

As a catalyst for design, the ideation cards play a crucial role in constructing a clear framework for data physicalization and supporting the generation of design ideas. In this workshop, the ideation cards we designed are named as DataVisage, which are used to guide the process of embodying and visualizing health data.

2.1 The Mapping Strategy

By reviewing and integrating relevant researches, we have highlighted certain requirements: The need to focus on the self-reflection, in order to enhance the feasibility of integrating solutions into real life [20]; The cards should not only inspire creativity but also assist designers in selecting and refining solutions, providing logical support throughout the entire process from ideation generation to prototype [21–23]. Our goal is to achieve a structured solution generation process by providing support for different stages of design, enabling designers to propose and create more practical HCI interactive prototypes. Based on these, the design dimensions of physicalization process we propose are as follows:

1. **Task:** *Physical Health (prevention; rehabilitation...), Mental Health (Individual; cooperation; society...).* In the phase of seeking design direction, we segment the domain of health, thereby guiding users in establishing design goals.
2. **Design:** *Visual Coding (metaphor; simplification ...), Interaction (user experience...), Context (support reflection; scenarios...).* The mapping logic throughout the three phases ranges from shallow to deep, starting with the data encoding, followed by interaction, and finally practical application and operational scenarios, thus encompassing various aspects of design solutions.
3. **Evaluation:** *Usability, Interactive Feedback, Technical Support, Usage Scenarios.* Reviewing the practicality of the design.

2.2 The Ideation of DataVisage

DataVisage is used to host the design strategies. As shown in Fig. 1, it consists of a deck of 18 cards, categorized into *Task Cards*, *Design Cards*, and *Evaluation Cards*, providing supports for the three stages of a designer's work. The *Task Cards* serve the purpose of grasping the design direction and promoting divergent thinking. The *Design Cards* assist in the selection, refinement, and preliminary evaluation of design solutions. The *Evaluation Cards* aid in the refinement and optimization of the ideas. All 18 cards have undergone careful consideration, and have been discussed and determined by four researchers. The card design employs a concise color scheme and layout to focus attention and maximize information delivery. The color scheme distinguishes different categories. The content of the cards is presented through text, illustrations, and other forms to explain the themes and provide case illustrations. In actual production, the *Evaluation Cards* are designed to be A5 size for content writing, while all other cards are A6 size.

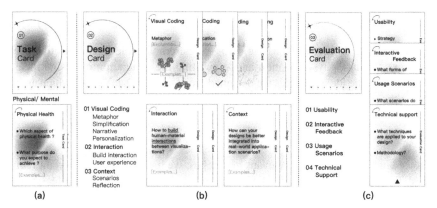

Fig. 1. Overview of DataVisage. (a) Task Cards. (b) Design Cards. (c) Evaluation Cards.

3   The Design of the DataVisage Workshop

3.1   Participants

The workshop was facilitated by researchers and implemented based on a graduate-level course in design studies. The participants consisted of the design students enrolled in the graduate-level course, who are regarded as novice designers, with a total of 19 participants (1 male, 18 females), aged between 23 and 27 (M = 23.42, SD = 1.07). All participants were graduate students majored in design, and possessed at least a basic knowledge of programming. They were divided into five design groups based on their preferences, with each group consisting of 3 to 4 individuals. The five groups were labeled as G1, G2, G3, G4, and G5. The participants were numbered as P1, P2,..., P19.

3.2   Procedure

As shown in Fig. 2, each group was given a set of toolkits. The activities were supported by DataVisage as well as additional creative ideation and prototyping tools such as paper and pencil, clay, etc. Participants were required to complete six steps within a limited time, following the workshop's arrangements, as shown in Fig. 3. The workshop process complemented DataVisage and introduced two rounds of individual brainwriting and group presentations within each group. Step 1 and Step 2 involve determining the design direction and framing design opportunities, while Steps 3 and 4 consist of 15-min brainstorming sessions using Task Cards and Design Cards separately, followed by 10-min group discussions with rotating speaking. Step 5 is for evaluation, and Step 6 is for prototype development. Throughout this process, participants engaged in thinking through ideations at various steps based on the prompts and case-specific guidance provided on DataVisage. For instance, prompts such as *"Which aspect of mental health?"* on *Task Cards*, *"Utilize metaphors to map data onto familiar concepts"* on *Design Cards*, and *"What techniques are applied to your design?"* on *Evaluation Cards*.

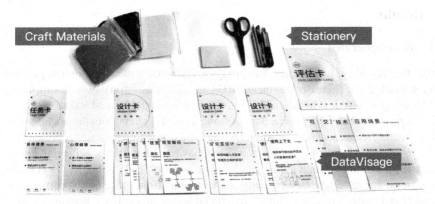

Fig. 2. Toolkits.

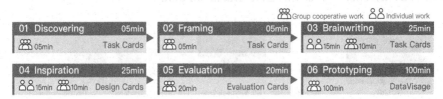

Fig. 3. Workshop procedure.

3.3 Data Collection and Analysis

A combined qualitative and quantitative approach was employed for data collection. Regarding qualitative data collection, firstly, we collected the creative artifacts and demonstration videos from the five groups. Throughout the workshop, researchers observed and documented the proceedings. Secondly, exit interviews were conducted with each participant individually, lasting for approximately 10 to 20 min, to gather their feedback on the workshop. The interview questions were designed based on double-diamond model [24], categorized into four sections: Discovery: decomposition of requirements based on Task Cards and creative divergence, Definition: refining and focusing of ideas through group discussions and individual brainwriting, Idea Generation: generate design concepts based on Design Cards, and Solution: selection of ideas and prototype production based on Evaluation Cards. The semi-structured interviews were audio-recorded and accompanied by note-taking for subsequent thematic analysis.

The questionnaire was employed to collect participants' feedback on DataVisage. The questionnaire design was inspired by [21] and focused on four aspects (see Appendix 1): Perceived Usefulness (PU1 ~ 5), Perceived Ease of Use (EU1 ~ 3), Ideation (ID1 ~ 3), and Evaluation (EV1 ~ 3). Perceived usefulness emphasizes the usefulness of the card information. Perceived ease of use refers to the comprehensibility and ease of mastery of the card information. The Ideation and Evaluation evaluate the divergent and convergent thinking process, respectively. The questionnaire utilized a 5-point Likert scale for rating the responses. Reliability and validity tests as well as data analysis were conducted using SPSS software [25].

4   Results

4.1   Ideas Generated

Under the pressure of limited time, five groups generated five ideations for data physicalization (see Fig. 4). These designs included G1 and G2 focusing on mental health, G3 and G4 focusing on physical health, and G5 encompassing both physical and mental health while ultimately addressing social data. Among these, G1 starts from the *Metaphor* and *Simplification* techniques suggested on *Design Cards*, mapping the stress represented by HRV to simplified synaptic dynamics. G2 emphasizes *Interactivity*, achieving human-material interaction through a dialogue between a person and the bottle. G5 considers the *Context* suggested by *Design Cards*, utilizing data from office coffee corners, such as voice and coffee times, to generate individual social data coffees. Building upon the integration of physical design and online gaming, G3 further harmonized the design style and interaction flow based on the *Evaluation Cards*.

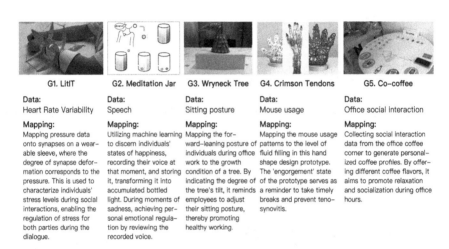

G1. LitIT	**G2. Meditation Jar**	**G3. Wryneck Tree**	**G4. Crimson Tendons**	**G5. Co–coffee**
Data:	Data:	Data:	Data:	Data:
Heart Rate Variability	Speech	Sitting posture	Mouse usage	Office social interaction
Mapping:	Mapping:	Mapping:	Mapping:	Mapping:
Mapping pressure data onto synapses on a wearable sleeve, where the degree of synapse deformation corresponds to the pressure. This is used to characterize individuals' stress levels during social interactions, enabling the regulation of stress for both parties during the dialogue.	Utilizing machine learning to discern individuals' states of happiness, recording their voice at that moment, and storing it, transforming it into accumulated bottled light. During moments of sadness, achieving personal emotional regulation by reviewing the recorded voice.	Mapping the for– ward–leaning posture of individuals during office work to the growth condition of a tree. By indicating the degree of the tree's tilt, it reminds employees to adjust their sitting posture, thereby promoting healthy working.	Mapping the mouse usage patterns to the level of fluid filling in this hand shape design prototype. The 'engorgement' state of the prototype serves as a reminder to take timely breaks and prevent teno– synovitis.	Collecting social interaction data from the office coffee corner to generate personal– ized coffee profiles. By offer– ing different coffee flavors, it aims to promote relaxation and socialization during office hours.

Fig. 4.   Outcomes of the workshop.

4.2   Quantitative Result

The reliability and validity of the questionnaire were examined using SPSS. The Cronbach's alpha value was 0.914, indicating excellent questionnaire reliability. The KMO value was 0.6, indicating an acceptable questionnaire validity.

Evaluation of Perceived Usefulness and Perceived Ease of Use.   As shown in Fig. 5a, the data from the questionnaire indicates that the cards demonstrate favorable performance in terms of Perceived usefulness (M = 4.19, SD = 0.66) and Perceived ease of use (M = 3.95, SD = 0.83). The results indicate that card design is effective in providing clear and useful instructions and guidance, and is good at promoting diverse and rapid ideations, as the card content is easily comprehensible.

The benefits of DataVisage as a Catalyst for Divergent and Convergent Thinking. The participants' ratings for *Ideation* (M = 3.83, SD = 0.78) and *Evaluation* (M = 4.10, SD = 0.61) reflect the role of DataVisage in stimulating creativity and assessing solutions (Fig. 5b). The results indicate that DataVisage contributes to various aspects of the design process, such as design positioning, ideation, and creative integration. Additionally, DataVisage has a positive impact on the selection, evaluation, and refinement of design ideations.

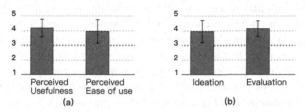

Fig. 5. Quantitative results. (a) Results of PU and PE. (b) Results of ID and EV.

4.3 Qualitative Result

The Balance between Individual Diversity and Group Collaboration. The DataVisage workshop process combines individual brainwriting and group discussions. Firstly, creative ideas are discussed using the cards, and then they are further refined and solidified through brainwriting. This approach facilitates rapid icebreaking and balances each individual's speaking rights (P8). The workshop process enables communication of creative ideas through two methods: direct discussions among group members and communications through writing. In particular, the unloading of individual thinking through brainwriting helps leverage each person's strengths and advantages. For example, P9 stated, *"Settling down to organize the logic helps clarify what the design is about. Moreover, everyone has different areas of focus, so we can each play to our strengths. After exchanging papers, we can complement each other's details."* P15 believed, *"Writing helps identify points that can be explored in depth."* P7 found reading others' ideas on paper fascinating: *"Everyone describes their ideas differently, some draw, some write long paragraphs. This transforms my way of thinking and inspires me more."* Additionally, brainwriting based on DataVisage creates an invisible social connection among group members. For example, P19 stated, *"I tend to add comments to others' ideas, and the next person can see the previous my comments. It's somewhat similar to leaving comments on a social networking site."*

Facilitating a Complete Divergent and Convergent Thinking Process. *Task Cards, Design Cards*, and *Evaluation Cards*, as tools throughout the workshop process, established a structured thinking framework for creative generation. Specifically, *Task Cards* serve as the starting point for exploring design directions for constructing group mind maps. As P9 pointed out, *"Task Cards assist in creative thinking, and the proposals diverge, filter, and evaluate based on the cards."*

Secondly, *Design Cards* facilitate the process of deriving and refining ideas. With a rough design direction and initial design proposals in place, using *Design Cards* helps quickly enhance understanding of data physicalization techniques and solidify solutions from multiple perspectives. For example, P2 suggested, *"The express of visual coding made me pay more attention to the form of visualization."* P16 stated, *"The illustration of data mapping further stimulated my thinking about coffee data extraction, such as color, coffee ground shape and texture, taste, etc."* P1 believed, *"The context illustrations made me consider aspects that I hadn't originally thought of."*

Evaluation Cards played a crucial role in evaluating and improving the final ideas, facilitating reflection on design choices and supplementing design details. For example, P12 stated, *"Evaluation Cards make the logic and structure of the design solution clearer, and unnecessary features and interactive operations were removed based on the evaluation cards."* P10 mentioned, *"Evaluation Cards prompted us to reconsider the connection between physical and web prototypes, and we added a tree image on the web page to maintain visual consistency."* P9 expressed, *"Evaluation Cards pushed me to think and clearly articulate the logical aspects involved on the cards."* P3 stated, *"Using Evaluation Cards, I supplemented some previously unconsidered aspects, such as technical means. It allows me to more comprehensively articulate that the design content is appropriate and reasonable."*

Practical Considerations for Embedding Data Physicalization into Real-World Scenarios. During the process of using DataVisage to assist creative design, participants were advised to consider their own proposals in the context of practical applications. The cards helped participants generate creative ideas sensibly and rationally select and improve design ideas from the perspective of data physicalization's performance, interaction, and practical usability. Ultimately, they generated comprehensive concepts based on daily life. P15 stated, *"The Interaction in Design Cards made me think about specific means, such as how to create a sense of immersion."* P6 mentioned, *"The Interaction in Design Cards helped me consider whether the design should be more entertaining or more rigorous and official."* P14 pointed out, *"When considering the context, I brought in the user's perspective and thought about my needs before and after using this prototype and what reflections I expect. Through this approach, I can create a real scenario to design a complete usage process."*

Benefits to the Details and Layout of the Card Design. Clear and concise design aided participants in quickly grasping information within limited time. For instance, participants indicated that the metaphor with example images serve as a means of "instant understanding" (P9), allowing for an intuitive comprehension of the intended meaning. The categorization and case descriptions on the *Design Cards* effectively stimulated divergent thinking, including association. For instance, P19 stated, *"The plant pattern on the Design Cards made me think about whether animal images like pufferfish or hedgehogs could also be used to represent psychological emotions."* P1 stated, *"The examples on the Context Cards provided excellent suggestions for the potential effects, thereby elevating our design. "*

Challenges. Participants provided constructive suggestions for the design of the cards. For example, there is room for improvement in the elaboration of data mapping. For instance, P8 pointed out that *"Instead of relying solely on text and graphics, creativity generation can be stimulated by variations in the texture, and even scent of the cards."*

5 Discussion

This paper proposes a card-based design workshop method as a means to construct the process of data physicalization, assisting designers in logically designing prototypes for data physicalization and enabling subsequent refinement and improvement. In this process, the groups utilize means such as physical sculptures and computer modeling to realize the production of data physicalization solutions. By combining qualitative and quantitative data, we present some indications to guide the process of creating data physicalization.

5.1 Full Utilization of Individual and Teamwork

Group collaboration and individual capabilities need to be balanced and utilized effectively, especially for new designers who tend to favor teamwork while overlooking the importance of individual independent thinking [26]. In this study, in order to balance the power dynamics among designers and avoid a leader prevailing, brainwriting exercises and rotating speaking method were introduced to enhance individual expression, ensuring that everyone's thoughts are equally represented. Additionally, the use of DataVisage further subdivided task details, providing each team member with a starting point for divergent thinking, enabling everyone to participate in the refinement and decision-making process of the final solution [21].

5.2 Establishing Suitable Mapping Strategies of Data Physicalization

In this study, a data physicalization strategy was constructed through DataVisage, by categorizing *Visual Coding, Interaction*, and *Context*, which supported participants in considering the content of prototype construction. Throughout this process, participants were guided to create design solutions that align with logical thinking by providing concepts, questions, and case studies. Enabling designers to think about the bottom and top layers of prototypes from shallow to deep. Additionally, prior research suggests the creation of more rigorous design frameworks through iterative approaches [8]. Building upon the integration and iteration of previous research, our work proposes the design strategy for designers, serving as a and further exploration of previous experiences. The evaluation of participants' feedback on the DataVisage highlighted the importance of card-guided thinking logic, such as framing design directions and encouraging creative divergence. Additionally, other methods such as involving participants in the formulation of design frameworks [8] and integrating interdisciplinary knowledge [9] may also effective ways to enhance and refine design approaches.

5.3 Guarantee a Fluid Design Thinking Process

Previous researches have emphasized the importance of creating a fluent thinking process [22]. DataVisage establishes the entry, process, and output of design thinking to ensure logical and smooth thinking within a limited time. Participants can focus on the scope and specific directions defined by the *Task Cards*, combine them with their own practical insights to propose meaningful design opportunities and solutions, and purposefully refine and select solutions based on *Design Cards* and *Evaluation Cards*. This approach prevents participants from feeling lost or stuck in one direction. By combining exploratory thinking with hands-on construction and integrating workshop procedures, cards, and physical materials, DataVisage facilitates a multidimensional and practical design exploration process. Further exploration can be conducted from a technological standpoint, utilizing 3D printing techniques [27], VR [28]. AR [29], to enable rapid prototyping and more extensive multi-sensory interactions with data. Alternatively, the integration of different tools, such as creating multi-modal design cards, may stimulate design creativity.

6 Limitations and Future Work

In this workshop, the participants did not achieve a well-balanced gender ratio, which may raise concerns about the generalizability of the results. We will address this issue in subsequent iterations and validation of the workshops. Besides, the design and prototyping process of the workshop took place within a laboratory environment, where participants' creativity and ideas were based on their own experiences rather than real-life exploration. Therefore, when considering the application of data physicalization in real-world scenarios, although participants engaged in thoughtful reflection and review using the ideation cards, there may still be a tendency for design ideas to remain detached from practical contexts. To optimize this situation, we can further integrate and improve design concepts in everyday life. Our future designs aim to integrate the workshop with daily life, helping designers identify problems and design opportunities from real-life experiences.

7 Conclusion

This paper proposes a card-based design workshop to support the creation of design ideations for data physicalization. By designing a data mapping strategy and integrating it with the workshop process, a fluent and efficient structured artifact creation process is achieved. 19 designers engaged in this workshop, aiming at promoting users' self-reflection and health promotion in the domain of proactive health, resulting in the creation of 5 design concepts. The quantitative results demonstrated the role of the ideation cards in standardizing the design process and promoting creative generation. The qualitative results highlighted the effectiveness of organizing design thinking and balancing individual and group collaboration. Our contribution lies in providing a design method for data physicalization, and gains insights for future related researches.

Acknowledgements. We would like to thank all the participants. This work is supported by The National Social Science Fund of China (21CG192) and Ministry of Education of China's First Batch of New Humanities Research and Reform Practice Project (2021160005).

Appendix 1. Questionnaire

Dimensions	Items	
Perceived Usefulness (PU)	PU1	The cards provide clear-cut usage instructions
	PU2	The cards have well-defined design keywords and descriptions
	PU3	The cards provide clear examples
	PU4	The cards have clear and easy-to-understand visual design
	PU5	The cards improved the quality of design ideas
Perceived Ease of Use (EU)	EU1	The content is easy to understand
	EU2	The presented knowledge can easily inspire design ideations
	EU3	The examples and guidance can help quickly generate ideas
Ideation (ID)	ID1	The cards can help identify and dig out design problems
	ID2	The cards can help generate more ideas
	ID3	The cards can help in the selection and integration of creative design proposals
Evaluation (EV)	EV1	The cards can help evaluate and inspect ideas
	EV2	The cards can help evaluate creative ideas from different perspectives
	EV3	The cards can help refine and improve ideas

References

1. Djavaherpour, H., et al.: Data to physicalization: a survey of the physical rendering process. Comput. Graph. Forum. **40**, 569–598 (2021). https://doi.org/10.1111/cgf.14330
2. Peschke, J., Göbel, F., Gründer, T., Keck, M., Kammer, D., Groh, R.: DepthTouch: an elastic surface for tangible computing. In: Proceedings of the International Working Conference on Advanced Visual Interfaces, pp. 770–771. ACM, Capri Island Italy (2012). https://doi.org/10.1145/2254556.2254706
3. Zuckerman, O., Gal-Oz, A.: To TUI or not to TUI: evaluating performance and preference in tangible vs. graphical user interfaces. Int. J. Hum.-Comput. Stud. **71**, 803–820 (2013). https://doi.org/10.1016/j.ijhcs.2013.04.003

4. Jansen, Y., et al.: Opportunities and challenges for data physicalization. In: Proceedings of the 33rd Annual ACM Conference on Human Factors in Computing Systems. pp. 3227–3236. Association for Computing Machinery, New York, NY, USA (2015). https://doi.org/10.1145/2702123.2702180

5. Wang, Y., et al.: An emotional response to the value of visualization. IEEE Comput. Graph. Appl. **39**, 8–17 (2019). https://doi.org/10.1109/MCG.2019.2923483

6. Lallemand, C., Oomen, M.: The candy workshop: supporting rich sensory modalities in constructive data physicalization. In: CHI Conference on Human Factors in Computing Systems Extended Abstracts, pp. 1–7. ACM, New Orleans LA USA (2022). https://doi.org/10.1145/3491101.3519648

7. Karyda, M., Wilde, D., Kjarsgaard, M.G.: Narrative physicalization: supporting interactive engagement with personal data. IEEE Comput. Graph. Appl. **41**, 74–86 (2021). https://doi.org/10.1109/MCG.2020.3025078

8. Khot, R.A., Hjorth, L., Mueller, F.: Shelfie: a framework for designing material representations of physical activity data. ACM Trans. Comput.-Hum. Interact. **27**, 1–52 (2020). https://doi.org/10.1145/3379539

9. Bae, S.S., Zheng, C., West, M.E., Do, E.Y.-L., Huron, S., Szafir, D.A.: Making data tangible: a cross-disciplinary design space for data physicalization. In: CHI Conference on Human Factors in Computing Systems, pp. 1–18. ACM, New Orleans LA USA (2022). https://doi.org/10.1145/3491102.3501939

10. Hull, C., Willett, W.: Building with data: architectural models as inspiration for data physicalization. In: Proceedings of the 2017 CHI Conference on Human Factors in Computing Systems, pp. 1217–1264. ACM, Denver Colorado USA (2017). https://doi.org/10.1145/3025453.3025850

11. Offenhuber, D., Telhan, O.: Indexical visualization—the data-less information display. In: Ekman, U., Bolter, J.D., Diaz, L., Sondergaard, M., Engberg, M. (eds.) Ubiquitous Computing, Complexity, and Culture, pp. 288–302. Routledge (2015). https://doi.org/10.4324/9781315781129-31

12. Forlizzi, J., Battarbee, K.: Understanding experience in interactive systems. In: Proceedings of the 5th conference on Designing interactive systems: processes, practices, methods, and techniques, pp. 261–268. ACM, Cambridge MA USA (2004). https://doi.org/10.1145/1013115.1013152

13. Lin, J.J., Mamykina, L., Lindtner, S., Delajoux, G., Strub, H.B.: Fish'n'Steps: encouraging physical activity with an interactive computer game. In: Dourish, P., Friday, A. (eds.) UbiComp 2006. LNCS, vol. 4206, pp. 261–278. Springer, Heidelberg (2006). https://doi.org/10.1007/11853565_16

14. Yu, B., Arents, R., Hu, J., Funk, M., Feijs, L.: Heart calligraphy: an abstract portrait inside the body. In: Proceedings of the TEI '16: Tenth International Conference on Tangible, Embedded, and Embodied Interaction, pp. 675–680. ACM, Eindhoven Netherlands (2016). https://doi.org/10.1145/2839462.2856341

15. Stusak, S., Tabard, A., Sauka, F., Khot, R.A., Butz, A.: Activity sculptures: exploring the impact of physical visualizations on running activity. IEEE Trans. Vis. Comput. Graph. **20**, 2201–2210 (2014). https://doi.org/10.1109/TVCG.2014.2352953

16. Evergreen, S., Metzner, C.: Design principles for data visualization in evaluation: design principles for data visualization. New Dir. Eval. **2013**, 5–20 (2013). https://doi.org/10.1002/ev.20071

17. Sauvé, K., Sturdee, M., Houben, S.: Physecology: a conceptual framework to describe data physicalizations in their real-world context. ACM Trans. Comput.-Hum. Interact. **29**, 1–33 (2022). https://doi.org/10.1145/3505590

18. Sauvé, K., Verweij, D., Alexander, J., Houben, S.: Reconfiguration strategies with composite data physicalizations. In: Proceedings of the 2021 CHI Conference on Human Factors in Computing Systems, pp. 1–18. ACM, Yokohama Japan (2021). https://doi.org/10.1145/341 1764.3445746

19. Panagiotidou, G., Görücü, S., Moere, A.V.: Data Badges: Making an Academic Profile through a DIY Wearable Physicalisation. https://doi.org/10.1109/MCG.2020.3025504

20. Thudt, A., Hinrichs, U., Huron, S., Carpendale, S.: Self-reflection and personal physicalization construction. In: Proceedings of the 2018 CHI Conference on Human Factors in Computing Systems, pp. 1–13. Association for Computing Machinery, New York, NY, USA (2018). https://doi.org/10.1145/3173574.3173728

21. Mora, S., Gianni, F., Divitini, M.: Tiles: a card-based ideation toolkit for the Internet of Things. In: Proceedings of the 2017 Conference on Designing Interactive Systems, pp. 587–598. ACM, Edinburgh United Kingdom (2017). https://doi.org/10.1145/3064663.3064699

22. Huron, S., Gourlet, P., Hinrichs, U., Hogan, T., Jansen, Y.: Let's get physical: promoting data physicalization in workshop formats. In: Proceedings of the 2017 Conference on Designing Interactive Systems, pp. 1409–1422. ACM, Edinburgh United Kingdom (2017). https://doi. org/10.1145/3064663.3064798

23. Deng, Y., Antle, A.N., Neustaedter, C.: Tango cards: a card-based design tool for informing the design of tangible learning games. In: Proceedings of the 2014 conference on Designing interactive systems. pp. 695–704. ACM, Vancouver BC Canada (2014). https://doi.org/10. 1145/2598510.2598601

24. Ferreira, F.K., Song, E.H., Gomes, H., Garcia, E.B., Ferreira, L.M.: New mindset in scientific method in the health field: design Thinking. Clinics **70**, 770–772 (2015). https://doi.org/10. 6061/clinics/2015(12)01

25. IBM SPSS Statistics I IBM, https://www.ibm.com/products/spss-statistics. Accessed 20 Jul 2023

26. Truong, K.N., Hayes, G.R., Abowd, G.D.: Storyboarding: an empirical determination of best practices and effective guidelines. In: Proceedings of the 6th conference on Designing Interactive systems, pp. 12–21. ACM, University Park PA USA (2006). https://doi.org/10. 1145/1142405.1142410

27. Mueller, S., et al.: WirePrint: 3D printed previews for fast prototyping. In: Proceedings of the 27th Annual ACM Symposium on User Interface Software and Technology, pp. 273–280. ACM, Honolulu Hawaii USA (2014). https://doi.org/10.1145/2642918.2647359

28. Seth, A., Vance, J.M., Oliver, J.H.: Virtual reality for assembly methods prototyping: a review. Virtual Real. **15**, 5–20 (2011). https://doi.org/10.1007/s10055-009-0153-y

29. Freitas, G., Pinho, M.S., Silveira, M.S., Maurer, F.: A systematic review of rapid prototyping tools for augmented reality. In: 2020 22nd Symposium on Virtual and Augmented Reality (SVR), pp. 199–209. IEEE, Porto de Galinhas, Brazil (2020). https://doi.org/10.1109/SVR 51698.2020.00041

Portable Interactive Nebulizer Design for Children

Cheng Zhai[1], Xinlin Chen[1(✉)], Zhangkai Cheng[2], Yousheng Yao[1(✉)], and Jie Zhang[3(✉)]

[1] Zhongkai University of Agriculture and Engineering, Guangzhou, China
`lanwdesign@163.com`, `120752037@qq.com`
[2] The First Affiliated Hospital of Guangzhou Medical University, Guangzhou, China
[3] Guangzhou Academy of Fine Arts, Guangzhou, China
`870010925@qq.com`

Abstract. The article designs a portable interactive nebulizer for children with a corresponding App application to increase children's engagement and interest in performing nebulization treatments. The design and prototyping of the interactive nebulizer were then completed using a combination of Arduino hardware and App software based on an analysis of current children's nebulizer products and gamification designs, as well as research and observation of children using nebulizers in the field.

Keywords: Children's nebulizer · Interactive product design · Medical product design · App application

1 Introduction

In recent years, urban industrialization in China has significantly impacted air quality and living environments, leading to a noticeable increase in asthma incidence, especially in children under 14, with an asthma prevalence rate as high as 3. 02% [1]. Asthma in children aged 3–14 is called 'childhood asthma.' Compared to infants and toddlers under the age of 3 who cannot independently use medical products, children aged 3–14 have gradually maturing organs and can consciously cooperate with treatment [2]. Effective treatment and self-management are essential for bronchial diseases such as asthma, as they can otherwise affect children's physiological and psychological development. Therefore, this article designs a portable interactive nebulizer for children aged 3 and above with bronchial diseases to assist them in nebulization therapy and recovery.

1.1 Theoretical Basis

Nebulizer therapy is a treatment method to assist children with respiratory infections, coughs, bronchitis, asthma, and other diseases. Due to the immature development of children's upper respiratory tract, they are prone to bronchial infections causing mucosal

P. Ciancarini et al. (Eds.): ICEC 2023, LNCS 14455, pp. 484–496, 2023.
https://doi.org/10.1007/978-981-99-8248-6_46

swelling and mucus blocking the airway during seasonal changes or viral infections. Using a nebulizer device to disperse the medication into tiny droplets or particles suspended in the air, the child can inhale them into the respiratory tract and lungs, depositing them in the airways to achieve therapeutic effects [3]. Since nebulization inhalation therapy is painless, children only need to breathe normally to naturally inhale the medication, making it very suitable for home nebulization treatment, avoiding cross-infection in the hospital, and saving transportation and time costs. However, several factors affect the efficacy of home nebulization therapy, including parents' choice of nebulization devices, assistance in the correct use and operation of the nebulization device for the child, recording the nebulization course, and regular follow-up visits [4]. The child's compliance with treatment is also an indicator of the effectiveness of the nebulization process [5]. Due to the child's young age and lack of concentration, they may develop resistance and fear of nebulization treatment, often interrupting the treatment process, which affects the effectiveness of nebulization therapy. Suppose the child cannot be effectively comforted when crying or is forced to undergo nebulization therapy incorrectly. In that case, it will increase the child's negative emotions, lower treatment compliance, and thus affect the treatment results. Personalized nursing plans based on routine clinical care, and the child's physiological and psychological needs can improve treatment compliance and effectiveness [6]. Effective interventions in nebulization inhalation therapy have significant implications for improving the treatment outcomes of children [7].

1.2 Field Research on Nebulizer Therapy for Children

To better understand the behavioral performance of children during nebulization treatment, the author conducted user observations at Guangzhou Children's Hospital and Guangzhou Women and Children Medical Center. Figure 1 shows the performance of third-party caregivers (parents/medical staff) and children of different age groups before, during, and after the nebulization treatment and the design elements derived from the observations.

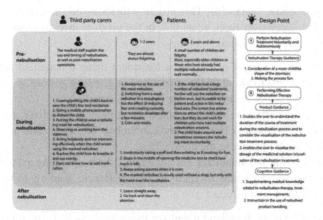

Fig. 1. Field research results of nebulization treatment for children.

During the observations, it was found that there were too many pediatric patients and limited healthcare personnel in both hospitals, resulting in the inability to arrange nebulization treatment promptly. In one hospital, the area was crowded with people, but each nebulization treatment station had a display screen playing cartoons to attract children's attention. The animated videos attracted most children receiving nebulization treatment. During the observation, a 6-year-old boy initially removed the device unconsciously but gradually became interested in the nebulization medical knowledge played in the video. The field research summarized two main issues with the current nebulization treatment: (1) Fear of nebulization treatment and medical products, and lack of understanding of the treatment, leading to children's resistance to nebulization treatment. (2) The nebulization treatment process is lengthy and tedious, and the product cannot make users perceive the duration of the treatment, lacks interactivity, and children's attention is easily distracted, resulting in poor treatment compliance and unsatisfactory treatment effects. Based on these problems, two design points can be derived: (1) Children should be encouraged to undergo nebulization treatment willingly, with the help of interesting guidance for the process. One design point is extracting the children's interest in animated videos observed to attract their attention. (2) To ensure effective nebulization treatment for children, it is essential to have guidance on both product and cognitive aspects. For the product aspect, the visualization of the nebulization treatment process and the amount of medication can be considered, allowing users to understand the relevant progress fully. Users can acquire relevant medical knowledge, management, and operation guidance for the cognitive aspect before or during nebulization treatment.

1.3 Existing Pediatric Nebulizers Analysis

Many portable handheld medical nebulizers are suitable for parents to accompany their children in nebulization treatment and recovery at home. However, the design of related products lacks specificity for the needs of children as the target group. According to the form, there are currently two types of nebulizers suitable for children: A pacifier-type nebulizer (suitable for children under three years old) and a mask-type nebulizer (ideal for children over three years old). This article will focus on the design of mask-type nebulizers for children over three years old. In the product investigation, some parents provided the following feedback:

(1) During the 15–20 min of nebulization treatment using a handheld nebulizer, it is difficult for parents to maintain the supporting or gripping gesture or state for a long time, and they cannot do anything else during this period.
(2) Since all the nebulization components of the handheld nebulizer are at the front when the mask is attached, the headband cannot bear the weight and falls downward, causing the mask to squeeze the child's face.
(3) If the child holds the nebulizer for treatment, their operating posture gradually becomes non-standard due to their limited patience, leading to unsatisfactory nebulization treatment effects.

Based on the existing handheld nebulizer usage process and structural constraints, and combined with the previous field research on children's nebulization treatment, the home nebulization treatment process is broken down into eight usage steps, with design guidelines for nebulizers in each step as shown in Table 1.

Table 1. Nebulizer Design Guidelines.

Usage Steps	Design Guidelines
1. Remove the liquid medicine container	1. The liquid medicine container is detachable 2. The liquid medicine container must be connected to the nebulization sheet, and the liquid medicine filling part is above the nebulization sheet 3. Not prone to dripping 4. Not easily breakable
2. Install the liquid medicine container to the overall nebulization	Children Cannot easily open the Mask
3. Check battery capacity	1. Display the power prompt signal and whether the charging device is nearby (the power prompt signal can be part of the interactive experience) 2. Whether the power location should be visible within the user's usage time
4. Wearing	1. Easy for children to wear
5. In use	1. Product volume and weight should not be concentrated only on the face 2. Alleviate children's resistance and fear (through interaction and diversion of attention) 3. Allow users to observe the duration of nebulization and whether nebulization treatment is in progress
6. Repeat step 1 and clean	1. Easy disassembly of the liquid medicine container 2. Easy cleaning of the liquid medicine container
7. Charging	1. Charging port location considers child safety 2. Allow users to understand the charging status
8. Storage	1. Nebulizer is easy to store 2. Nebulizer is easily portable

1.4 Gamification of Nebulization Therapy

When designing nebulizers for children, it is important to consider their psychological requirements. Relevant studies have shown that clinical nebulization therapy interventions can adapt to children's psychological needs by playing animated videos and books during the treatment process to distract children's attention or by selecting decorations that cater to children's psychology to create a warm and comfortable nebulization therapy environment [8]. Children are curious about things, and gamification can fully arouse their enthusiasm, cater to their interests and cognitive habits, make knowledge easy to understand and remember and guide them to learn independently [9]. The gamification reward mechanism has been applied in medical health, lifestyle intervention, and nursing education [10]. Gamification uses game thinking to solve non-game problems and influences people's behavior and motivation through game experiences. In Jane McGonigal's book "Reality is Broken", the core characteristics of gamification are summarized into four factors: (1) Goals: goal-oriented, such as eliminating a certain number of monsters to level up; (2) Rules: constraints and obstacles of the game, such as limited time, enemies, or prescribed operation methods; (3) Feedback: feedback systems can provide real-time feedback on the player's status and progress, such as levels, scores, or progress bars; (4) Voluntary participation, players are willing to complete the game independently [11]. Therefore, by using a gamification method that meets children's cognitive needs, gamification can be integrated into the design of children's nebulizers, enhancing emotional appeal. Medical knowledge can be incorporated into the nebulization therapy, using accompanying character design to give children a sense of participation and companionship, reducing anxiety and tension. In the preliminary observation, some children refused to nebulize and would not open their mouths to breathe, resulting in the medication not entering the bronchus. Therefore, when children use a face mask nebulizer for treatment, an APP mini-game with bronchial medical knowledge as the background can be interacted with, guiding the children to open their mouths.

2 Design of a Portable Nebulizer for Children

2.1 Target Users

Based on the above theories and practical observation research, the target population for designing children's face mask nebulizers is children aged three years and above. The product is portable, meaning that it can be used at any time without the constraint of a fixed scene, assisting in the treatment and recovery of the child. The problems and design directions addressed by the product are shown in Fig. 2.

2.2 Concept Designs

Considering the constraints of product structure and component positions, the following sketches present feasible solutions for details suitable for children to wear (see Fig. 3).

In designing the mask nebulizer's appearance (see Fig. 4), we incorporated elements that align with the psychological needs of children, such as biomimicry, emotionally interactive operation, color, texture, material variations, rhythmic sound, and

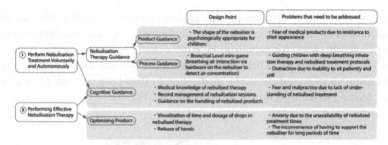

Fig. 2. Product Positioning.

Fig. 3. Product Positioning.

light effects. The main concept of this design is based on the frequency of a child's respiration during nebulization treatment, which drives changes in the appearance of the nebulizer. For instance, the mask may undergo biological changes, such as imitating the gill-breathing of a frog, or when the medicine container is attached, the nebulizing mask might exhibit light changes akin to a superhero mask.

These design features aim to provide a more engaging interactive experience for children using the product, thereby reducing any resistance or negative emotions associated with its use.

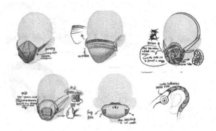

Fig. 4. Sketch of Face Mask Nebulizer Appearance Design Scheme.

2.3 Product Principle Tests

The author selected three relatively feasible sketch schemes for basic principle testing experiments.

(1) The first test scheme involves placing the medication box next to the ear, with an additional medication tube connecting to the face mask nebulizer (container carrying the nebulizing sheet) for nebulization. After examining the prototype, it was found that vertical misalignment between the medication box and the container having the nebulizing sheet would cause the medication to flow back through the medication tube, leading to the rejection of this scheme (see Fig. 5).

Fig. 5. Nebulizer Prototype Test One.

(2) The second test scheme involves the medication box being removable from the nebulization mask through a pressing mechanism, with the battery box located on one side of the ear and the connecting circuitry hidden within the headgear. The appearance of the nebulization mask is in a cartoon image, complemented by two eyes. The eye area is designed to be transparent, allowing caregivers to intuitively observe the amount of medication used (see Fig. 6). After examining the prototype, 3D model, and structure, it was discovered that simplification was possible, and the current design was unsuitable for future production.

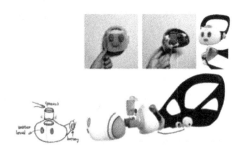

Fig. 6. Nebulizer Prototype Test Two.

(3) The third test scheme involves embedding the battery box in the headband and positioning it at the back of the head and neck, along with a detachable medication box and separable face mask. Using a child's head model with a 55cm head circumference, a 3D printing pen was used for prototype size exploration, and copper wire/strip

and nebulizing sheet kit (nebulizing sheet and nebulizing sheet drive module) were used for prototype production (see Fig. 7). After examining the prototype and conducting experiments on structural principles, further development of this scheme is possible.

Fig. 7. Nebulizer Prototype Test Three

2.4 Product Design and Innovation

2.4.1 Mock-Up

The integrated medication storage and face mask design of the children's nebulizer allows children to free their hands during nebulization therapy, improving comfort during use. The children's nebulization mask in this scheme is based on a child's head model, with the mock-up size as the standard. The breathing mask, medication container, and corresponding decorative shell can all be separated. The modular design allows for easy disassembly and cleaning of components. The feasibility of power component connections is explored through rapid mock-up construction using 3D printing technology (see Fig. 8).

Fig. 8. Final Scheme 3D Printed Prototype Mock-up.

2.4.2 Detailed Explanations of the Specific Design Elements and Features

The final components of the children's face mask nebulizer include the headband, battery box, connecting key, silicone face mask, face mask assembly, nebulizing sheet, medication container, and silicone decorative shell (see Fig. 9 and 10). The power connection wire is hidden within the headband, connecting the battery box and connecting assembly (connecting to the face mask assembly); the face mask assembly contains the power connection wire (connecting the connecting assembly and nebulizing sheet). The medication container includes a silicone flip-top and a partially translucent material. The silicone decorative shell corresponds in color and interaction with the accompanying character of the interactive App. It is available in multiple colors, with hollowed-out sections corresponding to the shape of the translucent part of the medication container. When the child uses the nebulizer, caregivers can see the remaining amount of medication. The face mask is detachable and made of silicone material, allowing easy removal for boiling, and sterilization.

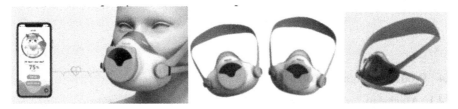

Fig. 9. Design Visualiser.

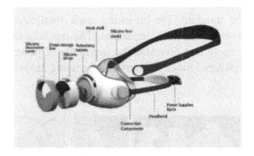

Fig. 10. Children's Face Mask Nebulizer Components.

2.5 APP Interaction Design

2.5.1 Overall Design Framework

Self-management of nebulization therapy helps children improve their health status and adhere to treatment. To increase children's participation in their daily treatments, we created an app to be used with a pediatric nebulizing mask. The interface consists of three levels of pages primarily: the nebulization process display interface, the nebulization diary interface, and the medical interaction mini-game interface. Making the nebulization treatment process more engaging can reduce anxiety and uneasiness caused by uncertainty for children. A nebulization diary can help parents of children with chronic conditions record regular treatment situations (see Fig. 11).

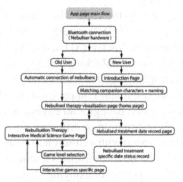

Fig. 11. APP Framework.

2.5.2 Interaction Interface Design

The author used Adobe Illustration, Adobe Photoshop, and Adobe XD for high-fidelity interaction interface design.

(1) Nebulization process visualization interface (see Fig. 12, left). When the child uses the nebulization face mask, the Bluetooth connection allows the APP homepage to display the ongoing nebulization process directly. By using percentages and visualizing the circle, users can understand the overall time of the nebulization treatment, reducing the anxiety caused by waiting. The homepage has two buttons pointing to the other two primary functional interfaces: one is the nebulization diary interface, and the other is the medical mini-game.

(2) Nebulization diary interface (see Fig. 12, center). This interface shows the number of times the child has undergone nebulization treatment. The accompanying character has different expressions for different completion times (see Fig. 12). Clicking on the corresponding nebulization treatment data allows users to view the accompanying character's energy (see Fig. 12, right). If the child completes the entire nebulization process for the day, the accompanying character's energy will be fully charged.

Fig. 12. Interaction Interface Design. (left: Nebulization Process Visualization Interface; center: Nebulization Diary Interface; right: Nebulization Record Interface)

Based on the four core characteristics of gamification theory, the nebulization game within the APP is designed with respiratory medical knowledge as the main background, matching the breathing frequency of the child while using the nebulization face mask. That is, (1) Goal: eliminate germs; (2) Rules: perform deep breathing within a limited time to operate the accompanying character; (3) Feedback: elimination completion adds energy to the accompanying character, unlocking and upgrading to the next level; (4) Voluntary participation: the accompanying character's energy drives children's emotions, increasing the sense of participation and companionship. Medical knowledge is conveyed to the child through the game background environment, corresponding text, and the accompanying character's incarnation in different game scenes. The first interface within the game is a game-level menu with a children's respiratory tract background (see Fig. 13, left one). The game's second level features a mini-game set against a bronchial backdrop (see Fig. 13, left two). The accompanying character transforms into a 'germ-eliminating' warrior. Its every move is controlled by the child's every breath, with the movement speed matching the breathing frequency. The green color represents germs, and the child needs to operate the character (i.e., breathe evenly for nebulization treatment) to 'eliminate' (knock down) the germs through the game. Each ascending game level unlocks more detailed medical knowledge (from the trachea to the lungs to the alveoli, etc.) (see Fig. 13, left three, level 3 alveoli game).

Fig. 13. Medical Interactive Game Interface.

2.5.3 Prototype Development

During the prototype construction, the initial mini-game interactive function prototype is created using APP Inventor (see Fig. 14). Subsequently, the designed APP is connected with Arduino hardware to implement the interactive production (see Fig. 15).

Fig. 14. App Prototype Production.

The electronic components selected for prototype construction include a Bluetooth module, pressure sensor, nebulizing sheet, nebulizing sheet driver board, Arduino Nano (mainboard), and battery box (two-button batteries). The APP controls character movement by detecting breathing frequency with a pressure sensor.

Fig. 15. Interaction between hardware and App

3 Conclusion

Researchers can make the following improvements can be made to the pediatric nebulizer in the future:

(1) As a prototype, the respiratory detection parameters are not high due to the breathing sensor's hardware limitations. The average respiratory curve of children varies with age, gender, and weight. In the future, suitable respiratory rates must be found through user testing to achieve the best interactive effect. (2) The mobile application requires optimization and improvement, such as adding a user-customized schedule recording function to achieve integrated nebulization therapy monitoring. (3) In the production process of a nebulizer, consideration must be given to the structural design of the power connection.

This portable interactive pediatric mask nebulizer proposes a design direction for pediatric nebulizers to incorporate the gamified interaction and increase the emotional design consideration for the psychology and emotions of the affected children. That will have a positive significance for assisting children with asthma or bronchial diseases in long-term rehabilitation treatment. The researchers are still optimizing the project for testing and plan to conduct user tests to demonstrate the product's usability or effects of maintaining children's attention while using this product.

References

1. National Pediatric Asthma Collaborative Group, Environmental and Health-related Product Safety Institute, Chinese Center for Disease Control and Prevention.: The third epidemiological survey of asthma in urban children in China. Chin. J. Pediatr. **51**(10), 729–735 (2013)
2. Miaodi, G.: Research on the Design of Children's Asthma Medical Care Products Based on Service Design Concept. Hubei University of Technology (2020). https://doi.org/10.27131/d.cnki.ghugc.2020.001007

3. Kunling, S., Guocheng, Z.: Emphasizing the standardization and clinical application of nebulized inhalation therapy in children. Chin. J. Pract. Pediatr. **29**(11), 837–839 (2014)
4. Jidong, T., Bing, L., Yaping, C., Bin, H.: Application of home nebulized inhalation therapy in children under 5 years old with bronchial asthma. Contemp. Nurse (early issue) **28**(08), 91–93 (2021). https://doi.org/10.19791/j.cnki.1006-6411.2021.22.034
5. Yuanzhen, Q., Lingfa, Z., Liyun, L.: Application effect of whole-process nursing in home nebulized inhalation. Contemp. Nurse (late issue) **27**(02), 81–83 (2020). https://doi.org/10.19793/j.cnki.1006-6411.2020.06.031
6. Lijuan, F., Jiao, Z.: Application effect of individualized whole-process nursing in outpatient nebulized inhalation children. Med. Equip. **33**(16), 167–168 (2020)
7. Xingming, H.: Clinical effect of ultrasonic nebulization inhalation therapy in patients with acute exacerbation of chronic bronchitis. Med. Equip. **32**(17), 106–107 (2019)
8. Lihua, G., Helan, Q., Faxiu, D., Yan, X.: Relevant influencing factors of nebulization inhalation compliance in children with bronchial asthma. China Med. Innovation **18**(35), 97–100 (2021)
9. Hongming, S., Panpan, Z., Xiao, S.: Gamification - the development trend of children's education. Digital Fashion (New Visual Arts) **2014**(01), 75–77 (2014)
10. Feng, J., Jin, H., Meicun, Z., Hejing, L., Ting, Z.: Current status of gamification application in medical health field abroad. PLA J. Nurs. **37**(11), 63–66 (2020)
11. McGonigal, J.: Reality is Broken: How Gamification Makes Reality Better.20–2. Zhejiang People's Publishing House, Hangzhou (2012)

Wryneck Tree: Designing a Multimodal Interactive System for Sedentary Office Forward Head Postures Correction

Chunman Qiu⬛, Fangfei Liu, Haina Wang, Yueming Xin, Xiaoyu Zhang⬛, and Xipei Ren⁽✉⁾⬛

School of Design and Arts, Beijing Institute of Technology, Beijing, China
x.ren@bit.edu.cn

Abstract. Sedentary office workers who lean their necks forward can easily lead to physical health problems such as posture and neck and shoulder pain. The purpose of this study is to integrate health technologies into sedentary office hours to help workers become aware of forward head posture and subsequently promote neck exercises. We have designed the Wryneck Tree interactive system, which consists of three parts: A physical interactive device that mimics the form of a tree, which can monitor forward head posture and subtly change its shape; A digital exergame that motivates users to perform neck relaxation exercises, and a data visualization interface that presents the head posture data. Preliminary user experiments have validated that the interactive system can encourage users to actively improve forward head posture, encouraging us to optimize the Wryneck Tree interactive system further.

Keywords: Neck Forward · Forward Head Posture · Interactive Design · Sedentary Work Environments · Health

1 Introduction

Forward head posture is one of the most common postural problems among office workers who sit for long periods. It is associated with postural imbalance and can increase the strain on the neck and back [1], leading to muscle tension, headaches, dizziness, difficulty breathing, and chest tightness [2]. Sitting at a computer for long periods of time can easily lead to poor posture [3]. Office workers who spend long periods in front of a computer often find it difficult to be aware of their forward head posture, and even if they are aware, it is difficult to maintain the correct posture for long periods. Proper activities such as head rotation, extension, and flexion can alleviate the discomfort caused by forward head posture [4,5]. Therefore, providing opportunities for office workers to become aware of their forward head posture and promoting neck exercises is crucial.

Research has shown that using interactive devices and sensors to monitor users' neck posture and provide real-time feedback or reminders can effectively help users adjust their posture. For example, using smart or wearable devices to provide visual,

© IFIP International Federation for Information Processing 2023
Published by Springer Nature Switzerland AG 2023
P. Ciancarini et al. (Eds.): ICEC 2023, LNCS 14455, pp. 497–506, 2023.
https://doi.org/10.1007/978-981-99-8248-6_47

auditory, or tactile feedback can effectively help users maintain proper neck posture [6–9]. Corrective exercises can effectively reduce forward head posture [10, 11], and allowing users to engage in neck relaxation training through games can increase their interest and motivation to exercise [12, 13].

In light of these findings, we have integrated the design of a multimodal feed-back monitoring system, game incentives, and data visualization to encourage reflection among office workers. We present the Wryneck Tree interactive system, which consists of three components: The Wryneck Tree interactive device, the Wryneck Tree interactive game, and the Wryneck Tree data visualization interface. The Wryneck Tree interactive system can monitor office workers' forward head posture, provide reminders for posture correction, provide game-based incentives for corrective exercises, integrate forward head posture data throughout the workday, and present it through data visualization to encourage user reflection and action.

2 Design of Wryneck Tree

2.1 Concept of Wryneck Tree Interactive System

Placed in sedentary work environments facing the computer, the interactive system integrates posture monitoring data to provide visual feedback and remind users to adjust their posture when it is incorrect. Every 40 min during work, visual cues encourage users to take breaks and relax while performing neck exercises through the interactive game. At the end of the day, the data on head forward posture and neck exercises are consolidated and visualized on the computer interface. The Wryneck Tree interactive system uses the metaphor of a tree to represent office postures, with a straight tree representing correct posture and a bent tree representing a wryneck posture, encouraging users to become naturally aware of their postural state (Fig. 1).

Fig. 1. Storyboard for the Wryneck Tree interactive system

2.2 Wryneck Tree Interactive Device

Function and Concept of the Wryneck Tree Interactive Device. The Wryneck Tree interactive device is placed next to the computer at the workstation, positioned to the front left of the user (Fig. 2a). During office work, the Wryneck Tree interactive device monitors the user's forward head posture. In its initial state, the device is upright. If the user cranks their neck forward, a light bar at the bottom of the device flashes once and the tree swings from side to side (Fig. 2b), reminding the user to correct their posture. The device will continue to sway until the user maintains the correct posture, at which point the Wryneck Tree interactive device will stop swaying and return to an upright position.

a. The Wryneck Tree interactive device is placed next to the computer on the workstation   b. The light band located at the bottom of the unit will flash once   Wryneck Tree sways from side to side

Fig. 2. Scenarios of Wryneck Tree interactive device

Function Realization of the Wryneck Tree Interactive Device. *Circuit Design of the Wryneck Tree Interactive Device.* The Wryneck Tree interactive device consists of an Arduino UNO board, an ultrasonic sensor, an infrared sensor, a servo motor and a LED strip. The ultrasonic and infrared sensors are positioned at the bottom of the Wryneck Tree device. By measuring the difference between the horizontal distance X from the user's body to the computer screen and the inclined distance Y from the user's head to the computer screen, the degree of forward head posture can be determined. The two distance sensors are placed at an angle. The angle is set at 27 degrees, taking into account the average increase in sitting posture and the typical distance between the user and the device. Each data set consists of two measurements: the first horizontal distance is defined as X1, the first inclined angle distance as Y1, the second horizontal distance as X2 and the second inclined angle distance as Y2. By calculation, the forward head posture distance for each data set is obtained as:

$$Y1\cos27° - Y2\cos27° - X1 + X2 \tag{1}$$

where X2-X1 is used to eliminate interference caused by changes in the user's sitting position (Fig. 3).

The Exterior Design of the Wryneck Tree Interactive Device. The outer shell of the current version of the Wryneck Tree interactive installation, used for experimental testing, has a transparent structure to show the internal circuits and mechanical components in action. The upper part of the Wryneck Tree interactive installation, known as the swinging tree crown, is designed with a three-part segmented structure based on considerations of range of motion. This design allows for smooth movement of the tree body as it swings, and the segments are connected and actuated by springs (Fig. 4a).

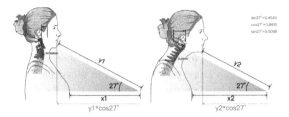

Fig. 3. The Wryneck Tree interactive device monitoring calculation method

Due to the thickness limitations of the manufacturing materials, the thickness of the tree crown increases progressively from top to bottom, creating a nested structure to increase stability during swinging.

The swinging motion of the top of the tree is controlled by servomotors pulling traction cables attached to the top of the tree. If the user is seated correctly, the Wryneck Tree interactive installation will stand upright and the two side cables will remain in a relaxed state. However, if the user adopts an incorrect forward head posture, the servo motors on each side operate at opposite angles (Fig. 4b). As a result, the tethers on each side are pulled to different lengths, causing the Wryneck Tree interactive installation to maintain a stable posture while leaning to one side. After being reminded to correct their posture, the user returns to a normal sitting position. The two servomotors operate to return to their initial state, and at the same time the traction ropes on the tree's crown relax. The body of the tree, assisted by the spring deformation, naturally returns to its upright position.

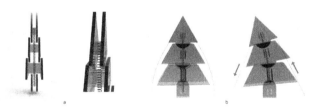

Fig. 4. Appearance of the Wryneck Tree interactive device

Wryneck Tree Interactive Game. The Wryneck Tree interactive game encourages users to perform neck relaxation exercises. When working continuously for more than 40 min, the Wryneck Tree interactive device will swing from side to side to attract the user's attention and draw the user's attention to the Wryneck Tree relaxation pop-up window in the bottom right corner of the work screen. The user clicks on the pop-up window to enter the Wryneck Tree interactive neck relaxation training game. The Wryneck Tree interactive game takes 1 min and the game requires the user to move their neck from side to side to maneuver the character to catch the sun falling from random left and right positions on the top and accumulate points (Fig. 5). The game is implemented using processing and OpenCV with a horizontally tilted camera. The game works by detecting the position and offset of the user's head and determining the speed of the tree's movement based on the offset. If the sun overlaps with the tree, the sun disappears and the score increases by 1; if the sun doesn't overlap with the tree, the sun continues to fall without affecting the score. After 1 min the game ends and the final score is displayed.

Click the pop-up window in the bottom right corner   Neck extension in the left and right direction controls the movement of the tree to catch the sun   Game interface   Score interface

Fig. 5. The interface display of the Wryneck Tree game

Wryneck Tree Visualization. At the end of a day's work, users can click on the data visualization module in the Wryneck Tree interface to access the data visualization page. The horizontal axis represents the working time and the vertical axis represents the deviation value of the sitting posture. The higher the deviation value, the more severe the forward head posture. On the corresponding line graphs for each 40-min interval, it is possible to see the number of forward head postures that occurred during this time and the score of the neck exercise game (Fig. 6).

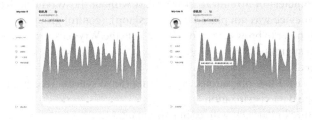

Fig. 6. The interface display of the Wryneck Tree visualization

3   User Test

Based on the functional prototype, we plan to have people who sit for long periods of time use it to investigate whether the Wryneck Tree System can effectively improve the neck forward problem through controlled experiments. At the same time, we hope to explore the experience of using different modules of the Wryneck Tree system through interviews. Specifically, we want to know: (1) The appearance elements, interaction elements, and perception elements of the Wryneck Tree interactive device; (2) The visual elements, interactive elements, and action elements of the Wryneck Tree interactive game; (3) The visual elements, interactive elements, and reflective elements of the Wryneck Tree interactive interface;

3.1 Participants

We recruited 10 volunteers (2 males and 10 females) to participate in the preliminary experiment, aged between 21 and 25 years (M = 23, SD = 1.26), with a mean age of 23 years. We numbered the subjects as "P1, P2...P10". These volunteers are office workers who spend a lot of time in front of a computer, which meets our research needs.

3.2 Setup and Procedure

Before the experiment began, each participant was asked to complete a 20-min control experiment and a 20-min experience experiment with the Wryneck Tree interactive system. The control experiment consisted of two parts. The control group completed a 10-min observation experiment in which participants used the computer to browse text without the Wryneck Tree interactive device. The experimental group conducted a 10-min observation experiment with the Wryneck Tree interactive device installed. We aimed to investigate whether the Wryneck Tree system could effectively improve forward head posture by analyzing changes in the proportion of time spent in a normal posture within 10 min. After completing the control experiment, participants had a 10-min break before proceeding to the 20-min Wryneck Tree interactive system experience experiment. At the end of the experiment, a semi-structured interview was conducted to address the research questions. The specific steps of the experiment were as follows.

1. Sign the informed consent form.
2. Use the computer for 10 min to browse text without the Wryneck Tree interactive device (the device was not placed on the desktop). (control group)
3. Use the computer to browse text for 10 min with the Wryneck Tree interactive device installed. (test group)
4. 10-min relax.
5. 20 min of Task Flow operations, completing the Wryneck Tree training game and exploring the data visualization.
6. Semi-structured interview with each participant.

3.3 Data Collection and Analysis

During the experiment, we collected qualitative and quantitative data, in the data collection for controlled experiments, we recorded the duration of head forward posture behavior of participants in the control group and the experimental group, using the statistical software SPSS to analyze the data collected from the control group and the experimental group to the proportion of normal posture within 10 min, the data were analyzed by repeated measures t-test to explore whether the Wryneck Tree Interactive System is effective in improving the neck forward tilt problem. To ensure accurate recording of the duration of head forward behavior in the experimental participants, simultaneous observational recordings and video recordings of the participant's sides were made at the same time during the experimental process, and the total duration of the participants' head forward tilt.

In terms of qualitative data, participants' evaluations of their experiences with the Wryneck Tree interactive system were captured through semi-structured interviews.

The interviews were recorded in the form of audio recordings and notes, and the audio recordings were later converted to text for subsequent coding and analysis, in order to understand the participants' perceptions, needs and suggestions about the system from their perspective.

4 Results

4.1 Quantitative Findings

Repeated measures t-test showed that participants' head forward posture duration was significantly shorter after using the Wryneck Tree interactive device (M = 69.90, SD = 68.501) compared to the control group who did not use the Wryneck Tree interactive device (M = 168.70, SD = 124.521), with a p-value of 0.035, which is lower than the significance level of 0.05 (Fig. 7). This suggests that after using the device, participants were able to correct their forward head posture more effectively and reduce the duration of poor posture.

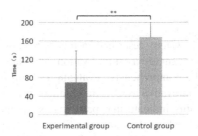

Fig. 7. Data Analysis Results

4.2 Qualitative Findings

Through qualitative analysis and coding of interview data, we identified three themes that encompassed participants' perspectives on user experience, their specific needs and requirements for certain features, as well as suggestions for design improvements.

Perspectives on User Experience. 70% of participants expressed positive attitudes towards the use of the system. Participants described their feelings of use in terms of personal fulfilment, proof of competence, monitoring and anxiety. For example, "The monitoring of the device subconsciously makes me more aware of my posture, even if no cues are triggered." (P2) "I would like to get a higher score in the game." (P4) "The device wobbling causes me anxiety as I don't want it to move, so I will consciously sit upright." (P7) This suggests that the system increased the participant's attention to self-posture to a certain extent, and was effective in helping the participants to reduce neck leaning behaviors through supervision, fun, and satisfying the sense of personal achievement.

Meeting Autonomous Needs. Participants expressed a desire to have the autonomy to choose accessories to decorate the product according to their personal preferences and different holiday requirements. For example, "During holidays, I can use accessories to decorate the small tree, like having a Christmas tree for Christmas." (P4) "It would be more interesting if I could choose the type of tree for the installation." (P5).

Challenges. Participants offered some helpful suggestions for the Wryneck Tree. They pointed out that the placement and appearance of the game prompt could affect the user's perception. Specifically, some participants noted that the sudden appearance of the prompt in the lower right corner, like a pop-up window, made it easy to ignore. Participants felt that the visualization interface was a little difficult to understand and that the information was not clear enough, indicating the need to improve the design of the visualization to ensure the accuracy and clarity of the information conveyed. Furthermore, they recommended taking into account individual work habits, such as allowing for personalized adjustments of sensitivity. For example, one participant mentioned that being too sensitive can sometimes discourage them from taking a break. (P3).

5 Discussion

The integrated interactive system described in this paper combines multimodal feedback monitoring reminders, game-based motivation, and data visualization to promote reflection. We conducted a comprehensive evaluation of the Wryneck Tree interactive system and discussed its innovative aspects and limitations.

The experimental results indicate that participants are able to effectively correct forward head posture and reduce the duration of poor posture. Participants showed a positive attitude towards using the Wryneck Tree interactive system. The innovative aspects of the Wryneck Tree interactive system encompass a multimodal approach, real-time monitoring, and gamification. The adoption of a multimodal approach allows the system to integrate real-time monitoring, gamification and data visualization, thus providing a novel and comprehensive solution to the problem of forward head tilt in sedentary office workers. The real-time monitoring feature tracks users' neck posture continuously, offering instant feedback and reminders to enhance user awareness and prompt timely posture correction. The integration of gamification encourages users to engage in neck exercises through interactive games, making the process more appealing and enjoyable, thereby motivating users to adopt healthier habits.

The Wryneck Tree system also has certain limitations. Firstly, there are individual differences in user responses to reminders, gamification, and visualization, which might result in variations in the system's effectiveness among users. Secondly, user engagement is a concern; although gamification can enhance engagement, users may lose interest over time. To address this issue, the introduction of incentive mechanisms, such as enhancing the social attributes [14] of the game, could further motivate users. In terms of future design and development of the Wryneck Tree system, we are considering enhancing the alignment between the system's functionality and specific usage scenarios. For instance, in the hardware design, we need to consider the relationship between different office space layouts and sensor placement forms. We are also considering enhancing the personalization and adaptive feedback of the interactive system, such as providing tailored interventions and support based on individual user characteristics, such as neck strength or flexibility.

6 Conclusions

In this paper, we propose the Wryneck Tree interactive system, which aims to address the issue of sedentary office workers with forward necks. This system offers real-time monitoring, game incentives, and data visualization to comprehensively tackle the problems faced by sedentary office workers. Our preliminary experiments examine the user experience of the Wryneck Tree interactive system and provide directions for improvement. In the future, we plan to make adjustments based on test feedback and conduct user research to verify the effectiveness of the system. We look forward to further in-depth research to help us develop new health and welfare projects.

Acknowledgements. Thanks to the participants in this study. This work is supported by The National Social Science Fund of China (21CG192) and Ministry of Education of China's First Batch of New Humanities Research and Reform Practice Project (2021160005).

References

1. Kang, J.-H., Park, R.-Y., Lee, S.-J., Kim, J.-Y., Yoon, S.-R., Jung, K.-I.: The effect of the forward head posture on postural balance in long time computer based worker. Ann. Rehabil. Med. **36**(1), 98–104 (2012). https://doi.org/10.5535/arm.2012.36.1.98(2012)
2. Fawzy Mahmoud, N., Hassan, K.A., Abdelmajeed, S.F., Moustafa, I.M., Silva, A.G.: The relationship between forward head posture and neck pain: a systematic review and meta-analysis. Curr. Rev. Musculoskelet Med. 12(4), 562–577 (2019). https://doi.org/10.1007/s12 178-019-09594-y
3. Black, N., DesRoches, L., Arsenault, I.: Observed postural variations across computer workers during a day of sedentary computer work. In: Proceedings of the Human Factors and Ergonomics Society Annual Meeting, vol. 56(1), pp. 1119–1122 (2012). https://doi.org/10. 1177/1071181312561243
4. Beneka, A., Gioftsidou, P.M.A.: Neck pain and office workers: an exercise Program for the workplace. ACSM s Health Fitness J. **18**(3):18–24 (2014). https://doi.org/10.1249/FIT.000 0000000000034
5. Louw, S., Makwela, S., Manas, L., Meyer, L., Terblanche, D., Brink, Y.: Effectiveness of exercise in office workers with neck pain: A systematic review and meta-analysis. S Afr J Physiother. 73(1), 392 (2017). https://doi.org/10.4102/sajp.v73i1.392(2017)
6. Kim, J., Lee, N.H., Lee, N.H., Cho, J.D.: A feedback system for the prevention of forward head posture in sedentary work environments. In: ACM Conference Companion Publication. https://doi.org/10.1145/2908805.2909414 (2016)
7. Hong, J., Song, S., Cho, J., Bianchi, A., Awareness, B.P.: Through flower-shaped ambient Avatar. In: TEI, Stanford. CA, USA (2015). https://doi.org/10.1145/2677199.2680575(2015)
8. Du, J., Wang, Q., de Baets, L., Markopoulos, P.: Supporting shoulder pain prevention and treatment with wearable technology. In: The 11th EAI International Conference (2017). https://doi.org/10.1145/3154862.3154886

9. Mironcika, S., Hupfeld, A., Frens, J., Asjes, J., Wensveen, S.: Snap-Snap T-Shirt: posture awareness through playful and somaesthetic experience. In: TEI 2020, Sydney, NSW, Australia (2020). https://doi.org/10.1145/3374920.3375013

10. Abdollahzade, Z., Shadmehr, A., Malmir, K., Ghotbi, N.: Research paper: effects of 4 week postural corrective exercise on correcting forward head posture. Jmr. 11(2), 85–92 (2017)

11. Lee, J., et al.: Effectiveness of an application-based neck exercise as a pain management tool for office workers with chronic neck pain and functional disability: a pilot randomized trial. Euro. J. Integrative Med. 12, 87–92 (2017). https://doi.org/10.1016/j.eujim.2017.04.012. (2017)

12. Markopoulos, P., Shen, X., Wang, Q., Timmermans, A.: Neckio: motivating neck exercises in computer workers. Sensors (Basel). 20(17), 4928 (2020). https://doi.org/10.3390/s20174928

13. Kloster, M.: Master's Thesis. University of Bergen; Bergen, Norway: Leveraging Virtual Reality Technology in Developing Neck Exercise Applications (2019). http://hdl.handle.net/1956/20818

14. Hamari, J., Koivisto, J.: Working out for likes: An empirical study on social influence in exercise gamification. Comput. Human Behav. 50, 333–347 (2015). https://doi.org/10.1016/j.chb.2015.04.018

Crimson Tendons: Designing a Mouse Usage Visualization System to Prevent Mouse Overuse Behaviors

Tiantian Zhao⊙, Anna Sui, Jiale Shi, Ting Hu, Xiaoyu Zhang⊙, and Xipei Ren⁽✉⁾ ⊙

School of Design and Arts, Beijing Institute of Technology, Beijing, China
x.ren@bit.edu.cn

Abstract. Overuse of the mouse is one of the possible behaviors that trigger carpal tunnel syndrome (CTS). In this study, we designed Crimson Tendons, a mouse use behavior visualization system. The system consists of a physical visualization device and a data canvas that records mouse usage data. The physical device uses flowing red liquid to map the mouse usage state. We proposed a preliminary user test and performed qualitative and quantitative analyses. The experimental results indicated that the device was attractive to users. They would choose to take active breaks to watch the flowing effect of the device, and this feedback would help us iterate on the design concept. The system has a novel design and contributes to the promotion of office health by helping to improve people's work habits and reduce the risk of CTS and other related diseases.

Keywords: Mouse Use · Interaction Devices · Visualization · Office Health

1 Introduction

Carpal tunnel syndrome (CTS) is one of the most common musculoskeletal disorders and technical disorders [1, 2]. The main symptoms of CTS are pain, numbness, a cold sensation, and paresthesia. The effectiveness of pharmacological and surgical treatments for CTS remains controversial [3, 4], so prevention and timely intervention are particularly important to reduce the prevalence of CTS. Studies have shown that computer work and prolonged operation of a computer mouse are associated with an increased risk of carpal tunnel pressure, and that tingling and numbness in the right hand are associated with time spent using the mouse device [5, 6]. Therefore, mouse use behavioral interventions for students and office workers working with highly exposed computers are essential to reducing the prevalence of CTS in this group.

Various interventions have been suggested by previous studies to prevent or alleviate CTS, with a primary emphasis on ergonomic factors [3], including the use of vertical mice and wrist supports. However, there is insufficient evidence to confirm their effectiveness [7]. In addition, studies have shown that rest may be used as activation or recovery time, so increasing rest time could aid in preventing CTS [8, 9].

Published by Springer Nature Switzerland AG 2023
P. Ciancarini et al. (Eds.): ICEC 2023, LNCS 14455, pp. 507–517, 2023.
https://doi.org/10.1007/978-981-99-8248-6_48

In summary, this paper proposes Crimson Tendons, a system to visualize mouse usage behavior. The system consists of a physical device and a data visualization canvas. The users can interact with the device while using the mouse. We hope that the visualization system will provide visual impact and intuitive data to draw users' attention and trigger their reflection, thus increasing the rest time during mouse use, preventing the occurrence of diseases like CTS, and promoting office health.

2   The Presentation of Data

2.1   Visualization Strategy

Considering the usage scenario of the users, the main visualization strategy of Crimson Tendons is to encourage users to take active breaks through visual feedback. Therefore, we created a more appealing physical device inspired by the microscopic blood vessels of the hand. We focus on physical visualization since other windows often block the canvas, and physical devices provide an immersive experience that cannot be replaced by an interface. We also added a data visualization canvas to complement the physical device, enabling users to intuitively monitor their mouse usage data and use it as a basis for health analysis (see Fig. 1). Compared to the physical device, the canvas uses a simple and intuitive data presentation.

Fig. 1. Crimson Tendons system usage scenario.

2.2   Canvas Data Visualization

The data canvas records and visually presents mouse usage data. It was created using processing (see Fig. 2). Considering the influence of the touch panel and other factors, we take the cursor state instead of the mouse use state and call Java's Robot class in

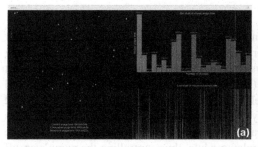

Fig. 2. Crimson Tendons' visual data canvas: (a) overall usage interface; (b) real-world usage scenario.

processing to monitor the cursor's position and movement state on the whole screen, so as to calculate the mouse's use length and movement rate.

The canvas consists of three parts: recording the user's current mouse usage time, segmented usage time, and mouse movement rate in the form of polka dots, bars, and lines, respectively (see Table 1). The reason for the inclusion of mouse movement rate is that dragging tasks also have a significant effect on wrist pressure [10]. Considering that users may pause their mouse movement while reading pages or performing other tasks on the computer, we used the criterion of whether the cursor position remains unchanged for 60 s; if yes, this period of mouse use continues to be timed; if not, this period pauses until the next time the cursor moves to start a new period.

Table 1. Data visualization interface related data indicators and their interpretation.

Data indicators	Specific explanation
Number of wave points	Number of wave points (pcs) = current usage time (sec)
Current usage time	Current usage time is the usage time of the current number of changes
Cumulative usage time	Cumulative usage time is the sum of the current usage time for all changes, also called total mouse usage time
Maximum usage time	Maximum usage time is the maximum of the current usage time
Mouse segmentation usage time	Mouse segmentation usage time is the data set of the current usage time
Number of changes	Every continuous pause up to 60s is a change
Mouse movement rate	The mouse movement rate is the data set of the single mouse movement rate

2.3 Physical Visualization

Crimson Tendons' physical interaction device is visualized in the form of a liquid flow mapping the state of mouse use. We crafted the main body of the hand prototype using lightweight white clay and wrapped transparent tubing around it, and then connected it to the water reservoir and the circuitry (see Fig. 3). The system's interactivity is achieved through an Arduino UNO board, a relay module, a self-priming pump, batteries, and the program in Processing. Specifically, when users use the mouse, Processing monitors the cursor's movement and communicates with Arduino in a serial port, transmitting the cursor's state as digital signals to the relay module, thus controlling the pump's on-off switch. When the mouse is in use, the liquid in the device flows, and only when the mouse is out of use for a period of 3 s does the relay stop working and the liquid in the device becomes stationary.

using clay to hold hands   winding water pipes   preparing red liquid   connecting circuits   perfecting the details   (a)   (b)

Fig. 3. Realization of the physical device: (a) prototyping process for physical device; (b) circuit realization.

Regarding the presentation effect of this device (see Fig. 4), we controlled the water level in the reservoir to allow a certain amount of air to enter the pipe, ensuring a clear flow effect. The twisted pipe mimics hand blood vessels, with red liquid inside symbolizing blood flow, creating a distinct contrast against the white hand-shaped body, making users facilitate their association with their hand's health status, prompting self-reflection, and serving as a reminder. In terms of the interaction experience, the flowing liquid provides real-time visual feedback, accompanied by subtle water flow sounds, contributing to alleviating workplace stress.

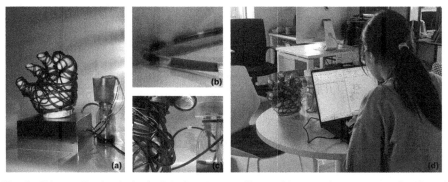

Fig. 4. Crimson Tendons' physical device: (a) overall part; (b) water pipe; (c) reservoir; (d) real use scenario.

3   User Test

3.1   Experiment Walkthrough

Participants. Three subjects were recruited for the experiment walkthrough. All of them were graduate students in design, so we could get some professional feedback. We numbered the participants as P1, P2, and P3.

Setup and Procedure. The subjects were first required to experience the data canvas under the guidance of the researchers and then watch a video of the process of using the physical device (see Fig. 5). After watching the video, we conducted semi-structured interviews (see Table 2).

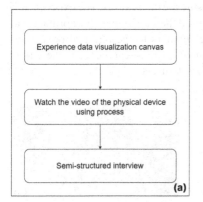

Fig. 5. Process of experiment walkthrough: (a) experimental flow chart; (b) interview process.

Table 2. Semi-structured interview question categories and interview directions.

Question category	Interview direction
Basic personal information	Gender, age, occupation, etc
The use of the mouse	Use of equipment, habits, frequency of symptoms of CTS, etc
Data canvas experience	Experience, impact on behavior, willingness to use, etc
Physical device experience	Feelings of using (watching videos), willingness to use, influence on behavior, linkage with interface, etc
Suggestions for the system	Suggestions for presentation, data types, user experience, etc

Data Collection. The data we collected was mainly from the semi-structured interviews. When subjects were interviewed, the main questions focused on their experience and feedback. During the interview process, we recorded the whole process in audio, and after the interview, we transformed it for organizing and coding analysis.

3.2 Pilot Study

Participants. Three subjects were recruited for a pilot study, all of whom were heavy mouse users with a fixed office location and graduate students in design. We numbered the participants as P4, P5, and P6.

Setup and Procedure. We assumed that during the pilot study mouse use time and movement rate decreased and the frequency of breaks increased when the user used the physical device. Unlike the walkthrough experiment, users actually used the physical device and the data canvas. The experiment was set up as a within-subjects experiment because we wanted to minimize the effect of individual differences.

The experiment was divided into two phases (see Fig. 6): in Phase 1, the subjects only used the data canvas to display data in real time and record data, and in Phase 2, the computer connected to the physical device while using the data canvas. The experimental time for both phases was 30 min, and the subjects used their computers for normal office work. The process of connecting the subjects' computers to the physical device and displaying the canvas was done under the guidance of the researchers. At the end of Phase 2, we conducted semi-structured interviews with users.

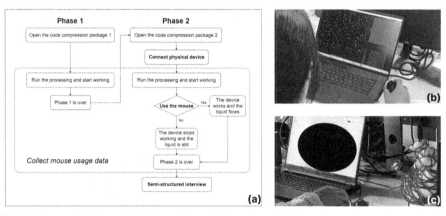

Fig. 6. Process of pilot study: (a) experimental flow chart; (b) Phase 1 experimental process; (c) Phase 2 experimental process.

Data Collection. Two types of data were collected. The data for quantitative analysis was collected through the program in processing, the data from user phases 1 and 2 will be calculated and analyzed in comparison. The data for qualitative analysis was collected through the user interview, which focused on the users' real feelings and suggestions for the system, and the rest was the same as the experiment walkthrough.

4 Results

4.1 Quantitative Findings from Pilot Study

Through the pilot study, we collected 30 min of mouse use data for each of the three subjects before and after using the physical device (see Table 3), and the length of mouse use was greater in Phase 2 than in Phase 1 for all of the subjects (see Fig. 7(a)), which is contrary to our hypothesis. P6 did not take a break in Phase 2 (see Fig. 7(c)). Subjects' Phase 2 mouse movement rate means were all smaller than Phase 1 (see Fig. 7(b)), which is consistent with our hypothesis.

Table 3. Mouse use data of subjects in Phase 1 and Phase 2 during 30 min.

	Mouse segmentation usage time (unit: minutes)		Total mouse usage time (unit: minutes)		Mean value of mouse movement rate		Peak value of mouse movement rate	
	Phase 1	Phase 2	Phase 1	Phase 2	Phase 1	Phase 2	Phase 1	Phase 2
P4	0.16	3.89	13.19	**20.63**	34.99	**25.98**	1643.35	892.11
P5	4.03	10.71	15.56	**19.34**	60.74	**32.17**	1588.95	2175.83
	6.79	6.80						
	3.32	1.75						
	1.41	0.01						
		0.08						
P6	0.23	**24.01**	21.17	**24.01**	69.34	**38.35**	1701.17	1227.83
	1.50							
	9.14							
	2.09							
	3.40							
	1.67							
	3.14							

4.2 Qualitative Findings

In the user interviews for the walkthrough experiment and the pilot study, we obtained basic information about mouse usage habits and some feedback about the product from the subjects. All six subjects used the mouse more frequently and generally for studying, and their recent usage lengths reached more than 8 h, making them heavy users of the mouse with short rest periods during continuous use of the mouse. All six subjects in the user test had a high frequency of mouse use, with recent usage lengths of 8 h or more, were heavy users of the mouse, and had short breaks during continuous mouse use.

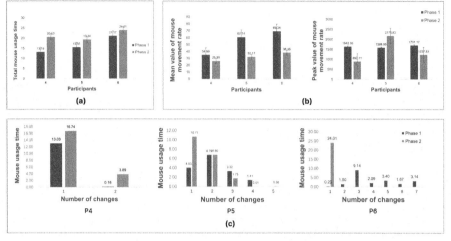

Fig. 7. Data of pilot study: (a) total mouse usage time (unit: minutes); (b) mean value and peak value of mouse movement rate data; (c) mouse segmentation usage time data for P4, P5 and P6 (unit: minutes).

The data collected through semi-structured interviews in both the walkthrough experiment and the pilot study was coded (see Table 4). Users of the data canvas mainly pay attention to the mouse usage time data, and most users express a willingness to record their own data to remind themselves regularly. Some users said they would like to clear the screen of the wave point and rest. For physical devices, some users feel afraid and think of their hands, which causes them to reflect. Additionally, some people find the devices intriguing, which could potentially divert their attention and disrupt their work. Users are interested in physical devices. P6 used the mouse consistently to observe the liquid flow, which may account for her lack of rest in Phase 2. Moreover, the participants provided suggestions to improve the system, requesting that the physical device be more connected to the data canvas. They also expressed a desire for interventions and long-term feedback.

Table 4. Users experience and feedback on data canvas, physical device and the whole system.

Categories	Experience and feedback	Examples
Visual canvas	Canvas attention	**"…paid more attention total time." (P1, P2, P3, P4, P5, P6)**
	Behavior influence	"…concentrate on not loafing on a job." (P5), "…deliberately stop when I see point." (P6) and "…take a look as a relaxation." (P4)

(continued)

Table 4. (*continued*)

Categories	Experience and feedback	Examples
	Intention to use	"…give me a general understanding of my work status." (P1), "…not limited to the computer screen." (P3)
Physical device	Physical device attention	"…the device attracts me more than the interface." (P1, P2, P3, P4, P5, P6)
	Reflection of the device	"amazing" (P6), "very artistic" (P1), "too concrete" (P3), "a little scary" (P4), "life is passing" (P2), "let me divert attention, will make me afraid" (P5)
	Behavioral influence	**"it reminds me of my own hands." (P2, P5), "it will make me want to see." (P1, P6),** "…ignore it after I get into work." (P3)
	Intention to use	**"…help people decompress or relieve their mood." (P2), "it can make the harm more serious and cause more reflection." (P2, P5)**
The whole system	User experience	"…very creative…" (P4), "water flows when the mouse is stationary, and it will be better to explain that water is stationary when it is used." (P5)
	Improvement suggestions	"…change the water flow rate according to the number of clicks." (P4), "on the screen, the flowing state echoes in color." (P3)

5 Discussion

Firstly, this paper proposes a physical visualization for mouse usage data. By quantitative analysis, we find that the subjects' mouse movement rate means in Phase 2 is lower than in Phase 1, which indicates that the physical device has a certain intervention on the user's mouse movement rate. As previous studies have shown that the wrist movement speed is smaller under pressure conditions [11], and the use of water sounds has a good effect on the users' psychological healing [12, 13], the sound of water in the physical device may have a certain effect on the user's stress relief. In addition, a part of the quantitative analysis results did not conform to the hypothesis, after adding the physical device, the total mouse use time was more than that in Phase 1, and the number of breaks was less, which was contrary to the hypothesis. One of the reasons for this may be due to the fact that we only designed a pilot study with a shorter and fewer number of subjects, and some chance occurred. Another reason could be that the subjects were more interested in the flow state of the device and thus appeared to use the mouse. Based on this result, we conjecture that it may be more beneficial to change the mouse state corresponding to the physical device state in order to make the user take a break to look at the flow state.

The effectiveness of the system is difficult to account for statistically due to the limited number of participants in the current user test. In the future, we will expand the scope of the experiment and validate the method's effectiveness in conjunction with further iterations of the prototype.

Secondly, during the user test, semi-structured interviews were conducted with participants from both the experiment walkthrough and the pilot study. Through qualitative analysis, the feedback provided by the users was collected on the system and mouse usage related health. Participants were found to pay more attention to the physical device than to the canvas. The reason for this observation may be that the physical visualization is more effective in visualizing the state of mouse usage while the user is working compared to the canvas. The majority of the existing research focuses on collecting mouse usage data with the aim of predicting health problems [14]. Additionally, a few studies concentrate on providing real-time user feedback to prevent health problems. As a result, this paper proposes an improved direction for visualizing mouse usage data, and possibly other types of health and behavioral data as well, by pairing physical with canvas visualization. Furthermore, users have provided feedback on the product system, and we plan to continue iterative optimization in future research.

6 Conclusion and Future Work

This paper describes Crimson Tendons, a mouse behavior visualization system, including the design and implementation of a liquid flow device to visualize the user's mouse behavior and an associated data visualization canvas. We also conducted a preliminary user test to verify its effectiveness. Mouse behavior is visualized through the red liquid flow in the device. Firstly, the device has an exaggerated but figurative shape, which directly reminds the user of the state of the hand when using the mouse and causes the user to reflect on the situation, thus preventing diseases such as CTS. At the same time, through the flow of water and the state of the mouse, the mapping relationship shifts the user's attention and soothes the user's stress and emotions. Secondly, the data canvas displays and records mouse usage data in real time, allowing the user to track long-term mouse usage behavior and providing a data record of their own office health behavior. We obtained valuable user feedback through user test, and in future research, we will iterate based on the test results and conduct large-scale and longer-term user tests with the updated and iterated system for a new round of product iteration.

Acknowledgements. Thanks to the participants in this study. This work is supported by The National Social Science Fund of China (21CG192) and Ministry of Education of China's First Batch of New Humanities Research and Reform Practice Project (2021160005).

References

1. Da Costa, J.T., Baptista, J.S., Vaz, M.: Incidence and prevalence of upper-limb work related musculoskeletal disorders: a systematic review. Work **51**(4), 635–644 (2015)
2. Tiric-Campara, M., et al.: Occupational overuse syndrome (technological diseases): carpal tunnel syndrome, a mouse shoulder, cervical pain syndrome. Acta Informatica Medica **22**(5), 333 (2014)
3. Schmid, A.B., Kubler, P.A., Johnston, V., Coppieters, M.W.: A vertical mouse and ergonomic mouse pads alter wrist position but do not reduce carpal tunnel pressure in patients with carpal tunnel syndrome. Appl. Ergon. **47**, 151–156 (2015)
4. Ali, K.M., Sathiyasekaran, B.W.C.: Computer professionals and carpal tunnel syndrome (CTS). Int. J. Occup. Saf. Ergon. **12**(3), 319–325 (2006)
5. Eleftheriou, A., Rachiotis, G., Varitimidis, S.E., Koutis, C., Malizos, K.N., Hadjichristodouloul, C.: Cumulative keyboard strokes: a possible risk factor for carpal tunnel syndrome. J. Occup. Med. Toxicol. **7**(1), 1–7 (2012)
6. Andersen, J.H., Thomsen, J.F., Overgaard, E., et al.: Computer use and carpal tunnel syndrome: a 1-year follow-up study. JAMA **289**(22), 2963–2969 (2003)
7. Trillos-Chacón, M.C., Castillo-M, J.A., Tolosa-Guzman, I., Medina, A.F.S., Ballesteros, S.M.: Strategies for the prevention of carpal tunnel syndrome in the workplace: a systematic review. Appl. Ergon. **93**, 103353 (2021)
8. Galinsky, T., Swanson, N., Sauter, S., Dunkin, R., Hurrell, J., Schleifer, L.: Supplementary breaks and stretching exercises for data entry operators: a follow-up field study. Am. J. Ind. Med. **50**(7), 519–527 (2007)
9. Charpe, N.A., Kaushik, V.: Reducing symptoms of carpal tunnel syndrome in software professionals. Stud. Ethno-Med. **6**(1), 63–66 (2012)
10. Keir, P.J., Bach, J.M., Rempel, D.: Effects of computer mouse design and task on carpal tunnel pressure. Ergonomics **42**(10), 1350–1360 (1999)
11. Wahlström, J., Hagberg, M., Johnson, P., Svensson, J., Rempel, D.: Influence of time pressure and verbal provocation on physiological and psychological reactions during work with a computer mouse. Eur. J. Appl. Physiol.ur. J. Appl. Physiol. **87**, 257–263 (2002)
12. 김진숙, 신원섭, 김명종. 치유의숲 소리, 경관, 소리경관 (soundscape) 에 따른 선호도 및 심리적 회복감 분석. 한국환경과학회지 **30**(3), 267–277 (2021)
13. Song, I., Baek, K., Kim, C., Song, C. Effects of nature sounds on the attention and physiological and psychological relaxation. Urban Forestry Urban Green. **86** 127987 (2023)
14. Andersen, J.H., Harhoff, M., Grimstrup, S., et al.: Computer mouse use predicts acute pain but not prolonged or chronic pain in the neck and shoulder. Occup. Environ. Med. **65**(2), 126–131 (2008)

Tutorials

Fashion in the Metaverse: Technologies, Applications, and Opportunities

Gustavo Marfia[1]([⊠]) [iD] and Lorenzo Stacchio[2] [iD]

[1] Department of the Arts, University of Bologna, Bologna, Italy
`gustavo.marfia@unibo.it`
[2] Department for Life Quality Studies, University of Bologna, Bologna, Italy
`lorenzo.stacchio2@unibo.it`

Abstract. This tutorial will provide participants with an overview of how academia and industry are applying Metaverse-related technologies to the entertainment sector, with an emphasis on fashion. Fashion, in fact, appears as an interesting use case, as it integrates: (a) entertainment and storytelling aspects, (b) creativity, (c) industrial production, and, (d) large customer bases. In the last three decades, different research products and experiences have been proposed based on augmented and virtual reality technologies, but the advent of a Metaverse ecosystem deploying non-fungible tokens, artificial intelligence paradigms, and advanced interfaces is opening completely new scenarios. The material will be presented adopting a methodological approach, proposing taxonomies and analyses which connect to consumer needs, use cases, hardware technologies, and software architectures. The target audience that would most benefit from this tutorial would be entertainment professionals in academia and industry, with a particular interest in cultural heritage preservation, creative aspects, brand identity, and xCommerce. By the end of this tutorial, an attendee could develop a drafted project proposal for future funding applications or outline a research and development agenda.

Keywords: Metaverse · Fashion · Creativity · xCommerce

1 Background on the Theoretical Approach

In the recent past, the Metaverse emerged as one of the disruptive sets of technologies, including eXtended Reality (XR), Artificial Intelligence (AI), Non-Fungible Tokens (NFT) Human-Computer Interaction (HCI), and the Internet of Things (IoT) allowing to define digital immersive experiences that could augment, simulate or re-define real-world environments and interactions [8, 9].

At the intersection of such technologies, Digital Twins (DT) [2] emerge as a core technology, able to validate, visualize, and manipulate the digital counterpart of physical objects.

Moreover, among the most important features often provided in Metaverse experiences, the collaborative aspect emerges as key, since enables entertaining

© IFIP International Federation for Information Processing 2023
Published by Springer Nature Switzerland AG 2023
P. Ciancarini et al. (Eds.): ICEC 2023, LNCS 14455, pp. 521–523, 2023.
https://doi.org/10.1007/978-981-99-8248-6

and engaging experiences for consumers while at the same time empowering creative and production processes for professionals [8, 9].

All of such paradigms and technologies are generating novel opportunities for both the research and the industrial world, in the entertainment field, and in particular in the field of fashion [4, 7–9, 11, 12].

In the field of entertainment, well-establish practices such as gaming, virtual concerts, and artistic performance are part of the everyday life of Metaverse users [9].

Concerning fashion instead, a large user base can experience several features related to (a) entertainment and storytelling aspects, (b) creativity, and (c) industrial production. For example, consumers can collaboratively interact, and customize the digital counterparts of real garments, try-on garments, buy items in digital marketplaces, and participate in fashion catwalks [8]. From an industrial perspective, users and professionals can exploit Metaverse paradigms to design, even with collaborative approaches, and promote their work with artistic performance, implementing marketing and brand identity strategies [8].

In all of these different use cases, integration of XR, AI, and NFTs paradigms is often applied to guarantee experience realism, and flexibility while guaranteeing intellectual properties and business exchanges [8].

2 Description of Tutorial Content

The first hour will be an introduction to the Metaverse, related technologies, and state-of-the-art systems from both academic and industrial point-of-view [7–9, 11, 12]. In particular, a discussion about XR, NFTs, AI, and DT, and how they can be composed in several contexts to create effective experiences for both business-oriented applications and academic ones.

For example, we will contextualize xCommerce, AI, and NFTs integration with recent works on the topic regarding business applications, storytelling, and collaborative approaches [3, 5–7, 12]. An overview of XR, AI, and DT paradigms in industrial use cases will be provided, focusing on topics like item validation, supply chain, and generative design [1, 10].

Participants will then be broken up into small groups or pairs to work with their colleagues (if present). After that, participants will work for 1.5 h to develop a brand new idea or work on mapping an existing idea/project into a novel solution for integrating Metaverse technologies into innovative or existing use-case. After the 'hands-on' working session, 30 min will be allocated for groups to report back on and present their ideas.

References

1. Alkhammash, E.H., Karaa, W.B.A., Bhouri, N., Abdessalem, S.B., Hassanien, A.E.: Digital twin solutions for textile industry: architecture, services, and challenges. In: Hassanien, A.E., Darwish, A., Snasel, V. (eds.) Digital Twins for Digital Transformation: Innovation in Industry. Studies in Systems, Decision and Control,

vol. 423, pp. 171–186. Springer, Cham (2022). https://doi.org/10.1007/978-3-030-96802-1_9

2. Barricelli, B.R., Casiraghi, E., Fogli, D.: A survey on digital twin: definitions, characteristics, applications, and design implications. IEEE Access **7**, 167653–167671 (2019)

3. Cheng, R., Wu, N., Chen, S., Han, B.: Reality check of metaverse: a first look at commercial social virtual reality platforms. In: 2022 IEEE Conference on Virtual Reality and 3D User Interfaces Abstracts and Workshops (VRW), pp. 141–148. IEEE (2022)

4. Far, S.B., Rad, A.I.: Applying digital twins in metaverse: user interface, security and privacy challenges. J. Metaverse **2**(1), 8–15 (2022)

5. Joy, A., Zhu, Y., Peña, C., Brouard, M.: Digital future of luxury brands: metaverse, digital fashion, and non-fungible tokens. Strateg. Chang. **31**(3), 337–343 (2022)

6. Luna-Nevarez, C., McGovern, E.: The rise of the virtual reality (VR) marketplace: exploring the antecedents and consequences of consumer attitudes toward V-commerce. J. Internet Commer. **20**(2), 167–194 (2021)

7. Morotti, E., et al.: Exploiting fashion x-commerce through the empowerment of voice in the fashion virtual reality arena. Virtual Reality , 1–14 (2021). https://doi.org/10.1007/s10055-021-00602-6

8. Park, H., Lim, R.E.: Fashion and the metaverse: clarifying the domain and establishing a research agenda. J. Retail. Consum. Serv. **74**, 103413 (2023)

9. Periyasami, S., Periyasamy, A.P.: Metaverse as future promising platform business model: case study on fashion value chain. Businesses **2**(4), 527–545 (2022)

10. dos Santos, C.H., Gabriel, G.T., do Amaral, J.V.S., Montevechi, J.A.B., de Queiroz, J.A.: Decision-making in a fast fashion company in the industry 4.0 era: a digital twin proposal to support operational planning. Int. J. Adv. Manufact. Technol. **116**, 1653–1666 (2021)

11. Stacchio, L., Angeli, A., Marfia, G.: Empowering digital twins with extended reality collaborations. Virtual Reality Intell. Hardw. **4**(6), 487–505 (2022)

12. Stacchio, L., et al.: Who will trust my digital twin? Maybe a clerk in a brick and mortar fashion shop. In: 2022 IEEE Conference on Virtual Reality and 3D User Interfaces Abstracts and Workshops (VRW), pp. 814–815. IEEE (2022)

Exploring New Frontiers at the Intersection of AI and Art

Giovanna Castellano[ID], Nicola Fanelli, Raffaele Scaringi[ID],
and Gennaro Vessio[✉][ID]

Department of Computer Science, University of Bari Aldo Moro, Bari, Italy
{giovanna.castellano,raffaele.scaringi,
gennaro.vessio}@uniba.it

Abstract. This tutorial explores how AI advancements can enrich the understanding, enjoyment, and accessibility of art, offering new and intriguing ways to engage with artistic works (Tutorial website: https:// sites.google.com/view/aiarttutorial.).

Keywords: Computer vision · Cultural heritage · Digital humanities · Deep learning · Generative AI · Knowledge graphs

1 Background and Motivation

In recent years, the digitization of artistic heritage has witnessed significant progress, offering a wealth of opportunities for computational solutions in art exploration and analysis. Digital archives, online collections, and high-resolution imaging have made artworks more accessible and available for in-depth examination. These digitized resources are valuable inputs for AI-based algorithms and techniques, enabling novel computational approaches to analyze, understand, and derive insights from this heritage [2, 3].

This tutorial paper aims to delve into the intersection of AI and art, specifically focusing on how recent AI advancements can be harnessed to explore art in new intriguing and transformative ways. The primary audience for this tutorial includes researchers, practitioners, and enthusiasts in AI, digital humanities, and e-heritage. By exploring topics such as knowledge graphs, large language models for artwork captioning, and diffusion models for artwork inpainting, we aim to demonstrate the potential of AI to enrich art appreciation, promote inclusivity, and facilitate cultural exchange.

2 Tutorial Outline

The tutorial encompasses three core topics, briefly described in the following paragraphs.

© IFIP International Federation for Information Processing 2023
Published by Springer Nature Switzerland AG 2023
P. Ciancarini et al. (Eds.): ICEC 2023, LNCS 14455, pp. 524–526, 2023.
https://10.1007/978-981-99-8248-6

2.1   Art and Knowledge Graphs

Knowledge graphs are powerful tools for organizing and encoding historical and contextual information related to artworks. In the context of this tutorial, attendees can delve into the concept of knowledge graphs and explore *ArtGraph*, a specific knowledge graph developed by the tutorial team [1]. *ArtGraph* is implemented using Neo4j, a NoSQL database, which provides a robust graph query language for information retrieval and knowledge discovery. With knowledge graphs, attendees can navigate and explore art-related information in a structured and interconnected manner. *ArtGraph* allows for the organization of diverse data, including artist biographies, movements, stylistic characteristics, and relationships between artworks and artists. By leveraging the capabilities of knowledge graphs, attendees can gain insights into how to harness the power of structured data to enhance art exploration, contextual understanding, and analysis in the digital humanities domain.

2.2   Artwork Captioning

Artwork captioning is an essential task in art exploration and appreciation, aiming to generate descriptive textual descriptions that capture the essence of an artwork, its visual elements, and underlying concepts [4]. In this tutorial, attendees can delve into the emerging field of artwork captioning and explore how it can be achieved using large language models, such as ChatGPT. When applied to artworks, traditional image captioning models often face challenges due to the unique characteristics and complexities of artistic creations. Traditional captioning models may struggle to accurately describe artworks' intricate details, emotional nuances, and underlying meanings. However, large language models have the potential to go beyond the surface-level visual features and incorporate broader contextual knowledge, art history, and cultural references. Artwork captioning has significant potential to enrich art experiences, promote inclusivity, and facilitate cultural exchange. Furthermore, it can allow individuals with visual impairments or limited artistic knowledge to access and understand artworks more comprehensively.

2.3   Artwork Inpainting

Artwork inpainting is an application of AI that involves restoring and completing missing or damaged parts within an artwork [5]. It is a challenging task due to the fine-grained details, textures, and artistic styles present in artworks. In this tutorial, attendees can explore the application of recent advances in diffusion models, inspired by techniques such as DALL-E, for artwork inpainting. By leveraging these models, attendees can learn how to generate realistic and coherent content seamlessly integrating with the original artwork. Artwork inpainting does not involve simple image interpolation; it aims to capture the artistic intent and style, ensuring that the generated content aligns harmoniously with the existing elements of the artwork. Artwork inpainting has significant implications for the restoration of damaged artworks, the completion of unfinished pieces, and the preservation of artistic heritage.

3 Concluding Remarks

Our work is ongoing, and our research on developing new art exploration and appreciation models is a work in progress. We are committed to actively exploring innovative approaches and refining our models to improve their performance and effectiveness. The tutorial aims to showcase the current advancements and potential of existing methods while also acknowledging the evolving nature of this research area and the stimulating possibilities.

References

1. Castellano, G., Digeno, V., Sansaro, G., Vessio, G.: Leveraging knowledge graphs and deep learning for automatic art analysis. Knowl.-Based Syst. **248**, 108859 (2022)
2. Castellano, G., Vessio, G.: Deep learning approaches to pattern extraction and recognition in paintings and drawings: An overview. Neural Comput. Appl. **33**(19), 12263–12282 (2021)
3. Castellano, G., Vessio, G.: A deep learning approach to clustering visual arts. Int. J. Comput. Vis. **130**(11), 2590–2605 (2022). https://doi.org/10.1007/s11263-022-01664-y
4. Cetinic, E.: Towards generating and evaluating iconographic image captions of artworks. J. Imaging **7**(8), 123 (2021)
5. Cipolina-Kun, L., Caenazzo, S., Mazzei, G.: Comparison of CoModGans, LaMa and GLIDE for art inpainting completing MC Escher's print gallery. In: Proceedings of the IEEE/CVF Conference on Computer Vision and Pattern Recognition, pp. 716–724 (2022)

Author Index

© IFIP International Federation for Information Processing 2023
Published by Springer Nature Switzerland AG 2023
P. Ciancarini et al. (Eds.): ICEC 2023, LNCS 14455, pp. 527–529, 2023.
https://doi.org/10.1007/978-981-99-8248-6

Printed in the United States
by Baker & Taylor Publisher Services